Springer Series on

Behavior Therapy and Behavioral Medicine

Volume 1 **Multimodal Behavior Therapy**
Arnold A. Lazarus

Volume 2 **Behavior-Therapy Assessment**
Eric J. Mash and Leif G. Terdal, editors

Volume 3 **Behavioral Approaches to Weight Control**
Edward E. Abramson, editor

Volume 4 **A Practical Guide to Behavioral Assessment**
Francis J. Keefe, Steven A. Kopel and Steven B. Gordon

Volume 5 **Asthma Therapy**
A Behavioral Health Care System for Respiratory Disorders
Thomas L. Creer

Volume 6 **Behavioral Medicine**
Practical Applications in Health Care
Barbara G. Melamed and Lawrence J. Siegel

Volume 7 **Multimodal Handbook for a Mental Hospital**
Designing Specific Treatments for Specific Problems
Lillian F. Brunell and Wayne T. Young, editors

Volume 8 **Eating and Weight Disorders**
Advances in Treatment and Research
Richard K. Goodstein, editor

Volume 9 **Perspectives on Behavior Therapy in the Eighties**
Michael Rosenbaum, Cyril M. Franks and Yoram Jaffe, editors

Volume 10 **Pediatric and Adolescent Behavioral Medicine**
Issues in Treatment
Patrick J. McGrath and Philip Firestone, editors

MICHAEL ROSENBAUM, Ph.D., is a Senior Lecturer in Clinical Psychology in the Department of Psychology at Tel-Aviv University, Israel. He is the cofounder and past president of the Israeli Association for Behavior Therapy. He was the principal organizer and chairperson of the First World Congress on Behaviour Therapy (Jerusalem, 1980). He is the past director of the psychology departments at Geha Psychiatric Hospital and at Lowenstein Rehabilitation Center. He is on the International Advisory Board of the journal *Child and Family Behavior Therapy*. His major research interests are in the areas of self-control, coping behaviors, and behavioral medicine. Dr. Rosenbaum received his Ph.D. from the University of Illinois at Urbana-Champaign where he was also a Visiting Associate Professor in 1980/81.

CYRIL M. FRANKS, Ph.D., is Professor of Psychology in the Graduate School of Applied and Professional Psychology at Rutgers University, Piscataway, New Jersey. He is cofounder and first president of the Association for Advancement of Behavior Therapy, founder and first editor (1970–1979) of the journal *Behavior Therapy*, senior author of the series *Annual Review of Behavior Therapy: Theory and Practice*, founder and coeditor of the Springer Series on Behavior Therapy and Behavioral Medicine, editor-in-chief of the journal *Child and Family Behavior Therapy*, the author of some 300 articles and chapters, and the editor of numerous books. Professor Franks received his Ph.D. from the University of London Institute of Psychiatry (Maudsley Hospital) in 1954. He also holds a B.Sc. from the University of Wales and an M.A. from the University of Minnesota.

YORAM JAFFE, Ph.D., received his B.A. from the University of California, Berkeley, and his Ph.D. in clinical psychology from the University of California, Los Angeles in 1974. Dr. Jaffe taught at Tel-Aviv University and is now on the psychology faculty at Bar Ilan University in Israel. For the past two years he has been Visiting Associate Professor in the Department of Psychology, UCLA. His research has been in areas of personality and psychopathology, and his current interest is focused on theoretical and clinical issues in cognitive therapy. Dr. Jaffe is one of the founders of the Israel Association for Behavior Therapy and was cochairperson of the First World Congress on Behaviour Therapy (Jerusalem, 1980).

Perspectives on Behavior Therapy in the Eighties

Michael Rosenbaum, Ph.D.
Cyril M. Franks, Ph.D.
Yoram Jaffe, Ph.D.
Editors

SPRINGER PUBLISHING COMPANY
New York

Springer Publishing Company, Inc.
200 Park Avenue South
New York, New York 10003

83 84 85 86 87 / 10 9 8 7 6 5 4 3 2 1

Library of Congress Cataloging in Publication Data

Main entry under title:

Perspectives on behavior therapy in the eighties.

(Springer series on behavior therapy and behavioral medicine ; 9)
Revised papers originally prepared for the First World Congress on Behaviour Therapy, held in Jerusalem in July 1980.
Includes bibliographies and indexes.
1. Behavior therapy—Congresses. I. Rosenbaum, Michael. II. Franks, Cyril M. III. Jaffe, Yoram. IV. Series. [DNLM: 1. Behavior therapy—Congresses. W1 SP685NB v.9/WM 425 P467 1980]
RC489.B4P464 1982 616.89'142 82-16797
ISBN 0-8261-4070-X
ISSN 0278-6729

Printed in the United States of America

To the memory of
Park O. Davidson

Contents

Preface

All contributors to this book attended the First World Congress on Behaviour Therapy, which convened in Jerusalem in the second week of July 1980. Following the Congress, selected participants were invited to submit chapters for the present volume. Most revised their presentations extensively to make them suitable for publication, others elected in consultation with us to prepare a different manuscript, reflecting prevailing research interests while retaining the "spirit" of the Congress. We set out to capture an integrated perspective for behavior therapy in the 1980s as seen through the eyes of selected Congress participants.

As explained more fully in our opening chapter, this volume was conceived during the preparations for the Congress. The bulk of the organizational work was carried out by Rosenbaum in Israel and Franks in the U.S.A. To help with the seemingly never-ending flow of details, Yoram Jaffe of Bar-Ilan University was later coopted by Rosenbaum as Congress Cochairperson, with the agreement that he would be listed as the third editor of the volume that would later emerge. With two of the editors in the U.S.A.—Franks at Rutgers University and Rosenbaum as Visiting Associate Professor at the University of Illinois—during the academic year 1980/81, the gestation period for this book began virtually as soon as the Congress ended. As always in such matters, our endeavour involved much more than originally bargained for and culminated in a final fortnight of frenetic but satisfying in-residence joint editorial activity by Franks and Rosenbaum in Princeton, New Jersey.

Accountability is one hallmark of behavior therapy, and it is for this reason that we detail the genesis of this volume. Rosenbaum and Franks assume primary responsibility for those deficits that are undoubtedly present. It is our hope that this volume gives as much reward in the reading as we had in its preparation. As part of the process we learned much about contemporary behavior therapy throughout the world.

Those who helped organize the Congress helped indirectly in the publication of this book. The list is too long to be published, yet we owe these individuals our deepest gratitude. In particular, we would like to thank Attorney Frederick L. Simmons, the First Trustee of the Schwartz Memorial Fund, Los Angeles, for the provision of financial support for the Congress through the Schwartz Institute in Israel. (All of us willingly agreed to contribute full royalties to the newly formed World Association of Behaviour Therapy, a precedent that we hope and anticipate will become an established tradition.)

We recognize with gratitude the counsel and encouragement received from Ursula Springer, Barbara Watkins, and other members of Springer Publishing Company throughout the preparation of this book. That is has been selected for inclusion in the Springer Series on Behavior Therapy and Behavioral Medicine, coedited by Cyril M. Franks and Frederick J. Evans, gives us considerable gratification. We are grateful to the secretarial staff of the Department of Psychology and the Institute for Child Behavior and Development at the University of Illinois, Urbana-Champaign; to Alleen Pusey, secretary to the Carrier Foundation Psychology Department, Belle Mead, New Jersey; to Gloria Johnson of the Graduate School of Applied and Professional Psychology, Rutgers University; and to Cynthia Smith and Diane Brodahl of the UCLA Department of Psychology, Word Processing Center.

All of us were shocked and saddened to hear of the sudden and tragic deaths in a car accident of Park O. Davidson and his wife in December of 1980. Professor Davidson of the University of British Columbia had been one of the key figures in the Congress and was engaged in the preparation of an invited contribution to this book at the time of his death. We share the grief of his many colleagues and offer the present volume as homage to his memory.

Michael Rosenbaum

Cyril M. Franks

Yoram Jaffe

Contributors

Andrea B. Ackerman, Ph.D.
Adjunct Assistant Professor
University of California
Los Angeles, California
Currently at New School for Child Development
Van Nuys, California

Kenneth D. Craig, Ph.D.
Professor and Director
Graduate Programme in Clinical and Community Psychology
Department of Psychology
The University of British Columbia
Vancouver, B.C. Canada

W. Edward Craighead, Ph.D.
Professor of Psychology
Department of Psychology
The Pennsylvania State University
University Park, Pennsylvania

Michael E. Dawson, Ph.D.
Associate Professor of Medical Psychology
UCLA School of Medicine
Los Angeles, California

Albert Ellis, Ph.D.
Director
Institute for Rational-Emotive Therapy
New York, New York

Ian M. Evans, Ph.D.
Professor
Department of Psychology
State University of New York
Binghamton, New York

Hans J. Eysenck, Ph.D.
Professor
Department of Psychology
Institute of Psychiatry
De Crespigny Park
London, England

Melanie J. V. Fennell, M.A., M.Sc.
Department of Psychiatry
University of Oxford
Oxford, England

Iris E. Fodor, Ph.D.
Professor
School of Education, Health, Nursing, and Arts Professions
New York University
New York, New York

Harry Hoberman, M.S.
Psychology Department
University of Oregon
Eugene, Oregon

Arie Kruglanski, Ph.D.
Professor
Department of Psychology
Tel Aviv University
Tel Aviv, Israel

Gloria Leon, Ph.D.
Professor
Department of Psychology
University of Minnesota
Minneapolis, Minnesota

Peter M. Lewinsohn, Ph.D.
Professor
Psychology Department
University of Oregon
Eugene, Oregon

Robert P. Liberman, M.D.
Professor
Neuropsychiatric Institute
Camarillo State Hospital
Camarillo, California

Perry London, Ph.D.
Professor
Department of Psychology
Tel-Aviv University
Tel-Aviv, Israel

O. Ivar Lovaas, Ph.D.
Professor
University of California
Department of Psychology
Los Angeles, California

Isaac Marks, M.D.
Professor
Institute of Psychiatry
De Crespigny Park
London, England

Susan M. McHale, Ph.D.
Assistant Professor of Human Development
The Pennsylvania State University
University Park, Pennsylvania

Barbara G. Melamed, Ph.D.
Professor
Department of Clinical Psychology
University of Florida
Gainesville, Florida

Andrew W. Meyers, Ph.D.
Associate Professor of Psychology
Memphis State University
Memphis, Tennessee

Keith H. Nuechterlein, Ph.D.
Assistant Professor of Medical Psychology
UCLA School of Medicine
Los Angeles, California

Ernest G. Poser, Ph.D.
Professor
Department of Psychology
McGill University
Montreal, Canada

A. John Rush, M.D.
Professor
Health Science Center
University of Texas
Dallas, Texas

Mitchell T. Taubman, Ph.D.
Research Psychologist
University of California
Los Angeles, California
Currently at Marilyn Ruman Clinic and Consulting Associates
Encino, California

John D. Teasdale, Ph.D.
Department of Psychiatry
University of Oxford
The Warneford Hospital
Oxford, England

Linda Teri, Ph.D.
Psychology Department
University of Oregon
Eugene, Oregon

Matisyohu Weisenberg, Ph.D.
Professor
Department of Psychology
Barr-Ilan University
Ramat-Gan, Israel

Linda Wilcoxon-Craighead, Ph.D.
Assistant Professor of Counseling and Educational Psychology
The Pennsylvania State University
University Park, Pennsylvania

Edwin P. Willems, Ph.D.
Associate Dean
College of Social Sciences
University of Houston
Houston, Texas

Frances E. Wilson, Ph.D.
Post Doctoral Fellow
Johns Hopkins School of Medicine and the John F. Kennedy Institute
Baltimore, Maryland

Robin Winkler, Ph.D.
Associate Professor
Department of Psychology
University of Western Australia
Perth, Australia

Joseph Wolpe, M.D.
Professor
Department of Psychiatry
Temple University
Eastern Pennsylvania Psychiatric Institute
Philadelphia, Pennsylvania

PART I

Introduction

CHAPTER 1

Behavior Therapy: Overview and Personal Reflections

Cyril M. Franks, Ph.D.
Michael Rosenbaum, Ph.D.

Every book has its unique developmental history. This book's history is closely associated with the genesis of a world association for behavior therapy and with the convening of the first World Congress on Behaviour Therapy in Jerusalem in 1980.

Since 1970, the European Association for Behaviour Therapy (EABT) has organized annual conferences in various European countries. At the seventh EABT conference, convened in Uppsala, Sweden, in the summer of 1977, the EABT representatives agreed to hold their tenth annual convocation in 1980 in Jerusalem. Since the Uppsala meeting was attended by many representatives from the United States of the Association for Advancement of Behavior Therapy (AABT),[1] a joint EABT–AABT meeting was called. At that meeting, Cyril Franks, cofounder and first president of AABT, proposed that the EABT's Jerusalem conference be expanded to the First World Congress on Behaviour Therapy, and that such world congresses be convened every three years in different parts of the globe. Despite some strongly expressed initial reservations by certain European delegates, the joint EABT and AABT meeting in Uppsala eventually endorsed this proposal unanimously, and a small organizing committee was formed. The effective working constituents of this committee were as follows: Cyril Franks (repre-

[1] The AABT was formed in 1966 as a multidisciplinary interest group by Dorothy Susskind, Edward Dengrove, Joseph Wolpe, Andrew Salter, Cyril Franks, and a few others. For further details about the origins and development of this organization, now well over 3,000 strong, readers are referred to Kazdin's (1978) 468-page *History of behavior modification.* This comprehensive volume is essential reading for those who seek an understanding of the historical and conceptual underpinnings of contemporary behavior therapy. Those whose concern is primarily with the scientific and philosophical foundations of behavior therapy and their implications for ongoing theory and practice would do well to read Erwin (1978).

senting AABT); Ron Ramsay (then EABT president); and Michael Rosenbaum (Congress chairperson). Yoram Jaffe of Israel was later appointed a cochairperson of the Congress.

Preparations for the Congress took three years. During this period, Michael Rosenbaum, and to a lesser extent Cyril Franks, corresponded with executives of virtually all behavior therapy associations in the world. The extent to which behavior therapy was found to be practiced and thriving in different parts of the globe was unexpected. In addition to AABT and EABT, there are a number of large behavior therapy associations in Australia, Japan, and Latin America, not to mention smaller groups elsewhere. The need for a world-wide organization became increasingly apparent as planning for the Congress proceeded.

During the week of July 13-17, 1980, behavior therapists from some 30 countries gathered in Jerusalem for the first World Congress on Behaviour Therapy. The participants included most of the founding fathers of behavior therapy, many second-generation leaders in the field, plus hundreds of research scientists, clinical investigators, practicing professionals, and students. All in all, some 1,200 practicing or student psychologists, psychiatrists, social workers, and members of other mental health professions attended the Congress. The participants came from as far afield as Japan, Australia, and South America. It was, indeed, the largest international meeting of its kind and, by many accounts, a success with respect both to content and the spirit of international cooperation that was fostered. Representatives of the various participating countries agreed to take active steps toward the establishment of a world association of behavior therapy associations. It was further decided that the second Congress would convene in Washington in 1983.

Twenty-four prominent behavior therapists who participated in the Jerusalem Congress were invited to write chapters for this book. These individuals represent a variety of interests and points of view. It seems to us that, despite certain geographical overrepresentation, topical exclusions, and other unavoidable biases, when combined into one volume, their collective writings offer a selective sample of significant developments in contemporary behavior therapy and point to some of the directions in which we seem to be moving.

Behavior therapy is now entering its third decade. The first decade (the 1960s) was the pioneering era, an era of unswerving ideology and polemics in which behavior therapists tried to present a united front against the common psychodynamic "foe." It was a period during which, despite much resistance, behavior therapy began to establish itself as a respectable method of treatment. Then, in 1972, Perry London wrote: "The borders are secure now, the settlers are thriving, the dark untrampled forests are trampled and cut down, the stumps blown, the fields plowed. It is time now to build this domain, not defend it." As the second decade unfolded, this was indeed what happened. Behavior therapy gradually but progressively deemphasized and largely abandoned its missionary zeal and searched for new horizons within its own domain. Concepts, methodologies, and ways of viewing data beyond those of traditional learning theory were introduced. More sophisticated methods of treatment and outcome evaluation were developed. The "cognitive revolution" swept into behavior therapy as it did into certain other areas of psychology. New frontiers were established, and new facets of behavior therapy came into being: behavioral medicine, behavioral psychopharmacology, biofeedback, behavioral ecology, community behavior therapy, a variety of systems approaches to behavior therapy, and the development of so-called self-control procedures, to name but a few. Throughout all of these, the cognitive trend became increasingly apparent.

Although behavior therapy has now abandoned the more messianic aspects of its disagreement with alien forces, considerable schism is developing within its own house. Behavior therapists argue among themselves rather than with others. But, in the main, it is a constructive and nonacrimonious discourse that is now moving the whole field into its present more mature and sophisticated stage. Nevertheless, certain critics of behavior therapy, and even a few naive friends, still make the erroneous assumption that behavior therapy is some kind of monolithic entity, a unitary treatment system that may readily be compared and contrasted with other therapeutic modalities. To demonstrate the falsity of this extraordinary notion, it is necessary to outline briefly the many and diverse historical, conceptual, and empirical streams that make up the complexity that characterizes contemporary behavior therapy.

No one country can lay valid claim to behavior therapy, and, as the very breadth of the Jerusalem Congress testifies, both its roots and present scope are truly international. In Russia, and later the Soviet Union, there was the remarkable systematization of the principles and data of classical conditioning under the leadership of Pavlov and his associates. Later, primarily in the United States, this became translated into practice by way of such techniques as conditioned reflex therapy and aversion conditioning. In South Africa, Wolpe's early research into the elimination of "neurotic" behavior in cats paved the way for the first viable "talk therapy" alternative to psychodynamic intervention, namely systematic desensitization. Two other South African pioneers in behavior therapy who achieved world prominence, at first in South Africa and then in the United Kingdom and the USA respectively, are Stanley Rachman and Arnold Lazarus. Lazarus, although firmly recognizing an allegiance to a broadly behavioral tradition, no longer calls himself a behavior therapist. By his own affirmation, he is a "multimodal therapist" (Lazarus, 1981).

In the United Kingdom, the search for a viable alternative led

Eysenck and his associates at the University of London Institute of Psychiatry (Maudsley Hospital) to Hullian learning theory and the generation of testable predictions as a laboratory-originated data-base for cautious and controlled extrapolation to the clinical situation. It is such reliance upon the data and methodology of experimental psychology as a basis for intervention, rather than clinical impression alone, that characterizes behavior therapy as a whole. But of equal importance to the Maudsley tradition, if not to all of behavior therapy, is Eysenck's emphasis upon, on the one hand, the constitutional and genetic determinants of behavior and, on the other hand, personality traits as enduring factors governing human behavior.

Inspired by his leadership, students of Eysenck established Maudsley enclaves throughout North America, Europe, Australia, India, Egypt, Israel, and other regions. Populated by students rather than disciples, many of these centers gradually took on individualities of their own, and differences of opinion emerged. For example, in Australia, Yates—incorrectly, we think—still regards the contribution of Shapiro (an enduring Maudsley citizen but ideologically rather separate from the mainstream) and his development of a methodology for the intensive study and treatment of the single subject as one of the forerunners of behavior therapy as we know it today. To our way of thinking, Shapiro's contribution, such as it is, is to experimental clinical psychology at large rather than to behavior therapy per se.

Meanwhile, in the United States, perhaps as part of the pioneering belief that the environment is there to be conquered and that there are few limits to our capacities for so doing, the emphasis upon external variables and Skinnerian operant conditioning reigned supreme until the advent of cognition, Bandura, and reciprocal interactionism. This operant emphasis led naturally to techniques such as token economies and the development of the sophisticated methodology of applied behavior analysis. Early applied behavior analysists were notoriously atheoretical, and many were radical behaviorists in their philosophic predilections. Few behavior therapists today are radical behaviorists. Metaphysical or radical behaviorism, with its denial of the very existence of mental states, and its non-mediational, antimentalistic bias, is incompatible with the everyday practice of clinical behavior therapy in the eighties, involving, as it does, cognition, awareness of self, and the like. The majority of behavior therapists today would probably not describe themselves as behaviorists at all. If forced to give themselves a philosophical label—in the unlikely event that they thought about such matters—they would probably call themselves methodological behaviorists, subscribing to the methodology of the behavioral scientist while recognizing the utility of mediational processes and inferences. But even within the latter camp there is much diversity. For some, data-based interventions go far beyond S-R mechanisms and overt behavior to implicate covert mental processes, cognition, affect, and more, culminating in such broad (if not always data-based) positions as Lazarus' multimodal therapy and his acronymic BASIC ID (behavior, affect, sensation, imagery, cognition, interpersonal relations, and drugs.) Others, such as Bandura, Mahoney, and Meichenbaum, recognize the potential relevance of mediational as well as more overt and directly measurable processes and devote considerable clinical and research acumen to the development of data-based strategies for their investigation.

Mahoney views the "cognitive connection" as a paradigm shift, a leap forward into a new mode of scientific exploration. As documented in more detail elsewhere (Franks & Wilson, 1973–1979; Franks, 1980; Wilson & Franks, 1982), we are inclined to view such a step as premature. Behavior therapy, like much of psychology, is still in a preparadigmatic stage, somewhat analogous to physics in the sixteenth or seventeenth century. There is no paradigm to shift. It is our contention that cognitive behavior therapy is not, as some would have it, an entity in itself. It is an integral component of behavior therapy per se, to be investigated by the methodology of the behavioral scientist (adapted if need be), utilizing in the first instance the explanatory concepts of S-R learning theory and some form of conditioning. With the good Bishop Occam, if not certain leading cognitivists, we are more inclined to postpone the introduction of additional explanatory concepts to account for the phenomena of cognition until we have explored all reasonable proposals to account for the data in terms of existing formulations. (With all its limitations, Eysenck's courageous conditioning-based model of neurosis provides an excellent example in this respect. The various components of his complex model are very amenable to experimental testing. More cannot be expected of any plausible scientific theory.)

This, of course, is not the position of those who call themselves behavior therapists but espouse neither some form of conditioning or learning theory model nor the methodology of behavioral science. Unlike the majority, who do, indeed, regard behavior therapy as an approach, such individuals are technique-oriented and view behavior therapy as a series of procedures to be applied as the whim dictates. For such individuals, the combination of such (to us) incompatible viewpoints as psychoanalytic and behavior therapy is both conceptually and practically possible. For reasons documented fully elsewhere (see especially Franks and Wilson, 1973–1979), we regard this as a totally untenable position.

Finally, we draw brief attention to two additional issues that remain bones of contention for those who care to think about such matters. For some behavior therapists, a primary goal of therapy is the attainment of self-control stemming from an inner-directed awareness of self based upon "free-will" and "self-determinism." For other behavior therapists, free-will is an illusion, and we are bound by circumstances beyond our control even when we proceed as if this were not so (whatever this means). Then there is the notion of conditioning itself, still fundamental to behavior therapy but under suspicion in certain experimental psychology circles. It is argued, often persuasively, that conditionability as a general factor, a property of the nervous system, has not as yet been adequately demonstrated. This complicates both research and clinical practice. Furthermore, even if a general factor of conditioning were to be demonstrated, if such a factor were to account for but a small portion of the variance in any specific situation, its predictive utility would be severely limited. Add to these such unresolved issues as the conceptual and the empirical relationships between classical and operant conditioning and even the very existence of conditioning as a concept at all, and it becomes increasingly obvious upon what uneasy foundations the so-called conditioning therapies rest.

It is apparent from the foregoing that behavior therapy is no longer the simplistic, cut-and-dried matter of the clinical application of something called "modern learning theory" that it was in the early 1960s. Provided that we stay firmly data-based, accept (but be prepared to update) the methodology of the behavioral scientist, and adopt a preference for working within some broadly conceived S-R learning theory model, the many new faces of third-decade behavior therapy will continue to reflect an aura of health and vitality rather than disease and decline. Of several feasible systems our present inclination is toward Bandura's social learning theory model. Like its much-neglected precursor, social behaviorism (Staats & Staats, 1963), social learning theory is learning-based but outcome-oriented. Additional strengths lie in its intrinsic amenability to systematically controlled investigation and replication in terms of the ready generation of testable hypotheses. In the long run, empiricism is best served if provisionally cast in some theoretical, prediction-testing mold, and social-learning theory falls squarely into this category (see Wilson, 1978, for a more extensive discussion of these and related issues). Our major problem with social learning theory is philosophical rather than scientific: it pertains to certain reservations about the role given to cognition as a partly independent agent in the shaping and interplay between environment and person (Franks & Barbrack, in press).

Behavior therapy as it now stands, then, is healthy despite, or perhaps because of, its variations and complexity. But it does present certain problems for the practitioner as well as the researcher. How the behavior therapist practices, what techniques to use, the approach to problems of strategy, and even the matter of patient/therapist relationships will inevitably depend upon the explicit theoretical orientation of the clinician concerned and the implicit philosophical and cultural milieu prevailing at the time (Franks, 1969).

Consistent with the broadening compass of behavior therapy, our domain has expanded from the brief S-R statements of the early 1960s to the complicated, some would say ponderous, all-embracing preambles of the 1980s. Consider, for example, the widely accepted definition currently advocated by the AABT:

> Behavior therapy involves primarily the application of principles derived from research in experimental and social psychology for the alleviation of human suffering and the enhancement of human functioning. Behavior therapy emphasizes a systematic evaluation of the effectiveness of these applications. Behavior therapy involves environmental change and social interaction rather than the direct alteration of bodily processes by biological procedures. The aim is primarily educational. The techniques facilitate improved self-control. In the conduct of behavior therapy, a contractual agreement is usually negotiated, in which mutually agreeable goals and procedures are specified. Responsible practitioners using behavioral approaches are guided by generally accepted ethical principles. (Franks & Wilson, 1975, p 1).

Such a definition offers the obvious advantage of breadth, the capacity to contain with ease many diverse positions, different strategies, and seemingly disparate techniques. Certainly, the advances in behavior therapy over the past two decades are remarkable. And yet the very pace of these advances, coupled with the vastness of the canvas under which behavior therapy shelters, could contain within it the seeds of its own destruction. Well may one ask: Will the coming years see behavior therapy fragmented into numerous self-contained fields? Or will some common underlying behavioral theme be found to encompass them all? The many facets of the above definition may not conform to a common behavioral theme or principle, but they are certainly all-inclusive. Little is excluded: provided that a finding is data-based and consistent with the dictates of behavioral science as we know it today, someone, somewhere, is likely to call it behavior therapy. Behavior therapy and applied behavioral science are becoming synonymous, and it is in this sense that certain present trends in behavior therapy may contain within them the seeds of their own destruction. Some would even go so far as to declare that this is not necessarily a bad thing. We are, after all, committed to the advancement of knowledge and to therapeutic benefit, rather than to any label or party line.

The second potential hazard is, to our way of thinking, much more serious and perhaps more likely to occur. The rapid advance of behavior therapy has led to a remarkable increase in technological know-how in a short time and to a proliferation of powerful techniques embracing an expanding spectrum of medical, psychological, educational, and sociological areas. Regrettably, much of this has been accomplished at the expense of time and inclination to reflect about what is going on, a disregard for replication and the consolidation of knowledge, and a failure to develop theoretical models capable of yielding testable predictions. The gap between theoretical development and application is widening. Behavior therapy began as a concerted attempt to generate theoretically and empirically sound alternatives to clinical folklore as a basis for therapeutic intervention. It is the potential for the abandonment of this foundation that we see as the greatest threat to behavior therapy in this coming decade.

What, then, lies in store for behavior therapy in the eighties? As far as we can ascertain, there is no immediately visible new area on the horizon demanding exploration, nor is any major conceptual revolution in sight. If we are fortunate, and in direct contrast to views expressed by London (1972), there will be a movement away from techniques as ends in themselves, toward theoretical consolidation and the values that started us off in the first place. If this does not occur, in our opinion the outlook for behavior therapy is bleak.

A number of recurrent issues and themes run through the present volume. Founding fathers of behavior therapy, such as Eysenck and Wolpe, still subscribe to a basic, if now more elegantly formulated, conditioning model. Eysenck presents a sophisticated new theory based on a bolstered-up version of classical conditioning in an ambitious, if not entirely successful, attempt to explain the development of neurotic behavior. Second generation behavior therapists are more inclined either to reject classical conditioning as sufficient in itself to account for the facts (such as modeling data) or to build systems based on other than S-R learning theories, Marks, for instance, questions the validity of classical conditioning in explaining neurotic symptoms and goes so far as to explain away the belief that behavior therapy is based on experimental psychology as a superstition "derived from the understandable struggles of clinical psychologists for identity and status."

Some clinicians who claim an affinity with behavior therapy look to experimental social psychology for their theoretical models. Kruglanski and Jaffe's chapter is an example of the direction in which extrapolation from cognitive social psychology *could* lead. It is clearly a far cry from behavior therapy as we know it or even from "cognitive" behavior therapy. The authors themselves note that "while the cognitive behavioral framework includes innovative concepts and . . . promising treatment methods, it still lacks the foundation of an integrative, coherent theory of general process of cognitive change." Craighead et al.'s knowledgeable discussion of issues in cognitive behavior therapy with children is more in accord with our hopes for the future. Also of relevance in this respect, Evans and Wilson advocate the use of data-based decision-making models in evaluating assessment procedures in behavior therapy. We are likely to hear more of such attempts in the coming decade. In a related vein, we further predict an increasing liaison between operationally formulated behaviorally sympathetic systems theory—not the largely antibehavioral version of an earlier era—and behavior therapy.

Both constitutional factors and individual differences were deliberately ignored by most early behavior therapists (Eysenck was and is a notable exception) and, more often than not, treatments were applied uniformly to all clients with similar behavioral disorders. At last, the former trend shows signs of reversal, and there is also a distinct increase in awareness of the need to match treatment and patient characteristics. This is a recurrent theme in many of the chapters in this book. For example, Dawson, Nuechterlein, and Liberman suggest that "attentional and information processing deficits and autonomic hyperresponsivity to stressors may be enduring trait-like characteristics of at least some individuals vulnerable to future schizophrenia." Our ability to detect these characteristics at an early stage may have important implications both for prevention and for treatment. Craig also draws attention to large individual differences in response to pain, and both Eysenck and Marks note that individuals differ in their vulnerability to the development of neurotic behavior patterns.

Rosenbaum introduces the concept of "learned resourcefulness" that describes the enduring repertoire of behaviors and skills by which a person self-regulates internal events—emotions, certain pains, and cognitions—interfering with the smooth execution of behavior. This type of behavioral repertoire may well determine in part whether an individual will develop severe anxiety or depression and how well he or she will respond to treatment. Although concepts such as "trait" and "personality" are still not well accepted among behavior therapists, we expect that in the 1980s greater effort will be invested in delineating the enduring behavioral characteristics of individuals. Once it is more generally acknowledged that individuals differ in this fashion, behaviorally compatible models of "personality" are likely to be developed.

Although only Poser deals directly with the issue of prevention, this subject is referred to in a number of chapters. Marks proposes the teaching of coping skills to children in order to prevent future development of phobic and obsessive-compulsive behaviors. Lewinsohn, Teri, and Hoberman advocate a psychoeducational approach to prevent severe depressions. Dawson, Nuechterlein, and Liberman list various treatment strategies to prevent psychotic episodes in schizophrenic patients who are at high risk for relapse.

In the newly developing area of behavioral medicine, the issue of prevention plays a significant role. Melamed's chapter focuses on preparing children for dental procedures in order to prevent an exaggerated emotional response to these procedures. Craig and Weisenberg both deal specifically with factors that determine how individuals control acute and chronic pains. Their work suggests many ways in which individuals may be trained to cope more effectively with pain. As Poser implies, program goals for the 1980s should include both the prevention of behavioral problems and the enhancement of physical and psychological well-being. As part of this program, it is clearly important to develop strategies for the early detection, optimizing, and maintaining of coping and related skills. Behavior therapy in the 1980s may, indeed, shift its focus in this direction—toward the teaching of individuals to be more resourceful and better able to cope with severe life events.

To evaluate the effectiveness of various prevention and health-promoting programs, there is a need for longitudinal studies over larger spans of time. Such studies are not very popular, perhaps because of the "publish or perish" atmosphere that prevails in many institutions. However, it seems to us that researchers in behavior therapy will have to engage in carefully conceived and executed longitudinal studies if they are to be seriously concerned with the design of preventive programs. We suspect that primary prevention might be more effective and more rewarding than the many short-term treatment outcome studies reported in the literature.

In sharp contrast to the 1960s, behavior therapists of the 1980s seem more aware of the limited effectiveness of their methods and of possible dangers in the inappropriate use of certain procedures. Marks suggests that behavioral methods may be effective only for certain well-specified problems and not for others. Ellis points out that some behavioral techniques may achieve good results in the short run but, by bolstering irrational beliefs, be deleterious over the long haul. Changing behavior without changing the individual's basic belief system may be inefficient and even harmful. Thus, the client might be led to such beliefs as "I can control my anxiety" rather than "I do not have to make myself anxious by insisting that I *must* do well and *have to* be approved by others." We await with interest the experimental investigations of Ellis' challenging belief system pertaining to these matters.

Both Leon and Fodor, dealing with two different eating disorders, emphasize the need to select appropriate treatment goals. In the past, behavior therapists tended to focus on the disorder itself (such as increasing or decreasing food intake) rather than the client's body-image and self-esteem. As Leon suggests, to increase the efficacy of the total program, the treatment of anorexia nervosa should also focus on changing the client's body-image. Perhaps a better therapeutic goal in the treatment of moderately overweight women who have failed in the past to reduce their weight might be to help them live comfortably with the sizes of their bodies rather than to be concerned about weight reduction per se. Since the probability of success in reducing weight permanently is low, therapists should focus on self-acceptance rather than changing eating habits or weight control.

From two different vantage points, Willems and Winkler stress the fact that changes in target behaviors may have desired and undesired effects on nontargeted behaviors and, in some instances, on the whole social network of the individual. Winkler suggests the use of principles derived from economics in order to study these interdependencies, whereas Willems approaches these issues from an ecobehavioral point of view.

Behavior therapy, with its focus on the present, tends to ignore developmental issues. Behavioral problems and their treatment are hardly ever related to the developmental state of the individual. Lewinsohn, Teri, and Hoberman raise a new perspective by discussing the development and occurrence of depression at three different stages of development: childhood, adolescence, and old age. The nature and treatment of depression at these stages are different. Is the treatment of other behavioral disorders different at different developmental stages?

When all is said and done—or said and not done, for that matter—and despite the many complexities, seemingly incompatible positions and potentially hazardous developments in the offing, behavior therapy is in a stronger position now than 20 years ago. If the gap between theory and application is now large, this is because 20 years ago theory was rudimentary and application limited. While laying no claim to comprehensiveness—the Congress itself was not comprehensive—we have tried to reflect these developments in our choices of author and topic areas to represent the status of contemporary behavior therapy. If the melange of voices resounds with friendly discord, this is no accident. It is our hope that, despite limitations and omissions, for which we and we alone take full responsibility, the present volume both reflects the current status of behavior therapy and offers a perspective for the future.

REFERENCES

Erwin, E. *Behavior therapy: Scientific, philosophical and moral foundations.* Cambridge, MA: Cambridge University Press, 1978.

Franks, C. M. *Behavior therapy, appraisal and status.* New York: McGraw Hill, 1969.

Franks, C. M. & Barbrack, C. R. Behavior therapy with adults: An integrative perspective. In M. Hersen, A. E. Kazdin, & A. S. Bellack (Eds.). *The Clinical Psychology Handbook.* New York: Pergamon Press (in press).

Franks, C. M. On behaviourism and behaviour therapy—not necessarily synomymous and becoming less so. *Australian Behaviour Therapist*, 1980, 7, 14-23.

Franks, C. M. 2001: Will we be many or one—or none? *Behavioural Psychotherapy*, 1981, *9*, 287–290.

Franks, C. M., & Wilson, G. T. *Annual review of behavior therapy: Theory and practice*, Volumes I–VII. New York: Brunner/Mazel, 1973–1979.

Kazdin, A. E. *History of behavior modification: Experimental foundations of contemporary research.* Baltimore, MD: University Park Press, 1978.

Lazarus, A. A. *The practice of multimodal therapy*. New York: McGraw-Hill, 1981.

London, P. The end of ideology in behavior modification. *American Psychologist*, 1972, *27*, 913–920.

Staats, A. W., & Staats, C. K. *Complex human behavior: A systematic extension of learning principles.* New York: Holt, Rinehart & Winston, 1963.

Wilson, G. T. The importance of being theoretical: Comments on Bandura's "self-efficacy: Toward a unifying theory of behavior change. *Advances in Behaviour Research and Therapy*, 1978, *1*, 217–230.

Wilson, G. T., & Franks, C. M. Introduction. In G. T. Wilson, & C. M. Franks (Eds.). *Contemporary behavior therapy: Conceptual foundations of clinical practice.* New York: Guilford Press, 1982.

PART II

A Divergent Perspective on the Nature and Practice of Behavior Therapy

CHAPTER 2

Science, Culture, and Psychotherapy: The State of the Art

Perry London, Ph.D.

The state of an art means two things: First, it means the level of skills involved in the current exercise of a craft, and, second, it means what is going on between the artisans, their patrons, their teachers, their students, their clients, and their customers. This essay aims to examine the current technical state of the psychotherapeutic arts and their role in contemporary Western culture.

Psychotherapy is an art (arts, really) because it is the exercise of skilled craft on some of the problems that make people nervous, unhappy, and badly behaved. The state of the psychotherapeutic arts is such that behavior modification is becoming, in some respects, a dominant specialty within them. This, in turn, is happening because behavior modification has established its credibility in ways that give it high marketability, even when economic conditions are unfavorable. It has done so, in part, by hooking up with learning theory, perhaps the best-studied topic in all of scientific psychology, but even more by making empirical measurements of treatment itself.

Psychotherapy is the same kind of art as clinical medicine or surgery. When people say it ought to be a science instead of an art, I think they mean it ought to be more a "scientific" than a "fine" art. I think there are at least two big differences between them. One is that fine art cherishes more personal skills, while scientific art aims to be more depersonalized, more automated. Another is that science largely depends on the *cumulability* of the information it collects, whereas fine art depends on other things. When we talk about scientific precision, we are implying maximum cumulability of information. The more measurement precision possible in a science, the more dependably information accumulates, and the faster grows the information pile or data base (to use the jargon) of the science.

Psychotherapy is an art, not a science, but it is a technical or scientifically based art. The technical goal of most clinical work in psychotherapy is *specificity*, here meaning the relatively precise application of specific treatments to specific conditions. One should be able to index technical progress in psychotherapy by counting new techniques and new problem catalogues. For a long time, these have been hard to come by in psychotherapy.

In that framework, it is easy to see why, since the late 1960s, more and more of the "action" in psychotherapy journals is in behavior modification and why psychoanalysis now occupies a somewhat smaller segment, relatively. The first time I made such a survey, late in 1975, Ray London (1977) then a graduate student (you can bet it was not me), examined all issues of 75 different journals published between 1973 and 1975. Psychoanalysis, he concluded, was in much the same state it had been a generation earlier with respect to who was being treated and how. M. Royden C. Astley (1974), in the presidential address to the American Psychoanalytic Association in 1970, described training in psychoanalysis, criticism of psychoanalysis, and the applications of psychoanalysis in practically the same terms as Freud had done 30 years earlier, and with no arguments for changing anything in training or in practice.

This is less true of *psychoanalytic therapy*, which psychoanalysts distinguish carefully from psychoanalysis itself. Attempts were made to relate psychoanalytic methods more-or-less differentially to different diagnostic entities, a kind of specification much needed throughout the psychotherapy business. For example, Klerman et al. (1979) developed the *Interpersonal Therapy* (IPT), which is a standardized dynamic therapy used chiefly for depression. Another example is the *Time-Limited Psychotherapy* of James Mann (1973), which treats disturbed behavior connected with feelings of abandonment, loss, and rejection in a systematic twelve-session psychodynamic regimen.

The development of therapeutic novelty is far more typical, however, of behavioral therapists than of psychodynamic ones. New techniques and applications of behavior therapy are being reported all the time. The growing catalogue of treatment methods makes the skill training involved in behavior modification different in 1980 from the way it was in 1970. There is simply more to learn. Token economy, shaping, modeling, overt and covert sensitization and desensitization, aversive control in the form of punishment and in the form of the removal of positive reinforcement, sex therapy and assertiveness training, self-instruction, mental rehearsal, stress inoculation training, and cognitive restructuring, each involves a different technology for different conditions.

The proliferation of topics is also reflected in the rate of increase in books, journals, and articles on behavior therapy during the

1970s. Its literature is becoming larger and growing faster than that of any other kind of psychological treatment. It is now a gold mine of doctoral dissertations (cynics would say a cesspool), where a generation ago many academic mentors discouraged psychotherapy dissertations of any kind as too difficult to be practical. The difference comes from the relatively tidy experimental character of so much of behavior therapy, which makes it easier to design rigorous dissertations.

In 1951, according to O'Leary and Wilson (1975), only four articles were published on what we would now call behavior therapy, distributed among two major psychology and two major psychiatry journals. In 1970, those same four journals carried 70 articles on behavior therapy. In the first *Annual Review of Psychology* chapter on this topic, Leonard Krasner (1971) references almost 400 of what he says were by then 4,000 articles on behavior therapy. Between 1973 and 1974, at least six journals entirely devoted to behavior therapy began publication. David Barlow, moreover, counted two behavior therapy journals in 1969 and 21 in 1979, not including journals on biofeedback or programmed instruction, which many scholars nowadays would consider parts of behavior therapy (Barlow, 1979).

In a final burst of obsessional vicarious journal counting, I persuaded my wife, Beverly London, to examine carefully the entire list of 1,011 journal titles that the National Institute of Mental Health routinely reviews for its computer abstracting system and to classify the psychotherapy journals. Before she stopped speaking to me, she reported that, by title alone, the list contained 23 psychoanalytic journals (including all varieties of psychoanalysis) and 26 behavior therapy journals (including biofeedback). A lot more behavior journal literature is spread across 35 other psychotherapy journals that are either general in their coverage or completely specialized (by such topics as hypnosis, family therapy, and so forth), the 101 psychiatry journals, and the many journals of clinical psychology, social work, abnormal psychology, and so forth, which she did not classify as psychotherapy journals.

This tally does not, of course, include anything but the professional and scientific literature—no popular articles or magazines or self-help books. David Barlow (1979) claims that the current popularity of behavior therapy is causing a lot of self-help books to advertise that they are behavioral when they really are not.

Those of you who sat through the long "winter of our discontent" in the 1960s waiting for behavior therapy to be socially acceptable cannot help but be pleased by this. Before you become too pleased, however, remember that general popularity is not always a good indicator of credibility or value. Publications in astrology are still far more numerous than those in behavior therapy.

SCIENCE, ART, AND ORTHODOXY

In fact, academic acceptance of behavior therapy was quite fast, dating from, let us say, Wolpe's 1958 volume. Most therapies, and psychoanalysis in particular, had to wait a great deal longer and, in fact, had tougher sledding on the way. The reason for this speed, I think, has something to do with the relationship of science and art to orthodoxy.

Rudolph Ekstein (cited in R. London, 1977) argues that psychotherapies go through social evolutionary or developmental stages somewhat like those of individuals. Psychoanalysis, he said, had gone through its growth stages and was mature (in 1974). The behaviorists were going through them at that time (in 1974), and Ekstein felt it was inevitable that they would reach a point where they, too, bogged down in their own orthodoxy.

Actually, behavior therapy had already had its share of orthodoxies by 1974, not too unlike psychoanalysis. Some of these are embodied in the demand for personal loyalty to professional institutions. I am told, for instance, that in the early days of the Association for the Advancement of Behavior Therapy, prospective members were required to sign a statement that they believed in the efficacy of learning. Even now, I have noticed some otherwise fine behavior therapy essays referring to it as "our science" in what sounds like Freud's famous dismissal of psychoanalysis' antagonists with the remark that psychoanalysts had their own science.

On the whole, behavior therapists have not done this very much. If they had gone in much for professional orthodoxies, it would have prevented their becoming part of the academic establishment and inhibited acceptance of their work. What spread them, I believe, was the lucky accident of their method of working, which saved them from the curse of being too tied to theory.

A science is defined more by its method than by its subject matter. In my opinion, the scientific difference between psychoanalysis and behavior therapy, in this connection, is that behavior therapy is identified mainly by its methodology, while psychoanalysis rests more on its underlying content assumptions. Behavioral methodology has nothing to do with learning or conditioning as such but, I think, with a single principle: *What you can do to alter behavior systematically depends upon how good a functional analysis you are able to make of it.*

There are orthodoxies among scientists, too, of course, but that is a quality of *people* involved, as is true in fine art, not of the material being dealt with, as in orthodox religion. There are fads aplenty in science, and fads may be transitory orthodoxies. But the scientific method, by its nature, promotes a kind of activity that makes it hard for people engaged in science to cling to their scientific orthodoxies. The operational deities of science *require* change, if anything, rather than prevent it—because the fundamental ritual of science is accumulating information.

Scientific method also tends to separate scientific art from fine art by deliberately dissociating progress from the personality and practice of the discoverers and inventors. Here I borrow from Bertrand Russell's *Physics and Experience* (1946) to make the same point: It is in the character of scientific work that you do not have to be very smart to do it, you just have to be careful. That means that it is possible for a great many more people to get into it. And it is possible for me to add to the body of knowledge that you have built, even though I may not be very smart and you may be a genius, by the method of science, which criticizes itself both empirically and logically and builds on itself cumulatively. The failure to encourage, or even to permit, deviance in technique or theory was, for a long time, one of the most legitimate scientific criticisms against psychoanalysis, and one that certainly delayed its general acceptance.

A fine art form, on the other hand, like a religious or social movement, may get enduring social impetus from the power of *people* who create or promote it rather than from the material itself. It is the work of art of those people. (That may account largely for the decline in the human potential movement—its gurus are dead.) A scientific modality, however, gets its durability as a result of being replicable and public and common, that is, *vulgar.* The literal *vulgarity* of science fuels it. The *artistry* of religion, or art, on the other hand, is largely the power of the art form to inspire.

In the case of psychotherapy, the practical demands of the market place also served to inhibit orthodoxies and speed up the development of novelties because they forced therapists to work on problems they were unprepared to deal with from their theories. Since behavior therapists were already schooled in the pragmatic, that is, in functional analysis of behavior problems, these pressures further discouraged preoccupation with learning theory and allowed them to be more interested than they otherwise might have been in the useful possibilities in old-fashioned and offbeat treatments. It diluted the behavioristic brew of learning theory ideas a lot, with more-and-more people using the functional concepts, terms, and methods of Gestalt therapy, rational-emotive therapy, and insight therapy, with specificity, with scientific vulgarity, and without so much as batting an operant in apology.

In doing so, some behaviorists recognized how much it is a mistake to dismiss other psychotherapies out of hand. Even psychoanalysis, with its apparent technical narrowness, has more variety in the hands of real practitioners than one might think. And Gestalt therapy and its offshoots within the human potential movement have produced ingenious techniques that are useful to a variety of problems. The old insight therapies have much to say about teaching people to do the things that are necessary to produce the changes that behavior therapists want—the social skills of being nice to people, of fostering relationships that elicit trust, of wanting to do the homework assignments of the modifying therapeutic regimen, of overcoming or undermining resistances, here meaning the anxieties or conflicting motives that prevent adherence to therapeutic regimens or prevent people even from understanding what those regimens are.

Functional specificity is not a matter of polemics, or politics, or labels, or intellectual party lines, but of relating antecedents to consequences in ways that best solve problems. Calling something "behavior modification" does not meet the standards of that specificity, any more than labeling it "relationship therapy" fails to do so.

Intellectual purists who dislike behavior therapy but agree with my analysis might say that it demonstrates the lack of scientific and intellectual rigor of behavior therapy, since I am saying, in effect, that its operations are really more eclectic than they may claim to be. People who like behavior therapy and agree with my analysis might say that any more intellectual rigor would cause *rigor mortis* for the practical usefulness of behavior therapy. Some might even say that that is what happened to psychoanalysis.

At all events, it is plain that what is called behavior therapy by 1980 included a lot of things that could not have been included in 1960, that cannot completely fit the mold of learning theory, that make behavior therapy look much more like eclectic therapy than it used to, and that still depend on functional analysis. For better or for worse.

THE TECHNICAL STATE OF BEHAVIOR THERAPY NOW

Despite its intellectual struggles with psychoanalysis and insight therapy, behavior therapy today is continuous with them as a scientific art. From today's perspective, it represents theoretical and practical refinements of insight therapy but not an intellectual revolution against it.

The continuity is evident in three ways: (a) the main enterprise remains talking, now more than ever; (b) the results of most outcome studies tend to be the same for most problems through both types of treatment; (c) the latest "fad" in behavior therapy, cognitive behavior therapy, is frankly and openly interested in the thought processes in people's heads as well as in their overt behavior and their emotional states (see, for instance, any issue of *Cognitive Therapy and Research*, NY: Plenum Press).

An underlying intellectual continuity across these treatments is the commitment to scientific method, which has been credible enough to make all of them mainstream members of the intellectual and social Establishment.

The demand for intellectual rigor according to the conventions of experimental science was a constant theme and great contribution of behavior therapists. Once those standards had been accepted, however, it was not so necessary for them to be hugely successful therapeutically in order to be acceptable, but only to be systematically sensible and not to seem too deviant in their treatment methods. It is for the same reasons that psychoanalytic projects get funded today.

Scientific method has imposed itself on psychotherapy largely, but not entirely, through the behavior therapists. Scientific theory of psychotherapy started with Freud's attempt to translate entropy theory and homeostatic theory into an explanation of mental life. The splendid studies of the Yale group in the 1930s and 1940s were intended to test *psychoanalytic* theory, not conditioning theory. The 1941 Knight outcome study tried to validate psychoanalytic methods; the process studies of insight therapies after World War II were aimed at the scientific understanding of the therapies already in wide use (P. London, 1964).

Even so, behavior therapy might have been better off intellectually from the beginning by starting from the premises and data base of a laboratory science instead of working backwards from clinical methods to attempt a scientific understanding of them.

It also came at a time when *operationalism* was widely talked about in the philosophy of science—so that *functional analysis*, its key concept, could blossom, virtually from the beginning, as a clinical tool for diagnosis and treatment.

But scientific method, religiously pursued, eventually laid bare a systemic weakness of behavior therapy, namely, that the theoretical structure was not able to carry gracefully all the practical approaches that functional analysis was developing for clinical problems. The treatments were often better than the explanations given for them. The general explanatory principles of S-R learning theory were useful as far as they went, but they did not go very far in some important ways. The principles of classical conditioning, the law of effect, successive approximation, observational learning, and the whole bundle of behavior theory concepts then extant, valuable as they were, could not satisfy the need of many therapists to explain to themselves how they managed to work mostly by talking and listening, which is what they did. Eventually, they rationalized what is now called cognitive behavior therapy in terms of elegant information processing and computer models. Sophisticated psychoanalysts had done that very thing 20 years before, and for the same reason (see Blum, 1961). So it goes with rationalizing.

The merits of either side in the theoretical debate about the value of cognitive concepts in behavior therapy is beside the point of this essay. The point is that the scientific character of behavior therapy is in the scientifically artful application of techniques, not in the adequacy of its theory. From that point of view, nothing is lost conceptually by the use of cognitive principles, and something is gained.

It legitimizes *necessary* procedures (what therapist can function without talking, and why should one have to disregard its irrelevance to strict S-R theory?), it permits inventiveness; it incorporates verbal methods such as rational-emotive therapy into behavior therapy; and it allows intelligent discourse about what is going on inside the "black box." It does not sacrifice functional analysis at all, but simply allows it to cover more ground, that is, to be more comprehensive. Stated mischievously, it cleans up insight therapy by making it functionally analytic!

This argument implies that cognitive behavior therapy is not only continuous with the scientific and technical tradition of insight and behavior therapy, but that, by its tendency to integrate them, it improves upon them in some important way. It does not address the fact, of course, that cognitive behavior therapy did not arise as a treatment of the conditions to which either insight or behavior therapy were most widely applied nor over which they were most disputed, such as phobias and anxiety states. Cognitive behavior therapy was developed, if not originated, as a treatment for *depression*, as the latter condition has apparently become more-and-more epidemic in modern society. This raises some serious questions that cannot be dealt with here, such as the relationship between therapeutic novelty and therapeutic progress. What is most important, for our present purpose, however, is that cognitive behavior therapy represents a domain of harmonious discourse, so to speak, between insight and behavioral orientations, making it abundantly clear that both of them are on the same side of the intellectual fence when considered from the vantage of what Barry Wolfe (1977) has labeled "the cultural context of psychotherapy." To examine this, we must now pass from the technical to the social or cultural state of the art.

THE CULTURAL STATE OF BEHAVIOR THERAPY

Behavior therapy is now established. That means that it is part of the academic, scientific, medical bureaucratic establishment, which approves, recommends, teaches, researches, and funds the public enterprises of the society.

"Establishment" is not meant here as a metaphor. In the United States, it refers to a budget that has been as large as two billion dollars per annum in the Alcohol, Drug Abuse and Mental Health Administration alone, not counting the rest of the Federal government, the States, the municipalities, the private organizations, the insurance companies, and everyone else involved with psychotherapy.

Membership in the establishment means status and prestige

among the institutional pillars of society. It also means direst access to institutional funds. In the mental health business, this has meant increasing research and training funds since 1945, but now it has been expanded in the United States to include insurance that reimburses therapists for providing service to patients (Parloff, 1980).

The scientific establishment is part of the political, social, and economic establishment. Behavior therapy, despite some early trouble and bad press, has become part of the scientific establishment. This was due, in part, to the behavior therapists' claim to scientific rigor. But it was also due to the fact that the claim could be used to support activities that themselves support the conventional social enterprise, without alarming it.

In fact, the early social consciousness and utopean tendencies of behavior therapy, extending it beyond the clinic and consulting room into the broader domains of the classroom, the prison, and potentially the reconstruction of society, à la Skinner and the radical behaviorists of the late 1960s, did it far more harm than good. Retreating from those positions did more for the establishment's good will than undertaking them ever could have. Psychoanalysis did not have this trouble because it was never connected with social reform.

Psychoanalysis has also been part of the establishment since the end of World War II. The humanistic psychotherapy movement, by-and-large, is not. This supposed third force—as Abraham Maslow saw it—against both psychoanalysis and behaviorism, is at once a non-establishment therapy system and, not coincidentally, one in which the therapeutic product, by virtue of its antimechanistic bias, is almost intentionally a piece of inspirational art (Wertheimer, 1978).

I believe that until the mid-1970s there were three clear trends within psychotherapy (see P. London, 1974). The first was psychoanalysis, which tried to treat the modal neurosis of what I think could be called the Age of Repression. It dominated psychotherapy until after World War II. Then behavior modification and crisis intervention became popular, both aimed at treating the ills of a push-button technological era that has been called, appropriately, the Age of Anxiety. And the third trend in psychotherapy was represented by encounter or, as it is now called, the growth or human potential movement. I have catalogued its many variants as "therapeutic games," not in contempt, but because they were not aimed at symptom relief and therefore did not signify disorder as much as recreation in the broadest sense. They are a therapeutic modality aimed at reducing the discomfort of what has become, I think, an age of malaise and of existential preoccupation, where the predominant neuroses are boredom, loneliness, and depression.

These three modes of treatment borrowed from each other, but mostly they competed with each other, leading what Morris Parloff called a "dogma-eat-dogma" existence (as quoted in Marshall, 1980).

The nature of the competition was not entirely technical—that is, it did not revolve only around the question of which therapy "worked better" but also around the question of what "working" meant. The issue was confused, moreover, by the fact that there were more sides than one could easily count. Wolfe (1977) believes, in fact, that the reason there are now so many different named schools of psychotherapy (there were 130 at his count) is because ". . . the social confusion regarding values . . . is found in the definitional confusion of what constitutes psychotherapy" (p. 10).

To illustrate: the competition between behavior therapy and classical psychoanalysis was originally entirely technical, which is why the lines of battle could be drawn neatly around things like the interpretation and reinterpretation of Freud's case of Little Hans, or, more generally, around the meaning of symptoms (P. London, 1972). Both of them, however, were united in technical opposition to humanistic psychology, which opposed both of them in turn for ideological, not technical reasons. Existential *psychoanalysis*, despite the surname, was allied with humanistic psychology in ideological opposition to both classical psychoanalysis and behavior therapy. The human potential movement opposed behavior therapy because, as Wolfe (1977) put it, behavior therapy

> served as . . . cultural defender of the faith in the experimental method of science and the technological approach to the solution of human problems. . . . By contrast, many of the humanistic psychotherapies extolled the virtues of spontaneity, of the experiential, and the personal, and saw solutions to human problems deriving from an awareness of and a freedom in experiencing one's feelings. . . . (pp. 10-11)

But behavior therapists never extended humanists the same courtesy of ideological opposition. On the contrary, their opposition was chiefly technical. They argued that humanistic psychotherapies did not "work," that is, they did not relieve the symptoms for which people sought help, because their lack of functional analysis and systematic approach made the pursuit of spontaneity, freedom, and the experience of feelings an exercise in futility.

In fact, the dispute is not only about what Wolfe calls "the relative merits of technique and spontaneity in therapeutic practice." It is a reflection also, in his view, of "the technologism/personalism dispute." There are other terms that can be used for it as well, like Apollonian/Dionysian. Borrowing from Gordon Allport and Edward Sampson (1978) on the one hand, and from Nathan Adler (1972) on the other, I would call this the *nomothetic/antinomian* dispute. It is primarily a dispute about religious and social values, but it has important implications for scientific psychology and for the practice of psychotherapy.

The *nomothetic* view of things is what most of us mean by "scientific." It means "lawful." In science, it implies that there are universal truths, scientific laws, and, with respect to human behavior, general principles that govern it. The nomothetic view of reality supports a normative approach to society, that is, one that emphasizes the common condition of humanity and one that is commonly associated with supporters of existing social institutions. This has always been the dominant viewpoint underlying modern science and, therefore, is the characteristic view of scientific psychotherapists.

The *antinomian* view of the world is eccentric and highly personal. It emphasizes the uniqueness of experience, values spontaneity above self-control and feeling above reason, and, in its approach to "social and political values," according to Nathan Adler (1972), "repudiates established ways . . ." and stands ". . . against the lawful or legitimate institutions of the particular society" (p. xix). After studying the hippies, drug cultures, and other countercultures of the late 1960s and comparing them to the aims and practices of the human potential movement, Adler named the latter "antinomian therapies."

Scientifically oriented psychotherapists, as members of the establishment, are particularly vulnerable to the interests of the political sectors of the establishment, because both their money and their sanctions for practice come from there. This explains the happy response of many behavior therapists to the efforts of the United States Federal Government, in preparing National Health Insurance legislation (a process temporarily suspended by the Reagan administration) and in anticipating the huge costs of mental health insurance, to require good evidence that psychotherapy works. Presumably, such evidence is to be produced by *outcome research.*

It is understandable that this effort should please behavior therapists. When Hans Eysenck first challenged the field, in 1952, with the claim that there was no evidence that psychotherapy worked, nobody ran for evidence. They responsed with contempt. When Rubinstein and Parloff (1962) edited the proceedings of a 1958 conference entitled "Research in Psychotherapy," they noted that people hardly mentioned outcome research at that conference. Indeed, outcome studies have long been the stepchild of other therapies, but they have been the touchstone for the claims of behavior therapists, far more than theory has. Behavior therapy "works," said behavior therapists, and its working is the decisive piece of evidence that outweighs all other arguments, pro or con, from scientific theory. It also works fast, they said, adding the power of economics or, in current bureaucratic jargon, of "cost effectiveness," to that of efficacy.

David Barlow, in his 1979 presidential address to the American Association for Advancement of Behavior Therapy, is delighted at the possibilities for outcome research. He believes, first of all, that more and better outcome research will "close the scientist/practitioner gap" and "multiply the data base on which our true advances are made by a factor far greater than we have thought possible." He also believes that, ". . . if there is one crystal clear trend in the next decade, it is accountability; which will be achieved by demonstrating unambiguously . . . that what we do is effective" (p. 16).

I respectfully disagree. We will never completely close the scientist/practitioner gap (though I trust we will narrow it), because the efficacy question can be answered empirically for some things that psychotherapy is used for, but not for others. More important, the *empirical* question, "Does psychotherapy do any good?" cannot be asked very sharply without thinking about the *ideological* question, "Good for what?" For a political establishment that is footing the bill, effective psychotherapy might be that which successfully promotes socially desired behavior, so treatments that reduce absenteeism from work and excessive use of medical facilities (whatever the means—see Parloff, 1980, p. 285) would be considered splendid. One could imagine, on the other hand, that therapies that encouraged people to strive less, achieve less, or drop out of the social system to follow their conscience to God, income tax evasion, or polymorphous perversion would not get the same happy patronage.

In fact, I am not too concerned about what American health insurance will cover psychotherapy for, nor even about the fact that only mainstream nomothetic therapies are likely to qualify for establishment support under outcome research rules. There are plenty of human miseries for which nomothetic psychotherapy should be provided, from any compassionate point of view, and outcome research demonstrating its value should certainly be supported.

What does concern me, in trying to understand the true state of today's psychotherapeutic arts, can be phrased in two questions:

First, to what extent do my nomothetic colleagues allow themselves to realize that, as psychotherapists, they are up to their ears in idiosyncratic, uninsurable nonefficacy, and maybe antinomian human problems?

And, second, to what extent might we be creative participants in history by listening to or dismissing such problems?

Almost everyone recognizes that the problems people bring to psychotherapy today include many that are not pathological or disordered by any professional convention. Many of them are problems of indecision and conflict about people's *wishes*, their *values*, and their *guesses* about what the future will be like. They arise because people are complicated, not because they are disordered, and because life is hard and painful. Needing somebody to just listen, drinking from the well of loneliness, struggling with the suitability of life styles are not symptomatic questions. Should I change wives, careers, friends, sex practices, gender, schools, consorts? These are consulting-room questions, but they are not medical, not disorders, and not, by current convention, insurable.

People who can ask one question, can ask all: "Cure my phobia, fix my premature ejaculation, and tell me whether adultery is really a sin or not."

One simple reason people bring psychotherapists such troubles is that they are already talking to them about their other troubles, and, finding them intelligent and helpful with one problem, it is plain good sense to ask for help with another. The reason therapists listen to them, behavior therapists included, is largely the same—having undertaken to help people with one problem and having been somewhat successful, it is plain good sense to try to help them with something else psychological, even if the therapist has no special technology for helping.

Besides, who else are they going to talk to? In the past, maybe they would have relied more on family, or physician, or priest, rabbi, or minister for guidance. But modern societies are more mobile than they used to be, and more anonymous, and more secular.

Indeed, some people probably ask psychotherapists such questions precisely because they value the *lack* of traditional parochial, moral, or religious commitments, which, they fear, would prejudice the counsel or earn the contempt of others. This is not a religious age, and psychotherapists are easily seen as secular priests by people who see themselves as secular parishioners. It is an uncomfortable role, but perhaps there is no good way of avoiding it.

By the same token, there is no good rule for handling it. As far as I can tell, mainstream therapists, even the most nomothetic and conventional, listen to antinomian and existential concerns. Along comes a heterosexual wanting to become celibate, or homosexual, or to marry his sheep, or perform some other victimless act of nonconformity. What does Dr. Mainstream do? "Go for" social conformity or professional hypocrisy? Refuse to listen? Lie to the insurance company about what the problem was in order to get paid and lie to his colleagues in order to get published? The answer is not obvious. But it is obvious that many therapists render more comprehensive efforts to help than can appear in outcome studies, and that they use treatment methods that are less systematic than they appear to be in scientific papers.

Finally, a nod to history. To what extent is it likely that today's antinomian may feed tomorrow's conventional wisdom, and that some of whatever progress there may be in human civilization may come from such dissidents tearing at the fabric of society. I think the history of Western civilization is full of examples in which the tensions between established order and individual searching for fulfillment, in whatever form, gave rise to later syntheses that enriched the life of later times. The prophets of the First Jewish Commonwealth, 3,000 years ago, were such antinomian wrestlers with the kings and priests of Israel. Christianity might have been another transitory Jewish heresy without Paul's antinomian vision of grace. Hassidism was an antinomian response to Rabbinic restrictiveness and grinding poverty and foiled messianism; so were the Quakers; so, too, the Methodists.

Antinomian movements of the past have generally been frankly religious, as the societies from which they sprang have been religious societies. More important, they have been the products of troubled times and conditions in which people have been shaken loose from their traditional identities and could not find fulfilling new ones in the mainstream of society. Those conditions obtain today, perhaps more than ever before. I have no idea what the outcome of such turmoil may be, short of the end of civilization, but it is sensible to think that social movements, like religious ones, begin with individual dissidence, just as it seems true that creative acts of every kind are generally individual and often idiosyncratic.

I am not, in any case, advocating the "cultivation of idiosyncrasy," which is Adler's (1972) characterization of humanistic psychotherapy, but of cautious respect for it, of concern with it. The ambiguity of the human condition will not diminish, I think, no matter how much money goes into how many outcome studies. As long as it does not, the tension between nomethetic and antinomian dispositions will remain in people's individual lives as well as in society.

Modern psychotherapists have a privileged private view of such events, as few others can. They cannot measure it, I think, or cure it. But they can watch it and sometimes maybe soothe—unsystematically and unscientifically—some of the suffering that comes from it. The sanction for doing it might be called "artistic license."

SUMMARY

Behavior therapy has become increasingly important in psychotherapy, because it succeeds so well in meeting the canons of a "scientific art," namely the development of relatively measurable and specific treatment applications. This is reflected more in behavior therapy than, for instance, in psychoanalysis, in three ways: (1) A relatively greater burgeoning of clinical literature; (2) a relatively larger catalogue of new treatment techniques; and (3) a relatively greater freedom, after some false starts, from institutional orthodoxies of ideology and practice. Cognitive behavior therapy represents a kind of integration of technical aspects both of insight and behavior therapy, and makes clear that both of them are part of the contemporary Establishment of Nomothetic rather than Antinomian psychotherapies. The ultimate virtues of any psychotherapy, in any case, will not be established even by the best outcome research, because many of the most important problems dealt with in psychotherapy are not finally subject to formal evaluation.

REFERENCES

Adler, N. *The underground stream: New life styles and the antinomian personality.* New York: Harper & Row, 1972.

Astley, M. R. C. Psychoanalysis: The future. *Journal of the American Psychoanalytic Association*, 1974, *22*, 83-96.

Barlow, D. H. Behavior therapy: The next decade. Presidential address to the Association for Advancement of Behavior Therapy, San Francisco, CA, December 1979.

Blum, G. *A model of the mind.* New York: Wiley, 1961.

Eysenck, H. J. The effects of psychotherapy: An evaluation. *Journal of Consulting Psychology*, 1952, *16*, 319-324.

Klerman, G. L., Rounsaville, B., Chevron, E., Neu, C., & Weissman, M. *Manual for short-term interpersonal psychotherapy (IPT) of depression.* Unpublished manuscript, 1979. (New Haven: Collaborative Depression Project, Yale University Medical School).

Krasner, L. Behavior therapy. In P. H. Mussen & M. R. Rosenzweig (Eds.). *Annual review of psychology*, Volume 22. Palo Alto, CA: Annual Reviews, 1971.

London, P. *The modes and morals of psychotherapy.* New York: Holt, Rinehart & Winston, 1964.

London, P. The end of ideology in behavior modification. *American Psychologist*, 1972, *27*, 913-920.

London, P. The psychotherapy boom. *Psychology Today*, 1974, *8*, 62-68.

London, R. W. The lonely profession: A study of the psychological rewards and negative aspects of the practice of psychotherapy. (Doctoral dissertation, University of Southern California, 1976.) *Dissertation Abstracts International*, 1977, *37*, 4691B.

Mann, J. *Time-limited psychotherapy.* Cambridge, MA: Harvard University Press, 1973.

Marshall, E. Psychotherapy works, but for whom? *Science*, 1980, *207*, 506-508.

O'Leary, K. D., & Wilson, G. T. *Behavior therapy: Application and outcome.* Englewood Cliffs, NJ: Prentice-Hall, 1975.

Parloff, M. B. Psychotherapy and research: An anaclitic depression. *Psychiatry*, 1980, *43*, 279-293.

Rubinstein, E. A., & Parloff, M. B. (Eds.). *Research in psychotherapy: Proceedings of a conference, Washington, D.C., April 9-12, 1958.* Washington, DC: American Psychological Association, 1962.

Russell, B. *Physics and experience.* Cambridge, England: Cambridge University Press, 1946.

Sampson, E. E. Scientific paradigms and social values: Wanted—a scientific revolution. *Journal of Personality and Social Psychology*, 1978, *36*, 1332-1343.

Wertheimer, M. Humanistic psychology and the humane but tough-minded psychologist. *American Psychologist*, 1978, *33*, 739-745.
Wolfe, B. The cultural context of psychotherapy. Unpublished manuscript, 1977. (Available from the National Institute of Mental Health, Parklawn Building, 5600 Fishers Lane, Rockville, MD).
Wolpe, J. *Psychotherapy by reciprocal inhibition.* Palo Alto, CA: Stanford University Press, 1958.

PART III

Assessment and Self-Regulation

CHAPTER 3

Behavioral Assessment as Decision Making: A Theoretical Analysis

Ian M. Evans, Ph.D.
Frances E. Wilson, Ph.D.

INTRODUCTION

With two new journals and a number of major texts devoted exclusively to the topic, behavioral assessment is clearly flourishing. Much of the output can be categorized into two types: the liturgy of behavioral assessment, a rather loose collection of admonitions and current wisdoms, and the measurement of clinically relevant phenomena—emotional arousal, social skills, excess behaviors, self-statements, and so forth. Obtaining accurate measurement of our dependent variables is indeed important and is perhaps the definitive feature of behavior therapy, particularly when therapy outcome research is focused on the retrospective evaluation of some completed program- the traditional experimental model. Clinical practice, however, uses measures interactively, in that treatment decisions are adjusted by client feedback; clinical evaluation, in other words, is formative rather than summative. Empirical knowledge is seldom organized into an informational framework to help the clinician *identify* and select the important dependent variables (target behaviors). In the experimental method that behavior therapists wish to emulate, the choice of dependent variables follows logically from the theory under investigation, whereas the phenomena of interest to a practicing clinician are always unique, idiopathic. Realistically, then, clinical assessment is an information-gathering, problem-identifying and revising, and goal-selecting and reselecting activity. These are the most critical features and also the most neglected.

One reason there has been little research on the discovery processes of behavioral assessment is the lack of a conceptual analysis of what actually transpires in the clinical setting. Kanfer and Saslow's (1969) "SORKC" model of behavioral diagnosis provided one possible framework, namely a series of logically related questions to be posed by the clinician. Goldfried and Sprafkin (1974) classified the variables to be examined in behavioral assessment, as did Kanfer and Grimm (1977), with respect to organizing client information during the interview. Lazarus (1976) formulated a multimodal model for exploring the fundamental domains of assessment, the "BASIC ID" (see also Nay, 1979). However, there is some indication that therapists are not particularly rigorous in following such guidelines (Swan & MacDonald, 1978; Wade, Baker, & Hartmann, 1979), nor is there any empirical evidence that doing so would lead to the design of the most effective treatment directed at the most central problem. Shapiro's (1951) interesting model of assessment as a series of hypotheses that are tested by the clinician in an experimental fashion failed to deal adequately with the source or origin of the hypotheses. Learning theory has provided the basis for suppositions regarding the functional analysis (or causal explanation) of behavior often relied upon in behavioral assessment and has exerted strong influence on the types of measures favored, encouraging direct measurement (Ciminero, 1977) but permitting indirect methods (Burns, 1980; Staats, 1975), although the latter are seldom reported (Bornstein et al., 1980). But there is nothing in learning theory to guide the choice of behavior (clinical phenomena) to measure or analyze functionally. Not even the most general behavior theory provides a conceptual model for determining the deviance, abnormality, or changeworthiness of behavior. One possible exception is the sociopsychological orientation (Ullmann & Krasner, 1975) that argues that the abnormality of behavior is entirely a socially determined dimension, that professional helpers are strongly influenced by deviancy labels, and that implicit biases inevitably influence clients' therapeutic goals even when therapists espouse a contractual, "repairman" (Bakan, 1967) model of their role. It is our contention that these issues, as well as many other common concerns in behavior therapy, such as ethics, outcome evaluation, and the therapist's social role, can readily be integrated by a simple theoretical proposition, namely that behavioral assessment, in contrast to the usual interpretation (as in Nelson & Hayes, 1979), can be conceived of as a decision-making activity, reducible to processes of clinical judgment.

Like so many theoretical positions, this one is not entirely original. Hawkins (1975) eloquently described the fundamental dilemma in behavioral assessment as one of identification, not of modification, and Lanyon and Lanyon (1976) considered the steps required for intervention decisions. Kanfer and Grimm (1977) have emphasized the necessity for clinical value judgments in determining clients' central problems, and occasionally therapeutic programs have been described in very appropriate conditional rather than prescriptive terms (such as McLean, 1976). Unfortunately, however, the growth of interest in clinical judgment and decision making that might have occurred within behavioral assessment was stunted by the over-identification of these concepts with only one aspect of the clinical endeavor—improving the reliability of a highly suspect psychiatric nosology by psychometric and subjective evaluation. Furthermore, many of the formal studies of clinical decision making, with their attendant mathematical models, have been conducted not to study the behavior of clinicians, but to analyze general human cognitive processes. These efforts, therefore, no matter how worthy, have not been perceived as significant to behavioral assessment, and the behavioral emphasis on what is directly observable seemed to reduce, if not obviate, the need for concern with clinical inference, intuitive knowledge, judgment based on signs, the detection of the secondary or underlying meaning of communications, and so forth (Goldfried & Kent, 1972). Thus there has been no systematic attempt to view behavioral assessment from a decision-making perspective. The purpose of this paper is to make a beginning in that direction.

MODELS OF DECISION MAKING

It is not a straightforward matter to cast behavioral assessment within the idiom of decision making or judgment. (These terms, together with problem solving, are used in a variety of ambiguous and often overlapping ways in the literature—a convenient tradition that we will respect.) It is useful to remember that clinical judgment is essentially an orientational framework and not a unitary phenomenon that transcends the context or the form of the specific judgmental activity. Clinical psychologists, whether behaviorally oriented or not, are required to make a variety of very formal decisions such as whether a client represents a serious suicide risk, or is competent to stand trial, or is mentally retarded. These activities lend themselves very obviously to analysis as decisions, but, as mentioned, the predominant context for judgment research has been diagnosis or, more accurately, the selection or choice of a psychiatric diagnostic label. There is no counterpart to this task in behavioral assessment, and while we have argued (Wilson & Evans, 1982) that from the point of view of reliability, selecting a target behavior is not terribly different from selecting a diagnosis, the cognitive realities are quite different.

Controlling the nature and amount of client information available, as we did, enables one to study clinicians' choice of targets and also provides a focus for determining the manner in which client information is initially conceptualized and organized. In summarizing the "major difficulty" that could be deduced from a brief child clinical case description, some behavior therapists listed specific, observable behaviors to be modified, others inferred negative social or environmental influences, particularly those attributable to parents, while still others suggested dynamic descriptors (such as "need for control"), specific diagnostic labels, or categories of organic dysfunction. If behavioral clinicians are, in practice, relying upon differing implicit constructs for determining and assimilating the critical features of client information, then it is not surprising that, given identical client data, discrepant target selections emerge. This represents, then, an entirely different cognitive activity from selecting a diagnostic label, in which the critical, defining features of each category are predetermined and specified.

The contextual issue can be further illustrated by reference to the empirical analysis of jury decision making, where one could focus on the implicit rules individual jurors use, or on the ability of jurors to comply with judges' instructions to ignore information, or on the social influences of group persuasion that result in a verdict (see Davis, Bray, & Holt, 1977, for a general review of such research). The situation most similar to this latter one in behavioral assessment is when treatment goals are established by an interdisciplinary group such as at a case conference or a meeting to develop an Individualized Educational Plan (IEP). Other parallels exist, but for the moment the important point is to dispel any misconception that decision making can be considered independently of a careful logical analysis of the task elements under consideration.

The nature of the task, or the form of the decision-making activity, also influences the type of theoretical decision model that might be applied. In the clinical judgment literature, readers may remember, it was relatively easy to demonstrate that the application of mathematical models for weighting and combining information —for example, the application of Bayes' theorem or linear aggregation of weights—could improve diagnosis, so that clinicians were urged to be actuarial (Meehl, 1954). If, as it was often argued, clinical judgment tends to be configural—that is to say, the weight or value given to some information is partly a function of the weights of other information—models are available for such processes, too, notably Anderson's (1974) information integration theory. Ostensibly such approaches can capture or model the cognitive processes actually used in a clinical decision. In one recent study, Vogelmann-Sine (1980) demonstrated that males' judgments of females' responses as indicating consent to sexual intercourse were an interactive function of specific variables, such as attitudes toward sex-role stereotypes and the degree of physical intimacy to which the woman was responding. But conclusions from this approach are totally reliant upon the fact that the subjects are given fixed information such as might be true of a rape trial, where rules of evidence and the activities of the defense and prosecution attorneys as interviewers control the information to which the jury has access. In life situations, a male wishing to avoid misunderstanding a female's intentions can gain a great deal more information, and so, too, can the clinician trying to understand the client's problems. If distortions in judgment occur, it may not be because the decision-maker was unable to calculate probabilities according to Bayes' theorem, but because, as Tversky and Kahneman (1974) suggested in their important paper, natural decision behavior is probably dominated by informal, heuristic models of utilizing knowledge. Thus there has grown up in recent years a more realistic, though possibly more vague, paradigm for investigating decision making, relying less on formal probabilistic rules and more on the use of dynamic cognitive processes such as memory, multiple versus sequential thinking, and so on (for an example, see Fox, 1980).

A similar, and also most useful, distinction between models of research has been made by Elstein, Shulman, and Sprafka (1978). They distinguish between the process-tracing approach, the object of which is to describe the reasoning processes used by subjects as they make judgments or solve decisional problems, and attempts to represent—usually with mathematical paradigms such as the lens model or linear regression—the cognitive operations involved in judgment by studying input-output relations. The primary problem with the latter procedure is that the successful matching of the output by some equation is not in itself proof of its being the veridical model of the judge's strategies for combination. However this approach is of special value when trying to construct, or reconstruct, a picture of what clues were relied upon by the subject. A problem with process-tracing methods is that by asking people to report on how they make a decision, one is probably influencing the process, and that, as will be well known to cognitive behavior therapists, the rationales a person provides to account for past or future action may be quite irrelevant from a causative standpoint.

Watts (1980) has provided an excellent summary of evidence supporting the notion that there exist two cognitive modes for making use of information to arrive at decisions, the intuitive and the "conscious" or rational. Since these processes are supposedly based upon different criteria and organized according to different conceptual frameworks, one would not expect the rationale-based verbal report of a subject describing how decisions were or will be made to replicate the intuitive, tacit mode of reasoning that may actually have been employed in reaching a decision. Both modes of thinking will have to be investigated independently, perhaps utilizing a variety of research models, so as not to influence inadvertently the judgment process under study. It will be especially important to understand the relative contributions of processes such as these in the various types of decisions required of the behavioral assessor, if, as Watts (1980) has proposed, the quality of clinical judgments can be improved by combining intuitive styles of thinking with the more objective, rational modes usually emphasized in clinical training. This is particularly relevant to behavioral assessment, in which only the latter mode is even recognized, and in which neither has been investigated.

In the long run, some creative integration of the existing decision models is likely to be advantageous for studying the range of complex judgments inherent in behavioral assessment. However, the present discussion will be oriented toward process tracing, since it seems to represent a more valuable heuristic strategy for generating descriptive interpretations of what transpires in assessment, as well as initial hypotheses about the variables involved. The various mathematical models may prove more appropriate in the context of what Levy (1963) has called "bounded" clinical judgments, which occur at a single point in time under known conditions and involve discrete, specifiable alternatives. These features are perhaps more representative of traditional psychiatric diagnosis than the interrelated sequences of target-selecting, goal-setting, and treatment-planning decisions expected of the behavioral clinician.

APPLICATION TO BEHAVIORAL ASSESSMENT

Without being able to analyze every feature of assessment, let us try to illustrate some of the prospects as well as the problems of decision-making concepts applied to behavioral assessment by considering a few examples of commonly recurring issues in the literature.

The Clinical Interview

Haynes and Jensen (1979) state that the behavioral interview is an assessment instrument demanding demonstration of reliability and validity. Unfortunately, this is a logical impossibility, as one of the purposes of the interview is to gather illusive and subtle information. The observer (clinician/interviewer) influences the content by the style and, more specifically, by the nature of the questions, which may, in turn, be influenced by the client's responses. Thus one could examine only the reliability of the conclusions, that is, agreement between two interviewers on some matter relating to the client, and not of the "instrument" itself, which is a mutually interactive process. The reliability of some predefined parameter could be assessed either by giving judges access to the same content (as in Berg & Fielding, 1979, where one of a pair of judges actually conducted the interview, and both rated the child on the presence or absence of ten characteristics such as fidgety, sad, and so forth), or by having judges collect their own information, potentially yielding different content for each (as in Hay et al., 1979). The purpose of the latter type of study is not clear, since, in effect, the judges would be using different instruments. For instance, the dependent variable in the Hay et al. study was target behaviors, or life problems expressed by the client, and whether agreement is reached depends, minimally, on two things: whether the interviewers asked the same questions and whether, when asked the same questions on more than one occasion, the clients provided the same answers. As one might expect, both sources of variability were found to be present by Hay et al. (1979).

As for validity, it would again depend on what was designated as the correct or appropriate type of outcome data from the interview before one could determine the availability of comparison criteria. Further, if the ultimate purpose of the behavioral interview is to arrive at a set of treatment goals—or targets—ordered in some fashion in terms of priority and of their relationship one to the other, then neither the obtained outcome nor the criterion outcome would have the properties of an exactly comparable metric, such as a score or a rating. Instead, we would be comparing imprecise categories of behavior that would have the properties of "fuzzy sets" (Zadeh, 1971). Fuzzy set theory allows for some ambiguity or lack of precision in such intuitively convincing categories as childhood autism, alcoholism, learning disability, or similar by allowing gradations of membership in a set or category. Also to be considered is whether nonagreement of subsets represents agreement on broader sets. For example, one clinician's goal of reducing self-critical statements might represent agreement with another's goal of increasing the range of rewarding activities if the global criterion purpose was reducing depression. Using an open-ended answer format, we found that calculating agreement among clinicians' treatment goals was complicated by the fact that not all clinicians based their decisions upon the same dimensions of behavior change (Wilson & Evans, 1982). Thus, for goals conceptualized in terms of change in specific target behaviors, some clinicians simply focused upon increasing a desired response, others emphasized decreasing an undesired response, while still others suggested teaching alternative or incompatible behaviors in order to accomplish both objectives. A number of clinicians focused upon the remediation of specific problem behaviors but proposed some hierarchical sequence of behavior change, whereas some goals were conceptualized in terms of global or long-term improvement. Of these global goal statements, however, some emphasized the general level of functioning that would be expected at the successful completion of therapy, while other respondents expressed global change by reference to the amelioration of moral problem classes or maladaptive response styles.

Therefore, in addition to goals that may be best understood as subsets of broader categories, goal decisions may also reflect a variety of points along the short-term/long-term or hierarchical/independent change dimensions, so that, pursuing the previous example, teaching communication skills to improve a relationship, to increase exchange of positive social interactions, to reduce self-critical statements, to ultimately minimize depression, represents a perfectly logical goal/method interactional treatment plan. If clinicians vary as to the conceptual dimensions utilized in arriving at goal specifications, and if these are interwoven with differing treatment method preferences, then identical constructs are likely to be labeled and expressed accordingly, making the straightforward comparison of the results of this process—such as the goal statements—difficult, if not impossible. Consider the situation in which a particular treatment method may be immediately suggested to the clinician presented with a client for whom, among other more intricate problems, some relatively discrete and easily modifiable behavior can be targeted. The availability of a proven method or preferred treatment strategy may heavily influence initial decisions about therapeutic goals, in contrast to the usual assumption that once both immediate objectives and global goals have been specified, only then can individualized strategies be designed and implemented to accomplish the desired results. What is needed for clarification is a process model in which goal setting is seen as a series of interrelated decision steps dependent upon the above dimensions and individual clinicians' implicit criteria for weighting and combining the various sources of information available at any given point in the assessment sequence.

Probably the most useful way of evaluating the quality of behavioral interviews will be to consider, and rate, their formal properties as problem-solving tasks. One such analysis has been presented by Clavelle and Turner (1980), who found that compared to social workers and paraprofessionals, clinical psychologists obtained information from clients "in the order of its influence on their decisions"—regarding suicide risk, need for hospitalization, or need for medication—and that they were, therefore, appropriately more confident about their decisions earlier in their interviews.

Information Value in Behavioral Assessment

This issue of confidence brings to mind the manner in which various types of information actually affect clinical judgment, a matter that has thus far been ignored within the context of behavioral assessment schemas. Of the many possible interesting aspects of information usage, we will consider here only a few key ones, and we will discuss the closely related question of outcome decisions in a later section.

First, assumptions about the way behavior can and should be modified will influence the importance assigned by the assessor to certain categories of information, which, in turn, affect the salience of information available during complex information presentations such as the interview. An informal example of this is provided in unpublished data we gathered from behaviorally trained clinical psychology students asked to think aloud about segments of case material presented to them sequentially. These students were not responsive to information that might have been suggestive of neurological or physical problems. Behavior therapists do not just ignore information having little value according to their theoretical predilections: they also tend to read into the situation, and form conclusions, about information that was not actually presented—the important role parents might be playing in child behavior problems, for example (Wilson & Evans, 1982).

A second, probably more pressing, concern, is the relationship between amount and consistency of information—however selectively it may be received by the clinician—and significant decisions affecting the design, timing, and nature of the intervention. In medicine, the classic study was performed by Oskamp (1965). After clinicians reached a diagnosis and treatment plan based on little information (few test findings), the accuracy of their diagnosis and the quality of their treatment plans were not much influenced by additional information. More testing information did, however, increase confidence in their diagnoses. (Notice that the test results originally presented may have provided the most critical cues necessary for deciding among alternative options; we have no analogy for this in behavioral assessment.) Of course one should be wary of overgeneralizing these findings, since contrary evidence also exists. For example, with teachers, Shavelson, Cadwell, and Izu (1977) did find that subjects were sensitive to the reliability of information and would alter their predictions (of pupil achievement) when given further information. Interestingly, however, the availability of new, *contradictory* information does not necessarily result in reappraisal or a desire to improve one's predictive powers: at least, experimental subjects will claim to have anticipated surprising, unpredictable outcomes all along (Fischoff & Beyth, 1975). Even subjects made aware of this bias still maintain an exaggerated sense of what they know (Fischoff, 1977).

The availability of increased information also has other interesting effects. It has been well demonstrated that irrelevant additional information affects judgments about probabilities, which can best be made by attention to known base rates. Behavior therapists seem to have shown themselves *not* to be particularly sensitive to the importance of such base rates. In a study by Langer and Abelson (1974), which is often cited with some delight, it was shown that behavior therapists were less influenced by labeling a person a patient as opposed to a job applicant than were psychoanalytically oriented clinicians. But, as Davis (1979) has pointed out, this actually indicated an inappropriate judgment by behavioral clinicians since, in the absence of any other information, simple base-rate data would suggest that a designated patient is more likely to have behavior problems than is an applicant for a job.

Distortion in Decision Making

Although these issues all relate to bias, it is important to remember that there are many different sources of bias. So far we have been discussing information acquisition and utilization, areas in which behavioral assessment has made efforts to be sensitive to potential sources of bias, but there may be additional distortions in the decision-making processes in which this information is used. Suggestive evidence for this arises from the techniques and methods for improving *clients'* decision making that have been available for some time and have become increasingly popular. Janis and Mann (1977) and Janis (1980) have suggested that in addition to common influences such as information overload, prejudice, group pressure, or lack of information and ignorance, the stress engendered by decisional conflict leads to erroneous decisions or vacillation. Conflict arises when opposing courses of action have far-reaching and vital consequences. Although not perhaps as threatening as crucial life decisions confronting clients, clinical decisions do sometimes have considerable social significance—such as the client's likelihood of homicide or child abuse—or personal hazard—to self-esteem, professional reputation, and so forth—which undoubtedly contributes to stress. There is as yet no empirical work on this topic, but Feldman (1976), in an important paper based on dissonance theory, has described some of the attitudes toward the client that may be engendered by failure, and these are rather similar to defensive avoidance, one of Janis and Mann's (1977) proposed patterns of coping with stress occasioned by difficult choices. Another coping pattern they describe, excessive vigilance and overly conscientious gathering of information, has also been ascribed to professionals, in the form of inexperienced physicians calling for too many diagnostic tests (Elstein et al., 1978), and can certainly be seen in some of the criticisms of psychological assessment, which often relies too heavily on repeated testing.

Nezu and D'Zurilla (1979) reported the positive results of a study in which undergraduates successfully improved their decision making after having been taught criteria for estimating the likelihood and value of different outcomes. In their model, the value to be attached to an outcome must be judged both by personal and by social criteria, which, for a clinician, would be comparable to factors affecting both the individual client and others in the community as a whole. For clinical psychologists, therefore, these represent the pragmatic and ethical issues involved in deciding on appropriate goals for the client. In Nezu and D'Zurilla's (1979) model, it is recommended that personal decisions should be made not just on the value of the outcome, but also on the likelihood of achieving it, which is a function of whether a particular course of action will produce the goal and whether such a course of action can be implemented by the individual. For the clinician, the analogous issue is whether the therapy, if successful, will produce the requisite results, and whether the therapist is capable, given available resources or the character of the client, of implementing the therapy. Thus some very old issues about whether "YAVIS" clients get favored over "HOUNDS," for instance, becomes a matter, often not clearly articulated, of therapists' assumptions regarding their potential effectiveness. The belief that the therapist can produce significant change reflects the perceived self-efficacy (Bandura, 1977) of the clinician. Unlike the usual assumptions regarding the overriding loftiness of ethical *decisions* per se, it seems that ethical concerns enter as one consideration in complex, pragmatic clinical judgments.

Judgments of Change

A major influence on assumptions regarding one's personal efficacy would be feedback both from the literature evaluating a given therapy technique (the believability of the scientific findings), and the clinician's own personal experience with the method. Experimental clinicians are wont to present treatment studies as though the outcomes were truths. It is assumed that as long as proper attention has been paid to external validity, new research findings will immediately cause clinicians to drop old methods and to initiate the new ones. At best, however, empirical findings merely inform the clinical decision. This is what critics are trying to communiate when they ask whether the results were "clinically" rather than just "statistically" significant. They are trying to give a weight to the information for making pragmatic clinical decisions and at the same time questioning their relevance for decisions regarding individual clients. Research findings have only relative believability to the clinicians who are the consumers of these findings.

That research outcomes are really probabilistic statements is well illustrated in the most basic judgment of behavior change. Traditionally, greatest emphasis has been placed on the *accuracy* of the behavioral baseline, while the equally crucial determination—whether there was a change in the dependent variable from baseline to treatment and whether it was clinically significant—was left to subjective impression. While there were a number of indications (e.g., Kent et al., 1974), in addition to common sense, that this was not a healthy state of affairs, it is only recently that the biases resulting from visual inference have been investigated. Wampold and Furlong

(1981) have demonstrated that experts in the behavioral assessment field are not likely to take relative variation into account when judging the degree of change from time-series baselines. Statistical criteria for aiding such judgments represent preset standards and are therefore not subject to the same types of bias, and yet these, too, have not met with much interest in the research field, and it is unlikely that clinicians will adopt such criteria with any greater enthusiasm.

Even more fascinating issues are raised if one starts to question the relevance of the measure employed to the change one wishes to observe. Here the clinician concerned with the individual client has had the upper hand because there are some very simple and obvious (though sometimes deceptive) criteria—basically consumer satisfaction indices—for determining the significance of change for the client. As data worthy of professional dissemination, however, the significance of most reported measures is less easy to judge.

Of course these arguments refer to a posteriori judgments of an intervention, based on outcome data. Unfortunately, behavioral assessment has tended to neglect the equally important clinical need for routinely gathered data to aid the day-to-day decisions the clinician must inevitably make with respect to changing, dropping, or initiating some treatment program. Clinicians are frequently exhorted to be "empirical" as though the use of current single-subject research designs would be of any real value to them. In this respect education seems well ahead of clinical psychology: a number of proposals have now been offered (supported empirically) that assist teachers using data-based instruction to make appropriate modifications to the educational plan. One example is the construction of "aim lines" to determine the value of continuing a particular program when the daily records show performance failing or exceeding the requirements of the program guidelines (such as McGuigan, 1980; White & Haring, 1980).

The areas covered in this section together reflect one of the oldest concerns in psychometrics, that is, the relevance of any measure to the ultimate criteria of interest (Thorndike, 1949). If, for instance, teachers judge some children to be hyperactive, and objective measurement of motor activity selects other children as the more active (as in Kivlahan, Siegel, & Ullman, 1980), which is the more correct? The failure to find agreement could mean either that the teachers do not consider motor activity to be an important feature of hyperactivity (the weighting they give the cue), or that they are poor in estimating it (measuring the cue). Such distinctions are not always made in behavioral assessment, yet they are fundamental. Furthermore, if teachers are to be accorded the status of expert and influential judges, the implication is that regardless of correctness, the objective monitoring of motor behavior in hyperactive children will be of little relevance to other clinical criteria, such as grades, avoidance of later social problems, and so on. Similarly, that clinicians are more influenced by verbal reports from parents than by direct observation of the child (McCoy, 1976) may be interpreted not as *bias* so much as a tendency to give more weight to parental summaries. Many studies of labeling bias and discrepancies between parents', teachers', and psychologists' appraisals of children's behavior can be reinterpreted this way.

CONCLUSION

This section might have been more appropriately called "cliffhanging," for, like the Saturday matinee, we are not going to leave the reader with a sense of completion. There are so many unresolved conceptual issues in what we hope has been a challenging perspective (if not quite as arousing as the approaching locomotive), that we propose to end not with conclusions but with a discussion of the evaluation of behavioral assessment, which, for some time, has presented a knotty logical problem. Behavioral measures can and should be evaluated by the traditional psychometric criteria, and also by their utility, cost, and effectiveness when the assessor provides data that will influence others' decisions. The available evidence on the non-utilization of psychological test data by, for instance, teachers is eye-opening, and the resulting vista is depressing (Shulman, 1980).

Similarly, when the outcome of assessment is to be a placement decision or a diagnostic category (with predictive, prognostic implications), there exist a number of criteria against which individual clinical decisions can be evaluated, at least on a retrospective basis. However, judgments about treatment priorities and therapeutic direction are difficult to evaluate independently, as there is no way of discovering how matters might have progressed if some other behavior had been the focus of intervention or whether some more insightful functional analysis would have shortcircuited a laborious or unsuccessful treatment program. While Nelson and Hayes (1979) have argued that there are ways of making such evaluations, such as determining, in general, whether a detailed assessment is worth the effort compared to simply starting a powerful intervention, this would be a cost/benefit analysis of the functional investigation of controlling variables and would not address the issue of problem selection, which, of course, precedes the functional analysis. We would argue that it is not possible to evaluate the quality of the decision, but that it is possible to evaluate the quality of the decision making.

This position has important implications for some of the most important controversies in behavioral assessment. Cone (1981) has recently argued that much behavioral assessment research is conducted along traditional psychometric lines that produce nomothetic descriptions of average behaviors and their typical environmental influences, which may not be of much relevance to the specific, idiosyncratic needs of an individual client. The obvious counterargument is that without developing general principles and generalizable relationships, the accumulation of knowledge is prevented, and each new client must be assessed de novo. The decision-making model solves such debates by acknowledging that each client has unique and sometimes novel needs, but that the clinician's thinking about such problems is influenced, among other things, by the accumulation of personal experience with similar cases and by the availability of research findings that then become the source of key hypotheses about the client. Many practicing clinicians (as Fishman, 1980) have complained that behavioral assessment has little practical applicability; such criticism must be attended to most seriously, as it implies that the consumers of research findings do not recognize how empirically established principles do, or should, influence their thinking about clients who obviously present unique constellations of problems.

Furthermore, and this might also be important in helping to bridge the gap between clinical practice and research innovation, there has been insufficient attention paid by behavior therapists to the role of the expert, which is a necessary feature in the development of an applied clinical science where demonstrable facts are few. The much-touted concept of the "empirical clinician" turns out to be, in essence, advice on how clinicians could become researchers if they really tried. Recognition of expertise, as we are advocating, recommends the study of experienced practitioners in order to formulate better the skills and strategies that a novice might need. This notion will not be foreign to behavior assessors who study the behavior of, for instance, socially skilled individuals in order to define the training goals for those less competent. Chi and Glaser (1980) have recently outlined a program of research designed to investigate the "stages and processes involved in the changes from novice to expert performance [in order] to devise achievement measures more directly focused at efficient educational strategies" (p. 38). There is, regrettably, no such research program in behavioral assessment, and the primary question of how to assess the assessors remains not only unanswered but also unasked in our field.

SUMMARY

It has not been generally recognized that the process of behavioral assessment occurs within the broader context of clinical judgment. In practical assessment it is the gathering of client information and the use of behavioral measures to effect treatment decisions that is of the essence, but it is the adequacy of the measures themselves that tends to dominate the activities of researchers in this field. Representing behavioral assessment as clinical decision making not only shifts emphasis back to the clinical purposes of assessment but integrates in a single conceptual framework many of the issues, problems, and controversies extant in the area. As such, the decision-making metaphor represents a theoretical synthesis that could have important implications for guiding future research.

The decision-making literature has, in the past, tended to emphasize only one facet of clinical judgment, formal diagnosis. The theories and models developed to account for the cognitive processes required of the diagnostician may be too limited to account for the reasoning strategies of the behavioral assessor, whose decisions take place in a different context and involve a number of different types, or forms, of judgment task. Of the available decision models we suggest that a "process-tracing" strategy is most likely to be fruitful at this early stage of inquiry. The activities of behavioral assessment must first be conceptualized according to their various cognitive demands and processes; then research models can be brought to bear that will explicate the complexities of clinical reasoning that are implicit or extemporaneous.

Rather than attempting to analyze all the various forms of judgment and decision making that are involved in behavioral assessment, we selected instead a few components of assessment to show how otherwise disparate issues can be encompassed within a common theoretical framework. The clinical interview, for example, may be understood as a highly complex opportunity for the clinician to engage in interactive problem solving. It is not analogous to an instrument for gathering data. How different types of information affect clinicians' decisions was also considered, followed by a brief mention of how decision processes themselves can be distorted. Within our model, it was argued that traditional views of the impact of data on applied science are somewhat suspect. For the clinician, it is the believability of empirical results that is the major influence on the judgment of change and its social significance for any given client.

Finally, we attempted to examine the advantages of the decision-making approach for clarifying the evaluation of behavioral assessment. We concluded that clinical decision making can be independently evaluated—not in terms of the specific outcomes (the judgments themselves), but in terms of criteria for the adequacy of the methods used to arrive at the decisions. These ideas have potential implications for the training of behavior therapists, who seem to be predominantly instructed in the psychometric properties of behavioral measures rather than in the selection and use of information pertinent to their decision-making requirements.

REFERENCES

Anderson, N. H. Information integration theory: A brief survey. In D. H. Krantz, R. C. Atkinson, R. D. Luce, & P. Suppes (Eds.), *Contemporary developments in mathematical psychology*, Volume 2. San Francisco, CA: Freeman, 1974.

Bakan, D. *On method: Toward a reconstruction of psychological investigation*. San Fransciso, CA: Jossey-Bass, 1967.

Bandura, A. Self-efficacy: Toward a unifying theory of behavioral change. *Psychological Review*, 1977, *84*, 191-215.

Berg, I., & Fielding, D. An interview with a child to assess psychiatric disturbance: A note on its reliability and validity. *Journal of Abnormal Child Psychology*, 1979, *7*, 83-89.

Bornstein, P. H., Bridgwater, C. A., Hickey, J. S., & Sweeney, T. M. Characteristics and trends in behavioral assessment: An archival analysis. *Behavioral Assessment*, 1980, *2*, 125-133.

Burns, G. L. Indirect measurement and behavioral assessment: A case for social behaviorism psychometrics. *Behavioral Assessment*, 1980, *2*, 197-206.

Chi, M. T. H., & Glaser, R. The measurement of expertise: Analysis of the development of knowledge and skill as a basis for assessing achievement. In E. L. Baker & E. S. Quellmalz (Eds.), *Educational testing and evaluation: Design, analysis, and policy*. Beverly Hills, CA: Sage, 1980.

Ciminero, A. R. Behavioral assessment: An overview. In A. R. Ciminero, K. S. Calhoun, & H. E. Adams (Eds.), *Handbook of behavioral assessment*. New York: Wiley, 1977.

Clavelle, P. R., & Turner, A. D. Clinical decision-making among professionals and paraprofessionals. *Journal of Clinical Psychology*, 1980, *36*, 833-838.

Cone, J. D. "Psychometric" considerations in behavioral assessment. In M. Hersen & A. S. Bellack (Eds.), *Behavioral assessment: A practical handbook*, Second edition. New York: Pergamon, 1981.

Davis, D. A. What's in a name? A Bayesian rethinking of attributional biases in clinical judgment. *Journal of Consulting and Clinical Psychology*, 1979, *47*, 1109-1114.

Davis, J. H., Bray, R. M., & Holt, R. The empirical study of social decision processes in juries. In J. Tapp & F. Levine (Eds.), *Law, justice, and the individual in society*. New York: Holt, Rinehart & Winston, 1977.

Elstein, A. S., Shulman, L. S., & Sprafka, S. A. *Medical problem solving: An analysis of clinical reasoning*. Cambridge, MA: Harvard University Press, 1978.

Feldman, M. P. Social psychology and the behaviour therapies. In

M. P. Feldman & A. Broadhurst (Eds.), *Theoretical and experimental bases of the behaviour therapies.* London: Wiley, 1976.

Fischoff, B. Perceived informativeness of facts. *Journal of Experimental Psychology: Human Perception and Performance*, 1977, *3*, 349-358.

Fischoff, F. B., & Beyth, R. "I knew it would happen": Remembered probabilities of once-future things. *Organizational Behavior and Human Performance*, 1975, *13*, 1-16.

Fishman, S. T. *Things aren't always what they appear to be—a clinician's view of assessment.* Paper presented at the meeting of the Association for Advancement of Behavior Therapy, New York, November 1980.

Fox, J. Making decisions under the influence of memory. *Psychological Review*, 1980, *87*, 190-211.

Goldfried, M. R., & Kent, R. N. Traditional versus behavioral assessment: A comparison of methodological and theoretical assumptions. *Psychological Bulletin*, 1972, *77*, 409-420.

Goldfried, M. R., & Sprafkin, J. N. *Behavioral personality assessment.* Morristown, NJ: General Learning Press, 1974.

Hawkins, R. P. Who decided that was the problem? Two stages of responsibility for applied behavior analysts. In W. S. Wood (Ed.), *Issues in evaluating behavior modification.* Champaign, IL: Research Press, 1975.

Hay, W. M., Hay, L. R., Angle, H. V., & Nelson, R. O. The reliability of problem identification in the behavioral interview. *Behavioral Assessment*, 1979, *1*, 107-118.

Haynes, S. N., & Jensen, B. J. The interview as a behavioral assessment instrument. *Behavioral Assessment*, 1979, *1*, 97-106.

Janis, I. Personality differences in decision making under stress. In K. R. Blankstein, P. Pliner, & J. Polivy (Eds.), *Assessment and modification of emotional behavior.* New York: Plenum, 1980.

Janis, I., & Mann, L. *Decision making: A psychological analysis of conflict, choice, and commitment.* New York: The Free Press, 1977.

Kanfer, F. H., & Grimm, L. G. Behavioral analysis: Selecting target behaviors in the interview. *Behavior Modification*, 1977, *1*, 7-28.

Kanfer, F. H., & Saslow, G. Behavioral diagnosis. In C. M. Franks (Ed.), *Behavior therapy: Appraisal and status.* New York: McGraw-Hill, 1969.

Kent, R. N., O'Leary, K. D., Diament, C., & Dietz, A. Expectation biases in observational evaluation of therapeutic change. *Journal of Consulting and Clinical Psychology*, 1974, *42*, 774-780.

Kivlahan, D. R., Siegel, L. J., & Ullman, D. G. *Relationships among measures of activity in children.* Paper presented at the meeting of the Association for Advancement of Behavior Therapy, New York, November 1980.

Langer, E. J., & Abelson, R. P. A patient by any other name . . . : Clinician group difference in labeling bias. *Journal of Consulting and Clinical Psychology*, 1974, *42*, 4–9.

Lanyon, R. I., & Lanyon, B. J. Behavioural assessment and decision-making: The design of strategies for therapeutic behaviour change. In M. P. Feldman & A. Broadhurst (Eds.), *Theoretical and experimental bases of the behaviour therapies*. London: Wiley, 1976.

Lazarus, A. A. *Multimodal behavior therapy*. New York: Springer, 1976.

Levy, L. H. *Psychological interpretation*. New York: Holt, Rinehart & Winston, 1963.

McCoy, S. A. Clinical judgments of normal childhood behavior. *Journal of Consulting and Clinical Psychology*, 1976, *44*, 710–714.

McGuigan, C. A. Analysis and use of performance data. In C. L. Hansen (Ed.), *Child assessment: The process & the product*. Seattle, WA: Program Development Assistance System, University of Washington, 1980.

McLean, P. Therapeutic decision-making in the behavioral treatment of depression. In P. O. Davidson (Ed.), *The behavioral management of anxiety, depression and pain*. New York: Brunner/Mazel, 1976.

Meehl, P. E. *Clinical versus statistical prediction*. Minneapolis, MN: University of Minnesota Press, 1954.

Nay, W. R. *Multimethod clinical assessment*. New York: Gardner Press, 1979.

Nelson, R. O., & Hayes, S. C. Some current dimensions of behavioral assessment. *Behavioral Assessment*, 1979, *1*, 1–16.

Nezu, A., & D'Zurilla, T. J. An experimental evaluation of the decision-making process in social problem solving. *Cognitive Therapy and Research*, 1979, *3*, 269–277.

Oskamp, S. Overconfidence in case study judgments. *Journal of Consulting Psychology*, 1965, *29*, 261–265.

Shapiro, M. B. An experimental approach to diagnostic psychological testing. *Journal of Mental Science*, 1951, *97*, 748–764.

Shavelson, R. J., Cadwell, J., & Izu, T. Teachers' sensitivity to the reliability of information in making pedogogical decisions. *American Educational Research Journal*, 1977, *14*, 83–97.

Shulman, L. S. Test design: A view from practice. In E. L. Baker & E. S. Quellmalz (Eds.), *Educational testing and evaluation: Design, analysis, and policy*. Beverly Hills, CA: Sage, 1980.

Staats, A. W. *Social behaviorism*. Homewood, IL: Dorsey, 1975.

Swan, G. E., & MacDonald, M. L. Behavior therapy in practice:

A national survey of behavior therapists, *Bahavior Therapy*, 1978, *9*, 799-807.

Thorndike, R. L. *Personnel selection: Test and measurement techniques.* New York: Wiley, 1949.

Tversky, A., & Kahneman, D. Judgment under uncertainty: Heuristics and biases. *Science*, 1974, *185*, 1124-1131.

Ullmann, L. P., & Krasner, L. *A psychological approach to abnormal behavior.* Englewood Cliffs, NJ: Prentice-Hall, 1975.

Vogelmann-Sine, S. *Implicit consent and rape: An integration theory analysis of female responses in a dating context.* Doctoral dissertation, University of Hawaii, 1980.

Wade, T. C., Baker, T. B., & Hartmann, D. P. Behavior therapists' self-reported views and practices. *The Behavior Therapist*, 1979, *2*, 3-6.

Wampold, B. E., & Furlong, M. J. The heuristics of visual inference. *Behavioral Assessment*, 1981, *3*, 79-92.

Watts, F. N. Clinical judgement and clinical training. *British Journal of Medical Psychology*, 1980, *53*, 95-108.

White, O. R., & Haring, N. G. *Exceptional teaching*, Second edition. Columbus, OH: Charles E. Merrill, 1980.

Wilson, F. E., & Evans, I. M. The reliability of target-behavior selection in behavioral assessment. *Behavioral Assessment*, 1982, *4*, in press.

Zadeh, L. A. Toward a theory of fuzzy systems. In R. E. Kalman & N. DeClaris (Eds.), *Aspects of network and system theory.* New York: Holt, Rinehart & Winston, 1971.

CHAPTER 4

Learned Resourcefulness as a Behavioral Repertoire for the Self-Regulation of Internal Events: Issues and Speculations

Michael Rosenbaum, Ph.D.

Behavior therapists, like other clinicians of different persuasions, subscribe to various theoretical notions in explaining the development of abnormal behaviors such as phobias and depression. Early behavioral etiological formulations assumed that anxieties and depressive behaviors were acquired by classical or instrumental conditioning. More recently, cognitive mediators were introduced to explain why phobic behavior persists over time (as in Bandura, 1977) or why depression develops (Beck et al., 1979). The basic assumption is that specific environmental conditions, in concert with specific cognitions employed by the individual in his or her interpretation of these conditions as well as expectations for the future, serve as critical factors in developing phobias or depressions. Most of the evidence that supports this assumption is based on

This chapter was written while the author was a visiting professor at the University of Illinois at Urbana-Champaign during the academic year 1980–81. The many hours of discussion that I had with Frederick H. Kanfer during this year helped me in formulating the concept of learned resourcefulness. The writing of this chapter was partially supported by the Department of Psychology and by the Institute for Child Behavior and Development at the University of Illinois. Special thanks are extended to M. L. Maehr and R. L. Sprague for providing me the intellectual atmosphere and the facilities for pursuing my scholastic interests during my stay at Illinois.

treatment outcome studies and/or laboratory and correlation studies of anxious or depressed individuals.

However, as a number of authors in this volume have pointed out, this basic formulation may have shortcomings and is in need of revision. For example, Marks (Chapter 7) suggests that "maybe we should think not in terms of why phobias and rituals are acquired in the first place, but rather why once these are acquired, patients have failed to extinguish them" (p. 115-116). He points out that many individuals acquire trivial fears and rituals at some point in their lives but are able to overcome them. Social learning theory (Bandura, 1977) would argue that what makes phobias persist are the person's self-generated expectancies that traumatic events may occur again and that he or she would not be able to cope with them effectively (low belief in "self-efficacy"). Why certain individuals develop these expectancies is not completely clear from the social learning theory. Lewinsohn (see Chapter 9, this volume), in two rarely performed longitudinal studies, found that depression-related cognitions and a reduced rate of engagement in pleasant activities arise concurrently with a depressive episode but do not precede it. Both of these variables were hypothesized to be the antecedents of depression (Beck et al., 1979; Lewinsohn, 1975). It is clear that only in a few cases do individuals develop depression because of environmental changes and cognitive distortions. I believe the most interesting question is why most individuals who suffer occasionally from depressive moods do not develop a full-blown depressive episode.

Behavior therapists were naturally more inclined to study deviant patterns of behavior than to investigate how "normal" individuals cope with situational and cognitive factors that presumably cause phobias and depressions. In understanding how most individuals cope with these high-risk factors, we will understand better the behavioral deficits of the depressed or anxious client.

In this chapter, I will suggest that most individuals have acquired throughout their lives a basic behavioral repertoire (Staats, 1975), which enables them to cope effectively with factors that were often assumed to cause depressive or phobic behavior. I have labeled this repertoire "learned resourcefulness." Many of the behaviors subsumed under this label were previously labeled "self-control" or "coping" skills. Since both "coping" and "self-control" already have multiple definitions and considerable surplus meaning, I chose a new label to describe this specific repertoire of behaviors.*

*Meichenbaum (1977) uses the concept of *learned resourcefulness* to describe attitudes developed by clients following a stress inoculation training procedure. These attitudes facilitate the generalization of newly learned coping skills beyond the original treatment situation. However, in the present paper the concept of learned resourcefulness describes a behavioral repertoire of coping skills and not just perceptions or attitudes.

I will first present the concept of learned resourcefulness and how it might be assessed. Then I will relate this concept to its antecedent concepts: self-control, coping, and learned helplessness. Finally, I will discuss the implications of this concept for future research and treatment. The constraints of space will not enable me to elaborate extensively on various points, yet I hope the basic concept of learned resourcefulness will be clear to the reader.

DEFINING THE CONCEPT OF LEARNED RESOURCEFULNESS

The concept of learned resourcefulness has certain similarities with Staats' concept of a basic behavioral repertoire or personality repertoire (Staats, 1968). Despite the fact that Staats presented this concept over a decade ago, it received little attention among behavior therapists. The following quotation from Staats' most recent paper can best describe the interactional properties of the basic behavioral repertoires.

> The individual begins from birth to learn systems of "skills" according to the principles of conditioning. . . . These systems are called basic behavioral repertoires (or personality repertoires) and are considered to be the basic constituents of personality in several ways. First, the way the individual *responds* in a situation is not only a function of the behaviorally significant aspects of the situation but a function (in part) of the individual's personality repertoires. Second, this is true for what the individual *experiences* in a situation as well as for what he or she *learns*. Each behavioral occurrence depends in part on the situation and in part on the individual's own personality repertoires" [italics added] (Staats, 1981, p. 244).

I differ from Staats in my assumption that learned resourcefulness, as a basic behavioral repertoire, is learned not only through conditioning but also through modeling and instructions.

Staats (1981) proposes that there are three general areas of personality: language-cognitive, emotional-motivational, and sensorimotor systems. Intelligence, for instance, is considered a basic behavioral repertoire in the language-cognitive system of the personality (Staats, 1975). In Staats' theory, there is a continuous interaction among the three personality systems; a change in one system will affect the others. Staats' concept of interaction is highly similar to Bandura's reciprocal determinism (Bandura, 1978). The "self-system" according to Staats (1975) consists of parts of the emotional-motivational and language-cognitive personality repertoires.

The basic behavioral repertoire that I have labeled *learned resourcefulness* belongs to the self-system. This repertoire constitutes a compendium of skills by which an individual controls the interfering effects that certain internal events (such as emotions, pain, or undesired thoughts) have on the smooth execution of a desired behavior. By learned resourcefulness, I do not mean the total elimination of these events, but the self-regulation of internal events in order to minimize the undesirable effects of these events on behavior. The following example will clarify what is meant by learned resourcefulness. There is considerable evidence that test anxiety is related to test performance. Hill (1980), in a detailed review of the literature, reported a correlation of −0.50 between test anxiety and achievement test performance in children in the last grade of school. There is obviously not a one-to-one correspondence between test anxiety and test performance. A considerable number of students who are anxious about tests nevertheless perform well on them. The test-taking behavior of these students has never been studied, as far as I know. In the context of the present discussion, it is hypothesized that these children have a basic behavioral repertoire of resourcefulness that enables them to perform well on tests despite their anxiety. It is assumed that for these children early signs of anxiety during a test function as cues to employ their resourcefulness, such as taking a deep breath or self-verbalizing coping statements that reduce the interfering effects of their anxiety.

In a recent study we found some support to this hypothesis (Shalev & Rosenbaum, 1980). We found that a measure of learned resourcefulness (Rimon & Rosenbaum's Children's Self-Control Scale: Rimon, 1980) and study habits correlated strongly with level of achievement in fifth-graders while there was only a small, but significant, correlation between test anxiety and achievement. These findings are in line with Meichenbaum and Butler's (1980) model of test anxiety.

In sum, a behavior will be included in the category of learned resourcefulness: (1) if it is cued by an internal event ("under the skin"), and (2) if it reduces or eliminates the interfering effects of this internal event on the performance of target behavior. Hence, learned resourcefulness is defined by its function as a skill, mainly a cognitive skill, for the self-regulation of emotions, pain, and cognitions. Learned resourcefulness does *not* refer to intellectual motoric or social resourcefulness.

Learned resourcefulness may involve a number of "enabling skills," such as the ability to self-monitor internal events, verbal abilities to label feelings, and self-evaluative skills.

Staats (1981) stated that in the theoretical-experimental investigation of a basic behavioral repertoire it is necessary: (1) to specify what the repertoire consists of; (2) how and by what principles the repertoire is learned; and (3) how and by what principles the repertoire interacts with other behavioral repertoires and situational variables. At this point, our research focused mainly on the assessment of learned resourcefulness. During the course of developing an assessment instrument, we had to deal with the interaction of learned resourcefulness with certain situational variables. However, we did not study, yet, the relationships of learned resourcefulness with other basic behavioral repertoires such as intelligence or scholastic achievement.

THE ASSESSMENT OF LEARNED RESOURCEFULNESS

Stating that a basic behavioral repertoire such as learned resourcefulness exists is useless unless we find ways of specifying and assessing this repertoire. Research in this area has just begun and so far comes under the rubric of "self-control" (e.g., Rosenbaum, 1980a, b).

There are several problems in the assessment and evaluation of a learned resourcefulness repertoire.

1. What is the specific nature of learned resourcefulness?—I conceive of learned resourcefulness as a specific skill. A skill is defined as a unit of behavior composed of one or more classes of behavior (Fischer, 1980). Fischer recently proposed a "skill theory" in order to explain cognitive development. Although he does not deal specifically with self-control or coping skills, his concept of skill might be a useful theoretical tool. Like other behavioral theoreticians (Bandura, 1978; Kanfer, 1970; Staats, 1975) he develops an interactional theory that states that the concept of skill always involves an integrated function of actions, cognitions, and the environment. He views cognitions as part of the self-regulatory system: ". . . cognitions refer to the process by which the organism exercises operant control . . . *over sources of variation in its own behavior* . . ." [italics added] (Fischer, 1980, p. 481). In that sense, learned resourcefulness consists of a repertoire of cognitive skills (verbal and nonverbal behaviors) directed at regulating internal events. The major problem is that most of these skills are not amenable to direct behavioral observations and can be assessed mainly through verbal reports or inferred through behaviors exhibited under specific conditions that require learned resourcefulness.

Recently two excellent collections of papers dealing with the various issues of cognitive assessment were published (Kendall & Hollon, 1981; Merluzzi, Glass, & Genest, 1981). The assessment methods suggested by the various contributors to these books provide fine guidelines for how learned resourcefulness could be assessed. For example, Genest and Turk (1981) make a convincing argument for the use of verbal reports to assess cognitive skills and processes. They suggest various procedures in which subjects are required to provide reports of ongoing thoughts, images, and feelings that they are experiencing or have just experienced while engaging in tasks that may require learned resourcefulness (such as pain-producing tasks). Verbal reports are dealt with as a legitimate source of data, as are observational data. It is beyond the scope of this paper to deal in any depth with the exciting developments in cognitive assessment. It should be emphasized, however, that it is possible today to assess the cognitive skills involved in learned resourcefulness.

2. The second major issue in the assessment of learned resourcefulness is the question of generalizability across time and situations. The assessment of learned resourcefulness involves, in principle, the same procedures as the assessment of intelligence, scholastic achievement, or motor skills. The behavioral-analytic approach to assessing competence proposed by Goldfried and D'Zurilla (1969) may be used. This involves three phases: (a) the establishment of a representative sample of tasks or situations in which the behavior in question is likely to occur; (b) the sampling of typical responses to these situations; and (c) the evaluation of these responses with regard to their effectiveness. Thus, in assessing the person's resource skills in coping with a painful event, we may expose him or her to a number of painful stimuli presented under different conditions and ask him or her to recount the cognitive skills he or she used to cope with the various pain-producing stimuli. Subjective and independent evaluations could then be obtained as to the relative effectiveness of the various responses to the pain stimuli. The type of situations chosen (contrived laboratory situations or natural events) and the methods used to assess the subjects' responses to these situations have important bearing on the generalizability of our measures across time and situations. The assessment of learned resourcefulness should be subjected to the appropriate psychometric tests of validity and reliability, as are other assessment procedures (Nay, 1979).

3. The general domain of learned resourcefulness might be divided into subdomains according to the internal event to be controlled (such as mood, anxiety, anger, pain). Is there a *general* repertoire of resourceful behaviors, or is resourcefulness specific to a specific internal event? This issue is reminiscent of the question of a general *g* factor in intelligence versus specific *s* factors in intelligence. This is an empirical question that calls for research. At this point, we assume that when an individual has a rich repertoire of resource skills to regulate certain internal events, he is likely to be effective in regulating other internal events. The exception to this assumption would be in a case when an individual had experienced a certain internal event (for example, pain) considerably more than any other internal event. Such an individual might be more resourceful in pain control than, for instance, in the control of his or her anxiety.

These and other issues that were not discussed here still await solution. It is clear that several concurrent approaches to data collection should be used. Further, in cases where the interest lies in assessing a specific resource skill, such as pain control, specific methods should be employed to assess that skill. Our current research just reflects the initial steps toward the assessment of learned resourcefulness.

Our starting point was the growing literature on the various self-management and coping skills therapies proposed by the cognitively oriented behavior therapists (such as Goldfried & Goldfried, 1980; Mahoney, 1974; Meichenbaum, 1977 and recent review of the literature; Rosenbaum & Merbaum, in press). These therapies are characterized by their emphasis on *general* coping strategies to deal more effectively with stressful life events, in contrast to situation-specific responses, as was usually the case in the more traditional behavior approaches. On the basis of this literature and the theoretical conceptualization of learned resourcefulness, I developed a self-report scale that I labeled the Self-Control Schedule (SCS) (Rosenbaum, 1980a), which should have been more appropriately labeled Learned Resourcefulness Scale. The behaviors assessed by the SCS cover the following content area: (a) use of cognitions and self-instructions to cope with emotional and physiological responses; (b) application of problem-solving strategies (such as planning, problem definition, evaluating alternatives, and anticipation of consequences); (c) ability to delay immediate gratification; and (d) a general belief in one's ability to self-regulate internal events. Most of the 36 items of the SCS depict specific behaviors in specific situations. Yet, the situations are described in general terms to make them applicable to a wide range of individuals. The psychometric properties of the SCS are described elsewhere (Rosenbaum, 1980a). Subjects scoring high on the SCS are assumed to have a rich repertoire of resourceful behavior, while subjects scoring low on the SCS are considered to be subjects with a low level of resourceful behavior.

The basic research strategy focused on the differential performance between high and low resourceful subjects on tasks requiring the use of learned resourcefulness. The situations and the tasks that were studied were either a contrived laboratory situation or a real-life event. In most of these studies the subjects' specific coping responses to the situation at hand were also assessed. The results of of a number of studies so far indicate that the SCS can serve as a useful tool in measuring general learned resourcefulness. A short summary of some of these studies will be presented in this section as well as in the following sections.

In one of our earliest studies (Rosenbaum, 1980b), we found that although high resourceful subjects did not differ from low resourceful subjects in their reported pain when exposed to a cold pressor (ice water), they tolerated the pain significantly longer than low resourceful subjects. Confirming our basic hypothesis, high resourceful subjects reported using specific coping methods more often and more effectively while exposed to the cold-pressor than low-resourceful subjects. The data of this study suggest that highly resourceful individuals are not necessarily less affected by internal events such as pain but that they are able to function despite their painful or emotional experience.

These findings were extended to a "real-life" situation, namely, seasickness (Rosenbaum & Rolnick, in press). Seasickness is a major problem in individuals who have to work on relatively small high-speed boats in a stormy sea. The typical physiological symptoms of seasickness include malaise, pallor, cold sweating, nausea, and vomiting. In our study (Rosenbaum & Rolnick, in press), we chose sailors who were most prone to suffer from seasickness. Our findings indicated that although the performance of seasick sailors was in general worse than that of not seasick sailors when sailing in a stormy sea, high resourceful seasick sailors still showed significantly less performance deficits in a stormy sea than low resourceful seasick sailors. Further, high resourceful seasick sailors reported using more extensively specific cognitive methods in coping with seasickness than low resourceful seasick sailors.

Considerable attention has been directed recently at training acute and chronic patients to cope with physical illness and disability (Melamed & Siegel, 1980). It would be reasonable to assume that a considerable number of persons already have these coping skills in their behavioral repertoire. The applications of the concept of learned resourcefulness in the general area of behavioral medicine has just begun. Palmon (1980) studied the effects of learned resourcefulness and the severity and frequency of seizures on the general adjustment level of epileptic patients. Her findings were strongly supportive of the learned resourcefulness hypothesis. She found that severity and frequency of seizures were unrelated to general adjustment, yet the epileptics' scores on the SCS correlated highly with the epileptics' ability to cope effectively with the debilitating effects of epileptic seizures. High resourceful epileptics were less depressed and less anxious and functioned better in everyday life than low resourceful epileptics, regardless of the severity of their illness. It is interesting to note that high resourceful epileptics did not differ from low resourceful epileptics in their assessment of their anxiety and depression levels immediately after a seizure. The Palmon study was a correlational and retrospective study, and it is subject to all the methodological problems of these kinds of studies. In the future we plan to investigate whether scores on the SCS and other measures of learned resourcefulness can predict patients' ability to cope effectively with various stressful medical procedures.

The assessment of learned resourcefulness is still in its developmental stage, and additional measures beyond the SCS are needed. The experimental evidence so far is very encouraging and supportive of the utility of the concept of learned resourcefulness.

LEARNED RESOURCEFULNESS AND SELF-CONTROL

The concept of learned resourcefulness is a natural extension of the early work done in behavior therapy under the heading of "self-control." Since over the years different meanings were associated with the term "self-control" by different behavior therapists, a new term was needed to indicate the special meaning I have attached to self-control in my previous research (as in Rosenbaum, 1980a, 1980b). In addition, the concept of learned resourcefulness, in contrast to self-control, does not connote any constraint of inner desire.

The interest in self-control among behavior therapists is pursued by two different lines of research: a "conceptual" and an "applied" line. The "conceptual" approach is characterized by constructing a theoretical model of the self-control *process*, followed by laboratory research to test the validity of the proposed model. The major proponents of this approach are Kanfer and Bandura. The "applied" approach to self-control takes an atheoretical stand and focuses on self-control *procedures* as a vehicle for improving existing therapeutic techniques. Goldfried's treatment-outcome studies are a prime example of this line of research (Goldfried & Goldfried, 1980).

Kanfer's (1970, 1980) theoretical model is the most sophisticated and well-researched model of self-control in behavior therapy. I will only highlight the major features of this model and how it relates to learned resourcefulness. Kanfer follows the interactional theories by postulating that behavior at a specific time is determined by three interacting variables: situational, self-generated, and biological variables. Kanfer (1970, 1980) views self-control as a special case of self-regulation. The term "self-regulation applies to the general case in which a person directs his own behavior, while the term self-control is reserved to the case when the behavior to be executed or avoided is conflictual" (Kanfer, 1980, p. 338). Kanfer (1970) postulated that self-regulation proceeds through three stages: self-monitoring, self-evaluation, and self-reinforcement. In Kanfer's revised model of self-regulation (Kanfer & Hagerman, 1981), the self-regulatory process will be initiated only if the individual believes that he or she could change the situation by his or her own actions. Similarly, movements from one self-regulatory stage to the other depend on various cognitive activities such as causal attributions, expectations for future outcomes, and evaluations of current behaviors and concerns.

While the concept of learned resourcefulness refers to a behavioral repertoire that is employed by an individual to self-regulate internal events, Kanfer's concept of self-control describes "a person's actions in a specific situation, rather than a personality trait . . . or his experience in learning to control his actions and impulses" (Kanfer, 1980, p. 342). Kanfer's revised self-regulatory model (Kanfer & Hagerman, 1981) is basically directed at explaining how individuals are *self-motivated* to regulate their own behavior. This model can explain when a person is most likely to employ his or her resource skills. Since the concept of learned resourcefulness does not deal with the issue of when and why the resource skill will be accessed, the present model and Kanfer's model can be viewed as being complementary to each other.

Bandura (1978) also proposed an interactional model of self-regulation. He postulates that human actions are determined by a reciprocal interaction between cognitions, situations, and behavior. The "self-system" in his theory refers to "cognitive structures that provide reference mechanisms and to a set of subfunctions for the perception, evaluation, and regulation of behavior" (Bandura, 1978, p. 348). Like Kanfer's model, Bandura's model focuses mainly on the motivational aspects of the self-regulatory system.

Bandura's concept of "self-efficacy" (Bandura, 1977) is receiving considerable attention in the current behavioral literature. Expectations of self-efficacy constitute one of the cognitive structures of the self-system that guide and direct behavior and are in turn also modified by behavior and situational variables. They "determine whether coping behavior will be initiated, how much effort will be expended, and how long it will be sustained in the face of obstacles and aversive experiences" (Bandura, 1977, p. 191). Bandura stresses that "expectation alone will not produce desired performance if the component capabilities are lacking" (p. 194). One of these capabilities is learned resourcefulness.

The relationship between learned resourcefulness (having the capabilities) and expectations for self-efficacy is of considerable importance in treatment. Are expectations for self-efficacy always necessary before the client attempts to apply his newly learned coping skills to previously stressful situations? Bandura's theory would indeed suggest so (assuming that adequate incentives are available). However, in the clinic we often encounter clients who have the appropriate skills and who are doing things that initially they felt they were not capable of doing. At this point there are no research reports that address this question directly. Smith (1979) dealt with it indirectly. He assessed expectations for self-efficacy and learned resourcefulness (using the SCS) in a group of women who entered a weight-reduction program based on self-management techniques. He found that the SCS was a far superior predictor both of dropping out of treatment and of success in effecting weight and habit changes than were the self-efficacy measures. However, the SCS scores did correlate with measures of self-efficacy. Having resourceful skills will most probably lead to increased belief in self-efficacy, but not in all cases. This problem calls for further research that will apply additional measures of learned resourcefulness.

In summary: the major conceptual models of self-control and self-regulation are concerned mainly with the issue of self-motivation and only indirectly with the specific skills needed in the process of self-regulation of internal events. Their major contribution to learned resourcefulness is in specifying when and where this basic behavioral repertoire will be used by the individual.

On the other hand, the "applied" approach to self-control is less concerned with explaining the nature of self-regulation, but is directed at the application of self-control methods and techniques to increase the effectiveness of behavior therapy. One pervasive, yet currently unsupported, conviction is that self-control interventions are likely to be more effective than therapies based on environmental manipulations (see recent reviews: Merbaum & Rosenbaum, 1980; Rosenbaum & Merbaum, in press).

Initially, the assumption was that clients can change their own behavior by the same methods that were formerly used successfully by the therapists. Thus, for example, since systematic desensitization was found to be effective in eliminating phobic behavior (Wolpe, 1969), a self-directed desensitization procedure was introduced (for example, Rosen, Glasgow, & Barrera, 1976). As our review of the literature (Rosenbaum & Merbaum, in press) has indicated, this approach was not very effective, mainly because of the large number of clients who were either not motivated or not capable of applying therapeutic methods on their own. A more promising approach to therapy was the introduction of specific self-control techniques into an essentially therapist-directed treatment program (see, for example, Fuchs & Rehm, 1977; Goldfried & Trier, 1974; Suinn & Richardson, 1971). This was applied with reasonable success to the treatment of anxiety and depression (see review by Rosenbaum & Merbaum, in press).

Another significant development in the "applied" approach to self-control was the development of stress inoculation methods. Meichenbaum (1977) and Goldfried (1980) suggest that clients and nonclients can be taught specific skills (such as self-relaxation, problem-solving, self-instructions, and similar) that will enable them to cope more effectively with future stressful life events. Goldfried (1980) even proposed to substitute the term "coping skill" for "self-control skills." He defines a coping skill in very vague terms as "any class of cognitive or overt behavior patterns that would deal effectively with problematic situations" (Goldfried, 1980, p. 111).

The unstated assumption in Meichenbaum's and Goldfried's work is that individuals who lack specific stress-handling skills are more likely to be affected by stressful environmental events. This assumption is very similar to my current concept of learned resourcefulness. Unfortunately, these researchers do not define the scope and the domain area of these skills. Yet their work is extremely valuable in suggesting what specific skills may be involved in learned resourcefulness. As I have already indicated, my initial attempt in developing a measure for learned resourcefulness was based on their findings.

LEARNED RESOURCEFULNESS AND LAZARUS' COPING THEORY

Richard Lazarus made probably the most important contribution to the theory of coping. While most models of coping have focused on the motivational aspects of the coping process, Lazarus is almost unique in his attention to the variety of coping strategies that may be employed by individuals who encounter stressful life events (Silver & Wortman, 1980). With the development of cognitive behavior therapy, Lazarus' two decades of research on coping was "discovered" by behavior therapists (such as Goldfried, 1980). In a number of recent publications (Lazarus, Kanner, & Folkman, 1980; Roskies & Lazarus, 1980) Lazarus calls for a rapprochement between his theoretical research on coping and cognitive behavior therapy, since both focus on the role of cognitions in emotional responses. The clinical work in behavior therapy could provide an excellent ground to test some of the general principles of Lazarus' coping theory.

It will be impossible to provide an extensive overview of Lazarus' theory in this chapter, and I want only to point out how and where the concept of learned resourcefulness can fit into his general theory of coping.

Lazarus follows suit with other interactional positions by viewing coping as an active mediating process between an environmental event and an emotional response (Lazarus et al., 1980). "Coping is a reaction to stress, but also a shaper of the stress experience, and in determining whether or not a given event will be evaluated as potentially stressful, the appraisal of the person's coping resources is as important as the appraisal of the environment. Coping and stress are but two faces of the same coin and any model of stress must also be viewed as a model of coping" (Roskies & Lazarus, 1980, p. 45). The coping process may involve either direct action to change a stressful situation or a change in the emotional reaction to this situation (Lazarus & Launier, 1978).

For the purpose of present discussion, the most important aspect of Lazarus' coping theory is his concept of coping resources. "If coping modes or strategies are conceptualized as the currency expended in a specific stress transaction, coping resources constitute the bank account from which this currency is drawn" (Roskies & Lazarus, 1980). These resources may exist within the person (as physical health, psychological skills) or within the environment (as social support, material resources). My concept of learned resourcefulness as a basic behavioral repertoire for the self-regulation of internal events could be viewed as one of the coping resources available for the individual when faced with a stressful situation. This concept has the same dynamic qualities as those suggested by Roskies and Lazarus (1980) for coping resources in general: "Coping resources . . . affect outcome not only by regulating feeling and hence behavior, but also in the reverse sequence. Greater resources may permit us to function with less behavioral disruption and, in maintaining habits, we also avoid mood disturbances" (p. 50).

Research on coping resources is just in its beginning stages. Most of the research has so far focused on social support systems and very little on intraindividual resources. Current and future research on learned resourcefulness is and will be focusing on the latter variables.

LEARNED RESOURCEFULNESS AND LEARNED HELPLESSNESS

During the past decade, Seligman's (1975) learned helplessness model of depression received considerable attention in the psychological literature. Since this model is well known and numerous books and review papers discussed this model (for example, Abramson, Garber, & Seligman, 1980; Seligman, 1981; see also Lewinsohn, Chapter 9, this volume), I will not describe it in any detail.

Initially, the learned helplessness model of depression postulated that learning that outcomes are uncontrollable produces the motivational, cognitive, and emotional components of depression (Seligman, 1975). More recently, with the cognitive spirit in the air, the model was reformulated to include attributional and expectancies components (Abramson, Seligman, & Teasdale, 1978). Thus, Seligman (1981) stated that "depression will occur when the individual expects that bad events will occur, expects that he or she can do nothing to prevent their occurrence, and construes the cause of this state of affairs as resulting from internal, stable and global factors" (p. 124). Thus, perception of uncontrollability and tendencies to attribute failure to global, stable, and internal factors are sufficient, but not necessary, conditions to produce depression.

The reformulated model of learned helplessness does not explain how individuals develop specific attributional styles, nor has it been convincingly proven that such styles are antecedent factors to depression. There is some evidence, however, that such attributional styles occur concurrently with depression (Seligman et al., 1979).

In certain respects the concept of learned resourcefulness is the antithesis of learned helplessness. While the learned helplessness model seeks the answer to the question: "What are the environmental contingencies and the cognitive styles that lead to depression?" I am interested, from a learned resourcefulness point of view, in "what are the behavioral skills that enable an individual to 'snap out' of a low mood and not develop a depressive episode despite situational and cognitive variables that might induce depression?"

In a recent study (Rosenbaum & Jaffe, in press), we investigated the relations between a person's resourcefulness as assessed by the Self-Control Schedule (SCS, see section on the assessment of learned resourcefulness) and his/her ability to cope with uncontrollable aversive stimulation so as to minimize adverse effects. The experimental paradigm most often used to produce cross-modal helplessness (see Hiroto & Seligman, 1975), was used for this purpose. Subjects were divided into high resourceful and low resourceful according to their scores on the SCS and were then administered a treatment with inescapable, escapable, or passively received noise. The degree of debilitation produced by these conditions was subsequently measured on a solvable anagram test. As predicted from the learned resourcefulness point of view, the results replicated the learned helplessness phenomenon only with the low resourceful subjects but not with the high resourceful subjects; that is, only the low resourceful subjects exhibited deficits in solving the anagrams following exposure to the inescapable noise. The differences between high and low resourceful subjects were not paralleled by differences in perceived aversiveness of the tone, perceived control over the tone, felt helplessness, and in the type of causal attributions made for the outcome of the performance on the noise task. In general, little relationship was found between subjects' causal attributions for their performance on the noise tasks and their subsequent performance on the anagrams, as would be predicted from the reformulated model of learned helplessness (Abramson et al., 1978). However, high resourceful subjects rated their ability to cope with "disturbing environmental stimuli" significantly higher than did low resourceful subjects. These findings add cogency to the suggestion made by Wortman and Dintzer (1978) that one's attributions regarding one's ability to cope with the adverse effects of the outcome may be more important than attributions of causality for the outcome itself.

Although the results of the above study provide support to the concept of learned resourcefulness, it is quite limited in generality because it deals with normal subjects in a contrived laboratory situation. Only longitudinal studies, in which measures of learned resourcefulness and attributional styles are used as predictors for depression, can resolve some of the issues raised in this section.

SUMMARY AND IMPLICATIONS FOR RESEARCH AND APPLICATION

This chapter introduced a new concept: learned resourcefulness. This concept describes an acquired repertoire of behaviors and skills by which a person self-regulates internal events—such as emotions, pain, and cognitions—that interfere with the smooth execution of behavior. For example, two individuals may be equally anxious when asked to perform before an audience, however they may differ in their learned resourcefulness. The resourceful individual may employ various skills to minimize the effects of her anxiety on her performance in public, while the less resourceful person may succumb to her anxiety.

Learned resourcefulness is similar to what Staats (1968) labeled a basic behavioral repertoire or a personality repertoire. These repertoires are learned from the moment of birth and serve as a basis for further learning. The concept of learned resourcefulness is a natural growth from the theory and application of self-control and self-regulation concepts in behavior therapy. The large body of literature that describes the application of a variety of self-control methods in treatment and in prevention of emotional problems—such as "stress inoculation"—provides the basis for understanding what the behavioral repertoire of learned resourcefulness may consist of. The conceptual models of self-regulation developed by Kanfer (1970; Kanfer & Hagerman, 1981) and Bandura (1978) provide the general theoretical framework in which the concept of learned resourcefulness is embedded. These models contribute to our understanding when and where an individual may be self-motivated to use his or her learned resourcefulness.

The concept of learned resourcefulness is also similar to a "coping resource," a term used within the general framework of Lazarus' theory of coping (as, for example, in Lazarus & Launier, 1978). On the other hand, the concept of learned resourcefulness is an antithesis to Seligman's (1975) concept of learned helplessness. I have hypothesized that highly resourceful individuals would not be affected by those environmental and cognitive factors that were presumed to cause depression according to the learned helplessness model. Some research evidence was cited in support of this hypothesis.

A concept such as learned resourcefulness is useless unless it can be measured. I have raised three major issues involved in the assessment of learned resourcefulness: (1) defining the specific nature of the behavioral repertoire involved in learned resourcefulness; (2) the question of generalizability across time and situations; and (3) the question of a general repertoire of learned resourcefulness versus a specific repertoire associated with specific internal events (such as the self-regulation of anxiety). Although I have suggested partial solutions to these questions, considerably more research is needed.

The assessment of learned resourcefulness is still in its infancy. Rosenbaum's Self-Control Schedule (Rosenbaum, 1980a) was found to be a useful instrument in assessing the general repertoire of learned resourcefulness. I have also reported studies in which specific behavior repertoires related to specific internal events—such as pain—have been assessed. I think that we might eventually be able to measure learned resourcefulness in the same way that we are now able to measure scholastic achievement. Recent developments of assessment procedures in cognitive behavior therapy (Kendall & Hollon, 1981; Merluzzi et al., 1981) provide promising leads for future research in this area.

The concept of learned resourcefulness and its assessment can have significant applications in the practice of behavior therapy. Kanfer and Saslow (1969), in their pioneering work on behavioral assessment, suggested that the behavioral repertoire of a client should be evaluated in terms of behavioral excesses, behavioral deficits, and behavioral assets. Kanfer (1981) has noted that assessment efforts in behavior therapy focus mainly on behavioral excesses and deficits while ignoring behavioral assets. Learned resourcefulness is a behavioral asset that could assist the therapist in designing a specific treatment program for his/her clients. The behavior therapist could guide clients to employ the resource skills that are already in their repertoire to solve their behavioral problems rather than attempting to teach them new skills. The acquisition of a new skill could be facilitated if it is based on the existing competencies of the clients.

Beyond the clinical practice, the assessment of learned resourcefulness can be useful in the selection of individuals for jobs that may tax their emotional resourcefulness.

Future research on learned resourcefulness should focus on at least some of the following areas: (1) assessment and quantification; (2) longitudinal studies in which resourcefulness will be used as a predictor variable for the development of behavioral problems; (3) analyzing the relationship between learned resourcefulness and coping with specific stressful situations (such as painful medical procedures); (4) analyzing the relationship between motivational concepts such as perceived control and self-efficacy and learned resourcefulness; (5) investigating the developmental aspects of learned resourcefulness across different age groups; and (6) study of the relationship between learned resourcefulness and other behavioral repertoires such as intelligence and scholastic achievement.

The researchers' skillfulness, imagination, and resourcefulness will determine whether learned resourcefulness will become a useful concept in behavior therapy.

REFERENCES

Abramson, L. Y., Garber, J., & Seligman, M. E. P. Learned helplessness in humans: An attributional analysis. In J. Garber & M. E. P. Seligman (Eds.), *Human helplessness.* New York: Academic Press, 1980.

Abramson, L. Y., Seligman, M. E. P., & Teasdale, J. Learned helplessness in humans: Critique and reformulation. *Journal of Abnormal Psychology*, 1978, *87*, 49–74.

Bandura, A. Self-efficacy: Toward a unifying theory of behavioral change. *Psychological Review*, 1977, *84*, 191–215.

Bandura, A. The self-system in reciprocal determinism. *American Psychologist*, 1978, *33*, 344–358.

Beck, A. T., Rush, A. J., Shaw, B., & Emery, G. *Gognitive therapy of depression.* New York: Guilford Press, 1979.

Fischer, K. W. A theory of cognitive development: The control and construction of hierarchies of skills. *Psychological Review*, 1980, *87*, 477–531.

Fuchs, C. Z., & Rehm. L. P. A self-control behavior therapy program for depressions. *Journal of Consulting and Clinical Psychology*, 1977, *45*, 206–215.

Genest, M., & Turk, C. D. Think-aloud approaches to cognitive assessment. In T. Merluzzi, C. Glass, & M. Genest (Eds.), *Cognitive assessment.* New York: Guilford Press, 1981.

Goldfried, M. R. Psychotherapy as coping skills training. In M. J. Mahoney (Eds.), *Psychotherapy process: Current issues and future directions.* New York: Plenum, 1980.

Goldfried, M. R., & D'Zurilla, T. J. A behavioral-analytic model for assessing competence. In C. D. Spielberger (Ed.), *Current topics in clinical and community psychology.* New York: Academic Press, 1969.

Goldfried, M. R., & Goldfried, A. P. Cognitive change methods. In F. H. Kanfer & A. P. Goldstein (Eds.), *Helping people change*, second edition. New York: Pergamon, 1980.

Goldfried, M. R., & Trier, C. S. Effectiveness of relaxation as an active coping skill. *Journal of Abnormal Psychology*, 1974, *83*, 348–353.

Hill, K. T. Motivation, evaluation, and educational testing policy.

In L. J. Fyans (Ed.), *Achievement motivation: Recent trends in theory and research.* New York: Plenum, 1980.

Hiroto, D. S., & Seligman, M. E. P. Generality of learned helplessness in man. *Journal of Personality and Social Psychology*, 1975, *31*, 311-327.

Kanfer, F. H. Self-regulation: Research issues and speculations. In C. Neuringer & J. I. Michael (Eds.), *Behavior modification in clinical psychology.* New York: Appleton-Century-Crofts, 1970.

Kanfer, F. H. Self-management methods. In F. H. Kanfer & A. P. Goldstein (Eds.), *Helping people change*, Second edition. New York: Pergamon, 1980.

Kanfer, F. H. Personal communication, May 1981.

Kanfer, F. H., & Hagerman, S. The role of self-regulation. In L. P. Rehm (Ed.), *Behavior therapy for depression: Present status and future directions.* New York: Academic Press, 1981.

Kanfer, F., & Saslow, G. Behavioral diagnosis. In C. M. Franks (Ed.), *Behavior therapy: Appraisal and status.* New York: McGraw-Hill, 1969.

Kendall, P. C., & Hollon, S. T. *Assessment strategies for cognitive-behavioral interventions.* New York: Academic Press, 1981.

Lazarus, R. S., Kanner, A. D., & Folkman, S. Emotions: A cognitive-phenomenological analysis. In R. Plutchik & H. Kellerman (Eds.), *Theories of emotion.* New York: Academic Press, 1980.

Lazarus, R. S., & Launier, R. Stress-related transactions between person and environment. In L. A. Pervin & M. Lewis (Eds.), *Perspectives in interactional psychology*, New York: Plenum, 1978.

Lewinsohn, P. M. The behavioral study and treatment of depression. In M. Hersen, R. M. Eisler, & P. M. Miller. *Progress in behavior modification*, Volume 1. New York: Academic Press, 1975.

Mahoney, M. *Cognitive and behavior modification.* Cambridge, MA: Ballinger, 1974.

Meichenbaum, D. *Cognitive-behavior modification: An integrative approach.* New York: Plenum Press, 1977.

Meichenbaum, D., & Butler, L. Toward a conceptual model for the treatment of test anxiety: Implications for research and treatment. In I. G. Sarason (Ed.), *Test anxiety: Theory, research, and applications.* Hillsdale, NJ: Lawrence Erlbaum Associates, 1980.

Melamed, B. G., & Siegel, L. J. *Behavioral medicine: Practical applications in health care.* New York: Springer, 1980.

Merbaum, M., & Rosenbaum, M. Self-control theory and technique in the modification of smoking, obesity, and alcohol abuse. *Clinical Behavior Therapy Review*, 1980, 2, 1-20.

Merluzzi, T., Glass, C., & Genest, M. (Eds.). *Cognitive assessment.* New York: Guilford Press, 1981.

Nay, R. W. *Multimethod clinical assessment.* New York: Gardner Press, 1979.

Palmon, N. *The relations between self-control, the severity of the disease and the every-day functioning of epileptic patients.* Unpublished M.A. thesis, University of Haifa, 1980.

Rimon, D. Children's assessment of their self-control: Development of a scale. Unpublished M.A. thesis, Tel Aviv University, 1980.

Rosen, G. M., Glasgow, R. E., & Barrera, M. A controlled study to assess the clinical efficacy of totally self-administered systematic desensitization. *Journal of Consulting and Clinical Psychology*, 1976, *44*, 208–217.

Rosenbaum, M. A Schedule for assessing self-control behaviors: Preliminary findings. *Behavior Therapy*, 1980, *11*, 109–121. (a)

Rosenbaum, M. Individual differences in self-control behaviors and tolerance of painful stimulation. *Journal of Abnormal Psychology*, 1980, *89*, 581–590. (b)

Rosenbaum, M., & Jaffe, Y. Learned helplessness: The role of individual differences in learned resourcefulness. *British Journal of Social Psychology*, in press.

Rosenbaum, M., & Merbaum, M. Self-control of anxiety and depression: An evaluative review of treatments. *Clinical Behavior Therapy Review*, in press.

Rosenbaum, M., & Rolnick, A. Self-control behaviors and coping with seasickness. *Cognitive Therapy and Research*, in press.

Roskies, E., & Lazarus, R. S. Coping theory and the teaching of coping skills. In P. Davidson & S. Davidson (Eds.), *Behavioral medicine: Changing health life styles.* New York: Brunner/Mazel, 1980.

Seligman, M. E. P. *Helplessness: On depression, development, and death.* San Francisco, CA: W. H. Freeman & Co., 1975.

Seligman, M. E. P. A learned helplessness point of view. In L. Rehm (Ed.), *Behavior therapy for depression.* New York: Academic Press, 1981.

Seligman, M. E. P., Abramson, L. Y., Semmel, A., & C. von Baeyer. Depressive attributional style. *Journal of Abnormal Psychology*, 1979, *88*, 242–247.

Shalev, S., & Rosenbaum, M. *The relationship between self-control behavior and test anxiety among elementary school children.* Unpublished manuscript. University of Haifa, 1980.

Silver, R. L., & Wortman, C. B. Coping with undesirable life events. In J. Garber & M. E. P. Seligman (Eds.), *Human helplessness: Theory and applications.* New York: Academic Press, 1980.

Smith, T. V. G. *Cognitive correlatives of response to a behavioral weight control program.* Unpublished doctoral dissertation, Queen's University, Kingston, Canada, 1979.

Staats, A. W. *Learning, language and cognition.* New York: Holt, Rinehart & Winston, 1968.

Staats, A. W. *Social behaviorism.* Homewood, IL: Dorsey Press, 1975.

Staats, A. W. Paradigmatic behaviorism, unified theory, unified theory construction methods and the zeitgeist of separatism. *American Psychologist*, 1981, *36*, 239-256.

Suinn, R. M., & Richardson, F. Anxiety management training: A nonspecific behavior therapy for anxiety control. *Behavior Therapy*, 1971, *2*, 493-510.

Wolpe, J. *The practice of behavior therapy.* New York: Pergamon, 1969.

Wortman, C. B., & Dintzer, L. Is an attributional analysis of the learned helplessness phenomenon viable? A critique of the Abramson-Seligman-Teasdale reformulation. *Journal of Abnormal Psychology*, 1978, *87*, 75-90.

PART IV

Origin and Treatment of the Neuroses

CHAPTER 5

Classical Conditioning and Extinction: The General Model for the Treatment of Neurotic Disorders

Hans J. Eysenck, Ph.D.

There exists an incredibly large number of different types of therapy for the treatment of neurotic disorders. Apart from the age-old suggestion and hypnotic method of treatment, we have Freudian psychoanalysis, probably the oldest of the modern treatments and in essence the model on which any later ones are fashioned. We have many different types of psychotherapy, just as we have many different kinds of psychoanalysis; most originated from attempts to modify the classical Freudian model, but more recently many go off in directions that seem to have little to do with Freud (Gestalt therapy, scream therapy, and so forth). Then we have behavior therapy, or rather the different kinds of behavior therapy that have been worked out by psychologists—desensitization, flooding or "implosion" therapy, modeling, and so forth. In a kind of no-man's land between psychotherapy and behavior therapy we have Rogers' client-centered therapy, Albert Ellis's rational-emotional therapy, logotherapy, and many others. Last but not least we have the relative newcomer, namely the so-called cognitive behavior therapies, of the making of which again there seems to be no end.

The fact that there are many different kinds of behavior therapy has caused many critics (such as Locke, 1971; London, 1972; Breger & McGaugh, 1965) to maintain that behavior therapy has not lived up to its pretentions. Eysenck (1959), in his original contribution inaugurating the term "behavior therapy" in its current meaning, suggested that it was differentiated from all other types of therapy by its reliance on a solid, experimentally demonstrable and laboratory-based theory, namely that of conditioning and extinction, and that consequently it had a scientific status altogether lacking in the various types of psychotherapy. A discussion of some of the issues raised by the critics has been given by Eysenck (1976), but the fact remains that there are many different methods of behavior therapy in existence, that there are many anomalies in the application of the theories of learning to the improvement of our methods of treatment, and that little effort has been made by behavior therapists to explain the apparent success of spontaneous remission and psychotherapy in alleviating the distress of the neurotic patient.

It will be suggested here that it is possible to develop a unified theory of behavior therapy, one that embraces all the different methods that have been used. It will be further suggested that this fundamental theory also explains the successes that have been claimed by their adherents for their various methods of psychoanalysis, psychotherapy, cognitive behavior therapy, and so forth. And, finally, it will be suggested that the same mode of explanation will suffice to account for the very real successes of spontaneous remission, that is, the recovery of patients without explicit psychiatric intervention. The theory in question is based on a model of neurosis that has been developed by the writer over a period of years (Eysenck, 1976; 1979), based on laboratory-type evidence gathered from work with animals and humans and also supported by large-scale clinical experiments. The theory will be developed in brief outline, and the reader must be referred to the papers mentioned above for a more detailed account of the theory and the experiments that support it.

It will be necessary first of all to state the conditioning theory of neurosis adopted by the writer, because unless this is clearly understood, the extension of the theory to embrace methods of treatment will not be readily comprehended. Essentially, the writer's model is based on the Watsonian theory, later modified by Mowrer and others, according to which neurotic symptoms are essentially classical conditioned autonomic (emotional) responses or behaviors originating in attempts to reduce the conditioned anxiety so generated. Thus, to take an example, the hand-washing rituals of the obsessive-compulsive patient would be regarded as attempts to reduce the conditioned anxiety attaching to "contamination" by dirt. Watson's original theory, while clearly along the right lines, has been criticized on many grounds and is not adequate to deal with the complex set of circumstances it set out to encompass. The major criticisms that have been made of Watson's original theory (Watson & Rayner, 1920) are as follows:

1. Watson's theory assumes equipotentiality among conditioned stimuli, that is, he assumed that one stimulus can be conditioned as readily as any other. This presumption is also made by Pavlov (1927,

p. 86). If we consider phobias as examples of neurotic reactions, we see that equipotentiality does not seem to hold. As Seligman (1971) has pointed out, phobias "comprise relatively non-arbitrary and limited set of objects; agoraphobia, fear of specific animals, insect phobias, fear of heights, and fear of the dark, and so forth. All these are relatively common phobias. And only rarely, if ever, do we have pyjama phobias, grass phobias, electric-outlet phobias, hammer phobias, even though these things are likely to be associated with trauma in our world" (p. 312).

The set of potentially phobic objects thus seems to be nonarbitary and to be related to the survival of the human species through the long course of evolution, rather than to recent discoveries and inventions that are potentially far more rational sources of phobic fears, such as cars, airplanes, and guns (Geer, 1965; Landy & Gaupp, 1971; Lawlis, 1971; Rubin et al., 1968; Wolpe & Lang, 1964). The nonarbitrary and limited choice of objects and situations that predominantly produce phobic fears in humans is difficult to explain along traditional lines of Pavlovian conditioning theory, or any of its behaviorist and near-behaviorist successors; Watson's theory seems to break down in relation to this well-documented phenomenon.

2. Single-trial conditioning, which seems to be basic to Watson's conception of neurosis, is sometimes, but certainly not universally or even frequently, reported in connection with the genesis of phobic fears; yet single-trial conditioning is very rare in the laboratory (Kamin, 1969; Seligman, 1968), and it is by no means clear how events that usually do not appear very traumatic in the life of the patient can lead to such very clear-cut consequences as severe phobias. There appears to be something in the nature of the CS that makes it particularly easy to associate with the UCS and thus produce a single-trial conditioning where another CS might not have done so. These facts present another considerable difficulty for the Watsonian model.

3. Laboratory CS-UCS connections are very dependent on precise experimental conditions, particularly the time relations involved. In eyeblink conditioning, for instance, the interval between CS and UCS must be something between 500 msecs and 2500 msecs; longer and shorter intervals do not normally generate conditioned responses. Similar limitations are observed in other types of laboratory conditioning experiments. However, such precision is of course unattainable (except by chance) in ordinary life events, and it is difficult to see how a conditioning paradigm can be applied to such everyday life events where conditions are clearly unfavorable to the development of conditioned responses. If neurotic fears are to be explained in terms of Pavlovian conditioning, then some way around this difficulty must be found.

An explanation of these difficulties, making it possible to retain a form of conditioning model, can be found in Seligman's hypothesis of "Preparedness" (Seligman, 1970, 1971). The theory maintains that "Phobias are highly prepared to be learned by humans, and, like other highly prepared relationships, they are selective and resistant to extinction, learned even with degraded input, and probably non-cognitive" (Seligman, 1971, p. 213). Seligman gives many examples of the fact that some contingencies are learned much more readily than others, that is, with highly degraded input, such as single-trial learning, long delays of reinforcement, and so forth; the work of Garcia, McGowan, and Green (1971) has become a classical example of this.

The notion of preparedness integrates well with the hypothesis of innate fears (Seligman, 1972; Hinde & Stevenson-Hinde, 1973; Breland & Breland, 1966); presumably *degree* of fear experienced separates the two concepts. When the fear upon first encountering the stimulus object is strong, it is considered innate; when it is weak but easily conditioned, we think of preparedness. The underlying physiological connection produced by the hypothetical evolutionary development is identical in the two cases; the difference is one of strength. The concept is a valuable one and appears necessary for full understanding of phobic neuroses in particular; it explains the nonarbitrary and limited choice of objects and situations involved, the possibility of single-trial conditioning, and the lack of precise temporary relationships between CS and UCS found in ordinary life events.

Preparedness is not a concept simply invented to account for obscure phenomena and hence involved in a circular argument; there are several laboratory studies carried out in an attempt to verify the failure of equipotentiality in laboratory situations also and to give support to the notion of preparedness. These are reviewed by Eysenck (1979) and strongly support the hypothesis.

There are, however, other objections to the Watsonian model hardly less damaging than those already considered.

4. Thus it is well known that unreinforced conditioned reactions extinguish quickly (Kimble, 1961), and neurotic reactions should be no exception to this rule. Typically, the patient who has acquired a conditioned anxiety reaction to certain situations or persons will encounter these situations or persons under conditions of no reinforcement; it should follow from traditional learning theory that extinction would take place. In other words, the growth of neurotic conditions should in fact be impossible in the great majority of cases; even though we might have a conditioning process responsible for conditioned emotional responses, these should soon extinguish. However, as is well known, neurotic phobias and fear reactions are relatively long-lasting, and although extinction of this type may account for many of these continuous remissions found in the literature (Rachman & Wilson, 1981), there are many records of long-lasting neuroses that clearly cannot be accounted for in terms of traditional theory.

5. A further difficulty arises because the growth of neurotic disorders is quite different to that which would be predicted on traditional learning theories. Instead of starting with a traumatic event, which produces strong conditioned responses that extinguish over time as a result of the presentation of CS-only experiences, what happens seems to be that the neurosis is initiated by a relatively low-key, nontraumatic conditioning experience, and that over time the strength of the conditioned anxiety reaction grows in an insidious fashion until after a sometimes very lengthy period of time a full-blown neurotic reaction arises.

6. The absence of a traumatic UCS referred to above is thus another difficulty in the traditional account. Traumatic events are of course sometimes found at the beginning of a neurotic disorder, particularly in wartime (Grinker & Spiegel, 1945), but even their experience has shown that many more neurotic breakdowns occur through separation from the family than through enemy action. In peacetime neuroses, traumatic UCS are distinctly rare (Gourney & O'Connor, 1971), and traumatic events initiating this sequence are distinctly rare, even by lenient standards (Rachman, 1968; Marks, 1969).

There are other objections to the Watsonian model, which are listed by Eysenck (1979), but these will suffice to indicate the difficulties the model encounters. Essentially the difficulties arise from the application of classical extinction theory to the development of neurotic disorders, and the writer has suggested that there are by now sufficient experimental data to justify a rewriting of the law of extinction. It is this newly developed law of extinction that makes possible the retention of the conditioning model of neurosis, and it will be used to explain the application of learning theory to all the different types of psychotherapy and behavior therapy mentioned in the first few paragraphs.

To help in the understanding of this reformulation, it is essential to make a distinction between what Grant (1964) identified as Pavlovian A conditioning (which is nothing but the familiar type of experiments in which a bell, as a conditioned stimulus, becomes associated with food, the unconditioned stimulus, finally resulting in the ringing of the bell by itself producing salivation), and Pavlovian B conditioning, which differs in many important ways from the A type. As Grant points out, in relation to Pavlovian deconditioning: "The subclass of classical conditioning could well be called Watsonian conditioning after the Watson & Rayner (1920) experiment conditioning fear responses in little Albert, but Pavlov has priority. The reference experiment for Pavlovian deconditioning might be that in which an animal is given repeated injections of morphine. The UCR to morphine involves severe nausea, profuse secretion of saliva, vomiting, and then profound sleep. After repeated daily injections, Pavlov's dogs showed severe nausea and profuse secretion of saliva at the first touch of the experimenter (Pavlov, 1927, pp. 35-36). In Pavlovian B conditioning, stimulation by the UCS is not contingent on the subject's instrumental acts, and hence there is less dependence upon the motivational state of the organism, and the CS appears to act as a partial substitute for the UCS. Furthermore, the UCS elicits the complete UCR of Pavlovian B conditioning, whereas in Pavlovian A conditioning the organism emits the UCR of approaching and ingesting the food. A great deal of interoceptive conditioning (Bykov, 1957) and autonomic conditioning (Kimble, 1961) apparently follows the Pavlovian B paradigm." (See also Kalat & Rozin, 1973.)

We thus have two major differences between Pavlovian A and Pavlovian B conditioning. In Pavlovian B conditioning the UCS supplies the motivation; in Pavlovian A conditioning the motivation (hunger) has to be present already if the experiment is to have any chance of success. Anxiety and other autonomic reactions clearly fall in line with Pavlovian B conditioning; Miller and others have shown abundantly that anxiety acts as a drive.

The second important point is that in Pavlovian B conditioning the CR is similar to the UCR; in other words, the two responses are to some degree interchangeable. This leads to a very important difference between Pavlovian A and Pavlovian B conditioning as far as their extinction is concerned. The writer has suggested (Eysenck, 1976) that extinction always follows unreinforced CS production, but that while in Pavlovian B conditioning the production of the unreinforced CS may be followed by extinction, it *may also be followed by incubation/enhancement of the conditioned response.* (The conditions under which extinction or enhancement follows will be outlined presently.) The reason why extinction may not occur in Pavlovian B conditioning, when the CS-only is presented, is simply that the CS is followed by the CR, and because of the similarity of the CR to the UCR, the presentation of the CS-only is not, strictly speaking, unreinforced; the CR, by virtue of its similarity to the UCR, acts as reinforcement, thus producing a positive feedback cycle leading to the continuous growth of the CR with CS-only presentations.

What are the conditions under which we would expect incubation/enhancement? The writer has suggested that the main one would be the strength of the UCS, the duration of CS presentation, and the personality of the subject involved in the experiment. The stronger the UCS, the more likely is the occurrence of incubation of the anxiety response. Personality variables are involved because objectively identical stimuli are experienced differentially by, say, individuals having high or low neuroticism (emotionality) scores (Eysenck & Rachman, 1965). The importance of the duration of CS-only presentation will become apparent presently.

Consider Figure 5-1, which is a diagrammatic illustration of some data presented by Napalkov (Eysenck, 1967). In these studies

Figure 5-1. Habituation of UCR and Incubation of CR, Following CS-Only Presentation. (Eysenck, 1979)

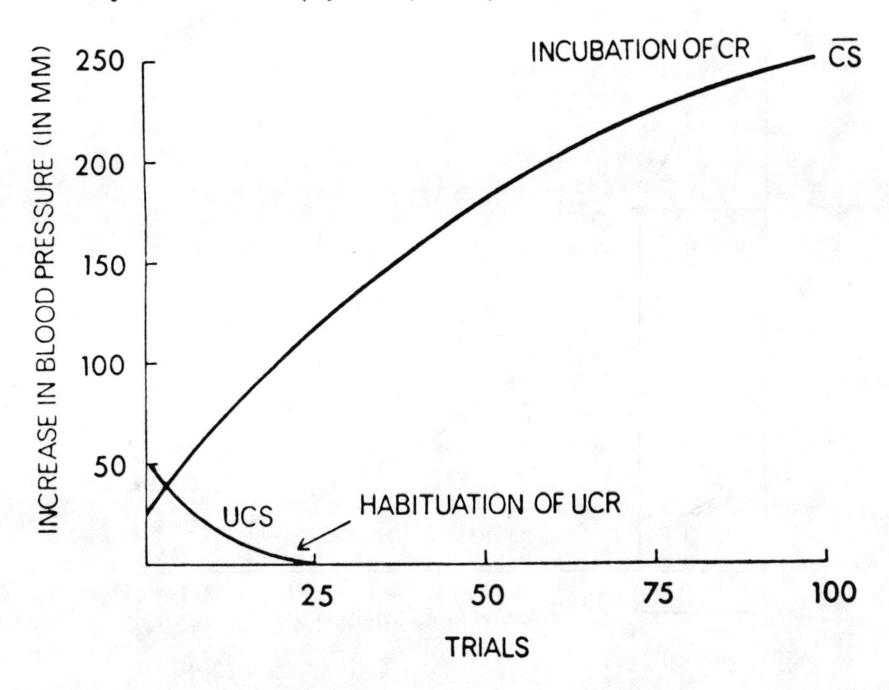

carried out with dogs, a pistol shot fired behind the ear of the dogs constituted the UCS, and increase in blood pressure in millimeters constituted the response. Repeatedly producing the UCS produced habituation, as shown in the lower part of the diagram. Experiments with conditioning were carried out using only one single trial conditioning; in other words, the shot was only paired with the CS response once, and after that only the CS was produced. As demanded by our restatement of the law of extinction, we observe an incrementation of these CR, going from a low value of about 50 mm to a very high value of 250 mm; the latter condition often became chronic, according to Napalkov, suggesting that the theory covers not only neurotic reactions, but also psychosomatic ones. Figure 5-1 clearly illustrates the incubation phenomenon; for proof, the many references given in Eysenck (1979) should be consulted.

Figure 5.2 gives a diagrammatic statement of the general law that, in the writer's submission, replaces the simple law of extinction, at least when Pavlovian B conditioning is involved. On the ordinate we plot strength of the CR, which in the case of human conditioning may be indexed in terms of psychophysiological measures, the fear thermometer reading, or some similar subjective estimate, or in terms

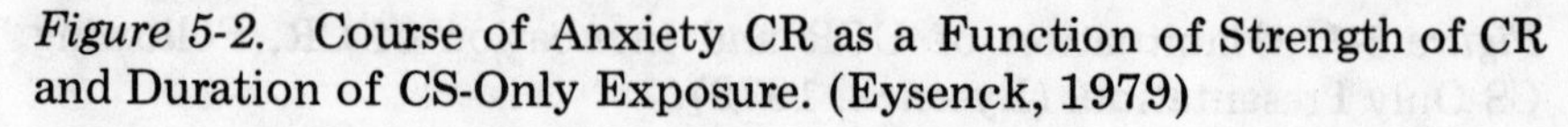

Figure 5-2. Course of Anxiety CR as a Function of Strength of CR and Duration of CS-Only Exposure. (Eysenck, 1979)

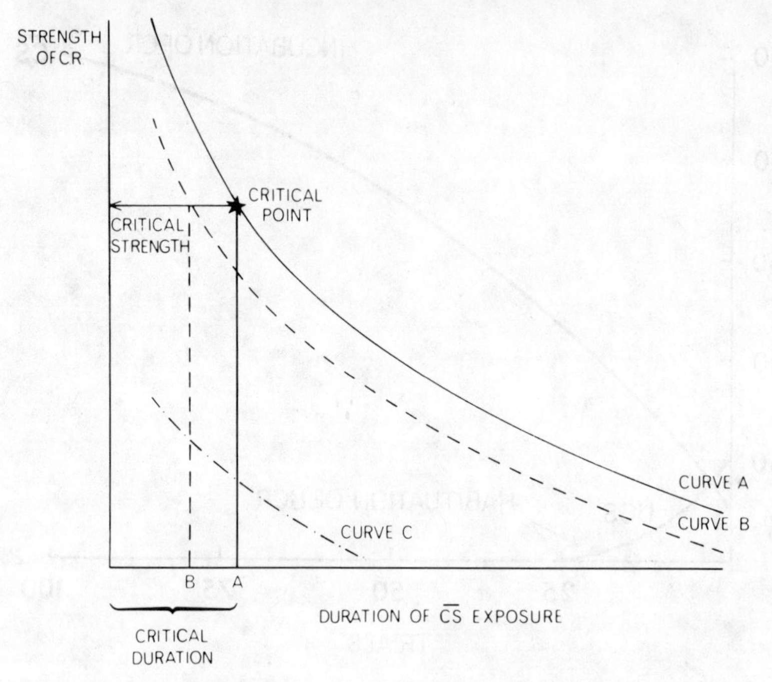

of behavior. The abscissa shows duration of CS-only exposure, and curve A indicates the decline of CR strength over time. The critical point is marked on curve A. When the CR is stronger than indicated by this point, then incubation/enhancement occurs; when it is below this point, then extinction occurs. If extinction is involved, then on the next presentation of the CS response strength will be weaker, and events as indicated in curve B will follow. Curve C illustrates the situation after several extinction trials have been given.

The critical nature of the duration of the S exposure is also indicated in this diagram. Given the events illustrated by curve A, then durations *shorter* than A will lead to incubation of anxiety, durations *longer* than A to extinction. For curve B, point B would be the critical point marking off durations producing incubation from those producing extinction.

There is evidence concerning all these points in the experimental and the clinical literature; details are given in Eysenck (1979). The theory also explains why at times flooding (that is, exposure above the critical point) leads to a positive therapeutic outcome, while at other times it leads to exacerbation of the neurotic anxiety. The difference lies simply in the duration of the CS exposure; where this is long, amelioration results, where it is too short, exacerbation results. Flooding treatment is typically initiated at a high point on curve A, that is, above the critical point; desensitization is typically carried out well below the critical strength, that is, along the lines of curve C. The theory thus explains not only the anomaly that sometimes flooding leads to one outcome, sometimes to another; it also shows that flooding and desensitization, although apparently proceeding along quite different and indeed contrary lines, are subject to the same explanation as far as their curative effects are concerned.

Strength of the CR and duration of CS-only exposure are not the only relevant variables; as mentioned before, personality is also very important. There is strong evidence to indicate that personality dimensions of extraversion-introversion and neuroticism-stability are closely involved with the origins of neurosis (Eysenck & Rachman, 1965; Eysenck, 1967) in the sense that people who are high on N and low on E are much more likely to develop neurotic disorders than are people not in that quadrant of the personality space. Neuroticism as a personality factor is produced largely by overreactivity of the limbic system, exerting a steering action on the autonomic system, while E is mediated by the ascending reticular formation, which in turns governs the arousal level in the cortex, producing a lower resting level in extraverts and a high resting level in introverts (Eysenck, 1967, 1981). Thus in theory the high N/low E person is predisposed to neurosis, because he reacts strongly to emotionally arousing stimuli and conditions such stimuli more readily. Also introverts extinguish conditioned responses more slowly than extraverts (Hemming, 1979). Such personality differences as these (or, in animal work, comparable differences) interact with the parameters already mentioned; the evidence is reviewed in Eysenck (1979). The prediction here is of course that weaker UCS are required to produce the same effect in high N scorers or low E scorers than would be required for low N or high E scorers. Similarly, duration of CS only would need to be longer for high N or low E scorers to get below the critical point, as compared with low N or high E scorers. The possibility of "trading" personality variables against experimental variables has been discussed in relation to experimental evidence by Savage & Eysenck (1964); the hypothesis is supported both at the animal and at the human level. Unfortunately, clinical psychologists have not shown much interest in the systematic investigation of personality parameters, despite the promise these hold out of a more accurate prediction (Di Loreto, 1971), so that on this point the evidence is rather meagre. We suggest, nevertheless, that personality interacts strongly with situational parameters and cannot be left out of any theory purporting to encompass the total situation.

The importance of such individual differences is clearly indicated by Hugdahl et al. (1977). These authors used spontaneous electrodermal responses, which are known to correlate with introversion and anxiety (Eysenck, 1967). Using neutral and "prepared" CS and electrodermal conditioning, they found "that arousal and fear relevance are additive factors in conditioning" (p. 353). They go on to say that "If the present situation can be taken as a model of real life phobic conditioning, the results suggest that persons with a habitual high arousal level are more susceptible to acquired phobias than are people with low arousal levels, and that fear relevance is an important factor in the content of the phobias. Furthermore, fear relevance and activation seem to interact so that a high habitual arousal level is increased even more than when potentially phobic stimuli are encountered, since the number of spontaneous fluctuations was higher in the high phobics than in the high neutral group. At such high levels of arousal, there is the danger that the habituation mechanism becomes inoperative, which might lead to unselective, diffuse responding to all stimuli. For instance, in the present study, the high phobic group did not differentiate between the significant C+ and the insignificant C— during acquisition" (p. 352).

As Eysenck (1979) has pointed out, "Spontaneous electrodermal fluctuation is a good measure of personality to use in this context, because it is correlated both with introversion and with neuroticism-anxiety (Lader, 1967; Lader & Wing, 1966). The results of the Hugdahl et al. work fit in well with the general theory here proposed and illustrate the importance of individual differences, the "preparedness" of CS, and the interaction between the two factors. Clearly, habituation and extinction are very much attenuated when suitable CS are used with suitable personality types, that is, types showing high arousal whether this arousal is indexed directly by means of psychophysiological measures, such as spontaneous electrodermal fluctuations, or by means of personality questionnaires (Crider & Lunn, 1971; Bohlin, 1971; Lader, 1967).

Figure 5-2, in principle, exemplifies our general theory according to which all neurotic disorders are produced by classical conditioning and all successful treatment of neurotic disorders proceeds by classical extinction. We have already seen how the diagram illustrates the clinical applications of behavior therapy known as desensitization and flooding. In the former, the patient is protected against any strong anxiety arising during therapy by a procedure in which he is kept in a relaxed state and is presented the unreinforced conditioned stimulus, whether in vivo or in imagination, only at points on the hierarchy that are relatively little arousing (that is, well below the critical point, as in curve C on our diagram). If the critical point is ever exceeded, the CS is immediately withdrawn; it has often been demonstrated that when the critical point is reached or exceeded in desensitization, the success of treatment is in peril, and the patient is actually made worse (Wolpe, 1958). In flooding, on the other hand, the patient is immediately confronted with the most frightening CS, that is, one at the top of the hierarchy; this procedure, which includes explicitly an element of response prevention, is continued for periods of an hour and more. Both desensitization and flooding are successful in practice (Kazdin & Wilson, 1978), although they appear to proceed in contradictory directions; the answer to this anomaly, as we have already pointed out, lies in the duration of exposure.

As an example, useful to illustrate the relevance of the theory diagrammed in Figure 5-2, we may quote the work of Rachman & Hodgson (1980) on obsessive-compulsive disorders. Figure 5-3 shows some of the results reported by these authors. Given are the ratings for urge (motivation for hand-washing after contamination) and discomfort suffered across various occasions. It will be seen that BE (before exposure to provoking stimulus) urge and discomfort ratings are low; they rise to a high point AE (after exposure), and return again to the starting point AR (after ritual, that is, after hand-washing). This part of the diagram illustrates the anxiety-reducing properties of the symptom, namely the ritual. The second part of the diagram shows the high rise of urge and discomfort after exposure, that is, at the beginning of the "flooding" treatment. Also shown is the gradual reduction in urge and discomfort over time, corresponding to curves A and B in Figure 5-2. Similar curves are available for psychophysiological and other measurements of the anxiety experienced by the individuals.

It is not only desensitization and flooding that can be explained in terms of our model; modeling itself also clearly falls in this paradigm. What is done there is to expose a patient to the feared object or situation, keeping his anxiety rather low by having the model coping successfully with the objective situation and clearly not implicating the patient directly. Much the same comment can be made about Ellis's rational-emotional type of therapy, or Rogers client-centered type of therapy. In both cases what happens is that the patient is exposed, in imagination and through a process of talking, to the feared objects or situations, thus being forced to expose himself to the unreinforced CS, which is in relatively weak form, thus preventing it from producing CR above the critical point. The presence of the therapist, encouraging the patient and generally serving to relax him, acts as an additional variable reducing the strength of the CS in these situations.

As far as psychotherapy is concerned, it seems clear that something very similar is taking place there also. The patient is encouraged to discuss his difficulties and his anxieties and to confront the objects or situations producing his fear responses, at least in imagination. He does so against a background of a sympathetic, helpful listener, who is usually supportive in his attitude, thus reducing generalized anxiety. The critical strength level of the CS is therefore not usually exceeded, and consequently all these encounters should be capable of being symbolized by curve C in our diagram. It is suggested that all successful methods of psychotherapy (and by success we do not necessarily mean that their effectiveness exceeds that of spontaneous remission, but merely that after therapy the patient is better than he was before therapy) follow this paradigm, and are therefore examples of classical extinction of Pavlovian B type conditioned responses.

Spontaneous remission, as the writer pointed out long ago (Eysenck, 1963) is also subject to a similar type of explanations. It is well known that people suffering from neurotic disorders who do not consult a physician, a psychiatrist, psychoanalyst, or a clinical psychologist will consult other people to discuss their troubles (priests, teachers, friends, relatives, and so forth). The conditions for extinction are therefore very similar to those that obtain under psychotherapy, and an exactly similar explanation may therefore be given for the occurrence of extinction. We thus end up with the parsimonious theory that is in good accord with the experimental facts ascertained in the laboratory and explains all phenomena of successful treatment.

It also seems that our theory can explain the relative success of behavioral therapies and the relatively lower level of success of psychotherapy and spontaneous remission (Kazdin & Wilson, 1978; Rachman & Wilson, 1981). The methods of behavior therapy explicitly use the mechanism of extinction and have been worked out so as to make for optimum effectiveness of this mechanism. The methods of psychotherapy have been worked out on different theoretical principles, and these interfere with the quickest method of extinction. The same is probably true of spontaneous remission: the people to whom the neurotic turns have no explicit theory to guide them, and hence their conduct will not be optimal as far as extinction of their conditioned responses is concerned. We would therefore expect, and we do find, that the methods of behavior therapy tend to work best, followed by psychotherapy, followed by spontaneous remission.

Psychoanalysis in general may be assumed to follow the same explanatory principles as psychotherapy, as far as psychotherapeutic effectiveness is concerned. The analysis gives ample opportunity for extinction to occur, but the occasions are not properly planned, and hence the effectiveness is much less than when proper care is taken to facilitate extinction, as in behavior therapy. There is, however, one additional phenomenon in psychoanalysis (and sometimes also in nonpsychoanalytic psychotherapy) that has given particular difficulties to theoreticians trying to account for it, but which can be explained very readily in terms of the theory he outlined. According to Strupp, Hadley, and Gomes-Schwartz (1977) psychotherapy and psychoanalysis in particular can produce not only positive but also negative effects; a point also made by Bergin (Garfield & Bergin, 1978). The evidence is strong, but not entirely conclusive (Rachman & Wilson, 1981); on the whole, it does seem likely that negative effects do occur and require an explanation. Such an explanation may readily be found in terms of our theory. Psychoanalysts in particular often adopt an unhelpful, pseudo-objective, interpretative attitude, which does not help the patient to relax or encourage him in any way; under these conditions his anxiety may easily exceed the critical point and thus lead to incrementation of anxiety, rather than improvement in his clinical condition. The evidence presented by Bergin (1963), Bergin and Jasper (1969), Bergin and Solomon (1970), Carkhuff (1967), and Carkhuff and Truax (1965) suggests that the hypothesis linking the personality and therapeutic manner of the therapist with success or failure along the lines of our theory may be correct, although the evidence they provide is not as firmly established as one would like to think.

We thus see that our theory is capable of accounting for most, if not all, the recognized features of modern therapeutic practices, of whatever kind. We have not discussed all the hundreds or even thousands of methods and theories that have been put forward (Gossop, 1981); the reader will readily be able to demonstrate to his own satisfaction that all of these methods involve the exposure of the patient to the unreinforced CS, whether in vivo or imagination, and that all attempt to get below the critical point by adopting some kind of hierarchical presentation of stimuli, as in desensitization, by relaxation or other methods of reassurance of the patient, or in some other way. These universally present features accord well with the theory, and it would seem that the relative success of the different methods (which seldom exceed that of spontaneous remission!) is due entirely to successful Pavlovian extinction of conditioned emotional responses. The point is sometimes made by critics that the theory leaves out entirely all cognitive factors, and that a more cognitively oriented theory would be preferable. Such an objection may be countered along two lines. The first of these is that there is in fact no proper cognitive theory applicable to the phenomena of neurosis. As Allport (1975) has pointed out, in concluding his examination of the field, "it is characterized by . . . uncritical, or selective, or frankly cavalier attitudes to experimental data; a pervasive atmosphere of special pleading; a curious parochialism in acknowledging even the existence of other workers, and other approaches, to the phenomena under discussion; interpretations of data relying on multiple, arbitrary choice points; and underlying all else, a near vacuum of theoretical structure within which to interrelate different sets of experimental results, or direct the search for significant new phenomena." Theories of this type are not likely to help us in gaining a scientific understanding of the phenomena of neurosis and treatment.

Equally convincing to the writer is another answer, namely that the relevance of cognitive phenomena was recognized already by Pavlov in his notion of the "second signalling system," and that these phenomena are just as subject to the laws of conditioning as are those already considered. As Pavlov pointed out: "The word is as real a conditioned stimulus for man as all the other stimuli in common with animals, but at the same time more all-inclusive than any other stimuli." And in another place: "Owing to the entire preceding life of a human adult a word is connected with all the internal and external stimuli coming to the cerebral hemispheres, signals all of them, replaces all of them, and can, therefore, evoke all the actions and reactions of the organisms which the stimuli produce." Thus, these cognitive factors are not omitted by conditioning theory; as Eysenck (1979) has pointed out, the conditioning theory includes consideration of cognitive factors, as in concepts such as semantic generalization, all mediational theories (McGuigan, 1978), and evaluative conditioning.

One of the reasons why cognitive psychotherapy has been so widely and uncritically accepted and welcomed is probably because it makes a clear distinction between animal work and human behavior and seems to recognize specific human features of behavior that orthodox behavior therapy may seem to neglect. It seems to be more humanistic and acceptable to people who still fail to appreciate the importance of evolutionary concepts in the explanation of human behavior. It may be useful to spell out in detail how successfully behavior therapists can utilize work with animals and principles thus established in their search for new and better methods of treatment, and what precisely would be required of the cognitive behavior therapist in order to establish superior claims to acceptance of his principles.

To acquire a proper understanding of the issues at stake, it is necessary to consider the particular model of man that protagonists of different points of view have to offer. The present writer (Eysenck, 1980a, 1980b) has argued for a biosocial model of man that recognizes equally the biological, genetic, evolutionary aspects of human nature and the cognitive, social, developmental aspects. Such a model—as MacLean pointed out in his theory of the triune brain—is graphically illustrated in the three-fold division of the human brain into what he calls the reptile brain, the paleocortex or limbic system, and the neocortex. These divisions are equally clear on the morphological and the functional plane, and although the different parts are not of course completely separate, there is little intercommunication between them. The neocortex is primarily the organ of rational thinking, information processing, and problem solving; it is this part of the cortex that has developed into a unique extent in human beings and separates them from the animal kingdom (with the doubtful exception of the apes). Ordinary language is a proper means of communication with this system, which is also characterized by the development of consciousness and introspective ability. Cognitive theorists are primarily concerned with this system, to the exclusion of the paleocortex and the reptile brain.

However, it seems clear now that neurotic disorders are primarily dysfunctions of the limbic system, that is, the paleocortex and/or the reptile brain. Furthermore, the language of the paleocortex is that of the *conditioned response*, and consciousness and ordinary language have little if any possibility of communicating with and influencing the paleocortex. It is for this reason that the mechanism of conditioning is crucial in the development of neurotic disorders and the mechanism of extinction is equally crucial in the treatment of neurotic disorders. Cognitive theorists would deny this and implicate cognitive processes in a very prominent fashion. How can such an argument be resolved?

As an example of how experimental and clinical events may clarify the issue, consider the recent work in our department on obsessive-compulsive disorders (Rachman & Hodgson, 1980). These disorders have been investigated exhaustively by psychoanalysts and other cognitive theorists, but as far as treatment is concerned success has been nugatory. Milan (1979), a well-known British psychoanalyst, points out that "even through the psychopathology in such cases appears perfectly intelligible, accumulated practical experience suggests that often the symptom itself develops an autonomy, and no matter how extensively the pathology is interpreted and apparently worked through, the symptom remains untouched. It is apparently true, for instance, that there is no known authenticated case of an obsessional hand-washer being cured by psychoanalytic treatment. In my view, therefore, the treatment of choice immediately becomes *behaviour therapy*" (pp. 218–219). This failure of cognitive methods to make any impression on the disorder is confirmed by a survey of clinical records of past cases at the Maudsley Hospital; the success of psychotherapeutic methods of all kinds has been trifling, as has the success of psychopharmacological methods and of physical methods such as lobotomy and electro-shock therapy. Thus this disorder is apparently impervious to a large variety of different types of psychiatric interference.

The treatment recently developed for disorders of this type, originally suggested by Eysenck and Rachman (1965), is explicitly based on an animal analogue, namely the behavior of dogs in a shuttlebox (Solomon et al., 1955). The shuttlebox consists of two large compartments separated by a hurdle that can be jumped by the dogs; the floor of each compartment can be separately electrified to give a shock to the paws of the dogs. Also included is a flickering light that acts as the conditioned stimulus, the shock being the unconditioned stimulus. The dog soon learns to jump from one compartment to the other after exposure to the light, followed by shock; he then quickly learns to jump to the conditioned stimulus

Figure 5-3. Urge and Discomfort Ratings BE (Before Exposure), AE (After Exposure), and AR (After Ritual Handwashing); on Right, Course of Urge and Discomfort after Exposure to CS-Only, with Response Prevention. (Rachman & Hodgson, 1980)

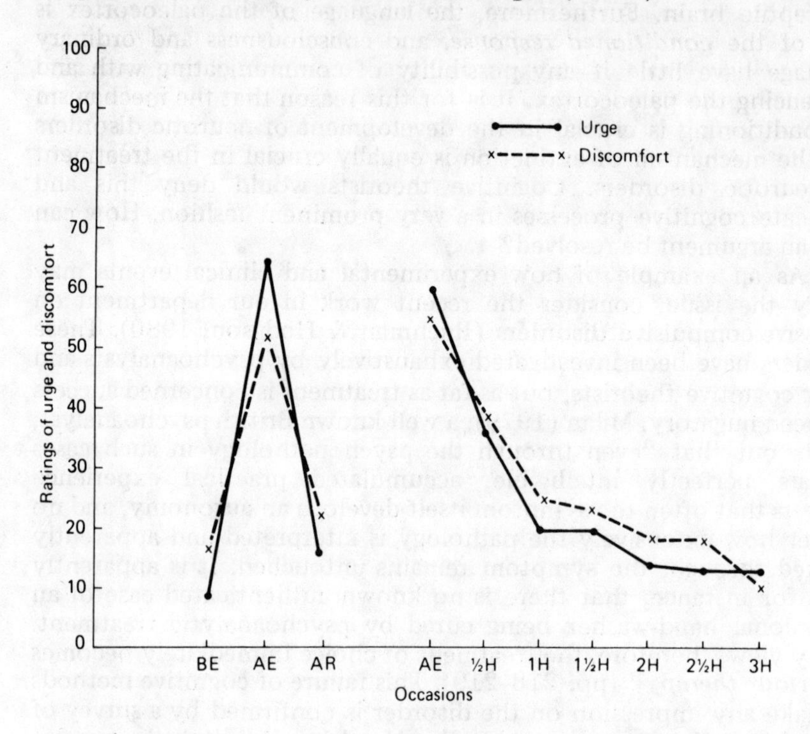

alone. When the conditioned response is well established, the electricity supply is disconnected so that the dog is *never shocked again.* Nevertheless he continues to jump; the hypothesis being that the jumping relieves his anxiety. The analogy with hand-washing in order to relieve anxiety seems very straightforward, and so does the use of methods of treatment for both "disorders."

In the case of the dogs, the best, and indeed the only effective method was found to be that of response prevention and flooding. The height of the hurdle was increased so that the dog could no longer jump across it, and he was then exposed to the CS-only. The dogs exposed to this condition showed strong emotions of fear, urinating and defecating; after a while the emotions subsided, very much as shown in Figure 5-3 on the right side, and several repetitions of this experience completely "cured" the dogs of their obsessive-compulsive behavior.

Similar methods were introduced in the treatment of human patients suffering from obsessive-compulsive disorders, but by making the patient immerse his hands in an urn filled with dirt and rubbish and then instructing him not to wash his hands but sit quietly for several hours in a room with the therapist. The typical response pattern is shown in Figure 5-3; "flooding" with emotion is followed by the gradual decrease below the critical point, and hence extinction occurs. Just as in the case of the dogs, a number of repetitions very much reduce and finally cure the disorder in something like 90% of all cases (Rachman & Hodgson, 1980). Follow-ups disclosed no symptom substitution or relapse, but rather a gradual improvement in all work, family, and sex aspects of the individual's life style.

Let us now consider this example of behavior therapy in the light of criticism and suggestions made by cognitive theorists. They suggest that cognitive methods involving understanding, coping mechanisms, and interpretation would either be sufficient by themselves to treat the patient and cure him, or would, if added to simple behavioral treatment, improve the extent or rate of cure of the patient. As we have seen, there is no evidence that such methods as have been tried have had any effect whatsoever on the symptom involved, and if cognitive theorists are to be taken seriously, then they would indeed have to show that either a higher proportion than 90% could be treated successfully by using their methods, or that the cure could be effected more quickly; needless to say, neither demonstration has so far been given, and it seems highly unlikely, from our experience, that anything of the kind could indeed be shown. The claims made by cognitive theorists are entirely on the theoretical plane. There is no evidence, as could only be derived from clinical trials, of the superiority of their methods, or even of the equivalence of their methods to orthodox behavior therapy of a noncognitive kind. Other examples could be given, but this one must suffice for the present. Cognitive behavior therapy, so called, relies on extinction of the classical kind for its effectiveness, just as do all other methods, and there is no evidence that the addition of cognitive features improves the rate or extent of amelioration.

If it be true, as suggested here, that all methods of therapy use Pavlovian extinction as an active ingredient, then in what way do the methods differ? Extinction essentially means the presentation of the CS only, at the level of strength of the CR, which, at the cessation of exposure, is below the critical point. Clearly, this exposure can be done in many different ways; for instance, it can be done in vivo, or in imagination; it may be done by imagery, verbal description, pictorial representation, film, or in many other ways. Furthermore, the general level of anxiety of the patient can be reduced by training in relaxation, by sympathetic understanding and kindliness, by drugs, or in many other ways. There are thus a myriad ways in which all these elements can be combined, but this does not affect the major point of this paper, namely, that what is basically responsible for successful treatment is the presentation of the CS-only on repeated occasions, below the critical point, with the patient in a state of relatively low anxiety at the point of termination of exposure of the CS-only. The closer the method adopted follows the procedure described, the better will the results be. Departures, such as the anxiety-provoking behavior of the orthodox psychoanalyst, will retard the success of treatment and may in fact make the patient worse. Proper understanding of this fundamental rule of treatment is essential for the successful application of psychological methods to the treatment of neurotic patients.

SUMMARY

Psychotherapy and behavior therapy have generated many different types of treatment, and there is very little agreement as to the causal mechanisms that mediate their effectiveness, or even the effectiveness of spontaneous remission (or whatever factors may mediate spontaneous remission). In this paper I suggest that it is possible to formulate a general theory that covers all the different types of treatment and accounts for their respective effectiveness, including that of spontaneous remission. This theory is based on Watson's original view that neurotic disorders are produced by Pavlovian conditioning, and that they can be cured by Pavlovian extinction. This theory has a long history, but many difficulties and anomalies have accumulated that have made it unacceptable to experimentalists and clinicians alike. The present paper seeks to rescue the theory from the criticisms that have been made of it by introducing certain novel concepts and views relating particularly to Seligman's notion of "preparedness" and the writer's notion of "incubation of anxiety," which effectively necessitates the rewriting of the law of extinction.

Given that the theory can be revitalized by making these necessary changes, and that the usual criticisms can be obviated in this manner, the rest of the paper is concerned with the application of the theory to different methods of treatment, including psychotherapy, psychoanalysis, different methods of behavior therapy, and spontaneous remission. It is argued that all these methods have in common the essential mechanism of extinction, namely the introduction of the unreinforced conditioned stimulus under conditions of reduced autonomic arousal. It seems possible to unify the vastly different methods that have been used for treatment using this conception, and it is suggested that the views here advocated may lead to an improvement in the methods of experimental investigation and clinical trial that have been used in this field. Recent work on obsessive-compulsive neuroses carried out in our laboratories is used to exemplify the application of these views to the clinical and experimental study of neurotic treatment.

REFERENCES

Allport, D. A. The state of cognitive psychology. *Quarterly Journal of Experimental Psychology*, 1975, *27*, 141-152.

Bergin, A. E. The effects of psychotherapy: Negative results revisited. *Journal of Counseling Psychology*, 1963, *10*, 244-250.

Bergin, A. E. & Jasper, L. G. Correlates of empathy in psychotherapy: A replication. *Journal of Abnormal Psychology*, 1969, *74*, 477-481.

Bergin, A. E., & Solomon, S. Personality and performance correlates of empathetic understanding in psychotherapy. In T. Tomlinson & J. Hart (Eds.). *New directions in client-centered therapy.* Boston, MA: Houghton Mifflin, 1970.

Bohlin, G. Monotonous stimulation, sleep onset and habituation of the orienting reaction. *Electroencephalography and Clinical Neurophysiology*, 1971, *31*, 593-601.

Breger, L., & McGaugh, J. Critique and reformulation of "learning theory" approaches to psychotherapy and neurosis. *Psychological Bulletin*, 1965, *63*, 338-358.

Breland, K., & Breland, M. *Animal behavior.* New York: Macmillan, 1966.

Bykov, K. M. *The cerebral cortex and the internal organs.* Trans. by W. H. Gantt. New York: Chemical Publishing Co., 1957.

Carkhuff, R. R. Toward a comprehensive model of facilitative interpersonal processes. *Journal of Counseling Psychology*, 1967, *14*, 67-72.

Carkhuff, R. R., & Truax, C. B. Lay mental health counseling. *Journal of Consulting Psychology*, 1965, *29*, 426-431.

Crider, A., & Lunn, R. Electrodermal lability as a personality dimension. *Journal of Experimental Research in Personality*, 1971, *5*, 145-150.

DiLoreto, A. *Comparative Psychotherapy.* New York: Aldine-Atherton, 1971.

Eysenck, H. J. Learning theory and behaviour therapy. *Journal of Mental Science*, 1959, *105*, 61-75.

Eysenck, H. J. Behaviour therapy, spontaneous remission and transference in neurotics. *American Journal of Psychiatry*, 1963, *119*, 867-871.

Eysenck, H. J. Single-trial conditioning and the Napalkov phenomenon. *Behaviour Research and Therapy*, 1967, *5*, 63-65.

Eysenck, H. J. Behaviour therapy—dogma or applied science? In M. P. Feldman & A. Broadhurst (Eds.). *Theoretical and experimental bases of the behaviour therapies.* London: Wiley, 1976.

Eysenck, H. J. The conditioning model of neurosis. *The Behavioral and Brain Sciences*, 1979, *2*, 155-199.

Eysenck, H. J. The bio-social model of man and the unification of psychology. In A. J. Chapman & D. M. Jones (Eds.). *Models of man.* Leicester, England: The British Psychological Society, 1980. (a)

Eysenck, H. J. Man as a biosocial animal. *Political Psychology*, 1980, *2*, 43–51. (b)

Eysenck, H. J. *A model for personality.* London: Springer Verlag, 1981.

Eysenck, H. J., & Rachman, S. *Causes and cures of neurosis.* London: Routledge & Kegan Paul, 1965.

Garcia, J., McGovan, B., & Green, K. Sensory quality and integration: constraints on conditioning. In A. H. Black & W. F. Prokasy (Eds.). *Classical conditioning.* New York: Appleton-Century-Crofts, 1971.

Garfield, S., & Bergin, A. E. *Handbook of psychotherapy and behavior change.* New York: Wiley, 1978.

Geer, J. H. The development of a scale to measure fear. *Behaviour Research and Therapy*, 1965, *3*, 45–53.

Gossop, M. *Theories of neurosis.* London: Springer Verlag, 1981.

Gourney, A. B., & O'Connor, P. J. Anxiety associated with flying. *British Journal of Psychiatry*, 1971, *119*, 159–166.

Grant, D. A. Classical and operant conditioning. In A. W. Mepton (Ed.). *Categories of human learning.* New York: Academic Press, 1964.

Grinker, R., & Spiegel, J. *Men under stress.* London: Churchill, 1945.

Hemming, J. H. Personality and extinction of a conditioned electrodermal response. *British Journal of Social and Clinical Psychology*, 1979, *18*, 105–110.

Hinde, R. A., & Stevenson-Hinde, J. *Constraints on learning.* London: Academic Press, 1973.

Hugdahl, K., Frederikson, M., & Ohman, A. "Preparedness" and "arousability" and determinants of electrodermal conditioning. *Behaviour Research and Therapy*, 1977, *15*, 345–353.

Hughdahl, K., & Ohman, A. Effects of instruction on acquisition and extinction of electrodermal responses to fear-relevant stimuli. *Journal of Experimental Psychology: Human Learning and Memory*, 1977, *3*, 608–618.

Kalat, J. W., & Rozin, P. You can lead a rat to poison but you can't make him think. In M. E. P. Seligman & J. L. Hager (Eds.). *Biological boundaries of learning.* New York: Appleton-Century-Crofts, 1973.

Kamin, L. J. Predictability, surprise, attention and conditioning. In B. A. Campbell & R. M. Church (Eds.). *Punishment and aversion behavior.* New York: Appleton-Century-Crofts, 1969.

Kazdin, A. E., & Wilson, G. T. *Evaluation of behavior therapy.* New York: Ballinger, 1978.

Kimble, G. *Hilgard & Marquis' "Conditioning and learning."* New York: Appleton-Century-Crofts, 1961.

Lader, M. H. Palmar skin conductance measures in anxiety and phobic states. *Journal of Psychosomatic Research*, 1967, *11*, 271-281.

Lader, M. H., & Wing, L. *Physiological measures, sedative drugs and morbid anxiety.* Oxford: Oxford University Press, 1966.

Landy, F. J., & Gaupp, L. A. A factor analysis of the fear survey schedule III. *Behaviour Research and Therapy*, 1971, *9*, 89-93.

Lawlis, G. F. Response styles of a patient population on the fear schedule. *Behaviour Research and Therapy*, 1971, *9*, 95-102.

Locke, E. A. Is "behavior therapy" behavioristic? *Psychological Bulletin*, 1971, *76*, 318-327.

London, P. The end of ideology in behavior modification. *American Psychologist*, 1972, *27*, 913-920.

Malan, D. H. *Individual psychotherapy and the science of psychodynamics.* London: Butterworths, 1979.

Marks, I. M. *Fears and phobias.* London: Academic Press, 1969.

McGuigan, F. J. *Cognitive psychophysiology: Principles of covert behavior.* Englewood Cliffs, NJ: Prentice Hall, 1978.

Pavlov, I. P. *Conditional reflexes.* Trans. by G. V. Anrep. London: Oxford University Press, 1927.

Rachman, S. *Phobias—their nature and control.* Springfield, IL: C. C Thomas, 1968.

Rachman, S. J., & Hodgson, R. J. *Obsessions and compulsions.* Englewood Cliffs, NJ: Prentice-Hall, 1980.

Rachman, S. J., & Wilson, T. *The effects of psychological therapy*, second edition. London: Pergamon Press, 1981.

Rubin, B. M., Katkin, E. S., Weiss, B. W., & Efran, J. S. Factor analysis of a fear schedule. *Behaviour Research and Therapy*, 1968, *6*, 65-75.

Savage, R. D., & Eysenck, H. J. The definition and measurement of emotionality. In H. J. Eysenck (Ed.). *Experiments in movitation.* London: Pergamon Press, 1964.

Seligman, M. E. P. Chronic fear produced by unpredictable electric shock. *Journal of Comparative and Physiological Psychology*, 1968, *66*, 402-411.

Seligman, M. E. P. On the generality of the laws of learning. *Psychological Review*, 1970, *77*, 406-418.

Seligman, M. E. P. Phobias and preparedness. *Behavior Therapy*, 1971, *2*, 307-320.

Seligman, M. E. P. *Biological boundaries of learning.* New York: Appleton-Century-Crofts, 1972.

Solomon, R., Kamin, L., & Wynne, L. Traumatic avoidance learning: The outcomes of several extinction procedures with dogs. *Journal of Abnormal and Social Psychology*, 1953, *48*, 291-302.

Strupp, H., Hadley, S. W., & Gomes-Schwartz, B. *Psychotherapy for better or worse.* New York: Jason Aronson, 1977.

Watson, J. B., & Rayner, R. Conditioned emotional reactions. *Journal of Experimental Psychology*, 1920, *3*, 1–14.

Wolpe, J. *Psychotherapy by reciprocal inhibition.* Stanford, CA: Stanford University Press, 1958.

Wolpe, J., & Lang, P. J. A fear survey schedule for use in behaviour therapy. *Behaviour Research and Therapy*, 1964, *4*, 27–30.

CHAPTER 6

Neurotic Fears: Two Origins, Two Classes of Treatment

Joseph Wolpe, M.D.

The now vast literature of behavior therapy impressively documents its efficacy in the treatment of the neuroses—the whole range of conditioned unadaptive anxiety response habits—and the disabilities secondary to them, such as psychosomatic disorders, sexual inadequacies, and neurotic depressions. Individual reports of cases showing a relationship between interventions and change are numerous. Their testimony is supported by the better-controlled studies, among which that of Paul (1964) is to this day the most impressive. Good evidence of the superiority of behavior therapy over brief psychoanalytically oriented therapy appears in the study by Sloane et al. (1975), although these authors gloss over it (see Giles, 1981). Much attention has lately been directed to the question of the best method for a particular syndrome; and many investigations have been undertaken to seek answers. In these investigations, the practice has been to compare different treatments for unselected clinical populations with the same diagnosis, such as insomnia or agoraphobia. The investigator collects the cases (within stated limits of age, duration, and so forth) and then randomly assigns them to the treatments to be compared.

This is a revision of a version that appeared in the *Journal of Behavior Therapy and Experimental Psychiatry*, Volume 12, 1981 under the title, "The Dichotomy Between Directly Conditioned and Cognitively Learned Anxiety."

This is, in its general outlines, the accepted procedure in medical research. But a crucial feature of such research is that the population to be treated must be ill in the same specific way. For example, in comparing antibiotics for the treatment of pneumonia, it would be necessary to have the same causal organism in all cases.

Similarly, in comparing behavioral treatments, there should be uniformity in the stimulus-response structure of the cases. A variety of conditionings may produce the same manifestation—activate the same final common path—in an organism as complex as a human being. This variability is the central reason why responsible practice requires careful behavior analyses before behavior therapy. Such analyses are equally necessary in research. The first question is whether a particular fear is cognitively based or due to autonomic conditioning.

THE TWO MODES OF ORIGIN OF HABITS OF FEAR

The mode of origin of a fear habit determines its stimulus-response structure. There are two basic modes: autonomic conditioning and cognitive learning.

Classical Autonomic Conditioning

The severe fears of animals known as experimental neuroses (Pavlov, 1941; Masserman, 1943; Wolpe, 1952) are clearly a matter of classical conditioning. The experimenter, using either conflict or noxious stimulation, elicits strong fear in an animal confined in a small cage. These responses are characterized by attempts to escape, combined with a variety of autonomic responses, of which the most consistent are dilatation of the pupils, piloerection, and rapid respiration. After several repetitions, the autonomic response pattern is found to be independently elicitable by the environmental stimuli, such as the experimental cage and the experimental room. And there is fear in other rooms according to how much they have in common with the experimental room.

Classical conditioning is frequently the basis of human neurotic fear as well. It may be conditioned to a high intensity by a single event (single trial learning) or may be progressively built up in a series of related events. The classic example of single trial fear conditioning is the war neurosis. A soldier has great anxiety aroused in him by the mutilation of comrades beside him in a situation in which machine-gun fire predominates; and after that he is found to be extremely anxious, not only on the battlefield, but also back home when he hears any sound that resembles machine-gun fire, such as a motorcycle going uphill. His anxiety is automatically aroused by the sound: no cognitive error is involved. He does not for a moment believe that danger threatens in the sounds of a motorcycle.

Civilian examples of single-trial fear conditioning are also common. A 34-year-old man's severe fear of being in an automobile had started four years previously, when his car had been struck from behind while he was waiting for a red light to change. He had been thust forward so that his head had struck the windshield. The injury was slight, and he had not lost consciousness; but he had been terrified, thinking that his last moment had come. Since then, he was fearful not only of driving a car, but even of sitting inside one, even if stationary. That fear was purely a matter of classical autonomic conditioning—he had no expectation of danger when he sat in a car.

Many instances of "single incident" causation are without the "traumatic" feature that the foregoing case shares with the war neuroses. It is not uncommon for a fear of public speaking or public scrutiny to begin from a single overwhelmingly distressful experience. A woman of 21 dated the onset of a very severe fear of this kind to an occasion in a classroom when she was 11 years old. While standing up and reading, she mispronounced a word, so that it gave a sentence an obscene meaning. The class burst into ribald laughter, to her intense embarrassment. After this, being the center of attention always made her very anxious.

Severe neurotic anxiety may also develop in steps, sometimes in many steps (see Table 6-1). Public speaking fears are probably usually based on numerous anxiety-arousing experiences. Similarly, neurotic fears of disapproval mostly develop from the repeated anxiety arousals caused by parents or teachers who are excessively punitive or critical.

It is important to realize that the causal anxiety is not necessarily aroused by an *external* stimulus. In a physician whose sexual interest was unequivocally confined to women, fear of homosexuality was conditioned in the following way. While reading, in a novel, a description of the sexual behavior of a homosexual man, he became aware of a spontaneous erection (which actually happened to him quite often without discernible relation to thoughts or circumstances). However, the thought now crossed his mind, "Does the fact that this is happening right now mean that I am unconsciously homosexual?" This thought (for which his knowledge of psychoanalysis was responsible) aroused great anxiety; and from that time onward he had anxiety when seeing a homosexual or reading about one, or when making physical contact with *any* male, as when sitting beside one on a bus. Similarly, in some cases of agoraphobia, the classical conditioning of anxiety has had a cognitive source. An unhappily married woman low in self-sufficiency may have fantasies of getting out of her marriage, which, while partly gratifying, are also anxiety-arousing because she dreads aloneness. The anxiety arousal leads to anxiety being conditioned to the fantasies (see Wolpe, 1958, p. 64) and with repetition the anxiety becomes so strong that there is generalization from social aloneness to isolation in space.

When fear conditioning is strong, it is remarkably resistant to extinction (Wolpe, 1958, p. 66), presumably because no other responses can compete with it successfully. Recent research (as in Amsel, 1962) points to response competition being the main basis of extinction. Experimental neuroses are reliably overcome by arranging systematically for weak anxiety responses to be inhibited by the competition of feeding. It was the similarity of classically conditioned human fears to those of animal neuroses that led to the treatment of human neuroses by response competition (reciprocal inhibition) (Wolpe, 1958). Recent literature in the behavior therapy field shows a widespread forgetfulness of the fact that not only the calmness produced by deep muscle relaxation, but also sexual responses, anger, and other responses can overcome anxiety response habits through systematic competition with anxiety (Wolpe, 1973).

The treatment of a classically conditioned anxiety response habit calls for desensitization or flooding or other deconditioning procedures; and efforts toward the correction of misconceptions are entirely off the point, since there are no relevant misconceptions to correct.

Cognitively Based Neurotic Fears

Other neurotic fears are due to erroneous cognitions. As a matter of background, most of our *noneurotic fears*—that is, those that have a basis in reality—are cognitively based; they have been acquired through information. We fear a snarling dog or the speeding, swerving driver of our taxi, not because we have had painful previous experiences with them or their like, but because we know them to be dangerous.

Misinformation can bring about fears that are as powerful and enduring as those based on the truth. A man may fear masturbation because he has been led to believe that it will injure his health, and a woman may be afraid of sexual arousal because her mother has told her it is disgusting and dirty or because she has gathered from religious teaching that to be excited by any man who is not actually her husband is a "mortal sin." People may fear worms, flying insects, doctors, or hospitals because they have observed a parent consistently showing fear of these. A family I encountered had three adolescent daughters with widespread fears of insects, because they had seen their mother go into a panic every time she saw one. Some wrong beliefs are based on erroneous inferences and not on wrong messages. A person who has a bizarre and unusual sensation may infer that his personality is disintegrating. Fears based upon faulty cognitions, however these may have originated, call for cognitive solutions.

Not infrequently, the very contiguity of the feared object and the cognitively aroused fear of it leads to the addition of classical conditioning of fear of the object. When that happens, adequate treatment requires *both* cognitive correction and emotional reconditioning.

The Distribution of Classically Conditioned and Cognitively Based Fears

In order to get a rough idea of the distribution of classically conditioned and cognitively based neurotic fears, I recently made a retrospective survey of cases from my files where the central complaint was unadaptive fear.

In each case, I first decided whether the fear was automatically conditioned or cognitively based and then whether its origin could be traced to single or multiple events. Twenty-six fears were found to be autonomically conditioned and 16 cognitively based. Both bases were manifest in two cases. The mean age of the subjects was 33.9 years; and the mean age at onset in those in whom it could be dated was 22.3 years. The data are presented in Table 6-1 and summarized in Table 6.2. As far as possible, similar cases are grouped together in Table 6-1.

CASES ILLUSTRATING THE CONTRASTING THERAPEUTIC REQUIREMENTS OF CLASSICALLY CONDITIONED AND COGNITIVELY BASED ANXIETY

I shall illustrate the different therapeutic requirements with reference to two cases of agoraphobia, and then describe a case that needed both kinds of treatment.

Agoraphobia Based on Emotional Conditioning

A 35-year-old married woman, an ex-nurse, and in general a very stable person, had been afraid to be alone for the past three years, following a terrifying experience. Her husband had gone off on a business trip, and because she was four months pregnant, an 18-year-old nephew was staying at the house during his absence. One evening, when the nephew went out on a date, she went to bed early to read. Suddenly, she became aware of a warm sensation around her thighs, and on pulling the covers off, saw the sheets sodden with blood.

Table 6-1. Breakdown of 40 Cases of Unadaptive Fear

	Nature of fear	Present age	Age at onset	Fear basis		Single event causation	Multiple event causation
				autonomically conditioned	*cognitively based*		
1	Death	31	7		x		x
2	Death	43	39		x	x	
3	Death	10	8	x			x
4	Death	14	8	x		x	
5	Death	46	3		x		x
6	Death and loss of control	39	11	x		x	
7	Being alone	30	29	x		x	
8	Being alone	31	childhood	x			x
9	Being alone	29	23	x		x	
10	Being alone	26	20	x		x	
11	Being alone	47	24	x			x
12	Driving	45	41	x		x	
13	Driving	36	34		x	x	
14	Driving	41	30		x		x
15	Driving	25	16		x	(undetermined)	
16	Public speaking	28	15	x		x	

17	Public speaking	39	21	x		x	
18	Public speaking	28	18		x	x	
19	Related to health	36	22	x		x	
20	Self-destruction	42	31		x	x	
21	Harming self	26	12		x		x
22	Blacking out	48	39	x		x	
23	Own blood	23	18	x		x	
24	People	31	11	x			x
25	Strange men	25	25	x		x	
26	Dentists	25	12	x		x	
27	Eye contact	30	8	x		x	
28	Automobiles	39	37	x		x	
29	Accidents	49	44	x		x	
30	Travel	36	25	x		x	
31	Agoraphobia	28	14	x	x	x	
32	Going to town	36	32	x			x
33	Flying	49	39		x	x	
34	Acrophobia	34	4	x		x	
35	Snakes	24	16		x		x
36	Mice	45	6	x		x	
37	Storms	58	childhood		x		x
38	Examinations	22	20		x	(undetermined)	
39	Sexual inadequacy	25	20		x		x
40	War guilt	35	26	x	x	x	

TABLE 6–2.
Analysis of bases of 40 neurotic fears.*

Autonomic conditioning	
Single event causation	21
Multiple event causation	5
Total	26
Cognitively based	
Single event causation	7
Multiple event causation	7
Undetermined	2
Total	16

*The presence of both autonomic and cognitive bases in two cases brings the total to 42.

In terror, she phoned her doctor, who arranged for an emergency transfer to the hospital, where an operation was performed. From that time onwards, she could never be alone in the house without anxiety, although she realized that only in the special circumstances of pregnancy could there be a reason for her fear. Careful questioning showed no misconception of any kind to be contributing to this fear. She was therefore treated by systematic desensitization, in which were counterposed the calmness of deep muscle relaxation and increasing durations of aloneness at home. She made a complete recovery in eleven sessions. At a three-year follow-up her recovery was found to have been fully maintained.

Agoraphobia Based on Misconception

A 29-year-old married woman was afraid to venture out alone because she believed that her frequent attacks of dizziness and tingling of the hands were early signs of "going crazy." Because she had an aunt who had been in a mental hospital and two cousins who were "flaky," she had concluded that she was hereditarily predisposed to mental instability. Once I had demonstrated to her that her dizziness and tingling were due to hyperventilation and then strongly assured her that there was no possibility of her going crazy, she rapidly lost her fearfulness. After seven sessions she was able to go out comfortably on her own anywhere she wished. She was still well a year later. It was clear from the behavior analysis that systematic desensitization would not have met the requirements of this case.

Agoraphobia Involving Both Habit Patterns

A single woman of 23 had become fearful of being alone ever since a disturbing experience six years previously in a college dormitory. Her heart had raced and her head had felt numb. She believed that if these symptoms increased she would lose her mind—a thought that terrified her. A variety of treatments had been ineffective, except for some tranquilization that drugs had produced. A year before I saw her, a therapist had attempted systematic desensitization and afterwards exposure in vivo, but she had not benefited at all. As happens all too commonly, he had assumed that she had a straightforward fear of separation. At the second session I established that her fear of being alone depended on the idea that the numbness in her head and other sensations were precursory to her losing her mind. Because such sensations are often due to hyperventilation, I got her to hyperventilate; and the sensations duly appeared. She readily understood that they could thus have nothing to do with "losing her mind," and felt great relief. However, during these six years, conditioned fears of lone excursions had developed through the contiguity of aloneness and the cognitively aroused fear. In consequence, she still feared to go out; but I could now treat the conditioned fear effectively by in vivo desensitization—which I could not have done as long as the fearful belief was uncorrected.

In sum, therapeutic operations can weaken an anxiety response habit only if they act upon the stimulus-response relations that underlie that habit. In every case, the antecedents of the anxiety must be precisely defined if one is to apply paradigms of learning successfully to unadaptive anxiety response habits. It should, of course, always be remembered that neurotic anxiety responses diminish in some patients because of the unplanned anxiety-inhibiting effects of emotional responses to the therapist (Wolpe, 1958, pp. 193–195). These are the main reason for the 40 to 50% of good results obtained by nonbehaviorists. They are also the probable reason why analogue studies with *weak fears* show control groups doing as well as groups receiving systematic desensitization (as in D'Zurilla, Wilson, & Nelson, 1973; Wilson, 1973).

COMPARATIVE OUTCOME RESEARCH

It is an unfortunate fact that the stimulus-response structure of the individual case has been much neglected in outcome research, and in consequence most of this research in behavior therapy is of little value. In a previous publication (Wolpe, 1977) I cited how in outcome studies on the treatment of homosexuality, unselected cases are bundled together, though some are based on general timidity, others on conditioned fear of closeness to women, and yet others on approach conditioning to males. Similarly, in the treatment of depression, investigators do not even, as a rule, separate endogenous from reactive depressions, let alone distinguish in the latter category between depressions that are cognitively based and those that are based on emotional conditioning.

In the commonest subject matter of outcome research—the treatment of phobias—the same erroneous assumption is made of uniformity of subject matter. Most important is the failure to distinguish between fears that are cognitively based and those due to direct emotional conditioning. This failure clouds the picture when the efficacy of any treatment is being assessed. Consider the example of systematic desensitization. Since this method contains little corrective information, it cannot be expected to have much effect on phobic cases that call for cognitive solutions. Therefore, such cases should be excluded when desensitization is being evaluated, just as viral pneumonias would be excluded in testing an antibiotic for use in pneumonia.

Inadequacy of behavior analysis has its most serious consequences in studies that compare desensitization with cognitive correction procedures. An example of such inadequacy is to be found in the widely quoted experiments of Bandura and his colleagues (for example, Bandura, Grusec, and Menlove, 1967; Bandura, Blanchard, and Ritter, 1969) that compared desensitization with two other treatments in phobias for dogs or snakes. The other treatments were graded exposure to films of fearless models and live modeling with guided participation. In the outcome, the films were found to be somewhat more effective than desensitization, while live modeling with guided participation clearly achieved the best results. In live modeling, the fearful person copies a fearless model's approaches step by step. Since Bandura et al. did not realize the variability of phobic problems, they did not consider that their treatments might influence their subjects in a variety of ways. It is obvious that the films and the modeling provided information; and it can reasonably be argued that a fearless model's proximity might produce reciprocal inhibition of anxiety in much the same way as the presence of a therapist does (Wolpe, 1958, pp. 193-195).

If subjects were subdivided according to whether their fears called for cognitive correction or emotional reconditioning, some precise predictions could be made. Subjects with fears resulting from misconceptions would be expected to do quite well with filmed modeling and poorly with desensitization. Those with conditioned anxiety would do rather poorly with filmed modeling and much better with desensitization. Modeling with guided participation would be successful with both groups because, in addition to being highly informative, this method might produce desensitization in vivo—through the model, a surrogate therapist, inhibiting conditioned anxiety.

SCIENTIFIC STUDY OF THE DICHOTOMY IN NEUROTIC ANXIETY

Formal studies of the cognition/autonomic conditioning dichotomy are now necessary. First, we need to know the distribution of the two kinds of cases in different populations of fearful subjects; second, we need controlled studies to test the prediction that cognitively based anxiety yields specifically to cognitive correction and classically conditioned anxiety specifically to deconditioning methods.

In surveying clinical populations, it is not satisfactory to rely solely on the idiosyncratic decisions of individual investigators. It is desirable to have instruments that anyone can use and that lend themselves to replication. In our department, a start has been made in this direction as the first stage of a therapeutic study of the classical conditioning/cognition dichotomy in two common phobias, one simple—claustrophobia—and one complex—fear of physiological symptoms as indications of insanity or loss of control. Lande and Turner (1980) have formulated questionnaires in these two areas and refined them by clinical use. In respect of each area, three questions are posed in relation to each of 20 situations. The questions are: (1) How fearful are you of this experience? (2) How often do you say to yourself that this is a sign of some real danger (other than anxiety)? (3) How much do you truly *believe* this is a sign of some real danger (other than anxiety)?

Examples of the 20 claustrophobic situations are: (1) stopped in a closed elevator; (2) in the middle of a crowd; (3) using an oxygen mask.

Examples of the 20 sensation situations are: (1) muscle twitching; (2) giddiness; (3) blurred vision. Each question is on a 5-point scale.

In a pilot run of these inventories, Lande and Turner (1980) found that 35 subjects indicated high fear in at least one item of the Closed Spaces Inventory and 49 subjects indicated it in the Sensations Inventory. Graphic representation showed the expected bimodal distribution for both closed space fears and sensation fears.

We shall go on to test the prediction that conditioned fears respond to deconditioning and cognitively based fears to cognitive correction.

In the meantime, the results of a retrospective study of 25 cases of neurotic depression (Wolpe, 1979) has provided a straw in the wind. Of these cases, 19 were found on analysis to be due predominantly to conditioned anxiety and 6 to be cognitively based; 17 of the 19 conditioned cases recovered or improved greatly by the use, primarily, of reconditioning methods and 5 of the 6 cognitive cases by means of cognitive correction.

We thus see deflated to a nonissue the current controversy whether psychotherapeutic change is a cognitive matter or a conditioning matter. Some fears are rooted in cognitive habit, others are a matter of direct emotional conditioning, and yet others have roots of both kinds. Every patient must be treated according to what his behavior analysis reveals.

SUMMARY

Fears develop on the basis of one or another of two distinct processes —autonomic classical conditioning or the establishment of new cognitive associations to already existing fears. This dichotomy relates both to the appropriate fears of everyday life and to neurotic fears. In the case of the latter, the appropriate treatment procedure should be dictated by the fear basis that behavior analysis reveals. Failure to carry out such analysis is the reason for much confusion and inconclusiveness in therapeutic outcome studies. A retrospective survey of anxiety cases revealed that one-third of the fears were cognitively based and two-thirds due to classical conditioning. A study of a clinical population on the basis of a questionnaire designed to separate between cognitively based and conditioned fears has shown the expected bimodal distribution.

REFERENCES

Amsel, A. Frustrative nonreward in partial reinforcement and discrimination learning: Some recent history and a theoretical extension. *Psychological Review*, 1962, *69*, 306–328.

Bandura, A., Blanchard, E. D., & Ritter, B. Relative efficacy of desensitization and modeling approaches for inducing behavioral, affective and attitudinal changes. *Journal of Personality & Social Psychology*, 1969, *13*, 173–199.

Bandura, A., Grusec, J., & Menlove, F. Vicarious extinction of avoidance behavior. *Journal of Personality & Social Psychology*, 1967, *5*, 16–23.

D'Zurilla, T. J., Wilson, G. T., & Nelson, R. N. A preliminary study of the effectiveness of graduated prolonged exposure in the treatment of irrational fear. *Behavior Therapy*, 1973, *4*, 672–685.

Giles, T. Behavior therapy vs. psychotherapy (part II): A review of the Sloane et al. study and behavior therapy outcome: The probable superiority of behavioral interventions. Manuscript in preparation, 1981.

Lande, S. D., & Turner, R. M. Cognitive habit inventories: A method of differentiating phobic types. Unpublished manuscript, 1980.

Masserman, J. H. *Behavior and neurosis.* Chicago, IL: University of Chicago Press, 1943.

Paul, G. L. *Insight versus desensitization in psychotherapy.* Stanford, CA: Stanford University Press, 1966.

Pavlov, I. P. *Conditioned reflexes and psychiatry* (Trans. by W. H. Gantt) New York: International Publishers, 1941.

Sloane, R. B., Staples, F. R., Cristol, A. H., Yorkston, N. H., & Whipple, K. *Psychotherapy versus behavior therapy.* Cambridge, MA: Harvard University Press, 1975.

Wilson, G. T. Effects of false feedback on avoidance behavior: "Cognitive" desensitization revisited. *Journal of Personality and Social Psychology*, 1973, *28*, 115-122.

Wolpe, J. Experimental neuroses as learned behavior. *British Journal of Psychology*, 1952, *43*, 243-268.

Wolpe, J. *Psychotherapy by reciprocal inhibition.* Stanford: Stanford University Press, 1958.

Wolpe, J. *Practice of behavior therapy*, Second edition. New York: Pergamon Press, 1973.

Wolpe, J. Inadequate behavior analysis: The achilles heel of outcome research in behavior therapy. *Journal of Behavior Therapy and Experimental Psychiatry*, 1977, *8*, 1-3.

Wolpe, J. The experimental model and treatment of neurotic depression. *Behaviour Research and Therapy*, 1979, *17*, 555-565.

CHAPTER 7

Behavioral Concepts and Treatment of Neuroses

Isaac Marks, M.D., F.R.C.Psych., D.P.M.

This paper concerns the development of behavioral concepts about the origin and treatment of neuroses, their current state of play, and some useful future directions the field might take. It should be clear at the outset that ideas about the genesis of a problem may have little to do with its remedy. One cannot argue that because a particular treatment is effective that this necessarily throws light on the etiology of a condition or even on its maintaining factors. We cannot conclude that digoxin's valve for cardiac failure indicates why the heart is failing. Even if operant methods assist the teaching of skills to subnormal children they tell us little about the causes of subnormality. The same is true for the treatments of neuroses.

The commonest neuroses presenting for treatment are those dominated by mild depression and/or anxiety, and these are unfortunately the least amenable so far to behavioral treatment. In Table 7-1 an asterisk indicates those problems where good research evidence suggests that behavioral psychotherapy is currently the approach of choice. These include phobic and obsessive-compulsive disorders, social skills problems, sexual dysfunction, and enuresis. Together, these make up about 25% of neurotic patients who present to psychiatric outpatient clinics.

CONDITIONING AND NEUROSES: SIMILARITIES AND DIFFERENCES

As Eelen (personal communication) noted, the term "conditioning" can refer to an experimental procedure, to the effect of this procedure, or to the process thought to explain these effects. In this paper, the term indicates behaviors presumed to have been acquired in conditioning-type situations. Perhaps the closest experimental model for any of the neuroses is the way in which one obtains extinction of conditioned avoidance responses in animals and phobic and obsessive-compulsive avoidance in humans. How phobias and obsessions are related to other neuroses is not clear. My own work on flooding, which later led to exposure in vivo, was partly stimulated by Baum's (1969) experiments with conditioned avoidance responses in rats. He used a simple cage with an electrifiable grid floor and a rectractable platform half-way up one side. The rat was dropped on the grid floor through which a few seconds later an electric current was passed. The rat soon learned to escape shock by jumping onto the platform and eventually to avoid shock completely by jumping onto the platform as soon as it was dropped on the cage floor. Once this conditioned avoidance response was readily established, even if the electric current was switched off, the rat, when placed on the cage floor, never stayed there long enough to learn that the current had been switched off. However, if, at this stage, after the current was switched on, the platform was retracted, giving the rat no "safe"

Table 7-1. Varied meanings of "NEUROSES"

Anxiety state

*Obsessive-compulsive disorders

Hysteria—conversion
—historic behavior
—chronic multiple complaints
Briquet's syndrome
illness behavior
hypochondriasis

*Phobias

Depression (neurotic)
morbid grief

*Social skills problems
abnormal personality

*Sexual dysfunction

Habit disorders
*enuresis, encopresis
hairpulling
tics, occupational cramps

*Behavioral psychotherapy is the preferred treatment.

platform to land on any longer, it would jump about frantically for a few minutes, but the jumps became steadily less frantic and then ceased. The conditioned avoidance response of jumping was abolished rapidly by the mere expedient of removing the platform onto which the rat had been jumping.

Perhaps this situation is analogous to exposure treatment in humans, where patients are persuaded to remain in contact with their phobias or ritual-evoking situations without avoiding them (reviewed by Marks, 1977). In time, and this usually takes several hours, the discomfort dies down, and the patient learns that there is no need to avoid phobic situations for discomfort to subside. Avoidance is no longer necessary for anxiety reduction.

Although this might explain the extinction of avoidance, what is not explained either in the rat or the human is why anxiety or conditioned fear usually extinguishes too, eventually, on continued contact with the evoking stimulus. There are four main measures of conditioned fear in animals (Mineka, 1979). The first is a decrease in ongoing operant responses that have been maintained by positive reinforcement; this was initially called "conditioned anxiety" by Estes and Skinner (Mineka, 1979) and later the "conditioned emotional response" (CER) by Hunt and Brady (Mineka, 1979). The second is an increase in ongoing operant responses that have been maintained by aversive stimulation (Sidman, Herrnstein, & Conrad, 1957). The third is passive avoidance of the locus of previous aversive stimulation. Lastly, the fourth is conditioned heart rate, which shows species variability, the rate increasing in dogs and monkeys and decreasing in rats. There are many discrepancies between the ways in which these various measures change, and commonly there is dissociation between changes in measures of fear and avoidance in animals, just as there are in humans during behavioral treatment.

There are also important differences between aversive conditioning experiments and human phobias and rituals (Table 7–2). First, conditioning experiments usually last only a few days at most, whereas human phobias and rituals have generally been present for years before they come for treatment. Moreover, repeated series of reacquisition and reextinction are rarely studied in aversive conditioning experiments, whereas these are the rule in clinical phenomena; repeated series of events may well differ substantially from those that have only occurred once (Akiyama, 1968). A third difference is that the initiating trauma is usually planned and clearly identifiable in animal experiments but generally absent in human phobias and rituals (Marks, 1977; Rimm, Janda, Lancaster, Nahl, & Dittmar, 1977). A related point is that with clinical phenomena it is not usually possible to say what events constitute the CS, US, CR, or UR

Table 7-2. Differences Between Aversive Conditioning Experiments and Human Phobias and Rituals

Differential Feature	*Aversive Conditioning*	*Human Phobias and Rituals*
1. Usual duration of phenomenon	days	years
2. Repeated reacquisition and reextinction	rarely studied	common
3. Initiating trauma	planned, identifiable	usually absent
4. CS, US, CR, UR	planned, identifiable	not usually identifiable
5. "Meanings" of S and R	less important	? more important

(conditioned [C] and unconditioned [U] stimuli [S] and responses [R]). Finally, the meanings of stimuli and responses are more varied in humans, especially for obsessive-compulsive problems.

PATHOLOGY: FAILED EXTINCTION OR ENHANCED ACQUISITION?

Although the exposure approach predictably and reliably helps most phobics and ritualizers who comply with treatment, and these are the majority, total cure is still the exception rather than the rule. Many patients have been shown time and again how to overcome their discomfort yet are unable to apply exposure principles in the absence of the therapist; they do not internalize the therapeutic rules. If there is a recrudescence of phobias or rituals, patients often do not generate therapeutic strategies from their previous successful experiences until they have had further advice from the therapist. Such patients are not good problem solvers, at least in this area.

When we consider that most people have trivial fears and rituals at some time or another but have managed to nip these in the bud before the problem grew to invade their lifespace, the question inevitably arises whether the patients we see are those who failed to inhibit the growth of such minor phobias and rituals. Maybe we should think, not in terms of why phobias and rituals are acquired in the first place, but rather why once these are acquired, patients have *failed to extinguish them.* Proof of this point would require longitudinal studies of cohorts, which would be time-consuming and expensive.

FROM A CONDITIONING TO A CLINICAL PARADIGM

Successful exposure treatment can ignore assumptions about unconditioned stimuli and responses. The language and theory of conditioning that evolved from laboratory experiments in animals can be modified in favor of a simpler paradigm that emerges in clinical experiments and has clear implications for theory and practice.

It is unnecessary to make the untestable etiologic assumption that phobias and obsessions have been acquired by conditioning and so should be regarded as conditioned stimuli (CSs). To do so would initiate a fruitless search for an unknowable unconditioned stimulus (US). Instead, we can speak simply of the ES, the evoking stimulus that triggers phobias and obsessions (Marks, 1977). The phobias and obsessions are the ERs, evoked responses, which can themselves become further ESs in a vicious circle, as with anticipatory fear of fear.

The ES/ER paradigm has a major advantage for clinicians. It indicates at once the therapeutic strategy that research has shown to be effective for the reduction of phobias and rituals—continued exposure to the ES's until the ER subside. The clinician needs to search for those situations (ES) that evoke the phobias and obsessions and then to maintain the patient in contact with them until he becomes used to them. In an agoraphobic this ES may be complex—panic while being out alone in public places, crowds, elevators, stores, and the like. The ER this evokes is a cluster of events such as avoidance and its autonomic concomitants. In compulsive ritualizers the ES might be the discomfort brought on by the perception of dirt, disarray, or uncertainty. This evokes the ER of compulsive washing, tidying up, or checking. The therapist's task is to seek components of the ES that evoke any ER, so that exposure of the patient to the appropriate ES complex can be contrived and continued until the ER no longer occurs. An agoraphobic can be persuaded to remain in a crowded store for an extended time, despite his or her panic; the compulsive tidier and checker of windows might be asked to untidy his possessions and deliberately refrain from checking rituals. With continued exposure to the ES, the discomfort gradually subsides, as do the urges to avoid or ritualize. This response decrement could be called habituation, adaptation, extinction, satiation, or boredom. These various labels overlap in their meanings and theoretical connotations, and this is not the place to enter into them.

CLINICAL ISSUES WITH PHOBIC AND OBSESSIVE-COMPULSIVE DISORDERS

Table 7-1 indicated that research has found only some neuroses to be amenable to behavioral psychotherapy. The value of exposure treatments in various forms has been reviewed in detail elsewhere (Marks, 1977; Emmelkamp, 1979; Foa & Steketee, 1979). A general shift has been away from fantasy exposure methods such as systematic desensitization to that of in vivo exposure approaches. Emmelkamp (1979) concluded that "the routine use of systematic desensitization in phobic patients seems unwarranted," and the same might apply with compulsive rituals. A fairly typical example of the result of in vivo exposure is shown in Figure 7-1. This shows the outcome in 124 phobics treated by nurse-therapists. Improvement was obtained in a mean of 10 sessions lasting an average of $1\frac{1}{2}$ hours each. Improvement was maintained until one year follow-up not only in the main phobia, but also in a more broad-scan fear survey schedule, in non-phobic anxiety and depression, and in work adjustment, that is, improvement in fear generalized so that patients were freed to lead more normal lives.

For compulsive rituals, good evidence is available of lasting improvement with exposure in vivo and self-imposed response prevention. Using similar measures workers in England, Greece, and the United States found comparable improvement up to three years follow-up after exposure in vivo (Boulougouris, 1977; Foa & Goldstein, 1978; Marks, 1975). Moreover, as with phobias, this improvement generalized to work adjustment.

The exposure paradigm of treatment may be useful not only for phobias and compulsive rituals, but also for other conditions such as nightmares and morbid grief, although the evidence here is still of a more preliminary kind. With nightmares, exposure treatment takes the form of repeated rehearsal of the content of the nightmare (Marks, 1978; Cellucci & Lawrence, 1978), and for morbid grief, exposure treatment consists of forced mourning (Ramsay, 1976).

Although most patients who are cooperative (and those are the great majority) improve with exposure in vivo, few of them are totally cured, and patients are generally told that they need a coping set to deal with tendencies to ritualize that might recur after discharge. Occasionally brief booster treatment is needed for this. It is not known to what extent improvement within sessions predicts improvement between sessions, but gains after a few sessions are a good predictor of outcome at follow-up (Marks, Rachman, & Hodgson, 1975; Robertson, 1979). In general, improvement in ritualistic behavior seems to be greater than that in obsessive ideation, but systematic observations of the speed of decrement of various com-

Figure 7-1. Improvement in 124 Phobics Treated with Exposure in Vivo by Nurse-Therapists (Marks, et al., 1978. Reprinted by permission of the Institute of Psychiatry)

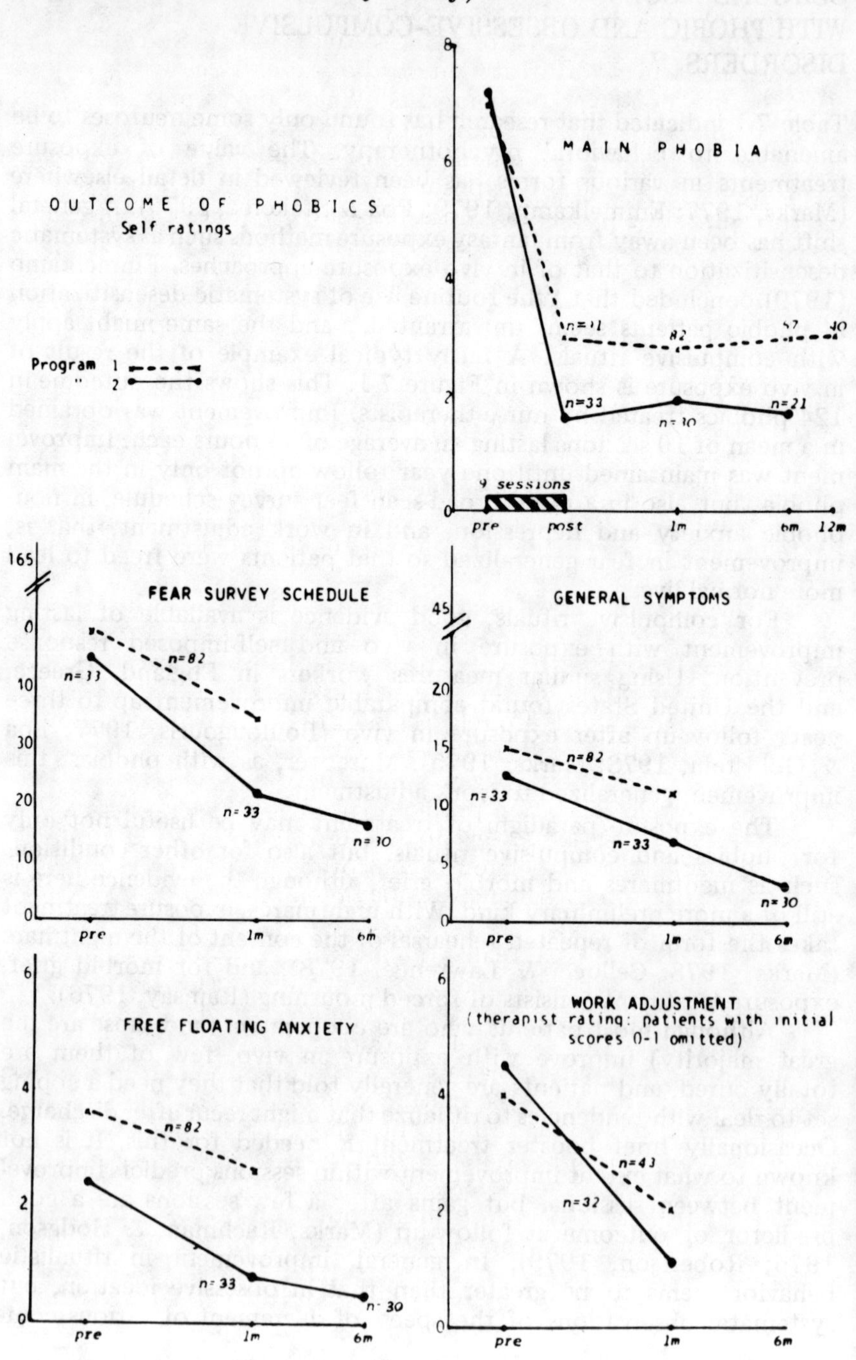

ponents of compulsive rituals remain to be carried out. In many obsessive-compulsive patients, treatment at some state needs to be carried out in the home or work settings that evoke rituals, and an essential aspect of treatment is the patients' carrying out of self-exposure homework assignments. Where the family have been involved in the patient's rituals, they need to be brought in, with the patient's consent, as cotherapists for supervising exposure treatment. Role rehearsal of exposure exercises and withholding of reassurance may be necessary. In a few cases treatment is impossible because the family members are incapable of carrying out these instructions.

AROUSAL DURING EXPOSURE

Many experiments have revealed that the outcome to desensitization in fantasy is not impaired by omitting relaxation training, which is also unnecessary for the reduction of rituals or phobias, either alone or paired with exposure in vivo (summarized by Marks, 1975; 1977).

A clear example where relaxation alone did not help rituals comes from a study carried out at the Maudsley Hospital (Marks et al., 1980) (Fig. 7-2). All patients were on placebo medication throughout the study. After four weeks they were admitted and assigned at random either to relaxation or to daily (five times a week) hour-long exposure in vivo. Patients complied similarly with each treatment. Improvement began soon after exposure in vivo was introduced, while relaxation produced negligible change. When after three weeks the relaxation group was crossed over to exposure in vivo, their rituals and associated discomfort reduced as in the originally exposed group. Improvement was not potentiated by the experience of preceding relaxation.

Less evidence is available about the value of high anxiety evocation during exposure treatment, but the evidence so far is that high anxiety yields no better results than low anxiety during fantasy exposure (Mathews et al., 1974) or during in vivo exposure (Hafner & Marks, 1976). Thus phobias and obsessions improve with exposure treatment, but it does not matter whether patients are relaxed, neutral, or anxious during subsequent exposure.

A more important variable is *duration of exposure*. Exposure in vivo gave significantly better results when carried out for two continuous hours rather than four interrupted half-hour periods in one afternoon, whether in agoraphobics (Stern & Marks, 1973) or in compulsive-rituals (Rabavilas, Boulougouris, & Stefanis, 1976).

Figure 7-2. Rituals Improve with Exposure in Vivo but not with Relaxation. (Marks et al., 1980)

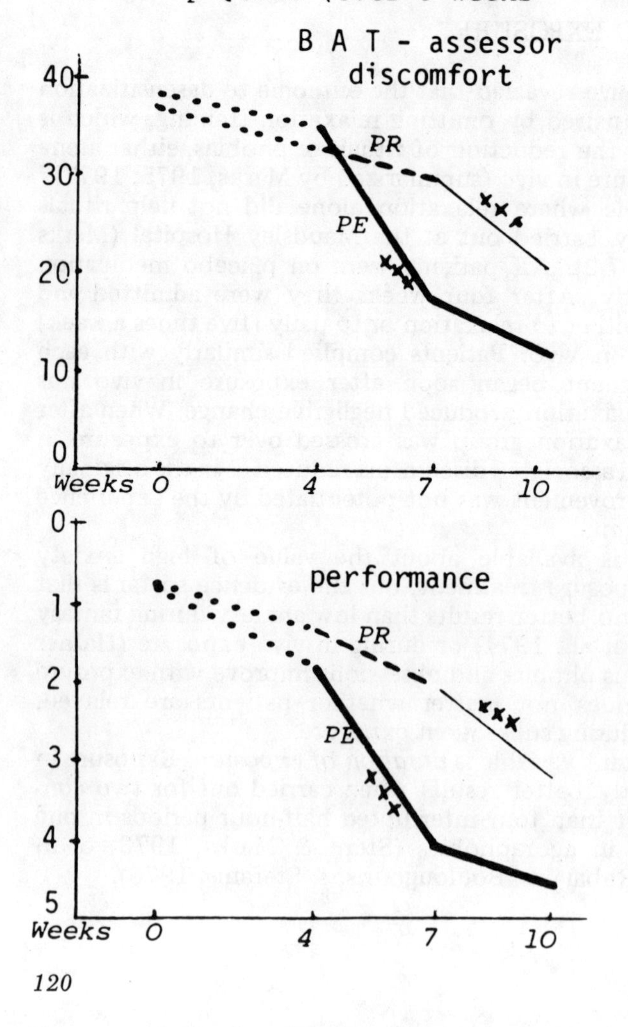

SELF-EXPOSURE HOMEWORK

It has become increasingly apparent that much behavioral treatment consists of teaching patients what to do between treatment sessions in structuring their homework exercises. There are now two controlled experiments that have found that self-exposure homework has a significant though small effect in reducing phobias and rituals. In the first study (McDonald et al., 1979), agoraphobics in one condition had no therapist-assisted exposure, only exposure-homework instructions; patients were asked to expose themselves to their phobic situations as much as possible while recording their efforts in a diary. Control patients were asked to keep a diary of important emotional events; exposure was not mentioned. All patients were seen only three times over six weeks, each time for 15 minutes only. Only those patients who were given exposure instructions improved significantly, or any more than those in the control condition (see Figure 7-3).

A second study (Greist et al., 1980) used a different control group to make a critical test of the exposure hypothesis. Thirteen phobic and four compulsive patients were seen briefly twice a week for two weeks in a balanced crossover design. They were told at the start that they would receive a week each of two contrasting approaches, to see which would be better for them. During one week they were to confront their phobic situation as long as possible until their anxiety died down and to record these confrontations in a diary. In the contrasting week they were told to avoid all possible sources of anxiety so that they could have a complete rest from tension. At the end of the two weeks they would continue with whichever treatment had suited them best. The results were unequivocal and could not be attributed to expectancy, because patients had similar expectations from each approach before treatment began. During the exposure week phobics and ritualizers improved significantly, whereas they worsened slightly on some measures during the week of avoidance (Figure 7-3). At the end of two weeks, patients again had exposure treatment, and improvement was resumed. This suggests that instructions to avoid phobia or ritual-inducing situations may actually be antitherapeutic.

It is possible that for some patients exposure-homework instructions are all that is required, whereas for others a therapist is necessary to accompany the patient at first for exposure treatment to get under way. Relatives, too, can be taught to act as cotherapists after being suitably primed in conjoint interviews with the patient. Agoraphobics have been treated effectively at home with the help of spouses as cotherapists and the use of appropriate instruction manuals; in this way, therapist time has been cut down to a mean of only three to five hours per patient (Jannoun et al., 1980). An example

Figure 7-3. Self-Exposure Homework—Effect in Two Studies. (McDonald et al., 1979; Greist, 1980. Reprinted from Michael Shepherd, Cure and Care of Neurosis, *Psychological Medicine*, 1979, *9*, 629–660. Reprinted by permission of Cambridge University Press)

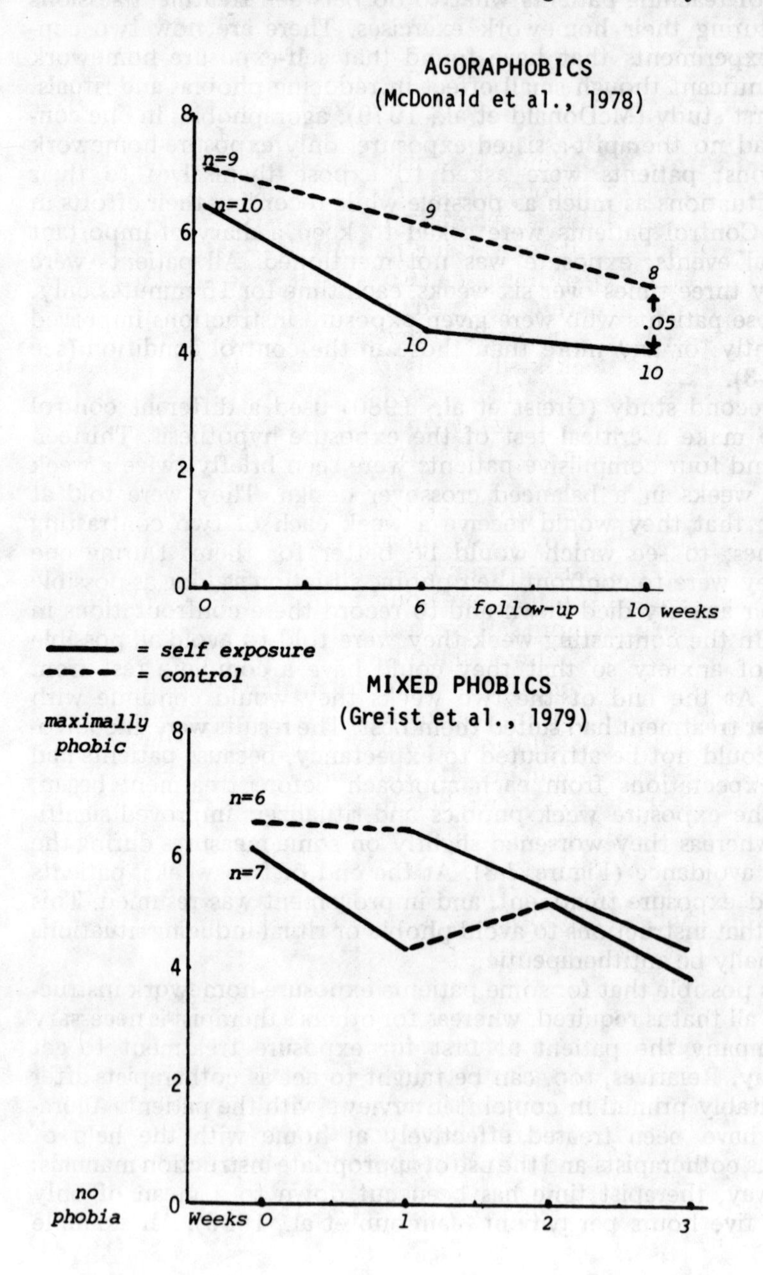

of a self-instruction manual appears in "*Living with Fear*" (Marks, 1978), and the kind of diary patients need to keep of their exposure homework is seen in Table 7-3.

RESPONSE PREVENTION WITH RITUALS

Exposure for obsessive-compulsives usually includes instructions to patients to stop carrying out their rituals ("response prevention"). This response prevention is generally unsupervised, although some have closely monitored it for varying periods. In the only long-term controlled investigation of this issue (Robertson, 1979), 20 obsessive-compulsive ritualizers were assigned at random to two weeks of exposure in vivo, with response prevention supervised for either 24 hours round the clock, or for only one hour daily. Although the 24-hour supervised patients had a significant short-term advantage at day four, this was no longer significant at two-weeks' follow-up and had disappeared completely by two- to four-years follow-up. If anything, the one-hour-supervised group did better in the long-term. The only case who was worse at long-term follow-up had been inadvertently instructed by a well-meaning social worker to resume cleaning activities. Robertson wondered whether the slightly greater long-term improvement in the one-hour group might be attributable to their having learned more self-control procedures during treatment than those who had continuous supervision.

Response prevention could be construed as a method that inevitably produces exposure; for example, if I feel my hands are dirty and am then not allowed to wash, exposure to the evoking stimulus of feeling contaminated will continue until washing is allowed unless habituation occurs before then.

SEVERE MARITAL PROBLEMS COMPLICATING PHOBIAS OR RITUALS

Marital problems are not a contraindication to exposure treatment. Stern and Marks (1973) reported a patient whose ritualistic checking failed to benefit from exposure but improved after subsequent marital contract therapy. In further study of this point, Cobb et al. (1980) treated 12 patients manifesting both phobic or obsessive-compulsive symptoms and marital discord. Couples were randomly assigned to ten sessions of either marital or exposure treatment, with

Table 7-3. Patient's diary of self-exposure homework (Marks, 1978. Reprinted by permission of the publisher.)

*DIARY RECORD OF EXPOSURE TASKS**

Day	*Date*	*Began*	*Ended*	*The exposure task I performed was:*	*(0 = complete calm, 100 = absolute panic) My anxiety during the task was:*	*Comments, including coping tactics I used:*	*Name of Co-therapist if any: J. Smith (Co-therapist's signature that task was completed*
Sunday							
Monday							
Tuesday							
					Example from an agoraphobic		
Wednesday		2:30 p.m.	4.30 p.m.	Walked to local supermarket and surrounding shops, bought food and presents for family, had coffee at drugstore	75	Felt worse when shops were crowded, practiced deep-breathing exercises	J. Smith (husband)
Thursday		10 a.m.	11.30 a.m.	Walked to local park, sat there for 1/2 hour till I felt better, then caught a bus downtown and back home	70	Felt giddy and faint, practiced imagining myself dropping dead	J. Smith

Friday	2 p.m.	4 p.m.	Rode a bus downtown and back 3 times till I felt better about it	60	Worst when bus was crowded—did deep breathing exercises	J. Smith

Plan for next week: Repeat exposure exercises in bus, park and shops every day until my anxiety is no higher than 30. Thereafter start visits to my hairdresser, and short surface train journeys.

Saturday	
Sunday	
Monday	
Tuesday	
Wednesday	

*from I. M. Marks, *Living with Fear*, McGraw Hill Book Co., New York, 1978, p. 258–9 a crossover after three-months' follow-up. Results indicated that marital therapy did not affect obsessive-compulsive or phobic problems but did improve the marital interaction. Exposure, on the other hand, ameliorated both the compulsive and phobic symptoms and the marital relationship. The authors concluded that the case reported by Stern and Marks was not representative and advised exposure treatment where marital discord coexists with obsessions or phobias. In contrast, Cobb and Marks (1979) found in a pilot study where compulsive rituals centered on morbid jealousy that exposure treatment was not of much benefit, but that broad-spectrum behavioral treatment including marital therapy was of more use.

TREATMENT FAILURES

The commonest reason for failure to improve is noncompliance with treatment instructions. There is an impression that patients who hold to their obsessive-compulsive beliefs with delusional intensity do less well in treatment (Foa & Steketee, 1979); this might be mediated through less compliance on the part of such patients with exposure instructions that would clash more with fixed than with malleable beliefs. Whether delusional fixity of ideas directly affects outcome remains to be tested. On a related theme, experimental evidence shows that far from obsessions warding off psychotic decompensation, in fact gains in compulsive rituals usually generalize to social adjustment.

Another impression among workers using the behavioral approach is that depressed phobics and ritualizers fail to habituate to exposure treatment, but this remains to be demonstrated experimentally. In two double-blind controlled trials (Marks, et al., 1980; Thoren et al., in press) compared to placebo, clomipramine was significantly beneficial for depressed ritualizers, but there was a strong tendency to relapse within several months of stopping the drug. On restarting the drug remission occurred again, so the effect of the drug seems to be to damp down the preexisting tendency to depression, to reduce the amplitude of its oscillations rather than to cure it, although the improvement that exposure in vivo produces in rituals and in social adjustment is usually long-lasting. In patients with depressed mood there is justification for combining clomipramine with exposure in vivo.

A small number of patients in several series (such as Marks, et al., 1975; 1980; Foa & Goldstein, 1978) are cooperative with treatment, do not avoid the ES, and are not depressed, yet they fail to habituate during exposure in vivo. Such patients are of critical importance for the exposure hypothesis, but it is not yet known how they differ from the majority of their fellows who do habituate and show improvement.

CURRENT THEORETICAL ISSUES

Ten topical considerations for research are summarized in Table 7–4. The most important theoretical task for exposure theory today is to specify the differences, which are so far largely unknown, between exposure that is traumatic or sensitizing (EX_s) and exposure that is therapeutic or habituating (EX_h). We do not understand why repeated experience of similar events before treatment leads to avoidance and increased fear, whereas continued exposure to similar events during treatment leads eventually to loss of discomfort. Our very definitions of exposure and avoidance need to be tightened.

The conditions that separate EX_s (sensitizing exposure) from EX_h (habituating exposure) are likely to be multivariate. The type and meaning of ES and ER may be relevant. This may partly depend on the patient's genetic make-up and developmental history. Some differences may depend on duration of exposure to the ES, or on the length of time between exposure trials or sessions. Studies of patients who fail to habituate might reveal other clues.

Table 7-4. Ten Considerations for Exposure Theory

1. What separates sensitizing exposure from habituating exposure?
2. What defines (i) exposure (ii) avoidance?
3. Role of type and meaning of evoking stimulus, evoked response
4. Why is longer exposure usually better?
   trials, within sessions
   sessions
   intervals between trials/sessions
5. Some patients fail to habituate despite:
   no avoidance (i.e. comply)
   no depression
   no sedation (alcohol, drugs)
6. Antidepressant drugs, phobias, and rituals in depressed patients
7. Biochemical/physiological influences on exposure
8. Exposure vs. coping (stress immunization)
9. Role of subjective state during exposure
   commitment
   positive versus negative self-instruction, escape
   resignation, submission versus despair, helplessness
10. Role of therapist's license, aid, instructions

It is crucial to explore those treatments that may improve phobias and rituals without any exposure. Antidepressant drugs can do this in patients with depressed mood (Marks et al., 1980). These may point to relevant biochemical and physiological factors. Patients can also improve with exposure to frightening scenes that are irrelevant to their phobias (Watson & Marks, 1971). This could be explained by saying that exposure acts by teaching patients how to cope with unpleasant feelings in general, not merely with their phobias. This widening of an exposure theory to a coping theory would have many implications.

The patient's subjective state during exposure could be critical. The patient's commitment to change could decide whether there is change in the meaning of the ES during exposure. The license of the therapist to treat may help the patient define the exposure situation as therapeutic instead of noxious and engage in contact with the ES instead of being distracted or trying to avoid it. Exposure theory predicts little about self-regulatory processes in fear reduction as yet. While some patients find value in "psyching themselves up" by thinking positive thoughts such as "I can beat this fear; I must take deep breaths slowly, and approach the thing I am scared of," others are helped by negative thoughts of the kind used in paradoxical intention (such as "I know I might die at any minute of a heart attack; I ought to get out of this situation"). We need to compare the effects of positive with those of negative self-statements during treatment and indeed with the effects of any self-statements.

Exposure theory has little to say about why the therapeutic license of the therapist often enables patients to do so much more than they can achieve on their own. How does the therapist's license to treat help the patient bear with the otherwise unbearable? Is this related to the attitude of resignation and submission that helps religious people? How does therapeutic resignation differ from the despairing helplessness seen in depression? To accommodate such important issues, exposure theory may need to be expanded into a wider paradigm that will replace it, but that would be in accord with the march of science.

RESEARCH STRATEGY: VOLUNTEERS VERSUS PATIENTS

Issues about behavioral treatment of neuroses can be confused because of incautious extrapolation of findings from analogue volunteer populations to those of patients. As Emmelkamp (1979) noted, "The clinical effectiveness of treatments can only be studied in clinical patients as subjects." The differences between clinic and other populations is emphasized by the findings of Lieberman and Gardner (1976). They gave questionnaires to large samples of prospective clients in psychiatric clinics, growth centers, and a national training laboratory, and compared scores among these populations and with a normative sample obtained from Uhlenhueth. The questionnaires concerned (1) life stress, based on the scale of Holmes and Rahe; (2) neurotic symptoms, based on the Hopkings Check List; (3) intensity of motivation for help to deal with life problems, solve personal hangups, or get relief from troublesome feelings. The results were clear. Clinic patients were significantly more disturbed than the other populations, having more life-stress and neurotic symptoms and more intense need for help. These disturbances complicate treatment programs much more for clinical populations than for analogue volunteers, so results from volunteers cannot be assumed to apply to clinical populations.

DELIVERY OF BEHAVIORAL TREATMENTS FOR NEUROSES

Now that we have effective behavioral treatments for some neuroses, how can they be delivered on the scale required to sufferers who can benefit from them? The demand for behavioral treatment far outstrips the supply of qualified therapists. The question is how to train them with the shortest training compatible with becoming effective.

It is by no means necessary to have a Ph.D. or an M.D. to be an effective behavioral psychotherapist, or indeed any other therapist. There is a general tedency for people to work with higher credentials than are needed for their tasks. Historically, the prestige of professions has depended more on the length and complexity of training than on competence at the end of training. McGregor (1976) pointed out that clinical schools of universities have to fulfill two quite different roles, which are often in conflict. First is the university role, where knowledge is sought after in study, discussion, and research. Success in this university role depends upon research productivity and scientific evaluation, and training for it is necessarily prolonged and expensive. The second contrasting role is clinical training, to produce manpower with appropriate *clinical* skills and in sufficient numbers to fulfill society's needs. Success depends on the numbers of graduates and their skill. Training for this clinical role could be much shorter than is required for the university role.

It could be argued that the expensive training of highly educated doctors and psychologists is not justified by their clinical role, but rather by their university role, by their abilities to consult on difficult problems, to teach, to research, and to organize. Such professionals also have a crucial role in developing better methods of training without feeling restricted by established roles and norms. In contrast, it is ludicrously wasteful to train masses of high-powered professionals to carry out routine clinical care, when this can easily be given by clinicians with much shorter and less expensive training.

What is the evidence that less-trained workers can do a good clinical job? In the general medical field there is ample evidence that nurses and paraprofessionals can give as good care as doctors in primary care (Sackett & Spitzer, 1974; Spitzer, Roberts, & Delmore, 1976; Chambers & West, 1978), for medical outpatients (Lewis, Resnick, & Schmidt, 1969), for general psychiatric outpatients (Climent, DeArango, & Plutchnick, 1978), and in giving dynamic psychotherapy to neurotic outpatients (Liberman & True, 1978).

In the behavioral fields there is abundant testimony that nurse-therapists obtain as good results as do psychiatrists and psychologists with behavioral treatment of phobias, compulsive rituals, and sexual disorders (Marks, 1977; McDonald, et al., 1979). In the behavioral treatment of obesity, Stunkard and Brownell (1980) have found significantly less attrition of obese subjects treated in groups by lay therapists than in groups treated by professional, experienced,

Figure 7-4. Lay Therapists Had Significantly Less Attrition of Treated Obese Subjects Than Did Ph.D. Trained Psychologists. (From Stunkard & Brownell, 1980)

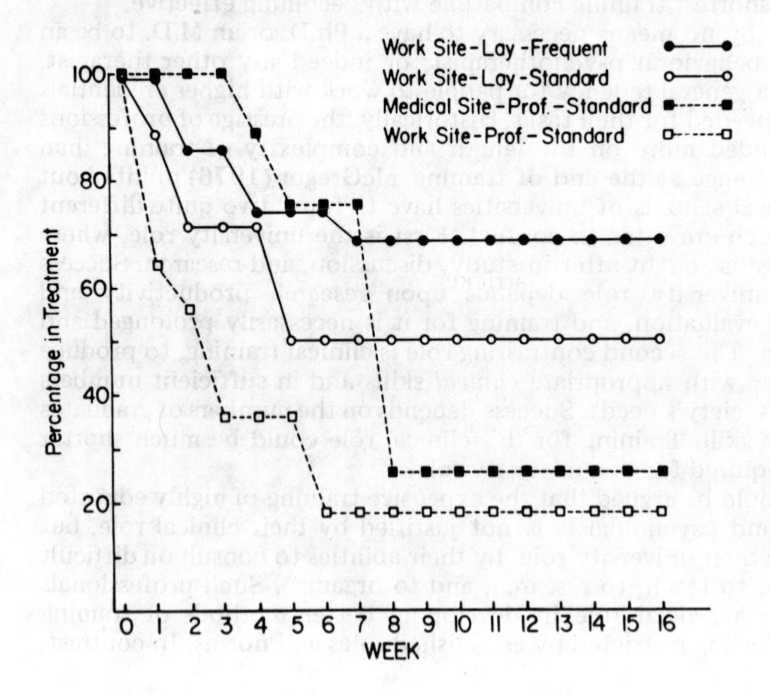

Ph.D.-trained psychologists (Figure 7-4) (Stunkard & Brownell, 1980). These results are not surprising when one considers Peter Lang's (1977) comments that "it is not a knowledge of chemistry that guides the chef to a good bouillabaisse, but knowing which fish to use and how to cook them." One does not need a Ph.D. in biochemistry to treat biochemical problems, or a Ph.D. in psychology in order to treat psychological problems. Maxmen (1976) recently forecast the advent of a "postphysician era" in which routine medical treatment will be given not by physicians but by briefly trained medics with the help of computers. The same might apply to some psychological treatment.

It is inevitable that professionals will resist changes in their roles. Bernard Shaw quipped that "all professions are a conspiracy against the laity." All have a tendency toward restrictive professionalization. A World Health Organization report commented that "Clinical psychology as a profession has in many countries tried to emulate the attributes of medicine. It has sought to enforce its own ethical standards; it has developed private practice and generally striven to obtain the rewards of high status and prestige. However there is also concern that clinical psychology might adopt too high a degree of professionalization too early in its development, and might emulate some of the worst features of the medical model: rigidity, exclusiveness, protective legal titles, and excessive concern with status, prestige and emoluments of private practice. It is hoped that the profession will *not* seek a rigidly defined role or legally protected label, in the interests of greater flexibility and openness to role changes, bearing in mind that our primary concern is for the patient's welfare" (cited by Fichter & Wittchen, in press).

Recent moves in some countries to restrict the practice of nonmedical psychotherapy only to those with psychology degrees is an instance of restrictive professionalization. The tendency of professional therapists to present themselves as experts in emotional problems can unduly degrade the valuable role that can be played by everybody in helping stricken relatives, friends, or neighbors (Chabot, 1979). If we are interested in treating as many neurotic patients as effectively and cheaply as possible, then we need to demystify behavioral technology, to state simply what we can do so that all can understand and help design a behavioral service based upon society's human values (Mahler, 1975).

The least expensive care is self-help. Exposure treatments ultimately work by teaching patients coping skills, and some of these can be acquired without direct professional intervention. Many can help themselves by working alone or in self-help groups, and manuals are beginning to be available for this purpose. Earlier I mentioned a preliminary manual for this kind of anxiety (Marks, 1978). Other self-help manuals are available for the treatment of sexual disorders (Kass & Stauss, 1975). In time, those who can help themselves will benefit from such texts, and only those who fail will need to go on to seek professional help.

However low the cost of cure, the prevention of disorder is always better. There are several ways in which we can begin to think of measures to prevent neuroses. We might teach children more coping skills to prevent the development of subsequent fear and depression. Perhaps children who are social isolates at school can at that stage be taught social skills to avoid them getting into the vicious circle begun by social isolation. Better sex education in schools might reduce later sexual dysfunction more than any number of sex therapy clinics. Selective remediation for a different problem—schoolchildren at risk for academic failure and behavioral difficulties—led to greater subsequent improvement in reading ability and in behavior than that obtained in a control group (Arnold et al., 1977). Prevention of some adult neuroses may also be feasible. Recently bereaved widows at risk for morbid grief were identified and given preventive counseling with a behavioral component; this led to less morbidity at one-year follow-up than in similar control subjects (Raphael, 1977).

A problem in developing preventive services for neurosis is our ignorance about where to apply the appropriate levers of change. Another difficulty is that as in medicine in general, so in behavioral treatments, cure is valued more highly than prevention. Freymann (1975) reminded us how old this attitude is. Hygeia, the ancient Greek goddess of health, was subservient in the Olympian hierarchy to Aesculapius, the god of healing. Although it may seem obvious common sense to extol the virtues of short training, flexible professional roles, and prevention before cure, common sense is not yet all that common, to quote Voltaire.

The canvas from which this sketch has been drawn is the same as that employed by Jaspers (1925/1962). There is no comprehensive hard picture of truth in this area that we can construct; all we can do is to point to many perspectives and directions, to movement on various planes that constrains us to remain alert and look far afield while we try to keep a firm grasp on the systematized knowledge that we have won so far. In the behavioral field the knowledge we have gained has led to tangible advances in theory and in clinical practice and points to paths we may follow with profit in the future.

SUMMARY

The diverse roots of behavioral psychotherapy for neuroses are emphasized, and experimental psychology is noted to be but one of the many "idols of origin," and to be little used in practice by most behavior therapists. The conditioning model of neurosis has shortcomings, and it may be necessary to think in terms of failed extinction of phobias and rituals rather than enhanced acquisition. For the therapist, clinical paradigms are more useful than experimental paradigms for reducing phobias and compulsive rituals. Exposure treatment is effective and arousal level during exposure has not been found to affect outcome. To reduce time needed by professional therapists, exposure treatment can often be carried out by patients themselves as "exposure homework," and relatives can act as cotherapists. Marital discord does not contraindicate exposure methods. Treatment failure can occur from lack of compliance, depression, or, rarely, nonhabituation. Ten theoretical problems for exposure research are detailed. The advent of effective behavioral psychotherapy for some neuroses has led to a demand for treatment that exceeds the supply of therapists, and paraprofessionals and self-help methods can help to bridge the gap, while preventive measures may prevent the development of some pathology.

REFERENCES

Akiyama, M. Effects of extinction techniques on avoidance response. *Bulletin of the Faculty of Education.* Hiroshima University, Japan, 1968, *17*, 173.

Arnold, L. E., Barneby, N., McManus, J., Smeltzer, D. J., Conrad, A., Winer, G., & Desgranges, L. Prevention by specific perceptual remediation for vulnerable first-graders. *Archives of General Psychiatry*, 1977, *34*, 1279-1294.

Barraclough, G. History and the Common Man. Presidential address to the Historical Association of Great Britain, London, 1966.

Baum, M. Extinction of an avoidance response following response prevention: Some parametric investigations. *Canadian Journal of Psychology*, 1969, *23*, 1.

Boulougouris, J. C. Variables affecting the behavior of obsessive-compulsive patients treated by flooding. In J. C. Boulougouris & A. Rabavilas (Eds.), *Studies in phobic and obsessive-compulsive disorders*, Oxford: Pergamon, 1977, pp. 73-84.

Bregman, E. O. An attempt to modify the emotional attitudes of infants by the conditioned response technique. *Journal of Genetic Psychology*, 1934, *45*, 169-198.

Cellucci, A. J., & Lawrence, P. S. The efficacy of systematic desensitisation in reducing nightmares. *Journal of Behavior Therapy and Experimental Psychiatry*, 1978, *9*, 109-114.

Chabot, B. The right to care for each other and its silent erosion. *Tidschrift voor Psychotherapie*, 1979, *5*, 199-216.

Chambers, L. W., & West, A. E. The St. John's randomized trial of the family practice nurse: Health outcomes of patients. *International Journal of Epidemiology*, 1978, *I*, 153-161.

Climent, C. E., De Arango, M. V., Plutchick, R., & Leon, C. A. Development of an alternative, efficient, low-cost mental health delivery system in Cali, Colombia, Part 1: The auxiliary nurse. *Social Psychiatry*, 1978, *13*, 29-35.

Cobb, J., & Marks, I. M. Morbid jealousy featuring as obsessive-compulsive neurosis: treatment by behavioural psychotherapy. *British Journal of Psychiatry*, 1979, *134*, 301-305.

Cobb, J. P., McDonald, R. M., Marks, I. M., & Stern, R. S. Which behavioural approach? Marital versus exposure treatment for combined marital and phobic obsessive problems. *Behaviour Analysis and Modification*, 1980, *4*, 3-16.

Cochrane, R., & Sobol, M. P. Myth and methodology in behaviour therapy research. In M. P. Feldman & A. Broadhurst (Eds.), *Theoretical and experimental bases of the behavior therapies*, New York: Wiley, 1976.

Emmelkamp, P. M. G. The behavioral study of clinical phobias. In: M. Hersen, R. M. Eisler, & P. M. Miller (Eds.), *Progress in behavior modification*, Volume III. New York: Academic Press, 1979.

Fichter, M. M., & Wittchen, H. V. (Eds.). *Clinical psychology and psychotherapy: A survey of the present state of professionalisation in 23 countries*, in press.

Foa, E. B., & Goldstein, A. Continuous exposure and complete response prevention treatment of obsessive-compulsive neurosis. *Behavior Therapy*, 1978, *9*, 821-829.

Foa, E. B., & Steketee, G. In M. R. Hersen, R. M. Eisler, and P. M. Miller (Eds.), *Progress in behavior modification*, Volume III. New York: Academic Press, 1979.

Foa, E. B., Steketee, G. S., & Milby, J. B. Differential Effect of exposure and response-prevention in obsessive-compulsive washers. *Journal of Consulting and Clinical Psychology*. In press.

Freud, S. The justification for detaching from neurasthenia a particular syndrome: the anxiety neurosis. In S. Freud, *Collected Works*, Volume I. London: Hogarth Press and International Psychoanalytical Press, 1894, pp. 76-106.

Freud, S. Turnings in the ways of psychoanalytic therapy. In S. Freud (Ed.), *Collected papers*, Volume 2. London: Hogarth Press and International Psychoanalytical Press, 1919.

Freyman, J. G. Medicine's great schism: Prevention v. cure. An historical interpretation. *Medical Care*, 1975, *13*, 525-536.

Greist, J., Marks, I. M., Berlin, F., Gournay, K., & Noshirvani, H. Avoidance versus confrontation of fear. *Behavior Therapy*, 1980, *11*, 1-14.

Hafner, J., & Marks, I. M. Exposure in vivo of agoraphobics: The contributions of diazepam, group exposure and anxiety evocation. *Psychological Medicine*, 1976, *6*, 71-88.

Hartmann, D. B., Baker, T. B., & Wade, T. C. The professional reading practices of behavior therapists. *The Behavior Therapist*, 1978, *5*, 13.

Hunter, R., & MacAlpine, J. *Three hundred years of British psychiatry*, London: Oxford University Press, 1963.

Janet, P. *Psychological healing*, Volume II. New York: Macmillan, 1925.

Jannoun, L., Munby, M., Catalan, J., & Gelder, M. A home-based treatment program for agoraphobia, replication and controlled evaluation. *Behavior Therapy*, 1980, *11*, 294-305.

Jaspers, K. *Allgemeine psychopathologie*. Manchester, England: Manchester University Press, 1925/1962.

Kass, D. J., & Stauss, F. F. *Sex therapy at home*. New York: Simon and Schuster, 1975.

Kazdin, A. E. *History of behavior modification: Experimental foundation of contemporary research*. Baltimore, MD: University Park Press, 1978.

Kimmel, H. D. (Ed.). *Experimental psychopathology: Recent research and theory*. New York: Academic Press, 1971.

Knoff, W. F. Abstracts of the Fifth World Congress of Psychiatry, 1969.

Lang, P. J. Imagery in therapy. An information processing analysis of fear. *Behavior Therapy*, 1977, *8*, 862-886.

Leonhard, K. *Individual Therapie und Prophylaxe der hysterischen, anankastichen und sensohypochendrischen Neurosen*. Jena: Gustav Fischer Verlag, 1963.

Lewis, C. E., Resnick, B. A., & Schmidt, G. Activities, events and outcomes in ambulatory patient care. *New England Journal of Medicine*, 1969, *280*, 645-649.

Liberman, B. L., & True, J. E. Evaluation of the comparative effectiveness of professionals, mental health associates, and other professionals in therapeutic interventions with psychiatric outpatients. Unpublished manuscript, 1978.

Lieberman, M. A., & Gardner, J. R. Institutional alternatives to psychotherapy. *Archives of General Psychiatry*, 1976, *33*, 157-162.

Mahler, J. Health—a demystification of medical technology. *The Lancet*, 1975, *2*, 829-833.

Marks, I. M. *Fears and phobias*. New York: Academic Press, 1969.

Marks, I. M. Behavioral treatments of phobic and obsessive-compulsive disorders: a critical appraisal. In M. R. Hersen, R. M. Eisler, & P. M. Miller (Eds.), *Progress in behavior modification*, Volume I. New York: Academic Press, 1975.

Marks. I. M. Exposure treatments. In S. Agras (Ed.), *Behavior modifi-*

cation: Principles and clinical applications, Second edition. Boston: Little, Brown and Co., 1977.

Marks. I. M. *Living with fear:* New York: McGraw-Hill, 1978.

Marks. I. M., Bird, J., & Lindley, P. Behavioural nurse-therapists-developments and implications. *Behavioural Psychotherapy.* 1978, *6*, 25–36.

Marks, I. M., Rachman, S., & Hodgson, R. Treatment of chronic obsessive-compulsive neurosis by in vivo exposure. *British Journal of Psychiatry*, 1975, *127*, 349–364.

Marks, I. M., Stern, R. S., Mawson, D., Cobb, J., & McDonald, R. Clomipramine and exposure in vivo for obsessive-compulsive rituals: I & II. *British Journal of Psychiatry*, 1980, *136*, 1–25 and 161–166.

Mathews, A. M., Johnston, D. W., Shaw, P. M., & Gelder, M. G. Process variables and the prediction of outcome in behaviour therapy. *British Journal of Psychiatry*, 1974, *125*, 256–264.

Maxmen, J. S. *The Post physician era: Medicine in the 21st century.* New York: Wiley, 1976.

McDonald, R., Sartory, G., Grey, S., Cobb, J., Stern, R., & Marks, I. M. The effects of self-exposure instructions on agoraphobic outpatients. *Behaviour Research and Therapy*, 1979, *17*, 83–85.

McGregor, M. Impact of health care legislation on the medical school. In P. W. Kent (Ed.), *International aspects of the provision of medical care.* London: Oriel Press, 1976, pp. 68–78.

Mineka, S. Role of fear in theories of avoidance learning, flooding, and extinction. *Psychological Bulletin*, 1979, *86*, 895–1010.

Rabavilas, A. D., Boulougouris, J. C., & Stefanis, D. Duration of flooding session in the treatment of obsessive-compulsive patients. *Behaviour Research and Therapy*, 1976, *14*, 349–355.

Ramsay, R. Grief: Film presented to EABT, Spetsae, Greece. Columbia Broadcast Co. 1976.

Raphael, B. Prevention intervention with the recently bereaved. *Archives of General Psychiatry*, 1977, *34*, 1450–1454.

Rimm, D. C., Janda, L. H., Lancaster, D. W., Nahl, M., & Dittmar, K. An explanatory investigation of the origin and maintenance of phobias. *Behaviour Research and Therapy*, 1977, *15*, 231–238.

Robertson, J. R. Controlled investigation of treatment of obsessive-compulsive disorders. Personal communication, 1979.

Sackett, D. L., & Spitzer, W. O. The Burlington Randomized Trail of the Nurse Practitioner. *Annals of International Medicine*, 1974, *80*, 137–142.

Seligman, M. Phobias and preparedness. *Behavior Therapy*, 1971, *2*, 307–320.

Seligman, M., & Hager, J. *Biological boundaries of learning.* New York: Appleton-Century Crofts, 1972.

Sidman, M., Herrnstein, R. J., & Conrad, D. G. Maintenance of avoidance behaviour by unavoidable shocks. *Journal of Comparative and Physiological Psychology*, 1957, *50*, 553-557.

Spitzer, W. O., Roberts, R. S., & Delmore, T. Nurse practitioners in primary care. VI: Assessment of their deployment with the litigation and Financial Index. *Canadian Medical Association Journal*, 1976, *114*, 1103-1108.

St. John, J. A. (Ed.), *The philosophical works of John Locke*. London: Bell, 1913.

Stern, R. S., & Marks, I. M. Contract therapy in obsessive-compulsive neurosis with marital discord. *British Journal of Psychiatry*, 1973, *123*, 681-684.

Stunkard, A. J., & Brownell, K. D. Workside treatment for obesity. *American Journal of Psychiatry*, 1980, *137*, 252-253.

Thoren, P., Asberg, M., Cronholm, B., Jornestedt, L., & Traskman, L. Clomipramine treatment of obsessive-compulsive disorder. I: A controlled clinical trial. *Archives of General Psychiatry*, in press.

Thorndike, E. L. *The psychology of wants, interests and attitudes*. London: Appleton-Century Crofts, 1935, pp. 195-196.

Usa, G., & Usa, I. A case of a nun who suffered from visionary obsessions of snakes treated by Morita therapy. *Psychologia*, 1958, *1*, 226.

Watson, J. B., & Rayner, R. Conditioned emotional reactions. *Journal of Experimental Psychology*, 1920, *3*, 1-14.

Watson, J. P., & Marks, I. M. Relevant and irrelevant fear in flooding —A crossover study of phobic patients. *Behavior Therapy*, 1971, *2*, 275-293.

Wolpe, J. *Psychotherapy by reciprocal inhibition*. Stanford, CA: Stanford University Press, 1958.

CHAPTER 8

The Philosophic Implications and Dangers of Some Popular Behavior Therapy Techniques

Albert Ellis, Ph.D.

Although behavior therapy at first avoided cognitive theories and practices and confined itself largely to classical conditioning and operant conditioning techniques, it has become increasingly receptive to cognitive variables and has indeed undergone something of a cognitive revolution (Beck, 1976; Ellis, 1962; Eysenck, 1964; Lazarus, 1971, 1976; Mahoney, 1974, 1977; Meichenbaum, 1977). Even staunch "conditionists" such as Eysenck (1980) and Wolpe (1958) have, if somewhat reluctantly and unenthusiastically, acknowledged the importance of cognition in the creation and improvement of behavioral disorders; and Skinner (1971), while still taking an atheoretical stance, has for a considerable period of time acknowledged the relevance of verbal or cognitive factors in conditioning and reconditioning.

If the cognitive revolution in behavior therapy is on the right track, and if some of the fundamental assumptions of rational emotive therapy (RET) and cognitive behavior therapy (CBT) have a measure of validity, it would appear that humans at least in part feel and behave the way they think—and also think the way they behave (Beck, 1976; Ellis, 1957, 1958, 1962; Ellis & Abrahms, 1978; Ellis & Greiger, 1977; Ellis & Whiteley, 1979; Goldfried & Davison, 1976; Rimm & Masters, 1974). If this is true, then all the major behavior therapy (BT) techniques have cognitive or philosophic implications. For not only do people tend to change their ways of emoting and behaving when they are helped, by cognitive behavior therapists, to modify their ideas; but they also change their ways of thinking (and, consequently, of *later* behaving) when they are helped by "pure" behavior therapists to modify their actions.

The theory that cognitions and behaviors interactively or transactionally affect each other, in other words, strongly implies that virtually all behavioral changes, whether made by individuals on their own or under the guidance of therapists, lead to significant kinds of cognitive changes, and vice versa. Moreover, if John Jones and Mary Smith change their "catastrophizing" or "awfulizing" attitudes toward, say, riding on elevators, they will tend first to begin to ride instead of phobically avoiding the use of elevators; they will, secondly, begin to feel relaxed or even enjoy it when riding elevators; they will, thirdly, "automatically" or "unconsciously" acquire a less fearful philosophy about elevators (and perhaps about several other conveyances, such as escalators and trains); and they will, because of this new, confirmed or stronger philosophy, "automatically" or "unconsciously" keep taking elevators and enjoying their use.

If this is so, then certain therapeutic problems will often arise in the employment of "pure" behavioral methods. For one of the main characteristics of thinking is that humans not only use it constructively to generalize but also are easily prone to use it unconstructively (that is, against their own best interest) to overgeneralize (Ellis, 1962, 1973, 1976; Korzybski, 1933). Thus, once John and Mary "realize" or "conclude" that riding in elevators is not "dangerous" or "catastrophic," they may also easily "realize" that other forms of transportation, such as escalators and trains, are equally "undangerous" and that they need not be in any way cautious or concerned about riding on or in them—which is not quite accurate or true (since, unless one carefully watches one's step, one may easily hurt oneself on an escalator). If John and Mary, therefore, are provided with the BT in vivo desensitization technique of forcing themselves to take many rides in elevators, they may indeed get over their elevator phobias; but they may also later harm themselves by using escalators without sufficient caution.

The main theme of this paper is that a good many BT methods work very well when used to help clients with behavioral problems to overcome their phobias, obsessions, compulsions, and addictions; but that when they are employed cavalierly and uncautiously, they may easily encourage these clients to overgeneralize or to philosophize self-defeatingly and thereby ultimately produce considerable harm as well as good. Even when these techniques tend to bring immediate benefits and are gratefully used by neurotic individuals, they may also influence their users (as well as the therapists who encourage their use) to acquire or exacerbate self-sabotaging philosophies that, in the long run, do more harm than good. This may, of course, be said of virtually all therapy methods—cognitive, emotive, and behavioral—since one never knows, when a given technique is endorsed by a therapist and utilized by a client, exactly what cognitions or conclusions such a client will make about this technique and about the results to which it leads. So all therapy has dangerous implications and potentials, and behavior therapy is of course no exception to this general rule (Bergin and Garfield, 1979). But the theme of this paper is that certain BT methods are especially likely to lead many clients into pathways of crooked thinking; and that therefore behavior therapists and cognitive behavior therapists had better be aware of the dangers of these particular methods and do something about minimizing these dangers.

Which BT "dangerous" methods am I particularly talking about? Let me now consider some of them that I have found, in my clinical practice, especially vulnerable in this respect.

SOCIAL REINFORCEMENT

Pavlov's (1927) theories and practices regarding the conditioning of dogs and other animals led ultimately to Skinner's (1953, 1971) operant conditioning and particularly to the advocacy by behavior therapists of social reinforcement to help change the dysfunctional feelings and behaviors of humans (Bandura, 1969, 1977). These therapeutic techniques work very well, as hundreds of experiments have shown, and they are employed regularly in BT, CBT, and RET (Ellis, 1962; Ellis & Harper, 1961; Ellis & Whiteley, 1979; Wolfe & Brand, 1977). The reason why they are so useful, in RET terms, probably is that most people find the approval of others—including their therapists—so reinforcing or rewarding that they are willing to change their basic irrational beliefs—for example, that they *can't* do well at certain tasks or that they *must* not undergo the hardship of dieting in order to lose weight—when they receive sufficient approval from their therapists and friends for surrendering these ideas.

In general, moreover, humans seem to become emotionally disturbed largely because of their low frustration tolerance or short-range hedonism. When deprived of something that they strongly want (and that they irrationally think they need or must have), they desperately strive for the pleasure of the moment (such as extra food) rather than for the pleasure of the future (such as thinness and good health), and they frequently succumb to immediate gratification rather than future gain (Ellis, 1979). When the contingencies of reinforcement are arranged so that they receive immediate gratification (such as approval from their therapists or parents) every time they go for long-range satisfactions (thinness) rather than short-range pleasure (extra food), they frequently substitute the former for the latter and give up their self-defeating addictive behavior (overeating). Knowing this, behavior therapists and cognitive behavior therapists frequently use social reinforcement to help change the neurotic behavior of children and adults; and, as noted above, they often get good results thereby, at least in the form of symptom removal.

Is there anything pernicious about the "good results" achieved by using social reinforcement? Indeed, there often is! For one of the strongest and most pervasive of all neurotic disturbances in people's firm belief that they absolutely *must* have others' approval and that they are rotten or worthless individuals if they do not merit it (Ellis, 1957, 1958, 1962; Ellis & Abrahms, 1978; Ellis & Grieger, 1977; Ellis & Harper, 1975; Ellis and Whiteley, 1979). When, therefore, therapists deliberately arrange social reinforcement to help clients change their disturbed feelings and behavior, they often tend to reinforce beneficial behavior (such as dieting) but they *also* reinforce the idea that these clients *need* (and not merely feel good about) the therapists' and others' approval; and consequently, many "cured" clients of BT probably end up less addicted to one form of self-defeating behavior (such as overeating) and more addicted to an equally or even more damaging form of behavior (such as addiction to love). Is their consequent gain really worth it?

Not that BT is alone in this respect. The great majority of modern psychotherapies seem to reinforce clients with their therapists' love (Berne, 1971; Freud, 1965; Rogers, 1961; Truax & Carkhuff, 1967), and thereby include the same philosophic implications as behavior therapists often do: namely, that these clients cannot accept themselves and function effectively *unless* they have distinct love gratifications. But BT, although not noted as a relationship-type therapy, does so even more systematically than some of the other therapies; and consequently it may be suspected of contributing significantly to human harm as well as good.

GRADUAL DESENSITIZATION

Behavior therapy uses many therapeutic techniques, but perhaps none more than that of gradual desensitization and shaping. Skinnerian operant conditioning largely consists of the process of gradually reinforcing children and adults with presumably rewarding conditions until they acquire new self-helping behaviors and surrender old self-defeating ones; and Wolpe's (1958, 1973) reciprocal inhibition technique consists of having clients gradually and repetitively interrupt their phobias or other dysfunctional thoughts, feelings, and actions with relaxation methods, until they slowly become desensitized. Both these highly popular BT techniques try to make sure that clients acquire or give up old behaviors almost painlessly and that, to this end, they very gradually institute behavioral changes.

These methods, as again considerable research evidence attests, often get excellent results—at least in the form of symptom removal. The difficulty is that they tend to endorse and reinforce a philosophy that states or implies that (1) emotional change has to be brought about slowly and cannot possibly occur quickly or suddenly; (2) that it must be practically painless as it is occurring; and (3) that it cannot occur with the use of jarring, painful, flooding methods of therapy. All these assumptions, however, seem to have a great deal of falseness, since emotional change can be dramatic and sudden (Ellis, 1957, 1962, Ellis & Abrahms, 1978; Ellis & Whiteley, 1979; Moreno, 1947; Perls, 1969; Small, 1979), and it often seems to be abetted by jarring, painful flooding techniques (Bard, 1980; Marks, 1978; Stampfl & Levis, 1967).

Since, moreover, one of the most important elements in human disturbance seems to be low frustration tolerance or what I have called discomfort anxiety (Ellis, 1979), and since this element largely consists of the philosophy, "I must not suffer from frustrating or unpleasant conditions!" and "I must be able to change my disturbed behavior easily and comfortably and must not be forced to go through pain to achieve emotional gain," it would appear that this basic self-defeating philosophy is often abetted or reinforced by psychotherapeutic gradualism. Consequently, any form of psychotherapy that helps clients feel better rather than get better is likely to do more harm than good (Ellis, 1968) and to be in some respects more antitherapeutic than therapeutic. This would sometimes seem to be the case when gradualism is promoted in behavior therapy.

THE USE OF COGNITIVE DISTRACTION

Many methods of psychotherapy, whether their practitioners realize this or not, are actually forms of cognitive distraction (Ellis, 1980a; Ellis & Abrahms, 1978). Thus, Jacobsen's (1942) muscular relaxation technique, Benson's (1975) relaxation response, and various forms of meditation and yoga (Shapiro, 1979) induce people to focus intently on their muscles, on their breathing, on their limbs, on their thoughts, or on something else; and, in so doing, they distract these individuals from focusing on how dreadful it is that they are not doing what they *must* do, or how terrible the world is because it is not as delightful as it *must* be. This kind of distraction stops them, at least temporarily, from creating anxious, depressed, or hostile thoughts that lead to emotional disturbance. Nearly all forms of cognitive distraction bring about therapeutic results, at least temporarily. For if, as rational emotive therapy and other cognitive behavior systems of therapy contend, human disturbance is largely created by self-defeating, *must*urbatory beliefs with which people strongly indoctrinate themselves and foolishly act upon, any effective form of intellectual diversion will interrupt and at least partly remove such irrational thinking (Ellis & Whiteley, 1979).

BT notably uses cognitive distraction in the form of reciprocal inhibition (Wolpe, 1958, 1973), thought stopping (Rimm & Masters, 1974), and skill training (Alberti & Emmons, 1979; Liberman et al., 1977), and in various other ways. In so doing, it creates harmful as well as beneficial effects because, first of all, such methods tend to be much more palliative than curative. Almost anyone who is anxious, for example, may learn Jacobsen's relaxation method and can use it to good effect—perhaps every single day of the week. But ten or twenty minutes after people who use it have relaxed and distracted themselves from their anxiety-provoking thoughts, they tend to return to the same basic thinking and to make themselves anxious all over again.

Worse yet, because cognitive distraction techniques like relaxation and thought stopping work so quickly, somewhat like tranquilizers, alcohol, biofeedback, and other means of interrupting anxiety, they are frequently employed *instead of* more elegant and more lasting methods of anxiety reduction. They therefore bolster many clients' low frustration tolerance (that is, taking the easy rather then the harder and more effective way out of their emotional dificulties); and they foster inefficient forms of therapy that will tend to keep people working at their anxiety forever, rather than once and for all eliminating most of it. Thus, one of my clients bypassed her dire need for approval by using transcendental meditation for years on many of the occasions that she felt very lonely without a male companion. But she never got rid of her neurotic need, nor did anything about acquiring a suitable companion, until I showed her that her TM exercises were mainly interfering with her showing herself that she did *not* need a lover but only strongly preferred one—and that she could get one if she stopped needing and stopped sidetracking herself by meditating!

UNSELECTIVE ECLECTICISM

Both BT and CBT have noneclectic theories about the acquiring and reducing of emotional disturbances, but they are both rather eclectic in their use of a variety of techniques of behavioral change. Behavior therapy, however, often tends to be unselectively eclectic, in that it employs a number of methods that have magical, mystical, or unscientific overtones and that therefore may help exacerbate rather than ameliorate emotional problems. Shapiro (1979), for example, espouses a combination of behavior therapy and oriental mysticism and favors clients reaching the Zen Buddhist state of nirvana. Palmer (1973) endorses bioenergetic and primal therapy techniques that are linked with systems of psychotherapy that include several antiscientific philosophies.

Here again the problem seems to be that BT is sometimes so interested in symptom removal that it ignores the negative philosophic connotations of some of the ways it uses to help remove these symptoms. Thus, although the Zen state of nirvana—assuming that anyone is really capable of achieving it for more than a few seconds—may well divert people from their feelings of anxiety or depression, it espouses a way of life, a desirelessness, that hardly facilitates human life or happiness and may even be seen as a state of severe withdrawal. And although some of the bioenergetic exercises may encourage people to let out their feelings, the Reichian philosophy on which they are based and which tends to go together with their usage leaves much to be desired as far as the achievement of mental health is concerned and may, especially in its espousal of the extreme abreaction of anger, lead to considerable individual and social harm.

Even without the philosophies that tend to go with them, moreover, the entrance of individuals into extreme states of withdrawal or into unusual expression of intense feelings tends to carry with it philosophic implications that are not necessarily "healthy." For if, encouraged by Zen Buddhist "therapists," I go into a state of exceptional withdrawal for an hour or so every day, I will, in all probability, whether or not I am aware of the Zen philosophy behind this withdrawal exercise, begin to tell myself things like, "I must not be very immersed in love, sex, family life, or business," "I can't stand people!" or "Life is a pretty awful state of being, and perhaps it would be better if I were dead!" And if, encouraged by a behavior therapist who employs bioenergetic exercises (or primal or screaming therapy), I pound pillows representing the head of my father, mate, or boss, I can easily figure out for myself (without the help of some of Wilheim Reich's extremist political notions), that people like by father really *are* bastards and truly *must* be punished; or that Hitler and other fascists *do* deserve to be roasted everlastingly in hell; or that my word *is* law and that my strong wishes *have to be* obeyed.

Caveat emptor! Whoever buys, at a behavior therapist's instigation, a set of emotive behavioral procedures to employ during therapy sessions or, especially, as homework assignments, tends to buy a stated or implied philosophy of living that significantly correlates with these procedures. Such a philosphy may, of course, be emotionally healthful and helpful; but it may also be self-sabotaging, especially in the long run. The main point is that behavior therapists and cognitive behavior therapists, if they employ various activity-oriented procedures, had better be intensely aware that these *do* almost invariably have important philosophic correlates; and that if, as rational-emotive therapy theory specifically suggests, the basic philosphy of people is one of the main reasons, and perhaps *the* most important, for what we call their "emotional disturbances," exactly which behavioral techniques are employed and are not employed with clients may be significantly related to the harm that therapists do. Clearly, therefore, behavior therapists had better be aware of the cognitive correlates of their procedures and give some serious thought to selecting such procedures with the goal of not merely helping but also of least harming their clients.

THE ROLE OF EFFICIENCY IN PSYCHOTHERAPY

Perhaps one of the most neglected values in psychotherapy is the value of efficiency (Ellis, 1980b). In the old days, it was wrongly assumed that if a few cases were reported which showed that a given form of therapy worked well with some clients, that "proved" that this treatment method was "valid" or "effective," and that was that. Recent corrective literature in this respect has tended to show that clinical impressions are not enough, and that, in addition, controlled experiments had better also be done to show that behavior therapy, or any other form of treatment, provides valid results (Mahoney, 1974; Meichenbaum, 1977; Thoresen & Coates, 1978).

Old myths, however, rarely die; and a good number of hardheaded investigators—such as Frank (1975)—still seem to hold that if a certain form of therapy sometimes or occasionally works, it is legitimate to keep using it despite its relative inefficiency. This is hardly clearheaded thinking (Ellis, 1975). No matter how many times it can be shown that certain kinds of behavior therapy work, I would still vigorously contend that if these methods (1) often do harm as well as good and (2) bring inefficient results instead of the more effective methods that might be used in their stead, they had better be abandoned or used only in exceptional instances.

I would more specifically contend that some forms of BT have been shown, in a good many controlled experiments, to help some clients, but that nonetheless they are often relatively inefficient or wasteful. Take, for example, Wolpe's (1958, 1973) popular method of systematic desensitization (SD) or reciprocal inhibition. I think there is little doubt that this method has a great deal of experimental evidence to support it (Kazdin, 1978; Kazdin & Wilcoxon, 1976; Wolpe, 1973). But I think that there is reason to believe that it is also (1) mainly distractive and palliative rather than philosophically "curative"; (2) inelegant, in the sense that it helps clients to think, "I can control my anxiety," instead of "I do not have to make myself anxious by insisting that I *must* do well and *have to* be approved by others"; (3) liked by clients for the wrong reasons: namely, that it is highly structured and relatively easy for them to learn; (4) overly favored by therapists for similar wrong reasons:

namely, that clients like it and it is relatively easy to teach; (5) sidetracking, in that it discourages clients from making profounder and more enduring changes; (6) productive of the philosophy of "Let's do something easily and quickly," which is the basic philosophy of low frustration tolerance (Ellis, 1979).

If these observations are correct (which may be experimentally determinable), then systematic desensitization, for all its popularity, is an "effective" but still rather "inefficient" method of behavior therapy. And if this is true, its usage will tend to arouse or exacerbate the *philosophy* of striving for minimal efficiency or inefficiency in therapy. For, unless all therapists, including behavior therapists, realize that helping clients is not enough, but that helping them in a manner that is quick, profound, lasting, and truly "deep" or "curative" is equally or more important than helping them in *any* way, psychotherapy will remain, as I think it now definitely is, somewhat effective but still highly inefficient. So the somewhat cavalier and unthinking employment of supposedly inefficient techniques such as SD may lead to results that are, in the short run, therapeutically "good" but in the long run philosophically unsound and somewhat "bad."

In the points I have just made, I have not, of course, exhausted the philosophic implications of behavior therapy nor completely shown how many of the popular and presumably "effective" techniques that are now employed may well lead to questionable results. But I hope that I have at least raised some issues that will be given serious consideration by behavior therapists and cognitive behavior therapists and that they will be used as hypotheses that may be experimentally tested.

PROPHYLAXIS AND TREATMENT OF THE PHILOSOPHIC DANGERS OF BEHAVIOR THERAPY

If some popular behavior therapy methods do, indeed, have philosophic dangers and if they therefore sometimes tend to be iatrogenic, what can be done to prevent and eliminate these dangers? Let me suggest some prophylactic and treatment precautions that may be taken.

1. As a behavior therapist, try to be fully aware of the possibility that some of the BT procedures that you use will have philosophic implications and dangers. Think about the possibilities of all the procedures you employ in this respect; but particularly give thought to certain of them, such as those mentioned in this article.

2. Check to see whether specific clients are likely to or are actually giving harmful meanings to the procedures that you are employing with them. If, for example, you use relaxation methods with a thirty-five-year-old alcoholic male who easily quits onerous

jobs and seems to have a serious degree of low frustration tolerance, check to see what conclusions he is making *about* his "successful" use of these methods. Is he telling himself that he has rid himself of practically all his anxiety through their use, and that he consequently does not have to work any longer at looking at its sources and extirpating it? Is he employing relaxation techniques instead of priming himself for looking for another job? Is he deifying you as a therapist for teaching him this fine relaxation procedure, or is he angrily condemning you for supplying him with a procedure that he has to keep using daily and that does not once-and-for-all rid him of his severe emotional problems? Check to see what his basic *attitudes* about the use of relaxation methods are and how these attitudes help or hinder him in his therapy.

3. If and when you observe that certain BT methods tend to result in harmful philosophic conclusions for many or some of your clients, ask yourself whether it is worthwhile continuing to employ these methods or to employ them unselectively. Consider dropping them for most or a few of your clients.

4. If you decide that, despite their liabilities, certain BT methods are worth using with many or a few of your clients, try to help these clients observe and dispute the irrational beliefs that they are constructing regarding these methods. Disputation of this kind is a key feature of rational-emotive therapy (RET) and as Phadke (1976) has outlined, it frequently includes the three-way process of detecting, discriminating, and debating:

a. Detect the irrational belief that your clients hold by looking for the absolutistic shoulds, oughts, and musts or demands and commands associated with this belief, as well as the awfulizing, I can't-stand-it-itis, and the damnation of self and/or others stemming from or going along with this belief. Thus, with regard to the use of relaxation methods of BT, a client may be telling himself, "I *must* find an easy way, such as relaxation, of solving my emotional problems! It is *awful* if I have to work hard to solve them! I *can't stand* having to continue to work hard at ridding myself of anxiety. I am a *rotten person* if I can't use this relaxation method correctly or if I continue to be anxious in spite of its use!" Help the client see that he is employing these irrational beliefs and that they will harm rather than help him, especially in the long run.

b. Show the client how to discriminate his irrational from his rational beliefs about the behavior therapy technique, such as relaxation, that you are teaching him to use. Thus, his rational beliefs, as distinct from his irrational ones, might be about the relaxation technique he is using: "I hope that this relaxation method works very well, since it is relatively easy to learn and apply. It is unfortunate, but not awful if I have to keep working at solving my problems of anxiety, and I can stand continuing to work hard at solving these problems. And even if I don't use this relaxation method correctly and still remain anxious, I am never a rotten person but only a person who is still behaving poorly in these respects."

c. Show the client how to debate his irrational beliefs about relaxation by using the scientific method of disputing his hypotheses concerning relaxation: "Where is the evidence that I *must* find an easy way, such as relaxation, of solving my emotional problems? Prove that it is *awful* (instead of merely inconvenient) if I have to work hard at solving them? How is it true that I *can't stand* having to continue to work hard at ridding myself of this anxiety? In what ways am I truly a *rotten person* if I can't use this relaxation method correctly or if I continue to be anxious in spite of its use?"

By helping this alcoholic client (or other clients) actively to think about and detect his irrational beliefs, to discriminate them from his rational beliefs, and vigorously to persist at debating and disputing these beliefs, you may well be able to help him (or them) give up these irrationalities and thereby be able to use relaxation methods (and other potentially harmful BT methods) without their arriving at the self-defeating philosophies that may accompany these methods. In this manner, you and your clients will be enabled to use BT methods that might otherwise prove inadvisable and to make better uses of somewhat questionable BT methods. You may expect no panaceas in this connection and may still at times feel it best to abandon some behavioral therapy procedures with certain clients. But you will at least arrange for minimal disadvantage or harm while maintaining a maximum number of effective BT procedures.

SUMMARY

If the cognitive revolution in behavior therapy (BT) is on the right track, it would appear that humans at least in part feel the way they think and also think and feel the way they behave. If so, then virtually all behavioral changes, whether made by individuals on their own or under the guidance of therapists, lead to significant kinds of cognitive or philosophic changes, and vice versa. Some of these philosophic changes that clients make through using behavior therapy (BT) techniques will tend to be beneficial and some will tend to be harmful. This chapter presents some of the dangerous philosophic implications that clients sometimes tend to make and by which they may harm themselves when they use certain BT methods, such as social reinforcement, gradual desensitization, cognitive distraction, unselective eclectic procedures, and other effective but in some ways inefficient behavior therapy procedures. These dangerous implications include: (1) the substantiation or exacerbation of clients' belief that they must win others' approval, or else they are worthless individuals; (2) the reinforcement of their irrational beliefs that emotional change must be brought about slowly, has to be practically painless, and cannot occur in a jarring manner; (3) the bolstering of the belief that if clients are distracted from anxiety-arousing thoughts, these thoughts will permanently ameliorate or disappear; (4) the supporting of their notions that anything that works in therapy is good and that the effectiveness of a technique is the same as its efficiency. These philosophic dangers of some behavior therapy procedures can be minimized if therapists will be aware of them, will use certain methods quite selectively, and will show clients how to dispute their irrational beliefs about therapy by teaching them the kind of scientific disputing that is intrinsic to rational emotive therapy (RET) and some other cognitive behavior therapies.

REFERENCES

Alberti, R. E., & Emmons, M. J. *Your perfect right*, Revised edition. San Luis Obispo, CA: Impact, 1979.

Bandura, A. *Principles of behavior modification.* New York: Holt, Rinehart & Winston, 1969.

Bandura, A. *Social learning theory.* Palo Alto, CA: Stanford University Press, 1977.

Bard, J. A. *A primer for mental health practitioners.* Champaign, IL: Research Press, 1980.

Beck, A. T. *Cognitive therapy and the emotional disorders.* New York: International Universities Press, 1976.

Benson, H. *The relaxation response.* New York: Morrow, 1975.

Bergin, A. E., & Garfield, S. L. (Eds.). *Handbook of psychotherapy and behavior change*, Revised edition. New York: Wiley, 1979.

Berne, E. *What do you say after you say Hello?* New York: Grove, 1971.

Ellis, A. Outcome of employing three techniques of psychotherapy. *Journal of Clinical Psychology*, 1957, *13*, 334–350.

Ellis, A. Rational psychotherapy. *Journal of General Psychology*, 1958, *59*, 35–49.

Ellis, A. *Reason and emotion in psychotherapy.* Secaucus, NJ: Lyle Stuart and Citadel Press, 1962.

Ellis, A. Is Psychoanalysis harmful? *Psychiatric Opinion*, 1968, *5*, 16–24.

Ellis, A. Helping people get better, rather than merely feel better. *Rational Living*, 1972, *7*, 2–9.

Ellis, A. *Humanistic psychotherapy: the rational-emotive approach.* New York: Crown Publishers and McGraw-Hill Books, 1973.

Ellis, A. Comments on Frank's "The limits of humanism." *Humanist*, 1975, *35*, 43–45.

Ellis, A. The biological basis of human irrationality. *Journal of Individual Psychology*, 1976, *32*, 145–168.

Ellis, A. Discomfort anxiety: A new cognitive-behavioral construct. *Rational Living*, 1979, *14*, 2–8; 1980, *15* (1), 25–30. (a)

Ellis, A. Rational-emotive therapy and cognitive behavior therapy: Similarities and differences. *Cognitive Therapy and Research*, 1980, In Press. (b)

Ellis, A. Values in rational-emotive therapy: The value of efficiency. *Psychotherapy: Theory, Research & Practice*, 1980. In press. (c)

Ellis, A., & Abrahms, E. *Brief psychotherapy in medical and health practice*. New York: Springer, 1978.

Ellis, A., & Grieger, R. (Eds.). *Handbook of rational-emotive therapy*. New York: Springer, 1977.

Ellis, A., & Harper, R. A. *A guide to rational living*. Englewood Cliffs, NJ: Prentice-Hall, 1961.

Ellis, A., & Harper, R. A. *A new guide to rational living*. Englewood Cliffs, NJ: Prentice-Hall and Hollywood: Wilshire Books, 1975.

Ellis, A., & Whiteley, J. N. (Eds.). *Theoretical and empirical foundations of rational-emotive therapy*. Monterey, CA: Brooks/Cole, 1979.

Eysenck, H. J. *Experiments in behaviour therapy*. Elmsford, NY: Pergamon, 1964.

Eysenck, H. J. The conditioning model of neurosis. *Behavioral & Brain Sciences*, 1980, *2*, 155–159.

Frank, J. The limits of humanism. *Humanist*, 1975, *35*, 40–52.

Freud, S. *Standard edition of the complete psychological works of Sigmund Freud*. London: Hogarth, 1965.

Goldfried, M. R., & Davison, G. C. *Clinical behavior therapy*. New York: Holt, Rinehart & Winston, 1976.

Jacobsen, E. *You must relax*. New York: McGraw-Hill, 1942.

Kazdin, A. E. *History of behavior modification*. Baltimore, MD: University Park Press, 1978.

Kazdin, A. E., & Wilcoxon, L. Systematic desensitization and non-specific treatment effects: A methodological evaluation. *Psychological Bulletin*, 1976, *83*, 729–758.

Korzybski, A. *Science and sanity*. Lakeville, CT: Institute of General Semantics, 1933.

Lazarus, A. A. *Behavior therapy and beyond*. New York: McGraw-Hill, 1971.

Lazarus, A. A. *Multimodal behavior therapy*. New York: Springer, 1976.

Liberman, R. P., King, L. S., DeRisi, W. J., & McCann, M. *Personal effectiveness: Guiding people to assert themselves and improve their social skills*. Champaign, IL: Research Press, 1977.

Mahoney, M. *Cognition and behavior modification*. Cambridge, MA: Ballinger, 1974.

Mahoney, M. Reflections on the cognitive learning trend in psychotherapy. *American Psychologist*, 1977, *32*, 5–14.
Marks, I. M. *Living with fear: Understanding and coping with anxiety.* New York: McGraw-Hill, 1978.
Meichenbaum, D. *Cognitive behavior modification.* New York: Plenum, 1977.
Moreno, J. L. *Theater of spontaneity.* Beacon, NY: Beacon House, 1947.
Palmer, R. D. Desensitization of the fear of expressing one's own inhibited aggression: Bioenergetic assertive techniques for behavior therapists. *Advances in Behavior Therapy*, 1973, *4*, 241–253.
Pavlov, I. P. *Conditioned reflexes.* London: Oxford University Press, 1927.
Perls, F. *Gestalt therapy verbatim.* Lafayette, CA: Real People Press, 1969.
Phadke, K. M. *Bull fighting: A royal road to mental health.* Bombay: Institute for Rational Education, 1976.
Rimm, D. C., & Masters, J. C. *Behavior therapy.* New York: Academic Press, 1974.
Rogers, C. R. *On becoming a person.* Boston, MA: Houghton Mifflin, 1961.
Shapiro, D. *Precision nirvana.* Englewood Cliffs, NJ: Prentice-Hall, 1979.
Skinner, B. F. *Science and human behavior.* New York: Macmillan, 1953.
Skinner, B. F. *Beyond freedom and dignity.* New York: Knopf, 1971.
Small, L. *The briefer psychotherapies.* New York: Brunner Mazel, 1979.
Stampfl, T. F., & Levis, D. J. Phobic patients: Treatment with the learning approach of implosive therapy. *Voices*, 1967, *3*, 23–27.
Thoresen, C., & Coates, T. What does it mean to be a behavior therapist? *Counseling Psychologist*, 1978, *7*, 3–21.
Truax, C. B., & Carkhuff, R. R. *Toward effective counseling and psychotherapy.* Chicago, IL: Aldine, 1967.
Wolfe, J. L., & Brand, E. *Twenty years of rational therapy.* New York: Institute for Rational Living, 1977.
Wolpe, J. *Psychotherapy by reciprocal inhibition.* Stanford, CA: Stanford University Press, 1958.
Wolpe, J. *The practice of behavior therapy.* New York: Pergamon Press, 1973.

PART V

The Understanding of Depression

CHAPTER 9

Depression: A Perspective on Etiology, Treatment, and Life Span Issues

Peter Lewinsohn, Ph.D.
Linda Teri, Ph.D.
Harry M. Hoberman, M.S.

INTRODUCTION

Systematic investigation of depression within a behavioral framework is a phenomenon of the very recent past. Early applications of behavioral treatments to depressed individuals were reported by Lazarus (1968), Burgess (1969), and Lewinsohn, Weinstein, and Shaw (1969). Yet, since these preliminary endeavors, a proliferation of clinical and theoretical developments has occurred. In a short period of time, both the number and the scope of behavioral studies of depression have increased dramatically and continue to do so. Several major reviews have appeared in recent years (Blaney, 1981; Craighead, 1981; Lewinsohn & Hoberman, 1981; Rehm & Kornblith, 1979; Rush & Beck, 1978). Stimulated by the accumulating evidence that a variety of structured behavioral and cognitive therapies are effective in ameliorating depression, this prolific activity is reflected in the increased acceptance of such approaches among clinicians.

It has been said that the behavioral study of depression has reached its adolescence (Lewinsohn & Hoberman, 1981). This advancing maturity is clearly visible in the growing sophistication in experimental design, the gradual refinement of therapeutic approaches, and the expanded concern for populations other than middle-aged adults. The aim of this chapter is threefold: first, contemporary theories of unipolar depression shall be reviewed, second, a number of cognitive behavioral treatments for depression in adults will be examined; and, lastly, an overview of the developing body of research on depression in children, adolescents, and elderly people shall be presented. In this way, an integrative review of the advances in the behavioral investigation of unipolar depression will be achieved.

THEORETICAL POSITIONS

Initially, behaviorists focused their attention on challenging intrapsychic and psychodynamic theories of depression. Slowly, operational definitions of depression emerged. Extensive advances in the area of assessment provided a more coherent base for researchers and clinicians alike (Lewinsohn & Lee, 1981) and allowed for communicability across studies. In conjunction with the improvement in assessment, a number of behavioral formulations developed to explain the phenomena of depression. All of these concern themselves with tracing the course of depression, including its genesis and maintenance. Each theory focuses on one central mechanism assumed to be causal in depression and only secondarily takes account of other symptoms and problematic behaviors. Some empirical support has been provided for each of the theories, although the kind of data typically presented is that derived from treatment outcome studies and/or correlations of studies using depressed individuals.

Currently, most influential theoretical approaches may roughly be divided into those that emphasize "reinforcement" and those that emphasize "cognitions" in the etiology of depression. While these two conceptualizations differ in where they place the locus of causation, it is important to recognize similarities. Both assume that the depressed patient has *acquired* maladaptive reaction patterns that can be *unlearned.* Symptoms are seen as important in their own right rather than as manifestations of underlying conflicts.

REINFORCEMENT POSITIONS

The first attempt at a behavioral analysis of depression is contained in Skinner's (1953) book *Science and Human Behavior*, in which depression is described as a weakening of behavior due to the interruption of established sequences of behavior that have been positively reinforced by the social environment. This conceptualization of depression as an extinction phenomenon, and as a reduced frequency of emission of positively reinforced behavior, has been central to all behavioral positions. Ferster (1965; 1966) provided more details by suggesting that such diverse factors as sudden environmental changes, punishment and aversive control, and shifts in reinforcement contingencies can give rise to depression, that is, to a reduced rate of behavior. The therapeutic implications of this conceptualization are relatively straightforward. Since the onset of depression is assumed to be preceded by a reduction in positive reinforcement, improvement should follow from an increase in positive reinforcement. Hence, the principal goal of treatment should be to restore an adequate schedule of positive reinforcement for the patient by altering the level, the quality, and the range of his/her activities and interpersonal interactions.

In their application of the term "reinforcement" to depression, Lewinsohn, Youngren, and Grosscup (1979) have advanced several general hypotheses about the relationship between reinforcement and depression. The primary hypothesis states that a low rate of response-contingent reinforcement constitutes a critical antecedent for the occurrence of depression. Reinforcement is defined by the *quality* of the person's interactions with his/her environment. Those person/environment interactions with positive outcomes (that is, outcomes making the person feel good) constitute positive reinforcement and strengthen the person's behavior. The term "contingent" refers to the temporal relationship between a behavior and its consequences. The reinforcement must follow the behavior. It is assumed that the behavior of depressed persons does not lead to positive reinforcement to a degree sufficient to maintain their behavior. Consequently, depressed persons find it difficult to initiate or to maintain their behavior, and they become increasingly passive. The low rate of positive reinforcement is also assumed to cause the dysphoric feelings so central to the phenomenology of depression.

A corollary hypothesis is that a high rate of punishing experience also causes depression. Punishment is defined by person/environment interactions with aversive (distressing, upsetting, unpleasant) outcomes. Punishing interactions with the environment may cause depression directly or indirectly by interfering with a person's engagement in, and enjoyment of, potentially rewarding activities. These notions, and research results consistent with them, are discussed elsewhere in more detail (Lewinsohn, Biglan, & Zeiss, 1976; Lewinsohn & Talkington, 1979; Lewinsohn, Youngren, & Grosscup, 1979). The absence of positively reinforcing events particularly relevant to the occurrence of depression falls into several clusters (Lewinsohn & Amenson, 1978): positive sexual experiences, rewarding social interactions, fun outdoor activities, solitude, and competency experiences. Punishing events particularly important for depression fall into three clusters: marital discord, work hassles, and receiving negative reactions from others.

COGNITIVE POSITIONS

Cognitive theorists such as Beck (1967), Rehm (1977), and Seligman (1974; 1975) have each advanced hypotheses that attribute a causal role to cognitions in the etiology of depression, but they differ with regard to the specific nature of the cognitions which are assumed to lead to depression.

Beck (1967, 1976) conceives of depression as a disorder of thinking. The signs and symptoms of depression are assumed to be a *consequence* of the activation of negative cognitive patterns. Several specific cognitive structures are postulated to be central for the development of depression: the cognitive triad, schemas, and cognitive errors (Beck et al., 1979). The cognitive triad consists of three cognitive patterns asserted to dominate ideation: a negative view of oneself, a negative view of the world, and a negative view of the future. Cognitive schemas are postulated to lead to systematic filtering or distortion of perception and memory. Such distortions are the cognitive errors. They are automatic and involuntary and include *arbitrary inference*, *selective abstraction*, *overgeneralization*, *magnification*, and *minimization* (Beck et al., 1979).

Rehm (1977) has developed a self-control theory of depression in which negative self-evaluations and low rates of self-reinforcement and high rates of self-punishment are seen as leading to the low rates of behavior that characterize depressed individuals. Three processes are postulated to be important in self-control: self-monitoring, self-evaluation, and self-reinforcement. Rehm suggests that depressed persons attend selectively to negative events, that they set stringent criteria for self-evaluation, and that the self-reinforcement of depressives is characterized by low rates of self-reward and high rates of self-punishment. Other self-control theories of depression have been proposed and are reviewed by Rosenbaum and Merbaum (1981).

Working from an experimental paradigm developed initially with dogs and other animals, Seligman (1974, 1975) has proposed a theory of human depression, the central tenet of which concerns the effect of the independence of behavior and outcomes. Learned helplessness is a laboratory phenomenon observed when dogs are exposed to uncontrollable trauma. The main psychological phenomena of learned helplessness are: (1) passivity; (2) retarded learning; (3) lack of aggressiveness and competitiveness; (4) weight loss and under-eating. The critical antecedent for learned helplessness is not trauma per se but rather lack of control over trauma. Depressed individuals are presumed to have been, or to be, in situations in which responding and reinforcement are independent. Recovery of belief that responding produces reinforcement is the critical attitudinal change theorized to cure of depression. Responding to criticisms (Eastman, 1976; Blaney, 1977), Seligman (in Abramson, Seligman, & Teasdale, 1978) has recently proposed a reformulation of the learned helplessness theory by incorporating extensions from attribution theory (Weiner et al., 1971). The revised theory suggests that the attributions the individual makes for the perceived noncontingency between his/her acts and outcomes are the source of subsequent expectations for future noncontingency. Dimensions of attributions argued to be particularly relevant to learned helplessness and depression include: internality/externality, generality/specificity, and stability/instability. A person is more likely to be depressed, it is hypothesized, if his or her attributions for failure and lack of control are internal (it's my fault), global (I'm incompetent), and stable (I'll always be like that), while his or her attributions for successes are external (I was lucky), specific (in this particular situation), and unstable (just this time).

Clearly, a rich and varied collection of theories of unipolar depression have been proposed by behaviorally oriented thinkers, each of them presenting certain data consistent with theoretical predictions. As noted earlier, evidence supporting theoretical models of depression is chiefly derived from two sources: treatment outcome studies and/or correlational studies of depressed individuals. Yet each of these empirical strategies is subject to several criticisms. In the first approach, if a theory-based treatment is successful in reducing depression level, the model of depression is said to be supported. Such a conclusion is problematic for several reasons. First, as is abundantly clear from a number of recent reviews (such as Rehm & Kornblith, 1979; Lewinsohn & Hoberman, 1981), a variety of cognitive or behavioral approaches are effective in ameliorating depression, obscuring any differential confirmation of theoretical predictions. Second, as Rehm and Kornblith (1979), and Rosenbaum and Merbaum (1981) have noted, these cognitive and behavioral therapies overlap considerably in the strategies and procedures employed in modifying depression level, further clouding the utility of such outcome studies in demonstrating empirical support for particular depression models. Finally, in a treatment study that attempted to compare the differential effects of theoretically derived therapeutic procedures (cognitive, pleasant activities, and social skill training), Zeiss, Lewinsohn, and Muñoz (1979) found that while all three treatments were equally effective in reducing depression level, changes on the intervening dependent measures (such as cognitive, activities and social skills) were *not* specific to the particular treatment received. The finding that relatively specific treatments did not selectively impact the relevant target behaviors suggests that perhaps treatment outcome studies as presently conducted are not necessarily an especially productive means of providing evidence for theories of depression.

Studies presenting findings that demonstrate covariation between depression level and other variables are also problematic. As is well known, correlation does not prove causation. While characteristic thought and behavior patterns of depression in adults have been identified, it is impossible to know whether these correlational findings are of etiological significance. As theorists suggest, certain critical phenomena may precede depression and in some way contribute to its occurrence, but, on the basis of research to date, it is equally possible that cognitive and behavioral problems are a consequence of depression.

In order to determine whether the distinguishing characteristics of depressives antedate or result from the disorder, there is a pressing need for longitudinal studies (Blaney, 1977). Such studies would monitor variables of potential etiological significance and the development of depression over time in order to investigate their temporal interrelationship. Recently, Lewinsohn and his associates have reported on the results of two prospective longitudinal studies of depression in large community samples. Lewinsohn et al. (1981) measured depression-related cognitions and self-esteem in a large sample (N = 998) at two points in time. Contrary to predictions from cognitive theories, subjects who were to become depressed during the course of the study according to Research Diagnostic Criteria (Spitzer, Endicott, & Robins, 1978) did not differ from controls on most of the cognitive measures. Rather, results suggest that depression-related cognitions arise concomitantly or immediately prior to an episode of depression. In any case, this study implies that a negative cognitive style may not be an enduring personality dimension of persons who become depressed. Similarly, Lewinsohn, Teri, and Hoberman (1981) studying the same community sample as above cited, found that a reduced rate of engagement in pleasant activities arises concurrently with an episode of depression but does not precede it. In addition, results suggested that stressful life events, young age, being female, a history of previous depression, marital status and adjustment, and employment status are all risk factors for unipolar depression at a high level of statistical significance.

Perhaps the most significant conclusion implied to date by the body of "behavioral" research is that more complete understanding of depression awaits more sophisticated and subtle empirical investigations. Over the last ten years, the theoretical reviews of the literature by Akiskal and McKinney (1973; 1975; Akiskal, 1979) have urged a synthesis of the variety of biological and psychological findings concerning depression. Their writings stress the importance of a perspective that depression as a clinical phenomenon may be multidetermined, and that its most common causes may neither be necessary nor sufficient but rather contributory (Susser, 1973). Recently, Craighead (1980) has also argued that depression be viewed as a polydimensional phenomenon, having a multiplicity of causes. In addition, he has suggested that despite global commonalities in the manifestation of depression, there may be greater clinical and theoretical utility in conceptualizing the expression of depression as nonunitary, with different depressions displaying different specific characteristics. In short, then, behavioral formulations of unipolar depression are moving toward progressively more inclusive and integrative positions; what remains is for theorists to continue to develop empirical investigations that match the maturity of their theories.

SELECTED COGNITIVE-BEHAVIORAL TREATMENT APPROACHES

While both cognitive and behavioral treatment approaches differ in where they place the locus of causation, it is important to recognize similarities. Both assume that the depressed patient has acquired maladaptive reaction patterns that can be unlearned. Symptoms are seen as important in their own right rather than as manifestations of underlying conflicts. Consequently, treatments are aimed at the modification of relatively specific behaviors and cognitions rather than a general reorganization of the patient's personality. All cognitive behavioral treatments are structured and time-limited. Finally, as noted before, the different cognitive and behavioral approaches manifest considerable overlap in the specific procedures and strategies employed in treating depression.

1. Decrease Unpleasant Events and Increase Pleasant Activities (Lewinsohn, Sullivan, & Grosscup, 1980). This approach evolved out of the "reinforcement" position and aims to change the quality and the quantity of the depressed patients' interactions in the direction of increasing positive and decreasing negative ones. The treatment is time-limited (12 sessions), highly structured, and a therapist manual is available. The general goal of this treatment is to teach depressed persons skills they can use to change problematic patterns of interaction with the environment and skills needed to maintain these changes after the termination of therapy. To accomplish the goals of treatment, the therapist makes use of a wide range of cognitive behavioral interventions such as assertion, relaxation training, daily planning and time management training, and cognitive procedures intended to allow the person to deal more adaptively with aversive situations. A more detailed description, case illustrations, and pre-, and post-, and follow-up data for three groups of depressed patients treated with this approach are presented elsewhere (Lewinsohn, Sullivan, & Grosscup, 1980).

2. Cognitive Therapy (Beck et al., 1979). Cognitive therapy aims to assist the patient in identifying the assumptions and schemas supporting recurrent patterns of stereotypical negative thinking and in pointing out specific stylistic errors in thinking. Detailed treatment protocols are presented in Rush and Beck (1978) and in Beck et al., (1979).

Cognitive therapy is short-term and time-limited: a maximum of 20 sessions spread over ten to twelve weeks. Therapy sessions consist of: (1) a discussion of previously assigned homework; (2) a focus on aspects of the patient's thinking; (3) homework assignments for the next session. Both behavioral and cognitive techniques are used. Activity schedules, mastery and pleasure ratings of activities, assertiveness training, and role-playing are all utilized to counteract the patient's loss of motivation, inactivity, and preoccupation with depressive ideas. By recognizing partial successes or accomplishments and small degrees of pleasure, the patient is helped to reevaluate his negative beliefs. Therapy then focuses on examining the close relationship between feelings, behavior, and thoughts.

Considerable evidence exists that cognitive therapy is an effective treatment for depression. Rush, Khatami, and Beck (1975) reported that cognitive therapy produced effective and lasting results for three severely depressed persons who had responded poorly to antidepressant chemotherapy. Similarly, Schmickley (1976) found that cognitive treatment resulted in significant improvement in 11 depressed outpatients. Shaw (1977) showed a cognitive approach was as efficacious as social skills training at follow-up. Finally, Rush et al. (1977) demonstrated that cognitive therapy was more effective than standard tricyclic medication with 41 moderately to severely depressed outpatients.

3. *Interpersonal Therapy* (McLean, 1976; McLean & Hakstian, 1979). The interpersonal disturbance theory of depression postulated by McLean (1976) considers depression to result when individuals lose the ability to control their interpersonal environment. Interpersonal therapy attempts to maximize the patient's competence in specific coping skills.

McLean stresses the importance of obtaining the patient's own criteria for improvement, and treatment maintains a focus on data management; explicit performance criteria are monitored by the patient. Emphasis on therapeutic decision making regarding appropriate intervention components is one unique aspect of interpersonal therapy, although behavioral and cognitive techniques are also employed. In addition, interpersonal therapy includes relevant social network members (such as spouse) as integral components of treatment. Six specific therapeutic components are suggested by McLean: communication training, behavioral productivity, social interactions, assertiveness, decision making and problem solving, and cognitive self-control.

McLean, Ogston, and Grauer (1973) found a therapeutic program based on the above to produce significant changes in problematic behaviors and in verbal communication style. More recently, in a large-scale treatment outcome study (N = 178), McLean and Hakstian (1979) reported interpersonal therapy as superior on nine out of ten outcome measures at the end of treatment and marginally superior at the three-month follow-up and with a significantly lower drop-out rate when compared to traditional psychotherapy, pharmacotherapy, and relaxation training.

4. *Self-Control Therapy* (Fuchs & Rehm, 1977). Rehm's (1977) self-control theory of depression emphasizes the importance of self-administered reinforcement and punishment. Treatment consists of six sessions, with two sessions devoted to each of the three self-control processes (self-monitoring, self-evaluating, and self-reinforcing skills) (Fuchs & Rehm, 1977).

Comparing a group behavior therapy program based on self-control principles to a nonspecific group therapy condition and waiting list control group, Fuchs and Rehm (1977) found that the self-control group showed significantly more improvement than the other conditions at termination and at six-months follow-up. Rehm et al. (1979) compared self-control therapy to a behavioral assertion training program. While both groups of subjects improved differentially in the expected direction on target measures, the self-control group improved more on behavioral and self-report measures of depression. In comparing self-control therapy with cognitive and nondirective treatment, Fleming and Thornton (1980) found significant improvements for all three groups at six-week follow-up. Rehm et al. (in press) recently dismantled the self-control therapy program to assess the relative contributions of the various components. All treated subjects showed significant improvement, although no differences were found among four therapy conditions; self-monitoring alone was as effective as the full self-control package.

5. *A Psychoeducational Approach to the Treatment of Unipolar Depression* (Brown & Lewinsohn, 1981; Steinmetz, Lewinsohn, & Antonuccio, 1981; Antonuccio, Lewinsohn, & Steinmetz, 1981). The most recent experimental development in the area of behavioral and cognitive treatment of depression has been the use of an explicit educational experience as the vehicle for treatment. A course entitled "Coping with Depression" is conducted over 12 two-hour class sessions spaced out over eight weeks, typically with eight participants. The course represents a multicomponent approach, emphasizing general self-help skills, self-control techniques relevant to thoughts, pleasant activities, relaxation, interpersonal interaction, and maintenance. A textbook (Lewinsohn et al., 1978), workbook, syllabus (Brown & Lewinsohn, 1979), and instructor's manual (Lewinsohn et al., 1979) have been developed for the course. The efficacy of the course was evaluated in an initial study (Brown & Lewinsohn, 1981;

Lewinsohn & Brown, 1979) designed to compare three different modes of teaching the course (class, individual tutoring, and minimal phone contact) with a waiting list control condition. Large and statistically significant clinical improvement was shown by all of the active conditions, which together were significantly superior to the waiting control condition. Improvement shown at termination of the course was maintained at the one-month and at the six-months follow-up.

The success of the psychoeducational approach was replicated and the dimensions of therapeutic outcome explored in two more recent studies. Antonuccio, Lewinsohn, and Steinmetz (1981) examined therapist differences related to course outcome. Results indicated that leaders differed significantly on behavioral and group process measures (for example, on group participation and cohesiveness, warmth, clarity, enthusiasm, and so forth) but not on depression outcome. Given the success of the treatment, their findings were taken as reflecting the competence of the therapists and the high degree of structure in the treatment format. This latter conclusion suggests that the structure of the psychoeducational approach may be somewhat robust to therapist differences. Relatedly, Steinmetz, Lewinsohn, and Antonuccio (1981) investigated participant variables related to course outcome. Individuals who had the best outcome in the course tended to be less severely depressed, to have higher expectations of treatment success, to be younger, and not to be taking antidepressant medication. In addition, regular course attendance and homework completion were positively associated with outcome. Since a number of psychosocial variables did not predict participant outcome and most participants improved markedly, it is postulated that the course is an effective intervention to override pretreatment individual differences.

In summary, it is clear that while cognitive behavioral approaches are characterized by certain differences, empirical support for the therapeutic efficacy of each has been provided. The question has been raised as to how all of these theoretically derived treatments can be similarly effective (Lewinsohn & Hoberman, 1981). A number of possibilities might account for these findings. As noted earlier, a considerable commonality exists among the various approaches regarding specific strategies employed to reduce depression level (Rehm & Kornblith, 1979; Blaney, 1981). Relatedly, treatment packages currently used may include some "common core." For example, Rosenbaum and Merbaum (1981) suggest self-control procedures, which may account for therapeutic success. In addition, the findings of Zeiss, Lewinsohn, and Muñoz (1979) suggest that even when particular treatments are utilized, they do not selectively impact the relevant target behaviors. These results are in keeping with Akiskal and McKinney's (1973; 1975) sense that there may be a common final pathway for depressions of varying causes. The variety of therapeutic approaches may impact on that same pathway in *reverse* to improve an individual's affective state.

Zeiss, Lewinsohn, and Muñoz (1979) hypothesized that the critical components for successful short-term cognitive behavioral therapy for depression include the following:

1. therapy should begin with an elaborated, well-planned rationale;
2. therapy should provide training in skills that the patient can utilize to feel more effective in handling his/her daily life;
3. therapy should emphasize independent use of these skills by the patient outside the therapy context and must provide enough structure so that the attainment of independent skill is possible for the patient;
4. therapy should encourage the patient's attribution that improvement in mood is caused by the patient's increased skillfulness, not by the therapist's skillfulness.

Similarly, McLean and Hakstian (1979) noted that high structure, a social learning rationale, goal attainment focus, and increasing social interaction were significant elements in the behavioral treatment of depression.

SPECIAL POPULATIONS

Considerable progress has been achieved in understanding depression in adults; the concept of depression has been operationalized, there is increased knowledge of the precipitants of depression, and a variety of therapies have proven successful in treating depression. Consequently, it is quite natural for researchers to begin to turn their attention to the dimensions of depression in particular age groups. At this point in time, the systematic investigation of depression in non-middle-aged persons is at a very early stage. Yet the preliminary studies of depression in children, adolescents, and elderly persons have important implications for a more general understanding of depression. Much of the work done with these populations reflects the progression of the knowledge of depression in adults; the application of assessment and treatment procedures found successful with adults have helped to illuminate both the consistencies and the variations of depressive phenomena within a developmental framework. Moreover, as the similarities and differences of depression in in different age groups are delineated, this information will direct more effective programs of treatment and prevention. We shall present here a selected review of the literature on these questions. For additional discussion, the reader is referred to Lefkowitz and

Burton (1978) for their review of childhood depression, Teri (1980c) for her review of adolescent depression, and Raskin (1979) for his review of depression in the elderly.

DEPRESSION IN CHILDREN

In the last ten years, several conferences concerning childhood depression have been held, and they have helped to focus many of the issues in this area (Annell, 1972; Schulterbrandt & Raskin, 1977; French & Berlin, 1979). Yet childhood depression remains an area marked by controversy, and at present very little is known about the etiology of depressive disorders in children (Cantwell & Carlson, 1979; Costello, 1980).

Until a short time ago, the very existence of childhood depression was subject to dispute. Both Rie (1966) and Graham (1974) questioned whether the concept of depression could appropriately be applied to children. Nonetheless, a substantial clinical literature accumulated attesting to the existence of childhood depression in a form similar to that of depression in adults (as in Anthony, 1975; Connell, 1972; Conners, 1976; Malmquist, 1975). Another group of writers argued that while depression is present in children, it does not exist as it does in adults. Rather, they argue that children manifest depression through a wide range of behaviors (such as headaches, enuresis, temper tantrums, delinquency) (see, for example, Glazer, 1968; Cytryn & McKnew, 1972; Toolan, 1962). These behaviors are considered "depressive equivalents" or masked depression, reflecting "underlying" depression. Kovacs and Beck (1977) provided a comprehensive review of the various descriptions of childhood depressive disorders and the issue of "masked" depressive behaviors in childhood. They concluded that ample evidence existed to support the existence of depressive behaviors in childhood comparable to those manifested by depressed adults.

However, Lefkowitz and Burton (1978) reported a lack of pertinent epidemiological evidence identifying a uniform syndrome of depressive behaviors in children and a lack of adequate assessment methods. They also suggested that depressive "symptoms" in childhood may be nonpathological, pointing to the results of longitudinal studies as indicating the transitory developmental nature of "symptom-behaviors" and the prevalence of many of these symptoms among normal children. While some of their conclusions have achieved consensus (Welner, 1978; Gittelman-Klein, 1977), others have not (Costello, 1980).

Disagreement also characterizes the evidence on the incidence and prevalence of depression in children. Prevalence figures have varied across studies as follows: 14% (Kovacs, 1977; Rutter, Tizard,

& Whitmore, 1970); 8.5% (Butler, 1979); 57% (Weinberg et al., 1973); 59-61% (Petti, 1978). Although the target populations have differed across these studies, obviously a considerable range of prevalences have been reported.

In view of the lack of consensus regarding the definition and prevalence of childhood depression, attention has been focused on generating instruments and procedures for assessing the presence of affective disorders in children, reviewed by Costello (1980). Lefkowitz and Tesiny (1980) reported on the development of a Peer Nomination Inventory of Depression (PNID) and demonstrated that it possesses good psychometric properties. Kovacs et al. (1976) showed that a Children's Depression Inventory (CDI) adapted from the Beck Depression Inventory (Beck, 1967) was highly correlated with clinical judgments of depression in children. A number of investigators have utilized adult diagnostic critieria to assess affective disorders in children (for example, Puig-Antich et al., 1978; Carlson & Cantwell, 1980a, b), with considerable success.

Beyond the development of assessment procedures, little experimental research has been conducted on depression in children. Both Herjanic, Moghaddas, and Prince (1978) and Poznanski, Krahenbuhl, and Zrull (1976) reported on longitudinal studies of children identified as depressed during childhood. In the latter study, 50% of the individuals studied at follow-up were found to be clinically depressed; the behavior style of these persons more closely resembled that of adult depressives. Lefkowitz and his associates (Lefkowitz & Tesiny, 1980, Lefkowitz, Tesiny, & Gordon, 1979) found correlations between depressed scores on the PNID and the following variables: low self-esteem, reduced intellectual fuctioning, school absence, externality, and families with lower income. Leon, Kendall, and Garber (1980) found that depressed children attributed positive events to external causes and negative events to internal causes significantly more than nondepressed children. Results of this study also suggested that depressed children manifest different types of problem behaviors at home and school. Concerning treatment, both Puig-Anrich et al. (1978) and Frommer (1968) report on the use of chemotherapy with depressed children. Successful teacher-mediated and parent-mediated interventions with depressed children were reported by Butler et al. (1980) and Butler and Miezitis (1979), respectively.

In summary, it seems clear that while preliminary work on the problem of childhood depression, work that lays the foundation for continued research in this area, has been done, virtually no empirical studies have examined the course or etiology of depression in children; neither the behavioral correlates of depression nor the antecedents of this condition have been explored in populations of children defined by rigorous assessment procedures.

DEPRESSION IN ADOLESCENTS

The potential importance of studying depressive phenomena in adolescents is highlighted by the rising rates of suicide in this group. As of 1975, suicide was the second leading cause of death among those aged 15 to 25, and this is increasing at a faster rate for adolescents than for any age group (Klagsburn, 1976; Toolan, 1971). As in the area of childhood depression, there is controversy about the existence of adolescent depression and the forms it may take, if it exists. In particular, notions of adolescence as a volatile and stressful period have produced much argument about whether depression can develop in this age group. On the basis of this conception, some have argued that "emotional turbulence" in adolescence may place adolescents at high risk (as Malmquist, 1971; Pornsand, 1967) while others have contended it is a natural aspect of adolescence (for example, Blos, 1962; Coleman, 1961). Such a conception of emotionality in adolescence has been found to be empirically unsubstantiated (as in Coelho, Siber, & Hamburg, 1962; Offer, 1969; Weiner & DelGaudio, 1977) and questions on the existence of depression in this age group have focused on other issues. Similar to childhood depression, adolescents are thought to manifest their depression through a wide range of behaviors (such as delinquency, drug addiction) seen as indicating "underlying" or "masked" depression (for example, Arajarvi & Huttunen, 1972; Masterson, 1970; Toolan, 1969). Taking a developmental perspective, others suggest that persons in "early" adolescence may experience "masked depression" and those in "late" adolescence exhibit more adultlike depressive behaviors (see Toolan, 1968; Weiner, 1975). Consistent with the gender differences observed in adult depression (Weissman & Klerman, 1977; Amenson & Lewinsohn, 1981), significantly more females than male adolescents are likely to be identified as depressed (Weiner, 1975; Teri, 1980).

Existing empirical studies on adolescent depression have often relied primarily on administering newly-devised, unvalidated assessment instruments to clinical samples (Hudgens, 1974; Inadamar et al., 1979; Mezzich & Mezzich, 1979a, b). Albert and Beck (1975) administered a modified form of the Beck Depression Inventory (BDI) (Beck, 1967) and a questionnaire tapping general adjustment to 63 junior-high-school students. They found that 33% of their sample reported moderate-to-severe depression, with 6% reporting severe depression. Self-reported problems in school and social adjustment were correlated with BDI scores. Depressive symptomatology among ostensibly depressed individuals resembled that of adult depressives.

To date, only one study has investigated depression in a large sample (N = 568) using the BDI. Teri (1980a, b) evaluated issues about the nature of depressive symptomatology and variables related to adolescent depression in a high-school population. High inter-item and item/scale correlations yielded a high measure of internal consistency on the BDI. Factor structure of the scale was similar to that obtained with adults. Four factors, consistent with theories of adult depression, were obtained: severe depression/sadness; psychomotor retardation/low tolerance; self-denigration; and vegetative signs. The mean BDI score of this sample was slightly higher than that obtained in general population studies of younger children or adults. However, only 5% reported severe depression, a figure similar to that of younger children but somewhat lower than that for adults. Results suggested that while depressed mood may exist normally for adolescents, depression also exists pathognomically in a small segment of the general adolescent population; depressed adolescents were easily differentiated from those not depressed.

In addition, a positive relationship was reported between depression and other measures of adjustment. In particular, although family and social relationships were related to depression, the primary predictor among the subscales of the Offer Self-Image Questionnaire (OSIQ) (Offer & Howard, 1972) was that measuring body and self-image. As this scale was designed to tap feelings of awkwardness and discomfort with one's body (such as dissatisfaction with recent body changes, feeling ugly and unattractive), this was considered to support the importance of pubescent physical changes and their psychosocial impact on the development of depression of this age group, as was suggested by Jersild, Brook, and Brook (1980).

The findings of Poznanski et al. (1976) cited earlier indicate that depressed behavior in childhood may persist into adolescence. More importantly, they reported that depressed adolescents increasingly came to resemble depressed adults. This suggests, as social learning theory implies, that individuals who experience severe dysphoria through time may be progressively shaped into a more consistent set of depressive behaviors. However, this information remains to be subjected to empirical investigation.

Finally, the importance of understanding depression in adolescence is accentuated by follow-up studies of disturbed adolescents. Pichel (1975), in studying 60 psychiatrically disturbed adolescent outpatients after ten years, found that adult disorders can be predicted on the basis of an individual's history of earlier adolescent difficulty. More particularly, Welner, Welner, and Fishman (1979) reported a follow-up of 16 depressed adolescents eight to ten years after inpatient discharge. Of these individuals, 63% (N = 10) were still suffering from unipolar depression, with a mean number of four hospitalizations from index hospitalization to follow-up. These results suggest that certain chronic patterns of depression may begin in adolescence, and they emphasize the significance of developing effective prevention and treatment programs for adolescents.

DEPRESSION IN ELDERLY PERSONS

Affective disturbances are the most frequent functional mental disorder in the later years of life (Busse & Reckless, 1961; Butler & Lewis, 1977; Epstein, 1976; Zung, 1980). A recent epidemiological study of elderly community-residing adults found the rate of significant dysphoric symptomatology was 14.7% (Blazer & Williams, 1980). Of these, 3.7% were diagnosed as experiencing major depressive disorders according to Research Diagnostic Criteria (Spitzer, Endicott, & Robins, 1978). Teri et al. (1981) reported the prevalence of depression in an elderly community sample as being comparable to that in middle-aged samples. However, surveys of psychiatrically hospitalized elderly and those seeking outpatient psychiatric treatment indicate that depression is diagnosed as the primary problem 40 to 50% of the time (Pfeiffer, 1980).

Diagnosis of depression in elderly persons presents a number of unique difficulties. First, numerous reports based on clinical studies of depression in the aged have documented strong associations with physical illness and disability among depressed populations, especially for elderly depressed (Gaitz, 1977; Epstein, 1976). Second, differentiating depression from dementia and other organic brain syndromes is a significant issue. As Post (1975) pointed out, many diagnosticians erroneously regard the appearance of depressive symptoms in later life as the beginning of senile organic mental changes; however, there is no necessary relationship between severe depression and dementia in old age. A third area of concern is the fact that a number of commonly prescribed medications such as antihypertensives may produce complaints and symptoms that can accentuate or produce depressive reactions. Consequently, in evaluating the possibility of depression in elderly persons, it is important to collect additional information regarding health conditions, medication, and mental status.

It is not clear to what extent current research findings for middle-aged adults can be generalized to the elderly. However, it is clear that elderly persons are more prone to the various factors considered influential in the development of depression in general. During the late adult years, individuals show a decline in cognitive processing abilities and physical health (Botwinick, 1978). There is a significant number of elderly suffering from some form of chronic medical disorder (Raskin, 1979). Beyond the high incidence of medical problems, the prevalent diseases are often of a serious nature (such as cancer). As a result of these characteristics many writers have suggested that physical health is a critical variable in explaining depression in elderly persons (Raskin, 1979; Salzman & Shader, 1972), perhaps by reducing their engagement in pleasant activities.

Teri et al. (1981), in a prospective community study of 2,848 elderly subjects, found that lack of physical health was the major category that predicted self-reported clinical depression. Income and certain physical and social activities were related to depression in elderly persons as well.

As individuals move into older age ranges, they are typically removed from roles that may have been critical in the maintenance of much of their behavioral repertoire and self-esteem. Changes in social networks may also strain the elderly person, particularly his or her social skills. Lewinsohn, Tursky, and Arconad (1980) found increased incidence of social exits and major life events (such as having close friends and relatives experiencing major illnesses) in the aged. More generally, work by Rodin and Langer (1980) has indicated that the aged perceive themselves and are perceived by others as helpless. The potential effect of these experiences and perceptions is certainly consistent with theories of depression discussed here.

Despite this, elderly persons do not frequently seek treatment (Blazer & Williams, 1980; Jacobson & Jathani, 1978), and resistance to treating older people has been noted (Butler & Lewis, 1977). Consequently it is very important to develop effective interventions to treat depression among older adults that will be acceptable and likely to be used by the depressed elderly.

Currently, there are very few published studies in the literature on effective treatment with elderly depressives, although several studies are in progress. Gallagher (1981) was the first to employ a modified behavioral procedure for use with elderly persons. Comparing structured behavioral therapy with nondirective psychotherapy in time-limited group formats, she found considerable improvement over time in several dependent measures. While no differential treatment effects on self-reported depression were obtained, observer ratings of in-group interaction patterns indicated significantly greater improvement for subjects receiving behavioral therapy. Similarly, those subjects reported greater satisfaction with treatment and improved overall functioning. Hedlund and Thompson (1980) reported on the initial results for 18 elderly subjects enrolled in a *Coping with Depression* course developed by Brown and Lewinsohn (1981). Subjects showed significant changes pre- to posttreatment on several depression and behavioral measures. Results indicated that elderly persons with a diagnosis of major depressive disorder were responsive to this approach in both individual and educational format. Given that elderly persons are reluctant to seek psychiatric or psychological treatment, the psychoeducational approach, by defining treatment as an educational enterprise, holds promise for the development of effective outreach programs for the elderly depressed.

CLOSING REMARKS

In conclusion, the past decade has been an especially productive period for behavioral researchers concerned with depression. Stimulated by recent theoretical developments, there has been an impressive proliferation of interventions for the psychological treatment of unipolar depression. Considerable empirical support for the therapeutic efficacy of each of those approaches has been established. The problem facing the practitioner at this point is one of choosing from among a range of promising conceptual formulations and therapeutic procedures. Buoyed by the progress in understanding and treating depression in middle-aged persons, researchers have begun systematically to investigate the phenomena of depression in more specialized age groups—namely children, adolescents, and elderly persons.

Looking ahead to the next ten years of behavioral research into depression, it is likely that more complete, albeit more sophisticated, conceptualizations of the etiology and course of depression among the varied age groups will be developed, that the characteristics of individuals most *and* least likely to respond to cognitive behavioral treatments will be identified, and that the effective components of these treatments for particular types of depressed individuals will be isolated and successfully employed.

SUMMARY

The study of depression by behavioral researchers began only recently. However, within a short period of time the number and scope of both theoretical and clinical investigations of depression have increased prolifically. The study of depression within a behavioral framework reflects its continuing maturity with increasing sophistication in the theories proposed to explain the etiology of unipolar depression, in the therapeutic procedures employed to ameliorate depression in adults, and its attempts to understand and treat depression in specialized populations (children, adolescents, and elderly persons).

The major theoretical approaches fall into one of two categories: those that emphasize "reinforcement" and those that emphasize "cognitions" in the etiology of depression. Lewinsohn's theory of response-contingent reinforcement and punishment falls into the first category. The second category includes a variety of cognitive theorists, Beck's theory of dysfunctional cognitive patterns and distortions, Rehm's theory of self-control, and Seligman's theory of learned helplessness. Important differences and similarities in the different theories are reviewed. A critique of the nature of the empirical strategies employed to test the theories of depression is presented.

A variety of cognitive behavioral therapies have been shown to be efficacious in ameliorating depression level. A number of these approaches are reviewed, including: decreasing unpleasant events and increasing pleasant activites, cognitive therapy, interpersonal therapy, self-control therapy, and a psychoeducational approach to treating unipolar depression. Therapeutic components, common across these approaches and thought to be critical for successful short-term cognitive behavioral therapy for depression are identified.

Given the progress achieved in understanding depression in middle-aged adults, it is perhaps natural that researchers have begun to turn their attention to the nature of depression in particular age groups. While systematic investigation of depression in children, adolescents, and elderly persons is at a very early stage, existing studies have helped to illuminate both the consistencies and variations of depressive phenomena within a developmental framework.

While the existence of childhood depression has been the subject of controversy, increasing clinical and empirical evidence provides support for such a psychopathological condition in children. The issue of whether or not children manifest "masked depression" is discussed, and a critique of current conceptions of childhood depression is evaluated. Assessment instruments and procedures for defining affective disorders in children, and the limited amount of experimental research on depression in children is presented.

Similarly, the area of depression in adolescence is marked by controversy. The concepts of depressive equivalents in adolescent populations and of heightened emotionality in adolescence are discussed. The few methodologically rigorous studies of depressed adolescents suggest that they manifest depression in manners similar to adults and that depressed adolescents are easily differentiated from those not depressed. The increasing rates of suicide in adolescents and studies showing the persistence of depressive behavior from adolescence into adulthood highlight the importance of further empirical investigations into the nature and treatment of depression in adolescence.

Finally, while there is no disagreement over the existence of depression in elderly persons, a number of considerations are unique to this age group. The diagnosis of depression is complicated by the high amount of physical illness and disability, the related effects of medication, and the increasing likelihood of organicity in the elderly. Evidence suggests that elderly persons are more prone to various factors implicated in the development of depression in middle-aged persons. Recent studies are discussed that investigate treatments for depression in the aged and have produced promising results.

REFERENCES

Abramson, L. Y., Seligman, M. E. P., & Teasdale, J. D. Learned helplessness in humans: Critique and reformulation. *Journal of Abnormal Psychology*, 1978, *87*, 49-74.

Akiskal, H. S. A biobehavioral approach to depression. In R. A. Depue (Ed.), *The psychobiology of the depressive disorders: Implications for the effects of stress.* New York: Academic Press, 1979.

Akiskal, H. S., & McKinney, W. T., Jr. Depressive disorders: Toward a unified hypothesis. *Science*, 1973, *182*, 20-29.

Akiskal, H. S., & McKinney, W. T. Overview of recent research in depression: Integration of ten conceptual models into a comprehensive clinical frame. *Archives of General Psychiatry*, 1975, *32*, 285-305.

Albert, N., & Beck, A. T. Incidence of depression in early adolescence: A preliminary study. *Journal of Youth & Adolescence*, 1975, *4*, 301-307.

Amenson, C. S., & Lewinsohn, P. M. An investigation into the observed sex difference in prevalence of depression. *Journal of Abnormal Psychology*, 1981, *49*, 1-13.

Annell, A. L. (Ed.), *Depressive states in childhood and adolescence.* Stockholm: Almquist and Wiksell, 1972.

Anthony, E. J. Childhood depression. In E. J. Anthony & T. Benedek (Eds.), *Depression and human existence.* Boston, MA: Little, Brown & Co., 1975.

Antonuccio, D. O., Lewinsohn, P. M., & Steinmetz, J. L. *Identification of therapists differences in a group treatment for depression.* Paper presented at the 89th Annual Convention of the American Psychological Association, Los Angeles, 1981.

Arajarvi, T., & Huttunen, M. Encopresis and enuresis as symptoms of depression. In A. L. Annell (Ed.), *Depressive status in childhood and adolescence.* Sweden: Almquist & Wiksell, 1972.

Barrera, M. An evaluation of a brief group therapy for depression. *Journal of Consulting and Clinical Psychology*, 1979, *47*, 413-415.

Beck, A. T. *Depression: Clinical, experimental, and theoretical aspects.* New York: Harper & Row, 1967.

Beck, A. T. *Cognitive therapy and the emotional disorders.* New York: International Universities Press, 1976.

Beck, A. T., Rush, A. J., Shaw, B. F., and Emery, G. *Cognitive therapy of depression.* New York: Guilford Press, 1979.

Becker, J. *Affective disorders.* Morristown, J. J.: General Learning Press, 1977.

Blaney, P. H. Contemporary theories of depression: Critique and comparison. *Journal of Abnormal Psychology*, 1977, *86*, 203-223.

Blaney, P. H. Cognitive and behavioral therapy of depression: A review of their effectiveness. In L. P. Rehm (Ed.), *Behavior therapy for depression: Present status and future directions.* New York: Academic Press, 1981.

Blazer, D., & Williams, C. D. Epidemiology of dysphoria and depression in an elderly population. *American Journal of Psychiatry*, 1980, *137*, 439–444.

Blos, P. *On Adolescence.* New York: Free Press, 1962.

Botwinick, J. *Aging and behavior.* New York: Springer, 1978.

Brown, R. A. & Lewinsohn, P. M. *Coping with depression course workbook.* Unpublished mimeo, University of Oregon, 1979.

Brown, R. A., & Lewinsohn, P. M. A psychoeducational approach to the treatment of depression: Comparison of group, individual and minimal contact procedures. Manuscript submitted for publication, 1981.

Burgess, E. The modification of depressive behaviors. In R. Rubin and C. Franks (Eds.), *Advances in behavior therapy*, 1968. New York: Academic Press, 1969.

Busse, E. W. Research on aging: Some methods and findings. In M. A. Berezin and S. H. Cath (Eds.), *Geriatric psychiatry: Grief, loss, and emotional disorders in the aging process.* New York: Ontario University Press, 1965.

Busse, E. & Reckless, J. Psychiatric management of the aged. *Journal of the American Medical Association*, 1961, *175*, 645–648.

Butler, L. Personal communication, 1979.

Butler, L., & Miezitis, S. *An investigation of parent-mediated intervention with depressed children; Final report: Research and development #3587.* Unpublished manuscript, Ontario Institute of Education, 1979.

Butler, L., Miezitis, S., Freeman, R., & Cole, E. The effect of two school-based intervention programs on depressive symptoms in pre-adolescents. *American Educational Research Journal*, 1980, *17*, 111–119.

Butler, R., & Lewis, M. *Aging and mental health, 2nd ed.* St. Louis: Mosby, 1977.

Cantwell, D. P., & Carlson, G. Problems and prospects in the study of childhood depression. *The Journal of Nervous and Mental Disease*, 1979, *167*, 522–529.

Carlson, G. A., & Cantwell, D. P. A survey of depressive symptoms, syndrome, and disorder in a child psychiatric population. *Journal of Child Psychology and Psychiatry*, 1980, *21*, 19–25. (a)

Carlson, G. A., & Cantwell, D. P. Unmasking masked depression in children and adolescents. *American Journal of Psychiatry*, 1980, *137*, 445–449. (b)

Coehlo, G. V., Silber, E., & Hamburg, D. A. Use of the student TAT to assess coping behavior in hospitalized, normal, and exceptionally competent college freshmen. *Perceptual Motor Skills*, 1962, *14*, 355-365.

Coleman, J. S. *The adolescent society*. New York: Free Press, 1961.

Conners, C. K. Classification and treatment of childhood depression and depressive equivalents. In D. M. Gallant & G. M. Simpton (Eds.), *Depression: Behavioral, biochemical, diagnosis, and treatment concepts*. New York: Spectrum Publications, 1976, 181-204.

Copeland, A. D. Textbook of adolescent psychopathology and treatment. Springfield, IL: Charles C Thomas, 1974.

Costello, Charles G. Childhood depression. In E. J. Mash, & L. G. Terdal (Eds.), *Behavioral assessment of childhood disorders*. New York, Guilford Press, 1980.

Craighead, W. E. Away from a unitary model of depression. *Behavior Therapy*, 1980, *11*, 122-128.

Craighead, W. E. Behavior therapy for depression: Issues resulting from treatment studies. In L. P. Rehm (Ed.), *Behavior therapy for depression: Present status and future directions*. New York: Academic Press, 1981.

Cytryn, L., & McKnew, D. H. Proposed classification of childhood depression. *American Journal of Psychiatry*, 1972, *129*, 63-69.

Eastman, C. Behavioral formulations of depression. *Psychological Review*, 1976, *83*, 277-291.

Epstein, L. J. Depression in the elderly. *Journal of Gerontology*, 1976, *31*, 278-282.

Ferster, C. B. Classification of behavior pathology. In L. Krasner & L. P. Ullmann (Eds.), *Research in behavior modification*. New York: Holt, Rinehart & Winston, 1965.

Ferster, C. B. Animal behavior and mental illness. *Psychological Record*, 1966, *16*, 345-356.

Fleming, B. M., & Thornton, D. W. Coping skills training as a component in the short term treatment of depression. *Journal of Consulting and Clinical Psychology*, 1980, *48*, 652-654.

French, A., & Berlin, I. *Depression in children and adolescents*. New York: Human Sciences Press, 1979.

Fuchs, C. Z., & Rehm, L. P. A self-control behavior therapy program for depression. *Journal of Consulting and Clinical Psychology*, 1977, *45*, 206-215.

Gaitz, C. M. Depression in the elderly. In W. Fann, I. Karacan, A. Pokorny, & R. Williams (Eds.), *Phenomenology and treatment of depression*. New York: Spectrum, 1977.

Gallagher, D. Behavioral group therapy with elderly depressives: An experimental study. *Annual Review of Behavioral Group Therapy*, Volume 3. Champaign-Urbana, IL: 1981.

Gerner, R. H. Depression in the elderly. In O. J. Kaplan (Ed.), *Psychopathology of Aging*. New York: Academic Press, 1979, pp. 97-148.

Gittelman-Klein, R. Definitional and methodological issues concerning depressive illness in children. In J. G. Schutterbrandt & A. Raskin (Eds.), *Depression in Childhood: Diagnosis, treatment and conceptual models.* New York: Raven Press, 1977.

Glazer, K. Masked depression in children and adolescents. *Annual Progress in Child Psychiatry and Child Development*, 1968, *1*, 345-355.

Graham, P. Depression in pre-pubertal children. *Developmental Medicine and Child Neurology*, 1974, *16*, 340-359.

Hall, R. C., Popkin, M. K., Devaul, R. A., Faillace, L. A., & Stickney, S. K. Physical illness presenting as psychiatric disease. *Archives of General Psychiatry*, 1978, *35*, 1315-1320.

Hedlund, B., & Thompson, L. W. *Teaching the elderly to control depression using an educational format.* Paper presented at meetings of the American Psychological Association, Montreal, Canada, September 1980.

Hendricks, D., & Hendricks, C. D. *Aging in mass society: Myths and realities.* Cambridge, MA: Winthrop Publishers, 1977.

Herjanic, B., Moghaddas, M., & Prince, R. Depression in children: 3 to 8 year follow-up. *World Journal of Psychosynthesis*, 1978, *10*, 16-21.

Hudgens, R. W. *Psychiatric disorders in adolescents.* Baltimore, MD: Williams & Wilkins, 1974.

Inamadar, S. C., Siomopoulos, G., Osborn, M., & Bianchi, E. D. Phenomenology associated with depressed moods in adolescents. *American Journal of Psychiatry*, 1979, *136*, 156-159.

Jacobson, S. B., & Jathani, N. The nursing home and training in geropsychiatry. *Journal of the American Geriatrics Society*, 1978, *26*, 408-414.

Jersild, A. T., Brook, J. S., Brook, D. W. *The psychology of adolescence.* New York: Macmillan, 1980.

Kazdin, A. E. Outcome evaluation strategies for the treatment of depression. In L. P. Rehm (Ed.), *Behavior therapy for depression: Present status and future directions.* New York: Academic Press, 1981.

Klagsburn, F. *Too young to die: Youth and suicide.* Boston, MA: Houghton-Mifflin, 1976.

Kovacs, M. *Children's depression inventory.* Unpublished test, 2nd version, 1977.

Kovacs, M., & Beck, A. T. An empirical-clinical approach toward a definition of childhood depression. In J. G. Schulterbrandt & A. Raskin (Eds.), *Depression in childhood: Diagnosis, treatment and conceptual models.* New York: Raven Press, 1977, 1-25.

Kovacs, M., Betoff, N. G., Celebre, J. E., Mansheim, P. A., Petty, L. K., & Raynak, J. T. *Childhood depression.* Unpublished data, University of Pennsylvania, 1976.

Lazarus, A. A. Learning theory and the treatment of depression. *Behavior Research and Therapy*, 1968, *6*, 83–89.

Lefkowitz, M. M., & Burton, N. Childhood depression: A critique of the concept. *Psychological Bulletin*, 1978, *85*, 716–726.

Lefkowitz, M. M., & Tesiny, E. P. Assessment of childhood depression. *Journal of Consulting and Clinical Psychology*, 1980, *48*, 43–50.

Lefkowitz, M. M., Tesiny, E. P., & Gordon, N. H. *Childhood depression, family income and locus of control.* Presented at the annual meeting of the American Psychological Association, New York, September 1979.

Leon, G. R., Kendall, P. C., & Garber, J. Depression in children: Parent, teacher, and child perspectives. *Journal of Abnormal Child Psychology*, 1980, *8*, 221–235.

Lewinsohn, P. M., & Amenson, C. S. Some relations between pleasant and unpleasant mood-related events and depression. *Journal of Abnormal Psychology*, 1978, *87*, 644–654.

Lewinsohn, P. M., Biglan, A., & Zeiss, A. M. Behavioral treatment of depression. In P. O. Davidson (Ed.), *The behavioral management of anxiety, depression, and pain.* New York: Brunner/Mazel, 1976.

Lewinsohn, P. M., & Brown, R. A. *Learning how to control one's depression: An educational approach.* Paper presented at the meeting of the American Psychological Association, New York, 1979.

Lewinsohn, P. M., & Hoberman, H. M. Depression. In A. S. Bellack, M. Hersen, & A. E. Kazdin (Eds.), *International handbook of behavior modification and therapy.* New York: Plenum Press, 1981.

Lewinsohn, P. M., & Lee, W. M. L. Assessment of affective disorders. In D. H. Barlow (Ed.), *Behavioral assessment of adult disorders.* New York: Guilford Press, 1981.

Lewinsohn, P. M., Muñoz, R. F., Youngren, M. A., & Zeiss, A. M. *Control your depression.* Englewood Cliffs, NJ: Prentice-Hall, 1978.

Lewinsohn, P. M., Steinmetz, J. L., Larson, D. W., & Franklin, J. Depression-related cognitions: Antecedent or consequence? *Journal of Abnormal Psychology*, 1981, *90*, 213–219.

Lewinsohn, P. M., Sullivan, J. M., & Grosscup, S. J. Changing reinforcing events: An approach to the treatment of depression. *Psychotherapy: Theory, research and practice*, 1980, *17*, 322–334.

Lewinsohn, P. M., & Talkington, J. Studies on the measurement of unpleasant events and relations with depression. *Applied Psychological Measurement*, 1979, *3*, 83–101.

Lewinsohn, P. M., Teri, L., & Hoberman, H. M. *Risk factors for unipolar depression.* Paper presented at the 89th Annual Convention of the American Psychological Association, Los Angeles, 1981.

Lewinsohn, P. M., Tursky, S. P., & Arconad, M. *The relationship between age and the frequency of occurrence, and the subjective impact, of aversive events.* Unpublished manuscript, University of Oregon, 1980.

Lewinsohn, P. M., Weinstein, M., & Alper, T. A behavioral approach to the group treatment of depressed persons: A methodological contribution. *Journal of Clinical Psychology*, 1970, *26*, 525–532.

Lewinsohn, P. M., Weinstein, M., & Shaw, D. Depression: A clinical-research approach. In R. D. Rubin & C. M. Franks (Eds.), *Advances in behavior therapy, 1968.* New York: Academic Press, 1969.

Lewinsohn, P. M., Youngren, M. A., & Grosscup, S. L. Reinforcement and depression. In R. A. Depue (Ed.), *The psychobiology of the depressive disorders: Implications for the effects of stress.* New York: Academic Press, 1979.

Malmquist, C. P. Depression in childhood and adolescence. I and II. *New England Journal of Medicine*, 1971, *284*, 887–893, 955–961.

Malmquist, C. P. Depression in childhood. In F. F. Flach & S. C. Draghi (Eds.), *The nature and treatment of depression.* New York: John Wiley & Sons, 1975.

Masterson, J. Depression in the adolescent character disorder. In J. Zubin & A. Friedman (Eds.), *The psychopathology of adolescence.* New York: Grune & Stratton, 1970.

McKnew, D. H., & Cytryn, L. Historical background in children with affective disorders. *American Journal of Psychiatry*, 1973, *130*, 1278–1279.

McLean, P. Therapeutic decision making in the behavioral treatment of depression. In P. O. Davidson (Ed.), *The behavioral management of anxiety, depression, and pain.* New York: Brunner/Mazel, 1976.

McLean, P. D., & Hakstian, A. R. Clinical depression: Comparative efficacy of outpatient treatments. *Journal of Consulting and Clinical Psychology*, 1979, *47*, 818–836.

McLean, P. D., Ogston, K., & Grauer, L. A behavioral approach to the treatment of depression. *Journal of Behavior Therapy and Experimental Psychiatry*, 1973, *4*, 323–330.

Mezzich, A. C., & Mezzich, J. E. A data-based typology of depressed adolescents. *Journal of Personality Assessment*, 1979a, *43*, 238–246.

Mezzich, A. C., & Mezzich, J. E. Symptomatology of depression in adolescence. *Journal of Personality Assessment*, 1979b, *43*, 267–174.

Offer, D. *The psychological world of the teenager.* New York: Basic Books, 1969.

Offer, D., & Howard, K. I. The Offer Self-Image Questionnaire for Adolescents. *Archives of General Psychiatry*, 1972, *27*, 529–537.

Petti, T. A. Depression in hospitalized child psychiatry patients: Approaches to measuring depression. *Journal of American Academy of Child Psychiatry*, 1978, *17*, 49–59.

Pfeiffer, E. The psychosocial evaluation of the elderly patient. In E. W. Busse & D. G. Blazer (Eds.), *Handbook of geriatric psychiatry*. New York: Van Nostrand Reinhold, 1980.

Pichel, J. I. A long term follow-up study of sixty adolescent psychiatric outpatients. *Annual Progress in Child Development*. New York: Brunner/Mazel, 1975, 189–198.

Pornsand, P. J. Psychiatric problems of adolescence. *Annals of the New York Academy of Sciences*, 1967, *142*, 820–823.

Post, F. *The significance of affective symptoms in old age*. London: Oxford, 1962.

Post, F. *The clinical psychiatry of late life*. Oxford: Pergamon Press, 1965.

Post, F. Dementia, depression, and pseudo-dementia. In D. F. Benson & D. Blumor (Eds.), *Psychiatric aspects of neurological disease*. New York: Grune & Stratton, 1975.

Poznanski, E. O., Krahenbuhl, V., & Zrull, J. P. Childhood depression: A longitudinal perspective. *Journal of American Academy of Child Psychiatry*, 1976, *15*, 491–501.

Puig-Antich, J., Blau, S., Marx, N., Greenhill, L. L., & Chambers, W. Prepubertal major depressive disorder. *American Academy of Child Psychiatry*, 1978, *17*, 695–707.

Raskin, A. Signs and symptoms of psychopathology in the elderly. In A. Raskin & L. Jarvik (Eds.), *Psychiatric symptoms and cognitive loss in the elderly: Evaluation and assessment techniques*. Washington, DC: Halstead Press, 1979.

Rehm, L. P. A self-control model of depression. *Behavior Therapy*, 1977, *8*, 787–804.

Rehm, L. P., Fuchs, C. Z., Roth, D. M., Kornblith, S. J., & Romano, J. M. A comparison of self-control and social skills treatment of depression. *Behavior Therapy*, 1979, *10*, 429–442.

Rehm, L. P., & Kornblith, S. J. Behavior therapy for depression: A review of recent developments: In M. Hersen, R. M. Eisler, & P. M. Miller (Eds.), *Progress in behavior modification*, Volume 7. New York: Academic Press, 1979.

Rehm, L. P., Kornblith, S. J., O'Hara, M. W., Lamparski, D. M., Romano, J. M., & Volkin, J. I. An evaluation of major components in a self-control therapy program for depression. *Behavior Modification*, in press.

Rie, H. E. Depression in childhood. *The Journal of American Academy of Child Psychiatry*, 1966, *5*, 653–685.

Rodin, J. & Langer, E. Aging labels: The decline of control and the fall of self-esteem. *Journal of Social Issues*, 1980, *36*, 12–39.

Rosenbaum, M., & Merbaum, M. Self-control of anxiety and depression: An evaluation review of treatments. *Clinical Behavior Therapy Review*, 1981.

Rush, A. J., & Beck, A. T. Behavior therapy in adults with affective disorders. In M. Hersen & A. S. Bellack (Eds.), *Behavior therapy in the psychiatric setting*. Baltimore, MD: Williams & Wilkins, 1978.

Rush, A. J., Beck, A. T., Kovacs, M., & Hollon, S. Comparative efficacy of cognitive therapy and imipramine in the treatment of depressed outpatients. *Cognitive Therapy and Research*, 1977, *1*, 17-37.

Rush, A. J., Khatami, M., & Beck, A. T. Cognitive and behavioral therapy in chronic depression. *Behavior Therapy*, 1975, *6*, 398-404.

Rutter, M., Tizard, J., & Whitmore, K. *Education, health and behavior*. London: Longmans, 1970.

Salzman, C., & Shader, R. I. Responses to psychotropic drugs in the normal elderly. In C. Eisdorfer & W. E. Fann (Eds.), *Psychopharmacology and Aging*. New York: Plenum Press, 1972.

Schmickley, V. G. The effects of cognitive behavior modification upon depressed outpatients. Dissertation Abstracts International, 1976, *37*, 987B-988B. (University Microfilms No. 76-18, 675.)

Schulterbrandt, J. G., & Raskin, A. (Eds.), *Depression in childhood: Diagnosis, treatment, and conceptual models*. New York: Raven Press, 1977.

Seligman, M. E. P. Fall into helplessness. *Psychology Today*, 1973, 7, 43-48.

Seligman, M. E. P. Depression and learned helplessness. In R. J. Friedman & M. M. Katz (Eds.), *The psychology of depression: contemporary theory and research*. New York: Wiley, 1974.

Seligman, M. E. P. *Helplessness: On depression, development, and death*. San Francisco, CA: Freedman, 1975.

Shaw, B. F. Comparison of cognitive therapy and behavior therapy in the treatment of depression. *Journal of Consulting and Clinical Psychology*, 1977, *45*, 543-551.

Skinner, B. F. *Science and human behavior*. New York: Free Press, 1953.

Spitzer, Robert L., Endicott, J., & Robins, E. Research Diagnostic Criteria. *Archives of General Psychiatry*, 1978, *35*, 773-782.

Steinmetz, J., Antonuccio, D., Bond, M., McKay, G., Brown, R., & Lewinsohn, P. M. *Instructor's manual for the Coping With Depression course*. Unpublished mimeo, University of Oregon, 1979.

Steinmetz, J. L., Lewinsohn, P. M., & Antonuccio, D. O. *Prediction of individual outcome in a group intervention for depression*. Paper presented at the 89th Annual Convention of the American Psychological Association, Los Angeles, CA, 1981.

Susser, M. *Casual thinking in the health sciences: Concepts and strategies of epidemiology.* New York: Oxford University Press, 1973.

Teri, L. *Depression in adolescence: An investigation of depression in adolescence and its relationship to social skills, assertion, and various aspects of self-image.* Unpublished dissertation, University of Vermont, 1980. (a)

Teri, L. The use of the Beck Depression Inventory with adolescents. *Journal of Abnormal Child Psychology*, in press, 1980. (b)

Teri, L. Depression in adolescence: A review of the literature. Unpublished manuscript available from author. 1980. (c)

Teri, L., Backus, B. A., Lewinsohn, P. M., Sundberg, N. D., & Hoberman, H. M. *Risk factors for unipolar depression in the elderly.* Paper presented at the 89th Annual Convention of the American Psychological Association, Los Angeles, CA, 1981.

Toolan, J. M. Depression in children and adolescents. *American Journal of Orthopsychiatry*, 1962, *32*, 404-414.

Toolan, J. M. Suicide in childhood and adolescence. In H. L. Resnick (Ed.), *Suicidal behaviors: Diagnosis and management.* Boston, MA: Little, Brown & Co., 1968, 220-227.

Toolan, J. M. Depression in children and adolescents. In G. Caplan & L. Lebovici (Eds.), *Adolescence: Psychosocial perspective.* New York: Basic Books, 1969.

Toolan, J. M. Depression in adolescence. In J. G. Howells (Ed.), *Modern perspectives in adolescent psychiatry.* England: Oliver & Boyd, 1971.

Weinberg, W. A., Rutman, J., Sullivan, L., Penick, E. C., & Dietz, S. G. Depression in children referred to an educational diagnostic center: Diagnosis and treatment. *Journal of Pediatrics*, 1973, *83*, 1065-1072.

Weiner, I. B. Depression in adolescence. In F. F. Flach & S. C. Draghi (Eds.), *The nature and treatment of depression.* New York: John Wiley & Sons, 1975, 99-118.

Weiner, I. B., & DelGaudio, A. C. Psychopathology in adolescence: An epidemiological study. In S. Chess & A. Thomas (Eds.), *Annual progress in child psychiatry and development.* New York: Brunner/Mazel, 1977, 471-488.

Weiner, B., Frieze, I., Kukla, A., Reed, L., Rest, S., & Rosenbaum, R. M. *Perceiving the causes of successes and failure.* Morristown, NJ: General Learning Press, 1971.

Weissman, M. W., & Klerman, G. L. Sex differences and the epidemiology of depression. *Archives of General Psychiatry*, 1977, *34*, 98-111.

Welner, Z. Childhood depression: An overview. *The Journal of Nervous and Mental Disease*, 1978, *166*, 588-593.

Welner, A., Welner, Z., & Fishman, R. Psychiatric adolescent inpatients: Eight to ten year follow-up. *Archives of General Psychiatry*, 1979, *36*, 698-700.

Yalom, I. D. *The theory and practice of group psychotherapy*, Second edition. New York: Basic Books, 1975.

Zeiss, A. M., Lewinsohn, P. M., & Muñoz, R. F. Nonspecific improvement effects in depression using interpersonal skills training, pleasant activity schedules, or cognitive training. *Journal of Consulting and Clinical Psychology*, 1979, *47*, 427-439.

Zung, W. W. K. Depression in the normal aged. *Psychosomatics*, 1967, *8*, 287-291.

Zung, W. W. K. Affective disorders. In E. W. Busse, & D. G. Blazer (Eds.), *Handbook of geriatric psychiatry*. New York: Van Nostrand Reinhold, 1980.

CHAPTER 10

Cognitions, Schemas, and Depressive Symptomatology

Donna E. Giles, M.A.
A. John Rush, M.D.

The cognitive theory (Beck, 1967, 1976; Rush & Beck, 1978; Beck & Rush, 1978; Beck et al., 1979) posits that three major psychological elements are central to the development and/or maintenance of depressive symptomatology. These elements include cognitions, referring to mental activity with verbal or pictorial content; schemas, referring to silent assumptions, dysfunctional attitudes, or maladaptive beliefs; and logical errors in thinking, including for example, selective attention, overgeneralization, personalization, magnification. The cognitive theory of depression explains depressive symptoms on the basis of the "cognitive triad": unrealistic, negatively biased views of the self, future, and world or "personal domain."

The cognitive triad is used to explain such symptoms as lack of motivation or will, suicidal ideation and/or action, excessive self-criticism, or guilty preoccupations. This triad is also used to account for vegetative symptoms. The depressed individual, sensing defeat and loss, assumes a protective posture, which includes increased muscle tension, sleep disturbance, appetite loss, psychomotor inhibition, apathy, fatigue, and low energy. A number of correlational and experimental studies (e.g. Velten, 1966; Loeb, Beck, & Diggory, 1971; Steiner, 1975; Hammen & Krantz, 1976; DeMonbreun & Craighead, 1977; Howes & Hokanson, 1979) provide support for this theory. Negative self-references lead to depressed mood, depres-

This chapter was supported in part by Grant MH 28459-01 to A. John Rush, M.D.

We wish to thank Marie Marks for providing secretarial support and for her forebearance throughout the many drafts of this chapter. Thanks are also due to Marilyn Thomas, Carol Laabs, and Karen Benedetto for their typing assistance. We would like to express our appreciation to Roland Dougherty, Dennis Sullivan, and Carl Fulton as well, for their groundwork in collecting and analysing data presented in this chapter.

sives tend to perceive and distort information negatively and engender negative social interactions. Persons who perceive their future as hopeless are more likely to entertain or enact suicidal notions (Beck et al., 1974; Wetzel, 1976).

Not only does the concept of the cognitive triad provide an explanation for the occurrence of the depressive syndrome, but cognitive theory also posits that a greater level of depressive symptomatology is associated with a greater frequency of, or belief in, negative views of the self, world, and future. As clinical improvement occurs, these negative views are predicted to be reduced or eliminated.

The second critical element, according to cognitive theory, is the concept of schemas. These cognitive structures represent the basis for classifying stimuli encountered on a moment-to-moment basis. According to theory, schemas reflect values and attitudes derived from early experiences. These silent assumptions consist of premises or beliefs that define which stimuli are salient and that organize the information into relevant conceptual networks. These beliefs, therefore, form the basis for attributing meaning to a given event that occurs in the individual's life. Unlike cognitions, schemas are not found in the person's moment-to-moment thinking or stream of consciousness. Rather, schemas are general rules that can be inferred from recurrent patterns of thinking or behavior.

Schemas are hypothesized to account for the ongoing vulnerability to recurrent depression in sensitized individuals. The theory states that different schemas are activated in different situations. A specific assumption becomes hypervalent in situations analogous to experiences initially associated with developing the belief. The theory predicts that increasing severity of depressive symptoms is associated with hypervalent schemas. These result in stereotyped, negatively-biased representations of a wider-and-wider range of stimuli. Through this mechanism, the process becomes a loop, with increasing depressive symptoms leading to increasingly potent schemas, which, in turn, lead to more negative views and, subsequently, to more severe depression.

The third element posited by cognitive theory consists of logical errors. These errors can be detected by comparing the individual's automatic thinking (cognitions) with associated stimulus conditions. That is, these errors are logical distortions of the information with which the individual is confronted. For example, a person who finds him or herself called in by a supervisor for correction in work performance may construe this event as evidence of being personally and globally ineffective and incompetent, while neglecting complimentary interactions with the supervisor on previous occasions. In this case, the individual has "selectively attended" to the negative interaction and has construed criticism and guidance as evidence of a personal defect that is both longstanding and unremedial.

To illustrate the application of this theory to a clinical situation, consider the case of a 69-year-old woman who developed a major depressive disorder following her daughter's announcement that she and her husband would be moving to another city. Her daughter and son-in-law were moving because of business demands. The patient began to think "I have nothing to live for without my daughter," "My daughter doesn't care about me anymore," "My son-in-law doesn't like me anyway." The patient has negative anticipations about her future in that there will be no change and has construed her relationship with her daughter and with her son-in-law to be antagonistic. In addition, she has indicated that she herself has no meaning without her daughter, implying a negative view of herself. Thus, the patient displays in this thinking pattern all three elements of the cognitive triad: a negative view of the self, world, and future.

In addition, the above thoughts are not logically related to the event of her daughter moving to a new city. She has arbitrarily inferred from this event that her life is without meaning; she has personalized, magnified, and displayed arbitrary inference again in her thought that neither her daughter nor her son-in-law care about her.

One might infer from this sequence of cognitions that the patient has an underlying belief that "I am nothing without my daughter"; beyond this inference, one might posit a schema such as "I am worthless unless someone cares about me." Superordinate schemas are deduced from these first-level inferences. They may consist of such notions as "I am not worthwhile unless those close to me show me that they care," or "I have nothing of value within my own self." Thus, this case illustrates the presence of the cognitive triad and a number of logical errors and implies the presence of specific schemas.

MEASUREMENT OF COGNITIONS, SCHEMAS, AND LOGICAL ERRORS

In order to operationalize the concepts presented by cognitive theory, one must derive a method to measure cognitions, the depressive's moment-to-moment thinking. In addition, measures of schemas and measures of logical errors must be developed. While the state of the art with regard to these measurements is rudimentary, several self-report measures have recently been or are being developed, to assess cognitions, schemas, and/or logical errors.

Perhaps the oldest defined self-report measure relates to view of the future. The Hopelessness Scale (Beck et al., 1974) is a 20-item true–false questionnaire with a range of 0 to 20. A higher score on this scale represents a greater negative bias in view of the future (that is, more hopelessness). Hopelessness has been found to account for the variance between depressives with and without suicidal intent in several studies (Beck, 1976; Wetzel, 1976). The authors demonstrated good internal consistency as well as adequate concurrent and construct validity (Beck et al., 1974).

The Automatic Thoughts Questionnaire (Hollon & Kendall, 1980) has recently been developed to measure each of three elements of the cognitive triad. This 30-item self-report lists cognitions. "I can't stand this anymore," "What's wrong with me?" and "Something has to change" are typical examples of cognitions assessed by this questionnaire. The respondent indicates the frequency during the past several days with which each of the 30 listed cognitions has occurred. The scores on this test range from 30 to 150. The ATQ reliably discriminated between depressed and nondepressed college students and showed high internal consistency (Hollon & Kendall, 1980).

Another instrument designed to measure cognitive distortions, using a multiple choice format, is the Hammen and Krantz (1976) Story Completion Test. This test consists of six stories. Each story is followed by three to four questions. For each question there are four responses, scored as "depressed distorted," "depressed nondistorted," "nondepressed distorted" and "nondepressed nondistorted." A sample story, question, and set of response alternatives is:

> Fred had started working in the main office last week. It felt like it had taken forever to find this job after he moved to L.A. He had grown up in a small town some distance away, and since he moved had met few people. The others who worked in the same office seemed friendly, although most of them were considerably older than he. One woman, Carolyn, was about his age, sort of pretty, but she worked down the hall and he saw her only occasionally. Taking his coffee break in the snack bar one afternoon, she came over and ate with him. They talked for a while. He found her fun and pleasant, and they seemed to enjoy each other. The break ended, and he had to get back to his office. He found himself thinking about her that afternoon—fantasizing about going out with her, wondering what she's like. He looked forward to seeing her the next day. At lunch the next afternoon, he sat alone in the snack bar and saw her come in. She saw him, smiled and waved, but she took her lunch to another empty table on the far side of the room.
>
> Put yourself in Fred's place and try to imagine as vividly as you can what he might think and feel.
>
> 1. Your first reaction was to think:
>   a. I might consider being a little assertive and pursue her.
>   b. I'm unhappy that she prefers to eat alone this afternoon.
>   c. She dislikes me and wants me to get the message.
>   d. She's playing hard-to-get.

This test was developed in a college student population and was cross-validated in a small sample of clinically depressed subjects. It showed moderate internal consistency and reliably distinguished depressed from nondepressed persons.

In order to reduce the face validity present in a multiple choice or true-false format, Watkins and Rush (1981) developed a sentence completion test to measure cognitions. This Cognitive Response Test consists of 36 items (CRT-36). Each item is an incomplete sentence or stem and must be completed by the subject to reflect his or her first "automatic" thought. For example, typical items in this test include: "My employer says he will be making some major staff changes. I immediately think . . ." or "At a social gathering, I meet a person to whom I am quite attracted. My immediate thought is . . ." Responses are scored as Rational (R), Irrational Depressed (ID), Irrational Other (IO), and Nonscoreable (NS). Scores may range from 0 to 36 for each subscale. The Irrational Depressed category has been shown to discriminate depressed from nondepressed subjects (Watkins and Rush, 1981). A recent report (Wilkinson and Blackburn, in press) provides evidence of concurrent validity for both the R and ID subscales.

There are fewer measures to assess schemas attributed to depressives. The Dysfunctional Attitude Scale (DAS) (Weissman, 1979) was developed explicitly to measure schemas proposed by cognitive theory. This is a 40-item inventory where each item is rated on a 7-point scale, defined by "totally agree" through "neutral" to "totally disagree." Scores on this test range from 40 to 280. Normal controls were found to have a mean DAS score of 117 ± 26. Items are of the type, "If I do not do well all the time, people will not respect me." This instrument was developed on a college student population and found to correlate moderately with Beck Depression Inventory ratings of severity. Test-retest scores separated by six to eight weeks rarely changed by more than 5 to 10 points. The DAS has also discriminated depressed outpatient subjects from nondepressed controls (Rush, unpublished data). The inventory has now been translated into German and is being utilized in several European studies as well.

There is currently no reliable and valid method to measure logical errors. Development of an operational definition of these logical errors has been difficult.

DEPRESSIVE SUBTYPES

Before discussing the relationship of symptoms to cognitions and schemas in depression, one must first confront the issue of the diagnosis of depressive disorders. While a number of studies providing support for the cognitive theory construe depression as a mood state (such as Velten, 1966), Beck (1967) views depression as a syndrome with various signs and symptoms. The syndrome of depression has been variously defined but perhaps most recently and consistently by DSM-III (APA, 1980). Major Depressive Disorder refers to a psychiatric episode characterized by self-reported dysphoria and at least four of the following symptoms: reduction or increase in appetite and/or weight; insomnia/hypersomnia; psychomotor agitation/ retardation; increased self-criticism or guilt; loss of pleasure, enjoyment, or libidinal drives; suicidal thinking, plans or action; impaired concentration and decision making; and decreased energy/increased fatigability. These symptoms must be present for at least two weeks. Finally, there must be no thought disorder suggestive of schizophrenia (as thought broadcasting, thought insertion).

While the episode of depression may be defined by such descriptive syndrome characteristics, there is considerable controversy as to the meaningfulness of categories making up depression subtypes. There seems to be a general agreement that major depressions are heterogeneous with regard to genetics, prognosis, and treatment response, however. Perhaps the two most commonly used and best-supported subdivisions consist of the unipolar/bipolar dichotomy and the endogenous/nonendogenous dichotomy.

The unipolar/bipolar dichotomy rests upon the presence by history of episodes of mania or hypomania in association with evidence of a major depressive episode. A manic episode is diagnosed if for a minimum of one week there is present an elevated, expansive, or irritable mood clearly different from normal; as well as three (if mood is elevated) or four (if mood is irritable) of the following: increased social/work/sexual/physical activity; increased talking or pressure to talk; flight of ideas/racing thoughts; inflated self-esteem/ delusions of increased self-worth; decreased need for sleep; distractibility; reckless involvement in activities (buying sprees, sex, business, driving). In addition, symptoms must result in serious impairment, prohibit meaningful conversation, result in hospitalization. Finally, there must be no evidence of thought disorders as found in Schizophrenia (APA, 1980).

Criteria for a hypomanic episode are similar to a manic episode except mood duration is two or more days and symptoms required are two with elevated mood and three with irritable mood.

There is evidence that at least some unipolar depressives are related genetically to those with bipolar depression. The majority of patients with unipolar depression seem genetically distinct from the bipolar group, however. Whether these two depressive types (bipolar versus unipolar) are psychologically distinct relative to cognitions, schemas, or logical errors during the depressive episode has not been evaluated.

The second dichotomy gaining significant attention is the endogenous/nonendogenous distinction. Endogenous depression is referred to as depression with melancholic features by DSM-III. Melancholia is diagnosed if the patient, during a depressive episode, has evidence of a major depressive disorder and, in addition, has the following symptoms: pervasive anhedonia, unreactive mood, and at least three of the following five: distinct quality to mood, mood worse in morning; marked psychomotor retardation/agitation; significant anorexia/weight loss; excessive/inappropriate guilt. Patients with Major Depressive Disorder that do not meet criteria for melancholia would be considered nonendogenous. Most patients with bipolar depression could be diagnosed endogenous or melancholic during the depressive episode if it is full-blown.

Other diagnostic subtyping schemes include the primary/secondary dichotomy (Robins & Guze, 1972) and the psychotic/nonpsychotic dichotomy. The latter refers to the presence of mood-congruent hallucinations and/or delusions (psychotic) as against their absence. With regard to the former dichotomy, primary depression is diagnosed if there is no major psychopathological syndrome other than mania or depression preceding the history of depression. Secondary depression is diagnosed when a major psychopathologic syndrome other than an affective disorder precedes the onset of the syndrome. Thus, for example, a person with alcoholism, who subsequently becomes depressed, would be diagnosed as depressed secondary to being an alcoholic. This is basically a research strategy designed to provide a more homogeneous group of depressions for research purposes. It does not have treatment selection or etiologic implications.

The endogenous/nonendogenous dichotomy has both etiological and treatment implications. Klein (1974) contends that the "endogenomorphic" or melancholic depressive suffers from a primary defect in the pleasure center, with concurrent disinhibition of the pain center. Thus, these depressions are associated with a neurochemical dysregulation of the limbic system, rendering the patient incapable of experiencing pleasure or anticipating enjoyment. These patients are said to respond nearly exclusively to psychopharmacological or electroconvulsive treatments and are presumed to be relatively unresponsive to psychosocial or psychotherapeutic interventions. The nonendogenous or nonmelancholic patients may be responsive somewhat to antidepressant medication but may also respond, according to Klein, to placebo or psychosocial treatments. These nonendogenous depressives have a pervasively pessimistic, negatively biased outlook, a characterization consistent with Beck's description of the cognitive defects of depressed persons. Thus, one could hypothesize that cognitive therapy would be more effective in nonendogenous patients than would medication, whereas the converse would be true with the melancholic group.

The cognitive model of depression, according to Beck (1967), describes and characterizes both unipolar and bipolar depressives. The issue of cognitive similarities between endogenous and nonendogenous depressions has not been explicitly addressed, but statement of a single cause in depression implies that these subtypes are indeed similar. It is not clear whether Beck endorses a single cause/single disease notion of depression in view of the recent research into subtypes.

Whether the form and content of the cognitive triad, schemas, and logical errors are specific to depression or whether they might apply to other psychopathologic symptoms has not been carefully studied. While considerable data support the specificity of negative distortions to depression (Loeb et al., 1971; Hammen & Krantz, 1976), it is not clear whether the logical errors or the "depressive" schemas are specific to depression. It is possible that they may be found in a variety of persons with different disorders and even in normal persons. One might speculate that logical errors are present in persons who are anxious or aroused from whatever condition, since they are similar to more primitive thought styles or cognitive errors found in children (Inhelder & Piaget, 1958).

MEASUREMENT OF SEVERITY OF DEPRESSIVE SYMPTOMATOLOGY

In order to relate cognitions and schemas to the depressive syndrome, one must have a method for assessing both the types of symptoms and their overall severity in a given individual. While a number of self-reports (such as Beck Depression Inventory, Carroll Rating Scale, Zung Depression Scale) and clinician-based ratings (as Hamilton Rating Scale, Raskin Depression Scale, Brief Psychiatric Rating Scale) provide means to assess treatment response in both psychotherapeutic and psychopharmacologic outcome studies, it is not clear whether any of these instruments is adequate for all persons with a depressive syndrome. Some of these instruments may be best suited for a particular depressive subtype. However, let us briefly review the most frequently utilized instruments.

The *Raskin Scale* requires the clinician to make a judgment on a 0-to-4 scale about the degree of symptomatology as evidenced by verbal report, interview behavior, and "secondary" symptoms (such as insomnia, lack of appetite). Thus, the scale ranges from 0 to 12, where 7 or greater is considered at least a moderate level of depressive symptoms. This scale is shown to be sensitive to psychotherapeutic as well as psychopharmacologic interventions. It skirts the problem of specific symptoms and uses global judgment.

The *Hamilton Rating Scale for Depression* (Hamilton, 1960; 1967) (HRS-D) is a 24-item scale. Items are rated along a continuum where categories vary generally from absent to severe. The scale is presented within a structured interview format. The interviewer questions symptoms of mood disturbance, guilt, sleep disturbance, somatic and psychological anxiety, nonspecific somatic complaints, suicidal ideation, weight loss, libidinal disturbance, insight into causes of depression, helplessness, hopelessness, and some thought disorder. The first 17, 21, or 24 items are used to calculate total scores. However, interrater reliability on only the first 17 items has been established (r = .90) (Hamilton, 1960). A score of 14 or greater on the first 17 items represents clinically significant depression. Scores of 0 to 10 are considered to vary along a continuum of normal to minor nondysfunctional disturbance. The maximum score on the 17-item HRS-D is 52.

The *Beck Depression Inventory* (BDI) (Beck et al., 1961) is a 21-item self-report test designed to measure severity of depression. A number of validity and reliability studies generally support the BDI as a measure of depression severity (Beck, 1967, pp. 189–207). Pearson biserial correlations between clinical judgments and test scores range between .65 and .67 (Beck, 1976, p. 197). Split-half reliability values range between .86 and .93. Symptom areas questioned are predominantly psychological, including mood, guilt, personal worth, interest, concentration, and suicidal preoccupation, as well as the more vegetative disturbance in sleep, appetite, and energy. A score of 10 or greater is considered depressed, with a range up to 63.

THE ROLE OF COGNITIONS

Beck's theory states that cognitions play a critical role in the development and maintenance of the depressive syndrome. That is, greater depressive symptomatology is associated with greater negative thinking about self, future, and the world. These views lead to greater dysphoria, and greater dysphoria, in turn, leads to more negative views. More recently, Beck (1976) has stated that cognitions cause depression. The relationship of depressive symptoms to cognitions has been assessed in a variety of studies. Most experimental studies rely on the induction of the mood state in normals through some cognitive maneuver, such as repeating negative statements or presenting the subject with situations over which she/he has no control (helplessness task, Seligman, 1975). These studies have recently been reviewed (Beck & Rush, 1978). While they support the notion that greater depressive symptomatology is associated with greater negative thinking, the majority of these studies have relied on nonclinically depressed subject groups, and the measurement of cognitions has been a difficult component to operationalize adequately.

An elegant test of the role of cognitions in depression would be to assess a group of persons longitudinally from an asymptomatic condition to a syndromatically ill condition, utilizing cognitive measures on a repeated basis. Such a study is as yet unavailable. The cognitive triad itself is related to measures of depressive symptomatology (such as BDI), however. Thus, a high correlation would be expected between depressive views of self, world, and future and overall rating of severity of depression. This question awaits measurement of depressive severity that is independent of view of self, world, and future. Such measures may be forthcoming, at least with regard to endogenous depression. For example, Gredon et al. (1980) have developed a speech pause methodology that appears to relate to the presence of endogenous depression. This method appears to be measuring psychomotor retardation. Again, while it falls short of measuring overall depressive symptoms, it does appear to assess a dimension of depression that may be quite independent of cognitive function.

Rush et al. (1981) recently studied a cohort of acutely depressed and subsequently largely remitted unipolar nonpsychotic depressed outpatients, including both endogenous and nonendogenous types. The mean age was 38.2 years, and the mean education was 11.4 years. The mean episode length was 12.6 months. Roughly 83% of the sample was female. When acutely depressed, these subjects endorsed more irrational depressed cognitions, according to the Cognitive Response Test (CRT-36) than when partially remitted (see Table 10-1). A similar finding was noted in samples of bipolar depressed outpatients studied when acutely ill and when remitted (see Table 10–2). Thus, in both unipolar and bipolar depressed outpatients, there is

Table 10-1. Cognitions (CRT-ID) and Attitudes (DAS) in Unipolar Depressives (n = 33)

Variable	*Symptomatic*	*Remitted*	*t*	*p*
HRS-D	22.8[a]	10.0[b]	10.19	.001
	(4.3)	(6.1)		
BDI	26.9	18.2	5.97	.001
	(7.3)	(10.6)		
CRT-ID	7.2	5.1	2.24	.032
	(6.1)	(4.2)		
DAS*	146.9	133.1	2.59	.014
	(39.8)	(33.5)		

*The DAS variable will be detailed later in the text.
a. n = 32; b. n = 30

Table 10-2. Cognitions (CRT-ID) and Attitudes (DAS) in Bipolar Depressives

Variable	*Symptomatic* (n = 10)	*Remitted* (n = 15)	*t*	*p*
HRS-D	24.7 (4.6)	5.9 (2.5)	11.81	.001
BDI	33.7 (10.0)	5.7 (4.2)	8.41	.001
CRT-ID	10.9 (4.9)	3.9 (2.8)	3.78	.001
DAS*	173.4 (39.1)	112.1 (40.1)	3.78	.001

*The DAS variable will be detailed later in the text.

evidence of greater cognitive distortion during periods of more severe depression.

When CRT-ID responses were correlated with depressive severity by the Hamilton Rating Scale, no relationships were found for the unipolar depressed, unipolar remitted, bipolar depressed, or bipolar remitted groups. A significant correlation ($r = .58$, $p < .01$) between cognitions (CRT-ID) and self-reported symptomatology (BDI) was found for the acutely depressed unipolar group, however, but not for the largely remitted unipolar group. No relationship between BDI and CRT-ID scores was found for the acutely depressed bipolar or remitted bipolar groups.

From these data, it appears that the relationship between cognitions and depressive symptoms is most salient in the unipolar group and then only during the episode of acute symptomatology. It also appears that the method for measuring depressive severity is critical in determining whether there is a correlation between cognitions and symptoms. The Beck Depression Inventory is a "cognitively loaded" self-report format that has only 5 of 21 items that inquire about vegetative symptoms (sleep, appetite, weight, and sexual drive), whereas the Hamilton Rating Scale is loaded toward vegetative items. Of its 17 items, 9 relate specifically to sleep, appetite, weight, sexual drive, and psychomotor activity. Thus, these data may be taken to suggest that vegetative symptoms in depression are relatively unrelated to cognitive distortions *per se* and that if cognitive distortions play a role in depressive disorders it is not clear that they are causal.

SCHEMAS

Cognitive theory predicts two relationships involving schemas that can be tested empirically. The first is that schemas should be correlated with the presence of negative cognitive distortions. With regard to the first contention, we (Rush et al., 1980) have studied a cohort of 54 unipolar endogenous and nonendogenous depressed patients utilizing the Beck Depression Inventory, the 17-item Hamilton Rating Scale for Depression, and the Dysfunctional Attitude Scale.

Figure 10-1 shows the frequency distribution of DAS responses in association with the depressive symptomatology by both HSR-D and BDI. What is striking is the lack of relationship between dysfunctional attitudes as measured by the DAS and severity of depression as measured by the HRS-D ($r = .25$, $p. < .10$). The BDI and DAS correlation is significant, however ($r = 53$, $p. < .01$). Visual inspection of the graph suggests that the correlation is accounted for by the direct relationship between BDI and DAS when a score of 146 on the DAS is selected. A third striking finding from this study is that a significant percentage of acutely depressed unipolar patients, who are clearly depressed and meet criteria for a definite diagnosis of Major Depressive Disorder, endorse no more dysfunctional attitudes than do normal controls previously recorded by Weissman (1979). Thus, 44% of the subjects fall within one standard deviation of normal or below a cutoff score of 143.

Further corroboration of this finding was noted in a study (Rush et al., 1981) in which DAS scores were compiled for a sample of 33 unipolar depressed patients when acutely symptomatic and later when largely remitted. As can be seen from Tables 10–1 and 10–2, DAS scores were for this group higher during the depressed than remitted times for both the unipolar and bipolar patients. On the other hand, this study showed that 14 of 33 patients scored within one standard deviation of normal by DAS when acutely symptomatic. In addition, there was no difference in depressive symptomatology between those with a normal DAS score and those with a high DAS score as defined by a median split in the sample of 146. For the normal DAS group, the HRS-D mean was 22.4, and for the high DAS group the HRS-D mean was 23.6. BDI scores were also equivalent for these two groups (normal DAS, BDI = 25.2; high DAS, BDI = 28.6). A finding of further interest is that when symptomatic improvement occurred, DAS scores showed significant reduction in the high DAS group, whereas no change occurred in the low DAS group (see Table 10–3).

Finally, according to the cognitive theory, cognitions proceed from schemas. Therefore, negative cognitions (CRT-ID scores) should directly relate to schemas (DAS scores). This hypothesis was assessed in the same cohort of unipolar and bipolar patients. During the symptomatic state, there was no significant relationship found

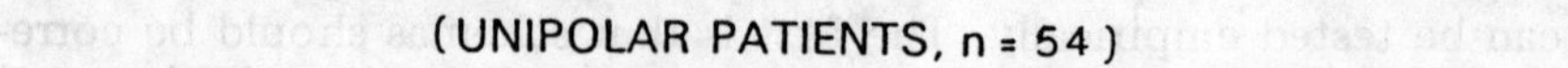

Figure 10-1. Frequency of DAS Scores and Corresponding Severity at Evaluation

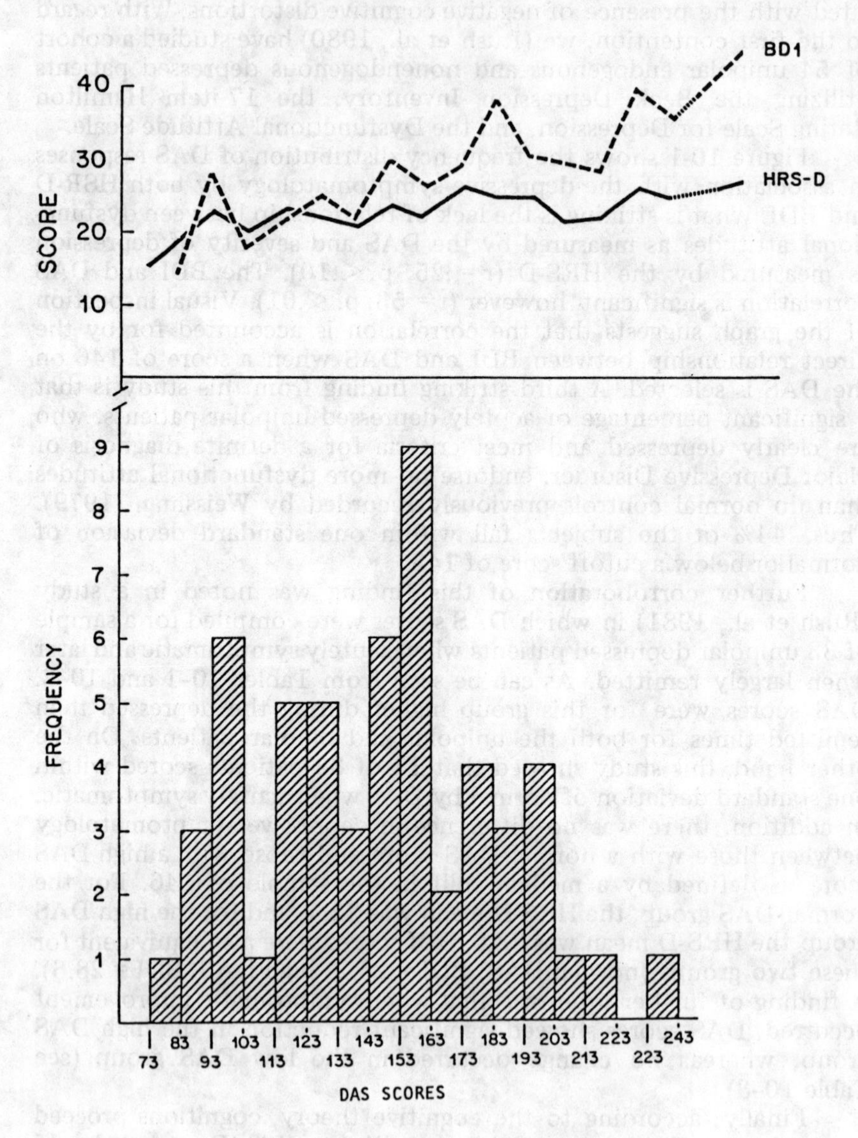

Table 10-3. Low DAS versus High DAS Unipolars

	SYMPTOMATIC			
Variable	*Low DAS (n = 16)*	*High DAS (n = 17)*	*t*	*p*
HRS-D	22.4 (3.8)	23.6 (4.9)	0.61	.550
BDI	25.2 (7.2)	28.6 (7.2)	1.02	.320
DAS	114.6 (24.1)	177.3 (24.5)	7.49	.011
CRT-ID	5.6 (3.9)	8.8 (7.4)	1.23	.219
	REMITTED			
Variable	*Low DAS (n = 16)*	*High DAS (n = 17)*	*t*	*p*
HRS-D	11.7 (6.4)	12.5 (6.2)	- .38	.705
BDI	17.1 (8.3)	19.4 (12.4)	- .62	.541
DAS	110.9 (31.0)	154.0 (19.6)	-4.81	.001
CRT-ID	4.8 (4.3)	5.5 (4.1)	- .49	.628

between attitudes (DAS) and cognitions (CRT-ID) in the bipolar group ($r = .11$). The unipolar group showed a positive although relatively weak relationship ($r = .37, p < .05$).

CONCLUSIONS AND SUMMARY

Cognitive theory (Beck, 1967, 1976) has provided an heuristic model of the origin, development, and maintenance of depression. Much research has focused on testing this theory, and from these studies, more has been learned about the vicissitudes of the disorder. However, many studies rely on nonclinical populations and/or correlational methods. Recent findings further support this theory in clinical populations. However, variability among depressed patients is great, and this variability does not relate strongly to symptom severity. Further, several findings are discrepant with predictions based on cognitive theory. Although negative cognitions discriminate depressed from remitted subjects, they do not appear to follow directly from schemas as predicted. Additional experimental and longitudinal studies are required to further test cognitive theory.

REFERENCES

American Psychiatric Association. *Diagnostic and statistical manual of mental disorders.* Third edition, Washington, DC: American Psychiatric Association, 1980.

Beck, A. T. *Depression: Clinical, experimental, and theoretical aspects.* New York: Harper & Row, 1967.

Beck, A. T. *Cognitive therapy and the emotional disorders.* New York: International Universities Press, Inc., 1976.

Beck, A. T., & Rush, A. J. Cognitive approaches to depression and suicide. In G. Serban (Ed.), *Cognitive defects in development of mental illness.* New York: Brunner/Mazel, 1978.

Beck, A. T., Rush, A. J., Shaw, B. F., & Emery, G. *Cognitive therapy of depression.* New York: Guilford Press, 1979.

Beck, A. T., Ward, C. H., Mendelson, M., Mock, J. E., & Erbaugh, J. K. An inventory for measuring depression. *Archives of General Psychiatry*, 1961, *4*, 561–571.

Beck, A. T., Weissman, A., Lester, D., & Trexter, L. The measurement of pessimism: The hopelessness scale. *Journal of Consulting and Clinical Psychology*, 1974, *42*, 861–865.

DeMonbreun, B. G., & Craighead, W. E. Distortion of perception and recall of positive and neutral feedback in depression. *Cognitive Therapy and Research*, 1977, *1*, 311–329.

Greden, J. F., Albala, A. A., Smokler, I. A., & Carroll, B. J. Speech pause time (SPT) as a marker of psychomotor deceleration among depressives: A follow-up report. Presented at the Society for Biological Psychiatry, Boston, MA, September 1980.

Hamilton, M. A rating scale for depression. *Journal of Neurology, Neurosurgery and Psychiatry*, 1960, *12*, 56–62.

Hamilton, M. Development of a rating scale for primary depressive illness. *British Journal of Social and Clinical Psychology*, 1967, *6*, 278–296.

Hammen, C. L., & Krantz, S. Effects of success and failure on depressive cognitions. *Journal of Abnormal Psychology*, 1976, *85*, 577–586.

Hollon, S. D., & Kendall, P. C. Cognitive self-statements in depression: Development of an automatic thoughts questionnaire. *Cognitive Therapy and Research*, 1980, *4*, 383–395.

Howes, M. J., & Hokanson, J. E. Conversational and social responses to depressive interpersonal behavior. *Journal of Abnormal Psychology*, 1979, *88*, 625–634.

Inhelder, B., & Piaget, J. (translated by A. Parsons and D. Milgram). *The growth of logical thinking: From childhood to adolescence.* New York: Basic Books, 1958.

Klein, D. F. Endogenomorphic depression. *Archives of General Psychiatry*, 1974, *31*, 447–454.

Loeb, A., Beck, A. T., & Diggory, J. Differential effects of success and failure on depressed and nondepressed patients. *Journal of Nervous and Mental Disease*, 1971, *152*, 106-114.

Robins, E., & Guze, S. Classification of affective disorders: The primary-secondary, the endogenous-reactive, and the neurotic-psychotic concepts. In T. A. Williams, M. M. Katz, & J. A. Shield, Jr. (Eds.), *Recent advances in the psychobiology of depressive illnesses.* Washington, DC: U.S. Government Printing Office, 1972.

Rush, A. J., & Beck, A. T. Cognitive therapy of depression and suicide. *American Journal of Psychotherapy*, 1978, *32*, 201-219.

Rush, A. J., Giles, D. E., Dougherty, R., & Sullivan, D. Cognitive distortions, schemas and depressive symptomatology. Unpublished manuscript, 1981.

Rush, A. J., Giles, D. E., Vasavada, N. V., & Weissenburger, J. Which depressions have cognitive distortions? Paper presented to The World Congress on Behavior Therapy, Jerusalem, Israel, July 1980.

Seligman, M. E. P. *Helplessness: On depression, development, and death.* San Francisco, CA: W. H. Freeman, 1975.

Steiner, R. E. A cognitive-developmental analysis of depression: Interpersonal problem solving and event interpretation among depressed and nondepressed women. Unpublished dissertation, Clark University, 1974, *Dissertation Abstracts International*, 1975, *35* (8-B), 4197.

Velten, E. A laboratory task for induction of mood state. *Behaviour Research and Therapy*, 1966, *6*, 473-482.

Watkins, J. T., & Rush, A. J. Cognitive response test. Unpublished manuscript, 1981.

Weissman, A. N. The dysfunctional attitude scale: A validation study. Unpublished dissertation, University of Pennsylvania, 1978. *Dissertation Abstracts International*, 1979, *40*.

Wetzel, R. D. Hopelessness, depression and suicide intent. *Archives of General Psychiatry*, 1976, *33*, 1069-1073.

Wilkinson, I. M., & Blackburn, I. M. Cognitive style in depressed and recovered depressed patients. *British Journal of Clinical Psychology*, in press.

CHAPTER 11

Investigating Immediate Effects on Depression of Brief Interventions: An Underused Tactic in Depression Treatment Research

John D. Teasdale, Ph.D.
Melanie J. V. Fennell, M.A., M.Sc.

The investigation of psychological treatments for depression has yielded results that are at present both encouraging and problematic. On the one hand, there is considerable preliminary evidence to suggest that a wide range of treatment packages are at least modestly effective. On the other hand, there is no clear indication of what constitutes the effective components or mechanisms of action of these treatments. Effective treatments often differ considerably both in their content and in their underlying rationale. This has led to a widespread suggestion that more attention should be directed toward the so-called "nonspecific" components shared by apparently diverse treatments (as in Zeiss, Lewinsohn, & Muñoz, 1979).

This work was supported by the Medical Research Council of the United Kingdom.

The historical development of other areas of behavior therapy suggests that rapid improvements in treatment effectiveness and efficiency can result from a two-fold strategy that attempts (1) to identify the active therapeutic components of effective treatments, and (2) knowing this, to develop treatment procedures that ensure that a given active component is implemented as effectively and efficiently as possible. In the treatment of agoraphobia, for example, the important component appears to be prolonged exposure to the phobic stimuli. This can be implemented very effectively and efficiently by a structured self-help program of graded exposure, with assistance from the spouse (Jannoun et al., 1980). As a result of this two-fold strategy this program, with only 4.5 hours of therapist time, achieves reductions in phobic severity approximately twice those once achieved as a result of 60 to 70 hours of systematic desensitization (Gelder & Marks, 1966).

A similar two-fold strategy might productively be used to develop improved psychological treatments for depression. In emphasizing as an initial step the identification of specific active therapeutic ingredients or processes, this approach contrasts with the growing emphasis placed on so-called nonspecific factors in the treatment of depression. However, as we shall discuss in more detail later, these approaches are not necessarily irreconcilable, despite the difference in emphasis: even "nonspecific" factors are likely to have their effects through specifiable processes.

How, then, can we achieve the first step of the two-fold strategy, the identification of active therapeutic components or processes in the alleviation of depression? Two related sources that may be of value are psychological theories of depression and the evaluation of pyschological treatments for depression. Let us consider as an example the cognitive model of depression and the cognitive behavioral treatment (CBT) that derives from it (Beck et al. 1979). The model suggests that the essential requirement of effective treatment is the reduction in frequency or intensity of thoughts with depressive content. CBT is a complex treatment package specifically designed to achieve this end.

To date most investigations of CBT have consisted of comparative clinical outcome trials (as in Rush et al., 1977). Unfortunately, superior outcomes for CBT in such trials provide only limited support for the notion that changing depressive thinking is *the* essential requirement of effective psychological treatment for depression. This is because CBT includes many components other than those uniquely directed at changing depressive thinking.

For this reason, the therapeutic effects of the CBT package could be attributed to its "nonunique" components rather than the thought-change procedures as such. One could, of course, attempt to compare the effects of CBT with other treatment packages designed to contain the same "nonunique" components as CBT but differing in the "unique" components. However, there are considerable difficulties in designing such treatments and in demonstrating convincingly that they are truly comparable in their nonunique components. A further complication in any clinical trial on depression is that differences between treatments are likely to be attenuated by the "noise" brought into the system by extratherapy factors such as "spontaneous" remission or the effect of positive or negative life events.

Overall, clinical outcome trials, while obviously invaluable in other respects, may not be the most productive way to test out the idea that changing depressive cognitions is the crucial factor in the treatment of depression. The main reasons for this are (1) the complexity of clinical treatment packages, (2) the difficulty of precisely specifying and implementing a treatment of intervention, and (3) the difficulty of measuring the changes actually attributable to treatment against the "noise" of changes resulting from extratherapy factors.

This general problem has, of course, been recognized for some time. Bergin and Strupp (1970), for example, suggested that, given the nature of traditional outcome research, the individual experimental case study and experimental analogue approaches were likely to be the primary strategies for improving knowledge of the mechanisms of change. In depression there are problems with both these approaches. As yet we have no satisfactory experimental analogue of clinical depression. We might study mild "normal" depression, but the considerable "spontaneous" variations in the phenomena under investigation pose problems for the design of sensitive analogue outcome studies. There is, of course, the additional difficulty inherent in extrapolating from "normal" to clinical depression. The "natural" variability of the state of depression also poses problems for the individual experimental case approach to the study of clinical depression. This usually relies on establishing a relatively stable baseline against which the effects of interventions can be compared. The advantage of the analogue and single case approaches lies in the greater precision they allow in the control and description of the treatment intervention, in the measurement of change in the condition, and in determining the relationship between change and the effects of the treatment. In depression, these advantages can be achieved if, instead of using conventional analogue or single-case study approaches, we study the immediate effects on the state of clinical depression of brief therapeutic interventions. By investigating change over brief intervals, we overcome the difficulties resulting from "natural" variations in depression and also allow the interventions to be described and measured with some accuracy. The relevance of such studies to the clinical treatment of depression depends, of course, on the assumption that the processes underlying short-term change are similar to those involved in the long-term changes that are of more obvious clinical interest. This assumption is quite consistent with the rationale of at least some aspects of CBT.

Thus, investigating the immediate effects on depression of brief interventions aimed at changing depressive thinking might be a useful way to discover whether this is indeed a particularly effective component in the treatment of depression. It could also provide evidence of the validity of the cognitive model of depression on which CBT is based. To date, experimental investigations of this cognitive model have taken two main forms. Correlational studies have shown significant associations between measures of depression and measures of depressive thinking (Beck & Rush, 1978). Experimental studies (for example, Teasdale & Bancroft, 1977) have shown that instructing subjects to think thoughts with depressive content can increase their depression. However, the support for the model from these two sources is somewhat limited. The existence of an association between depression and depressive thinking is not sufficient evidence that depressive thinking causes depression. Further, the fact that depression *can* be caused by negative thoughts in no way shows that these thoughts are the *normal* cause of clinical depression.

The most direct test of the hypothesis that depressing thoughts are the normal cause of clinical depression is to examine the prediction that reducing the frequency or intensity of such thoughts in depressed patients will alleviate their depression. Clearly, one way to do this is to examine the immediate effects on depression of brief interventions designed to modify depressive thinking. Thus, this type of investigation appears to hold promise both as a way of delineating effective therapeutic procedures and of testing a central hypothesis of the cognitive model of depression. More generally, the tactic of investigating immediate effects of brief interventions would appear to offer considerable advantages in depression treatment research, as a way both of isolating effective therapeutic ingredients and of testing the theoretical bases of treatments (see Teasdale, 1981, for a more detailed discussion of this issue). However, it is a tactic that has been relatively little used. M. B. Shapiro some time ago advocated the usefulness of this approach (Shapiro, 1966). His work may have had less impact than it deserved because he studied complex clinical interventions (such as an hour of client-centered therapy) rather than simple experimental manipulations, and also because it relied on a unique self-report measure of depression. As we shall discuss in detail later, there are at present no wholly satisfactory measures of short-term change in depression, and this may have been an important reason for the relative neglect of this approach.

The study we report investigated the immediate effects on

clinical depression of brief thought-change interventions. Two previous studies with the same aim (Teasdale & Rezin, 1978a and b) failed to obtain conclusive evidence, largely because the procedures used to reduce depressive thoughts, distraction and thought-stopping, did not achieve sufficient reduction in negative thoughts. The present study used some of the "cognitive" CBT techniques (Beck et al., 1979, Chapter 8) to change depressive thinking. Its purpose was, by studying the immediate effects of these procedures on depression, both to obtain evidence of their specific effectiveness in alleviating depression, and to test the prediction of the cognitive model of depression that reducing belief in depressive thoughts will alleviate depression. As this study is described in detail elsewhere (Teasdale & Fennell, in press), we will describe it only in outline here.

THE STUDY

The thought-change procedures studied were from the "cognitive" techniques of cognitive behavioral therapy described by Beck et al. (1979, Chapter 8). Periods devoted to such active thought-change procedures were compared with periods in which the therapist aimed to explore thoughts and to gain information relevant to them (as he normally would in therapy) but without directly trying to change the thoughts. A within-subject design was used in patients who were already receiving sessions of cognitive therapy. For each patient, the effects were measured of approximately 30 minutes devoted to each type of procedure within a normal cognitive therapy session. In this way general "nonspecific" factors, such as being in therapy, having a collaborative therapeutic relationship, credible overall treatment rationale, high treatment structure, and the like, were essentially similar for the two procedures. By embedding periods of the procedures to be compared within the same general therapeutic context of normal cognitive therapy, any differences in the effects of the two procedures could be reasonably interpreted in terms of differences in the specific content of the 30-minute periods.

Subjects chosen for the study were chronically moderately/severely depressed female patients who met the Research Diagnostic Criteria for Major Depression, who had currently been depressed for at least a year, and who had previously failed to respond to antidepressant medication. All but one had been previously hospitalized for depression. There were two reasons for choosing such a relatively difficult group:

1. because we were interested in identifying specific therapeutic factors, we wanted a group who would be unlikely to show

much response to very general aspects of therapy, such as having an opportunity to talk about their problems, to ventilate their feelings, and so on;

2. as they were a difficult group, they constituted quite a stringent test of the cognitive model.

We are reporting data on five patients. While this is a small number, in a within-subject design it meets the minimum necessary to use simple statistics (5/5 in the predicted direction is significant on a sign-test) and a prediction of strong effects had been made. As it turns out, the results are very clear-cut.

The experimental session began with measurement of the state of depression. A major difficulty in conducting this type of study is the shortage of measures appropriate for measuring changes in depression over brief periods. We employed a 100 mm. Visual Analogue Scale (VAS) as a self-report measure of depressed mood, and measured the time it took subjects to count from 1 to 10 "in their own time" as an index of the psychomotor component of depression (counting time, CT). We have previously shown (Teasdale, Fogarty, & Williams, 1980) that CT correlates quite highly with self-rated depression in some patients, and that it can be sensitive to changes over short intervals. However, we had not previously used it in this type of study. Subjects had previous experience with all the measures used in the study.

The session proceeded as usual with agenda-setting and the like and continued until a suitable thought had been identified. The criteria used to accept thoughts as suitable were: (1) they were depressive in content, containing distortions, and commensurate with the associated affect; and (2) they were judged to be central to the patient's depression and currently directly affecting the state of depression. As it was intended to modify the existing state of depression, it was important to use only thoughts judged to be currently contributing to that state. Examples of the thoughts used are "I am and always will be a cripple as a person," "I am never going to get over my depression," and "I am inadequate in relationships."

Once a suitable thought had been identified, the patient rated her belief in the thought on a 0–100 scale, as is usual in CBT (Beck et al., 1979, p. 403), and the VAS and CT measueres were administered. These constituted the preintervention assessments. Treatment condition was then randomly determined by the therapist noting the number on the taperecorder counter (all therapy sessions were routinely audiotaped). If the tens digit was even, the therapist proceeded with the Thought Change condition, if it was an odd number, the therapist proceeded with the Thought Exploration condition. In the *Thought Change condition* the therapist attempted to change the identified thought using "cognitive" CBT techniques as described by Beck et al. (1979, Chapter 8). These mainly involved encouraging the patient to reevaluate her thinking by helping her to consider all the evidence relevant to an issue rather than just a biased sample, to consider alternative explanations, to review alternative courses of action, and so on. In the *Thought Exploration condition*, the therapist proceeded to explore the identified thought by questioning and reflective statements, and to obtain more relevant information, much as in normal CBT practice.

Each condition continued for approximately 30 minutes. At the end of the period of Thought Exploration or Thought Change, belief in the identified thought was rerated and VAS and CT again administered. These constituted the postintervention measures. From then on, the session continued much as any other CBT session. If a thought had been explored, an attempt was made to modify it before the end of the session.

For each patient, the procedure was repeated, using the alternative experimental condition, at a later point in therapy.

RESULTS

To check that therapists had implemented the two procedures as intended, all sessions were audiotaped, and two raters blind to experimental condition and to the purpose of the study rated on visual analogue scales the amount of time the therapist spent attempting to change the identified thought and exploring and obtaining more information relevant to the identified thought. For all patients, both raters independently rated Thought Change sessions as having more time directed at changing thoughts (73%) than the Thought Exploration sessions (18%). Conversely, for all patients both raters judged more time to be spent in exploring and obtaining information in the Exploration condition (74%) than in the Thought Change condition (30%). Thus, the experimental conditions were satisfactorily implemented as intended.

Figure 11-1 shows the effects of the two procedures in changing belief in the identified thoughts. As intended, in each case the Thought Change exploration procedure produced more change in belief than the Thought Exploration procedure, mean belief change being 61 for Thought Change but zero for all but one patient in the Thought Exploration condition. Figure 11–1 also shows the effect of the Thought Change and Thought Exploration procedures on changes in self-reported depression as measured by the Visual Analogue Scale (VAS). Results conform to prediction for each of the five subjects, mean reduction in depression being 38 on the 0–100 VAS scale in the Thought Change condition, but only 3 in the Thought Exploration condition. This result is statistically significant by a sign test ($p<.05$,

Figure 11–1. Changes in Belief in Depressive Thoughts, Self-Rated Depression (VAS), and Percentage Change in Counting Time (CT) in the Thought Change and Thought Exploration Conditions. Positive scores indicate changes in the direction of reduced depression.

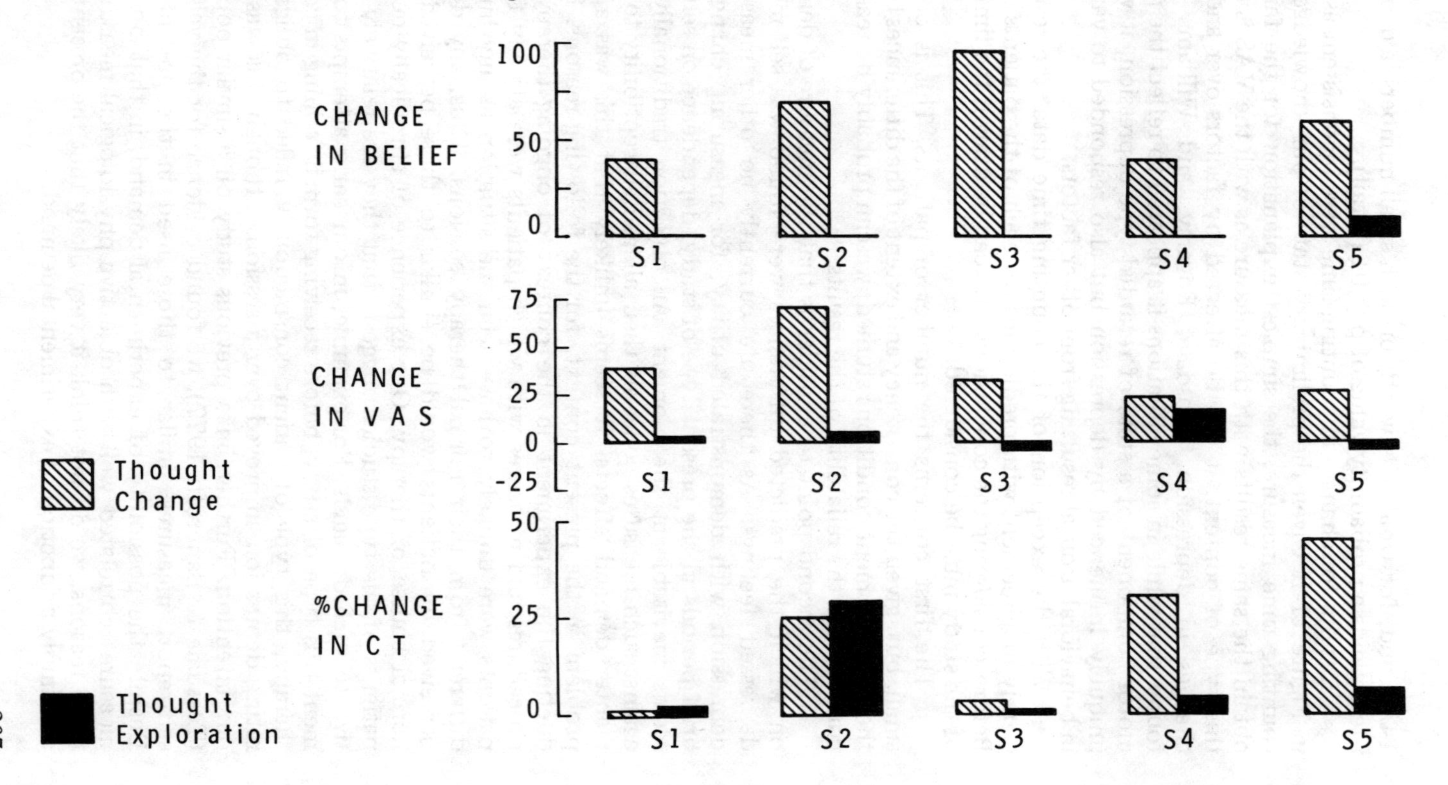

1-tail) and, for what it is worth on such small numbers, a dependent t-test yields a probability value of $p \triangleq .01$ (1-tail).

Results for changes in counting time were inconsistent as shown in Figure 11-1. Given the preliminary state of our knowledge of the counting time measure, the simplest explanation for the failure to obtain the same results with this measure as with the VAS is that, in this type of context, it can be affected by factors over and above changes in depression. Teasdale, Fogarty, and Williams (1980) found that while in some situations it appeared to reflect the psychomotor component of a state of retarded-type depression, it was not uniquely influenced by depression but also responded to variations in behavioral arousal resulting from other factors.

With the exception of the counting time data, the results are clearly in agreement with predictions for each of the patients studied. Before considering the conclusions that can be drawn, the limitations of the study must be considered.

The first concerns the number of patients. This is obviously small, but, given the consistency and extent of the differences between the two treatment conditions studied, we can probably be reasonably confident of the reliability of the results.

The second point to consider is that the measure of depression on which the predicted differences were found was self-report of depressed feelings. As there are currently no other measures of depression with demonstrated utility, for measuring changes over brief periods in the present type of study, dependence on self-report seems inevitable at the moment. An objection traditionally raised against such measures concerns their alleged susceptibility to experimenter demand effects. It seems unlikely that this was a serious problem in the present context, for the following reasons. By conducting the experiment in the context of ongoing therapy, using procedures and measures with which patients were already familiar, patients were unlikely to have seen the situation as anything very different from their normal therapy sessions. Thus, any demands perceived by patients would be similar to those perceived in the normal course of therapy. Our experience of chronically depressed patients of the type studied suggests that they are relatively insensitive to such demands. For example, in our early attempts to implement this type of study, before receiving formal training in cognitive therapy, this type of patient conspicuously failed to oblige us by rating depression improved over a session, although this was clearly our intention. Further, in a previous study on a similar population (Teasdale & Bancroft, 1977), we found evidence for the validity of self-report measures similar to those used in the present study. Despite the possibility of experimental demand, in that study such measures correlated well with objective physiological measures. For these reasons, we do not think it very likely that the present results are simply a function of experimental demand.

DISCUSSION

Within its limitations, this study has given support to a central prediction of the cognitive model of depression. The finding that modifying the depressive thinking of clinically depressed patients leads to immediate alleviation of their depression supports the hypothesis that such thinking normally contributes to the maintenance of that depression. It also provides evidence suggesting the specific effectiveness of certain "cognitive" CBT techniques as therapeutic agents.

Apart from sample size, the main areas where this investigation might be improved are the specification of the therapeutic intervention and the measurement of changes in belief and in the state of depression. Both these areas are problematic for research in general in this field. Although we are confident that other trained cognitive therapists could achieve similar results, we did not specify in advance as precisely as we would like the exact nature of the "cognitive" CBT interventions to be employed. As in current practice in CBT for depression, we specified clearly the therapeutic strategy to be employed but left the therapist a degree of flexibility on the tactics. We are currently attempting to specify more closely the therapeutic options permitted and the decision rules for choosing between them. This exercise, apart from improving this type of study, would be of obvious benefit in improving the replicability of CBT practice in outcome trials and in providing clearer guidelines in training.

The other major problem is measurement, particularly of the state of depression. As is widely recognised (for example, Rehm, 1981), there is a dearth of suitable instruments for measuring depression by means other than ratings by the patient or by a clinician. In part, of course, this reflects our current limited knowledge of the nature of the state of depression. The need for additional forms of measurement is even more pressing in investigations of the type we have reported here than in the normal clinical trial. Hopefully, the increased pressure to solve this problem that follows from adopting the present tactic of investigation might lead to more rapid progress in this area.

We have suggested that studies of the type reported here should form the first step in a two-stage research strategy in which specific therapeutic components are first identified and then incorporated into an efficient "delivery system." The potential utility of this approach is suggested by the contrast between the demonstrated effectiveness of the CBT techniques in producing immediate changes in depression in the present study, and the overall clinical results obtained on a small number of similar chronic treatment-resistant depressed patients (Fennell & Teasdale, in press); 20 sessions of CBT produced quite modest improvements in the clinical state of these patients. We believe the best explanation for this is that, because the treatment delivery system was not particularly designed for this group, patients, after leaving the clinic, made only limited use of the techniques that we have shown are effective within therapy sessions. The overall result of the usual form of clinical trial confounds the two separate issues of (1) the specific effectiveness of therapeutic techniques and (2) the effectiveness of the delivery system by which patients are trained to implement them in their day-to-day life. Knowing that cognitive CBT techniques can be effective in the short term in "difficult" patients leads us to think in terms of developing better delivery systems for this group rather than to look to radically different forms of intervention. We might well have adopted the latter course of action if we had only the results on overall clinical outcome to guide us. It will, of course, be necessary before conducting clinical trials incorporating improved delivery systems to check our assumption that getting patients to implement the CBT techniques themselves will lead to sustained improvement in depression.

The two-fold research strategy we are advocating is essentially one in which an overall treatment package is "assembled" by incorporating components, each of which has been shown to be specifically effective in the short term, into an efficient delivery system. The final stage, obviously, has to be the evaluation of the overall package by means of the traditional clinical trial.

How do we reconcile our emphasis on the identification of specific therapeutic components and processes with the importance attached to so-called "nonspecific" factors by a number of authors? We shall consider the report by Zeiss et al. (1979) as representative. In this study, depressed subjects responding to an announcement offering therapy for depression as part of a research project were randomly assigned to one of three treatment conditions. They were also randomly assigned to begin therapy either immediately or after a one-month waiting period. One treatment aimed at increasing the client's rate of mood-related pleasant activities. Another treatment aimed at increasing assertiveness, positive social impact, and social interaction. The third treatment aimed at changing depressive cognitions (cognitive modality). The effects on depression and on the behaviors assumed to be the specific targets of each type of approach were measured for a month of each treatment and for the one-month waiting period. Results showed that, overall, active treatments produced more improvement in depression than the wait condition. However, the advantage of active treatment was relatively modest, and there were no significant differences in effectiveness between the three treatments. Further, while measures of target behaviors generally showed improvement over time, improvement was not greater following active treatment than following the wait period. Most importantly, there was no specific effect of a particular treatment modality on the behaviors most obviously targeted in that modality.

Zeiss et al. concluded: "The major finding of this study is that all of the treatments had nonspecific effects" (p. 435). They go on to suggest, with Bandura (1977), that all treatments were equally effective to the extent that they increased self-efficacy: "The effectiveness of the treatments may, in this view, be unrelated to the specific skills trained in each module. Instead, by various routes, all patients began to have positive experiences in their daily lives, which they attributed to increased self-efficacy" (p. 437). Finally, they suggested that any treatment meeting the following criteria should be effective in overcoming depression:

1. Therapy should begin with presentation of an elaborated rationale, which should provide initial structure that guides the patient to believe that he or she can control his or her own behavior and, thereby, his or her depression.
2. Therapy should train the patient in skills he or she can use to feel more effective in handling daily life.
3. Therapy should emphasize the patient's independent use of these skills outside the therapy context and provide enough structure to allow the attainment of independent skill.
4. Therapy should lead patients to attribute their improvement in mood to their own increased skillfulness.

In fact, Zeiss et al. are proposing a specific mechanism by which treatments are effective in reducing depression. This is that treatments operate to increase patients' efficacy expectations that they can execute skills that they have been led to believe will alleviate depression. Their apparent emphasis on nonspecific factors appears when they consider the means by which this is to be achieved. Based on the lack of difference between treatments in their own study, they suggest that it may not matter particularly what skills are taught, as long as they can be plausibly related to relief of depression and are of a kind that the patient "can utilise to feel more effective in handling his or her daily life" (Zeiss et al., 1979, p. 438).

Our own interpretation is in many ways similar to that of Zeiss et al. but differs in a subtle but important way. Like them, we believe it probable that part of the effectiveness shared by their three treatments was mediated by patients acquiring the expectation that there was something that could be done to alleviate their depression and that they could learn skills to achieve this. However, our emphasis on the identification of specific therapeutic processes and components leads to different emphasis at two points, the second of more substance than the first. The first is that if one believes that acquiring the above expectation is a crucial ingredient of successful therapy (which is, of course, quite consistent with a cognitive model of depression), then it would be desirable both to check this assumption using short-term experiments, and, if the assumption is valid, explicitly to design one's treatment to modify such expectations rather than to rely on it happening "incidentally." The second, more important, point relates to the means by which the expectation is to be achieved. Zeiss et al. (1979) appear to suggest that it may not matter particularly whether the skills that patients are taught are, of themselves, actually capable of modifying depression. They seem to suggest that, as long as the skills can be plausibly related to a psychological model of depression and are "of some significance to the patient" (Zeiss et al., 1979, p. 438), then "the specific content of the skill training offered to depressed clients may be less important than has been previously assumed" (Zeiss et al., 1979, p. 437). In other words, Zeiss et al. appear to be suggesting that as long as patients believe that the skill they have learned and are practicing will relieve their depression, then it will, indeed, have that effect. Now, this may well be the case in certain situations: it may be that with relatively mildly depressed patients likely to show some degree of "spontaneous remission" anyway, any skill with face validity will have some effect. However, this appears to be a somewhat precarious position: if the magic only works as long as you believe it works, then occasional doubts may lead to the magic becoming ineffective, and this may quickly lead to a vicious spiral of doubt, ineffectiveness, and therapeutic pessimism. It would clearly be preferable, particularly with more "difficult" patients, to base attempts to increase patients' expectations that they can control their depression on procedures that are inherently effective in alleviating depression—that is, on interventions that relieve depression irrespective of whether patients believe they will or not. The tactic of investigating short-term effects of specific interventions is obviously relevant in two ways here, (1) to examine the immediate effects on depression of convincing patients that they can control their depression and (2) to examine the immediate effects on depression of a variety of interventions in the absence of a "therapeutic set." (It should be pointed out that the present investigation, very clearly, did not adopt this second strategy.) Thus, we would see the sequence of events in assembling effective treatments for depression something as follows:

1. demonstration of the short-term effectiveness of specific interventions in the absence of "therapeutic set";
2. demonstration of the short-term effectiveness of changing patients' expectations that they can control their depression;
3. demonstration that training the patient to engage frequently in the interventions shown to be effective in (1) and (2) can lead to longer-term benefit;
4. incorporation of the components shown to be effective in (1) and (2) into a treatment package designed (a) explicitly to impart the expectation that the patient can control his depression and (b) to implement antidepressive interventions of

demonstrated utility as effectively and efficiently as possible;
5. evaluation of the package by clinical trials, and continual evolution of more effective and efficient packages.

SUMMARY

1. Improvement in psychological treatments for depression could result from a two-fold strategy that seeks, first, to identify specific active therapeutic components and, second, to develop treatment procedures to implement the active components effectively and efficiently.
2. Traditional clinical outcome trials may be of limited value in identifying specific therapeutic components in the treatment of depression.
3. Investigations of the immediate effects on depression of brief discrete interventions may be a way both to identify active therapeutic components and to test psychological theories of depression.
4. In a small experiment on chronic moderate/severely depressed patients already receiving cognitive behavior therapy (CBT) for depression, periods devoted to changing identified depressive thoughts by "cognitive" CBT techniques led to greater improvement in depressed mood than periods devoted to exploring and obtaining more information concerning the thoughts. This supports (a) the specific therapeutic effectiveness of "cognitive" CBT techniques and (b) a central prediction of the cognitive model of depression.
5. The strategy advocated is contrasted with that suggesting the importance of "nonspecific" factors in the treatment of depression. The latter position does, in fact, propose a specific therapeutic process. It is suggested that this process is best realized using interventions with demonstrated short-term effectiveness in reducing depression.

REFERENCES

Bandura, A. Self-efficacy: Toward a unifying theory of behavioral change. *Psychological Review*, 1977, *84*, 191–215.

Beck, A. T., & Rush, A. J. Cognitive approaches to depression and suicide. In G. Serban (Ed.), *Cognitive defects in the development of mental illness.* New York: Brunner/Mazel, 1978.

Beck, A. T., Rush, A. J., Shaw, B. F., & Emery, G. *Cognitive therapy of depression.* New York: Wiley, 1979.

Bergin, A. E., & Strupp, H. H. New directions in psychotherapy research. *Journal of Abnormal Psychology*, 1970, *76*, 13–26.

Fennell, M. J. V., & Teasdale, J. D. Cognitive therapy with chronic drug refractory depressed out-patients: a note of caution. *Cognitive Therapy and Research*, in press.

Gelder, M. G., & Marks, I. M. Severe agoraphobia: a controlled prospective therapeutic trial. *British Journal of Psychiatry*, 1966, *112*, 309–319.

Jannoun, L., Munby, M., Catalan, J., & Gelder, M. G. A home-based treatment program for agoraphobia: replication and controlled evaluation. *Behavior Therapy*, 1980, *11*, 294–305.

Rehm, L. (Ed.). *Behavior therapy for depression: Present status and future direction.* New York: Academic Press, 1981.

Rush, A. J., Beck, A. T., Kovacs, M., & Hollon, S. Comparative efficacy of cognitive therapy and pharmacotherapy in the treatment of depressed outpatients. *Cognitive Therapy and Research*, 1977, *1*, 17–37.

Shapiro, M. B. The single case in clinical psychological research. *Journal of General Psychology*, 1966, *74*, 2–23.

Teasdale, J. D. What kind of theory will improve psychological treatments? In J. Boulougouris (Ed.), *Learning theory approaches in psychiatry*, Chichester and New York: Wiley, 1982.

Teasdale, J. D., & Bancroft, J. Manipulation of thought content as a determinant of mood and corrugator electromyographic activity in depressed patients. *Journal of Abnormal Psychology*, 1977, *86*, 235–241.

Teasdale, J. D., & Fennell, M. J. V. Immediate effects on depression of cognitive therapy interventions, *Cognitive Therapy and Research*, in press.

Teasdale, J. D., Fogarty, S. J., & Williams, J. M. G. Speech rate as a measure of short-term variation in depression. *British Journal of Social and Clinical Psychology*, 1980, *19*, 271–278.

Teasdale, J. D., & Rezin, V. The effects of reducing frequency of negative thoughts on the mood of depressed patients: Tests of a cognitive model of depression. *British Journal of Social and Clinical Psychology*, 1978, *17*, 65–74. (a)

Teasdale, J. D., & Rezin, V. Effect of thought-stopping on thoughts, mood and corrugator EMG in depressed patients. *Behaviour Research and Therapy*, 1978, *16*, 97–102. (b)

Zeiss, A. M., Lewinsohn, P. M., & Muñoz, R. F. Nonspecific improvement effects in depression using interpersonal skills training, pleasant activity schedules, or cognitive training. *Journal of Consulting and Clinical Psychology*, 1979, *47*, 427–439.

PART VI

The Nature and Role of Cognition

CHAPTER 12

The Lay-Epistemic Model in Cognitive Therapy

Arie W. Kruglanski, Ph.D.
Yoram Jaffe, Ph.D.

INTRODUCTION

In its efforts to apply itself to the treatment of emotional disturbances, behavior therapy has become increasingly concerned with cognitive change or cognitive therapy. In a keynote address to the First World Congress on Behavior Therapy in Jerusalem in July 1980 (the congress that produced the present volume), Wolpe (1980) asserted that unadaptive anxiety response habits may have a cognitive rather than a pure autonomic conditioning origin. Further, in some cases there may be a combined emotional and cognitive source for the anxiety. Anxieties with a cognitive origin have been acquired on the basis of misinformation and call for cognitive measures whereby the misconceptions involved are corrected. To illustrate what he means by "cognitive source" and "cognitive correction," Wolpe described the case of a patient who suffered from agoraphobia and would not leave her house by herself. Her mistaken belief was that the frequent spells of dizziness and tingling of the hands she experienced were early signs of "going crazy." The patient also described her aunt as "flaky" and believed that she was hereditarily predisposed to suffer from a similar mental illness. Treatment was fully effective within seven sessions in which Wolpe demonstrated to the patient that her dizziness and tingling sensations were due to hyperventilation and,

Kruglanski's work for this chapter was supported by Grant 9404 from the Ford Foundation received through the Israel Foundations Trustees and by Grant 9693 from the Israel Academy of Science.

in addition, persistently disputed any possibility of her "losing her mind."

The contemporary trend toward incorporation of cognitive concepts and procedures into behavior therapy has expanded the behavioral perspective into what is now commonly referred to as cognitive behavior therapy (cf. Bandura, 1977; Mahoney, 1974; Meichenbaum, 1977). Thus, Bandura (1977) now argues that "changes achieved by different methods derive from a common cognitive mechanism" (p. 191). He terms his pivotal cognitive concept "expectations of self-efficacy" and defines it as "the conviction that one can successfully execute the behavior required to produce the outcomes" (p. 193). The trend toward cognitive behavior therapy reflects at least two major sources of influence. One such influence emanates from the current wave of the so-called 'cognitive revolution" sweeping across a number of areas in academic psychology (cf. Arnkoff, 1980; Davison, 1980; Weimer, 1980). The other source of influence is represented by the systems of cognitive therapy developed by Ellis (1962), Beck (1976), Raimy (1975), and others. In a nutshell, these therapeutic systems may be represented by the following statements: "successful psychological treatment occurs when faulty ideas or beliefs are modified or eliminated" (Raimy, 1975, p. 4); "the cognitive therapist induces the patient to . . . correct his fallacious thinking. His problems are derived from certain distortions of reality based on erroneous premises and misconceptions" (Beck, 1976, p. 20); and,

> The rational-emotive practitioner . . . quickly pins the client down to a few basic irrational ideas which motivate much of his disturbed behavior. . . . he shows him that they are extralogical premises which cannot be validated. . . . he explains how they can be replaced with more rational, empirically based ideas, and he teaches the client how to think scientifically . . . so that he can observe, logically parse, and thoroughly annihilate any subsequent irrational ideas and illogical deductions that lead him to feel and act in a self-defeating manner. (Ellis, 1973, p. 185)

While the cognitive behavioral framework includes innovative concepts and what seem to be promising treatment methods, it still lacks the foundation of an integrative, coherent theory of the general process of cognitive change. Such a theory was developed recently by Kruglanski (1980; Kruglanski & Jaffe, in press) as a theory of lay epistemology. This theory concerns the rules that govern the acquisition and modification of all knowledge. It originated in cognitive-social psychology as an attempt to provide an integrative framework whereby diverse models of causal attribution and diverse cognitive-consistency formulations (such as dissonance or balance) can be synthesized into one overarching theory. Kruglanski's theory of lay epistemology is grounded in several assumptions about knowledge characteristic of a modern philosophical position called nonjustificationism (cf. Bartley, 1962; Weimer, 1977), a position whose major contemporary proponents are Popper (for example, 1972) and Kuhn (1970).

The present chapter applies the lay-epistemic model to cognitive therapy. First, the theory of lay epistemology is presented as a theory of the process underlying therapeutic cognitive change (that is, the "how" of such change). Then, the unique essence (that is, the "what") of such change is explicated, and implications for the conduct of cognitive therapy are drawn.

A THEORY OF LAY EPISTEMOLOGY: THE PROCESS OF COGNITIVE THERAPY

The Properties of Knowledge

Knowledge is assumed to be made of propositions. Propositions are made of concepts, and concepts are "universals": Each concept is infinitely divisible into its own particular instances. The distinction between universals and particulars is relative, not absolute. Each particular is, in turn, a universal, infinitely divisible, and so forth. For example, the term "Mary Jones" may be conceived of as a particular instance of the universal "human being." But "Mary Jones" may also be conceived of as a universal category divisible into its own particular instances: Mary Jones at time 1, time 2, place 1, place 2, and so on.

Any given bit of knowledge may be characterized on two dimensions or aspects: (a) the content of the proposition or its specific topic; (b) the confidence with which the proposition is being held, or the subjective probability of it being true. Some propositions—for example, that it is presently daytime—may be held with a great deal of confidence. This would be reflected in attaching to those propositions the label of *facts.* Other propositions are believed in less confidently. Those may be called *hypotheses.* Thus, the difference between "facts" and "hypotheses" would be in the level of confidence one has in the respective proposition. The confidence, or the subjective probability one attaches to a proposition, does not reflect the *objective truth* of a proposition: As we already know, each proposition is made of universals, and each universal is infinitely divisible. This means that for each concept there exist infinite items of relevant evidence, having to do with the infinite separate particular instances of the concepts in question. But at any given point one could only have checked a finite number of evidential items. Therefore, the *possibility* of having erred is everpresent in all knowledge, including scientific knowledge, and we may not estimate the degree to which our propositions represent the objective reality. Therefore, any knowledge that we may have constitutes a *bias*, that is, a subjectively-based preference for a given proposition over possible alternative propositions that could be accounting for the same past evidence in different ways and to have different implications regarding future, yet unchecked, items of relevant evidence.

The Epistemic Sequence

The epistemic sequence consists of two interwoven phases: the phase of hypothesis generation—or of problem formulation—and the phase of hypothesis evaluation—or of problem resolution. Little is known about the phase of hypothesis generation. It has to do with the stream of consciousness and the availability of ideas, or the ease with which they come to the knower's mind at a given moment. The phase of hypothesis evaluation is governed by the principle of logical consistency. The knower deduces from the competing hypotheses their noncommon implications and tests them against the available evidence. A hypothesis the implication of which turns out to be logically consistent with the evidence would be believed in more strongly. A hypothesis contradicted by the evidence would be believed in less strongly, unless the knower found good reasons to doubt the evidence in question. Logical inconsistency can only be resolved by denying one of the horns of the inconsistency. The horn to be denied is that which is initially held with the lower degree of confidence: The cognition labeled as "hypothesis" will give way if contradicted by a cognition labeled as "fact," because the latter term implies greater confidence on the part of the knower than does the former.

The Braking Mechanisms of Hypothesis Generation

Consistency with past evidence is only a necessary not a sufficient condition for the experience of confidence. For the individual might be motivated to generate further alternative accounts, incompatible with a current account, of the extant evidence. Several conditions may affect the individual's tendency to continue or discontinue the generation of alternative hypotheses on a given topic. We call them the braking mechanisms of hypothesis generation, and we identify two major categories of such mechanisms: (1) the epistemic authority of the source wherefrom a given cognition originated; (2) the knower's epistemically relevant motivations. There can be different kinds of epistemic authority lending credence to propositions ascribed thereto: religious authorities, scientific authorities, the authority of a collective, the authority of one's own senses, and so on. The construct of epistemic authority is considered a braking mechanism for the following reason: Ascription of a given hypothesis to a highly esteemed authority would inhibit the process of generating further alternative hypotheses, thus constituting a braking influence upon this process.

In addition to epistemic authority of the source of the hypothesis, the individual's tendency to inhibit or disinhibit the generation of alternative hypotheses is assumed to be influenced by three epistemically relevant motivations. We call those: (1) the *need of structure*; (2) the *fear of invalidity*; and (3) the *need of conclusional contents.* The need for structure is the need to have some knowledge on a given topic, any knowledge, as opposed to a state of ambiguity. The need for structure is assumed to exert an inhibiting or braking influence on the hypothesis-generation process because the generation of alternative hypotheses endangers the existing structure. The need for validity stems from the fear of making a mistake, given the price expected to be paid for one. The need for validity is assumed to exert a facilitating influence upon the hypothesis-generation process because of the fear of committing oneself to a given, possibly erroneous hypothesis. The need for conclusional contents refers to the individual's desire to fulfill a given wish or to attain a given goal. A conclusion signifying the fulfillment of a wish would be more pleasing to an individual than a conclusion signifying a frustration of a wish. The need for conclusional contents is assumed either to inhibit or to facilitate the process of hypothesis generation, depending on whether a currently considered hypothesis or proposition represents the satisfaction or the frustration of a given need.

MALADAPTIVE EPISTEMOLOGY: THE FRUSTRATIVE HYPOTHESIS

The What of Cognitive Therapy

The lay-epistemic model in cognitive therapy conceptualizes the essential distinction between neurotic and normal individuals in terms of content, not process. The epistemic process outlined above is assumed to be universal and to characterize alike people who suffer from emotional disorders and those who function relatively well. In other words, just as the present theory assumes that the lay and the scientific methods of inference represent the same knowledge-acquisition process, it sees no qualitative difference in the way mentally disturbed and normal individuals arrive at their inferences. The present assumption is that what does separate people who suffer emotionally from those who do not are the particular contents of the inferences made by the emotionally troubled individuals. These contents represent maladaptive knowledge resulting from the fact that they engender emotional distress for the individual. We call such dysfunctional cognitions, *frustrative hypotheses.* A frustrative hypothesis is *a belief* in the frustration of an important goal. Cast in cognitive terminology, suffering results from the belief that one has failed or will fail to obtain an important objective.

To illustrate the concept of frustrative hypothesis, let us consider a few examples. If a person's objective was to excel in absolutely everything, he or she would be likely to suffer upon finding out that he or she has failed on a given task. Similarly, if one's objective was to be well liked and adored by all, one would be likely to suffer on finding out that one was rejected by at least some individuals. The foregoing are examples of belief or types of knowledge pertaining to what Beck (1976) has called the states of loss leading to the depression syndrome. In present terms, "depression" may be thought of as evolving from past frustration, or a "loss" already experienced. By contrast, an anticipatory frustration could lead to what Beck has termed a "danger to personal domain" experienced as anxiety or fear. The anticipatory fear in the above example represents the belief that at some future time one's objective of maintaining positive esteem would be thwarted. Other cases of psychological disorders dealt with by the cognitive therapists (such as the variety of phobias) are also amenable to this analysis. It is possible to show that in all those instances the disorder refers to a sense of pain and discomfort attendant upon a belief that some of one's important objectives (of self-esteem, safety, physical welfare, or similar) have been or will be frustrated.

An example from one of our patients illustrates the unfortunate grip frustrative beliefs have on a person's emotional life, and the role of the epistemic authorities that have transmitted and backed up such beliefs. The patient, a 32-year-old religious housewife with three children, presented various anxiety symptoms and complained of fears, guilt feelings, dissatisfaction, and disappointment with her accomplishments in life. One of the more powerful self-statements she expressed, representing the belief that she never completes her undertakings, was: "I'm the unfinished symphony." It is significant to note that the metaphor she chose to articulate her frustrative hypothesis was borrowed word-for-word from her mother. Throughout the patient's life, her mother had frequently used this metaphoric expression to criticize her for failing to complete projects she had started. In addition, the patient complained that she had difficulties enjoying potentially pleasurable activities fully. For example, even such diverse pleasure experiences as joining an outdoor painting group on an idyllic spring day or engaging in sexual relationships with her husband would elicit strong feelings of guilt and remorse, and her enjoyment would be totally spoiled. This problem was easily traced back to her grandmother's puritanical philosophy. The grandmother, a hard-working religious woman, lost her husband at the age of 42, never remarried, and lived with the patient's family. The patient perceived her grandmother as the dominant figure in the house, admired her in many ways, and was tremendously influenced by her. Specifically, the grandmother proclaimed the virtues of a life of ardent work and would scold the patient when she saw her engaged in some self-indulgent, pleasurable activity such as relaxing with a book. The grandmother kept stating that "life is not meant for pleasure," a statement the patient apparently adopted as one of her frustrative, dysfunctional beliefs, which she voiced in therapy in such expressions as, "I cannot enjoy anything in life." The two sets of frustrative hypotheses described above for this patient illustrate the powerful impact of epistemic authorities—in the present case, the grandmother and the mother—and the emotional damage they can cause to a person by transmitting to him or her self-defeating knowledge.

The lay-epistemic model may be extended to the systems approach in family therapy (see, for example, Haley and Hoffman, 1967; Minuchin, 1974). As a system, family members may share in common a knowledge-acquisition process analogous to the epistemic process described here for individuals. While the pertinent literature discusses a number of characteristics of the family system such as structure, organization, rules, and other features, it has failed to articulate distinctly the epistemic functions of this system. For example, Minuchin (1974), who has developed Structural Family Therapy, argues that the family's "organization and structure screen and qualify family members' experience" (p. 7). However, he does not elaborate on the cognitive component of the family system as may be represented by an epistemic process and its possible contents.

Members of distressed families may share in common frustrative hypotheses as defined above from the individual perspective. As such, familial frustrative beliefs represent maladaptive contents of the familial epistemic process and are responsible for a good deal of the family's dysfunction and emotional misfortune. This often finds overt expression in the presenting symptoms of one of the family's children. The contents of familial frustrative beliefs can be illustrated by the following statements made in the course of family therapy sessions we have conducted: "We are a divided family," "Everything is planned, there is nothing spontaneous in our family," "We are always victims of some kind of social injustice," "We don't know how to play with each other and have fun together," "Michael is the 'black sheep' of our family."

In sum, frustrative beliefs constitute a major cognitive block to a person's or a family's happiness in life. It is the task of therapy to cull its utmost resources and lift this barrier.

The Three Therapeutic Shifts

According to the present analysis, then, the object of cognitive therapy is to persuade the patient to change his or her frustrative hypothesis. The therapeutically relevant changes that one could perform on the frustrative hypothesis can be naturally classified according to the conceptual structure of such hypothesis. A frustrative hypothesis contains the elements of a *goal*, a *means* to that goal, and a relation of *inefficiency* connecting the two (whereby is meant that the means is an inefficient way of getting to the goal). Accordingly, the frustrative hypothesis could be profitably modified via (1) an *assessment shift*, that is, a change in the perceived relation of inefficiency between the current means and goal to one of perceived efficiency: (2) a *goal shift*, that is, a change in the person's goal to a more readily attainable objective, given the individual's resources; (3) a *means shift*, that is, a change in the person's means of getting to the goal to a more efficient one. Let us elaborate.

As assessment shift concerns the case in which it may be possible to effect the required change in the frustrative hypothesis by getting the patient to take a new look at the relevant evidence, including "facts" not sufficiently attended to heretofore. In such a case no attempt is made to change the patient's goal or his/her particular means of reaching it; instead, an attempt is made to get the patient to perceive that contrary to former assessment the current means is an effective (rather than ineffective) way of attaining the goal in question. Just like an earstwhile ugly duckling may discover that he is actually a beautiful swan, a person whose suffering stems from believing that he/she is not respected by other people or is failing at his/her job may be introduced to evidence suggesting the contrary to be the case.

But sometimes all evidence available to the patient as well as the therapist may unequivocally support the patient's frustrative belief. It may appear that the patient is indeed failing to earn the approval of important others, is ignored, disliked, or ridiculed, or is poorly endowed to cope with a given category of tasks. Under those circumstances it would seem futile, besides being unethical, to convince the patient of the opposite or induce him/her to execute an assessment shift of the kind referred to. In such a case there seem to exist two principal tacks whereby the individual can be induced to abandon his/her dysfunctional, suffering-producing beliefs. Earlier we called them a means shift, and a goal shift. To reiterate, a means shift refers to the case in which a person substitutes a new, efficient means to the desired goal for the old inefficient one. Such a means shift could ultimately promote the belief that the end may indeed be attained and so eliminate the suffering founded on the contrary belief. For example, a person prevented from attaining his/her ends because of a lack of assertiveness may be induced to undergo an assertiveness training course and so improve his/her interpersonal relations; a person with frustrations in the sexual domain may be induced to attend a Masters & Johnson course in sexual techniques and ultimately abandon the negative beliefs about his/her sexual inadequacies. A means shift may be accomplished by a number of the commonly used behavioral methods, including deep muscular relaxation and biofeedback, imaginal or in-vivo systematic desensitization, prolonged exposure, covert sensitization, live, symbolic, or performance modeling, self-instruction, and various reinforcement and contingency management procedures.

But a means shift may not always seem an appropriate way of changing a person's frustrative belief. Firstly, regardless of the attempted means, some goals may appear unrealistic or unattainable for almost anyone. For example, the goal of succeeding at every single task, or of being admired by every single person, seem to belong in that unattainable category. Secondly, some goals may seem uniquely unattainable for some people; those would be people lacking the unique qualities necessary for the attainment of those particular goals. Many people could not hope to become successful writers, musicians, or businessmen, for a simple lack of talent indispensable for success in those areas. In cases where the goal would seem to lie beyond a person's reasonable means, an efficient way of dealing with frustration and suffering might be to induce the individual to abandon the goal in question and substitute for it a new, more readily achievable, objective.

Regardless of whether the tack selected by the therapist involves an assessment shift, a goal shift, or a means shift, there is a belief change that needs to be executed by the patient. A person comes to therapy with a given belief, for example, that his goal is unattainable, that it is a worthwhile, indispensable goal, that there is nothing the patient can do or no alternative means that he can try in order to achieve that goal. The therapist's task is to unfreeze some of those beliefs, to suggest more nearly functional alternatives in their stead, and to convince the patient to accept or refreeze the latter beliefs. In attempting to accomplish those objectives, the therapist might do well to rely on the lay-epistemic principles adumbrated earlier. For example, in attempting to unfreeze the patient's dysfunctional beliefs, the therapist could criticize the beliefs in question, thereby arousing the fear of invalidity. The therapist could make use of the patient's needs for conclusional contents in order to show that his current dysfunctional beliefs have detrimental consequences for the patient's interests. The therapist could evoke the patient's need for structure, in order to facilitate his acceptance of new, constructive ideas instead of the old, dysfunctional ones. Finally, the therapist could make an efficient use of the patient's esteemed epistemic authorities at all stages of the persuasion process.

DISTINCTIONS FROM ALTERNATIVE APPROACHES

The Misconception Issue

At this point we should like to note some important ways in which the present approach to cognitive therapy differs from major alternative approaches. One of the most important such differences is that the present view denies the assumption that the thinking of disturbed individuals is distorted, biased, or illogical, and that in order to alleviate the pain and suffering the distortion needs to be rectified and logic restored. As a reminder of the misconception position in cognitive therapy, one may recall Ellis' criterion-question for a cognition that calls for therapeutic intervention: "In which way does it have truth or falseness?" (1977, p. 20), and also Beck's therapeutic objective, which is, "to identify, reality-test, and correct distorted conceptualizations and the dysfunctional beliefs (schemas) underlying these cognitions" (Beck et al., 1980, p. 4).

Our first counterargument is that the implied relation between conceptual accuracy and well-being must be rejected. The naked truth is not necessarily pleasant; frequently it can be cruel and merciless in its consequences for the individual. Furthermore, some authors have suggested that individuals often use the so-called false or twisted conceptions in a way that enhances their coping and eventual adjustment. Thus, Lazarus (1980) has observed that well-adjusted individuals may at times function by "bending reality a bit to maintain certain illusions" (p. 123), and that "we often also need the luxury of some illusions" (p. 124). In this connection, Lazarus also asserts that adaptive appraisal can vary a great deal because much of life is indeed highly ambiguous. Hence he recommends that sometimes the therapist better help the patient "think more positively about his or her plight rather than fixate on the painful truth" (p. 124). In a similar vein, Mischel (1979) writes that it is doubtful whether realism can be considered the crux of appropriate affect, and that "to feel good about ourselves we may have to judge ourselves more kindly than we are judged (p. 752). This represents his conclusion from empirical findings showing that depressed patients were more "realistic" in their negative self-evaluations than nondepressed psychiatric and normal controls, in terms of a better match with evaluations by independent observers (see experiment by Lewinsohn et al., 1980).

While in some circumstances "truthful" ideas or beliefs may be beneficial and "false" ideas pernicious in their consequences, we believe that in general there is little basis for concluding that there exists a deterministic or a statistical relation between the veridicality of a belief or an inference and the happiness or unhappiness that it may engender.

The second point we wish to make in relation to the misconception issue is that according to the present conception there is no such inferential method in existence, including the scientific method, that can guarantee the truth of conclusions arrived at by its users, or that can reduce in some estimable sense the potentiality of error. Let us reiterate: The epistemic process delineated earlier is assumed to characterize to an equal degree the scientific and the lay methods of inference. Bias and the potentiality of error constitute inevitable features of such a process, as do "overgeneralizations," "selective abstractions," and "arbitrary inferences" noted by Beck (1976) as cognitive distortions typical of affective pathology. There is no known way of liberating the patient's inferential behavior from any of those characteristics; they are present to a comparable degree in the reasoning of the very best scientists that mankind has produced.

The present view is very much in line with the nonjustificationist position of Weimer (1980) regarding the relationship of science and psychotherapy; he sees them both as "fundamentally rhetorical processes that are primarily argumentative in nature" (p. 370). Any kind of knowledge, be it in science, therapy, or daily life, is a matter of argumentation and persuasion rather than "proof" (Weimer, 1980, pp. 386–388).

The Validity and Wisdom of Universal Lists of Frustrative Beliefs

Another unique feature of the present system is its lack of commitment to specific contents of frustrative hypotheses. Such a commitment has been typical of a good many extant systems of cognitive therapy. As a good illustration of what is claimed to be a universal list of maladaptive contents, one may consider the list of eleven "irrational beliefs" published by Ellis (1962, pp. 61–87) as part of the Rational-Emotive Therapy system he developed. This list has become a household word among many therapists. More recently, however, Ellis (1977) has distilled his original list into a much shorter one, holding only three "major irrational ideologies"—for example, "I *must* do well and *must* win approval for my performances, or else I rate as a rotten person" (p. 11).

According to the present conception, *any* belief denoting the frustration of a significant goal would induce suffering and thus be a proper object for cognitive therapy. It is assumed that what may constitute a list of significant goals may vary widely across individuals and situations so that, in principle, there can be an infinite number of frustrative hypotheses representing the thwarting of such goals. Therefore, no a-priori list of psychologically detrimental belief can be universally relevant, and any attempt to catelogue or categorize them would per force be *arbitrary* and *nonunique.* The hidden danger of such cataloging or categorization is that it might induce a cognitive set rendering the therapist insensitive to the patient's unique beliefs responsible for his suffering. By approaching the patient with this kind of a list of preconceptions, the therapist runs the risk of inadvertently constraining the range of therapeutically relevant interpretations of patient experience he may otherwise make, and would thus possibly undermine his own therapeutic as well as diagnostic endeavors.

The Primacy of Behavioral Performance Experiences as the Mediators of Cognitive Change

Finally, the lay-epistemic model differs from those analyses that regard the personal experience of performance outcomes as a particularly effective mediator of cognitive change. Kopel and Arkowitz (1975) are among the proponents of the primacy of a person's own behavioral performance in producing such a change. They thus state that "the therapeutic effects brought about by observing one's own behavior may be more powerful than the effects obtained from a verbal interchange which conveys the basic information to the client" (p. 195). Bandura (1977) similarly implied that expectancies or inferences arrived at via actual performance are superior to alternative modes of persuasion, such as verbal or based on vicarious experience, because the latter "do not provide an authentic experiential base for them" (p. 198). Therefore: "it is performance-based procedures that are proving to be most powerful for effecting psychological changes . . . (and) cognitive events are induced and altered most readily by experience of mastery arising from effective performance" (p. 191).

Within the present theoretic framework, personal experience is tantamount to the case in which the knower must rely on own epistemic authority in evaluating the validity of an inference. Whether or not such a reliance would be an effective mediator of cognitive change should depend on whether or not in the specific circumstances the knower adjudged his/her own authority as sufficient for clearly interpreting the experience. For example, a "success experience" at some task can hardly be expected to uplift one's feelings of self-efficacy if one seriously doubted one's own qualifications for pronouncing the "experienced outcomes" a success. Bandura (1977) does note that the efficacy of experiential methods is constrained by the interpretations imposed on the experiences. In the present scheme we propose to abolish the distinction between "experience" and "interpretation" and to regard both as equally conceptual or interpretative (see Popper, 1963; Weimer, 1977).

Furthermore, according to the present analysis, the knower's self-ascribed authority is merely one among several factors affecting his/her tendency to accept a given hypothesis. Other such factors are alternative authorities linked with this particular hypothesis, authorities associated with possible alternative hypotheses, the motivational significance of the hypothesis, and so on. From our perspective, the question of which of the above factors is the most effective mediator of cognitive change cannot be settled a priori. Rather, the answer would depend on the relative strengths (or levels) of those various factors in a particular set of circumstances, something that cannot be known in advance of specifying what those circumstances might be.

CONCLUSIONS

Let us conclude by briefly adumbrating the unique image of therapy implied by the present analysis. First and foremost, this would be a highly contingent kind of therapy that would derive particular treatment procedures from the patient's specific circumstances. Two separate aspects of those circumstances would have to be diagnosed: The patient's unique *epistemic characteristics* and his unique *frustrative hypotheses.* By epistemic characteristics we mean, for example, the epistemic authorities revered by the patient and his epistemically relevant needs. Those would furnish the basis for deciding *how* to conduct cognitive therapy with a particular patient. But one also would need to know *what* should be the aim of therapy in a particular instance. Thus, it is necessary to identify the patient's frustrative beliefs and to determine whether the most efficient way of their modification might involve an *assessment shift*, a *means shift*, or, perhaps, a *goal shift.*

Subsequent treatment would be closely tailored to the patient's epistemic style and the kind of cognitive shift that seems most indicated. For example, a patient with a particular respect for expert authority might be profitably exposed to individual sessions with the therapist. A patient with a high regard for group authority might more profitably be exposed to therapy in group settings. And a patient with high confidence in his/her own expertise or authority in a given area might be profitably exposed to relevant personal experiences. The patient's dysfunctional beliefs would be addressed from the viewpoint of the conclusional needs they might be tacitly serving. An attempt might be made to convince the patient that those very beliefs may lead to the frustration of other important beliefs and/or that the needs implicitly assumed to be served by the dysfunctional beliefs can be fulfilled more efficiently otherwise. An appropriate use would be made of the patient's validity and structure needs at the respective stages of unfreezing and refreezing of the appropriate beliefs, and so on.

Further analysis beyond the present scope would show that the lay-epistemic approach to cognitive therapy at once provides an integrative framework for disparate schools of cognitive therapy active today, and it identifies the limiting conditions under which different cognitive therapeutic techniques may or may not apply. Admittedly, so far the lay-epistemic model for cognitive therapy is at the blueprint state; to benefit from its potential, it is necessary to conduct research on its various derivations and to translate its theoretical constructs onto concrete procedures at the levels of diagnosis as well as treatment. Efforts in these directions are already underway.

SUMMARY

The task of cognitive therapy is to effect some kind of cognitive change in the patient. This chapter considers the "how" and the "what" of such change: The *process* whereby the required change may be brought about and the unique *essence* of such change, respectively. A basic assumption that we make is that there is nothing unusual or qualitatively special about the way in which the neurotic patient arrives at his/her inferences. Rather, his ills are assumed to stem from the particular contents of those inferences. It is they that need to be changed and the way in which they can be must follow from the rules that govern all cognitive change. Those rules are addressed from a theoretical perspective on lay epistemology developed recently by Kruglanski (1980). The present theory of lay epistemology is grounded in several assumptions about knowledge characteristic of a modern philosophical position called nonjustificationism.

As far as the process of cognitive change is concerned, the theory assumes that knowledge is made of propositions. Propositions are made of concepts, and concepts are "universals": Each concept is infinitely divisible into its own particular instances. Any given bit of knowledge may be characterized on two dimensions—(1) the content of the proposition; (2) the confidence with which the proposition is being held or the subjective probability of it being true. For each concept there exist infinite items of relevant evidence, having to do with the infinite separate particular instances of the concepts in question. But at any given point one could only have checked a finite number of evidential items. Therefore, the possibility of having erred is everpresent in all knowledge, and we may not estimate the degree to which our propositions represent the objective reality. Therefore, any knowledge that we may have constitutes a *bias*—that is, a subjectively-based preference for a given proposition over possible alternative propositions that could be accounting for the same past evidence in different ways and have different implications regarding future yet unchecked items of relevant evidence.

The theory postulates an epistemic sequence consisting of (1) the phase of hypothesis generation, which is related to the stream of consciousness and the availability of ideas, and (2) the phase of hypothesis evaluation, which is governed by the principle of logical consistency. A hypothesis the implication of which turns out to be logically consistent with the evidence would be believed in more strongly than a hypothesis contradicted by the evidence. However, consistency with past evidence is only a necessary, not a sufficient, condition for the experience of confidence. Two major categories of additional conditions, called the *braking mechanisms of hypothesis generation*, affect the individual's tendency to continue or discontinue the generation of alternative hypotheses on a given topic. One such category is the *epistemic authority* of the source wherefrom a given cognition originated; ascription of a given hypothesis to a highly esteemed authority would inhibit the process of generating further alternative hypotheses. The second category is made of the knower's *epistemically relevant motivations*, primarily: (1) the *need of structure*, which is the need to have some knowledge on a given topic, any knowledge, as opposed to a state of ambiguity; (2) the *fear of invalidity*, which is the fear of making a mistake, given the price expected to be paid for one; and (3) the *need of conclusional contents*, which refers to the individual's desire to fulfill a given wish or attain a given goal.

The "what" of cognitive therapy, according to the present conception, is called a frustrative hypothesis. This is the belief that one has failed or will fail to attain an important goal. Such a cognition is dysfunctional in that it causes suffering to the individual. From the present perspective, then, the object of cognitive therapy is to persuade the patient to change his/her frustrative hypothesis. A frustrative hypothesis contains the elements of a goal, a means to that goal, and a relation of inefficiency connecting the two. Accordingly, the frustrative hypothesis could be profitably modified via (1) an *assessment shift*, that is, a change in the perceived relation of inefficiency between the current means and goal to one of perceived efficiency; (2) a *goal shift*, that is, a change in the person's goal to a more readily attainable objective, given the individual's resources; (3) a *means shift*, that is, a change in the person's means of getting to the goal to a more efficient one.

Some important distinctions of the lay-epistemic model from alternative approaches to cognitive therapy are presently noted. Firstly, the model denies the assumption that the thinking of disturbed individuals is distorted and biased and that in order to alleviate the pain and suffering the distortion needs to be rectified; also, the implied relation between conceptual accuracy and well-being is rejected, and it is assumed that the "truth" of inferences can never be guaranteed. Secondly, the model stays uncommitted to specific contents of frustrative hypotheses. Since there can be an infinite number of such hypotheses, any attempt to list or categorize them would be arbitrary and nonunique and is likely to render the therapist insensitive to the patient's unique frustrative beliefs. Finally, unlike some other approaches, the model does not assume the primacy of behavior or personal experience in the mediation of cognitive change. Personal experience is tantamount to the case in which the knower must rely on own epistemic authority in evaluating the validity of an inference. Whether or not such a reliance would be an effective mediator of cognitive change should depend on whether or not in the specific circumstances the knower adjudged his/her own authority as sufficient for clearly interpreting the experience.

In conclusion, a scheme for the conduct of cognitive therapy is outlined as implied by the lay-epistemic model of the process and contents of therapy based on cognitive change.

REFERENCES

Arnkoff, D. B. Psychotherapy from the perspective of cognitive therapy. In M. J. Mahoney (Ed.), *Psychotherapy process: Current issues and future directions.* New York: Plenum, 1980.

Bandura, A. Self-efficacy: Toward a unifying theory of behavioral change. *Psychological Review*, 1977, *84*, 191–215.

Bartley, W. W., III. *The retreat to commitment.* New York: Knopf, 1962.

Beck, A. T. *Cognitive therapy and the emotional disorders.* New York: International Universities Press, 1976.

Beck, A. T., Rush, A. J., Shaw, B. F., & Emery, G. *Cognitive therapy of depression.* Chichester, England: Wiley, 1980.

Davison, G. C. And now for something completely different: Cognition and little r. In M. J. Mahoney (Ed.), *Psychotherapy process: Current issues and future directions.* New York: Plenum, 1980.

Ellis, A. *Reason and emotion in psychotherapy.* New York: Lyle Stuart, 1962.

Ellis, A. Rational-emotive therapy. In R. Corsini (Ed.), *Current psychotherapies.* Itasca, IL: Peacock, 1973.

Ellis, A. The basic clinical theory of rational-emotive therapy. In A. Ellis & R. Grieger (Eds.), *Handbook of rational-emotive therapy.* New York: Springer, 1977.

Haley, J., & Hoffman, L. *Techniques of family therapy.* New York: Basic Books, 1967.

Kopel, S., & Arkowitz, H. The role of attribution and self-perception in behavior change: Implications for behavior therapy. *Genetic Psychology Monographs*, 1975, *92*, 178–212.

Kruglanski, A. W. Lay epistemo-logic—process and contents. *Psychological Review*, 1980, *87*, 70–87.

Kruglanski, A. W., & Jaffe, Y. Lay epistemology: A theory for cognitive therapy. In L. Y. Abramson (Ed.), *An attributional perspective in clinical psychology.* New York: Guildford, in press.

Kuhn, T. S. Logic of discovery of psychology of research? In I. Lakatos & A. Musgrave (Eds.), *Criticism and the growth of knowledge.* Cambridge MA: Cambridge University Press, 1970.

Lazarus, R. S. Cognitive behavior therapy as psychodynamics revisited. In M. J. Mahoney (Ed.), *Psychotherapy process: Current issues and future directions.* New York: Plenum, 1980.

Lewinsohn, P. M., Mischel, W., Chaplin, W., & Barton, R. Social competence and depression: The role of illusory self-perceptions? *Journal of Abnormal Psychology*, 1980, *89*, 203–212.

Mahoney, M. J. *Cognition and behavior modification.* Cambridge, MA: Ballinger, 1974.

Meichenbaum, D. *Cognitive-behavior modification: An integrative approach.* New York: Plenum, 1977.

Minuchin, S. *Families and family therapy.* London: Tavistock, 1974.

Mischel, W. On the interface of cognition and personality: Beyond the person-situation debate. *American Psychologist*, 1979, *34*, 740–754.

Popper, K. R. *Conjectures and refutations.* New York: Basic Books, 1963.

Popper, K. R. *Objective knowledge: An evolutionary approach.* Oxford: Clarendon, 1972.

Raimy, V. *Misunderstandings of the self: Cognitive psychotherapy and the misconception hypothesis.* San Francisco, CA: Jossey-Bass, 1975.

Weimer, W. B. *Psychology and the conceptual foundations of science.* Hillsdale, NJ: Lawrence Erlbaum Associates, 1977.

Weimer, W. B. Psychotherapy and philosophy of science: Examples of a two-way street in search of traffic. In M. J. Mahoney (Ed.), *Psychotherapy process: Current issues and future directions.* New York: Plenum, 1980.

Wolpe, J. *The dichotomy between cognitive and emotional sources of anxiety.* Keynote address at the First World Congress on Behaviour Therapy, Jerusalem, July, 1980.

CHAPTER 13

Issues in Cognitive-Behavior Therapy with Children

W. Edward Craighead, Ph.D.
Andrew W. Meyers, Ph.D.
Linda Wilcoxon-Craighead, Ph.D.
Susan M. McHale, Ph.D.

Cognitive behavior therapy with children emerged out of the behavior therapy movement in the late 1960s and early 1970s. A number of factors interacted in a complex way during a brief time span to lead to its development. The influence of cognitive psychology was evident in cognitive explanations of modeling effects, in the role of the language development literature in self-instruction training, and in the development of clinical procedures based on problem solving. Additional influential factors were the evolution of cognitive explanations of self-control and the development of Ellis's and Beck's cognitive therapy (see Craighead, in press).

The rapid development of cognitive behavior therapy with children during the 1970s has spawned several summary reviews (Craighead, Wilcoxon-Craighead, & Meyers, 1978; Hobbs et al., 1980; Urbain & Kendall, 1980). These papers and the research upon which they were based have highlighted a number of issues. The purposes of this chapter are to provide an organization of those issues and to summarize the data germane to them. As will be obvious to the reader, the empirical data are frustratingly sparse, especially on some issues, and the proportion of speculation to data is large. However, a discussion of the issues seems warranted in order to bring them into clearer focus and to provide a heuristic framework for their further discussion and empirical evaluation.

The issues or problem areas appear to center around three main themes; additionally, there are several associated, overarching issues. Consequently, we will discuss the issues relevant to cognitive behavior therapy and research with children within the context of the following four problem areas: (1) identification of clinically relevant treatment targets; (2) development of adequate assessment devices; (3) fitting the level of the treatment program to the target behaviors; and, (4) overarching problems such as the developmental level of the client, generalization of treatment effects, locus of intervention, and the role of paraprofessionals in treatment.

IDENTIFICATION OF CLINICALLY RELEVANT TARGET BEHAVIORS

One of the major contributions of behavior therapy to clinical psychology has been its emphasis on the operational definitions of target behaviors—the specification of the variable whose modification will provide a solution to the client's problem. Cognitive behavior therapy has retained this emphasis on the necessity of a clear definition of the target for change; however, in contrast to the classical behavioral emphasis on overt, observable behaviors, the target behavior within this framework may be an internal or cognitive variable that only the client can observe.

Deciding what is to be changed is a complicated matter. To the neophyte the answer is easy—the therapist changes the problem behavior as the client has presented it. However, it takes only a little clinical experience to know that it is not that simple. When doing therapy with children, the therapist must decide whether the child's behavior is the problem, whether the parents' perception of a behavior is the problem, or whether the presenting problem is a reflection of deviant family dynamics, to mention only a few of the factors affecting this decision.

Current research in cognitive behavior therapy with children has focused on the treatment of specific target behaviors (Hobbs et al., 1980). Very little attention has been paid either to the rationale for the choice of treatment targets or to the use of these procedures in a preventive manner. This raises two issues: (1) the relationship of the treated targets to current psychopathology; and (2) the relationship of current targets to future adjustment.

Issue 1: The Relationship of Treatment Targets to Current Psychopathology

Reflecting societal concerns with children in general, little attention was devoted until this century to childhood psychopathology. The increased emphasis on children's problems is evident in the evolution of the Diagnostic and Statistical Manual of the American Psychiatric Association. DSM-I gave childhood disorders cursory treatment by including only a few of them with their respective adult syndromes. DSM-II (APA, 1968) listed "Behavior Disorders of Childhood and Adolescence" and "Transient Situational Disorders" (which included primarily problems of childhood and adolescence) among its ten categories of psychopathology. DSM-III (APA, 1980) carries the emphasis on childhood disorders a step further by retaining a separate category, entitled "Disorders Usually First Evident in Infancy, Childhood, or Adolescence," and additionally suggesting that most adult categories, such as affective disorders and schizophrenia, can be applied to childhood problems.

Although the expansion of diagnostic categories reflects an increased concern for children's problems, classification using standard nosologies such as DSM-III or the one recommended by the Group for the Advancement of Psychiatry (1966) has raised the same issues as those raised in diagnostic classification with adults. In the main, classification has been unreliable when specific subcategories are diagnosed, diagnoses do not have good predictive validity for treatment planning, and they may produce iatrogenic effects for the labeled child.

The picture is not quite so bleak, however, when one considers the recent empirical work regarding childhood psychopathology. An empirical approach to childhood disorders is consistent with the assumptions of methodological behaviorism, which characterize cognitive behavior therapy. The point is illustrated clearly in the following summaries of two investigations. These examples suggest simultaneously that: (1) there may be good reasons for the favorite treatment targets of cognitive behavior therapists; (2) additional target behaviors are urgently in need of study; (3) a methodology should be devised for determining empirically what behaviors need to be changed.

In a large-scale project, Achenbach and Edelbrock (1981) attempted to ascertain which childhood problems, as rated by parents, determine whether or not a child is brought to the attention of mental-health professionals. Their data were based on 1,300 children referred for treatment at outpatient mental health centers and 1,300 carefully matched, nonreferred children. The major behavior problems that discriminated between the two groups were "unhappy, sad, depressed" and "poor school work." The reported incidence of other commonly treated problems, such as "fears certain animals, situations, or places" and "wets the bed," did not differ for referred and nonreferred children. Although the categories need further differentiation for intervention planning, a point to be considered later, they do suggest categories of clinical significance. Since "poor school work" was one of the major discriminators between the two groups, it is probably not accidental that behavioral and cognitive-behavioral therapists have directed a great deal of effort toward the alleviation of academic problems. The recent increase in empirical investigations of childhood depression reflects the importance of the second problem area. These problem areas might have been addressed earlier and more systematically, had greater attention been paid to the general childhood psychopathology literature.

The second example, which is drawn from the area of social skills training with children, illustrates the effectiveness of an empirically based methodology for determining the targets of treatment. Using such a procedure, investigators identify groups of individuals who are disparate on some clinically significant problem and then identify the specific remediable behaviors and/or cognitions that differentiate those groups. By using sociometric data to define socially skilled children, Gottman, Gonso, and Rasmussen (1975) identified four variables that discriminated socially successful from socially unsuccessful subjects. Successful children exhibited higher rates of greetings, asking for and giving information, extending an offer for others to be included in an ongoing activity, and effective leave-taking behaviors. Thus, social skills training geared to these target behaviors would be more likely to produce socially skillful children than would social skills training that focused on other specific behaviors such as smiling, eye contact, voice volume, and speech fluency, which have characterized much of the previous work with children and adults (see Eisler & Frederikson, 1980). Although these latter behaviors may intuitively seem important, they have not been related empirically to social competence.

These examples suggest that cognitive behavior therapy could expand and enhance its contribution to the alleviation of childhood disorders by focusing on those behaviors directly associated with clinically relevant psychopathology research. We are not suggesting a return to a medical model classification system, but rather a greater awareness of and sensitivity to the empirical work in psychopathology—work that guides the clinician in the selection of appropriate target behaviors.

Issue 2: The Relationship of Treatment Targets to Preventive Interventions

As noted in Craighead's (in press) review of historical changes within the field of behavior therapy, the focus of therapeutic intervention has changed in recent years from an emphasis on correcting deviant behavior to a concern for instilling in individuals new behaviors or skills. This new approach magnifies the problem of selecting the appropriate target of intervention. A focus on pathology requires that the therapist identify current deviant behavior as the target of treatment. Adapting a skills training approach, on the other hand, involves an implicit assumption that the behavior or set of behaviors to be trained is related to future, positive adjustment. Not only must positive adjustment be defined, but skills predictive of it must also be identified. This approach is preventive because the client's employment of these trained skills is presumed to decrease the likelihood of future problematic behavior.

Furman (1980) has noted that choices of target behaviors for preventive intervention are often made on the basis of subjective judgments. Alternatively, more effective decisions could be based on empirical evidence derived from an understanding of child development; that is, from the knowledge of developmental precursors of adaptive behaviors in particular domains of functioning. Preventive interventions based on the skills training approach would be best established by making use of the predictive power inherent in developmental models of behavior and the empirically established relationships among behaviors exhibited at different points in development. For example, theorists focusing on the mother/child relationship have hypothesized that certain forms of mother/child social behavior predict the child's later social functioning, and these theorists have provided correlational evidence demonstrating that contingent responsiveness in mother/infant interaction is related to the child's problem-solving skill and peer competence at the ages of two and five (Arend, Gove, & Sroufe, 1979; Matas, Arend, & Sroufe, 1978; Sroufe, 1979). Similarly, popularity with peers during the school-age years appears to be related to adjustment in later life (Cowen et al., 1973). This approach is illustrated in the work of Gottman et al. (1975) who specified the behavioral correlates of peer popularity in devising a social skills training program for school-age children.

As an alternative to choosing behaviors predictive of later adaptive functioning, skills training procedures may take the approach of fostering behaviors to improve current functioning. Although such an approach may be preventive of future difficulty, the major emphasis is on enhancement of current levels of functioning in nonpathological children. Again, developmental models may be helpful in that they may define skills that are developmental precursors of a desired behavior. An essential component of self-control is, for example, the ability to employ personal standards to evaluate one's performance (Furman, 1980). This ability develops with age and may be related to another developing tendency that has been observed in children, namely, their shift from responding to social reinforcement (praise) to responding to the "correctness" of their behavior (Zigler & Kanzer, 1962). A third, simultaneously developing cognitive ability, means/end reasoning, may underlie both of these changes. That is, preschool children may fail to grasp the connection between their behavior (means) and a desired outcome (end) because of their underdeveloped reasoning ability, making the "correctness" of problem solutions meaningless as a reinforcer. Thus, before a child is reinforced by achieving a correct answer and before a child is capable of self-evaluation, it may be essential to train the requisite reasoning abilities. These reasoning abilities, in turn, may be prerequisites for the success of self-control training procedures. Further discussion of the appropriateness of a developmental approach for prediction across age and across behavioral domains is presented at a later point in this chapter.

DEVELOPMENT OF ADEQUATE ASSESSMENT INSTRUMENTS

During the 1960s the major emphasis in behavior therapy with children was operant; consequently, the major focus of assessment instruments was on observable behavior. As was noted earlier, behaviors were often defined in an arbitrary and idiosyncratic manner. Even though this problem may have affected the external validity of many studies, research employing such scales typically reported good interrater reliability and minimal effects of observer bias, experimental demand, and so on. With the advent of cognitive behavior therapy, however, the situation regarding assessment has changed. In addition to behavioral observational data, experimenters have employed more global teacher- and parent-rating scales and more "traditional" individual assessment devices. For example, attempts have been made to assess such internal variables as self-statements, mental imagery, and problem-solving processes. This approach has raised the following issues related to the appropriate use of adequate assessment devices.

Issue 3:
Psychometric Properties of Assessment Instruments

The development of assessment devices beyond observational scales necessitates the employment of a number of well-established measurement principles; adequate psychometric properties must be established for an assessment instrument before it can be appropriately employed. Even such fundamental issues as normative data and reliability have not been addressed for some frequently employed measures. Of course, cognitive behavior therapists do not have a corner on this market!

Two examples will clearly illustrate the point. First, minimal criteria for a reliable assessment instrument include a report of internal consistency of split-half reliability and stability (test-retest). Unless a measure possesses adequate reliability, it will not be systematically related to the variable it, in fact, purports to measure, nor can it vary systematically in response to treatment. With the exception of instruments borrowed from other areas of research (such as the MFFT in Egeland & Weinberg, 1976, and the Childhood Behavior Checklist in Achenbach, 1978 and Achenbach & Edelbrock, 1979), assessment instruments for which adequate reliability, validity, and normative data exist are generally not available; although recent recognition of this problem and research efforts in this area have produced some improvements (Achenbach & Edelbrock, 1978; Kendall & Hollon, 1981).

Second, several children's assessment devices employed by cognitive behavior therapists have been submitted to factor analysis with little or no attention paid even to basic issues such as the ratio of items to subjects, cross-validation, and gender and age of subjects (see Comrey, 1978). For example, Kendall and Wilcox (1979) developed a much-needed rating scale of self-control. It contains 33 items; the original factor analysis was based on teacher ratings of 106 children, and the factor structure was not cross-validated. However, good reliability, normative data, and external validity were reported for this scale.

It is not being suggested that such assessment instruments should not be used; on the contrary, they are essential to the development of the field on both practical and conceptual levels. Progress will be limited, however, until assessment measures with adequate psychometric properties are designed. If we are going to develop psychological tests, then this must be done according to well-established procedures of test construction (Wiggins, 1973).

Issue 4: Assessment of Target Behaviors

Once clinically-relevant, newly-identified target behaviors are identified, assessment instruments should be developed to measure them. If one predicts change in domains other than overt motor behavior, then it is imperative to measure change in those domains. Although adequate measures of cognitive/intellectual functioning have been developed, comparatively little effort has gone into the construction of measures of social/emotional development and dysfunction.

Several recently developed scales have been designed to measure variables that cognitive-behaviorists consider to be of clinical and conceptual importance. For example, the Hahnemann Medical College group (Spivack, Platt, & Shure, 1976), which was studying applications of problem-solving procedures with preschool children, developed measures for each of the levels of problem solving they attempted to train. These measures included the Preschool Interpersonal Problem-Solving Test (PIPS), to measure preschool children's ability to generate alternative solutions to problems, the "What Happens Next Game" (WHNG) to measure consequential thinking in preschoolers, and the Means-Ends Problem Solving Test (MEPS) to measure the ability of middle childhood youngsters to plan a route toward solving a problem.

As important findings from other areas of psychology such as developmental and psychopathology become available, relevant new measures must follow. For example, Achenbach and Edelbrock's

(1981) findings regarding the important role of depression in children referred to outpatient mental health centers underscores the need for research in that rapidly developing area (Schulterbrandt & Raskin, 1977). Before research in psychopathology and intervention can progress, however, adequate assessment instruments of childhood depression must be developed. The Kiddie-SADS, a structured interview based on the adult SADS (Endicott & Spitzer, 1978), and the Childhood Depression Inventory (Kovacs, personal communication, 1980), which is a downward extension of the widely used adult Beck Depression Inventory, are initial attempts to construct such measures (cf. Orvaschel, Weissman, & Kidd, in press). However, even basic information on reliability, validity, and normative data for these tests is not yet available.

Issue 5: Assessment Instruments Responsive to Treatment

Care must be taken to ensure that changes in the variables of interest will be reflected in changes in the data provided by the assessment instrument. Before such measures are used to evaluate clinical trials, it is important not only to identify their psychometric properties but also to demonstrate that clinical populations differ from normal and appropriate pathological control groups.

When dependent variables are conceptually related to treatment effects, the measures of the dependent variables should be responsive to treatment. If one evaluates a program designed to teach increasingly adaptive types of play activity, then it is important to define and measure each level of play. For example, one might use Rubin's (Rubin, Maioni, & Hornung, 1976; Rubin, Watson, & Jambor, 1978) combination of the Parten (1933) and Smilansky (1968) scales as a measure of play. Parten (1933) defined six levels of play: unoccupied, solitary, onlooker, parallel, associative, and cooperative. Smilansky's (1968) categories rated children's involvement with toys and games and included: functional, constructive, dramatic, and games or play with rules. Rubin's combination of these scales resulted in 24 categories, which have been validated against several measures of social and cognitive competence (Rubin & Maioni, 1975). This scale provides scores for each type of play and could be used to evaluate the effects of the treatment program designed to teach more adaptive play skills. Measures of this type should assist in the clarification of the relationship between outcome effects and the treatment variable.

Issue 6: Measurement of Independent Variables

In the analogy between conducting an empirical investigation and the cognitive-behavioral approach to clinical intervention, the independent variable corresponds to the treatment or therapy program

(Craighead, Kazdin, & Mahoney, 1981). It is in this correspondence between the treatment program and the independent variable that it is suggested that measures of the "independent variable" need to be developed.

It is by the satisfactory assessment of the treatment program itself that conceptually relevant conclusions can be drawn from clinical outcome studies. When such measures are taken and related to dependent measure changes, more satisfactory conclusions regarding the mechanisms of clinical change can be drawn. Such data might be used to rule out alternative explanations of treatment effects without resorting to the use of placebo control groups and the associated ethical and methodological problems (O'Leary & Borkovec, 1978).

Issue 7: Multimethod Assessment

Several methods exist for assessing childhood problems. These include behavioral observations, ratings by others such as parents and teachers, peer evaluations such as sociometric data, and individual standardized tests of social, emotional, behavioral, and cognitive (intellectual) functioning. Several examples of instruments exist for each of these measurement areas. Very little is known about the interrelationships of those instruments that presumably measure the same variable when they are obtained by these different methods. In fact, very little is known about the relationships of different measures of the same variable within the same general method of assessment—for example, no direct comparisons exist for the peer rating and peer nomination procedures of obtaining sociometric data (Foster & Ritchey, 1979).

The interrelationships among the various measures of specific variables need to be defined. Such information would be of significance in: (1) understanding the nature of the presenting problem—is the behavior problematic to the child him/herself or to the parents or teacher? (2) developing a treatment program germane to the identified problem; and (3) specifying the method of data collection for obtaining treatment outcome information. In the area of social skills with preschoolers, for example, the following assessment package might allow these measurement objectives to be obtained: behavioral observations based on the manual by Shapiro and Ogilvie (1976) and including measures of play behavior (cf. Rubin et al., 1976; Rubin et al., 1978); sociometric ratings based on all paired-comparisons of the subjects' social group (Vaughn & Waters, 1981); PIPS as a measure of interpersonal problem solving (Spivack & Shure, 1974); the Kendall and Wilcox (1979) Self-control Scale; a measure of intellectual functioning; the 39-item Conners Teacher Rating Scale (Conners, 1973); and the Child Behavior Checklist (Achenbach, 1978; Achenbach & Edelbrock, 1979) for parent ratings.

All these measures are relevant to current conceptual and treatment issues in social skills training with both normal and handicapped children (Asher & Hymel, in press; Gresham, 1981). Normative data on these, as well as other measures of interest to cognitive-behavior therapists, allow one to determine not only whether one treatment is comparatively more effective than another, but also the level of functioning of groups of subjects and individuals within groups. Understanding the interrelationships of these measures will provide a better operational definition of social skills, suggest appropriate treatment strategies, and identify relevant treatment outcome measures.

FITTING THE LEVEL OF THE TREATMENT PROGRAM TO THE TARGET BEHAVIORS

Issues confronting the clinician in two phases of therapeutic intervention, problem identification and assessment, have been examined. In the following section of this chapter, a third component of intervention—determining the target of cognitive behavioral treatments—will be considered. The basic issue to be discussed is the degree of specificity of intervention targets. Techniques in cognitive behavior modification range from teaching particular self-instruction strategies to modifying subjects' general cognitive style.

Issue 8: Specificity of Targets for Change

Meichenbaum and Asarnow (1979) suggested that the active use of self-instruction assists the subject in organizing task information and generating alternative problem solutions; provides verbal mediators enabling the subject to distinguish relevant task dimensions; facilitates the subject's retention of task demands in short-term memory; and enhances positive task orientation. These functions should improve the subject's problem-solving skills, and, indeed, evidence of self-instruction treatment efficacy is promising. However, as Meichenbaum and Asarnow (1978) indicated, evidence for treatment generalization across response modes and settings is equivocal. The failure to find generalization of self-instruction treatment gains is now widespread and raises the question of whether changes produced by self-instruction interventions are actual modifications of the child's cognitive style or superficial changes in specific task responses.

This question has prompted a number of recommendations to develop more impactful cognitive training strategies. Meichenbaum and Asarnow (1978) suggested that self-instruction interventions must focus directly on generalization training. Brown (1978) urged that we train children how to think rather than what to think. Brown hypothesized that training a set rule or procedure can produce significant task performance improvement without fostering an understanding of why a solution was effective or when and how to apply a particular strategy. Brown suggested that the child be trained in the use and maintenance of cognitive strategies, with an emphasis on teaching the child why and on which tasks the strategies are effective and when not to apply the strategies. That is, such an approach implies both generalization and discrimination training: generalization in that skills applicable in a variety of situations are learned, and discrimination in that appropriate contexts for the exhibition of a particular skill are recognized.

Generalized problem-solving strategies have been included in the category of metacognitive phenomena, which encompass the functions of self-awareness, prediction, planning, checking, and monitoring (Brown, 1978). Brown asserted that the individual must be aware of self as a thinking agent; must be able to assess situational and task demands and their interaction with his or her cognitive capacities in order to predict and plan the efficacious use of cognitive strategies; and must be able to monitor performance and be aware that the solution to a problem can be checked in a variety of ways and that all checks must agree. These introspective phenomena extend beyond the areas of problem solving and cognitive development to the domains of social cognition, role taking, interpersonal communication, self-concept, learned helplessness, and locus of control (Brown, 1978). Bandura's (1977) recent discussion of the concept of self-efficacy fits easily into a metacognitive framework. The importance of focusing explicitly on the development of these component behaviors in therapy is considered in a later section of this chapter.

Few studies have attempted to train directly metacognitive skills. Schleser, Meyers, and Cohen (1981), using six-year-olds, compared a task-specific (again, Matching Familiar Figures) self-instruction package with a meta or general problem-solving self-instruction strategy, a didactic instruction, and a no-treatment control group on a trained task (Matching Familiar Figures) and a nontrained generalization task (a perspective-taking task). Both self-instruction groups contained problem identification, self-guidance, monitoring and checking, self-reinforcement, and coping components. The didactic instruction contained the same task-relevant information except for the active rehearsal, self-instruction components. The results indicated that self-instructions were necessary for improvement on the trained task and that metacognitive self-instructions were necessary for improvement on the generalization task. The inclusion of a didactic instruction control group confirmed the necessity of active involvement of the child in the self-instruction intervention.

Schleser et al. (1981) argued that subjects in the specific self-instruction group showed no generalization, because they were asked to apply a cognitive strategy without a great deal of cognitive involvement—what Meichenbaum and Asarnow (1978) refer to as "mental transformation" of the task or what Piaget has referred to as "operative" knowledge. These subjects apply their strategies to tasks in a "blind rule" manner, and consequently they gain little experience in planning and modifying the strategy. The metacognitive self-instructions give the subject a general problem-solving approach, which they must modify and experiment with on the training task. This exposure and practice prepares them to modify their problem-solving strategies in response to the novel aspects of the generalization task.

The findings of Schleser et al. (1981) and a similar study by Kendall and Wilcox (1980) suggest directions for future research in this area. In both studies, metacognitive strategies force the child actively to manipulate problem-solving approaches. Piaget has often conceptualized understanding as the ability to manipulate a concept actively (the concept of operative knowledge). In empirically testing this concept, Blank and Solomon (1968) showed, for example, that socially disadvantaged preschool children who experienced an exploratory instructional dialogue performed better than didactic instruction groups on conflict resolution tasks. This leads us to conclude that subjects who "discover" problem-solving strategies should demonstrate more generalized task improvement.

In a second study with six-year-olds, Schleser et al. (1981) tested the efficacy of "learning by discovery" in the context of self-instruction training. These investigators compared a group that "discovered" task-relevant self-instructions through a dialogue with a specific self-instruction group (where instructions were delivered in the traditional fading manner), a didactic instruction, and a no-treatment control group. All groups were tested on a trained task (Matching Familiar Figures) and an untrained generalization task (a perspective-taking task). Furthermore, subjects were matched for age and then classified as Piagetian preoperational or concrete operational by their performance on two conservation tasks. The subjects in the two control groups showed no significant improvement on either task; the performance of subjects in the specific self-instruction group replicated earlier findings by showing significant improvements on the trained task but not on the generalization task. In the discovery condition, concrete operational subjects improved significantly on both tasks and performed significantly better than all other groups on the generalization task. Preoperational subjects did not show this improvement. These findings indicate that for those subjects with adequate cognitive capacity the discovery procedure was able to facilitate the development of a general problem-solving strategy. Research in this area should continue to develop such metacognitive training strategies for child-clinical, developmental-cognitive, and socioeconomic categories and groups.

OVERARCHING PROBLEMS

Thus far we have described a number of issues associated with the identification, assessment, and treatment phases of cognitive behavioral interventions with children. Additionally, there are several general issues that cut across all phases of intervention. The contributions of a developmental view of children's behavior to assessment and treatment procedures will be discussed in the next section. This will be followed by a consideration of the relationship of behavioral and cognitive skills and the more pragmatic concerns of the role of parents and other nonprofessionals in clinical interventions and decision making regarding the locus of intervention.

Issue 9: Adoption of a Developmental Approach

A predominant characteristic of childhood is change. In identifying problem behaviors, children are compared with others of their age group, but descriptions of a given child's relative strengths and weaknesses may vary considerably across childhood. Thus, the child who has temper tantrums or is more aggressive than her peers in preschool may not demonstrate an exceptional amount of aggression as an adolescent. Similarly, the shy and withdrawn toddler may play well with his peers when he enters school. This concept of continuity and change is one of the key issues confronting developmental psychologists. Taking a developmental-clinical perspective in assessment, one would determine where a certain behavior lies in a developmental sequence of immature to mature functioning in a given domain. Taking a developmental approach to treatment, one would attempt to foster in children those behaviors that have a demonstrated empirical relationship to later adaptive functioning.

1. Children's behavior is viewed within the context of normal development; the clinician should focus on the appropriate behaviors children exhibit within a particular domain of functioning.
2. Children's behavior is placed in the context of a developmental sequence that provides, implicitly, the knowledge of what skills children already possess and what skills they have yet to acquire.
3. Children's behavior in one domain of functioning is viewed in the context of other developmental achievements. The assumption that development within different domains of functioning occurs in synchrony (such that, for example, language, social, play, and motor skills typical of a four-year-old are exhibited concurrently) may not be valid in the case of a particular child.
4. Finally, a developmental approach focuses on the processes underlying a particular behavior or set of behaviors. Again, rather than viewing particular behaviors in isolation, the goal is,

instead, to define functional relationships both among behaviors occurring in sequence during development and among behaviors in different domains of functioning at any given point in development. Such a tack would allow for a preventive approach to treatment by identifying specific delays within behavioral domains or dissynchronies in rates of development across domains before these disturbances become problematic to the child.

The importance of a developmental approach in three steps of clinical intervention—identifying problems, assessing children's level of functioning, and determining the direction to be taken by imposed behavior changes, that is, deciding what new behaviors should be fostered—have each been discussed. An additional application of a developmental approach comes about in a fourth step in intervention, making decisions about intervention techniques. Although early theorists may have suggested—implicitly or explicity—that behavior modification techniques are applicable to nearly every subject (across age and even across species), more recent research suggests that the subject's cognitive level, in particular, must be taken into account as the clinician decides how to intervene. Furman (1980), for example, reviews evidence that suggests that children's responsiveness to certain reinforcement and punishment techniques, as well as their responsiveness to certain components of modeling procedures directed at modifying behavior, change developmentally. The importance of considering a child's developmental status in deciding upon treatment techniques is particularly salient in self-instruction training with children.

The impetus for much of self-instruction training came from Luria's (1961) work on the relationship between verbal and motor behaviors. Luria suggested a three-stage theory of language development, in which the child's verbal behavior gradually comes to control motor responses. In the first stage, from birth to age two, the child does not spontaneously emit self-directing verbalizations, and motor responses are controlled by external cues. From the age of two to five, the child spontaneously emits self-directing verbalization and exerts some control over gross motor responses, though this control is still largely dependent on external cues. During the final stage, from the age of five on, the child utilizes covert speech and regulates some behavior by internal verbal cues.

Theoretical discussions of the role of "private speech" and the relationships between language and thought have appeared in the literature (for example, Piaget, 1926 and 1962; Vygotsky, 1962) and critical tests of these conflicting views have provided equivocal results (as in Kohlberg, Yaeger, & Hjertholm, 1968). Clinical evaluations of self-instruction training based on Luria's model have also produced conflicting results (Craighead, Wilcoxon-Craighead, & Meyers, 1978). A study by Meichenbaum and Goodman (1969), however, illustrated the model's heuristic value. These authors found that kindergarten children given self-instruction cues on a motor task showed performance improvements when self-verbalizations were conducted aloud, but covert self-instructions had little functional control over task performance. First-graders demonstrated better performance when self-instructional cues were delivered covertly rather than overtly.

Positions such as Luria's (1961) and evidence such as Meichenbaum and Goodman's (1969) imply that, when designing self-instruction treatment programs, one must consider not only the presenting problem but also the child's initial developmental abilities and capacities. Developmental changes in areas such as memory, language, means-end reasoning, conditional thinking, categorization abilities, and children's perceptions of rules will all influence the effectiveness of cognitive behavioral strategies. White (1965) has reviewed at length some of the major changes in children's cognitive abilities between the ages of five and seven. These changes undoubtedly affect the child's responsiveness to cognitive behavioral techniques. In this regard, several authors have called for an assessment of the child's cognitive capacity in order to individualize self-instruction training (Furman, 1980; Kendall & Korgeski, 1979; Meichenbaum & Asarnow, 1978).

A most obvious tool for classifying the child's current developmental level is age. This approach is problematic, because, far from being an explanatory variable, age is only a marker variable and, as such, has no necessary relationship to aspects of the child's functioning. When one is confronted with a developmentally delayed child or a child with cognitive, motor, or emotional handicaps, the age marker itself becomes almost meaningless. For this reason, other investigators have turned to stage-dependent conceptions of child development, of which Piaget's (Inhelder & Piaget, 1964) is the most prominent. These approaches attempt to define functional relationships among skills exhibited at any period of development by postulating global processes that underlie such a set of abilities. As such, assessment of one such ability is thought to provide an indication of the child's functioning across domains. Stage theories have been criticized for adopting a nomothetic approach and thereby being unable to predict behavior on the level of the individual (see Bandura, 1977; Feldman & Toulmin, 1976). But even social learning theorists assume that the child possesses developing component cognitive functions that may be used to specify appropriate self-instruction interventions. In the following section we will briefly review several selected studies that demonstrate differential task performance resulting from age, cognitive stage, or cognitive skill.

Age-dependent performance has been found across a variety of tasks. Kagan et al. (1964) presented first- through sixth-graders with several tests of conceptual style (such as Matching Familiar Figures) and found that selections based on analytic concepts increased with age, while choices based on functional relationships between stimuli decreased with age. Such changes seem to parallel the child's shift from functional to analytic categorization, or from syntagmatic to paradigmatic word associations (White, 1965). In reviewing their concept learning experimentation, Kendler and Kendler (1962) found that college students executed reversal shifts more rapidly than nonshifts, kindergarten students performed both shifts at approximately the same rate, and preschoolers found nonreversal shifts easier. As White (1965) noted, this change may be part of the more global change in the five-to-seven period from color to form dominance.

Children's responses to instructions and models have also been influenced by subjects' ages. In addition, several investigators have reported an increasing planfulness as children mature (Appel et al., 1972; Cocking & Copple, 1978; White, 1965). Appel et al. instructed four-year-old preschoolers, seven-year-old first-graders and eleven-year-old fifth-graders either to look at or to memorize a set of slide-delivered stimuli with numbers of stimuli varied to equate task difficulty across ages. Only fifth-grade subjects showed significant differences on recall between the look and memory conditions. On two of four indices, fifth-graders also showed significantly more study behavior in the memory condition than in the look condition. Performance by first-graders was significantly different on one of four study indices, and preschoolers showed no differences between conditions. Appel et al. concluded that fifth-graders understood the memorize-look distinction both conceptually and behaviorally; first-graders understood that there was a difference but did not possess the behavioral skills to affect performance; and preschoolers did not understand the distinction conceptually or behaviorally. These developmental changes in children's performance on memory tasks reflect changes in the five-to-seven age range in children's spontaneous exhibition of covert rehearsal of, for example, word lists for memory recall tasks (Ornstein & Naus, 1978). Thus, whereas no developmental changes occur in children's performance on recognition memory tasks (a task thought to require no active covert rehearsal), when active cognitive processing is necessary for task performance (as in recall tasks) young children (of less than seven years) must be explicitly trained to use such strategies.

Laughlin, Moss, and Miller (1969) measured differences across age in modeled performance. First-, third-, and fifth-graders were shown a model who solved problems either through the use of hypothesis-scanning questions or more effective constraint-seeking questions. The constraint-seeking model decreased questions to solution, whereas the hypothesis-scanning model increased questions to solution. More importantly, there was a model by grade interaction that indicated that older children asked a greater percentage of constraint-seeking questions. Presumably, constraint-seeking questions require long-term planfulness on the part of the child, a skill the younger child may not possess. Thus, first-graders were less likely to imitate this form of problem solution.

Denney (1975) obtained similar results on problem-solving efficiency when he exposed six-, eight-, and ten-year-old children to an exemplary model, a cognitive model who verbalized problem-solving strategies, a self-rehearsal condition, and a no-model control. All three experimental treatments increased the percentage of constraint-seeking questions used by eight- and ten-year-old subjects, but only the cognitive model enabled six-year-olds to perform significantly better than controls. Denney hypothesized that eight- and ten-year-olds already possessed the strategies displayed by the cognitive model, but that six-year-olds required the cognitive model's strategy demonstration. Such changes in modeled behavior parallel changes in children's spontaneous employment of increasingly sophisticated hypothesis-testing strategies for problem solving (as in Levine, 1974).

This evidence clearly indicates that a child's age is an important consideration for constructing cognitive interventions, but as Bandura (1977) has pointed out, age may not be the best index of cognitive development. The use of developmental stages offers one alternative.

In a study detailed earlier, Schleser et al. (1981) used conservation tasks to identify the Piagetian developmental levels of first- and second-grade students. Two groups of same-age students were identified as either Piagetian preoperational or concrete operational. All subjects were given a training task (Matching Familiar Figures) and a generalization task (perspective-taking). The more developmentally advanced (concrete operation) children made more correct choices and had longer response latencies on both tasks than did preoperational children. However, only those concrete operational subjects actively involved in the training showed performance improvement on the generalization (untrained) task. The authors interpreted these results as indicating that even for same-age children, the child's cognitive capacity is a significant determinant of task performance. Whereas stage theories of cognitive development may not be able to account for all individual performance, these data indicate the importance of considering some measure of the child's cognitive capacity.

Gholson and Beilin (1979) have considered both cognitive level and cognitive skills in their presentation of a systhesis of Piaget's stage-dependent cognitive theory and conventional developmental learning theory. They hypothesized that the child brings to any task a set of sequentially organized cognitive subprocesses (for example, memory storage and retrieval, coding processes, attentional mechanisms) and an executive processor to integrate these subprocesses. Subprocesses are thought to change quantitatively with development and may be influenced by immediate training experiences. The executive processor corresponds to Piaget's operational stages and reflects the underlying cognitive schemes available to the child at a given developmental level, which, in turn, determine the kinds of solution plans the child can generate and execute. This processor changes only quantitatively, with development becoming increasingly logical and sophisticated (Gholson & Beilin, 1979).

The Gholson and Beilin model is difficult to test empirically, but it does alert us to the fact that any cognitive intervention must recognize the limits of the child's cognitive capacity and that cognitive skill development (such as improvement in retrieval from memory skills) must take place within these limits. Research on cognitive interventions should seek to operationalize the child subject's cognitive capacity and explore the interaction between intervention and cognitive skills.

Issue 10:
Relationship of Behavioral and Cognitive Skills

One implication of a developmental approach is the importance of ensuring that a child's behavioral repertoire includes the requisite skills for carrying out the tasks to be trained through cognitive behavioral techniques. That is, cognitive interventions may supply or expand the child's use of mediational strategies that facilitate skilled performance, but such interventions cannot supply those skills required for adequate performance. An experiment by Robin, Armel, and O'Leary (1975) illustrates this problem. They presented five- and six-year-old children with a novel letter-copying task and gave them either direct training that included practice, feedback, and reinforcement, self-instruction training that included direct training and self-instructional components, or no treatment. Results showed that both training groups performed significantly better than the control group and that the self-instruction group performed significantly better than the direct training group. However, none of the groups demonstrated generalization to a second, form-copying task.

Whereas the performance of the self-instruction group in this study is cause for some optimism, the experimenters reported that the self-instruction training was both difficult and time-consuming; that there was no relationship between a child's self-instruction behavior and eventual performance; and that self-instruction training accounted for only 17% of the performance variance. Robin et al. (1975) argued that these limited results may have been produced by the complicated and novel motor skill task that was not in the children's behavioral repertoire. They suggested that self-instruction strategies should help the child to overcome motor control deficiencies but are not adequate for teaching the child new motor skills. A similar point was made by Kendall (1977) when he stressed the necessity of pretraining in component task skills. This issue has been discussed in the developmental literature by Flavell and Wellman (1977), who distinguished between production and mediation deficiences. Mediation deficiencies imply a lack of competence on the part of an individual. In memory tasks, for example, young children have not yet acquired rehearsal strategies necessary for accurate recall. Production deficiencies, on the other hand, involve a failure to exhibit appropriate strategies already in the child's behavioral repertoire, even though the task requires such strategies for solution. Thus, young, school-age children will use rehearsal strategies in memory tasks when they are instructed explicitly to do so but fail to recognize spontaneously the situations in which such strategies are appropriate (Ornstein & Naus, 1978). It may be that cognitive behavioral procedures are more effective in the latter—production deficiency—than in the former—mediation deficiency—situation.

Bandura (1977) has argued that cognitive skills are developed by initially performing operations on actual objects and then translating external functions into covert symbolic ones of increasing complexity and abstraction. A further illustration of the necessity of component skills in cognitive interventions can be seen in Bandura's concept of observational learning. He stated that the amount of observational learning that will be exhibited behaviorally depends on the availability of component skills. He asserted that component cognitive (such as selective observation, memory encoding) and behavioral skills (that is, the subskills required for complex physical performance) must first be developed through maturation, modeling, and practice.

The necessity in self-instruction interventions of prior training of required physical skills is apparent, but Bandura's argument indicates that cognition as well as motor performance can be conceptualized in skill terms. This is, of course, an underlying assumption in much of the self-instruction training literature, and it suggests that component cognitive skills must also be present before mediational strategies can be utilized effectively. An example from the memory literature illustrates this point. Meacham's (1972) work indicates that children can rarely be trained, and then only temporarily, to engage in a mnemonic activity—such as clustering—that is not well formed and capable of being displayed spontaneously. Attempts to train for other kinds of cognitive operations from object permanence to conservation are, in general, equally unsuccessful.

Recognizing the need for prior training of physical and cognitive skills is central to designing productive self-instruction interventions. This recognition requires a comprehensive analysis of the cognitive and motor demands of the target tasks and an equally detailed assessment of the cognitive and motor abilities of the subject or client. Investigation in this area should identify viable task and subject assessment strategies and explore the interaction among skill deficits, task demands, skill training, and self-instruction interventions. It is clear that producing generalized behavior change in children depends on identifying those variables that contribute to this complex interaction.

Issue 11: Role of Paraprofessionals and Locus of Intervention

As we just noted, one of the potential advantages of self-instruction interventions with children is that such interventions may produce cognitive changes that enable the child to meet task demands across a variety of problems and situations (Meichenbaum, 1977). Similar generalization and maintenance of behavior change arguments have been made for the use of natural mediators as therapeutic agents. A logical addition, them to any cognitive behavioral program is the use of parents, teachers, and other natural mediators to further facilitate the generalization and maintenance of behavior change.

Douglas (1975) has argued that involving parents and teachers in the cognitive therapy process should encourage the generalization of treatment gains. Not only are new behaviors learned within the social context in which they should be exhibited, but inappropriate behaviors may also be extinguished in context, which would seemingly allow for a more rapid reduction in the occurrence of such behaviors (Guerney, Guerney, & Andronico, 1966). Similar arguments regarding speed of learning and extent of generalization may be made concerning the locus of intervention. In addition, Bandura's (1971) investigations of characteristics that make models more likely to be imitated (that is, when models are perceived as nurturant, competent, or similar to the subject) would suggest that parents and even teachers may effectively adopt the model's role in fostering new behaviors. Still another line of evidence has argued for the practicality of employing parents as agents of behavior change in their children. The positive effects of working with parents with regard to a particular child have been found to be transmitted to other children in the family (Gordon et al., 1978). Finally Flavel (1978) suggested that parents can actively facilitate the child's development of self-regulatory activity and generalized planning abilities. Despite such admonitions, few experimental efforts have actually evaluated the delivery of cognitive interventions by natural mediators.

To date, only two studies have attempted to teach parents and their children problem-solving skills. In a multiple-baseline design, Kifer et al. (1974) used rehearsal and social reinforcement training strategies to teach three parent/child pairs conflict resolution skills. An evaluation of the program revealed an increase in negotiation skills both in the experimental setting and during home observation. Robin et al. (1977) conducted a similar study in a group design. They employed instructions, modeling, feedback, and social reinforcement to teach 12 parent/adolescent dyads problem-solving communication skills. The treated dyads demonstrated significant increases in problem solving behaviors over waiting list control dyads both in real and in hypothetical conflict situations; however, self-reports indicated no improvement at home. In addition to parents, teachers and peers have been taught to deliver cognitive behavioral interventions. Douglas et al. (1976) worked directly with hyperactive eight-year-old boys and with the children's teachers and parents. Change agents used cognitive modeling, self-instruction, and contingency management strategies to focus and develop the child's attentional skills, problem-solving abilities, and social interaction skills. When compared to a no-treatment control group, results generally supported the effectiveness of the comprehensive training program across a variety of cognitive, academic, and social tasks at posttest and at a three-month follow-up.

Robin, Schneider, and Dolnick (1976) worked through the classroom teacher and peers to teach emotionally disturbed students to limit aggressive episodes. Children were taught to withdraw from potentially aggressive situations when cued by the teacher or a fellow student. When the child engaged in the nonaggressive response, he or she was taught to relax and problem solve. Although design problems preclude any causal statements, a significant decrease in aggressive behaviors was observed. In addition, peers have been used successfully to modify children's behavior by acting as models (for example, O'Connor, 1972; Evers & Schwarz, 1973), tutors (Allen, 1976; Allen & Feldman, 1973), reinforcers of specific behavior (as in Wahler, 1967; Solomon & Wahler, 1973), and partners in social interaction (as in Furman, Rahe, & Hartup, 1979).

As Glenwick and Jason (in press) point out, questions regarding the "who, what, when, how, and why" of intervention cannot be distinguished in a meaningful way from considerations of where such interventions occur. In reviewing the research literature on locus of intervention, these authors underscore the point that intervening in the natural environment (that is, making use of natural mediators such as teachers and parents in the context of children's daily activities, such as home and school) will increase the likelihood that behavior changes to be instilled in children will be maintained. Intervening in the context of the naturalistic environment may preclude a need for generalization training procedures, because environmental cues for the elicitation of a particular behavior are constant. Research must identify the most feasible target problems and program delivery modalities for the attention of natural mediators as well as selecting appropriate strategies for training these lay therapists.

SUMMARY

Cognitive behavior therapy with children emerged from the behavior therapy movement in the late 1960s and early 1970s. It has grown rapidly during the past decade. Research in cognitive behavior therapy with children and recent critiques of work in this area have produced a number of issues. This chapter identified and discussed the following issues, which were organized around three themes and additional overarching problems.

Theme 1: Identification of clinically relevant target behaviors
- Issue 1: The relationship of treatment targets to current psychopathology
- Issue 2: The relationship of treatment targets to preventive interventions

Theme 2: Development of adequate assessment instruments
- Issue 3: Psychometric properties of assessment instruments
- Issue 4: Assessment of target behaviors
- Issue 5: Assessment instruments responsive to treatment
- Issue 6: Measurement of independent variables
- Issue 7: Multimethod assessment

Theme 3: Fitting the level of the treatment program to the target behaviors
- Issue 8: Specificity of targets for change

Overarching Problems
- Issue 9: Adoption of developmental approach
- Issue 10: Relationship of behavioral and cognitive skills
- Issue 11: Role of paraprofessionals and focus of intervention

REFERENCES

Achenbach, T. M. The Child Behavior Profile, I: Boys ages 6–11. *Journal of Consulting and Clinical Psychology*, 1978, *46*, 759–776.

Achenbach, T. M., & Edelbrock, C. S. The classification of child psychopathology: A review and analysis of empirical efforts. *Psychological Bulletin*, 1978, *85*, 1275–1301.

Achenbach, T. M., & Edelbrock, C. S. The Child Behavior Profile, II: Boys aged 12–16 and girls aged 6–11 and 12–16. *Journal of Consulting and Clinical Psychology*, 1979, *47*, 223–233.

Achenbach, T. M., & Edelbrock, C. S. Behavioral problems and competencies reported by parents of normal and disturbed children aged four through sixteen. *Monographs of the Society for Research in Child Development*, 1981, *46* (1, Serial No. 188).

Allen, V. L. (Ed.). *Children as teachers.* New York: Academic Press, 1976.

Allen, V. L., & Feldman, R. S. Learning through tutoring: Low achieving children as tutors. *Journal of Experimental Education*, 1973, *42*, 1–5.

American Psychiatric Association. *Diagnostic and statistical manual: Mental disorders* (DSM-I). Washington, DC: American Psychiatric Association, 1952.

American Psychiatric Association. *Diagnostic and statistical manual of mental disorders*, second edition. Washington, DC: American Psychiatric Association, 1968.

American Psychiatric Association. *Diagnostic and statistical manual of mental disorders*, Third edition. Washington, DC: American Psychiatric Association, 1980.

Appel, L., Cooper, R., McCarrell, N., Sims-Knight, J., Yussen, S., & Flavell, J. Development of the distinction between perceiving and memorizing, *Child Development*, 1972, *43*, 1365–1381;

Arend, R., Gove, F., & Sroufe, L. Continuity in early adaptation: From attachment theory in infancy to resiliency and curiosity at age four. *Child Development*, 1979, *50*, 950–959.

Asher, S. R., & Hymel, S. Children's social competence in peer relations: Sociometric and behavioral assessment. In J. D. Wine & M. D. Smye (Eds.), *Social competence*. New York: Guilford Press, in press.

Bandura, A. Vicarious and self-reinforcement processes. In R. Glaser (Ed.), *The nature of reinforcement*. New York: Academic, 1971.

Bandura, A. *Social learning theory*. Englewood Cliffs, NJ: Prentice-Hall, 1977.

Blank, M., & Solomon, R. A tutorial language program to develop abstract thinking in socially disadvantaged preschool children. *Child Development*, 1968, *39*, 380–389.

Brown, A. Development, schooling and the acquisition of knowledge about knowledge. In R. Anderson, R. Spiro, & W. Montague (Eds.), *Schooling and the acquisition of knowledge*. Hillsdale, NJ: Erlbaum, 1978.

Cocking, R., & Copple, C. Change through exposure to others: A study of children's verbalizations as they draw. Paper presented at the Annual Conference on Piagetian Theory and the Helping Professions, Los Angeles, February, 1978.

Comrey, A. L. Common methodological problems in factor analytic studies. *Journal of Consulting and Clinical Psychology*, 1978, *46*, 648–659.

Conners, C. K. Rating scales for use in drug studies with children. *Psychopharmacology Bulletin* (Special Issue, Pharmacotherapy of Children), 1973, 24–84.

Cowen, E. L., Pederson, A., Babigian, H., Izzo, L. D., & Trost, M. A. Long-term follow-up of early detected vulnerable children. *Journal of Consulting and Clinical Psychology*, 1973, *41*, 438–446.

Craighead, W. E. A brief clinical history of cognitive-behavior therapy with children. *School Psychology Review*, in press.

Craighead, W. E., Kazdin, A. E., & Mahoney, M. J. *Behavior modification: Principles, issues, and applications*, Second edition. MA: Houghton Mifflin, 1981.

Craighead, W. E., Wilcoxon-Craighead, L., & Meyers, A. W. New directions in behavior modification with children. In M. Hersen, R. M. Eisler, & P. M. Miller (Eds.), *Progress in behavior modification*, Volume 6. New York: Academic, 1978.

Denney, D. The effects of exemplary and cognitive models and self-rehearsal on children's interrogative strategies. *Journal of Experimental Child Psychology*, 1975, *19*, 476–488.

Douglas, V. Are drugs enough? To treat or to train the hyperactive child. *International Journal of Mental Health*, 1975, *4*, 199–212.

Douglas, V., Parry, P., Marton, P., & Garson, C. Assessment of a cognitive training program for hyperactive children. *Journal of Abnormal Child Psychology*, 1976, *4*, 389–410.

Egeland, B., & Weinberg, R. A. The Matching Familiar Figures Test: A look at its psychometric credibility. *Child Development*, 1976, *47*, 483–491.

Eisler, R. M., & Frederikson, L. W. *Perfecting social skills: A guide to interpersonal behavior development*. New York: Plenum, 1980.

Endicott, J., & Spitzer, R. L. A diagnostic interview: The Schedule for Affective Disorders and Schizophrenia. *Archives of General Psychiatry*, 1978, *35*, 837–844.

Evers, W., & Schwarz, J. Modifying social withdrawal in preschoolers: The effects of filmed modeling and teacher praise. *Journal of Abnormal Child Psychology*, 1973, *1*, 248–256.

Feldman, C. F., & Toulmin, S. Logic and the theory of mind. In W. J. Arnold (Ed.), *Nebraska Symposium on Motivation*, Volume 23. Lincoln, NE: University of Nebraska Press, 1976.

Flavell, J. Metacognition. In E. Langor (Chair), *Current perspectives on awareness and cognitive processes*. Symposium presented at the meeting of the American Psychological Association, Toronto, August 1978.

Flavell, J. H., & Wellman, H. M. Metamemory. In R. V. Kail & J. W. Hagen (Eds.), *Perspectives on the development of memory and cognition*. Hillsdale, NJ: Erlbaum, 1977.

Foster, S. L., & Ritchey, W. L. Issues in the assessment of social competence in children. *Journal of Applied Behavior Analysis*, 1979, *12*, 625–638.

Furman, W. Promoting social development: Developmental implications for treatment. In B. B. Lahey & A. E. Kazdin (Eds.), *Advances in clinical child psychology*, Volume 3. New York: Plenum, 1980.

Furman, W., Rahe, D. F., & Hartup, W. Rehabilitation of socially withdrawn preschool children through mixed-age and same-age socialization. *Child Development*, 1979, *50*, 915–922.

Gholson, B., & Beilin, H. A developmental model of human learning In H. W. Reese & L. P. Lipsitt (Eds.), *Advances in child development and behavior*, Volume 13. New York: Academic Press, 1979.

Glenwick, D. S., & Jason, L. A. Locus of intervention in child cognitive behavior therapy: Implications of a behavioral community psychology perspective. In A. W. Meyers & W. E. Craighead (Eds.), *Cognitive-behavior therapy with children.* New York: Plenum, in press.

Gordon, I. J., Olmsted, P. P., Rubin, R. I., & True, J. H. Continuity between home and school: Aspects of parental involvements in follow through. Paper presented at the Fifth Biennial Meeting of the Southeastern Conference on Human Development, Atlanta, April 1978.

Gottman, J. M., Gonso, J., & Rasmussen, B. Social interaction, social competence, and friendship in children. *Child Development*, 1975, *46*, 709–718.

Gresham, F. M. Social skills training with handicapped children: A review. *Review of Educational Research*, 1981, *51*, 139–176.

Group for the advancement of psychiatry, Committee on child psychiatry. Psychopathological disorders in childhood: Theoretical considerations and a proposed classification. GAP report No. 62, June, 1966.

Guerney, B. G., Guerney, L. F., & Andronico, M. P. Filial therapy. *Yale Scientific Magazine*, 1966, *40*, 6–26.

Hobbs, S. A., Moguin, L. E., Tyroler, M., & Lahey, B. B. Cognitive behavior therapy with children: Has clinical utility been demonstrated? *Psychological Bulletin*, 1980, *87*, 147–165.

Inhelder, B., & Piaget, J. *The early growth of logic in the child.* New York: Norton, 1964.

Kagan, J., Rossman, B., Day, D., Albert, J., & Phillips, W. Information processing in the child: Significance of analytic and reflective attitudes. *Psychological Monographs*, 1964, 78 (Whole No. 578).

Kendall, P. C. On the efficacious use of verbal self-instructional procedures with children. *Cognitive Therapy and Research*, 1977, *1*, 331–341.

Kendall, P. C., & Hollon, S. D. (Eds.). *Assessment strategies for cognitive-behavioral interventions.* New York: Academic Press, 1981.

Kendall, P. C., & Korgeski, G. P. Assessment and cognitive-behavioral interventions. *Cognitive Therapy and Research*, 1979, *3*, 1–21.

Kendall, P. C., & Wilcox, L. E. Self-control in children: Development of a rating scale. *Journal of Consulting and Clinical Psychology*, 1979, *47*, 1020–1029.

Kendall, P. C., & Wilcox, L. E. Cognitive-behavioral treatment for impulsivity: Concrete versus conceptual training in non-self-controlled problem children. *Journal of Consulting and Clinical Psychology*, 1980, *48*, 80–91.

Kendler, H. H., & Kendler, T. S. Vertical and horizontal processes in problem solving. *Psychological Review*, 1962, *69*, 1–16.

Kifer, R. E., Lewis, M. A., Green, D. R., & Phillips, E. L. Training predelinquent youths and their parents to negotiate conflict situations. *Journal of Applied Behavior Analysis*, 1974, *7*, 357–364.

Kohlberg, L., Yaeger, J., & Hjertholm, E. Private speech: Four studies and a review of theories. *Child Development*, 1968, *39*, 691–736.

Kovacs, M. Personal communication. March 1980.

Laughlin, T., Moss, I., & Miller, S. Information processing in children as a function of adult model, stimulus display, school grade, and sex. *Journal of Educational Psychology*, 1969, *60*, 188–193.

Levine, M. The development of hypotheses testing. In Liebert, R. M., Poulos, R. W., & Strauss, G. D. (Eds.), *Developmental psychology*. Englewood Cliffs, NJ: Prentice-Hall, 1974.

Lord, C. A developmental approach to the social behavior of autistic children and youth: Focus on peer interaction. Paper presented at the meetings of the National Society for Autistic Children, Boston, July, 1981.

Luria, A. *The role of speech in the regulation of normal and abnormal behavior*. New York: Liveright, 1961.

Matas, L., Arend, R., & Sroufe, L. Continuity in adaptation in the second year: The relationships between quality of attachments and later competence. *Child Development*, 1978, *49*, 547–556.

Meacham, J. Development of memory abilities in the individual and society. *Human Development*, 1972, *15*, 205–228.

Meichenbaum, D. *Cognitive-behavior modification: An integrative approach*. New York: Plenum, 1977.

Meichenbaum, D., & Asarnow, J. Cognitive-behavior modification and metacognitive development: Implications for the classroom. In P. C. Kendall & S. D. Hollon (Eds.), *Cognitive-behavioral intervention: Theory, research, and procedures*. New York: Academic, 1979.

Meichenbaum, D., & Goodman, J. Developmental control of operant motor responding by verbal operants. *Journal of Experimental Child Psychology*, 1969, *7*, 533–565.

O'Connor, R. D. Relative efficacy of modeling, shaping and the combined procedures for modification of social withdrawal. *Journal of Abnormal Psychology*, 1972, *79*, 327–334.

O'Leary, K. D., & Borkovec, T. D. Placebo groups: Unrealistic and unethical controls in psychotherapy research. *American Psychologist*, 1978, *33*, 821–830.

Ornstein, P., & Naus, M. Rehearsal processes in children's memory. In P. Ornstein (Ed.), *Memory development in children*. Hillsdale, NJ: Lawrence Erlbaum Associates, 1978.

Orvaschel, H., Weissman, M. M., & Kidd, K. K. Children and depression: The children of depressed parents; the childhood of depressed patients, depression in children. *Journal of Affective Disorders*, in press.

Parten, M. B. Social participation among preschool children. *Journal of Abnormal and Social Psychology*, 1933, *27*, 243–269.

Piaget, J. *The language and thought of the child*. New York: Harcourt Brace, 1926.

Piaget, J. Comments on Vygotsky's critical remarks. In L. Vygotsky, *Thought and language*. Cambridge, MA: MIT, 1962.

Robin, A., Armel, S., & O'Leary, K. D. The effects of self-instruction on writing deficiencies. *Behavior Therapy*, 1975, *6*, 178–187.

Robin, A. L., Kent, R., O'Leary, K. D., Foster, S. L., & Prinz, R. An approach to teaching parents and adolescents problem-solving communication skills: A preliminary report. *Behavior Therapy*, 1977, *8*, 639–643.

Robin, A., Schneider, M., & Dolnick, M. The turtle technique: An extended case study of self-control in the classroom. *Psychology in the Schools*, 1976, *12*, 120–128.

Rubin, K. H., & Maioni, T. L. Play preference and its relationship to egocentrism, popularity, and classification skills in preschoolers. *Merrill-Palmer Quarterly*, 1975, *21*, 171–179.

Rubin, K. H., Maioni, T. L., & Hornung, M. Free play behaviors in middle and lower class preschoolers: Parten and Piaget revisited. *Child Development*, 1976, *47*, 414–419.

Rubin, K. H., Watson, K. S., & Jambor, T. W. Free play behaviors in preschool and kindergarten children. *Child Development*, 1978, *49*, 534–536.

Schleser, R., Cohen, R., Meyers, A. W., & Rodick, J. D. The effects of cognitive level and delivery procedures on generalization of self-instructions. Manuscript submitted for publication, 1981.

Schleser, R., Meyers, A. W., & Cohen, R. Generalization of self-instructions. Effects of general versus specific content, active rehearsal, and cognitive level. *Child Development*, 1981, *52*, 335–340.

Schulterbrandt, J. G., & Raskin, A. *Depression in childhood: Diagnosis, treatment, and conceptual models*. New York: Raven Press, 1977.

Shapiro, B., & Ogilvie, D. *Manual for assessing social abilities of one- to six-year-old children.* June, 1976. Available from Preschool Project, Laboratory of Human Development, Graduate School of Education, Harvard University, Cambridge, MA.

Smilansky, S. *The effects of sociodramatic play on disadvantaged children: Preschool children.* New York: Wiley, 1968.

Solomon, R. W., & Wahler, R. Peer reinforcement of classroom problem behavior. *Journal of Applied Behavior Analysis,* 1973, *6,* 49–56.

Spivack, G., Platt, J., & Shure, M. B. *The problem-solving approach to adjustment.* San Francisco, CA: Jossey-Bass, 1976.

Spivack, G., & Shure, M. B. *Social adjustment of young children: A cognitive approach to solving real-life problems.* San Francisco, CA: Jossey-Bass, 1974.

Sroufe, L. The coherence of individual development. *American Psychologist,* 1979, *34,* 834–841.

Urbain, E. S., & Kendall, P. C. Review of social-cognitive problem-solving interventions with children. *Psychological Bulletin,* 1980, *88,* 109–143.

Vaughn, B. E., & Waters, E. Attention structure, sociometric status, and dominance: Interrelations, behavioral correlates and relationships to social competence. *Developmental Psychology,* 1981, *77,* 275–288.

Vygotsky, L. F. *Thought and language.* New York: Wiley, 1962.

Wahler, R. Child-child interactions in free field settings: Some experimental analyses. *Journal of Experimental Child Psychology,* 1967, *5,* 278–293.

White, S. H. Evidence for a hierarchical arrangement of learning processes. In L. Lipsitt & C. Spiker (Eds.), *Advances in child development and behavior,* Volume 2. New York: Academic Press, 1965.

Wiggins, J. S. *Personality and prediction: Principles of personality assessment.* Reading, MA: Addison-Wesley, 1973.

Zigler, E., & Kanzer, P. The effectiveness of two classes of verbal reinforcers in the performance of middle and lower class children. *Journal of Personality,* 1962, *30,* 157–163.

PART VII

Schizophrenia and Childhood Autism

CHAPTER 14

Relapse in Schizophrenic Disorders: Possible Contributing Factors and Implications for Behavior Therapy

Michael E. Dawson, Ph.D.
Keith H. Nuechterlein, Ph.D.
Robert P. Liberman, M.D.

INTRODUCTION

Schizophrenic disorders have often been viewed as continuous and relatively stable in character, in contrast to the episodic course typical of bipolar and unipolar affective disorders. In recent years, however, increased attention has been focused on the fluctuations in the course of schizophrenic disorders and on the possible determinants of these changes in functioning (Wing, 1978; Zubin & Spring, 1977). The social importance of understanding the factors contributing to relapse in schizophrenia has increased markedly in the last three decades as antipsychotic medications have allowed most patients with a schizophrenic disorder to return to the community after the acute psychotic phase. Discharge from the hospital has, unfortunately, often been followed by readmission. Among patients treated with antipsychotics, nearly half relapse within two years after discharge. The parallel rate of relapse among placebo-treated patients is a discouraging 80% (Hogarty et al., 1974).

Ironically, while presenting signs and symptoms are of great importance in the diagnosis of schizophrenia, the characteristic symp-

Preparation of this paper was supported by NIMH Research Grant MH 30911, which funds the Mental Health Clinical Research Center for the Study of Schizophrenia (Robert P. Liberman, Principal Investigator).

toms of schizophrenic disorders have weak predictive power for the social, occupational, and overall course of these disorders (Carpenter et al., 1978; Strauss & Carpenter, 1972 and 1974). This evidence does not imply that signs and symptoms should not be carefully elicited and assessed. Indeed, many conflicting findings in the literature may be due to lack of specificity in diagnostic criteria and lack of systematic diagnostic interviewing techniques. However, the available evidence does suggest that effective prediction of overall schizophrenic outcome must include consideration of many factors beyond the symptoms that define the schizophrenic episode.

The purpose of this chapter is to examine some of the factors that may contribute to the high rate of schizophrenic relapse, to present a tentative heuristic model that describes the possible interactive role of the factors in producing relapse, and finally to identify some of the behavioral treatment implications of the proposed model. Relapse will be defined in the sense of clinical deterioration indexed by a return of incapacitating symptoms.

FACTORS RELATED TO RELAPSE

Four categories of factors related to schizophrenic relapse will be briefly reviewed: (1) family factors, (2) social factors, (3) attentional and information processing factors, and (4) psychophysiological factors.

Family Factors

A series of studies reported during the past decade, originating from the Institute of Psychiatry in London, has shown that the emotional climate within the families of schizophrenic patients has a strong influence on the course of the illness. The measures of emotional climate used in these studies were elicited by the Camberwell Family Interview (CFI), a semistructured interview conducted with the patient's family member at the time of the patient's hospitalization. The CFI inquires about the patient's behavior during the three months prior to hospitalization and the family member's attitudes and feelings toward this behavior.

The tape-recorded CFI is evaluated, based on both verbal and nonverbal indices (such as tone of voice), for several factors. The two factors that have proved to be the most predictive of future relapse are the number of critical comments and ratings of emotional overinvolvement. If the family member makes more than 6 or 7 critical comments and/or is rated 4 or higher on a five-point scale of emotional overinvolvement, he or she is designated high in "expressed emotion" (EE). Otherwise the family member is designated as low-EE.

Vaughn and Leff (1976) found that 48% of the patients from high-EE families relapsed within nine months after discharge from the hospital, whereas only 6% of the patients from low-EE families relapsed within the same time period. These results are consistent with earlier findings of Brown, Birley, and Wing (1972) who reported that 58% of patients from high-EE families relapsed, compared to 16% of the low-EE group. More recently, a replication of the EE research with 54 schizophrenic patients and their families conducted by Vaughn, Snyder, et al. at the Camarillo/UCLA Clinical Research Center revealed that 56% and 17% relapsed from high- and low-EE families, respectively (Liberman, 1981). This differential rate of relapse was not related to type or severity of symptoms or to features of the psychiatric history.

Since many of the high-EE patients (approximately 50%) did *not* relapse, it is clear that other factors besides EE are important. Both Brown et al. (1972) and Vaughn and Leff (1976) observed that drug therapy and the amount of face-to-face contact with family members are important moderating variables for patients from high-EE families. The rate of relapse among patients from high-EE families is significantly lower if the patients are maintained on neuroleptics and if contact with their relatives is limited. The highest relapse rate (92%) occurs among patients from high-EE families who have frequent contact with the family members and are not taking medication.

The results reviewed thus far indicate that the emotional climate within the family is a major factor in schizophrenic relapse. This conclusion rests upon the assumption that the CFI is a valid index of the emotional climate prevailing within the family and that the patients are sensitive, perhaps hypersensitive, to this emotional climate. The latter assumption has been supported by two recent studies, which measured autonomic arousal of patients while interacting with high-EE or low-EE family members. In both studies, the principal measure of autonomic arousal was the rate of spontaneous electrodermal responses, that is, responses that occur in the absence of known eliciting stimuli. In the first of these studies, Tarrier et al. (1979) measured the rate of spontaneous electrodermal response for 20 minutes while remitted schizophrenics were with the experimenter only, and then for 20 minutes while the patients were with the key family member. The high- and low-EE groups did not differ in rate of spontaneous electrodermal responses when tested in the presence of the experimenter. However, differences did emerge when the family member was brought into the situation. Patients with low-EE family members showed a gradual decline in the rate of spontaneous electrodermal responses, while patients with high-EE family members failed to exhibit this decline. Thus, autonomic arousal was maintained at a high level only in the presence of high-EE family members. More recently, these results have been largely replicated in a group of acute inpatients with florid symptoms (Sturgeon et al., in press). Thus, the results indicate that the family member's level of EE has a significant impact on the patient's continuing level of autonomic arousal, which may possibly contribute to the relapse process.

Life Events and Social Factors

Although the family is usually the most proximal, powerful, and constant source of social stimulation for the patients, other nonfamilial social factors have been implicated in the onset of schizophrenic symptoms. As with the study of family factors, seminal work in this area originated from the Institute of Psychiatry in London. Brown and Birley (1968) and Birley and Brown (1970) studied 50 recently hospitalized schizophrenic patients with symptom onsets that occurred within three months of hospitalization and could be accurately dated within a week. Both the patient and an informant were interviewed about events occurring within a 13-week period prior to symptomatic onset. The life events included dangers, disappointments, losses, damages, and fulfillments that could be specifically dated. They included events that would generally be considered pleasant (such as marriage), unpleasant (such as death of a loved one), or neutral (such as brother announces engagement). They were classified as "independent" of the patient's behavior (for example, burglary) or as "possibly independent" (for example, loss of job). The latter distinction is extremely important, since some types of life events may reflect consequences, not antecedents, of schizophrenic symptomatology. For example, divorce or loss of a job may be the result of early disruptive prodromal signs of the impending schizophrenic episode. In reviewing this area, we will therefore limit discussion to only those events that are "independent" of the patients' behaviors.

In the patient group, 46% reported at least one independent life event during the three weeks immediately preceding onset of the schizophrenic episode, as compared with an average of 12% during the three earlier three-week periods. In the normal control group, only 14% to 15% of the subjects reported life events during each of the four three-week periods. Thus, the proportion of normal subjects experiencing independent life events remained at a constant level across the reporting period, whereas the proportion of schizophrenics experiencing an independent life event increased markedly during the three-week period immediately preceding onset of the symptoms.

Jacobs and Myers (1976) found that 40% of recently hospitalized schizophrenics reported at least one independent life event during the year preceding symptom onset, compared to 29% of matched normal controls. While this difference is in the expected direction, it is small and not statistically significant. The most probable reason for these generally negative results would seem to be the use of a one-year period in which life events were recorded. Recall that Brown and Birley found significant differences between patients and controls only for life events that occurred within a few weeks of symptom onset. As Jacobs and Myers admit, "It is quite possible, therefore, that the annual period used as the basis for comparison with normals dilutes a real, greater, immediate difference" (p. 85).

More recently, Leff and Vaughn (1980) measured life events and family-expressed emotion (EE) in a group of recently hospitalized schizophrenic patients. The proportion of schizophrenic patients from high-EE families who experienced at least one independent life event within three weeks of symptom onset was only 5%. Among patients from low-EE families, the proportion experiencing an independent life event within the same time period was 56%. Thus, it appears that high-EE families produce stress that may by itself prove to be sufficient for schizophrenic relapse, while low-EE families are less stressing, hence additional stressful life events are required for relapse. These data suggest that stressors, either in the form of exposure to high-EE relatives or exposure to life events, will negatively affect the patient and possibly precipitate a symptomatic relapse.

It should be noted that the life event studies reviewed above relied upon retrospective verbal reports to index the occurrence of life events. Thus, the results may be influenced by the subjects' rationalizations and distorted memories. Prospective studies are needed to clarify the interpretation of these relationships. Rabkin's (1980) recent review of the literature discusses these and other methodological limitations in research on life events and schizophrenia.

It should also be noted that life events do not universally result in schizophrenic symtomatology, even among persons vulnerable to these disorders. Clearly, other factors must be involved. Among the most important of these "other factors" may be coping mechanisms and social support systems. A plausible sequence of events is the following: a vulnerable individual is exposed to a stressful life event, the individual's coping style proves to be inadequate to remove the stressor, and the individual avoids seeking support from his social network, which he perceives to be unwilling or unable to help (Tolsdorf, 1976). This scenario, while somewhat speculative at this time, emphasizes the importance of stressful life events, along with coping limitations and the lack of social support, in schizophrenic relapse.

Attentional and Information Processing Factors

Disturbances in attention and in the processing of information are among the most striking features of the subjective reports of schizophrenic patients. Indeed, in a review of over 50 books and articles written by persons who had had a schizophrenic episode, Freedman (1974) found that problems in focusing attention and concentrating were mentioned more often than any other perceptual or cognitive disorder.

These subjective accounts have been supplemented by a very

large body of literature examining the performance of schizophrenic patients on objective tasks that require certain information processing operations. While many controversies remain regarding the nature of the information processing deficits that are most specifically tied to schizophrenic disorders, a tentative listing of attentional deficits found among schizophrenic patients relative to normal individuals would include impaired maintenance of focused attention (Orzack & Kornetsky, 1966; Rodnick & Shakow, 1940; Shakow, 1962; Zahn, Shakow, & Rosenthal, 1961), distractibility when relevant and irrelevant stimuli are in sequence (Oltmanns, 1978; Oltmanns & Neale, 1975), and impaired detection and recognition of relevant stimuli embedded in simultaneous irrelevant noise (Rappaport, Hopkins, & Hall, 1972; Wishner & Wahl, 1974; Stilson & Kopell, 1964; Stilson et al., 1966). Investigations on the stages of information processing have revealed slow processing of information in the initial sensory memory stage, although sensory memory itself may be structurally intact (Davidson & Neale, 1974; Neale, 1971; Russell & Knight, 1977; Saccazzo, Hirt, & Spencer, 1974), and inefficiency in the control of information organization in short-term memory (Koh, 1978; Traupman, 1975). These deficiencies in attention and information processing among persons with schizophrenic disorders may contribute to a particular proneness to information or sensory overload.

Deficits in attention among schizophrenic patients have often been examined through studies of simple reaction time. Simple reaction time can be greatly influenced by a variety of factors, including motor speed and motivation (Nuechterlein, 1977). Nevertheless, to the extent that simple reaction time reflects attentional deficits among schizophrenic patients, there is evidence that such deficits have prognostic value. Cancro et al. (1971) examined simple reaction time in 30 recently hospitalized schizophrenic patients and then followed these patients for the next three years. Slow reaction time reliably predicted longer duration of hospitalization over the subsequent three-year period. This predictor was independent of social class, depressive mood, and the Phillips Prognostic Rating Scale. The Cancro et al. results are similar to the short-term prognostic data recently reported by Zahn and Carpenter (1978). These investigators measured the simple reaction time of drug-free acute schizophrenic patients about three weeks following hospital admission. The patients were divided into those who improved clinically over the next three to four inpatient months and those who did not improve. The subsequently improved group was characterized by significantly faster mean reaction time than the nonimproved group, despite comparable global symptomatic levels during the initial testing period. Thus, the results of these two studies suggest that simple reaction time may be a useful prognostic indicator, with slow reaction time associated with poor prognosis.

Recent work has also focused on whether the attentional and

information processing deficits are "state-like" reflections of current symptomatology or are "trait-like" indicators of an enduring vulnerability to schizophrenic disorders. Data relevant to this question have been obtained by examining individuals who are at risk for developing schizophrenia because of their genetic relatedness to schizophrenic patients as well as by examining persons in remission following a schizophrenic episode. Deficits in sustaining focused attention and in selective attention have been found among some children born to a schizophrenic patient (Asarnow et al., 1978; Erlenmeyer-Kimling & Cornblatt, 1978; Marcus, 1972; Neale, in press; Nuechterlein et al., in press) and among other first-degree relatives of schizophrenics (DeAmicis & Cromwell, 1979; Wood & Cook, 1979). A residual attentional deficit has also been found in persons who have had a schizophrenic episode but at the time of testing were nonpsychotic but medicated (Asarnow & MacCrimmon, 1978; Miller, Saccuzzo, & Braff, 1979) or nonsymptomatic and unmedicated (Wohlberg & Kornetsky, 1973). In addition, Cornblatt and Erlenmeyer-Kimling (1980) report that a composite attentional index drawn from several test scores of children born to a schizophrenic parent predicts overall level of psychological functioning some six or seven years later. Taken together, these studies suggest that some attentional and information processing deficits may reflect "trait-like," enduring characteristics of the individual, which, in turn, may reflect an individual's vulnerability to schizophrenic symptoms.

The studies reviewed above employed diverse measures of attentional and information processing abilities. Thus, the degree to which these reports are referring to the same deficit needs further clarification. Moreover, the specificity of these deficits to schizophrenia as compared to other psychopathological disorders has not yet received sufficient study (Neale, in press; Nuechterlein, in press). Nevertheless, the currently available data are consistent with the possibility that some deficits in attention and information processing are present before, during, and after schizophrenic episodes in some individuals.

Psychophysiological Factors

Some of the most interesting recent psychophysiological studies of schizophrenics have measured electrodermal orienting responses. The paradigm employed in these studies involved the repetitive presentation of an innocuous tone, to which the subjects were instructed merely to listen. Among normal subjects exposed to this paradigm, the typical result is that the tone initially elicits a phasic increase in skin conductance, referred to as the skin conductance orienting response (SCOR). The SCOR is considered to reflect an autonomic alerting response associated with attention to the novel stimulus. The SCOR of normal subjects typically habituates following 4 to 8 repetitions of the innocuous tone.

Schizophrenic patients have been found to exhibit abnormalities in the elicitation and habituation of SCORs. A number of studies reported during the past decade have found that between 40% and 50% of schizophrenic patients fail to exhibit any SCORs (as in Gruzelier & Venables, 1972). Only 5% to 10% of normals show such an absence of SCORs. In contrast to these schizophrenic *nonresponders*, the remaining patients display SCORs and are classified as *responders.* Among the schizophrenic responders, two types of abnormalities in SCOR habituation have been observed. Some patients show exceptionally *fast habituation* (as in Patterson & Venables, 1978) while others show exceptionally *slow habituation* (for example, Gruzelier & Venables, 1972). Both of these patterns of results differ from the normal, gradual rate of habituation.

While the results reviewed above have been obtained from medicated schizophrenic patients, the responder/nonresponder and the fast habituator/slow habituator distinctions do not appear to be artifacts of antipsychotic medications. Phenothiazines lower skin conductance levels and reduce the frequency of spontaneous electrodermal responding, but they appear to have minimal suppressing effects on SCORs to innocuous stimuli (Venables, 1975 and 1977).

The significance of the responder/nonresponder and the fast habituator/slow habituator distinctions is suggested by their relationships to other physiological, behavioral, and clinical measures. For example, it has been found that schizophrenic SCOR responders, compared to nonresponders, have higher heart rates, blood pressure, skin conductance levels, and higher frequencies of spontaneous electrodermal responses (Gruzelier & Venables, 1974 and 1975). In addition, symptomatic differences between schizophrenic responders and nonresponders have been observed. Based on ratings of ward behavior, responders are more anxious, manic, and assaultive (Gruzelier, 1976) while nonresponders are more withdrawn and conceptually disorganized and less excited (Bernstein et al., 1980; Straube, 1979). Thus, the responders appear to be autonomically and behaviorally hyperaroused, while the nonresponders appear autonomically and behaviorally hypoaroused.

Two recent studies have found that SCOR individual differences, particularly differences in rate of habituation, are predictive of short-term clinical prognosis. Frith et al. (1979) measured SCORs in a group of recently hospitalized unmedicated schizophrenics. The patients were divided into two groups based on their SCORs: (1) those who showed no habituation or slow habituation and (2) those who showed relatively fast habituation or no SCORs at all. While the two groups did not differ clinically, the nonhabituator group exhibited higher overall electrodermal arousal than did the habituator group. More important, the nonhabituators evidenced less clinical improvement following four weeks of drug or placebo treatments than did the habituators.

In a related study, Zahn, Carpenter, and McGlashan (1981) also recorded SCORs from a group of recently hospitalized unmedicated acute schizophrenics. After 3 to 4 months of treatment (principally psychosocial therapy), 17 of the patients had improved, while 18 had not improved. At the time of hospital admission, the two groups did not differ in global symptomatology, but the nonimproved group exhibited slower SCOR habituation than did those who had improved. These results, like those of Frith et al., indicate that slow SCOR habituation and high electrodermal arousal are predictive of poor short-term outcome.

Finally, as with the attentional measures reviewed previously, there remains the issue of whether the electrodermal measures are "state-like" reflections of current symptomatology or "trait-like" indicators of an enduring vulnerability of schizophrenic episodes. Data from the two studies reviewed above (Frith et al., 1979; Zahn et al., 1981) support the enduring vulnerability interpretation. Both of these studies found that clinical improvement was not accompanied by significant electrodermal changes, suggesting that the electrodermal abnormalities "are not merely secondary consequences of the psychotic state but may reflect more permanent dispositions which have important clinical consequences in terms of outcome" (Zahn, 1980, p. 93). Additional electrodermal data obtained from the offspring of schizophrenics suggest a similar conclusion. While these data are not entirely consistent, at least three studies have reported electrodermal hyperresponsiveness and/or slow habituation to mildly aversive stimuli among the offspring of schizophrenics (Mednick & Schulsinger, 1978; Salzman & Klein, 1978; van Dyke, Rosenthal, & Rasmussen, 1974). Thus electrodermal hyperresponsiveness and/or slow habituation may reflect a fundamental vulnerability characteristic of at least some individuals who are at risk for schizophrenia.

AN INTERACTIVE MODEL OF SCHIZOPHRENIC RELAPSE

The factors reviewed above are not likely to operate independently. Instead, we suggest that the critical processes leading to schizophrenic relapse involve interactions among these factors. In order to specify the nature of some of the most important interactions, we present a tentative and somewhat simplified model of schizophrenic relapse in Figure 14-1.

The first class of major variables in the model are the external environmental variables of "social stressor" and a "nonsupportive social network." It is proposed, based on the evidence reviewed earlier, that the presence of social stressors and a nonsupportive social network will increase the probability of a schizophrenic relapse. Social stressors include life events as well as exposure to high-EE family members. The existence of high-EE family members also contributes to the lack of support available from the social network, but the concept of a social network is more inclusive than the family, including friends, neighbors, coworkers, and professional help available. The effects of social stressor and social network variables are assumed to interact. For example, the effects of an independent life event (such as the death of a loved one) may be compounded by the lack of other social support or may be minimized by the presence of other supportive figures.

The second class of major variables in the model includes enduring trait-like characteristics of the individual. The specific characteristics shown in Figure 14-1 are "information processing dysfunctions" and "arousal dysfunctions." As mentioned earlier, not only do symptomatic schizophrenic patients exhibit these types of dysfunctions, but there is evidence that some subjects who are at high risk for developing schizophrenic symptoms also show these anomalies. These dysfunctions may be relatively permanent characteristics, which, in some cases, may not be easily detectable as long as the individual is not unduly stressed. In other cases, the dysfunction may be so extreme as to be easily detectable, as with the individual with poor premorbid adjustment. In either instance, the preexisting characteristics make the individual especially vulnerable to the negative effects of social stressors and a nonsupportive social network.

The nature, specificity, source, and modifiability of these vulnerability characteristics need to be better understood. What are the precise information processing and arousal dysfunctions and what are the best behavioral, psychophysiological, and biochemical indicators of these dysfunctions? How specific are these dysfunctions to schizophrenia? To what degree are these dysfunctions due to genetic inheritence, perinatal complications, and prior learning experiences? To what degree are they modifiable by chemical and behavioral interventions? These are only some of the questions that need to be addressed by future research.

The third class of major variables in the model are the transient intermediate states of "sensory overload and hyperarousal" and "deficient processing of social stimuli." These intermediate states occur when the vulnerable individual is stressed beyond a certain threshold. These intermediate states aggravate the already poor social environment by means of a feedback loop. An individual in the intermediate state, showing cognitive disorganization and irritability, is likely to elicit more criticism from family members and more rejection by members of the social network. Hence, a vicious cycle is created, the person feels overwhelmed and unable to cope, and a full-blown schizophrenic episode is imminent unless the cycle is broken. The episode may be associated with an abnormal lowering of autonomic arousal and electrodermal reactivity in some individuals ("the nonresponders" and "fast habituators"). In any event, as shown in Figure 14-1, the relapse would be associated with "schizophrenic symp-

Figure 14–1. A simplified Interactive Model of Schizophrenic Relapse. External environmental variables (indicated by oval circles) interact with enduring vulnerability characteristics (indicated by squares) to produce transient intermediate states (indicated by parallelograms). The transient intermediate states create a vicious cycle by feedback to the environmental variables. The end results of the vicious cycle are the outcome behaviors (indicated by rectangles).

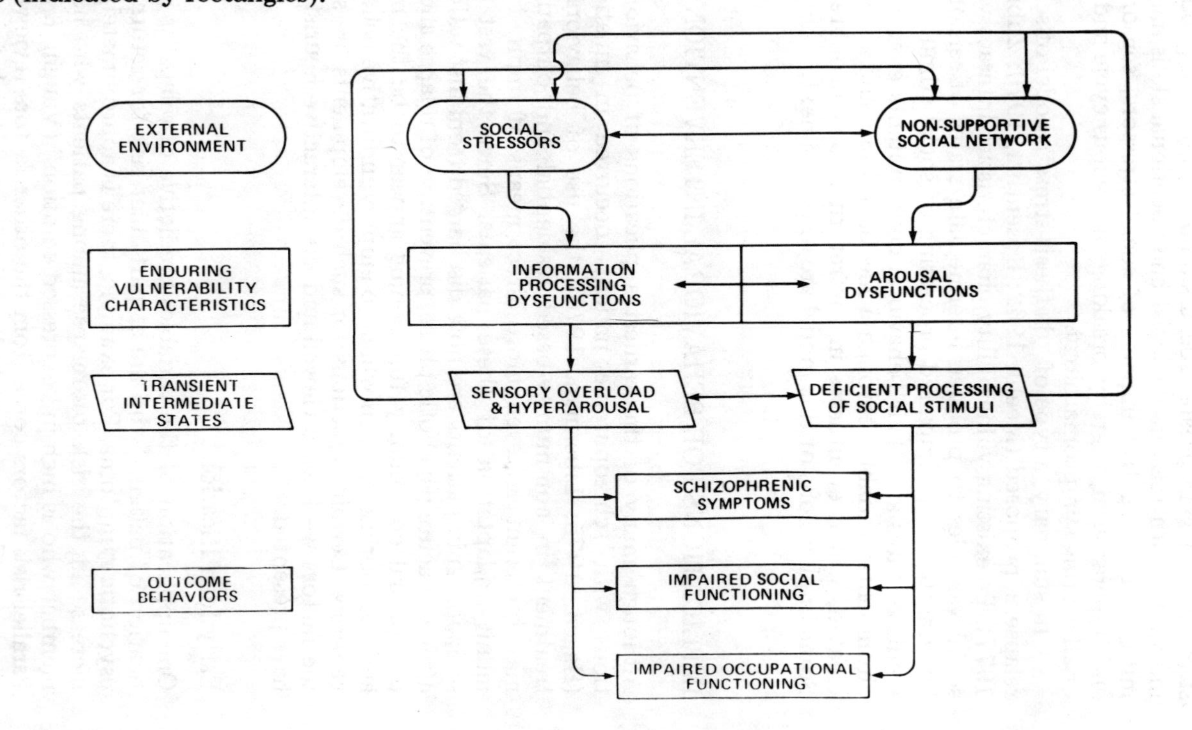

toms," "impaired social functioning," and "impaired occupational functioning." On the other hand, some patients at higher levels of psychosocial functioning may be able to cope actively to reduce stressors and gain greater social support. Thus, the good premorbid individual with reasonable social and vocational skills may be able to mitigate the negative impacts of social stressors, sensory overload, and hyperarousal, thereby breaking the vicious cycle and minimizing or alleviating symptomatology.

In summary, a type of "diathesis-stress" model of schizophrenic relapse is proposed (Meehl, 1962; Rosenthal, 1970; Zubin & Spring, 1977). Preexisting vulnerability characteristics interact with noxious social variables to produce intermediate states of sensory overload, hyperarousal, and impaired processing of social stimuli. These intermediate states and their behavioral concomitants exacerbate the environmental variables through a feedback loop, and a vicious cycle is created, which eventuates in the return of a schizophrenic episode. Some implications of this model are discussed next.

IMPLICATIONS FOR BEHAVIORAL INTERVENTION

Although many of the earliest applications of behavioral interventions with schizophrenic patients occurred in inpatient settings (Hagen, 1975; Liberman, 1976), the use of behaviorally-oriented treatment in community-based residential and outpatient settings may represent an even more direct means of improving the community adaptation of these patients. Since the vast majority of schizophrenic patients are now discharged from institutional settings after the acute psychotic phase, prevention of relapse and promotion of optimal community functioning appear to be the most fruitful and appropriate areas in which to employ innovative behavioral interventions. Certain directions for such developments are suggested by the factors we have reviewed and the interactive heuristic model we have presented.

Early Identification

One application of the variables predictive of relapse is in the identification of patients who are at particular risk for return of disabling psychotic symptoms. For example, there is approximately a four-fold increase in the risk of relapse among patients who have a family member who is high in "expressed emotion" (Vaughn & Leff, 1976). Parallel risk factors come from the other factors reviewed, although current evidence does not allow the increased risk for relapse to be quantified. Life events independent of the patient's control appear to be associated with a short-term increase in risk of symptomatic exacerbation, especially for those patients whose significant others do not in themselves impose an overstimulating environment (Brown & Birley, 1968; Birley & Brown, 1970; Leff & Vaughn, 1980). In the information processing domain, slow reaction time during the inpatient period apparently identifies a subgroup of schizophrenic patients who are not only likely to require more future hospitalization (Cancro et al., 1971; Weaver & Brooks, 1964), but also show less short-term improvement (Zahn & Carpenter, 1978). High autonomic arousal and slow electrodermal habituation are similarly associated with poor short-term prognosis (Frith et al., 1979; Zahn et al., 1981), although their relationship to relapse per se has apparently not been studied.

Intervention Strategies for Prevention of Relapse

Beyond identifying individuals who are at high risk of relapse, the proposed model also suggests certain preventive intervention strategies. Among patients with high expressed emotion relatives, maintenance neuroleptics and reduction of face-to-face contact with the relatives after discharge are especially promising therapeutic strategies. An alternative to reduction of contact with overstimulating relatives may be to intervene in the overstimulating behavior itself. Approaches to family education and family therapy that emphasize reduction of hostile criticism and emotional overinvolvement through better understanding of the nature of schizophrenia and improved social and communication skills are being evaluated by researchers at the Camarillo/UCLA Research Center, the University of Southern California, and the University of Pittsburgh (Anderson, Hogarty & Reiss, 1980; Falloon et al., in press; Liberman, Falloon, & Aitchison, in press).

Since stressful life events are ubiquitous in everyday community life and only some life events are likely to be under the patient's control, the impact of this source of potential overstimulation may be effectively altered through provision of personal "buffers" and social support networks. Behavioral approaches to increasing stress resistance or stress resiliency have not been extensively developed with schizophrenic patients, but the stress inoculation approaches (for example, Meichenbaum, 1977) that have been applied to the self-management of anxiety and anger may be worthy of adaptation for the nonpsychotic period following a schizophrenic episode. These adaptations might incorporate practice in coping with life stressors that are likely to be particularly frequent or potent for individual patients. It would appear that situations involving criticism, intrusiveness by others, and novel or complex information processing demands may be relevant to many remitted schizophrenic patients. Practice in the control of reactions to such stimuli might incorporate the use of covert self-statements, relaxation techniques and self-monitoring of arousal, feelings of overload, and symptom levels to abort development of sensory overload and hyperarousal.

Overt coping strategies may also allow the person prone to schizophrenic relapse to reduce the impact of stressors. Social skills training approaches have been applied with schizophrenic patients in an effort to increase their emotional expressiveness and social competence (as in Goldsmith & McFall, 1975; Hersen & Bellack, 1976; Liberman & Bryan, 1977). A review of these efforts to date suggests that some social skills training programs have been effective with schizophrenic patients during the training period, but the durability and generalization of these improvements have thus far been limited (Wallace et al., 1980). Further efforts need to focus on situational generalization, especially through interventions in the outpatient period directed toward living skills that will be readily reinforced by the patients' immediate social environment.

At the Camarillo/UCLA Clinical Research Center, Wallace (1981) has developed social skills training modules that focus on interpersonal situations that appear to be particularly relevant to the everyday life of outpatient schizophrenic patients. By teaching concrete skills involved in peer and family relations, independent community living, vocational rehabilitation, and symptom management, this program aims to help the postpsychotic schizophrenic patient actively to improve his community adaptation level. Success in developing such active coping efforts should help the patient to avoid undue social stressors connected with social and vocational failure and to develop a more adequate social network. Results of a controlled study have revealed less relapse and rehospitalization among schizophrenic patients who received social skills training than among patients randomly assigned to equally intensive holistic health therapy.

In addition to coping actively and assertively with difficult social and vocational situations, the model of schizophrenic relapse that we have outlined suggests that selective avoidance and withdrawal from certain overly stimulating situations may be particularly adaptive for schizophrenia-prone individuals. This view is consistent with that of Wing (1975), who posits that social withdrawal in schizophrenia may be an attempt to cope with information overload and hyperarousal. Thus, outpatient treatment for schizophrenic patients may include direct training in recognizing potential stressors and subjective stress, evaluating the likelihood of successful active engagement of the situation, consideration of intentional avoidance or escape if the danger of overstimulation is great, and role-playing of graceful withdrawal from certain stressful situations.

Response to Intervention: Possible Predictors and Indicators

As we have noted, certain information processing and psychophysiological measures appear to predict probably clinical improvement in schizophrenia. One theoretical interpretation of these predictors is that retarded responsiveness to relevant external stimuli, overresponsiveness to neutral stimuli, and autonomic hyperarousal may index tendency to relapse in these poor-responding patients. Perhaps these patients would be especially appropriate for interventions emphasizing stress reduction and relaxation in the face of unavoidable stressors rather than assertive, active coping strategies. Patients with relatively fast reaction time to relevant stimuli, faster electrodermal habituation to neutral stimuli, or lower autonomic arousal may be better candidates for approaches that involve active engagement of the environment and more complex information processing skills.

Measures of attention, information processing, and arousal may also be useful as intermediate indicators of treatment response. Based on the heuristic model we propose, reduction in autonomic arousal and improved information processing during the course of intervention would imply that the patient was moving away from the states of hyperarousal and sensory overload associated with poor outcome. Opposite changes during treatment might indicate that the intervention activities were themselves overstimulating and were exacerbating rather than reducing the patient's cognitive disorganization and autonomic arousal.

Altering Processes Underlying Vulnerability to Relapse

To extend the implications of the model one step further, we consider a possible future application of broad-based behavioral intervention. If the information processing and arousal dysfunctions that have been identified recently in persons at risk for schizophrenia and schizophrenics in relative remission prove to be reliable antecedents of schizophrenic symptomatology, efforts to alter these dysfunctions might provide a more direct means of reducing vulnerability to development of schizophrenic psychotic symptoms than the methods considered thus far. The extent to which behavioral or chemical interventions might change such underlying vulnerabilities is unknown, but the likelihood that some of these dysfunctions are genetically influenced does not necessarily imply that they are unalterable.

The development of behavioral and biofeedback approaches directed toward regulation of attentional and information processing strategies and reduction of autonomic arousal in outpatient schizophrenic patients might provide valuable information on the role of these anomalies in schizophrenic relapse. Current evidence is correlational in nature, making attribution of cause and effect very tentative. Successful alteration of attentional and arousal dysfunctions would provide critical data, therefore, on the casual contribution of such processes to development of schizophrenic thought disorder, hallucinations, and delusions.

SUMMARY

Four categories of factors contributing to the high rate of schizophrenic relapse were identified and discussed.

1. High "expressed emotion" among family members is associated with a high probability of schizophrenic relapse, especially if the patient has frequent face-to-face contact with the family and is not taking medication.
2. A sizable proportion of patients report the occurrence of an independent life event within a few weeks preceding the onset of schizophrenic symptoms, especially if the patient comes from a low "expressed emotion" household.

   Taken together, these two facts suggest that exposure to a social stressor, whether in the form of a life event or in the form of a critical or overinvolved family member, substantially increases the likelihood of a schizophrenic relapse.
3. Attentional and information processing deficits are prominent among schizophrenic patients and some have prognostic value regarding the course and duration of the symptoms. In addition, some attentional and information processing deficits are present among persons at risk for schizophrenia and remain following the disappearance of the symptoms in schizophrenic patients.
4. Schizophrenic patients exhibit a variety of electrodermal abnormalities, with slow habituation of the SCOR and high electrodermal arousal associated with poor short-term prognosis. In addition, there is some evidence that electrodermal hyperresponsivity and/or slow habituation to mildly stressful stimuli is present among the offspring of schizophrenics.

Taken together, the latter two conclusions suggest that attentional and information processing deficits and autonomic hyperresponsivity to stressors may be enduring trait-like characteristics of at least some individuals vulnerable to future schizophrenia.

Based on the factors described above, a tentative "diathesis-stress" model of schizophrenic relapse is presented. According to the model, information processing and autonomic dysfunctions are preexisting vulnerability characteristics. When an individual with these characteristics is exposed to social stressors, transient intermediate state of sensory overload, hyperarousal, and impaired processing of social stimuli result. These intermediate states exacerbate the already poor social environment. Hence, a vicious cycle may be created, which eventuates in a schizophrenic relapse unless the cycle is broken.

Finally, certain preventive treatment implications of the model are discussed. These include the early identification of patients who are at particularly high risk for relapse, selecting an appropriate preventive treatment for the patient, monitoring the effectiveness of the therapeutic strategy, and perhaps modifying the underlying vulnerability to schizophrenic relapse.

REFERENCES

Anderson, C. M., Hogarty, G. E., & Reiss, D. J. Family treatment of adult schizophrenic patients: A research based psycho-educational approach. *Schizophrenia Bulletin*, 1980, *6*, 490–505.

Asarnow, R. F., & MacCrimmon, D. J. Residual performance deficit in clinically remitted schizophrenics: A marker of schizophrenia? *Journal of Abnormal Psychology*, 1978, *87*, 597–608.

Asarnow, R. F., Steffy, R. A., MacCrimmon, D. J., & Cleghorn, J. M. An attentional assessment of foster children at risk for schizophrenia. In L. C. Wynne, R. L. Cromwell, and S. Matthysse (Eds.), *The nature of schizophrenia: New approaches to research and treatment*. New York: Wiley, 1978.

Bernstein, A. S., Taylor, K. W., Starkey, P., Juni, S., Lubowsky, J., & Paley, H., *Initial responsiveness and the effect of prolonged stimulus repetition on skin conductance, finger pulse volume, and EEG response in schizophrenics and controls.* Paper presented at the annual meeting of the Society for Psychophysiological Research, Vancouver, Canada, October, 1980.

Birley, J. L. T., & Brown, G. W. Crisis and life changes preceding the onset or relapse of acute schizophrenia: Clinical aspects. *British Journal of Psychiatry*, 1970, *116*, 327–333.

Brown, G. H., & Birley, J. L. T. Crisis and life changes and the onset of schizophrenia. *Journal of Health and Social Behavior*, 1968, *9*, 203–214.

Brown, G. H., Birley, J. L. T., & Wing, J. K. Influence of family life on the course of schizophrenic disorders: A replication. *British Journal of Psychiatry*, 1972, *121*, 241–258.

Cancro, R., Sutton, S., Kerr, J. B., & Sugerman, A. A. Reaction time and prognosis in acute schizophrenia. *Journal of Nervous and Mental Disease*, 1971, *153*, 351–359.

Carpenter, W. T., Bartko, J. J., Strauss, J. S., & Hawk, A. B. Signs and symptoms as predictors of outcome: A report from the international pilot study of schizophrenia. *American Journal of Psychiatry*, 1978, *135*, 940–945.

Cornblatt, B., & Erlenmeyer-Kimling, L. *Early attentional predictors of adolescent behavioral disturbances in children at risk for schizophrenia.* Paper presented at the Risk Research Consortium Plenary Conference, San Juan, Puerto Rico, March 1980.

Davidson, G. S., & Neale, J. M. The effects of signal-noise similarity on visual information processing of schizophrenia. *Journal of Abnormal Psychology*, 1974, *83*, 683–686.

DeAmicis, L., & Cromwell, R. L. Reaction time crossover in process schizophrenia patients, their relatives and control subjects. *Journal of Nervous and Mental Disease*, 1979, *167*, 593–600.

Erlenmeyer-Kimling, L., & Cornblatt, B. Attentional measures in a study of children at high-risk for schizophrenia. In L. C. Wynne, R. L. Cromwell, and S. Matthysse (Eds.). *The nature of schizophrenia: New approaches to research and treatment*. New York: Wiley, 1978.

Falloon, I. R. H., Liberman, R. P., Lillie, F., & Vaughn, C. E. Family therapy in schizophrenics with a high risk of relapse. *Family Process*, in press.

Freedman, B. J. The subjective experience of perceptual and cognitive disturbances in schizophrenia. *Archives of General Psychiatry*, 1974, *30*, 333–340.

Frith, C. D., Stevens, M., Johnstone, E. C., & Crow, T. J. Skin conductance responsivity during acute episodes of schizophrenia as a predictor of symptomatic improvement. *Psychological Medicine*, 1979, *9*, 101–106.

Goldsmith, J. G., & McFall, R. M. Development and evaluation of an interpersonal skill-training program for psychiatric inpatients. *Journal of Consulting and Clinical Psychology*, 1975, *84*, 51–58.

Gruzelier, J. H. Clinical attributes of schizophrenic skin conductance responders and nonresponders. *Psychological Medicine*, 1976, *6*, 245–249.

Gruzelier, J. H., & Venables, P. H. Skin conductance orienting activity in heterogenous sample of schizophrenics. *Journal of Nervous and Mental Disease*, 1972, *155*, 277–287.

Gruzelier, J. H., & Venables, P. H. Bimodality and lateral asymmetry of skin conductance orienting activity in schizophrenics: Replication and evidence of lateral asymmetry in patients with depression and disorders of personality. *Biological Psychiatry*, 1974, *8*, 55–73.

Gruzelier, J. H., & Venables, P. H. Evidence of high and low levels of physiological arousal in schizophrenics. *Psychophysiology*, 1975, *12*, 66–73.

Hagen, R. L. Behavioral therapies and the treatment of schizophrenics. *Schizophrenia Bulletin*, 1975, *1*, 70–96.

Hersen, M., & Bellack, A. S. Social skills training for chronic psychiatric patients: Rationale, research findings, and future directions. *Comprehensive Psychiatry*, 1976, *17*, 559–580.

Hogarty, G. E., Goldberg, S. C., Schooler, N. R., & Ulrich, R. F. Drug and sociotherapy in the aftercare of schizophrenic patients II. Two year relapse rates. *Archives of General Psychiatry*, 1974, *31*, 603–608.

Jacobs, S., & Myers, J. Recent life events and acute schizophrenic psychosis: A controlled study. *Journal of Nervous and Mental Disease*, 1976, *162*, 75–87.

Koh, S. D. Remembering of verbal materials by schizophrenic young adults. In S. Schwartz (Ed.), *Language and cognition in schizophrenia.* Hillsdale, NJ: Lawrence Erlbaum Associates, 1978.

Leff, J., & Vaughn, C. The interaction of life events and relatives expressed emotion in schizophrenia and depressive neurosis. *British Journal of Psychiatry*, 1980, *136*, 146–153.

Liberman, R. P. Behavior therapy for schizophrenia. In L. J. West & D. E. Flinn (Eds.) *Treatment of schizophrenia: Progress and prospects.* New York: Grune & Stratton, 1976.

Liberman, R. P. *The Camarillo/UCLA MHCRC for the study of schizophrenia: A progress report.* Paper presented at the annual meeting of the Mental Health Clinical Research Centers, Chicago, IL: March, 1981.

Liberman, R. P., & Bryan, E. Behavior therapy in a community mental health center. *American Journal of Psychiatry*, 1977, *134*, 401–406.

Liberman, R. P., Falloon, I. R. H., & Aitchison, R. A. Multiple family therapy for schizophrenia. *Schizophrenia Bulletin*, in press.

Marcus, L. M. *Studies of attention in children vulnerable to psychopathology.* Unpublished doctoral dissertation, University of Minnesota, Minneapolis, 1972.

Mednick, S. A., & Schulsinger, F. Some premorbid characteristics related to breakdown in children with schizophrenic mothers. In D. Rosenthal & S. Kety (Eds.), *Transmission of schizophrenia.* New York: Pergamon Press, 1968.

Meehl, P. E. Schizotaxia, schizotypy, schizophrenia. *American Psychologist*, 1962, *17*, 827–838.

Meichenbaum D. *Cognitive-behavior modification.* New York: Plenum, 1977.

Miller, S., Saccuzzo, D., & Braff, D. Information processing deficits in remitted schizophrenics. *Journal of Abnormal Psychology*, 1979, *88*, 446–449.

Neale, J. M. Perceptual span in schizophrenia. *Journal of Abnormal Psychology*, 1971, *77*, 196–204.

Neale, J. M. Information processing and vulnerability: High risk research. In M. J. Goldstein (Ed.) *Preventive intervention in schizophrenia: Are we ready?* Washington DC: U.S. Government Printing Office, in press.

Nuechterlein, K. H. Reaction time and attention in schizophrenia: A critical evaluation of the data and theories. *Schizophrenia Bulletin*, 1977, *3*, 373–428.

Nuechterlein, K. H. Specificity of deficits to vulnerability to schizophrenic disorders: Compared to whom and what when? In M. J. Goldstein (Ed.), *Preventive intervention in schizophrenia: Are we ready?* Washington DC: U.S. Government Printing Office, in press.

Nuechterlein, K. H., Phipps-Yonas, S., Driscoll, R. M., & Garmezy, N. The role of different components of attention in children vulnerable to schizophrenia. In M. J. Goldstein (Ed.), *Preventive intervention in schizophrenia: Are we ready?* Washington, DC: U.S. Government Printing Office, in press.

Oltmanns, T. F. Selective attention in schizophrenic and manic psychoses: The effect of distraction on information processing. *Journal of Abnormal Psychology*. 1978, *87*, 212–225.

Oltmanns, T. F., & Neale, J. M. Schizophrenic performance when distractors are present: Attentional deficit or differential task difficulty? *Journal of Abnormal Psychology*, 1975, *84*, 205–209.

Orzack, M. H., & Kornetsky, C. Attention dysfunction in chronic schizophrenia. *Archives of General Psychiatry*, 1966, *14*, 323–326.

Patterson, T., & Venables, P. H. Bilateral skin conductance and skin potential in schizophrenic and normal subjects: The identification of the fast habituator group of schizophrenics. *Psychophysiology*, 1978, *15*, 556–560.

Rabkin, J. G. Stressful life events and schizophrenia: A review of the research literature. *Psychological Bulletin*, 1980, *87*, 408–425.

Rappaport, M., Hopkins, H. K., & Hall, K. Auditory signal detection in paranoid and non-paranoid schizophrenics. *Archives of General Psychiatry*, 1972, *27*, 747–752.

Rodnick, E., & Shakow, D. Set in the schizophrenic as measured by a composite reaction time index. *American Journal of Psychiatry*, 1940, *97*, 214–225.

Rosenthal, D. *Genetic theory and abnormal behavior.* New York: McGraw-Hill, 1970.

Russell, P. N. & Knight, R. G. Performance of process schizophrenics on tasks involving visual search. *Journal of Abnormal Psychology*, 1977, *86*, 16–26.

Saccuzzo, D. P., Hirt, M., & Spencer, T. J. Backward masking as a measure of attention in schizophrenia. *Journal of Abnormal Psychology*, 1974, *83*, 512-522.

Salzman, L. F., & Klein, R. H. Habituation and conditioning of electrodermal responses in high risk children. *Schizophrenia Bulletin*, 1978, *4*, 210-222.

Shakow, D. Segmental set: A theory of the formal psychological deficit in schizophrenia. *Archives of General Psychiatry*, 1962, *6*, 1-17.

Stilson, D. W., & Kopell, B. J. Visual recognition in the presence of noise by psychiatric patients. *Journal of Nervous and Mental Disease*, 1964, *139*, 209-221.

Stilson, D. W., Kopell, B. S., Vandenberg, R., & Downs, M. P. Perceptual recognition in the presence of noise by psychiatric patients. *Journal of Nervous and Mental Disease*, 1966, *142*, 235-247.

Straube, E. R. On the meaning of electrodermal nonresponding in schizophrenia. *Journal of Nervous and Mental Disease*, 1979, *167*, 601-611.

Strauss, J. S., & Carpenter, W. T., Jr. The prediction of outcome in schizophrenia: I. Characteristics of outcome. *Archives of General Psychiatry*, 1972, *27*, 739-746.

Strauss, J. S., & Carpenter, W. T., Jr. Characteristic symptoms and outcome in schizophrenia. *Archives of General Psychiatry*, 1974, *39*, 429-434.

Sturgeon, D. A., Kuipers, L., Berkowitz, R., Turpin, G., & Leff, J. Psychophysiological responses of schizophrenic patients to high and low expressed emotion relatives. *British Journal of Psychiatry*, in press.

Tarrier, N., Vaughn, C. E., Lader, M. H., & Leff, J. P. Bodily reactions to people and events in schizophrenics. *Archives of General Psychiatry*, 1979, *36*, 311-315.

Tolsdorf, C. C. Social networks, support and coping: An exploratory study. *Family Process*, 1976, *15*, 407-418.

Traupman, K. L. Effects of categorization and imagery on recognition and recall by process and reactive schizophrenics. *Journal of Abnormal Psychology*, 1975, *84*, 307-314.

van Dyke, J. L., Rosenthal, D., & Rasmussen, P. V. Electrodermal functioning in adopted-away offspring of schizophrenics. *Journal of Psychiatric Research*, 1974, *10*, 199-215.

Vaughn, C. E., & Leff, J. P. The influence of family and social factors on the course of psychiatric illness. *British Journal of Psychiatry*, 1976, *129*, 125-137.

Venables, P. H. Psychophysiological studies in schizophrenic pathology. In P. H. Venables, & M. J. Christie (Eds.), *Research in psychophysiology*. New York: Wiley, 1975.

Venables, P. H. The electrodermal psychophysiology of schizophrenics and children at risk for schizophrenia: Controversies and developments. *Schizophrenia Bulletin*, 1977, *3*, 28–48.

Wallace, C. J. The social skills training project of the Mental Health Clinical Research Center for the Study of Schizophrenia. In J. P. Curran & P. M. Monti (Eds.), *Social skills training: A practical handbook for assessment and treatment*. New York: Guilford, 1981.

Wallace, C. J., Nelson, C., Liberman, R. P., Lukoff, D., & Aitchison, R. A. Review and critique of social skills training with schizophrenics. *Schizophrenia Bulletin*, 1980, *6*, 42–64.

Weaver, L. A., Jr., & Brooks, G. W. The use of psychomotor tests in predicting the potential of chronic schizophrenics. *Journal of Neuropsychiatry*, 1964, *5*, 170–180.

Wing, J. K. Impairments in schizophrenia. A rational basis for social treatment. In R. D. Wirt, G. Winokur, and M. Roff (Eds.), *Life history research in psychopathology*, Volume 4. Minneapolis: University of Minnesota Press, 1975.

Wing, J. K. Clinical concepts of schizophrenia. In J. K. Wing (Ed.), *Schizophrenia: Towards a new synthesis*. London: Academic Press, 1978.

Wishner, J., & Wahl, O. Dichotic listening in schizophrenia. *Journal of Consulting and Clinical Psychology*, 1974, *42*, 538–546.

Wohlberg, G. W., & Kornetsky, C. Sustained attention in remitted schizophrenics. *Archives of General Psychiatry*, 1973, *28*, 533–537.

Wood, R. L., & Cook, M. Attentional deficit in the siblings of schizophrenics. *Psychological Medicine*, 1979, *9*, 465–467.

Zahn, T. P. Predicting outcome from measures of attention and autonomic functioning. In C. Baxter and T. Melnechuk (Eds.), *Perspectives in schizophrenia research*. New York: Raven Press, 1980.

Zahn, T. P., & Carpenter, W. T., Jr. Effects of short-term outcome and clinical improvement on reaction time in acute schizophrenia. *Journal of Psychiatric Research*, 1978, *14*, 59–68.

Zahn, T. P., Carpenter, W. T., & McGlashan, T. H. Autonomic nervous system activity in acute schizophrenia II. Relationships to short term prognosis and clinical state. *Archives of General Psychiatry*, 1981, *38*, 260–266.

Zahn, T. P., Shakow, D., & Rosenthal, D. Reaction time in schizophrenic and normal subjects as a function of preparatory and intertrial intervals. *Journal of Nervous and Mental Disease*, 1961, *133*, 283–287.

Zubin, J., & Spring, B. Vulnerability—a new view of schizophrenia. *Journal of Abnormal Psychology*, 1977, *86*, 103–126.

CHAPTER 15

An Overview of Behavioral Treatment of Autistic Persons

O. Ivar Lovaas, Ph.D.
Andrea B. Ackerman, Ph.D.
Mitchell T. Taubman, Ph.D.

The last 30 years have seen a great amount of research attention to the disorder of childhood autism. The focus has been on understanding the etiology and nature of the disorder, as well as on developing and evaluating treatment procedures. This chapter will review the contributions and perspectives of behavioral researchers to this field. Recently developed innovative treatment procedures, programs, and settings also will be highlighted. Future directions and issues in the field of behavioral research and treatment of autism will be discussed.

BEHAVIORAL DESCRIPTION OF AUTISM

Leonard Kanner first described autism as a distinct type of childhood psychosis in 1943 (see Kanner, 1943 and 1949). The disorder varies in severity, shading into both the normal and retarded ranges of intellectual functioning (see Rutter, 1974; Wing, 1976). It also seems to overlap in symptomatology with other disorders of childhood, including language disorders, sensory impairments, and emotional disturbances. Efforts have therefore continued to define more precisely the essential features of autism using operational definitions of behavior. Since there is no physical, pathological, or psychological test that can confirm the diagnosis of autism, and since there is variability

The preparation of this chapter was supported by grants from USPHS MH 32803-02 and NIMH MH11440-13. We express our appreciation to Janet Klaner for her valuable assistance in the preparation of this chapter.

in the expression of the disorder, the use of precisely defined behavioral criteria in research and reporting is essential to progress in understanding and treatment. Some of the more salient behaviors will be reviewed below.

Severe Affective Isolation

Autistic children are usually dramatically unresponsive to the affectionate overtures of others. As infants, they do not seem to notice the comings and goings of caretakers; they fail to anticipate being picked up, and they do not cup and mold when held. As they develop, autistic children often isolate themselves both from adults and from children, and they usually continue to resist affection. Affectively, autistic children exhibit limited responsiveness to the feelings of others. They usually display little emotion but may exhibit extremes of emotional behavior at unpredictable times.

Apparent Sensory Deficit

Related to the autistic child's limited emotional responsiveness is the frequent report by parents of these children that they have suspected blindness or deafness. Autistic children often act as if they do not see people or objects, such as when they fail to return the gaze of others. They also act as if they do not hear voices or sounds, such as when they fail to respond to their names or to simple directions. However, the children usually display inconsistencies in their responding to sensory stimuli, suggesting to the parents that the children can actually see and hear. So, for example, an autistic child may not respond to a simple reprimand to stop, but may respond to the statement, "Let's go bye bye." This apparent sensory deficit can occur in other modalities. For example, many autistic children are reported to have high pain thresholds but may also be intolerant of any touching by people.

Both the affective isolation and apparent sensory deficit can be detected at an early age, perhaps even during the first few months of life. Many writers on autism consider early onset (onset before two years of age) as critical in making the diagnosis.

Insistence on Sameness

Autistic children often demand that little or no change be made in their daily routine, in the arrangement of the environment, or in the sequencing of actions. The child may become very angry, upset, or frightened if, for example, the furniture in the house is rearranged. The autistic child may also compulsively and repetitively arrange a group of objects and become upset if the display is altered or moved. This insistance on sameness is also evidenced in the frequency with which autistic children refuse the transition from soft to solid foods.

Self-Stimulatory Behavior

Autistic children are noted for the excessive amounts of time they spend engaged in repetitive, stereotyped behaviors that seem to be performed solely for the purpose of the sensory feedback they provide. These responses have been observed to involve all parts of the body as well as the child's interaction with objects. Some frequently reported self-stimulatory behaviors include gazing at lights, saliva swishing, hand and arm flapping, body rocking, finger flicking, toe walking, spinning objects, feeling surfaces, and playing in water. While all children and adults engage in some apparently self-stimulatory behaviors, autistic children are noted for the frequency, intensity, and visibility of these responses in their otherwise limited behavioral repertoire.

Tantrums and Self-Injurious Behaviors

Autistic children are frequently reported to engage in tantrumous and/or aggressive behavior toward people or objects in the environment. They may hit, bite, pinch, or kick adults and children, including family members. They may tear, break, or otherwise destroy household items. They also may simply cry, scream, and carry on for extended periods of time. These behaviors often occur without apparent provocation, and the children may be unconsolable. Some autistic children direct aggressive responses at themselves in the form of self-injurious behaviors. They may hit themselves with their fists, bite their skin and extremeties to produce open wounds, or hit their heads or other body parts against sharp objects. These behaviors vary in their severity from very mild to extremely severe. They are most distressing to observe and can be life threatening due to infection and actual physical damage. Also, they can result in the necessity of restraining the child, thereby limiting the child's access to new learning and to proper physical development.

Language

Approximately 50% of autistic children can be described as mute. They generally have no recognizable nor functional speech. Their verbalizations, if any, consist of various sounds and noises that may or may not be similar to infant babbling. Among those autistic children who do have recognizable speech, many engage in either immediate or delayed echolalia. That is, the child's speech is actually the repetition of some part or all of what has just been said or a repetition of something heard earlier. Only a few autistic children have some functional expressive language. Also, nearly all autistic children, whether mute or echolalic, are delayed and deficient in their understanding of and response to language. This is referred to as a receptive language deficit.

Other Behavior Problems

The self-stimulatory behaviors, the insistence on sameness, and the tantrumous, aggressive, and self-injurious behaviors can be characterized as the behavioral excesses associated with autism. The effective isolation, sensory variability, and receptive and expressive language problems can be characterized as behavioral or skill deficits associated with autism. A number of additional behavioral deficits are also frequently characteristic of autistic children. Most autistic children have few age-appropriate self-help skills. They may be unable or unwilling to dress or feed themselves. They may not be urine-/or bowel trained or able to attend to personal hygiene. Autistic children typically do not play with toys, or they may use toys only for self-stimulatory or compulsive purposes. Autistic children also exhibit deficits in social behaviors and may neither attend to nor interact with adults or children. Finally, autistic children have little apparent appreciation for the outcomes of their actions, and so they may fail to avoid dangerous or risky situations. An example would be climbing to a high and precarious position on a piece of furniture.

Normal-like Behaviors

Autistic children, since the time of Kanner's early writing (1943), have been noted to have unusual competencies or abilities, despite their overall delayed and unusual development. For instance, they may be adept at disassembling and reassembling puzzles or mechanical objects. They may show good auditory memory, as when they memorize the words or tunes to songs or commercials. They may show good visual memory, as when they insist that their environment remain the same, or they find their way to hiding places for food and other favorites. Many autistic children may show the "unusual fears" associated with normal young children, such as sudden fears of certain sounds or common everyday objects. While these "islets of intelligence" have been used in the past to infer potentially normal or intact intelligence, from a behavioral perspective these responses are best viewed as splinter skills, with no further inferences made. Autistic children often evidence motor development well within the normal limits. Normal motor development is sometimes used to assist in the differential diagnosis of autism and retardation. While delayed motor development and/or the presence of detectable brain damage are not incompatible with the presence of autism, they usually rule out a primary diagnosis of autism.

Diagnostic Criteria

To summarize the above descriptions into a more succinct diagnostic picture, the following behavioral descriptions may be offered:

A. *Behavioral deficiences:*

1. affective isolation;
2. apparent sensory deficit;
3. little or no language;
4. little or no play with toys;
5. little or no play with peers;
6. few or no social or self-help skills.

B. *Behavioral excesses:*

1. tantrumous and aggressive behavior, sometimes in the form of self-injury;
2. ritualistic, stereotyped, repetitive "self-stimulatory" behaviors.

C. *Normal-like behaviors:*

1. normal motor development;
2. good visual or auditory memory;
3. special interests in mechanical objects, numbers, music, etc;
4. unusual fears or phobic-like behaviors.

The more of these behavioral manifestations are shown, the more likely it is that the diagnosis of autism will be given. Special emphasis may be given to affective isolation, apparent sensory deficit, and one or more of the behaviors listed under "normal-like behaviors" above.

BEHAVIORAL CONCEPTUALIZATION OF AUTISM

A comprehensive discussion of the many theories regarding the etiology of autism would take more time and space than is alotted here, especially since the amount of theorizing about this population is out of proportion to its size. Briefly, much of the early theorizing emphasized the possible influence of parents who themselves had some unusual qualities (for example, Kanner, 1943; Bettelheim, 1967) or who utilized deviant child-rearing practices in producing the syndrome of autism. There has been very little by way of experimental examination of psychodynamic conceptualizations, primarily because the intrapsychic constructs of the theory do not lend themselves to objective analysis. The concept of deviant child-rearing practices is somewhat more accessible to research analysis, and the results of empirical studies have uniformly failed to support this notion (see McAdoo & DeMeyer, 1978; Pitfield & Oppenheim, 1964). Treatment approaches based on the recommendations of more dynamic theories have had little impact on the behaviors of autistic children (Brown, 1960; Creak, 1963; Kanner & Eisenberg, 1955; Rutter, 1966).

There is more support, however, for theories that suggest that autism arises on the basis of some type of organic brain disorder, in light of the data available regarding neurobiological, intellectual, perceptual, social, and language deficits and defects. Though various loci for such disorders have been hypothesized, there are currently no good grounds for placing the lesion in any particular area of the brain (Rutter, 1974). Likewise, it is not known whether autism is a single disease entity, a nonspecific syndrome of biological impairment, or a collection of symptoms arising from a heterogeneous group of both biological and psychosocial influences (Rutter, 1974). It is also the case that few of these theories have produced information that can aid in remediation, since the implications of research work on biological, psychological, and cognitive processes for treatment are obscure (Menyuk, 1978; Yule, 1978).

The first behavioral conceptualization of autism was formulated by Ferster (1961) following the failure of traditionally oriented approaches in remediating autism. While Ferster began by translating dynamic terms and concepts into a functional behavioral analysis, this quickly gave way to a more objective analysis of autism as a series of behavioral excesses and deficits. Ferster stated that the learning difficulties associated with the syndrome of autism were the result of a failure of social stimuli to gain functional properties for the children. Early research conducted by Ferster and DeMyer (1961, 1962) demonstrated that through systematic manipulations of contingencies, the rates of various behaviors could be modified and accelerated in several autistic children. Stimulus control and conditioned reinforcers were also established under highly controlled conditions. These early studies demonstrated that a functional relationship between autistic children's behavior and environmental events could be established and that learning and behavior change could occur.

Ferster's early work gave way to a flurry of therapeutically oriented behavioral research. In pioneer work, Wolf, Risley, and Mees (1964) were successful in producing dramatic improvements in the eating, social, and verbal skills of a young autistic child. Proceeding from research with normal children demonstrating the use of imitation to facilitate generalized learning (Baer & Sherman, 1964), Lovaas et al. (1967) taught autistic children nonverbal imitation and demonstrated how this could enhance the learning of other intellectual, social, and self-help skills. Subsequent research (Lovaas et al., 1966) demonstrated the effectiveness of a shaping and discrimination training procedure in establishing verbal imitation in previously mute autistic children.

From these early investigations have grown a substantial number of detailed and rigorous investigations demonstrating the effectiveness of behavioral procedures for the treatment of the range of deficits and excesses of autism. Over time these methodologies have been brought together to form comprehensive behavioral programs for the treatment of autism. The empirical foundations for current conceptualization and treatment strategies are reviewed below.

It is important to note that behavioral research into autism did not examine a hypothetical underlying entity like "autism" as such (whatever that is), but broke "autism" into separate behaviors and analyzed each behavior relatively separately. For example, the failure to develop language was researched relatively independent of self-injurious behaviors, even though these behaviors may, in a later analysis, show themselves to have certain overlapping areas. In all likelihood, such a research strategy greatly facilitated inquiry by making certain problems more "accessible." It is also noteworthy that such a strategy allows for a sharing of information (and skills) among researchers studying different kinds of childhood problems, such as mental retardation, aphasia, and so on. In other words, behavioral scientists did not become terribly obsessed by the merits of making certain—perhaps imaginal—fine and subtle discriminations regarding exactly what someone did or did not imply, in his or her diagnostic criteria of autism. The emphasis of the research efforts became primarily practical and minimally theoretical.

MANAGEMENT OF SELF-INJURIOUS BEHAVIORS

Self-Injury

Self-injurious behaviors are of special concern, because they can be harmful to the individual, to the environment, and/or to other people in the environment; and they may significantly reduce the individual's interactions with the environment, reducing opportunities for learning to occur (Forehand & Baumeister, 1976). The elimination of self-injurious behaviors thus becomes not only desirable, but is at times essential if other behaviors are to be established and extreme consequences such as institutionalization are to be avoided or postponed (Bucher & Lovaas, 1968; Forehand & Baumeister, 1976; Lovaas, Young, & Newsom, 1978).

Several early behavioral studies suggested that the withdrawal of social attention contingent on self-injurious behaviors might effectively reduce these behaviors in autistic and retarded children (Hamilton, Stephens, & Allen, 1967; Wolf et al., 1964). Subsequent studies also clearly demonstrated that the delivery of social attention (affection and concern) contingent on self-injurious behavior worsened the problem (Lovaas et al., 1965; Lovaas & Simmons, 1969). In other words, studies indicated that extinction procedures could eliminate self-injurious behaviors, while attention increased them. Lovaas and Simmons (1969) provided further support for the learned social nature of self-injurious behavior by demonstrating that such behavior occurred in environments where social reinforcement was available but not where such reinforcement or cues for such reinforcement were absent. A recent study by Carr, Newsom, and Binkoff (1976) also demonstrated such narrow social stimulus control over self-injurious behavior. Their study was also interesting because it demonstrated that the child's self-injury could serve as an escape response; self-injury increased when demands were placed on the child but decreased when demands ceased or when cues signaling the withdrawal of demands were presented. Similar findings are reported by Frankel and Simmons (1976) in their review of the literature on self-injury.

There are times when children are so severely self-destructive that extinction operations may result in permanent injury or even death (Lovaas et al., 1978). There are also times when extinction, withdrawal of reinforcement, time-out, and other procedures are contraindicated (see Carr et al., 1976) or ineffective (for example, Baroff & Tate, 1968). In such cases, the use of brief physically aversive stimuli, such as a slap on the thigh, may prove to be the most rapid, successful, and humane form of treatment (Bucher & Lovaas, 1968; Carr, 1976; Lovaas et al., 1965a; Lovaas et al., 1978; Simmons & Lovaas, 1969). Studies utilizing such a physically aversive stimulus contingent on self-injurious behaviors have reported rapid and usually complete elimination of these behaviors in very short periods of time (for example, Corte, Wolfe, & Lock, 1971; Lovaas & Simmons, 1969; Merbaum, 1973; Tate & Baroff, 1966). These studies are also quite consistent in reporting a high degree of discrimination of treatment effects across persons and environments (as in Lovaas, Schaeffer, & Simmons, 1965b) and an absence of negative side effects (see Lichstein & Schreibman, 1976).

More recently, research on the use of contingent aversives in the context of a comprehensive instructional and treatment program have demonstrated the benefits of the therapeutic use of such procedures in combination with rich schedules of positive reinforcement (Ackerman, 1979). When other procedures have failed, the therapeutic and professionally monitored short-term utilization of physical punishment, with the consent of parents and relevant others, has allowed for the successful avoidance of years of enduring pain and physical harm. However, despite the supportive evidence for its use, it should be emphasized that physical punishment as part of a comprehensive program should be utilized when it can be documented that all other reasonable and appropriate efforts have failed, when its employment is acceptable to all relevant individuals concerned, and only when administered by qualified professional staff. It is critical that physical punishment of self-destructive behavior be undertaken only when a considerable amount of time and effort is devoted to building and maintaining *adaptive* behaviors, which will have a chance of replacing self-injury as a means for obtaining social reinforcers. The extent to which positive reinforcement for behaviors incompatible with self-destruction increase the durability of the suppressive effects of punishment is not known with autistic or other human populations, although the basic research literature suggests that it greatly enhances both short- and long-term suppressive effects (Azrin & Holz, 1966).

SUPPRESSION OF SELF-STIMULATORY BEHAVIORS

Self-stimulatory behaviors represent a different sort of danger to autistic children. A variety of studies have demonstrated that self-stimulatory behaviors interfere with the learning of new, appropriate behaviors (Koegel & Covert, 1972; Lovaas et al., 1965b) and/or the performance of more appropriate responses already in the child's repertoire (Koegel, Firestone, Kramme, & Dunlap, 1974). An example of the blocking effect of self-stimulation is presented in a study by Lovaas, Litrownik, and Mann (1971). They compared the performance (approaching a candy dispenser at the sound of a tone) of mute autistic, echolalic autistic, and normal children when engaged in self-stimulation and when not engaged in such behavior. The results indicated increased response latencies in mute autistics when engaged in self-stimulation, decreased response latencies in mute autistics as training progressed, and decreased self-stimulation with increased reinforcement for other behaviors.

These studies suggest that self-stimulatory behavior decreases the autistic child's responsivity to the environment. The fact that autistic children frequently choose self-stimulation over behaviors leading to food or social reinforcement (Koegel & Covert, 1972; Koegel et al., 1974; Lovaas et al., 1971; Lovaas et al., 1965b) suggests that self-stimulatory behaviors may be equally rewarding to the child. The autistic child's deficiency in socially oriented, appropriate reinforcers also predicts the high rate of self-stimulatory behavior observed (Lovaas et al., 1978). To allow more socially appropriate reinforcers to become functional and to compete with the apparently strong sensory reinforcement provided by self-stimulatory behaviors, it appears necessary to suppress such behaviors (Lovaas et al., 1978). Foxx and Azrin (1973) provide a similar analysis of the functional properties of self-stimulation.

A variety of procedures have been used to suppress self-stimulatory behaviors, with varying degrees of effectiveness. Extinction and time-out procedures are generally ineffective in reducing self-stimulation, since such behavior is apparently not controlled by extrinsic or social reinforcers. Rather, the person himself seems to control the reinforcers that maintain self-stimulatory behaviors (Lovaas et al., 1978). Efforts to reduce self-stimulatory behaviors using differential reinforcement of other behaviors (for example, Hollis, 1968). reinforcement of low or zero rates of self-stimulation (as in Mulhern & Baumeister, 1969), and response cost contingent on self-stimulation (for example, Mattos, 1969) have met with some degree of effectiveness. However, these procedures usually achieve only some response reduction, are cumbersome to carry out, and have not addressed issues of generalizability or durability (Forehand & Baumeister, 1976). In many cases self-stimulation occurs at such high rates that reliable reinforcement of alternative behaviors is virtually impossible, and the autistic child's frequently deficient behavioral and reinforcement repertoires often rule out such procedures (Forehand & Baumeister, 1976; Foxx & Azrin, 1973). To date, punishment procedures in the form of shock (Baumeister & Forehand, 1973; Lovaas et al., 1965b), sharp slaps on the hands, arms, legs, or buttocks (Koegel & Covert, 1972; Koegel et al., 1974) and positive practice overcorrection (Azrin, Kaplan, & Foxx, 1973; Foxx & Azrin, 1973), paired with the teaching of more appropriate alternative patterns of responding, seem to produce maximal therapeutic benefit. Such procedures seem to decrease the reinforcement value of self-stimulation by pairing aversive events with the occurrence of such behaviors (Lovaas et al., 1978).

Recent and innovative work by Rincover et al. (1979) involved the development of a "sensory extinction" procedure for reducing self-stimulation. With the employment of this procedure, self-stimulation was effectively reduced through the removal of the auditory, visual, or proprioceptive consequences of the behavior (whatever was functional for that particular child). The authors also found that when toys that supplied sensory stimulation in preferred modalities were provided, self-stimulation was generally reduced while appropriate play increased. Once severely inappropriate behaviors such as self-destruction and self-stimulation are being effectively reduced, the major focus of behavioral treatment begins. It is at this point that efforts are directed at helping these children acquire appropriate, socially adaptive behaviors. The foundation of this strategy is behaviorally oriented language training.

LANGUAGE INSTRUCTION

The core of much of the behavioral work with autistic children has been language training. The absence of language can be seen as a broad and critical deficit in their repertoires. However, language training is viewed not only as a strategy for remedying this deficiency, but also as a means for eventually impacting other deficit areas. Language training provides the foundation for further instruction in social, play, and cognitive skills. And the acquisition of language permits access to the world of learning in the larger environment that often appears inaccessible to these children.

Given the pivotal importance of language instruction, much early behavioral work with autistic children was concentrated in this area. In these early interventions (Lovaas, et al., 1966; Risley & Wolf, 1967; Wolf, et al., 1964) a behavioral technique was developed to establish speech in mute and echolalic autistic children. Over time, increasingly comprehensive programs were developed to teach more complex aspects of language, such as pronouns, prepositions, verbs, and verb tenses (Lovaas et al., 1973; Schreibman & Carr, 1978; Stevens-Long & Rasmussen, 1974). Eventually, the collection and combination of language training procedures came to form a complete behaviorally oriented intervention program for building speech and language. A comprehensive description of this type of program is presented in Lovaas (1977) and in considerably more detail in Lovaas et al. (1981). What follows is an overview of the sequencing of such a comprehensive language training program.

Prerequisite Training

Language instruction must begin with preparing the child for the teaching situation. As discussed previously, the reduction of self-stimulation and self-destruction is a prerequisite to later instruction. Concurrent with the suppression of inappropriate behaviors, the therapist attempts to establish some initial forms of stimulus control. For instance, the child is required to comply with some very simple demands, such as sitting quietly in a chair or attending to the therapist's face for a short period of time. Instructions often evoke tantrums, noncompliance, self-destruction, or self-stimulatory behavior. Therefore, the establishment of stimulus control and the reduction of atavistic and self-stimulatory behaviors proceed concurrently.

Building a Verbal Topography

The teaching of verbal behaviors begins with the therapist and child sitting closely facing each other and with the child attending to the therapist's face. Verbal imitation training is the essential building block to teaching language. Imitation occurs when a response has the same topography as its controlling discriminative stimulus; that is, the response resembles its stimulus. For example, when the therapist says "Mm," the child says "Mm." The building of verbal imitation involves the establishment of various discriminations. In the first step with mute children, the therapist attempts to increase the child's vocalizations by providing reinforcement contingent upon any vocalizations. The child is fondled, tickled, and the like in order to increase the probability that sounds will be emitted. This is necessary with essentially mute children in order to produce some vocalizations with which to work. The second step involves teaching the child to make a temporal discrimination; vocalizations are reinforced only if they occur within about three seconds of the therapist's vocalizations. In the third step, successively closer approximations to the therapist's speech sounds are reinforced, until the child matches the particular sound given by the therapist (for example, emits "oh" after the therapist says "oh"). The sounds to be imitated are selected according to several criteria. Usually they are those sounds most frequently emitted by the child (for example, during step one). Also, sounds that have clearly observable visual components that can be exaggerated by the therapist are selected. Finally, some sounds are particularly conducive to manual prompting. The child can be assisted in holding the mouth in the appropriate shape when vocalizing. For example, the sound "mm" is prompted by pressing the child's lips together when vocalizing. In the fourth step, the process above is repeated with a second sound. This sound should be auditorily and visually very different from the first one. For example, if "oh" was the first sound, "mm" or "bee" would be an appropriate second sound. Once the child can reliably imitate the second sound, the therapist intermixes the presentation of the two sounds and reinforces the child only for correct responding. Increasingly finer discriminations are required as new sounds, syllables, words, and word combinations are added. Of course this extension of the process takes many months or even years of training.

Teaching Meaning (stimulus functions)

Although a child may imitate the vocalizations of others, the meaning of the vocalizations is not necessarily known. The acquisition of meaningful speech involves establishing a context for speech. This requires learning two fundamental discriminations. The first, the expressive discrimination, involves a nonverbal stimulus requiring a verbal response. An example would be holding up an object and requiring the child to label it. The second, the receptive discrimination, consists of a verbal stimulus and a nonverbal response. This refers to speech comprehension in which the child and his behavior come under the verbal control of others. An example would be giving the child the direction, "Go get your shoes." Most language situations involve components of both discriminations.

The language training program based on teaching these two discriminations begins with labeling objects and proceeds to labeling actions. These labeling programs are made functional as soon as possible. Once the child can label relevant objects and events in the environment, it is required that these labels be used to access what the labels denote. In this manner, speaking becomes rewarding for the child by gaining access to desired objects and events in the environment.

It should be pointed out that it is here that the time, energy, dedication, and skill of parents and others involved with the child is critical in substantially expanding the child's world through language.

The program gradually moves on to teaching the child to become increasingly proficient in language, including instruction on more abstract concepts and parts of speech such as pronouns, prepositions, and verb tenses. In time this may progress to the use of language in such activities as recall and story telling.

The high degree of behavioral complexity that has been achieved with some of these children is illustrated by the results of programs designed to teach grammar and abstract concepts, such as prepositional and time relationships (Lovaas, 1977). In these efforts, the children learned to generate their own sentences and to respond to stimuli they had not previously encountered. The behavioral technology for teaching language to autistic children has achieved an advanced stage of sophistication. Some autistic children acquire complex and complete language, although many children make less substantial gains.

AN OUTLINE OF THE TREATMENT PROGRAM

In addition to their language deficiencies, autistic children often have marked deficits in other areas of their behavioral repertoires. A guide to program planning and instruction to ameliorate the range of skill deficits present in autistic children is provided in Lovaas et al. (1981). In brief, when the parents first bring their child to our clinic, the child is usually indifferent to our efforts to intervene or reacts with tantrums, aggression, noncompliance, and/or self-destructive behaviors. The parents are often frustrated, anxious, and quite confused about what to do. We work closely with the parents to teach them our skills in detail (the parents work with us in an apprenticeship relationship at first). As a result, from the very first day of treatment the parents have learned some useful treatment skills and can see the beneficial effects of their new way of handling their child. Since we have found that tantrumous behaviors along with self-stimulatory behaviors interfere with the acquisition of more appropriate and adaptive ways of functioning, we attempt to suppress these pathological behaviors from the beginning. Extinction, time-out, and punishment procedures are used, depending upon whether the behaviors are maintained by social reinforcement, avoidance motivation, or are self-reinforcing. So, for example, self-stimulation, which has been demonstrated to be self-reinforcing, is best dealt with using punishment. On the other hand, some tantrums may be reinforced by the fact that they get people to reduce demands on the child. When this is the case, working through or punishment will be more successful than time-out or extinction, which may actually further reinforce the tantrum behavior.

Concurrent with efforts to reduce disruptive, inappropriate behaviors, the treatment team begins to teach more appropriate patterns of responding. This is essential if the child is to learn alternatives to inappropriate behaviors that can successfully gain access to positive reinforcement in the environment. Thus, we begin by teaching the child behaviors that can be lavishly praised and that will facilitate future learning. These behaviors include sitting in the chair, attending to the therapist's face, and suppressing self-stimulatory and other disruptive behaviors. The parents work together with the other therapists in order to provide the child with 24-hour-a-day treatment opportunities.

After the first phase of "Getting ready to learn," we start a second phase: "Early learning." In this phase, our treatment efforts center on the acquisition of three major categories of behavior. The first is nonverbal imitation, which becomes the foundation for future teaching of social, play, and self-help behaviors. Soon after the child has acquired several imitative motor responses, we begin to shift to verbal control over these behaviors, as in teaching receptive commands or compliance training. The child's understanding of simple requests and commands is critical to his or her maintenance in the home, school, and community. The third major emphasis is verbal imitation training, where the child learns to produce increasingly complex verbal responses from sounds to words to phrases and full sentences. This early language training is then made functional as the child learns the meaning of these speech sounds in relation to objects and events in the world.

The third phase centers on teaching the child basic self-help skills, such as adequate toileting, dressing, eating skills, appropriate behaviors in stores, cars, and so forth. The fourth major phase centers on teaching more complex language, as in using and understanding abstract speech, using language to obtain information, and so on.

Over time (anywhere from six months to several years), we introduce the child to more and more normalized community settings, such as school, church, restaurants, and parks. We continue to normalize the child's and the family's contacts in the community and give the child more and more responsibility for independent, age-appropriate behavior. The degree of independence achieved varies considerably in the children we have treated thus far, but all have made substantial gains over their level of functioning at intake and over their outcome as predicted by follow-up studies to date. Although this outline applies to the treatment provided by the UCLA Autism Project, similar programming is offered through other comprehensive projects. Other autism treatment programs that employ similar behavioral techniques include the May Institute, Project TEACCH (Lansing & Schopler, 1978), and the Princeton Child Development Center.

FOLLOW-UP STUDIES

Research has evaluated the outcome effectiveness of an initial attempt at a comprehensive behavioral treatment program. This study, conducted by Lovaas et al. (1973), examined a group of behaviorally treated autistic children and involved the measurement of several appropriate behaviors such as verbal, social, and play responding and inappropriate behaviors including self-stimulation and echolalia. The measures were collected before, immediately following, and one to fours years after the conclusion of treatment. The children were either released to their parents after treatment or, for those without family placements, to a state hospital.

The results of the investigation indicated that all children improved with treatment, with substantial increases in appropriate and decreases in inappropriate behaviors. The follow-up data were very significant: children who stayed with their parents either maintained or increased their gains; the institutionalized children showed a marked decrement in their performance. These results provide strong support for the importance of the development of conditions to facilitate the maintenance of treatment gains. Treatment of autistic persons is best planned as a life-long effort.

YOUNG VERSUS OLDER AUTISTIC INDIVIDUALS

The kinds of services delivered to young versus older autistic persons differ in certain important ways. Quite early in our work we discovered that young autistic children identified and initiated into treatment prior to 40 months of age made substantial gains in treatment, generalized those treatment gains better across environments, and showed less relapse at follow-up. Therefore, early identification and massive (more than 40 hours per week of individual) treatment is critical to maximize treatment gains. A main emphasis in the "Young Autism Project" is to facilitate the child's integration among normal peers, in normal schools, and a surprising number of children are able to accomplish such an adjustment. In such a project it is important *not* to publicize the child's diagnosis of autism, but to shield him or her from the pessimistic and abnormal interactions given to a child with such a label.—For many young autistic children, the diagnosis of autism virtually guarantees the child a "career" in autism. with special schools, institutions, and isolation from normal, more therapeutic invironments.

Until recently, for the treatment of older autistic individuals there has been little available as an alternative to institutionalization when natural home placement is not viable. However, within the last few years there has begun a movement toward the community-based residential treatment of autistic individuals. With time, it has become increasingly clear that while the development of these community-based group home facilities represents an important improvement in residential options for autistic individuals, these changes are not sufficient. Development of custodial care group home facilities in residential neighborhoods could amount to nothing more than the establishment of small local institutions.

This difficulty led to the establishment of Teaching Homes for autistic individuals in 1974. Such group homes employ the Teaching Home Treatment Model and are unique along a number of critical dimensions. In addition to complete care, these community-based homes furnish comprehensive behavioral instruction and treatment in language, social, play, self-help, and cognitive skill areas. Operated by a live-in couple referred to as Teaching Parents, these homes provide continuity in treatment and family style setting to facilitate instructional efforts. Staff at these homes participate in an extensive training program that provides them with the range of skills necessary to operate such a comprehensive program. Finally, perhaps the most unique feature of Teaching Homes is the emphasis on the use of empirically based procedures and on the ongoing evaluation of the model and its effects. Only through such research can the strengths and weaknesses of the program be identified and the model be continuously improved and refined. A project designed to provide such training on the Teaching Home Model and to conduct research on the programs' and their effectiveness is currently in operation (Lovaas, 1979). This project, while assisting in the nationwide initiation of Teaching Homes programs, is also generating evidence for the success and preferability of such a treatment alternative for older autistic persons.

CONCLUSIONS

Several implications can be drawn from the treatment approaches and research described. First, it is clear that major accomplishments have been achieved in the development of effective behavioral procedures for the treatment of autism. What began as rudimentary attempts at producing limited behavior change have grown into sophisticated, systematic treatment technologies. Comprehensive treatment programs based on these methodologies have been developed and demonstrate promising success. Although much has been done to evaluate the effectiveness of single behavioral procedures, little research has been conducted to evaluate the overall impact of comprehensive treatment programs. Also, continued formulation and investigation of treatment procedures is necessary for increasingly effective therapy to be provided. Additional investigations into the nature of autism and functional analysis of its behavioral components would generate further understanding of the disorder and clearly be facilitative to the development of relevant and efficient treatment.

The results from comprehensive autism treatment programs also offer several suggestions and precautions for future efforts. Concentration on parent and family training as well as attention to generalization would be essential strategies. Additionally, exploration of alternatives to institutionalization, such as community-based group homes, would be a pursuit of considerable value.

There remain many unanswered and critical questions relating to the treatment of autistic children. However, exceptional gains have been achieved. Results thus far obtained, as well as a commitment to ongoing research, evaluations, and development makes the behavioral treatment of autistic children a particularly unique and promising approach.

SUMMARY

In the recent past, considerable progress has been made in the behavioral treatment of autism. Autism has increasingly been conceptualized in behavioral terms, which include severe affective isolation, apparent sensory deficit, self-stimulatory behaviors, tantrums and self-destruction, mutism and echolalia, deficiency in play behavior, social skill deficits, and certain behaviors similar to those of more normal children. Traditional psychodynamic perspectives on the etiology of autism have received little empirical support, during a time when behavioral approaches to autism have generated a wealth of research and treatment efforts, which have demonstrated success in impacting the disorder.

Behavioral treatment efforts have been directed at several separate problem behaviors that comprise autism. In the area of aggressive and self-injurious behavior, extinction and time-out have, under certain circumstances, been successfully applied. In certain limited situations when the child's life was endangered, the utilization of physical punishment, in a controlled fashion and in the context of a comprehensive instructional program designed to build better communicative behaviors, has been strongly indicated. Self-stimulatory behavior, which has been found to attenuate new learning, has been reduced or eliminated through the use of punishment as well as overcorrection and sensory extinction.

While the reduction of interfering inappropriate behaviors is critical to successful treatment, the focus of good behavioral treatment programs centers on the building of appropriate, socially facilitating behaviors. The core of such instruction is language training. The initial step in this training is teaching the child to imitate sounds. Later, the child learns the meaning of speech and how to use it to express his or her own wants or to understand the demands of others. Behavioral treatment is also provided to overcome deficits in other areas such as social, cognitive, play, and self-help skills. One of the most significant developments centers on the dissemination of treatment technologies to all people involved in the autistic person's life, such as the parents, teachers, peers, and so on. Also of significance is the establishment of treatment environments that are available during most of the waking hours of the child and located as close to the natural (least restrictive) environment as possible. Normal children learn "on their own," autistic and retarded children learn only when explicitly and specifically taught.

Several issues requiring future attention also were raised in this paper. The more important issues center on the need for additional outcome evaluations, with special attention to generalization and maintenance of treatment effects, exploration of treatment alternatives to institutionalization, and continued development and investigation of other treatment methodologies. Overall, the results obtained through behavioral treatment of autistic individuals have been impressive and provide considerable encouragement for the prognosis of these children in the future.

REFERENCES

Ackerman, A. B. *The role of punishment in the treatment of preschool aged autistic children: Effects and side effects.* Unpublished doctoral dissertation. University of California, Los Angeles, CA: 1979.

Azrin, N. H., & Holz, W. C. Punishment. In W. E. Honig (Ed.), *Operant behavior: Areas of research and applications.* New York: Appleton-Century-Crofts, 1966.

Azrin, N. H., Kaplan, S. J., & Foxx, R. M. Autism reversal: Eliminating stereotyped self-stimulation of retarded individuals. *American Journal of Mental Deficiency*, 1973, *78*, 241–248.

Baer, D. M., & Sherman, J. Reinforcement control of generalized imitation in young children. *Journal of Experimental Child Psychology*, 1964, *1*, 37–49.

Baroff, G. S., & Tate, B. G. The use of aversive stimulation in the treatment of self-injurious behavior. *Journal of Child Psychiatry*, 1968, *7*, 454–470.

Baumeister, A. A., and Forehand, R. Stereotyped acts. In N. R. Ellis (Eds.), *International review of research in mental retardation*, Volume 6. New York: Academic Press, 1973.

Bettelheim, B. *The empty fortress: Infantile autism and the birth of self.* New York: The Free Press, 1967.

Brown, J. Prognosis from presenting symptoms of preschool children with atypical development. *American Journal of Orthopsychiatry*, 1960, *30*, 382–390.

Bucher, B., & Lovaas, O. I. Use of aversive stimulation in behavior modification. In M. R. Jones (Ed.), *Miami symposium on the prediction of behavior, 1967: Aversive stimulation.* Coral Gables: University of Miami Press, 1968.

Carr, E. G., Newsom, C. D., & Binkoff, J. Stimulus control of self-destructive behavior in a psychotic child. *Journal of Abnormal Child Psychology*, 1976, *4*, 139–153.

Carr, J. The severely retarded autistic child. In L. Wing (Ed.), *Early childhood autism: Clinical, educational, and social aspects*, Second edition. New York: Pergamon Press, 1976.

Corte, H. E., Wolf, M. M., & Locke, B. J. A comparison of procedures for eliminating self-injurious behavior of retarded adolescents. *Journal of Applied Behavior Analysis*, 1971, *4*, 201–213.

Creak, M. Childhood psychosis: A review of 100 cases. *British Journal of Psychiatry*, 1963, *109*, 84–89.

Ferster, C. B. Positive reinforcement and behavioral deficits of autistic child. *Child Development*, 1961, *32*, 437–456.

Ferster, C. B., & DeMyer, M. K. The development of performance in autistic children in an automatically controlled environment. *Journal of Chronic Diseases*, 1961, *13*, 312–345.

Ferster, C. B., & DeMyer, M. K. A method for the experimental analysis of the behavior of autistic children. *American Journal of Orthopsychiatry*, 1962, *32*, 89–98.

Forehand, R., & Baumeister, A. A. Deceleration of aberrant behavior among retarded individuals. In M. Hersen, R. M. Eisler & P. M. Miller, (Eds.),*Progress in behavior modification*, Volume 2. New York: Academic Press, 1976.

Foxx, R. M., & Azrin, N. H. The elimination of autistic self-stimulatory behavior by overcorrection. *Journal of Applied Behavior Analysis*, 1973, *6*, 1–4.

Frankel, R., & Simmons, J. Q. Self-injurious behavior in schizophrenic and retarded children. *American Journal of Mental Deficiency*, 1976, *80*, 512–522.

Hamilton, J., Stephens, L., & Allen, P. Controlling aggressive and destructive behavior in severely retarded institutionalized residents. *American Journal of Mental Deficiency*, 1967, *71*, 852–856.

Hollis, J. H. *Analysis of rocking behavior.* Working Paper No. 193, Parsons Research Center, Parsons, Kansas, 1968.

Kanner, L. Autistic disturbances of affective contact. *Nervous Child*, 1943, *2*, 217–250.

Kanner, L. Problems of nosology and psychodynamics of early infantile autism. *American Journal of Orthopsychiatry*, 1949, *19*, 416–426.

Kanner, L., & Eisenberg, L. Notes on the follow-up of autistic children. In P. H. Hock & J. Zubin (Eds.), *Psychopathology of Childhood.* New York: Grune and Stratton, 1955.

Koegel, R. L., & Covert, A. The relationship of self-stimulation to learning in autistic children. *Journal of Applied Behavior Analysis*, 1972, *5*, 381–387.

Koegel, R. L., Firestone, P. B., Kramme, K. W., & Dunlap, G. Increasing spontaneous play by suppressing self-stimulation in autistic children. *Journal of Applied Behavior Analysis*, 1974, *7*, 521–528.

Lansing, M. D., & Schopler, E. Individualized education: A public school model. In M. Rutter & E. Schopler (Eds.), *Autism: A reappraisal of concepts and treatment.* New York: Pergamon Press, 1978.

Lichstein, K. L., & Schreibman, L. Employing electric shock with autistic children: A review of the side effects. *Journal of Autism and Childhood Schizophrenia*, 1976, *6*, 163–173.

Lovaas, O. I. *The autistic child: Language development through behavior modification.* New York: Irvington Publishers, 1977.

Lovaas, O. I. *Teaching Homes for Developmentally Disabled Children* (Research Project MH32803). National Institute of Mental Health, 1979.

Lovaas, O. I., Berberich, J. P., Perloff, B. F., & Schaeffer, B. Acquisition of imitative speech by schizophrenic children. *Science*, 1966, *151*, 705–707.

Lovaas, O. I., Ackerman, A. B., Alexander, D., Firestone, P. B., Perkins, M., & Young, D. B. *Teaching developmentally disabled children: The me book.* Baltimore, MD: University Park Press, 1981.

Lovaas, O. I., Freitag, G., Gold, V. J., & Kassorla, I. C. Experimental studies in childhood schizophrenia: Analysis of self-destructive behavior. *Journal of Experimental Child Psychology*, 1965, *2*, 67–84. (a)

Lovaas, O. I., Freitas, L., Nelson, K., & Whalen, C. The establishment of imitation and its use for the development of complex behavior in schizophrenic children. *Behaviour Research and Therapy*, 1967, *5*, 171–181.

Lovaas, O. I., Koegel, R. L., Simmons, J. Q., & Long, J. S. Some generalization and follow-up measures on autistic children in behavior therapy. *Journal of Applied Behavior Analysis*, 1973, *6*, 131–165.

Lovaas, O. I., Litrownik, A. & Mann, R. Response latencies to auditory stimuli in autistic children engaged in self-stimulatory behavior. *Behavior Research and Therapy*, 1971, *9*, 39–49.

Lovaas, O. I., Schaeffer, B., & Simmons, J. Q. Experimental studies in childhood schizophrenia: Building social behavior in autistic children by use of electric shock. *Journal of Experimental Research in Personality*, 1965, *1*, 99–109. (b)

Lovaas, O. I., & Simmons, J. Q. Manipulation of self-destruction in three retarded children. *Journal of Applied Behavior Analysis*, 1969, *2*, 143–157.

Lovaas, O. I., Young, D. B., & Newsom, C. D. Childhood psychosis: Behavioral treatment. In B. B. Wolman, J. Egan & A. O. Ross (Eds.), *Handbook of treatment of mental disorders in childhood and adolescence*. Englewood Cliffs, NJ: Prentice-Hall, 1978.

Mattos, R. L. Operant control of facial ticing and finger sucking in a severely retarded child. Paper presented at the meeting of the American Association on Mental Deficiency, San Francisco, CA: May, 1969.

McAdoo, W. G., & DeMyer, M. K. Personality characteristics of parents. In M. Rutter & E. Schopler (Eds.), *Autism: A reappraisal of concepts and treatment*. New York: Pergamon Press, 1978.

Menyuk, P. Language: What's wrong and why. In M. Rutter & E. Schopler (Eds.), *Autism: A reappraisal of concepts and treatment*. New York: Pergamon Press, 1978.

Merbaum, M. The modification of self-destructive behavior by a mother-therapist using aversive stimulation. *Behavior Therapy*, 1973, *4*, 442–447.

Mulhern, T., & Baumeister, A. A. An experimental attempt to reduce stereotypy by reinforcement procedures. *American Journal of Mental Deficiency*, 1969, *74*, 69–74.

Pitfield, M., & Oppenheim, A. N. Child rearing attitudes of mothers of psychotic children. *Journal of Child Psychiatry*, 1964, *5*, 51–57.

Rincover, A., Cook R., Peoples, A., & Packard, D. Sensory extinction and sensory reinforcement principles for programming multiple adaptive behavior change. *Journal of Applied Behavior Analysis*, 1979, *12*, 221–233.

Risley, T., & Wolf, M. M. Establishing functional speech in echolalic children. *Behaviour Research and Therapy*, 1967, *5*, 73–88.

Rutter, M. Behavioral and cognitive characteristics of a series of psychotic children. In J. K. Wing (Ed.), *Early childhood autism; Clinical, educational and social aspects.* New York: Pergamon Press, 1966.

Rutter, M. The development of infantile autism. *Psychological Medicine*, 1974, *4*, 147–163.

Schreibman, L., & Carr, E. G. Elimination of echolalic responding to questions through the training of a generalized verbal response. *Journal of Applied Behavioral Analysis*, 1978, *11*, 453–463.

Simmons, J. Q., & Lovaas, O. I. Use of pain and punishment as treatment techniques with childhood schizophrenics. *American Journal of Psychotherapy*, 1969, *23*, 23–36.

Stevens-Long, J., & Rasmussen, M. The acquisition of simple and compound sentence structure in an autistic child. *Journal of Applied Behavior Analysis*, 1974, 7, 473–479.

Tate, B. G., & Baroff, G. S. Aversive control of self-injurious behavior in a psychotic boy. *Behaviour Research and Therapy*, 1966, *4*, 281–287.

Wing, L. Diagnosis, clinical description, and prognosis. In L. Wing (Ed.), *Early childhood autism: Clinical, educational, and social aspects*, Second edition. New York: Pergamon Press, 1976.

Wolf, M. M., Risley, T., & Mees, H. Application of operant conditioning procedures to the behavior problems of an autistic child. *Behaviour Research and Therapy*, 1964, *1*, 305–312.

Yule, W. Research methodology: What are the "correct controls"? In M. Rutter & E. Schopler (Eds.), *Autism: A reappraisal of concepts and treatment.* New York: Pergamon Press, 1978.

PART VIII

Behavioral Medicine

CHAPTER 16

A Social Learning Perspective on Pain Experience

Kenneth D. Craig, Ph.D.

INTRODUCTION

Individual differences in illness behavior pose substantial problems for health practitioners dealing with most forms of disease and injury. Given that expression of pain represents the cardinal symptom of tissue pathology for professionals and patients alike, variations in the means whereby patients communicate painful distress assume particular importance. The individual differences in pain expression are quite profound. Tissue damage or stress of a given amount can lead either to outright panic and intense suffering or to dispassionate acceptance and forbearance. These striking variations have led, in part, to rejection of exclusively sensory models of pain (Melzack & Wall, 1970), and acceptance of multidimensional formulations incorporating cognitive and affective dimensions, as well as sensory components (Sternbach, 1968). Sophisticated clinicians temper their use of self-reported pain as a source of diagnostic information with their knowledge of the patient's life history, current circumstances, and personal characteristics before making judgments of tissue stress or pathology.

The successes of social learning theory in explaining the development of many patterns of personal experience and social behavior (Bandura, 1977; Rosenthal & Zimmerman, 1978) have led to attemps to understand the origins of variations in pain experience and behavior in developmental histories and ongoing social experiences (Craig, 1978; 1980; Craig & Prkachin, 1980). Social learning theory provides a conceptual framework that integrates the regulatory functions of cognitive, affective, behavioral, and environmental events (Bandura, 1977; Rosenthal & Zimmerman, 1978; Wilson & O'Leary,

Support for the author's research reported here was provided by grants from The Canada Council and the Social Sciences and Humanities Research Council of Canada.

1980). Depending upon the circumstances, social learning analyses of developmental changes or therapeutic effects may disclose a primary role for: (1) contiguity learning of relationships between correlated experiences, (2) environmental consequences yielding operant conditioning effects, and (3) cognitive processes mediating the impact of both the former processes. From this perspective, pain expression would resemble other patterns of behavior subject to social influence. The sequence of change is one of observational learning, tentative trial and error when circumstances are appropriate, and corrective feedback leading to refinements in the skill.

ORIGINS OF INDIVIDUAL DIFFERENCES

Two interactive sources of formative influence on pain experience and behavior can be isolated, independent of differences in tissue pathology.

Variations in Genetic Endowment

Temperamental differences reflecting genetic, prenatal, and perinatal influences are observable in infants from birth (Wolff, 1959). Variations in spontaneous physical activity and in responsiveness to most forms of stimulation, noxious and innocuous alike, would be expected to affect pain responsiveness. Sex differences have been observed in the response to noxious stimuli, with female infants reacting more vigorously than males (Maccoby & Jacklin, 1974). There would seem to be biological dispositions to individual differences in the expression of pain as well as socialization influences. As with most patterns of behavior, an unequivocal means of separating the determinants has not been discovered. Undoubtedly there are interactions between genetically-determined dispositions to respond with pain to potentially noxious events and social learning events. The emphasis in the present paper is on the latter.

Socialization Experiences

A progressive transformation is observable in the development of pain expression and experience, ranging from innate patterns released by noxious events to complex patterns of cognitive, affective, and behavioral reactions (Craig, 1980). The transformation would reflect maturation of sensory/motor capabilities for interacting with the environment as well as emerging capacities for encoding and processing information. In addition, the changes directly reflect the child's experience of pain in a family context and, indirectly, a culture-specific context (Craig, 1978).

The family and community appear to have a substantial impact on all of the following components of the response to noxious events:

sensitivity to interoceptive and external events at a basic level of sensory experience, memories of prior pain experiences, the conceptual information necessary to deal with situational demands, the emotional reaction, the skills needed to communicate distress to others, and the coping techniques used to minimize further injury and enhance recovery. However, empirical demonstrations of the impact of socialization on developmental changes in the expression of pain are lamentably few (Craig, 1980). The exceptions have provided tantalizing but incomplete findings. For example, at about six months, children generally acquire a capacity to anticipate pain. Prior to this age, they usually do not recognize forthcoming needle punctures during inoculations. Thereafter, they respond to the needle, white coats, and restraint involved with expressions of fear and distress (Levy, 1960). In an interesting recent study using anatomical scoring techniques to distinguish facial emotional expressions, Izard et al. (1980) reported that at seven to eight months infants began to express fear in anticipation of an inoculation needle, reacted to the actual event with a distinct facial expression of physical distress, and expressed anger thereafter. Pain clearly becomes embedded in a complex network of thoughts and feelings at a very early age.

Ethnocultural variations in pain expression have provided a major basis for the belief that social learning represents a primary determinant of pain expression. In the classic study, Zborowski (1969) interviewed and observed in New York groups of surgical patients of Irish, Jewish, Italian, and "old-American" descent, along with their families, to determine their behavioral and attitudinal patterns of pain expression. In brief summary, the Jewish and Italian patients had a low tolerance for pain and were the most emotional and dramatic in their response. In contrast, the "old-Americans" tended to bear pain with a minimum of outward expression. Irish patients also were reluctant to admit pain and withdrew from family and friends. Tursky and Sternbach (1967) reported similar differences among subcultures in the United States in psychophysical reaction patterns to experimental pain, as well as parallel differences in physiological activity that suggested the behavioral variations were associated with differences in pain experience.

Weisenberg et al. (1975) used multiple discriminant analyses to distinguish among black, white, and Puerto Rican dental patients in the eastern United States on items reflecting anxiety and attitudes toward pain such as "The best way to handle pain is to ignore it," or "It is a sign of weakness to give in to pain," or "When I am sick I want the doctor to get rid of the pain even before he finds out what the trouble is." Puerto Rican patients endorsed these items most frequently, with whites the least likely to do so, and blacks in-between. The findings were described as consistent with the position that pain is a more ambiguous experience than is commonly believed to be the case, and sufferers would be expected to turn to others in their social environment to validate their experience and determine appropriate reactions. In consequence, people would learn to interpret and express their reactions by observing the reactions of others (Weisenberg, 1980).

While there are many reports of ethnocultural group differences, research in the area has many limitations (Wolff & Langley, 1968), and there have been reports of failure to find differences between ethnic groups in pain expression. For example, Flannery, Sos, and McGovern (1981) found no differences in self-report and behavioral measures of episiotomy pain among the same ethnic groups Zborowski studied, as well as Black Americans. It is noteworthy that differences between groups have been small, relative to within group variability, and there is considerable overlap across groups. Methodological problems are also found with poor group definition, limited sample sizes, questionable measures of clinical or experimental pain, failure to control for demographic variables, and overgeneralization. The latter problem seems crucial, since intergroup differences become smaller as successive generations of immigrant families acculturate to the modes of expression of the dominant majority (Zborowski, 1969).

Children have considerable opportunity to learn about pain. Many normal maturation processes involve pain, with teething perhaps the most prominent example. Disorders entailing pain are also commonplace—for example, colic, diaper rash, and ear infections. Pain may also be inflicted by others. Treatment-exacerbated discomfort is not uncommon in dental and medical settings. Further, parental discipline providing pain may range from a slap on the bottom to injurious child abuse. Finally, cuts, scrapes, bruises, and bites are the inevitable consequences of childhood inexperience, poor coordination, and skill deficits. There clearly is ample opportunity for pain of many kinds to acquire meaning in a culture-specific context and for the child to acquire protective skills reflecting the practical experiences of others.

LEARNING PROCESSES AND PAIN

Children rapidly learn through direct experience with pain and benefit from observing others experiencing pain.

Direct Experiences with Pain

Acute pain preempts attention and is a powerful motivator of action. Its urgency dictates that we learn to avoid, control, or minimize distress, and pain behavior usually represents the hurt person's best resolution of situational demands. Withdrawal reflexes rapidly become superseded by avoidance behavior as relevant skills develop.

Fordyce (1976) and others concerned with behavioral pain management (see Roberts & Reinhardt, 1980) have effectively demonstrated how reinforcement for pain behavior in the form of analgesics, rest, withdrawal from work responsibilities, attention, and sympathy can promote and maintain invalid roles in the chronic pain patient.

Other programs for the behavioral management of chronic pain have construed patients' problems as frequently the result of cognitive and behavioral skill deficits (Cameron, 1980; Meichenbaum, 1977). Substantial support is emerging for the use of direct instruction in adaptive skills using self-monitoring, relaxation, biofeedback, stress management, and self-instructional strategies. Treatment successes do not provide evidence on the manner in which problems develop, but they do suggest a need for exploration of the possibility that maladaptive cognitive and behavioral practices have been learned.

A powerful source of influence affecting the style of responding to noxious events is found in adults' attempts to teach children to avoid injury. With important exceptions, particularly child abuse, adults react to pain in children with distress and endeavor to minimize danger or to provide relief (Murray, 1979). While parents and others might not know precisely how to react when danger threatens, they can be expected to work hard to ensure that children conform to personal expectations about how to behave when in danger or experiencing pain or illness. Strict surveillance, physical guidance, explicit verbal instructions, modeling demonstrations, and corporal punishment for failure to abide by rules are all likely to be stringently applied.

It is noteworthy that oversensitive parents and other adults would appear susceptible to becoming unwittingly trapped or coerced into supporting abnormal illness behavior if the child learned to overreact to minimal sensations of distress (Latimer, 1979; Miller & Kratochwill, 1979). Parents of children suffering recurring abdominal pain without known organic origins have been characterized as overanxious (Hughes & Zimm, 1978) or overprotective (Apley, 1975) and having a common fear that the abdominal pain was a manifestation of cancer, leukemia, or some dangerous illness (Stone & Barbero, 1970). There appears to be potential for parents' apprehensions or inaccurate conceptions of their children evoking behavior that would conform to expectations and confirm faulty beliefs.

Vicarious Pain Learning

While direct, personal experiences of pain are important, observational learning about painful events and experiences from others may assume an even more central role (Craig, 1978). The very complex, important developmental task of learning about painful injury and disease would seem to be less often accomplished through personal experience than through viewing how others handle suffering and pain. Everyone must master such tasks as learning what is dangerous, how to react to the demands of physical threat, how pain is best expressed to avoid and minimize distress, and how to seek help from others. The process would be very hazardous and prolonged if we learned solely through direct personal exposure to risky situations. Fortunately, most often we are spared needless errors.

The impact of observational learning within the family is particularly prominent when children witness pain that is unduly persistent or severe (Craig, 1978). The intensity of these experiences seems to make children prone to modeling the dramatic forms of pain complaint representing the other family members' solutions to the problems of pain and chronic disease. For example, children who become particularly distressed or uncooperative during dental treatment tend to have other primary family members with unfavorable attitudes towards dental care and who report adverse experiences with dentists (Kleinknecht, Klepac, & Alexander, 1973). Similarly, children who have recurring abdominal pain without an established organic basis have a high probability of other family members who suffer chronic pain syndromes (Apley, 1975). Christensen and Mortensen (1975) presented evidence that it is the parents' current attitudes toward pain rather than past histories that affect their children's recurrent pain behavior. The incidence of parents' abdominal disorders during childhood was unrelated to their children's complaints, but concurrent problems were.

Overreaction to pain in these families may reflect a general failure to use adaptive coping skills. For example, tendencies to exaggerate the severities of painful experiences can provoke substantial distress. Imagining painful experiences leads to the patterns of physiological arousal that are ordinarily associated with the painful experiences themselves (Craig, 1968). Because children can apparently become predisposed to unusual patterns of pain complaint by chronic pain problems in other family members, the social learning perspective would appear to provide a reasonable approach to understanding and intervening with pain-prone families.

MODELING INFLUENCES ON EXPERIMENTAL PAIN

In evaluations of intentional modeling influence strategies in the experimental pain laboratory, exposure to the pain reports of tolerant or intolerant models has consistently yielded matching behavior in volunteer subjects' reactions to noxious stimuli. The impact has been demonstrated on a variety of self-report and pain-avoidance measures (cf. Craig & Weiss, 1971; Craig & Prkachin, 1978, Neufeld & Davidson, 1971) in such magnitude that situational determinants of pain behavior frequently appear to supercede the effects of personality factors (Craig & Best, 1977).

Less-than-optimal modeling influence strategies or unintentional modeling in the natural environment may yield less potent effects that interact with personality characteristics. For example, Chaves and Barber (1974) found that a single exposure to a different-sexed, older experimenter modeling tolerance for pressure-induced pain yielded reductions in reports of pain for observers only when they had displayed relatively great initial intolerance. Prkachin and Craig (1981) observed that those who displayed strong intolerance of pain were relatively refractive to efforts to influence their pain behavior when the models were peers preselected as relatively insensitive to pain. The task of teaching people to avoid high-risk situations would seem more readily accomplished than teaching them to tolerate the pain these situations provoke.

INFLUENCING PRIVATE PAIN EXPERIENCES

While research on modeling influences has focused on behavioral styles for expressing pain, there has been a continuing concern for measurement of the subjective experience of pain (Craig & Prkachin, 1978, 1980). The problem relates to the reactive nature of verbal report. Qualitative descriptions of experience and verbal rating scales are readily biased through personal intention and situational demand. While verbal reports of pain are generally sensitive, reliable, and discriminating of variations in patients' conditions (Hilgard, 1969), there is a risk of a discrepancy between subjective experience and verbal expression (Craig & Prkachin, 1980). Interpreting the findings of the impact of social models on pain has posed a problem not dissimilar to that encountered by health professionals who must decide how much pain patients genuinely are suffering. Perhaps palliative techniques are restricted in their impact to public displays, leaving private experiences unaffected. Most clinicians are familiar with patients who have faked great distress or suppressed admitting to severe pain.

Anecdotal evidence of malingering commonly leads to a distrust of verbal reports of pain, when there is evidence of reinforcing consequences for pain complaint. In contrast, there is evidence of considerable concordance between self-report of pain and measures of subjective pain experience in the laboratory (Craig & Prkachin, 1978; Hilgard, 1969). Further, Finneson (1976) had patients who were suspected of being malingerers surreptitiously observed and found that they continued to show evidence of disability. Thus, the evidence supports the conservative practice of accepting pain complaints as genuine expressions of subjective distress. Most attention has been devoted to malingerers faking illness or disabilities in the interests of personal benefit. It may be that a more serious problem exists with people who remain stoical despite great pain because the sick role is personally unacceptable or they greatly fear medical treatment or hospitalization.

In developing measures of private pain experience, we have focused on behavioral expressions that are either relatively unamenable to voluntary control or not ordinarily attended to, hence less likely to have been brought under voluntary control.

Deviations of Verbal Report

Several psychophysical scaling procedures concern experimental phenomena that are self-monitored only with difficulty and are not readily brought under purposeful control. For example, magnitude estimation can be used to assess the rate of growth in perceived discomfort as a function of physical characteristics of noxious stimulation (Craig, Best, & Ward, 1975). Various laboratories have reported that the perceived magnitude of experimentally-induced pain grows as a function of the physical value of the stimulus raised to a power. Most psychophysicists have accepted a sensory-based model of pain and construed the power function as an index of the operating characteristics of sensory transducers. However, recent formulations of the power law have included roles for cognitive moderating variables (Baird, 1970). Hence, demonstrations of the impact of the social environment on the exponent of the power function would indicate transformations in the nature of the experience. Our findings have indicated that the power exponent for electric shock derived through magnitude estimations was affected by exposure to a tolerant model. Its size was reduced, indicating a slower rate of increase in perceived discomfort (Craig, 1978; Craig, Best, & Ward, 1975). Thus, there was a systematic change in fundamental sensory properties of the pain experience as a result of the social influence strategy.

Sensory decision theory also can be used to extract from verbal reports independent measures of sensory sensitivity and willingness to report an experience (Clark, 1974), although there is concern over the meaning of the derived indices (Chapman, 1977; Rollman, 1977). Saying something is no longer painful could reflect either of two events. The first would be a genuine diminution of painful distress, indicating that sensory processes had been altered. The sensory decision theory index used to infer this state is based on a diminished capacity to discriminate between noxious events of different intensities. Analgesic medications, transcutaneous nerve stimulation, and acupuncture seem to achieve their effects by a dampening of neural input.

A second possibility would be that the individual becomes

reluctant to admit that the experience is painful. Investigations of psychological influence strategies most frequently have indicated their impact on pain is restricted to this response bias parameter. Thus, placebos and direct analgesic suggestions were found to have no effect on sensory sensitivity, but yielded a reluctance to admit to pain (Clark, 1974). In contrast, a substantial impact of social models on sensory sensitivity has been observed. Exposure to intolerant models increases sensory sensitivity. Somehow the models potentiate the experience of pain or produce hypervigilance (Craig & Coren, 1975). Further, exposure to tolerant models would appear to reduce sensory sensitivity. Tolerant modeling seems to reduce the distress associated with potentially painful stimuli (Craig & Prkachin, 1978). This latter study also yielded findings of decreased sympathetic nervous system arousal to painful stimuli as a result of exposure to the tolerant model, further supporting the position that fundamental qualities of the pain experience are under the control of the social context.

Nonverbal Expressions of Pain

People in pain usually display a complex pattern of responses interpretable as pain expression that extends well beyond verbal report. Pain expressions could include paralinguistic vocalizations, such as crying, screaming, or moaning, and nonvocal expressions, including vigorous physical withdrawal from the source of pain, facial grimaces or winces, and postural adjustments to ward off or prevent pain.

Nonverbal expression undoubtedly contributes to observers' evaluations of suffering. The classic studies of Zborowski (1969) on ethnocultural variations in pain included accounts of pain expression extending well beyond verbal report. For example, he stated, "The expressive behavior of Jewish and Italian patients, which suggested their desire to communicate their suffering to others, was manifested also in various motor responses to pain such as body movements, gestures, twisting, and jumping (p. 241)." Acculturation appeared to be responsible for these variations in inhibition or dramatic expression of pain states.

In a study of the cues nurses used to assess their patients' pain, Johnson (1977) reported that nurses tended to rely more on physiological signs, body movements, facial expressions, and other modalities of nonverbal communication than on self-report. This is consistent with findings that judgments of others are much more accurate when the observer has both verbal and nonverbal cues available, rather than just the former (Archer & Akert, 1977), and that greater credibility is attached to nonverbal signs of emotional experience than self-report when the different channels of information are contradictory (Harper, Wiens, & Matarazzo, 1978). It also has been reported that nonverbal emotional expressions are less subject to motivated dissimulation than self-report (Ekman & Friesen, 1969, 1974). Finally, it is noteworthy that many children and others who do not have extensive verbal repertoires can only be understood through nonverbal forms of communication. The diversity of behavioral events interpretable as signs of pain suggests that information may be lost in investigations restricted to verbally-based dependent measures.

Evidence has accumulated that nonverbal channels of information can be decoded to provide information about subjective experiences of pain, although the area is not without controversy. Hjortsjo (1970) and Ekman (1979) have provided anatomical descriptions of the involvement of the facial musculature in adult displays of pain, but systematic studies differentiating adult facial expressions of pain from other emotions do not appear to have been undertaken. Indeed, Leventhal (1979) recently asserted that the belief that pain shows in one's facial expression is a conceptual inaccuracy. In apparent contrast, in an earlier study Leventhal and Sharp (1965) found that during childbirth labor, raters of facial expressions observed increasing signs of discomfort. Nurse coders had been trained to rate nonverbal signs of discomfort using an a priori coding system. While signs of discomfort increased, independent signs of comfort decreased. The growth in magnitude of signs of discomfort was much more pronounced in primiparous women. Women with lower trait anxiety scores also showed fewer signs of discomfort.

Evidence of a distinctive facial expression of pain in infants is less equivocal. Izard et al. (1980) were able to identify a consistent pattern of facial muscle movements expressing physical distress in response to the pain of the penetration of an inoculation needle. The pattern could be reliably discriminated from the discrete facial expressions of seven different emotions. Subsequently Izard and his associates (Izard et al. 1981) concluded that the expression of physical distress provided a highly reliable indicator of pain in infancy, but it differs from adult pain expression. Hence, the latter appears to be the product of maturation and/or learning. Izard et al. (1981) observed changes in emotional expression between the ages of 2 and 19 months, with the pain expression decreasing in prominence with age, and anger expression increased. While genetic and learning/experiential determinants of the transition again cannot be untangled, it is clear that pain becomes embedded in complex emotions at a very early age.

In a recent study developmental changes in infancy were observed in a broader array of expressive reactions to immunization injections, using time-sampling and behavioral assessment (Craig, McMahon, Morrison, & Grantham, 1981). Infants aged between 2 and 12 months differed from those between 13 and 25 months by crying and screaming for longer periods of time, responding with more diffuse motor activity, and not visually attending to the site of the injection prior to or after the needle injection. The children aged between 13 and 25 months engaged in nonpain verbalizations to a much greater extent, carefully watched the nurse prior to and after the injection, cried for a shorter period of time, and protected themselves with arm movements or by pulling their torso away.

There were substantial individual differences at all ages, but the age differences and several sex differences seemed to highlight the potential for differential patterns of formative adult response to the children. Girls differed from the boys during the immunization session by talking more than boys and paying greater attention to the injection site on their arms. In turn, the children's mothers tended to use verbal distraction more often with the baby girls, while the boys were more likely to have details of the pain-producing procedures explained to them. While these observations provide only a preliminary account of the complexities of social transactions during an episode of acute pain, they suggest variations in child-rearing practices that could lead to substantial differences in the pattern of response to noxious events.

Studies of induced pain with adults provide a basis for understanding the impact of the social environment on stylistic expressions of pain, both verbal and nonverbal. Prkachin (1978) videotaped volunteer subjects accepting electric shocks while they were exposed to models expressing tolerance or intolerance. Untrained observers then viewed the tapes to judge the severity of induced pain. The observers were able to employ nonverbal expressive behavior reliably to discriminate among painful and nonpainful shocks. Further exposure of the subjects during painful stimulation either to tolerant or to intolerant social models reduced the judges' ability to discriminate the levels of shock delivered, with exposure to a tolerant model yielding substantially greater reductions.

Exposure to the intolerant model unexpectedly did not generate a greater display of distress. This outcome could have been the consequence of accepting shocks with a companion who rated them as yielding more distress than the subject, but in a dispassionate manner, or the findings could have reflected a substantial subject attrition in this group, leaving only relatively tolerant subjects. The outcome of exposure to the tolerant model was less ambiguous and confirmed expectations that there would be a generalized attenuation of pain expression both across verbal and across nonverbal indices. It further supports claims that variations in the social context influence fundamental components of experience, rather than just biasing verbal report, and is consistent with evidence that planned modeling therapies reduce expressions of pain and related behavior problems in clinical settings (Melamed et al. 1975; Melamed & Siegel, 1975; Vernon, 1974).

COGNITIVE MEDIATION OF MODELING INFLUENCES

The major thrust of the research program described here has been to examine the impact of exposure to social models displaying various styles of pain response on self-report and other behavioral manifestations of pain. The cognitive processes that mediate vicarious influences have remained unexamined, for the most part, although some evidence for their role is available. For example, modeling displays cannot influence behavior unless observers attend to them. There is evidence that expressions of pain readily grasp the attention of observers. Viewing others in physical distress instigates a pattern of physiological arousal identified with strong emotional reactions and attention to the external environment (Craig & Lowery, 1969). The provocative circumstances of witnessing physical distress in others may elicit attentional avoidance in some individuals (Bandura & Rosenthal, 1966), and provoke undesirable anxiety in others (Shipley, Butt, & Horwitz, 1979). Regardless of the individual differences in the impact, most people feel compelled to attend when others experience distress.

The manner in which observers encode and interpret others' pain experiences has received little attention. There is evidence that situational learning is substantially more efficient during vicarious as opposed to direct pain experiences (Craig, 1967). The affective response of the observer could range from sympathetic distress to sadistic pleasure (Baron, 1971), depending upon cognitive sets. The extent to which observers retain information provided by another's display of pain also remains unexamined, as is the case with pain memory in general (Hunter, Philips, & Rachman, 1979). Hunter et al. did find that, contrary to expectations that recall of pain is difficult or inaccurate, memories of acute head pain provoked during neurosurgical investigations remained accurate some five days subsequent to the procedures. Further study appears warranted of the assumption that observers retain memories of others' pain behavior, which, in turn, affect the observers' pain expression. Cognitive-behavioral intervention strategies for chronic pain (Turk & Genest, 1979) should yield further insights.

CONCLUSION

This research program has demonstrated the striking sensitivity of pain expression to the immediate social context, with the behavior of social models of particular importance. These findings support current formulations of pain that emphasize life history and environmental determinants as well as sensory phenomena (Melzack, 1973; Sternbach, 1978). The social learning perspective appears to provide novel contributions to our understanding of psychosocial influences on pain experience and behavior during the course of development and in states of painful illness.

SUMMARY

Tissue insult provokes substantial individual differences in pain expression that are most problematic when conventional medical treatment fails to provide lasting relief. Chronic pain currently represents an enormous social problem deserving of innovative approaches and intervention strategies. Social learning analyses indicate that personal backgrounds and current life circumstances represent important determinants of pain experience and behavior. During the course of development, there is a transition from innate patterns released by noxious events to complex cognitive, affective, and behavioral expressions of pain profoundly influenced by the family and cultural context. Family interaction patterns provide for the transmission of societal concepts, standards, and normative practices. Parental role modeling and precedents, children's propensities to attend to and emulate others' actions, and the use of strong controls to ensure conformity to expected roles yield pain behavior that is determined by social realities as well as tissue insult.

Investigations were described indicating that social models who are tolerant or intolerant of pain substantially influence pain experience and expressions in observers. Verbal reports of experimentally-induced pain indicate that observers match social models in the severity of pain reported. In addition, using indices of experience derived through psychophysical scaling and sensory decision theory, sensory sensitivity and the rate of growth of the perceived magnitude of pain were found to be similarly subject to the control of the social context. Nonverbal measures of pain have also been examined. Nonverbal expression is an important determinant of observer's reactions to an individual in pain, and many patients, including children, have limited verbal repertoires. Evidence indicates that nonverbal expressions correlate with noxious stimulus intensity and are influenced by the presence of companions. For example, exposure to tolerant models leads to reductions in painful expression.

REFERENCES

Apley, J. *The child with abdominal pains.* Oxford: Blackwell, 1975.

Archer, D., & Akert, R. M. Words and everything else: Verbal and nonverbal cues in social interpretation. *Journal of Personality and Social Psychology*, 1977, *35*, 443–449.

Baird, J. C. A cognitive theory of psychophysics, I, II. *Scandinavian Journal of Psychology.*, 1970, *11*, 35–46; 89–102.

Bandura, A. *Social learning theory.* Englewood Cliffs, NJ: Prentice-Hall, 1977.

Bandura, A., & Rosenthal, T. L. Vicarious classical conditioning as a function of arousal level. *Journal of Personality and Social Psychology*, 1966, *3*, 54–62.

Baron, R. A. Magnitude of victim's cues and level of prior anger arousal as determinants of adult aggressive behavior. *Journal of Personality and Social Psychology*, 1971, *17*, 236–243.

Cameron, R. Behavioral treatments for clinical pain. In R. Roy & E. Tunks (Eds.), *Chronic pain:. Psychosocial factors in rehabilitation.* Baltimore, MD: Williams and Wilkins, 1980, in press.

Chapman, C. R. Sensory decision theory methods in pain research: A reply to Rollman, *Pain*, 1977, *3*, 295–305.

Chaves, J. F., & Barber, T. X. Cognitive strategies, experimenter modeling, and expectation in the attenuation of pain. *Journal of Abnormal Psychology*, 1974, *83*, 356–363.

Christensen, M. F., & Mortensen, O. Long-term prognosis in children with recurrent abdominal pain. *Archives of Disorders of Childhood*, 1975, *50*, 110–114.

Clark, W. C. Pain sensitivity and the report of pain: An introduction of sensory-decision theory. *Anesthesiology*, 1974, *40*, 272–287.

Craig, K. D. Vicarious reinforcement and noninstrumental punishment in observational learning. *Journal of Personality and Social Psychology*, 1967, *7*, 172–176.

Craig, K. D. Physiological arousal as a function of imagined, vicarious and direct stress experiences. *Journal of Abnormal Psychology*, 1968, *73*, 513–520.

Craig, K. D. Social modeling influences on pain. In R. A. Sternbach (Ed.), *The Psychology of Pain.* New York: Raven, 1978.

Craig, K. D. Ontogenetic and cultural determinants of the expression of pain in man. In H. W. Kosterlitz & L. Y. Terenius (Eds.), *Pain and society.* Weinheim/Deerfield Beach Fl/Basal Verlag Chemie, 1980, 37–52.

Craig, K. D., Best, H., & Ward, L. M. Social modeling influences on psychophysiological judgments of electrical stimulation. *Journal of Abnormal Psychology*, 1975, *84*, 366–373.

Craig, K. D., & Coren, S. Signal detection analyses of social modeling influences on psychophysical judgments of electircal stimulation. *Journal of Psychosomatic Research*, 1975, *19*, 105–112.

Craig, K. D., & Lowery, H. J. Heart-rate components of conditioned vicarious autonomic responses. *Journal of Personality and Social Pyschology*, 1969, *11*, 381–387.

Craig, K. D., McMahon, R., Morrison, J., & Grantham, P. Variations in verbal and nonverbal pain expression during immunization injections in the first two years of life. Unpublished manuscript, 1981.

Craig, K. D., & Prkachin, K. M. Social modeling influences on sensory decision theory and psychophysiological indexes of pain. *Journal of Personality and Social Psychology*, 1978, *36*, 805–815.

Craig, K. D. & Prkachin, K. M. Social influences on public and private components of pain. In I. G. Sarason & C. B. Spielberger (Eds.), *Stress and anxiety*, Volume 7. New York: Hemisphere, 1980.

Craig, K. D., & Weiss, S. M. Vicarious influences on pain threshold determinations. *Journal of Personality and Social Psychology*, 1971, *19*, 53–59.

Ekman, P. About brows: Emotional and conversational signals. In M. von Cranach, K. Foppa, W. Lepenies, & D. Ploog (Eds.), *Human ethology*. London: Cambridge University Press, 1979.

Ekman, P., & Friesen, W. V. Nonverbal leakage and clues to deception. *Psychiatry*, 1969, *32*, 88–106.

Ekman, P., & Friesen, W. V. Detecting deception from the body or face. *Journal of Personality and Social Psychology*, 1974, *29*, 288–298.

Finneson, B. E. Modulating effect of secondary gain on the low back pain syndrome. In J. J. Bonica & D. Albe-Fessard (Eds.), *Advances in pain research and therapy*, Volume 1. New York: Raven, 1976.

Flannery, R. B., Sos, J., & McGovern, P. Ethnicity as a factor in the expression of pain. *Psychosomatics*, 1981, *22*, 39–50.

Fordyce, W. E. *Behavioral methods for chronic pain and illness*. St. Louis: C. V. Mosby, 1976.

Harper, R. G., Wiens, A. N., & Matarazzo, J. D. *Nonverbal communication*. New York: Wiley, 1978.

Hilgard, E. R. Pain as a puzzle for psychology and physiology. *American Psychologist*, 1969, *24*, 103–113.

Hjortsjo, C. H. *Man's face and mimic language*. Malmo, Sweden: Nordens Boktryckeri, 1970.

Hughes, M. L., & Zimm, R. Children with psychogenic abdominal pain and their families. *Clinical Pediatrics*, 1978, *17*, 569–573.

Hunter, M., Philips, C., and Rachman, S. Memory for pain. *Pain*, 1979, *6*, 35–46.

Izard, C. E., Dougherty, L. M., Coss, C. L. & Hembree, E. A. Age-related and individual differences in infants' facial expressions following acute pain. Unpublished manuscript, 1981.

Izard, C. E., Huebner, R. R., Risser, D., McGinnes, G. C., & Dougherty, L. M. The young infant's ability to produce discrete emotion expressions. *Developmental Psychology*, 1980, *16*, 132–140.

Johnson, M. Assessment of clinical pain. In A. K. Jacox (Ed.), *Pain: A sourcebook for nurses and other health professionals*. Boston, MA: Little, Brown, 1977.

Kleinknecht, R. A., Klepac, R. K., & Alexander, L. B. Origins and characteristics of fear of dentistry. *Journal of the American Dental Association*, 1973, *86*, 842–848.

Latimer, P. R. The behavioral treatment of self-excoriation in a twelve-year-old girl. *Journal of Behavior Therapy and Experimental Psychiatry*, 1979, *10*, 349–352.

Leventhal, H. A perceptual-motor processing model of emotion. In P. Pliner, K. R. Blankenstein, & I. M. Spigel (Eds.), *Perception of emotion in self and others.* New York: Plenum Press, 1979.

Leventhal, H., & Sharp, E. Facial expressions as indicators of distress. In S. S. Tomkins & C. E. Izard (Eds.), *Affect cognition and personality*. New York: Springer, 1965.

Levy, D. M. The infant's earliest memory of inoculation. *Journal of Genetic Psychology*, 1960, *96*, 3–46.

Maccoby, E. E., & Jacklin, C. N. *The psychology of sex differences.* Stanford: Stanford University Press, 1974.

Meichenbaum, D. *Cognitive-behavior modification.* New York: Plenum Press, 1977.

Melamed, B. G., Hawes, R., Heiby, E., & Glick, J. Use of filmed modeling to reduce uncooperative behavior of children during dental treatment. *Journal of Dental Research*, 1975, *54*, 797–801.

Melamed, B. G., & Siegel, L. J. Reduction of anxiety in children facing hospitalization and surgery by use of filmed modeling. *Journal of Consulting and Clinical Psychology*, 1975, *43*, 511–521.

Melzack, R. *The puzzle of pain*. Harmondsworth, Middlesex, England: Penguin, 1973.

Melzack, R., & Wall, R. D. Psychophysiology of pain. *International Anesthesiology Clinics*, 1970, *8*, 3–34.

Miller, A. J., & Kratochwill, T. R. Reduction of frequent stomachache complaints by time out. *Behavior Therapy*, 1979, *10*, 211–218.

Murray, A. D. Infant crying as an elicitor of parental behavior: An examination of two models. *Psychological Bulletin*, 1979, *86*, 191–215.

Neufeld, R. W. J., & Davidson, P. O. The effects of vicarious and cognitive rehearsal on pain tolerance. *Journal of Psychosomatic Research*, 1971, *15*, 329–335.

Prkachin, K. M. Interpersonal influences on pain expressions. Unpublished doctoral dissertation, University of British Columbia, 1978.

Prkachin, K. M., & Craig, K. D. Vicarious influences among people with natural variations in pain expression. Submitted for publication, 1981.

Roberts, A. H., & Reinhardt, L. The behavioral management of chronic pain: Long-term follow-up with comparison groups. *Pain*, 1980, *8*, 151–162.

Rollman, G. Signal detection theory measurement of pain: A review and critique. *Pain*, 1977, *3*, 187–211.

Rosenthal, T. L., & Zimmerman, B. J. *Social learning and cognition.* New York: Academic Press, 1978.

Shipley, R. H., Butt, J. H., & Horwitz, E. A. Preparation to re-experience a stressful medical examination: Effect of repetitious videotape exposure and coping style. *Journal of Consulting and Clinical Psychology*, 1979, *47*, 485–492.

Sternbach, R. A. (Ed.). *The psychology of pain.* New York: Raven Press, 1968.

Sternbach, R. A. *Pain: A psychophysiological analysis.* New York: Academic Press, 1978.

Stone, R. T. & Barbero, G. J. Recurrent abdominal pain in childhood. *Pediatrics*, 1970, *45*, 732–738.

Turk, D. C., & Genest, M. Regulation of pain: The application of cognitive and behavioral techniques for prevention and remediation. In P. C. Kendall and S. D. Hollon (Eds.), *Cognitive-behavioral interventions: Theory, research and procedures.* New York: Academic Press, 1979.

Tursky, B., & Sternbach, R. A. Further physiological correlates of ethnic differences in responses to shock. *Psychophysiology*, 1967, *4*, 67–74.

Vernon, D. T. A. Modeling and birth order in responses to painful stimuli. *Journal of Personality and Social Psychology*, 1974, *29*, 794–799.

Weisenberg, M. The regulation of pain. In F. L. Denmark (Ed.), *Psychology: The leading edge.* New York: The New York Academy of Sciences, 1980, 102–114.

Weisenberg, M., Kreindler, U. L., Schachat, R., & Werboff, J. Pain: Anxiety and attitudes in black, white and Puerto Rican patients. *Psychosomatic Medicine*, 1975, *37*, 123–135.

Wilson, G. T., & O'Leary, K. D. *Principles of behavior therapy.* Englewood Cliffs, NJ: Prentice-Hall, 1980.

Wolff, P. H. State and neonatal activity. *Psychosomatic Medicine*, 1959, *21*, 110–118.

Wolff, B. B., & Langley, S. Cultural factors and the response to pain: A review. *American Anthropologist*, 1968, *70*, 494–501.

Zborowski, M. *People in pain.* San Francisco: Jossey Bass, 1969.

CHAPTER 17

Behavioral Strategies in Pain and Its Control

Matisyohu Weisenberg, Ph.D.

INTRODUCTION

When discussing pain phenomena, especially clinically, at least two basic situations have been described: (1) acute and (2) chronic pain. In the acute situation the person is either about to be, or is presently being, exposed to pain stimulation. The duration of the problem is relatively short, lasting for a few moments to at most several days. Anxiety-like responses are strongly associated with the acute pain reactions. These include increases in heart rate, blood pressure, pupillary diameter, and striated muscle tone. In brief, these are the signs commonly connected with flight or fight reactions and anxiety. Autonomic reactions may be proportional to stimulus intensity. In turn, anxiety-reduction techniques seem to help a great deal in reducing the reaction to pain (Sternbach, 1968, 1974, 1978).

The chronic situation, in which patients have pain of several months' duration, involves a number of different conditions. There appears to be a habituation of autonomic signs. Sternbach (1974, 1978) has stressed depressive reactions such as disturbance of sleep, appetite, and libido. The use of antidepressive medication or otherwise treating the depression seems, in turn, to reduce the pain (Spear, 1967; Taub, 1975).

A commonly found description of a chronic-pain patient might be the following:

> No positive medical findings of a physiological nature can be found. The patient appears to be oriented, displays appropriate affect, with no evidence of a thought disorder. There is no display of *la belle indifference* of the classic hysteric. Yet, the patient complains of pain, has limited physical activity, consumes

countless pills each day, has a reduced social and sexual experience, has not been able to work at his usual job, has sought help from dozens of health care providers, has undergone several surgeries, has spent thousands of dollars for health care, and has yet to find relief from pain.

The above example illustrates one of the frustrating problems of pain control for which the medical profession has had limited success. Severing nerve connections does not produce lasting relief, and prescribing medication is not adequate. Psychologists have taken up the challenge and have demonstrated a reasonable degree of success in dealing with pain control by utilizing a variety of behavioral strategies and techniques (see Weisenberg, 1975, 1977, 1980b for a longer discussion).

PAIN AS A COMPLEX PHENOMENON

When examining reactions to pain and pain control it becomes vital to consider the complexity of the phenomenon. Pain perception is not synonymous with nociceptive stimulation (see Chapman, 1978; International Association for the Study of Pain (IASP), 1979). There is a great deal of processing that occurs from the mement of nociceptive stimulation at the periphery to the point of awareness. Recently the IASP has adopted a definition of pain that emphasizes the psychological aspects of pain: "An unpleasant sensory and emotional experience associated with actual or potential tissue damage, or described in terms of such damage" (IASP, 1979, p. 250). In their notes explaining their definition of pain, the IASP Subcommittee on Taxonomy has explicitly noted the psychological nature of pain and has separated the nociceptive stimulus from the perception of pain. "Activity induced in the nociceptor and nociceptive pathways by a noxious stimulus is not pain, which is always a psychological state, even though we may well appreciate that pain most often has a proximate physical cause" (IASP, 1979, p. 250).

Pain reactions can convey a great deal more than a signal that tissue damage is occurring. As Szasz (1957), Zborowski (1969), and others have pointed out in discussing human reactions to pain, communication aspects are frequently overlooked. Cultural aspects of the situation influence the expression of pain (see Weisenberg et al., 1975). Pain reactions can mean "Don't hurt me," "Help me," "It's legitimate for me to get out of my daily responsibilities," "Look, I'm being punished," "Hey, look, I am a real man," "I'm still alive." Much of the behavioral approach at pain control developed by Fordyce (1976, 1978) and his colleagues is based upon the meaning of the pain as seen through its behavioral consequences rather than upon the nociceptive stimulation. Patients can be taught that they can control and contain the influence of pain on their lives even when the sensation of pain itself cannot be eliminated completely. The amount of general anesthesia, surgical intervention, and the number of pills prescribed and consumed for pain and anxiety control have consequently gone down with the use of such behavioral approaches.

Theoretically, the gate-control theory of pain is still controversial regarding the existence of a gating mechanism (Melzack & Wall, 1965, 1970; Melzack, 1973; Melzack & Dennis, 1978). However, in its basic conceptualization of pain phenomena it is still most representative of current views. Pain has a sensory component similar to other sensory processes. It is discriminable in time, space, and intensity. However, pain also has an essential aversive–cognitive–motivational and emotional component that leads to behavior designed to escape or avoid the stimulus. Different neurophysiological mechanisms have been described for each system. The fibers that project to the ventobasal thalamus and somatosensory cortex are partly involved in the sensory-discriminative aspects of pain. Fibers that project to the reticular formation, medial intralaminar thalamus, and limbic system are related to the aversive–cognitive–motivational and emotional component of pain that leads to escape behavior. Higher cortical areas are involved in both discriminative and motivational systems influencing reactions on the basis of cognitive evaluation and past experience. More than any other theoretical approach, gate-control emphasizes the tremendous role of psychological variables and how they affect the reaction to pain. Especially with chronic pain, successful pain control often involves changing the motivational component while the sensory component remains intact. Hypnosis, anxiety reduction, desensitization, attention distraction, as well as other behavioral approaches can be effective alternatives and supplements to pharmacology and surgery in the control of pain. Principles of learning and social influence processes can be applied effectively to control pain. Their effect is felt mostly on the motivational component of pain.

In a more recent statement of gate-control theory, Melzack and Dennis (1978) have emphasized differences between chronic and acute pain. With acute pain there is usually a well-defined cause and a characteristic time course whereby the pain disappears after the occurrence of healing. The rapid onset of pain is referred to as the *phasic* component. The more lasting persistent phase is referred to as the *tonic* component. The tonic component serves as a means of fostering rest, care, and protection of the damaged area so as to promote healing.

However, with chronic pain the tonic component may continue even after healing has occurred. Melzack and Dennis (1978) refer to low-level abnormal inputs that produce self-sustaining neural activity. These inputs seem to be memory-like mechanisms related to pain.

They can occur at any level of the nervous system. Normally, these so-called inputs, referred to as *pattern generating systems*, are inhibited by a central control biasing system. When neuronal damage occurs, such as after amputation or after peripheral nerve lesions, the central inhibitory influence is diminished, thus allowing sustained activity to occur even as a result of nonnoxious input. Thus, for example, Loeser and Ward (1967) demonstrated abnormal bursts of firing in dorsal horn cells as long as 180 days after the sectioning of dorsal roots in the cat.

Melzack and Dennis (1978) propose that the abnormal prolonged bursting activity that occurs in deafferented or damaged neuron pools can be modulated by somatic, visceral, and autonomic inputs, as well as by inputs from emotional and personality mechanisms by means of the activation of descending inhibitory input. Short-acting, local blocks of trigger points or intense stimulation by dry needling, cold, injection of saline, or electrical stimulation can interrupt the abnormal firing and produce relief beyond the duration of the treatment.

On the other hand, memories of prior pain experiences at spinal or supraspinal levels can also trigger abnormal firing patterns. Thus, once the pain is under way, the role of the neuromas, nerve injury, or other physical damage begins to be of lesser importance. What is needed is therapy to affect the pattern-generating mechanisms. Once the person is free from the influence of the pattern-generating mechanisms, even temporarily, he can begin to maintain normal activity, which, in turn, would foster patterns of activity that inhibit abnormal firing. These abnormal firing mechanisms can be affected by multiple inputs. It is therefore preferable to use simultaneous multiple therapies, such as antidepressant drugs, electrical stimulation, anesthetic blocks, and realistic goals for the patient to achieve to make life worth living.

From a research point of view, several of the most exciting findings in recent years relate to the discovery of an endogenous neural humoral system of control of pain. There are three major sets of findings: (1) The finding of zones such as the midbrain periaqueductal gray matter from which stimulation-produced analgesia (SPA) can be obtained (Liebeskind, Mayer, & Akil, 1974; Liebeskind & Paul, 1978; Reynolds, 1969). (2) These same zones seem to be closely associated with the opiate binding sites and mechanisms of action of morphine in the nervous system (Liebeskind et al., 1974; Simon & Hiller, 1978). (3) Furthermore, it appears that the body produces its own group of endogenous morphine-like substances called endorphins (Hughes et al., 1975; Simon, Hiller & Endelman, 1975).

The discovery of endogenously produced endorphin has led to a series of studies relating a variety of pain control strategies to the production of these endogenous substances. Thus, it has been reported that the pain control effects of acupuncture, but not of hypnosis, have been blocked by naloxone (Mayer et al., 1976). Terenius (1978) reviewed evidence that lumbar cerebrospinal fluid from patients with chronic pain showed lower concentrations of endorphin. In turn, congenital insensitivity to pain may be related to a tonic hyperactivity of an endogenous pain system (Dehen & Cambier, 1978). Naloxone has been reported to have no effect (Mihic & Binkert, 1978) or a significant effect (Levine, Gordon & Fields, 1978) in blocking the effects of placebos.

A great deal is still unknown. However, studies dealing with the endogenous pain control system provide a neurohumoral basis for the behavioral and psychological control of pain. Ultimately, it might be possible to achieve the ideal nonaddictive pain control strategy, with the fewest side effects and complications, when we will be capable of behaviorally unlocking the body's own endogenous pain control system.

PROGRESS IN AND ISSUES OF PAIN PHENOMENA

Despite the success and progress of the past few years, there are some basic questions that have remained unresolved. Among these can be included: (1) pain measurement, (2) the relationship between pain and anxiety, (3) the role of control as a variable in pain perception. It will not be possible to review all of these issues in depth in this chapter. However, the basic problems will be summarized.

Pain Measurement

The measurement of pain phenomena in all of its many dimensions is a basic scientific and clinical problem. To date, there have been numerous laboratory and clinical procedures that have been used (see Weisenberg, 1977, 1980b for a detailed discussion). A great deal of progress has been made. However, the recent controversy over the applicability of signal detection procedures in the laboratory has raised numerous methodological questions concerning the legitimacy of many of the inferences previously drawn in a large number of pain studies.

Rollman (1976, 1977, 1979) has argued that *d'* does not measure sensory pain such that a reduction in *d'* need not indicate a reduction in experienced pain. In turn, a reduction of experienced pain need not indicate a reduction of *d'*. *Lx* cannot be said to be a measure of emotional change associated with pain. Rollman argues that signal detection theory can at best tell whether one stimulus is discriminable from another, but this is not the same as measuring sensitivity. Furthermore, a powerful analgesic need not cause a lack of discrimination of adjacent stimulus levels to be effective from a sensory point of view. It is possible for both stimuli to shift downward. Inability to discriminate adjacent levels, in turn, does not mean that severe pain has been relieved. Pain cannot be equated with discrimination.

Chapman (1977) dismisses much of Rollman's criticism as based upon an inaccurate view of how pain researchers have used signal detection theory. Differences in results between laboratories using signal detection theory are related more to differences in methodology and to other different parameters studied than to the inconsistency of signal detection theory. Despite Chapman's strong defense of signal detection theory, Wolff (1978) is of the opinion that Rollman raises questions showing the need for further clarification of the meaning of d' and Lx, especially at high levels of pain intensity.

Clinically, laboratory procedures are not always applicable. Studies of the McGill Pain Questionnaire (Melzack, 1975) or instruments similar to it are an encouraging step in the right direction. Additional research will obviously be required to clarify, sort, and replicate findings. There are, however, those who might argue that the use of scales such as the McGill Pain Questionnaire would be most appropriate for patients with good verbal skills but not for those without such skills (see Wolff, 1978).

One approach that has been used to overcome language barriers is the visual analogue scale. As described by Wolff (1978), a visual analogue scale is a straight line whose ends are fixed by a statement of the extreme limits of the sensation to be measured, such as No Pain/Excruciating Pain. The visual analogue scale has been found to be sensitive to changes in pain as a result of anesthetic. Scott and Huskisson (1976) report that visual analogue or graphic rating scales can readily be used by patients without any previous experience. These authors recommend these scales as the best available method for measuring pain or its relief.

Clinically, factors other than the description of the pain itself enter into the evaluation of the patient. Merskey (1974) recommends inclusion of an assessment of patient personality, as well as an assessment of severity of pain and responses of the patient to stimuli. Sternbach (1974) suggests careful observation of the manner in which the patient responds, as well as attention to what is said. Does the patient demand, whine, flatter? What emotional response does the patient elicit from the interviewer—bravery, sympathy, irritation? Major areas of information that are useful include an understanding of the role of the pain in the patient's life and the secondary gain obtained through the symptoms.

One area that clinicians are asked to judge is the potential success of surgery in eliminating the pain. Recently, Hendler et al. (1979) described an instrument to predict the outcome of contemplated surgery of low back patients. Their results are encouraging but indicate the need for additional refinement.

Pain and Anxiety

Pain and anxiety are usually associated with each other. The general conclusion is that the greater the anxiety, the greater the pain (Sternbach, 1968). Therefore, control and reduction of anxiety can help to reduce pain. Indeed, as already mentioned, many of the psychological approaches that are used with acute pain are based upon anxiety reduction. We have almost come to the point of equating anxiety and pain control. Included as treatments would be such anxiety-reducing techniques as desensitization, relaxation, biofeedback, hypnosis, suggestion, placebos, and stress-innoculation training (see Weisenberg, in press, for a fuller description).

However, the exact relationship of pain and anxiety is still not fully understood. Thus, prescribing diazepam or teaching muscular relaxation does not automatically by itself result in the absence of pain. Bolles and Fanselow (1980) have even taken the opposite position from those who work with pain patients. They openly state that fear *inhibits* pain. On the basis of their work with animals, Bolles and Fanselow postulate that there are two separate systems: (1) fear, and (2) pain. When an animal is stimulated nociceptively and the fear system is aroused, the pain system is inhibited via the activation of the endogenous control system's production of endorphins. The inhibition of pain permits the animal to perform those activities that are necessary to defend against or escape from the nociceptive situation.

Tissue damage activates the pain system once the animal has entered the recuperative phase. The pain system seems to (1) organize the perception of nociceptive stimuli arising from tissue damage; (2) organize recuperative behavior, including the search for suitable places of rest and care; and (3) inhibit other kinds of motivation. Bolles and Fanselow (1980) explain what appears, in their formulation, as the less common occurrence of increased reaction to pain as a consequence of fear as due either to prolonged muscle tension or to the confusion of fear and pain. That is, the person being provided with some amount of nociception is in reality reacting to fear while calling it pain. A person is really not feeling pain at the dentist's office after the injection of anesthesia into the tissue, only fear, which he has mislabeled as pain.

Wall (1979) has taken a somewhat different approach to pain perception. He has suggested that there are three basic phases of behavior in reaction to nociceptive stimulation. In the *immediate* phase, pain does not always occur in reaction to injury. The soldier in battle has other activities that are of more immediate concern. In the *acute* phase, anxiety is not as relevant. Only when the person is free to be concerned about his injury is pain felt. It is during this second, acute phase that pain and anxiety come together so that treating one results in the treatment of the other.

Wall (1979) emphasizes that not every injury requires the person to go through both the first and the second phase. When receiving medical or dental care, attention is not centered on escaping or fighting the doctor, but rather upon the immediate tissue damage and its consequences—that is, phase two, where pain and anxiety seem to work together.

There is a third phase involving a period of pain, lassitude, and inactivity that is commonly seen in injured men and animals. It is during the latter phase that the chronic-pain patient is encountered. However, this phase is not unique to pain. It can be seen following illness even in the absence of pain, such as following hepatitis. The chronic-pain patient is viewed by Wall as the extreme of a common condition.

Wall's view of chronic pain raises another important issue in the behavioral control of pain. As Fordyce (1976, 1978) views chronic pain, the basic problem is pain behavior—the grimacing, whining, complaining, inactivity, demanding surgery, medication. Once these cease, then there is no pain problem.

Acute, time-limited pain does lead to a variety of pain behaviors, such as grimacing, moaning, limping, and so forth. However, because of its short time duration, it is more readily tied to its nociceptive stimulus and less subject to learning and conditioning. Acute pain may require some life-style changes temporarily. However, it usually does not lead to a lasting change.

Chronic pain, however, persists for an extended period of time. Symptom behaviors continue to occur and are, therefore, more readily subject to learning and conditioning, independent of the nociceptive stimuli that led to their original occurrence. In addition, the chronicity often leads to major, lasting changes in life style, activities, and social relationships. Over time there is more and more rehearsal of sick-behavior and less of well-behavior. Once disability ceases, return to well-behavior can become a formidable task.

Fordyce's (1976) treatment program is the one most others have used as a prototype. Techniques such as stimulation or biofeedback are used for respondent pain. Operant techniques are used to extinguish pain behaviors such as moans, requests for medication, or lack of physical activity because of pain. Attention is given for health-related activity; inattention for pain-behavior. Well-behaviors including future activities are planned out. Medication is managed, to reduce or eliminate addiction. A time-contingent rather than complaint-contingent regimen is used, in which the active ingredient is masked. The goal is to reduce the amount of active ingredient as treatment progresses. A carefully planned exercise program is initiated. Exercise is viewed as a well-behavior in its own right as well as a building block to future behaviors. Rest and attention are used as reinforcers for meeting exercise quotas and are withheld for failure to meet the quota. A variety of graphs and records are kept to provide patients with feedback on progress. The spouse or family members are also trained. They are made aware of how they reinforce pain behaviors and are asked to become partners in reinforcing well-behaviors.

There is a great concern attached to generalization of well-behaviors beyond the hospital environment. This is done by teaching the patient self-control and self-reinforcement. The patient's natural environment is also programmed. New behaviors and goals are also established. Patients are given passes to go home during treatment, so that they can try out newly established behaviors in their natural environments. Following inpatient discharge, patients continue to come for treatment on a gradually reduced basis.

Long-term follow-up studies indicate that these programs utilizing a combination of procedures can be effective in dealing with chronic pain (Fordyce et al., 1973; Ignelzi, Sternbach & Timmermans, 1977; Newman et al., 1978). What remains unclear in these programs is just what the active ingredients are. Furthermore, a question that also remains unanswered is the type of actual change that occurs in the perception. Does the person no longer have pain, or is he behaving as if he has no pain? Fordyce (1976) has dismissed this latter question as unimportant. If the person behaves as if he has no pain, then that is all that counts.

Both theoretically and practically, however, these questions are extremely meaningful. Are we activating a pain-control system such as the endogenous endorphin system? If so, what does it take to do so? Is it necessary to include the full list of ingredients in a program such as Fordyce's (1976)? How much of it is required?

Is it possible, just as Stroebel and Glueck (1973) have stated with regard to biofeedback, that we are basically using placebo phenomena to deal with chronic pain? That is, are we essentially changing attitudes by *convincing* patients that they have the ability to function despite their pain? As a consequence, the person then proceeds to function whether or not we have actually relieved his pain, or is there something else in addition? Are the essential ingredients, then, any approach that leads to a change in belief and behavior?

Weisenberg (1980a) has previously related anxiety to the variable of control. That is, anxiety that is relevant to the feeling of control of the pain increases the reaction to pain. Anxiety that is not pain-related but related to another aspect of the situation does not necessarily lead to increased pain reaction. Thus, the patient at the dentist's office who is anxious regarding dental treatment would show an increased pain reaction, while the soldier whose anxiety is not related to a specific injury but to his actions in battle may not even feel the wound he receives.

As acute pain passes over to a state of chronicity without relief, anxiety seems to be reduced, while depression-like activity appears to increase. Perhaps here, too, the variable of control is also relevant.

There is the development of a feeling of learned helplessness as described by Seligman (1975). Perhaps what treatment essentially does is to restore the feeling of control. There are many examples in the pain literature (Gotteib et al., 1975; Melzack & Perry, 1975).

The Role of Control as a Pain Variable

As indicated earlier, providing a person with a feeling of control can be important in reducing the reaction to pain. In the laboratory, numerous studies have indicated that providing subjects with some degree of control over the pain stimulation can reduce stress and increase pain tolerance. Bowers (1968) has argued that lack of control increases anxiety and hence results in larger pain and stress reactions. Subjects informed prior to shock tolerance measurement that they would be able to avoid electric shock tolerated it at a level more than twice as high as those who thought shock was random. Postexperimental ratings of shock painfulness did not differ for each group.

Staub, Tursky, and Schwartz (1971) related control to predictability. Uncertainty increases anxiety and results in less pain tolerance, while reduction of uncertainty increases tolerance. Subjects given control over the intensity and timing of shocks tolerated higher levels of shock before rating them as uncomfortable than no-control subjects. Loss of control after it had been given to subjects resulted in lower intensities of shock being rated as uncomfortable. No-control subjects produced large heart rate responses at all levels of intensity, while control subjects made more differentiated responses, reacting mainly to the most intense shocks.

Clinically, Keeri-Szanto (1979) has described a technique whereby postsurgical patients are permitted to control the administration of their own narcotic medications. Demand analgesia avoids many of the difficulties that occur in nondemand situations. The required prescription has to be written once the patient indicates a need for pain relief. To accomplish this, the nurse must be summoned and convinced that the patient "really" is in pain and the drug must be signed out from the locked cabinet. The time it takes for the drug to be absorbed after injection must also be included. By the time all of the above has occurred, the drug level for which relief was originally requested is no longer the same, and the pain has intensified. In contrast, with a demand system, patients do not abuse the amount of drug used. It was also possible to identify approximately 20% of the patients who were placebo responders and for whom lesser concentrations of narcotic were indicated. Drug administration can thus be accomplished in a way that leads to greater satisfaction of individual needs without necessarily using the most potent maximal dosages.

The issue of control and predictability, as with many other areas of pain perception, is not entirely clear. Corah (1973) tried to replicate a study showing that a control device introduced into the dental operatory would produce more cooperative behavior. Twenty-four children aged 6 to 11 were provided with a green/red button device to use during treatment. The control device group showed less response to high arousal procedures, as measured by GSR, but slightly more response during low arousal procedures, as compared with a no-control group. Behavioral ratings of each group did not differ. Regarding the effectiveness of control, these results are not entirely clear.

Both the studies of Geer, Davison, and Gatchel (1970) and Glass et al. (1973) demonstrated that providing subjects with the perception of behavioral control of shock resulted in less sympathetic arousal as measured by GSR. However, the change in ratings of painfulness as a function of perceived control was equivocal. Once more the issue of control and pain reduction remains unclear.

In an analysis of control as a variable, Averill (1973) shows that it has been used to refer to behavioral control, cognitive control, or decisional control. He states that it is difficult to conclude that there is a direct relationship between stress and control. Reduction of uncertainty appears to be more important than maintaining behavioral control, per se. Use of a warning signal to increase predictability does not always result in reduced stress and reactions to pain. The meaning of a warning signal must also be taken into account, such as does it mean continuous vigilance or does it imply that the person can relax during nonsignaled tasks? Other factors that must be considered include the presence or absence of feedback that tells the subject how well he is controlling, the subject's ability to tolerate the information necessary for control, and what appears as larger short-term stress reactions but long-term adaptations.

It seems that control is an important variable in pain reduction. However, who should be given the control, the patient or the health provider, may vary depending upon the goals or circumstances. Long-term gain may require greater immediate arousal, as seen in the literature on preparation for surgery. However, an important ingredient in chronic pain tolerance appears to be a sense of control. As mentioned earlier, many pain control clinics strive to achieve this goal as part of their treatment strategy. The message is, "you can function and control your pain rather than let it control you."

CONCLUSION

We have made great progress over the past few years. The contribution of the psychologist in pain control has been accepted and has received deserved recognition. We are, however, at a point where we must begin to clarify just exactly what we are doing that seems to help, and why.

Three areas of concern have been discussed: (1) pain measurement, (2) the role of anxiety, and (3) the role of control as a variable in pain perception. Each of these areas is of basic concern in our understanding of pain and deserves continued study. I have merely touched the tip of the iceberg.

SUMMARY

Recently, it has been widely acknowledged that pain perception is always a psychological event. Clinically, pain can be described in two basic situations: (1) acute, and (2) chronic pain. In the acute situation, anxiety and anxiety-like responses are of central importance. In chronic pain, depression, behavioral gain, and a sense of control appear to be of prime importance.

Pain as conceptualized theoretically by theorists such as Melzack and Wall is seen as a complex phenomenon. Pain is a sensation. However, its perception involves a whole range of motivational, emotional, and cognitive variables. Therefore, psychological intervention can have a great impact upon pain perception. Principles of learning and social influence processes have been applied effectively to pain control. Behavioral techniques include greater use of stress- and anxiety-reducing procedures such as relaxation, desensitization, hypnosis, biofeedback, modeling, and a variety of cognitive strategies.

From a research point of view, some of the most exciting research has involved the discovery of endogenous pain control systems and the production of endogenous opiate-like substances called endorphins. This discovery raises a basic challenge to psychologists to uncover the behavioral keys to engage the body's own pain control system. Indeed, a series of studies has begun in this direction.

Although great progress has been made, there are still numerous issues that must be resolved. Three basic issues are: (1) pain measurement, (2) the role of anxiety, and (3) the role of control in pain perception.

Pain measurement is the basic requirement for a science of pain perception and for clinical diagnosis and assessment of intervention strategies. Pain measurement techniques should deal with the various components of pain. In the laboratory, substantial progress has been made. An important issue that must be resolved is the concern raised by the use of signal detection theory in pain measurement. Numerous conclusions have been made based upon its use.

Clinically, attempts have been made to develop both verbal and nonverbal assessment techniques. Not only is it necessary to assess levels of pain, but clinicians are also asked to assess the probable outcome of surgical intervention. We have only just begun in these areas.

Anxiety as a variable has been widely associated with pain reactions. Many pain reduction strategies, especially in acute pain situations, are based upon anxiety reduction.

However, exactly what the relationship of pain and anxiety are is not clear. Recently, Bolles and Fanselow and Wall have separately proposed that anxiety and pain do not necessarily have to be related. Weisenberg had related anxiety to pain only when the anxiety is relevant to the pain and its control, and not to some extraneous source, such as a battle in a war. Currently, there are no systematic data to resolve this issue. Yet, many of our clinical interventions are based upon anxiety reduction.

Another variable of importance is control. It has been widely shown in both laboratory and clinical study that subject control can reduce the reaction to pain. However, control, too, is a complex variable. Just how control is related to pain and just who should be given control is not clear. As a sense of control is basic to much of our treatment of chronic pain, it is important to clarify its relationship to pain reactions.

Psychology has received important recognition with regard to its role in pain perception and pain control. Although great progress has been made, numerous problems remain to be resolved; only a few of these have been mentioned in this chapter.

REFERENCES

Averill, J. R. Personal control over aversive stimuli and its relationship to stress. *Psychological Bulletin*, 1973, *80*, 286–303.

Bolles, R. C., & Fanselow, M. S. A perceptual-defensive-recuperative model of fear and pain. *The Behavioral and Brain Sciences*, 1980, *3*, 291–301.

Bowers, K. S. Pain, anxiety and perceived control. *Journal of Consulting and Clinical Psychology*, 1968, *32*, 596–602.

Chapman, C. R. Sensory decision theory methods in pain research: A reply to Rollman. *Pain*, 1977, *3*, 295–305.

Chapman, C. R. Pain: The perception of noxious events. In R. A. Sternbach (Ed.), *The psychology of pain.* New York: Raven Press, 1978.

Corah, N. L. Effect of perceived control on stress reduction in pedodontic patients. *Journal of Dental Research*, 1973, *52*, 1261–1264.

Dehen, H., & Cambier, J. Congenital indifference to pain and endogenous morphine-like system. *Pain Abstracts: Second World Congress on Pain*, 1978, 15.

Fordyce, W. E. *Behavioral methods for chronic pain and illness.* St. Louis, MO: C. V. Mosby, 1976.

Fordyce, W. E. Learning processes in pain. In R. A. Sternbach (Ed.), *The psychology of pain.* New York: Raven Press, 1978.

Fordyce, W. E., Fowler, R. S., Lehmann, J. F., DeLateur, B. J., Sand, P. L., & Treischmann, R. B. Operant conditioning in the treatment of chronic pain. *Archives of Physical Medicine and Rehabilitation*, 1973, *54*, 399–408.

Geer, J. H., Davison, G. C., & Gatchel, R. I. Reduction of stress in humans through nonveridical perceived control of aversive stimulation. *Journal of Personality and Social Psychology*, 1970, *16*, 734–738.

Glass, D. C., Singer, J. E., Leonard, H. S., Krantz, D., Cohen, S., & Cummings, H. Perceived control of aversive stimulation. *Journal of Personality*, 1973, *41*, 577–595.

Gottleib, H. J., Hockersmith, V. W., Koller, R., & Strite, L. C. *A successful treatment program for chronic back pain patients.* Symposium presented at the meeting of the American Psychological Association, Chicago, Ill., 1975.

Hendler, N., Viernstein, M., Gucer, P., & Long, D. A preoperative screening test for chronic back pain patients. *Psychosomatics*, 1979, *20*, 801–808.

Hughes, J., Smith, T. W., Kosterlitz, H. W., Fothergill, L. A., Morgan, B. A., & Morris, H. R. Identification of two related pentapeptides from the brain with potent opiate agonist activity. *Nature*, 1975, *258*, 577–579.

Ignelzi, R. J., Sternbach, R. A., & Timmermans, G. The pain ward follow-up analysis. *Pain*, 1977, *3*, 277–280.

International Association for the Study of Pain, Subcommittee on Taxonomy. Pain terms: A list with definitions and notes on usage. *Pain*, 1979, *6*, 249–252.

Keeri-Szanto, M. Drugs or drums: What relieves postoperative pain? *Pain*, 1979, *6*, 217–230.

Levine, J. D., Gordon, N. C., & Fields, H. L. Evidence that the analgesic effects of placebo is mediated by endorphines. *Pain Abstracts: Second World Congress on Pain*, 1978, 18.

Liebeskind, J. C., Mayer, D. J., & Akil, H. Central mechanisms of pain inhibition: Studies of analgesia from focal brain stimulation. In J. J. Bonica (Ed.), *Advances in neurology: International symposium on pain*, Volume 4. New York: Raven Press, 1974.

Liebeskind, J. C., & Paul, L. A. Psychological and physiological mechanisms of pain. *Annual Review of Psychology*, 1978, *28*, 41–50.

Loeser, J. D., & Ward, A. A., Jr. Some effects of deafferentation on neurons of the cat spinal cord. *Archives of Neurology* (Chicago), 1967, *17*, 629–636.

Mayer, D. J., Price, D. D., Barber, J., & Rafii, A. Acupuncture analgesia: Evidence for activation of a pain inhibitory system as a mechanism of action. In J. J. Bonica & D. Albe-Fessard (Eds.), *Advances in pain research and therapy*, Volume 1. New York: Raven Press, 1976.

Melzack, R. *The puzzle of pain*. New York: Basic Books, 1973.

Melzack, R. The McGill Pain Questionnaire: Major properties and scoring methods. *Pain*, 1975, *1*, 279–299.

Melzack, R., & Dennis, S. G. Neurophysiological foundations of pain. In R. A. Sternbach (Ed.), *The psychology of pain*. New York: Raven Press, 1978.

Melzack, R., & Perry, C. Self-regulation of pain: The use of alpha-feedback and hypnotic training for the control of chronic pain. *Experimental Neurology*, 1975, *46*, 452–469.

Melzack, R., & Wall, P. D. Pain mechanisms: A new theory. *Science*, 1965, *150*, 971-979.

Melzack, R., & Wall, P. D. Psychophysiology of pain. *International Anesthesiology Clinics*, 1970, *8*, 3–34.

Merskey, H. Assessment of pain. *Physiotherapy*, 1974, *60*, 96–98.

Mihic, D., & Binkert, E. Is placebo analgesia mediated by endorphine? *Pain Abstracts: Second World Congress on Pain*, 1978, 19.

Newman, R. I., Seres, J. L., Yospe, L. P., & Garlington, B. Multidisciplinary treatment of chronic pain: Long-term follow-up of low-back pain patients. *Pain*, 1978, *4*, 283–292.

Reynolds, D. V. Surgery in the rat during electrical analgesia induced by focal brain stimulation. *Science*, 1969, *164*, 444–445.

Rollman, G. B. Signal detection theory assessment of pain modulation: A critique. In J. J. Bonica & D. Albe Fessard (Eds.), *Advances in pain research and therapy*, Volume 1. New York: Raven Press, 1976.

Rollman, G. B. Signal detection theory measurement of pain: A review and critique. *Pain*, 1977, *3*, 187–211.

Rollman, G. B. Signal detection theory pain measures: Empirical validation studies and adaptation-level effects. *Pain*, 1979, *6*, 9–21.

Scott, J., & Huskisson, E. C. Graphic representation of pain. *Pain*, 1976, *2*, 175–184.

Seligman, M. E. P. *Helplessness*. San Francisco, CA: W. H. Freeman, 1975.

Simon, E. J., & Hiller, J. M. The opiate receptors. *Annual Review of Pharmacology and Toxicology*, 1978, *18*, 371–394.

Simon, E. J., Hiller, J. M., & Edelman, I. Solubilization of a stereospecific opiate-macromolecular complex from rat brain. *Science*, 1975, *190*, 389–390.

Spear, F. G. Pain in psychiatric patients. *Journal of Psychosomatic Research*, 1967, *11*, 187–193.

Staub, E., Tursky, B., & Schwartz, G. E. Self-control and pre-

dictability: Their effects on reactions to aversive stimulation. *Journal of Personality and Social Psychology*, 1971, *18*, 157-162.
Sternbach, R. A. *Pain: A psychophysiological analysis.* New York: Academic Press, 1968.
Sternbach, R. A. *Pain patients: Traits and treatment.* New York: Academic Press, 1974.
Sternbach, R. A. Clinical aspects of pain. In R. A. Sternbach (Ed.), *The psychology of pain.* New York: Raven Press, 1978.
Stroebel, C. F., & Glueck, B. C. Biofeedback treatment in medicine and psychiatry: An ultimate placebo? *Seminars in Psychiatry*, 1973, *5*, 378-393.
Szasz, T. S. *Pain and pleasure.* New York: Basic Books, 1957.
Taub, A. Factors in the diagnosis and treatment of chronic pain. *Journal of Autism and Childhood Schizophrenia*, 1975, *5*, 1-12.
Terenius, L. Endogenous peptides and analgesia. *Annual Review of Pharmacology and Toxicology*, 1978, *18*, 189-204.
Wall, P. D. On the relation of injury to pain. *Pain*, 1979, *6*, 253-264.
Weisenberg, M. (Ed.). *Pain: Clinical and experimental perspectives.* St. Louis, MO: C. V. Mosby, 1975.
Weisenberg, M. Pain and pain control. *Psychological Bulletin*, 1977, *84*, 1008-1044.
Weisenberg, M. The regulation of pain. *Annals of the New York Academy of Science*, 1980, *340*, 102-114. (a)
Weisenberg, M. Understanding pain phenomena. In S. Rachman (Ed.), *Contributions to medical psychology*, Volume 2. Oxford, England: Pergamon Press, 1980. (b)
Weisenberg, M. The use of behavioral techniques in the control of pain. In R. Daitzman (Ed.), *Clinical behavior therapy and behavior modification.* New York: Garland Press, in press.
Weisenberg, M., Kreindler, M. L., Schachat, R., & Werboff, J. Pain: Anxiety and attitudes in black, white and Puerto Rican patients. *Psychosomatic Medicine*, 1975, *37*, 123-135.
Wolff, B. B. Behavioral measurement of human pain. In R. A. Sternbach (Ed.), *The psychology of pain.* New York: Raven Press, 1978.
Zborowski, M. *People in pain.* San Francisco, CA: Jossey-Bass, 1969.

CHAPTER 18

The Effects of Preparatory Information on Adjustment of Children to Medical Procedures

Barbara G. Melamed, Ph.D.

Medical fears and phobias keep many people from pursuing diagnostic procedures, undertaking routine dental treatment, and complying with prescribed health care practices. This anxiety may lead to serious problems in face of inescapable situations such as illness, need for surgery, or painful tooth abscess. Individuals who have learned to avoid facing routine medical care are unprepared to cope with the stressors involved in responding to the demands of receiving treatment. This anxiety may interfere with their ability to understand the information that the physicians/dentists present to them regarding their needs. Without the basic knowledge of what to expect, the patient is not likely to be able to comply with the procedures or follow through with recommended health regimens.

In America, over 12 million people (more than 5% of the population) are estimated to avoid necessary dental treatment due to their fears of pain and discomfort (Friedson & Feldman, 1958).

We wish to acknowledge the support of the National Institute of Dental Research through grant DE-05305. The contributions of James Talbert, Bradley Rogers, Farhot Moazam and Dixon Walker, who participated as surgeons, Shirley Graves, who was responsible for pediatric anesthesiology, Carroll Bennett, Clem Hill, Sterling Ronk, and Frank Courts, who participated as dentists, Natalie Small and Patricia Cluff, pediatric patient educators, Stephanie Smith, Jan Faust, and Jesus Fernandez for data collection are gratefully acknowledged. Mitzi Dearborn was largely responsible for coordination and data analysis. Hospital and nursing staff of pediatric surgery units at Shands Teaching Hospital supported the research effort.

Children observe the reactions of their parents and siblings and learn what to fear. Studies suggest that past unpleasant experiences and negative family attitudes toward dentistry are primarily responsible for the development of those phobias.

Medical compliance in patients having to undergo noxious diagnostic or surgical procedures or take medications is also interfered with by medical fears. It is clear that previous experience in a stressful situation may influence the individual's reaction to future contacts with health care professionals. Whether or not the person has been able previously to cope with the experience may determine whether he or she is able to handle the current situation.

The hospital experience has been blamed for transient and long-term psychological disturbances in young children. The stress of hospitalization for a child includes fear of separation from the parents, the distress of unfamiliar surroundings, anxiety about painful procedures, the actual physical discomfort of surgery or recovery from illness, and loneliness precipitated by isolation from peers and the daily school routine. The estimates of behavioral disturbances resulting from the hospital experience range between 10 and 92% of all children hospitalized (Cassell, 1965; Chapman, Loeb & Gibbons, 1956; Gellert, 1958; Goffman, Buckman, & Schade, 1957). Although some children suffer severe transient and long-term disturbances, such as regressive behaviors, increased dependency, loss of toilet training, excessive fears, and sleep or eating disturbances, *not all* children are equally vulnerable to the negative effects of the hospital experience. It is necessary at this time to evaluate which factors enhance the emotional stress that can accompany hospitalization and to identify which children are at high risk for developing behavioral disturbances without psychological preparation for hospitalization.

In the past decade, there has been increased research demonstrating that psychological factors influence the course of illness and bodily response to stress (George, Scott, Turner, & Gregg, 1980; Melamed and Siegel, 1980). It is not surprising that this recognition has led to an increase in the use of psychological preparation in hospitals. A recent survey (Peterson & Ridley-Johnson, 1980) reported that over 70% of hospitals providing pediatric care for nonchronic conditions use psychological preparation routinely with patients undergoing diagnostic or surgical procedures.

It is often assumed that *all* children can benefit to some extent by receiving support and information about what to expect. However, children's prehospital adjustment and personality characteristics may make them more or less prone to psychological consequences resulting from the hospital experience. Some children may even benefit from the mastery of their fears and anxieties following a successful experience (Sipowicz & Vernon, 1965). Conversely, some youngsters may become more frightened or even overwhelmed by the presentation of hospital-relevant information if they are too young to understand it, if it is presented too far in advance, or if it is incompatible with their way of coping with stress (Melamed, Robbins, & Graves, 1981). Even adults have been shown to suffer negative consequences if the materials being presented are inconsistent with their coping styles or if they perceive themselves as inadequate in handling the threatening aspects of the medical procedure (Kendall, in press).

The goal of this review is to identify what preparation is appropriate for an individual child, given the requirements for his/her behavior, parental support, the hospital environment and policies, and the child's own coping resources.

The series of studies presented were carried out in settings where the patients, children between four and fifteen years of age, were exposed to stressors involved in receiving dental restorations or preparation for surgery. It is important to consider that stress may be appropriate and even adaptive to individuals' encountering noxious events; it helps them to pay attention to necessary events. It allows them to inhibit responses that may lead to dangerous circumstances (such as moving during oral injection or intravenous insertion). Factors that lead to distress likely to interfere with treatment need to be uncovered. Our hypotheses involve predictions about the interaction between the actual situation and the individual. We view this within an information processing model and predict that:

1. Information presented immediately prior to the noxious event reduces the patient's anxiety as measured by self-report, improved cooperation, and medical indices.
2. The patients' autonomic level of arousal mediates what information they can acquire in this context. Their nervous system must be sympathetically activated to ensure attention but set to "take in" information rather than to "reject" it (cardiac deceleration).
3. Peer modeling preparations are more effective than providing information through demonstration, because this facilitates attention to the relevant information.
4. The child's age influences how much information can be retained.
5. Prior experience influences:
    a. the initial level of anxiety the child brings to the situation.
    b. whether or not coping strategies have been learned.

In our earlier studies, we demonstrated that film modeling reduced anxiety in children with no previous hospital experience. Patients were 4 to 12 years of age, hospitalized for elective surgery, including urinary-genital tract, tonsillectomy, or herniorrapy. One group viewed a videotape providing hospital-relevant information depicted through the eyes of a 7-year-old white boy. A group, matched in age, sex, and type of surgery, saw a hospital-irrelevant film of a boy going on a fishing trip. The results of this manipulation were reflected by the Palmar Sweat Index behavior and self-report of reduced medical concerns.

Two findings were of particular interest. First, the immediate effect of viewing the hospital-relevant film was to raise significantly the level of sympathetic activation. Secondly, these children showed less sympathetic arousal at the preoperative and postoperative assessments than the control film group, even though all children received in-hospital preparation by the staff. The children who saw the peer modeling film were rated as more cooperative and received less pain medication, ate solids more quickly, and reported fewer postsurgery problems (Melamed & Siegel, 1975).

In a replication of this, the effects of age and time of preparation on youngsters viewing the hospital film, either one week in advance of admission or immediately prior to surgery (Melamed et al., 1976), were evaluated. Children 7 years of age or younger seemed to be sensitized by viewing the film in advance. It was interesting that these youngsters showed no habituation of their palmar sweat response from the time of viewing to admission, whereas older children arrived at the hospital with less arousal and were rated as more cooperative. Perhaps the younger child was too anxious and the high level of autonomic activation interfered with the processing of the information being presented. Unfortunately, we had failed to obtain any measure of what information the child had actually acquired during the film or what the autonomic reaction actually was during the observation.

The effects of previous hospital experience on the child's readiness to receive preparation prior to an impending second operation were investigated (Melamed & Siegel, 1980). The results of the previous work were crossvalidated for those children seeing the film prior to their first operation. However, in the group viewing the hospital film, who had already had at least one operation, we found that compared to a matched control group receiving a neutral film, these prepared children were no less anxious during the hospital experience. The mean level of palmar sweating immediately prior to film viewing was markedly higher in this previous-operation group than in that of children who had not had an operation. It was possible that the autonomic nervous system was at such a high level that new information was not able to be processed. Again, it seemed plausible that the children either already had information about what to expect, or were sensitized by seeing the film of another child undergoing the experience, and therefore did not pay attention to the information being presented.

In a current study at the University of Florida, this question is being examined in detail. Specific hospital-relevant material is presented to children while prefilm heartrate and sweat activity are recorded.

Table 18-1 summarizes the major population characteristics of these children, who were hospitalized at Shands Teaching Hospital of the University of Florida, Gainesville. Although the range of surgeries is very wide, including the removal of cysts, heart valve closure, diagnostic procedures such as catheterization and cystocopy, each child required inpatient hospitalization and general anesthesia.

Children between the ages of 5 and 15 hospitalized for elective surgery requiring general anesthesia and an inpatient stay in the hospital were assigned either to the relevant hospital slide tape or to the control film condition. They were matched for age, race, and sex. At the current time, we have data on 33 patients, consisting of 11 girls and 22 boys, of whom 22 had previous experience and 11 had not been hospitalized. Of these, 25 viewed the hospital preparatory film (Small, 1977) and 8 viewed a film about a boy going on a fishing trip.

Each child was seen individually the night before the scheduled surgery. At this time, many of the preoperative procedures, including blood tests and x-rays, had been completed. Table 18-2 illustrates the measures and times of the assessments.

Heart rate and palmar sweating were obtained at the onset of the procedure (baseline), immediately preceding, and following the

Table 18.1. Surgery Population Characteristics

	Experimental *(n = 25)*	*Control* *(n = 8)*
Sex		
Males	17	5
Females	8	3
Race		
White	19	6
Nonwhite	6	2
Experience		
Hospital experience	18	4
No hosp. experience	7	4
Surgery experience		3
No surgery exp.	9	5
Age	$\overline{x}$ = 9.44 *SD* = 2.66	$\overline{x}$ = 9.25 *SD* = 2.49

Table 18-2. Time of Assessment

Measures	*Baseline*	*Prefilm*	*During*	*Postfilm*	*O.R.*	*1 month post-discharge*
Child						
Heart Rate	X	X	X	X		
Palmar Sweat Index	X	X		X		
Peabody Picture Vocabulary Test		X				
Hospital Fears Rating Scale		X	X	X		
Observer Rating of Anxiety		X		X		
Operating Room Behavior Rating					X	
Hospital Information Test				X		X
Parent						
Anxiety Questionnaire	X					
Child Development Questionnaire	X					
Peterson Behavior Problem Checklist	X				X	
Hospital Information Test	X					X

film preparation. Palmar Sweat Index allows for the enumeration of the number of active sweat glands and is a clear index of the sympathetic nervous system activity. Pulse rate was recorded by means of radial pulse recorded for 30 seconds.

The Peabody Picture Vocabulary Test was administered to provide an index of intelligence, as it might covary with other measures. The child's self-reported medical concerns were obtained from the Hospital Fears Rating Scale, a 13-item survey that allows a report on a scale between "not at all afraid" and "very afraid" (Melamed & Siegel, 1975). The independent observer, who was unaware of group assignment, observed the frequency of verbal and nonverbal anxiety behaviors on the Observer Rating Scale of Anxiety. This scale has an interrater reliability of 91%. In addition, a questionnaire was designed to assess the amount of information children had about general hospital procedures related to surgery. The items were general, although the slide-tape hospital preparation was used to formulate the pertinent questions. Test-retest reliability of this measure was 60% ($p < .01$) for children between the ages of 5 and 15 years of age. A measure devised to be used in the operating room during the induction of anesthesia was adapted from Lindgren, Saarnivara, and Humberg (1979). It reflected the degree of cooperation the child exhibited during the anesthesia induction by intravenous or gas induction means.

Results indicated that the relevant slide-tape film produced differences in children's knowledge of hospital procedures and their children exposed to an unrelated film.

Figure 18-1 shows that those children who had viewed the experimental hospital slide tape had significantly more information about hospital procedures than those who saw an unrelated control film, $t(16) = 2.79$, $p < .05$. The children in the experimental group who were older (ages 8–15) achieved a higher percentage of correct information than those under 7 years, 11 months, $t(23) = 5.21$, $p < .01$ (see Figure 18-2).

The scores on the PPVT did reveal that more intelligent children were obtaining more information from the slide-tape, whereas the correlation between amount of information and IQ in the control group was not significant.

The influence of previous experience was examined within the group who received the hospital-relevant information. The children who had had previous surgery experience had a significantly higher percentage of information correct than those who had never been hospitalized, as seen in Figure 18-3, $r(20) = .58$; $p < .02$. This correlation was not true for the sample of children exposed to the control film. However, the size of the sample is too small to draw any definitive conclusions. One finding that may shed light on these results was derived from the physiological data. As predicted, those children who had lower prefilm heart rates had higher scores on the information test, $r(9) = -.63$, $p < .07$. The overall effect of heart rate

Figure 18-1. Percent Information Correct for Children Viewing Hospital Relevant of Unrelated Control Film.

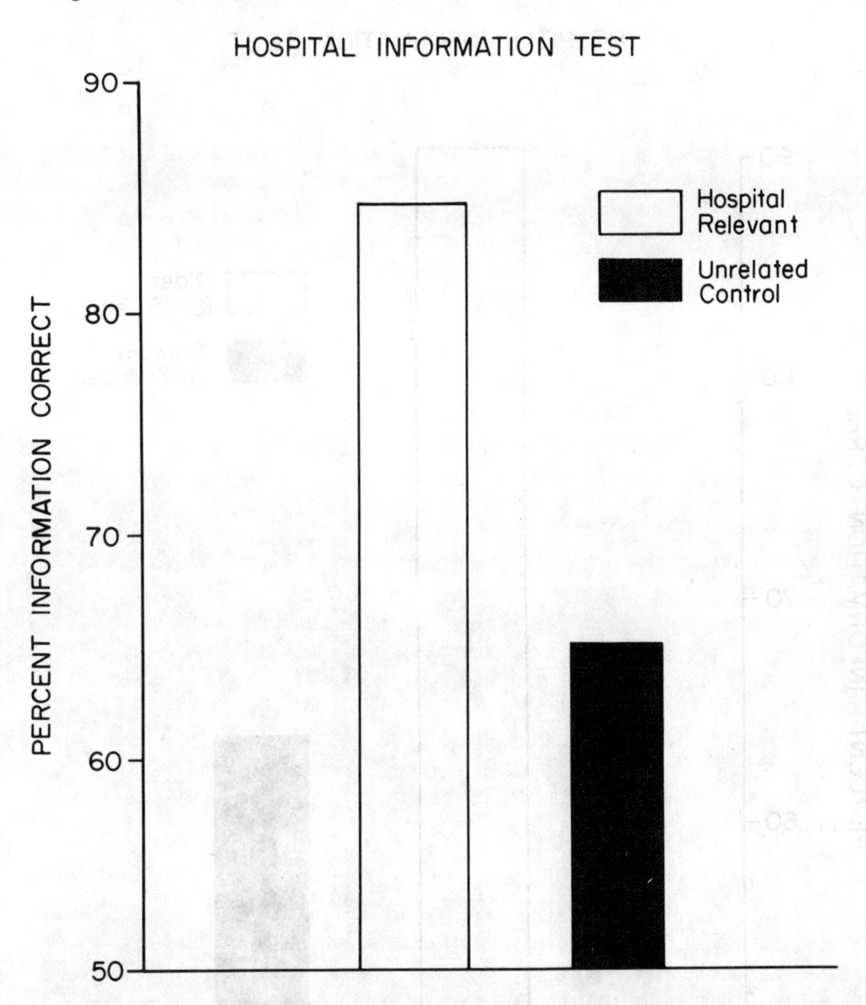

was an increase in heart rate for those children viewing the experimental hospital-relevant material as compared with those viewing the unrelated film (Figure 18-4). When the effect of previous experience was examined, the sensitization effect noted in the earlier study in the sweat gland measure was reflected in the heart rate data. Figure 18-5 revealed that the heart rate difference scores of children with previous surgery experience was significantly higher in response to the film than that of children with no prior experience. However, this relationship was also noted in children who had had previous experience who had not been exposed to the relevant film.

Other ratings of the child's and parents' anxiety also correlated

Figure 18-2. Percent of Information Correct for Older and Younger Children after Observing the Hospital Slide-Audiotape.

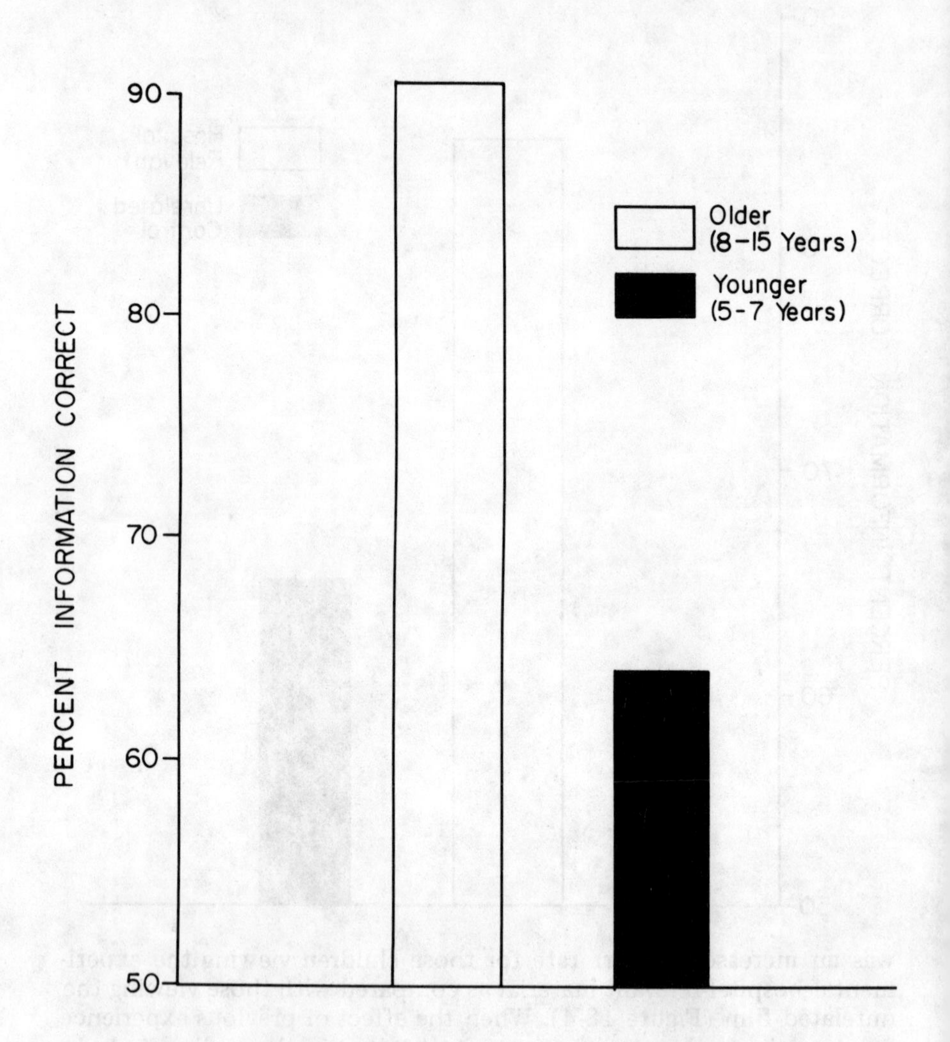

significantly with the amount of information obtained. Those children reporting higher self-concerns about medical procedures obtained less information from the film. Those children rated as more anxious prefilm also received less information from the slide-tape. Those children who had parents with higher anxiety about the surgery experience obtained lower scores on the information test. These results are correlational in nature and should not be interpreted as cause and effect prior to additional investigations. Table 18-3 reveals the extent of relationships that existed.

The direction of the heart rate was crucial in determining whether information was retained. It was found and predicted that lower heart rate facilitated the taking in of information. In both the pre-film and post-film assessment, lower heart rate levels were associated with greater acquisition of information. It is also interesting to note that individuals with high self-reports of anxiety retained less information. In addition, individuals with higher medical concerns also had lower levels of sweat gland activity. Perhaps this discordance

Figure 18-3. Percent of Information Correct for Children with Previous Hospital Experience or no Previous Experience after Observing the Hospital Slide-Audiotape.

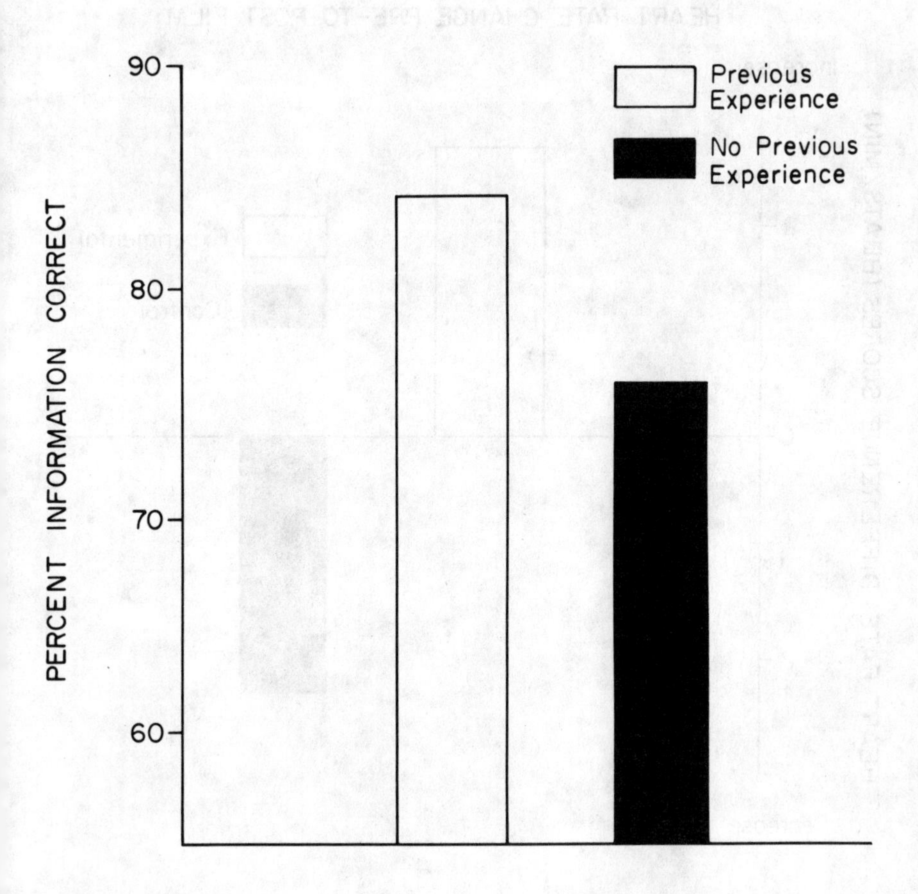

between the physiology and the subjective report underlies the mechanism that interferes with the patient's acquisition of relevant information. The individual is not set to attend to the information being provided. There is insufficient activation to promote orienting to the film. The child's anticipatory anxiety (subjective report) may prevent him or her from paying attention.

Age also affected a child's readiness to process information. Previous research in our laboratory (Melamed et al., 1976) suggested that children under the age of seven reported the highest medical concerns. In the current study, age alone accounts for a large amount of the variance, with younger children recognizing less information correctly and tending to report more fear.

The interpreting of the effectiveness of preparation by studying

Figure 18-4. Heart Rate Difference Scores for Children Observing Hospital Slide-Audiotape or Unrelated Control Film.

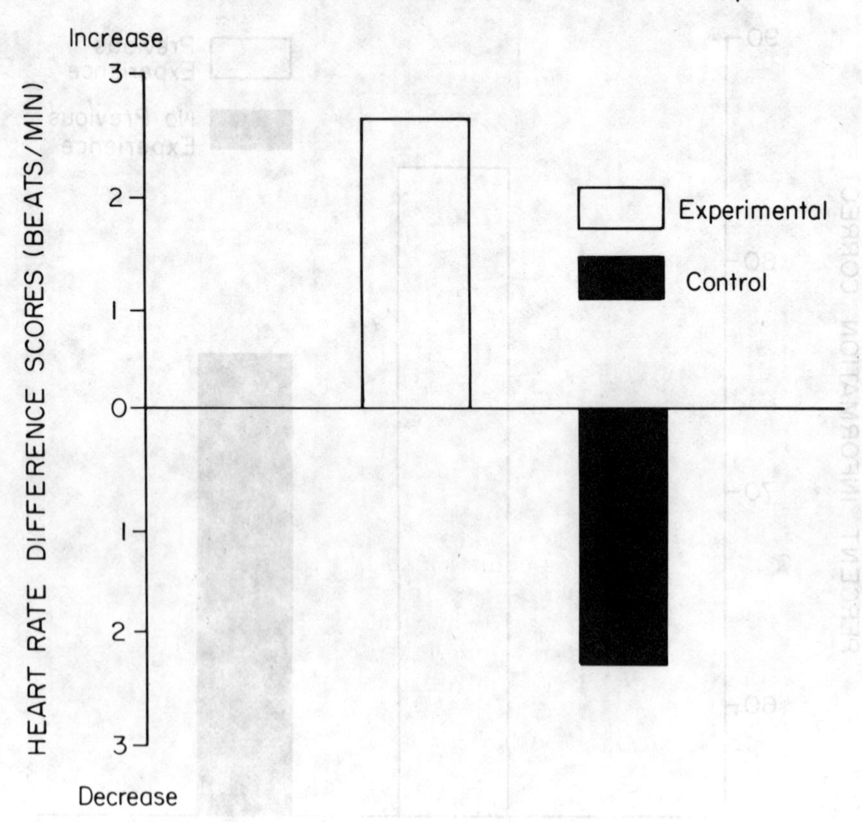

Figure 18-5. Heart Rate Difference (Base Level to Postfilm) Scores for Children with Previous Hospital Experience or No Previous Experience.

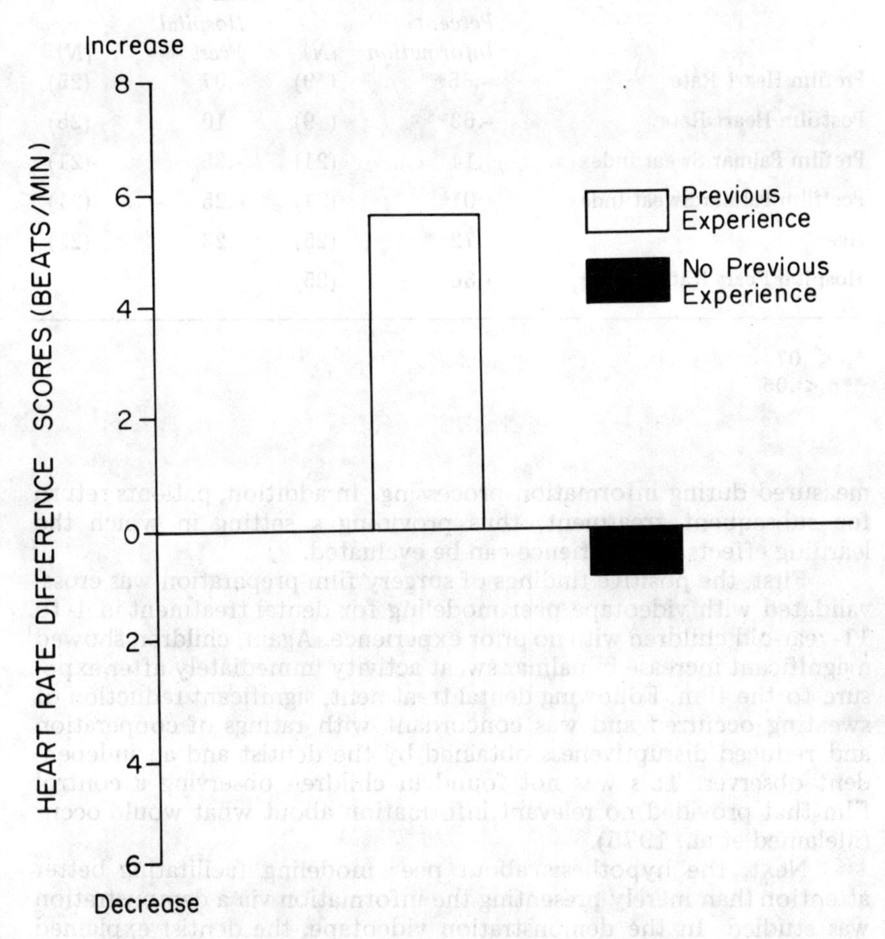

children in the hospital is complicated by (1) the fact that children have multiple contacts with health professionals, (2) different physicians' preferences regarding premedication, and (3) specific differences in medical procedures undertaken. Thus, these same questions were studied in a naturally controlled laboratory, "the dental operatory," in which there is sanction for noxious events, a predictable sequence of events (Novocaine, cavity preparation, drilling, amalgam placement), and a limited number of professionals involved. Also, since the patient is fairly immobile, concurrent physiology can be

Table 18-3. Intercorrelations between measures of autonomic arousal, self-report of hospital fears, age, and percent of information in children observing hospital-relevant information

	Percent Information	*(N)*	*Hospital Fears*	*(N)*
Prefilm Heart Rate	-.65**	(9)	-.07	(25)
Postfilm Heart Rate	-.63**	(9)	.10	(25)
Prefilm Palmar Sweat Index	.14	(21)	-.35	(21)
Postfilm Palmar Sweat Index	01	(21)	-.25	(21)
Age	.72**	(25)	-.23	(25)
Hospital Fears Rating Scale	-.36*	(25)		

*p < .07
**p < .05

measured during information processing. In addition, patients return for subsequent treatment, thus providing a setting in which the learning effects of experience can be evaluated.

First, the positive findings of surgery film preparation was cross-validated with videotape peer modeling for dental treatment in 4- to 11-year-old children with no prior experience. Again, children showed a significant increase in palmar sweat activity immediately after exposure to the film. Following dental treatment, significant reduction of sweating occurred and was concordant with ratings of cooperation and reduced disruptiveness obtained by the dentist and an independent observer. This was not found in children observing a control film that provided no relevant information about what would occur (Melamed et al., 1975).

Next, the hypothesis about peer modeling facilitating better attention than merely presenting the information via a demonstration was studied. In the demonstration videotape, the dentist explained the procedure without a child in the dental chair. Eighty children ages 4 to 11, with and without prior dental experience, viewed either the peer model or the demonstration videotape prior to restorative treatment. Peer modeling was found to be more effective in reducing subjective anxiety than the dentist merely providing information about what would occur. Figure 18-6 illustrates that viewing another child also resulted in fewer disruptive responses than merely observing the demonstration. The children had been provided with a model of how to behave.

The examination of autonomic response patterns allowed us to examine the second hypothesis regarding the possible mechanisms responsible for the advantage of peer modeling (Melamed et al., 1978). The palmar sweat index showed a pre/postfilm increase, regardless which videotape was viewed. This would be consistent with the notion that alertness was elicited by relevant information. However, differences in mean heart rate response were elicited by viewing the demonstration peer modeling videotapes. Figure 18-7 shows that there was greater deceleration in those children watching the injection segment via the peer model, as compared to children watching this on a demonstration tape with notions of orienting put forth by Lacey (1967) and Graham and Clifton (1966), which regard cardiac deceleration as reflecting a taking-in of information from the environ-

Figure 18-6. Degree of Disruptiveness during Dental Treatment and Type of Videotape Preparation. (Melamed, B.G., Yurcheson, R., Fleece, E.L., Hutcherson, S., & Hawes, R., "Effects of film modeling on the reduction of anxiety-related behaviors in individuals varying in level of previous experience in the stress situation." *Journal of Consulting and Clinical Psychology*, 1978, 46(6), 1360. Copyright © 1978 by the American Psychological Association. Reprinted by author's permission)

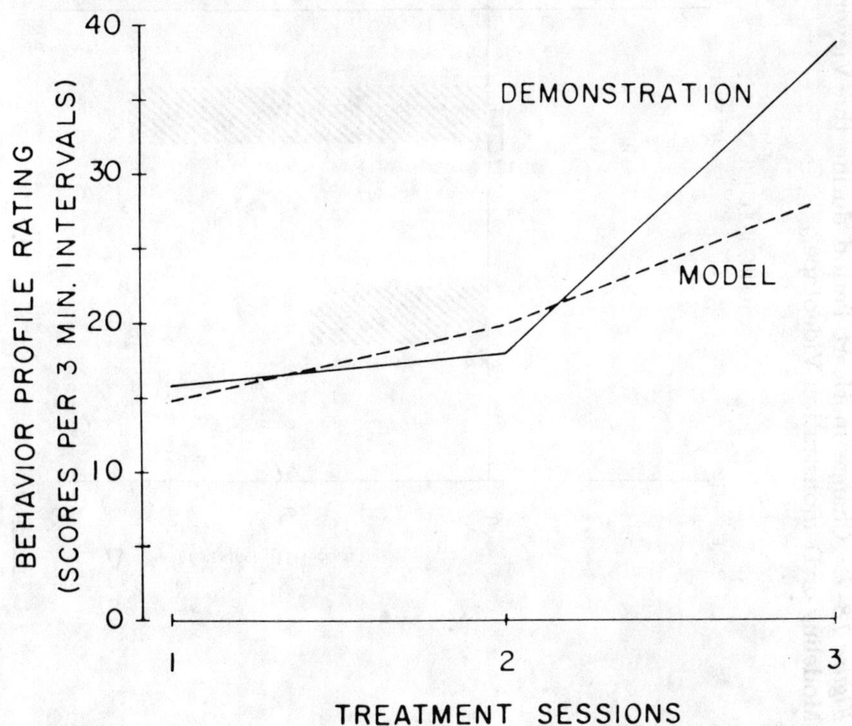

Figure 18–7. Change in Heart Period during the Viewing of Injection and Postinjection Segments of Peer Modeling or Demonstration Videotape.

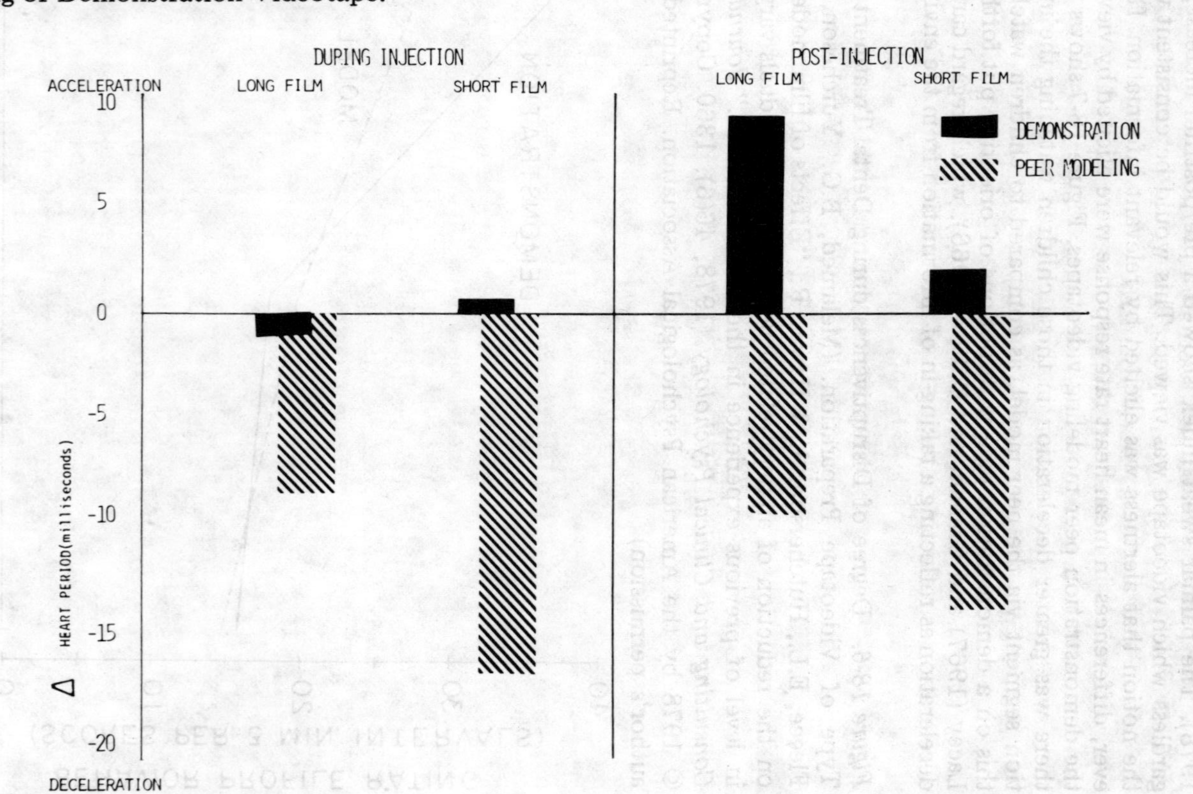

ment, whereas cardiac acceleration is associated with environmental rejection.

The increase in sweat gland activity is believed to be associated only with sympathetic activation and would be found in any situation (intake or rejection) that prompted individuals to be alert or aroused. Thus, it is only by examining the fractionation of arousal (cardiac deceleration, accompanied by increased sweat gland activity) that we find both an alert subject and one capable of taking in information from the environment. It seems plausible then that children watching the demonstration were sympathetically aroused but not functionally attentive and thus did not learn what they needed to know in order to cope with the medical environment, whereas the children who watched the peer model were functionally aroused and able to process the information necessary in learning what to expect and how to behave. In support of this, it was found that children viewing peer models recalled more of the information that had been presented than those seeing the demonstration.

Many of the previous results obtained in the surgery study regarding the importance of the child's age, fear level, and previous experience were also found to exist within the dental context. The children with high reports of dental anxiety benefited least from film preparation. Children between the ages of 6 and 8 benefited the most from viewing the peer demonstration or peer model. The children without previous experience, while benefiting from peer modeling, were sensitized (showed greater disruption) following brief exposure to a demonstration of the induction procedure. Children who had already had restorative treatment benefited more from seeing a cooperative peer model than from a demonstration of what would occur. It was noted, however, that children with previous experience also showed less disruptive behavior after a short demonstration of what would occur without a child model, perhaps indicating that they knew the expected behavior and were able to use previously learned coping strategies.

SUMMARY

The findings resulting both from the dental setting and from the hospital studies suggest that one cannot assume a beneficial effect from routinely presented preparatory material prior to a stressful event. One must view the preparation as a transaction between the individual and everything he/she brings to the situation (such as fear level, age, previous experience) and the type of information being presented. We need to consider not only the type of preparatory material but also whether the observer is properly attuned to receive this information. The results do suggest that autonomic patterns of response modulate the process of taking in information from exposure to advance preparations. Our research suggested that if patients were exhibiting a simultaneous pattern of increased palmar sweating and decreased heart rate during exposure, they were more likely to retain the information presented. The use of a peer model appeared to facilitate this "attentive" set in individuals. The age of the child was also a primary determinant of when and how to present the information. The child with high self-reports of fear and either a very low or a very high level of sympathetic activation may not be able to handle too much advance preparation. In fact, children under the age of 7 may be sensitized by presenting too much information; thus, it is important to assess whether or not the material provided is actually retained.

Future studies are needed to define the relationships between an individual's autonomic responsivity and previous experience to predict accurately whether preparation in advance of the stressful event will promote better coping behavior. It would be most critical to evaluate predisposing factors such as anxiety level, coping style, and age of the child prior to undertaking routine preparation for medical and dental procedures. If, in fact, we can predict the likelihood of attentiveness by an individual's autonomic patterning of responses to a stressor, then the development of a screening device should be encouraged. Perhaps autonomic patterning in response to a noxious loud tune would be predictive of response characteristics under other threatening situations. If certain formats of presenting information can facilitate attention, these should be developed and evaluated for the targeted population.

REFERENCES

Cassell, S. Effects of brief puppet therapy upon the emotional responses of children undergoing cardiac catheterization. *Journal of Consulting Psychology*, 1965, *29*, 1–8.

Chapman, A. H., Loeb, D. G., & Gibbons, M. J. Psychiatric aspects of hospitalization of children. *Archives of Pediatrics*, 1956, *73*, 77–88.

Friedson, E., & Feldman, J. The public looks at dental care. *Journal of the American Dental Association*, 1958, *57*, 325–335.

Gellert, E. Reducing the emotional stress of hospitalization for children. *American Journal of Occupational Therapy*, 1958, *12*, 125–129.

George, J. M., Scott, D. S., Turner, S. P., & Gregg, J. M. The effects of psychological factors and physical trauma on recovery from oral surgery. *Journal of Behavioral Medicine*, 1980, *3*, 291–310.

Goffman, H., Buckman, N., & Schade, G. The child's emotional response to hospitalization. *American Journal of Diseases of Children*, 1957, *93*, 157–164.

Graham, F., & Clifton, R. Heart rate change as a component of the orienting response. *Psychological Bulletin*, 1966, *65*, 305–320.

Johnson, J., & Dabbs, J. Enumeration of active sweat glands. *Nursing Research*, 1967, *16*, 273–276.

Kendall, P. C. Stressful medical procedures: Cognitive behavioral strategies for stress management and prevention. In D. Meichenbaum & M. Jaremko (Eds.), *Stress management and prevention: A cognitive behavioral perspective*. New York: Plenum, in press.

Lacey, J. Somatic response patterning and stress. In M. Appley & R. Trumball (Eds.), *Psychological stress: Issues in research*. New York: Appleton-Century-Crofts, 1967.

Lindgren, L., Saarnivaara, L., & Himberg, J. Comparison of I. M. Pethidine, Diazepam and Flunitrazepam as premedicants in children undergoing otolaryngological surgery. *Journal of Anesthesiology*, 1979, *51*, 321–326.

Melamed, B. G., Hawes, R., Heiby, E., & Glick, J. The use of film modeling to reduce uncooperative behavior of children during dental treatment. *Journal of Dental Research*, 1975, *54*, 797–801.

Melamed, B. G., Meyers, R., Gee, C., & Soule, L. The influence of time and type of preparation on children's adjustment to hospitalization. *Journal of Pediatric Psychology*, 1976, *1*, 31–37.

Melamed, B. G., Robbins, R. L., & Graves, S. Psychological preparation for surgery and medical procedures. In D. Russo & J. Varni (Eds.) *Behavioral Pediatrics: Research and practice*. New York: Plenum, in press.

Melamed, B. G., & Siegel, L. J. Reduction of anxiety in children facing hospitalization and surgery by use of film modeling. *Journal of Consulting and Clinical Psychology*, 1975, *43*, 511–521.

Melamed, B. G., & Siegel, L. J. *Behavioral Medicine: Practical applications in health care*. New York: Springer, 1980.

Melamed, B. G., Yurcheson, R., Fleece, E., Hutcherson, S., & Hawes, R. Effects of film modeling on the reduction of anxiety-related behaviors in individuals varying in level of previous experience in the stress situation. *Journal of Consulting and Clinical Psychology*, 1978, *46*, 1357–1367.

Peterson, L., & Ridley-Johnson, R. Pediatric hospital response to survey on prehospital preparation for children. *Journal of Pediatric Psychology*, 1980, *5*, 1–7.

Sipowicz, R. R., & Vernon, D. T. Children, stress and hospitalization. *Journal of Health and Social Behavior*, 1965, *9*, 275–287.
Small, N. (Producer) *You're going to have an operation*. Gainesville, FL: Learning Resources Center, J. Hillis Miller Health Center, 1977. (Slide-Audiotape)

CHAPTER 19

Anorexia Nervosa: The Question of Treatment Emphasis

Gloria R. Leon, Ph.D.

INTRODUCTION

Anorexia nervosa, literally translated, means a "nervous loss of appetite." This particular phrase was used in the late 1800s by the English physician Sir William Gull to describe the etiology of the body emaciation and other physical and behavioral characteristics noted in this disorder of self-starvation. In 1664, approximately 200 years earlier, Richard Morton had used the term "nervous phthisis" when describing the case of an 18-year-old girl with diminished appetite who, according to Morton, engaged in continuous studying both night and day and exhibited body emaciation "like a Skeleton only clad with skin" (cited in Bliss & Branch, 1960). It is striking that many of the primary behavioral features of this disorder have remained remarkably similar over almost three centuries, despite the many societal and cultural changes that have occurred over that extended period of time.

Major Features

The major criteria for the diagnosis of anorexia nervosa have been cited in DSM-III (the current revision of the American Psychiatric Association's diagnostic categories) as the following: an intense fear of becoming overweight, a disturbance in body image, significant weight loss to the point where 25% of the original body weight is lost, a refusal to maintain a minimal normal body weight, and, in females, amenorrhea with no known physical disorder that could account for the cessation of lack of onset of menstruation. A consistent cross-national feature of anorexia nervosa is its major prevalence among adolescent females, generally of middle- to upper-class socioeconomic status (Crisp, Palmer, & Kalucy, 1976).

Anorexia nervosa is manifested by a dieting pattern resulting in self-starvation, with the number of calories digested per day often varying between just 200 to 500 calories. Hyperactivity is also a common characteristic, frequently involving ritualized and extremely strenuous exercise activities that the youngster feels compelled to carry out. These exercise periods may occur during the night as well as the daytime, thus contributing to the reported disruption in sleep patterns. The premorbid behavioral and personality characteristics of anorexics have been described as perfectionistic, obsessive-compulsive, intelligent, achievement oriented, and shy and timid (Bemis, 1978).

Amenorrhea will generally occur in pubescent and postpubescent females when the percentage of body fat falls below a 17% level (Frisch, 1977). However, quite often the amenorrhea occurring in female anorexics will take place before significant weight loss has occurred (Halmi et al., 1977). Further, it is often the case that menses do not resume until a number of years after the normal body weight has been restored.

Eating Patterns and Hunger

The type of eating patterns manifested by a person suffering from anorexia nervosa may simply involve a severe restriction of the daily amount of food consumed. However, in some individuals a characteristic pattern may consist of moderate food consumption or occasional food binging, followed by vomiting. Some controversy exists as to whether the food restriction and the eating/vomiting behaviors are two distinct patterns with differing psychological concomitants or varying features of the same eating disorder. The latter conception suggests that either type of pattern might be manifested in the same individual within a given time period. No matter how this controversy is ultimately resolved, current outcome studies do indicate that the vomiting pattern is a poor prognostic indicator irrespective of the other eating behaviors that might be manifested (Halmi et al., 1977).

Although the term "anorexia nervosa" suggests that anorexics do not experience sensations of hunger, careful research has indicated that this assumption is not true, and that the term is a misnomer. Garfinkel's research (1974) demonstrated no differences between a group of anorexics and a normal weight control group in terms of physical sensations of hunger during a period of fasting. Indeed, clinicians have reported that many anorexics will comment that at times they feel desperately hungry, and that the intense exercise activity they engage in functions in part as a distraction from these feelings of hunger (Bruch, 1973). It seems more accurate, therefore, to conceptualize the disorder of anorexia nervosa as a weight phobia that has generalized to a fear of taking in food (Leon, 1977). Thus, the restriction in food intake is not due to a lack of hunger but to a phobic avoidance of the ingestion of food. Similarly, Crisp et al. (1977) referred to anorexia nervosa as a disorder of shape and discussed its etiology in terms of a phobic avoidance centering around the pubertal weight threshold. A strong desire for an extremely thin appearance rather than a diminishment or cessation of hunger would thus appear to be the primary characteristic of this eating disorder.

TREATMENT CONCERNS

Anorexia nervosa has proven to be an extremely difficult disorder to treat, irrespective of the specific treatment procedures used and the theoretical orientation of the therapist. The long-term prognosis for persons diagnosed as anorexic remains guarded, at best. Published death rate estimates have ranged from 3% (Dally, 1967) to 21% (Halmi, Brodland, & Rigas, 1975), while long-term treatment outcome studies report that only 33 to 39% of the patients followed up could be classified as manifesting a good outcome (Halmi, Powers, & Cunningham, 1975; Morgan & Russell, 1975).

The initial behavior modification programs for the treatment of anorexia nervosa focused almost exclusively on the modification of deviant eating patterns (such as Bachrach, Erwin, & Mohr, 1965; Leitenberg, Agras, & Thomson, 1968). The systematic evaluation and modification of family and other interpersonal relationships were not included as part of these programs. Further cognitive factors such as body image perception were studied but not considered to be relevant targets for change in any type of behavior modification procedure. Recently, there has been an increasing emphasis on evaluating treatment outcome from the perspective of the general adequacy of interpersonal functioning and the normalization of eating patterns, as well as from the perspective of the maintenance of the weight gain (Halmi, Powers, & Cunningham, 1975; Leon, 1979; Pertschuk, 1977). A broadening of the variables dealt with in behavior modification programs and also the criteria for treatment success may be particularly important in light of Pertschuk's findings that 37% of anorexics who had undergone a behavioral treatment program focused primarily on weight gain manifested a bulimia pattern at follow-up. None of these persons had engaged in binge eating followed by vomiting prior to hospitalization. These early programs were crucial in demonstrating the efficacy of behavior modification techniques in treating anorexia nervosa. However, hindsight suggests that programs that are not so exclusively oriented on reinforcement for weight gain might have better "quality of life" outcomes.

The extension of the intervention perspective from eating behaviors and pounds gained to more general issues of interpersonal relationships has direct implications for the further development of behaviorally oriented treatment programs. While it clearly does not seem appropriate to delve into presumed oral impregnation fantasies (Waller, Kaufman, & Deutsch, 1940/1964) in order to treat anorexia nervosa effectively, it does seem important to evaluate carefully the interpersonal concerns and conflicts expressed by these persons. The resolution of particular interpersonal problems may be crucial in ensuring the generalization of the treatment gains made while the individual was in an inpatient or outpatient treatment program. As Lazarus (1971) pointed out some time ago, behavior therapy must progress from an exclusive concern with the symptom to an evaluation and modification of the interpersonal reinforcers maintaining the problem behaviors in the natural environment.

Bruch (1978) has sharply criticized the behavior modification procedures developed for treating anorexics because of the issue of control. She feels that restrictive programs that force compliance in gaining weight in order to earn particular reinforcers confirm to anorexics that they do not have control over their bodies, an issue she feels that they are particularly concerned with. This iatrogenically induced experience is presumed to precipitate decompensation to psychosis.

Although reviews of treatment outcome follow-up studies using behavior modification techniques (Garfinkel, Moldofsky, & Garner, 1977; Van Buskirk, 1977) do not bear out Bruch's dire predictions of negative outcome, neither have these programs demonstrated strikingly favorable long-term results. Further, a recent multicenter investigation demonstrated no advantage of behavior modification over several other treatment programs in terms of in-hospital weight gain (Halmi, 1980). It seems to this author that in order to gain a better understanding of the etiology and treatment of anorexia nervosa, more knowledge has to be obtained about the personality and behavioral factors operating at the onset of the disorder and in the past history of the individual.

Interpersonal and Control Factors

The interpersonal issues relevant to anorexia nervosa may center around concerns about self-control and control within the family setting, sexual concerns expressed in the context of anxiety about growing up, and factors of body image and physical attractiveness. Current data from a long-range ongoing study of anorexics that we are conducting will be presented to illustrate the points made about the development of this particular eating disorder. The data presented in this chapter will function to illustrate or initially confirm some of the theoretical formulations developed. Although the data do not constitute a finalized investigation, the research findings to date are extremely promising. They appear to highlight interpersonal factors in anorexia nervosa in addition to eating patterns that would seem to be important to include in the development of more effective treatment programs. These findings are quite consistent for the subjects evaluated thus far, and we are currently in the process of confirming these findings with a greater number of subjects.

Our current results (Leon, Bemis, & Lucas, 1980) are based on an extensive evaluation of 18 female anorexics ranging in age between 16 and 20 years. The tests administered included a specially constructed History and Personality Questionnaire consisting of sections on family patterns, childhood history, present and past eating patterns, and body image attitudes. The Rosenbaum Self-Control Schedule (SCS) (Rosenbaum, 1980), the Minnesota Multiphasic Personality Inventory (MMPI), and the Family Environment Scale (FES) (1974) were also administered.

The results of this investigation have clearly indicated an association between factors of self- and environmental control and the onset and maintenance of the food restriction pattern. This association can be illustrated by the responses to a number of the questionnaire items; for example, "I liked the feeling of willpower and self-control" was chosen as a reason for wanting to lose weight by 71.6% of the anorexics. In addition, this enjoyment of the feeling of willpower and self-control was indicated as the most gratifying aspect of continued weight loss by 88.9% of the group. The reported precipitating factors for weight loss similarly appeared to be related to control issues; the dieting pattern was often reported to have begun during periods when the events occurring in the youngsters life were out of control. Among the events listed as occurring at the time the food restriction began were: parents' divorce, a brother moving out of the house, problems with boyfriend, mother nearly dying, and a tornado destroying the house. Concomitant with these findings, 61.1% of the group indicated that weight loss made them feel that they had more control over their lives. A behavior pattern of self-control as a generalized characteristic in a variety of situations was further suggested by the SCS findings. The mean score for the anorexic group on this generalized self-control scale was 34.9, in comparison to the scale score norm of 27.5 for females of approximately the same age (Rosenbaum, 1980). These results indicate a significantly greater degree of self-control attitudes and behaviors reported by the anorexic group in a variety of situations.

The body image distortions noted in anorexic patients can perhaps be better understood within the context of these self-control factors. The tendency for the anorexic to view herself as overweight may reflect an evaluative or labeling process rather than an actual perceptual distortion. Thus, when the emaciated and starving anorexic looks in the mirror and says "I look fat," the youngster may not be mistakenly perceiving a fat person in the mirror, but she may be communicating a self-evaluation that she would look better still if she lost a few more pounds. The reinforcer for the emaciated appearance and the weight loss may be a cognitive attribution that the emaciated appearance reflects self-control and, particularly, control over one's body. This confirmation of control over oneself then becomes extended to an experience of control over other persons as others are indeed thwarted in their often frantic efforts to induce the anorexic to eat and to gain weight.

Heterosexual concerns also seem to be related to the anorexic dieting and self-starvation pattern. Of the anorexics studied, 36.8% indicated that they felt they were the most physically attractive in terms of self-attractiveness at their present weight or at a lower weight. However, 55.5% indicated that they felt that they would be the most physically attractive to the opposite sex at a *higher* weight. Therefore, a discrepancy existed between the weight at which the anorexic felt that she would be most physically attractive to herself (the lower weight she continually strives for), and the weight at which she felt that she would be most attractive to the opposite sex. Uncertainties about heterosexual relationships may therefore be avoided by weight reduction, since the self-starvation results in the loss of the secondary sex characteristics such as breast development and the undoing of the generally more rounded, pubescent figure. The reinforcing nature of avoiding the physical and perhaps the heterosexual ramifications of puberty may be reflected by the fact that 33.3% of the anorexic group indicated that they were unconcerned about their primary amenorrhea or the cessation of menstruation. Further, an additional 16.6% indicated that they were pleased when their menstrual periods stopped with weight loss.

Family interaction processes may also be of importance in the development of the anorexic's eating pattern. The Family Environment Scale results indicated that the anorexic group and the fathers' and the mothers' groups each demonstrated the highest mean scores on the Organization subscale and, second, on the Cohesiveness subscale of the FES. Similar views of the family system by the anorexic and the parents were also noted in terms of the subscale with the lowest mean score. For all groups, the relatively lowest mean score was on the Conflict scale, suggesting that the family environment was seen as relatively free of disagreements. This particular combination of high organization and cohesivesness and low conflict (agreed upon by all family members evaluated) points to a tightly-knit family with prescribed roles and rules of conduct that all members adhere to. The severity and intractability of the dieting and self-starvation pattern can possibly be viewed as a passive and acceptable means of defiance and self-assertion within a rigidly defined family system.

The normal-range MMPI profiles for 16 of the 18 anorexics evaluated suggests that the bizarre and self-destructive eating patterns manifested by these individuals are not a result of generalized psychopathology. On the other hand, the data and discussion presented thus far suggests that the issues dealt with in treatment should probably include not only behaviors related to food consumption but also behaviors related to family, interpersonal and sexual issues, and self-control.

Anorexia Nervosa in Males

The incidence of anorexia nervosa in males has been reported at between 5 and 15% (Bemis, 1978). A greater severity of the disorder, in terms of a more generalized impairment in psychological functioning, has been reported for males and for lower socioeconomic-class females (Crisp, et al., 1977; Crisp & Toms, 1972). The greater overall severity of the disorder in these particular groups may be related to a markedly lesser degree of social reinforcement that is gained by having an exceedingly thin appearance. In the case of adolescent males, the peer group norms for ideal masculine body build have been demonstrated to be centered around the development of lean muscle mass (Huenemann et al., 1966). For low-socioeconomic-class females, food may be scarce and therefore one does not have the luxury of food refusal. Further, the body image ideals for lower socioeconomic groups appear to be formulated in terms of a relatively higher weight level (Huenemann, et al., 1966). Thus, when anorexia nervosa develops in persons from these groups, there is a greater degree of deviance from the cultural norms of ideal body build than occurs with higher-socioeconomic-class females. This greater degree of deviance may therefore be related to the greater degree of impairment demonstrated.

In light of the more generalized psychopathology that has been reported for males diagnosed as anorexic, the responses of the two male anorexics evaluated in the present investigation (Leon, Bemis, & Lucas, 1980, Note 2) appear significant. Similar concerns related to issues of self-control, heterosexual relationships, and their association with physical appearance were demonstrated. The greater degree of general psychopathology in males already commented upon was evident in the large number of MMPI scale elevations within the abnormal range on the test protocol of the 17-year-old male. These particular MMPI results reflect a high degree of confusion and defensiveness, as is often seen in persons who are in a state of acute distress.

The patient's history indicates that he lost 65 pounds in one year and weighed 100 pounds at the time he was hospitalized. He reported that the precipitating factors to his dieting behavior were that people had called him "chubby," his girlfriend had broken up with him, and he had "lost my virginity," describing this sexual event as a horrible experience. He also indicated that his mother had started drinking extremely heavily at about this same time. The relationship of body weight to heterosexual relationships can best be illustrated by the following responses to the questionnaire: he reported that he would be most physically attractive to the opposite sex "at a higher weight." However, he also responded that the idea of gaining 5 pounds was "frightening," while choosing "neutral" as his feeling about losing 5 pounds. He indicated that he feels "unhappy or frightened" when others comment that he has gained some weight; he chose "happy" as his feeling when others comment that he has lost weight. The patient indicated that he felt that societal standards of sexual behavior were "too permissive," and that the idea of sexual relationships "scares him and does not interest him." The self-control relationship to weight loss was nicely illustrated by the item, "In what areas of your life do you feel that you have best control?" His response was, "My weight."

The questionnaire responses given by this 17-year-old anorexic male seem indicative of the same kinds of conflicts and concerns that have been discussed in this chapter as relevant to the understanding and treatment of anorexia nervosa in females. It is significant that despite the male sex of this subject and the greater generalized disturbance suggested by the psychometric data and his behavior on the ward, the psychological problems and the function of the self-starvation as a means of solving these problems were consistent with the findings demonstrated by the anorexic females in this sample.

Body Image

Body image factors have not been considered to be important or relevant factors to deal with in the behavior modification procedures that have been developed for treating eating disorders. However, a number of treatment outcome studies have indicated that body size perception may be a significant prognostic indicator of treatment outcome in anorexia nervosa. Goldberg et al. (1977) found that a lesser in-hospital weight gain (irrespective of the specific treatment program used) was associated with a greater pretreatment tendency to overestimate the size of body parts such as the width of the face, chest, waist, and hips, the length of the foot and arm, and body depth. Garfinkel, Moldofsky, and Garner (1977) used a distorting photograph device that can be adjusted to make an actual photograph of the subject look thinner or fatter. They found that all anorexic patients rated as having a "poor" treatment outcome at a 28-month or longer follow-up initially overestimated their body size. In addition, self-estimates of body size were correlated with global clinical scores of improvement and the final weight at follow-up. Garner et al. (1976) further found that overestimation of body size was significantly related to degree of neuroticism and a lack of a feeling of self-control. It would therefore seem important to include in the treatment of anorexia nervosa some type of systematic analysis and modification of the cognitive factor of body image in order to increase the efficacy of these treatment programs.

General Societal and Cultural Factors

Western society appears to promote actively a physical attractiveness ideal for females oriented around being as thin as possible (Calden, Lundy, & Schlafer, 1959; Stewart, Tutton, & Steele, 1973). This striving for an exceedingly thin appearance seems directly related to the inordinate concern expressed in these societies about dieting and trying new methods of weight loss. The results of a number of investigations have demonstrated that a preoccupation with slimness and dieting is a widespread phenomenon even among nonanorexic adolescent females (such as Huenemann, et al., 1966; Nylander, 1971). This general cultural attitude about female physical appearance may therefore provide a reinforcing climate for persons who have focused on or defined a variety of personal concerns in terms related to their bodily appearance. They may then develop a pattern of dieting that becomes self-destructive in terms of its intensity and intractability.

Family Interrelationships

Particular patterns of family relationships may actively reinforce the development and maintenance of the self-starvation pattern in anorexic youngsters. According to Minuchin and his colleagues (see Minuchin, Rosman, & Baker, 1978, for example), the key factor maintaining the anorexic eating pattern is the child's involvement in the parental conflict. The parents are seen as denying their interpersonal difficulties with each other by defining the anorexic child as the family problem. The youngster therefore receives a great deal of reinforcement for dieting and engaging in unusual eating practices through the attention focused on him or her by the parents and other family members. The quiet, shy, nonassertive, "model child" thus becomes the focal point of an intense degree of concern and conflict, with the parents often antagonistic to and disagreeing with each other about the most effective strategy to use to induce the youngster to stop dieting and begin eating in a more regular manner.

In terms of the possibility of family pathology centered on the anorexic youngster's eating behavior, it is of interest that Crisp, Harding, and McGuinness (1974) found that the parents of anorexics became significantly more anxious and depressed as the anorexic youngster improved in treatment. Kalucy, Crisp, and Harding (1977) concluded that the recovering anorexic as she or he becomes more adolescent and less childlike in appearance challenges the family stability, particularly in terms of parental conflicts concerning the parents' sexual relationship. The anorexic adolescent is presumed to have attempted to cope with the family interpersonal conflicts through the modification of his or her shape. The anorexic may therefore be living in a family system in which the adolescent's physical appearance and eating behaviors are integrally enmeshed with a variety of family problems. Thus, it is not surprising that many anorexic youngsters do not maintain the treatment gains achieved while they were in the hospital.

While I do not espouse a particular type of family structure or family conflict situation as being crucial in the etiology of anorexia nervosa, it seems evident that any type of treatment program, in order to be effective, must take into account the interpersonal environment the individual lives in. This environment obviously includes both the family and the peer group. Modifications in the interaction patterns among the family members and a change in the types of behaviors that are reinforced within this family context would seem to be extremely important for long-term treatment success to occur. For the young adult anorexic not living at home, peer relationships may assume a relatively greater importance in comparison to specific family relationships as targets for modification.

Eating Disorders and a Control Continuum

One dimension in which the variety of eating disorders can be conceptualized is on a self-control continuum. As suggested in this chapter, the regulation of food intake may become associated with a multitude of intra- and interpersonal factors. In terms of the eating behavior, anorexia nervosa can be viewed as a manifestation of an excess of self-control. At the other end of the continuum, obesity, as an addictive behavior pattern, can be seen as a manifestation of a lack of self-control. The binge-eating/vomiting behaviors of the bulimia syndrome are often interspersed with periods of food restriction. These particular behaviors may reflect ineffective attempts to normalize food intake. Since regular eating patterns cannot be established, control is maintained through dieting and food restriction that alternates with breakthroughs of uncontrolled eating.

It is of interest that many "cured" anorexics, upon release from inpatient treatment programs, do not establish regularized food eating patterns, but instead develop bulimia and vomiting behaviors as a means of maintaining their weight at a borderline-normal level (Pertschuk, 1977). The factor of control and regulation of food intake thus remains a problem behavior despite participation in behavior modification treatment programs specifically designed to change eating patterns.

CONCLUSIONS

Issues of control over one's self and one's general environment along with control in relation to eating seem to be important factors to deal with in effectively treating anorexia nervosa. This broadened perspective of control implies an evaluation and modification in the treatment of family factors, heterosexual relationships and expectations, and cognitive factors such as body image. It is of interest that Bruch (1978) identified each of these topics as important areas of concern in the etiology and in the focus of treatment of anorexia nervosa. However, it would seem that one can deal with these concerns through particular treatment programs without abandoning the behavioral approach that she so vilified. Although exploration of these issues would not seem to result automatically in the normalization of eating patterns, their evaluation and inclusion in the treatment regimen may be a necessary step in improving the long-term outcome from this severe eating disorder. The intriguing relationship between body image overestimation and poor treatment outcome should also be studied further.

SUMMARY

Anorexia nervosa is an eating disorder that is most commonly manifested in adolescent females of middle- to upper-class socioeconomic status. Persons exhibiting this disorder appear to suffer from a food phobia and a fear of weight gain rather than a nervous loss of appetite. The term "anorexia nervosa" is a misnomer, since most individuals will experience feelings of hunger as long as they consume 200 or more calories per day. Severe food restriction, strenuous exercise activities, and amenorrhea in females are part of the symptom picture.

The premorbid behavioral and personality characteristics of anorexics have been characterized as achievement-oriented, intelligent, shy, and timid. The maladaptive eating pattern may consist of self-starvation through very limited daily food intake, or may involve a pattern of moderate food consumption with occasional food binging that is followed by vomiting. The presence of vomiting behavior has been found to be a poor prognostic indicator.

The early behavior modification programs for treating anorexia nervosa focused almost exclusively on the modification of the maladaptive eating behaviors. These pioneering programs were quite effective in increasing the quantity of food eaten by the anorexic and therefore promoting weight gain while that person was in treatment. However, quite often a regularization of eating patterns did not occur, and over time there was an erosion of the weight gain achieved during treatment. Recently, there has been an increasing recognition of the importance of evaluating treatment effectiveness from a number of perspectives, including the general adequacy of interpersonal functioning and the normalization of eating patterns, as well as the amount of weight gained. Cognitive factors related to body image evaluation, the perception of control over oneself and the environment, and interpersonal and family factors have received recent consideration as important variables to deal with in developing more effective programs for treating anorexia nervosa.

The findings of the investigation described in this chapter suggest that the perception of control over hunger and one's body appearance through self-starvation may be a powerful reinforcer maintaining the anorexic's self-starvation eating pattern. Further, the control over one's family and other persons in the environment achieved through food restriction also appears to be a potent reinforcer associated with the onset and maintenance of the maladaptive eating behavior. Our current data further suggest a relationship between general interpersonal and heterosexual concerns, the striving for an excessively thin appearance to avoid these problems, and the development of the anorexic eating disorder.

Anorexia nervosa is seen primarily in females, with only a 3 to 10% incidence reported in males. These findings may be related to the fact that an exceedingly thin appearance as a physical attractiveness ideal is a model for females rather than males in Western culture. The greater discrepancy of anorexic males from the cultural ideals of physical attractiveness may be a reflection of the finding that males exhibiting this eating disorder often manifest more severe generalized psychiatric disturbance than found in anorexic females. Nonetheless, the importance of self-control factors, heterosexual concerns manifested through the desire for extreme slimness, and self-starvation in response to uncontrolled life crises were demonstrated in the several males as well as the females evaluated in our study.

In order to increase the effectiveness of behavioral programs for treating anorexia nervosa, it would appear that factors in addition to intake and weight gain have to be dealt with during treatment and throughout the maintenance period. The importance of control factors should be recognized, and the anorexic can be helped to develop more effective ways of establishing a sense of self-control and attention from family and other persons than through food restriction. In addition, concerns about growing up and dealing with heterosexual relationships need to be addressed, and the development of more socially mature behaviors can also be a goal of the treatment program. An exploration of these variables and their relation to body image perception might increase the efficacy of currently existing behavior modification programs and improve their long-term outcome.

REFERENCES

Bachrach, A. J., Erwin, W. J., & Mohr, J. P. The control of eating behavior in an anorexic by operant conditioning techniques. In L. P. Ullmann & L. Krasner (Eds.), *Case studies in behavior modification.* New York: Holt, Rinehart & Winston, 1965.

Bemis, K. Current approaches to the etiology and treatment of anorexia nervosa. *Psychological Bulletin*, 1978, *85*, 593–617.

Bliss, E. L., & Branch, C. H. H. *Anorexia nervosa: Its history, psychology, and biology.* New York: Paul Hoeber, 1960.

Bruch, H. *Eating disorders: Obesity, anorexia nervosa, and the person within.* New York: Basic Books, 1973.

Bruch, H. *The golden cage. The enigma of anorexia nervosa.* Cambridge, MA: Harvard University Press, 1978.

Calden, G., Lundy, R. M., & Schlafer, R. J. Sex differences in body concepts. *Journal of Consulting Psychology*, 1959, *23*, 378.

Crisp, A. H., Harding, B., & McGuiness, B. Anorexia nervosa: Psychoneurotic characteristics of parents: Relationship to prognosis. *Journal of Psychosomatic Research*, 1974, *18*, 167–173.

Crisp, A. H., Kalucy, R. S., Lacey, J. H., & Harding, B. The long-term prognosis in anorexia nervosa: Some factors predictive of outcome. In R. A. Vigersky (Ed.), *Anorexia nervosa.* New York: Raven Press, 1977.

Crisp, A. H., Palmer, R. L., & Kalucy, R. S. How common is anorexia nervosa? A prevalence study. *British Journal of Psychiatry*, 1976, *128*, 549–554.

Crisp, A. H., & Toms, D. A. Primary anorexia nervosa or weight phobia in the male: Report on 13 cases. *British Medical Journal*, 1972, *1*, 334–338.

Dally, P. J. Anorexia nervosa: Long-term follow up and effects of treatment. *Journal of Psychosomatic Research*, 1967, *11*, 151–155.

Family Work and Group Environment Scales Manual. Palo Alto, CA: Consulting Psychologists Press, 1974.

Frisch, R. Food intake, fatness, and reproductive ability. In R. A. Vigersky (Ed.), *Anorexia nervosa.* New York: Raven Press, 1977.

Garfinkel, P. E. Perception of hunger and satiety in anorexia nervosa. *Psychological Medicine*, 1974, *4*, 309–315.

Garfinkel, P. E., Moldofsky, H., & Garner, D. M. The outcome of anorexia nervosa: Significance of clinical features, body image, and behavior modification. In R. A. Vigersky (Ed.), *Anorexia nervosa.* New York: Raven Press, 1977.

Garner, D. M., Garfinkel, P. E., Stancer, H. C., & Moldofsky, H. Body image disturbances in anorexia nervosa and obesity. *Psychosomatic Medicine*, 1976, *38*, 327–336.

Goldberg, S. C., Halmi, K. A., Casper, R., Eckert, E., & Davis, J. M. Pretreatment predictors of weight change in anorexia nervosa. In R. A. Vigersky (Ed.), *Anorexia nervosa.* New York: Raven Press, 1977.

Halmi, K. Direct and interactive effects of behavior therapy in anorexia nervosa. Paper presented at the World Congress on Behaviour Therapy, Jerusalem, Israel, July 1980.

Halmi, K., Brodland, G., & Rigas, C. A follow-up study of 79 patients with anorexia nervosa: An evaluation of prognostic factors and diagnostic criteria. In R. D. Wirt, G. Winokur, & M. Roff (Eds.), *Life history research in psychopathology*, Volume 4. Minneapolis, MN: University of Minnesota Press, 1975.

Halmi, K. A., Goldberg, S. C., Eckert, E., Casper, R., & Davis, J. M. Pretreatment evaluation in anorexia nervosa. In R. A. Vigersky (Ed.), *Anorexia nervosa.* New York: Raven Press, 1977.

Halmi, K. A., Powers, P., & Cunningham, S. Treatment of anorexia nervosa with behavior modification. *Archives of General Psychiatry*, 1975, *32*, 93–85.

Huenemann, R. L., Shapiro, L. R., Hampton, M. C., & Mitchell, B. W. A longitudinal study of gross body composition and body conformation and their association with food and activity in a teen-age population: Views of teen-age subjects on body conformation, food and activity. *American Journal of Clinical Nutrition*, 1966, *18*, 325–338.

Kalucy, R. S., Crisp, A. H., & Harding, B. A study of 56 families with anorexia nervosa. *British Journal of Medical Psychology*, 1977, 381–395.

Lazarus, A. A. *Behavior therapy and beyond.* New York: McGraw-Hill, 1971.

Leitenberg, H., Agras, W. S., & Thomson, L. E. A sequential analysis of the effect of selective positive reinforcement in modifying anorexia nervosa. *Behaviour Research and Therapy*, 1968, *6*, 211–218.

Leon, G. R. *Case histories of deviant behavior: An interactional perspective*, Second edition. Boston: Allyn and Bacon, 1977.

Leon, G. R. Cognitive-behavior therapy for eating disturbances. In P. Kendall & S. Hollon (Eds.), *Cognitive-behavioral interventions: Theory, research, and procedures.* New York: Academic Press, 1979.

Leon, G. R., Bemis, K. M., & Lucas, A. R. Family interactions, control, and other interpersonal factors as issues in treatment of anorexia nervosa. Paper presented at the World Congress on Behaviour Therapy, Jerusalem, Israel, July 1980.

Minuchin, S., Rosman, B. L., & Baker, L. *Psychosomatic families.* Cambridge, MA: Harvard University Press, 1978.

Morgan, H. G., & Russell, G. F. M. Value of family background and clinical features as predictors of long-term outcome in anorexia nervosa: 4 year follow-up study of 41 patients. *Psychological Medicine*, 1975, *5*, 355–372.

Nylander, I. The feeling of being fat and dieting in a school population: An epidemiologic interview investigation. *Acta Sociomed. Scand.*, 1971, *3*, 17–25.

Pertschuk, M. J. Behavior therapy: Extended follow-up. In R. A. Vigersky (Ed.), *Anorexia nervosa*. New York: Raven Press, 1977.

Rosenbaum, M. A schedule for assessing self-control behaviors: Preliminary findings. *Behavior Therapy*, 1980, *11*, 109–121.

Stewart, R. A., Tutton, S. J., & Steele, R. E. Stereotyping and personality: 1. Sex differences in perception of female physiques. *Perceptual and Motor Skills*, 1973, *36*, 811–814.

Van Buskirk, S. S. A two-phase perspective on the treatment of anorexia nervosa. *Psychological Bulletin*, 1977, *84*, 529–538.

Waller, J., Kaufman, M. R., & Deutsch, F. Anorexia nervosa: A psychosomatic entity. In M. R. Kaufman & M. Heiman (Eds.), *Evolution of psychosomatic concepts: Anorexia nervosa, a paradigm*. New York: International Universities Press, 1964. (Reprinted from *Psychosomatic Medicine*, 1940, *2*, 3–16.)

CHAPTER 20

Behavior Therapy for the Overweight Woman: A Time for Reappraisal

Iris E. Fodor, Ph.D.

INTRODUCTION

> Ms. VM enrolls for a behavioral weight control program. She says she is very unhappy. She also reports feeling fat and unattractive and says she hates her body. She has tried many diets before unsuccessfully and asks for help in losing weight. Ms. VM is five feet tall and weighs 140 pounds, with measurements of 37-27-38. We discover that she is classified as 33 pounds overweight according to the Metropolitan Life Insurance Tables for Recommended Weight (Bray, 1973, p. 7) and proceed to help her lose weight by designing a behavioral program for self-control of her presumed overeating behavior. Our client's full name is Venus Di Milo.

Ms. Di Milo in many respects represents the standard patient for most behavioral treatment programs. These programs have tended to attract a population of females who would be classified as moderately overweight. If Ms. Di Milo is typical, she may lose as much as a pound a week in the program lasting between two and six months, about 11 pounds in all, but unfortunately a year later she is likely to be close to her original weight again. From the follow-up we may also discover that she is even more unhappy with herself, for now she has failed at behavior therapy.

This author has been working with many patients like Ms. Di Milo over the past nine years, with some more successfully than with others. Out of this clinical work has come a conviction that standard behavioral packages for obesity fail many of our clients. This is not because we do not know how to design effective programs for overeating behaviors, but because we are too narrowly focused on overeating as the main target behavior to change and on weight loss as the desired goal. We do not take into account the multifaceted nature of our primarily female overweight population. We need to examine carefully other variables associated with overweight such as etiology, severity, negative self-image, and, most importantly, the meaning of overweight for a woman in a culture that overemphasizes thinness as desirable.

BEHAVIOR THERAPY AND THE OVERWEIGHT WOMAN

Women who are classified as overweight according to the Metropolitan Life Insurance Tables (1960) account for 20 to 30% of the female population (20 million American women) who, in turn, contribute to a billion-dollar medical, pharmaceutical, and publishing weight-reduction industry (Bray, 1973; Powers, 1980).

Until the beginning of behavioral work on obesity, there had been little change in the pessimistic prognosis for change described by Stunkard (1958):

> Most obese persons will not remain in treatment. Of those that remain in treatment, most will not lose weight, and of those that do lose weight, most will regain it (p. 79).

However, in 1962, Ferster, Nurnberger, and Levitt reported on an operant method for developing self-control of overeating behaviors. Stuart (1967), following this lead, devised a step-by-step behavioral curriculum to modify eating patterns and produced with Davis (Stuart & Davis, 1972) a primer for weight reduction (*Slim Chance in a Fat World*).

By the mid 1970s, there were numerous comprehensive, mostly positive reviews of what had become a vast behavioral clinical and research literature (Abramson, 1973, Hall & Hall, 1974, Stunkard, 1974, Leon, 1976, and Bellack, 1977). Stunkard and Mahoney's (1976) appraisal typifies the majority view:

> . . . behavioral techniques appear to offer the most promising and pragmatic approach to weight control (p. 61).

Stunkard (1974) was particularly optimistic about the implementation of programs for self-help organizations, and a cognitive component was added to the behavioral package (Mahoney & Mahoney, 1976).

However, doubts were also beginning to be raised (Mahoney,

1975, Yates, 1975). Stunkard retreated from his earlier endorsement in discussing follow-up:

> . . . enough follow-up studies have been conducted to permit a disturbing conclusion: Most obese people regain most of the weight they have lost in most treatments of obesity (Stunkard & Penick, 1979, p. 801).

Wilson (1979) is even more critical of behavioral treatments for obesity.

> First, most of the research is limited by severe methodological shortcomings . . . outcome is marked by substantial intersubject variability, attempts to identify accurate predictors of variables are unsuccessful . . . the magnitude of the weight loss has fallen short of clinical significance and long term evaluations are lacking (p. 199).

Thus, as we enter the 1980s, we see that behavior therapists have only been able, 19 years after Ferster, Nurnberger, and Levitt's work, to offer their predominantly female clients a slim chance at weight reduction and no permanent weight control, and we are almost back full circle to 1958.

A NEED TO REEVALUATE TARGET SELECTION

Part of the problem may relate to the social-learning bias of behavior therapists, which is in opposition to the medical model. Hence, behavior therapists emphasize patterns of eating as opposed to constitutional and metabolic aspects of obesity. However, other features of social learning theory have not been explored in this work, particularly the therapists' attitude toward overweight women and its influence on goal selection. There is now research to suggest that the helping professionals, particularly physicians who are still overwhelmingly male, are prejudiced against overweight people. In particular, physicians are found to hold an even more negative stereotyped attitude toward the obese than the obese reserve for themselves. They are reported to dislike obese patients and to view them as weak-willed and ugly (Powers, 1980). It may be that many behavior therapists share a similar attitude, since when they are confronted with a moderately overweight woman, they assume the problem is the overweight and typically set up a behavioral program to shape the patient into the cultural thin mold deemed appropriate for women in our culture. Other alternatives are rarely considered.

Unfortunately, the standard behavioral programs we have been working on during the past decade do not work for most overweight women. Despite the strong incentives to lose weight and the societal backup rewards for thin people, we have not succeeded. In many ways, what I am suggesting is an even more uphill battle, a program to enhance self-esteem in moderately overweight women.

This author feels that behavior therapists have a contribution to make in developing programs for self-esteem by borrowing cognitive behavior techniques developed for other target behaviors. One can speculate that the obsession to be thin derives from underlying negative beliefs about overweight that are shared by both the client and the rest of the culture. For example, Stunkard and Mendelson (1967) report that many obese persons appraise their bodies as grotesque and feel that others also view them with contempt.

In an attempt to help therapists to develop other types of programs and patients to accept other goals, it is proposed that we examine some of the underlying beliefs shared both by patient and by therapist that reflect the societal negative view of overweight. Again, it is important to emphasize that the strategies employed are aimed toward patients typically seen by behavior therapists (moderately overweight women).

COMMON ASSUMPTIONS SHARED BY OVERWEIGHT WOMEN CLIENTS AND MOST THERAPISTS

The client and the therapist both agree that it is undesirable to be moderately overweight and therefore adhere to the following beliefs:

1. it is undesirable to be overweight, and there is an ideal weight that is more desirable;
2. overweight is related to obesity;
3. a. it is unhealthy to be moderately overweight;
   b. weight loss is healthy;
4. overweight is caused by overeating (excess caloric intake);
5. one is unattractive and undesirable as a moderately overweight woman;
6. anybody with enough willpower can learn to control their overeating behavior; self-regulation is good.

EXAMINING THE BELIEFS UNDERLYING SELECTION OF WEIGHT REDUCTION AS A GOAL BY CLIENTS AND THERAPISTS

1. It Is Not Desirable to Be Moderately Overweight, and there Is an Ideal Weight that Is Desirable

Overweight is typically defined as a condition in the behavioral literature in which one's weight is greater than that of the average person of the same age, sex, height, and body frame, according to the Metropolitan Life Insurance Tables (Bray, 1973; Stuart and Jacobson, 1979). However, there are no universal criteria for overweight, nor is there an acceptable system for choosing frame size (Bray, 1973; Powers, 1980).

Silverstone (1968), in a survey sample of normal-weight people, reports that 10% of males and 33% of females consider themselves overweight. Behavior therapists report that as many as a third of applicants for behavioral overweight programs are of normal weight, while we know from the anorexia literature that the belief that one is overweight when one is thin is now a major health problem for female teenagers and young women (Wooley & Wooley, 1980).

If we accept the standard tables for weight developed by our culture, the Metropolitan Life Insurance Tables (1960, 1977), we find that males and females differ at various points in the life cycle in degree of overweight and obesity. Females have more body fat in general, with increases following puberty, childbirth, and again in the mid-thirties. If we consider 20% above the average weight according to Metropolitan Life Insurance Tables as overweight (the criteria used in most behavioral studies), we see that up to the age of 40, 32% of men and 40% of women are so classified, while by the age of 60, 29% of the men and 45% of the women are considered overweight. Furthermore, there are differential rates of overweight for white and black women. For example, for the over-45 age group, 24% of white and 32% of black females are considered overweight. (Stuart & Jacobson, 1979; Huenemann, Crawford, & Shapiro, 1980).

Overweight is also related to acculturation and ethnicity. Of first-generation females, 24% are reported to be overweight, compared to a rate of 4% overweight for fourth-generation females (Goldblatt, 1965). Furthermore, some ethnic groups have varying incidences of overweight for women, such as Czechoslovakians, 41%, Italians, 29%, and ethnic British, 9% (Herman, 1973; Stuart & Jacobson, 1979). In addition, standards of overweight vary by class for women, but not for men. The higher the socioeconomic class, the lower the probability of overweight (Goldblatt, Moore, & Stunkard, 1965).

So, what is a "normal" weight for a woman? What is "overweight" for a woman? The answer is, it depends on one's age, ethnic group, socioeconomic class, or race. The Metropolitan Life Insurance Tables for Desired Weights do not reflect women as they actually are. In following the guidelines suggested by these tables, we may be trying to shape a white, Anglo-Saxon, upper-class standard for all women, which may be unreasonable.

2. Overweight Is Related to Obesity

In most of the behavioral literature, the terms 'overweight' and 'obese' are used interchangeably. Yet, these terms have different meaning in the medical literature. Most behavior therapists use overweight as their selection criteria and weight loss as their goals, with the assumption that they are treating obesity. Yet there is disagreement on the degree of overweight that constitutes a presumption of obesity (Bray, 1973). Obesity is usually defined as a greater-than-average amount of body fat (Powers, 1980, Leon, 1976, Mahoney et al., 1979). Keys and Grande (1973) point out that body weight is not a reliable criterion for obesity. Skin fold thickness measurements may be more reliable as an index of body fat, yet few behavioral researchers use this measure.

Mahoney et al. (1979), in their comprehensive review on this subject, stress the low correlation between weight and body fat and weight loss and loss of body fat in the few carefully measured studies.

3a. It Is Unhealthy to Be Moderately Overweight

Perhaps the biggest incentive to lose weight is the belief that it is unhealthy to be overweight, which, in turn, leads to reduced longevity. This view is beginning to be challenged and may not be entirely relevant for females of moderate overweight.

There is no question that obesity is often associated with many diseases—hypertension, diabetes, cardiovascular disease, gallstones, and so on. However, as Powers (1980) states, "There is continuing debate about the etiological significance of obesity in these diseases" (p. 35).

Most of the research concerning health hazards and obesity cite differences between moderately and severely overweight people and between males and females. Generally, overweight is considered "a much greater hazard to the health of men than to the health of women (Stuart & Jacobson, 1979, p. 244). For example, women in particular are reported to be at low risk for cardiovascular diseases. When one examines the risk factor for moderately overweight women for other diseases, it is clear there are striking differences between the severely overweight (100% overweight) and the moderately overweight. Only severely overweight women are reported to be at high risk for diabetes and surgical mortality (Bray 1976).

Studies of longevity and overweight suggest that moderately overweight women may not jeopardize longevity. For example, women in the United States (who are reported to be consistently more overweight than men at every age) are reported to show greater longevity than men throughout the life cycle. Furthermore, this trend is continuing and holds for black women as well as white women (Metropolitan Life Insurance Company, 1960, 1977).

Generally, according to Bray (1976), there is agreement that mortality only becomes significant when body weight is more than 30% above "desirable" levels:

> Among men, the risk of death rises precipitously as a function of weight, while among women, mortality does not appear to be significantly affected by excessive weight gain before later life. . . . it is therefore clear that while women are more prone to overweight and obesity . . . they are far better able to bear its consequences (p. 244, Stuart & Jacobson, 1979).

Finally, a recent report from the National Institute of Aging reports that moderate overweight may actually have survival value in old age (*Obesity and Bariatric Medicine*, 1979).

3b. Weight Loss Is Healthy, Desirable

Linked to the assumption that overweight is unhealthy and deadly is the belief that it is desirable for health reasons to lose weight. Recent research by the USPH suggests that a person whose weight remains stable is better off than a person whose weight has fluctuated up and down a couple of times (Friedman, cited by Reichman, 1977; Wooley & Wooley, 1980).

While behavior therapists have focused on self-control of eating behavior, many clients still supplement the behavioral programs with fasts, liquid protein diets, and amphetamines. Liquid protein diets, in particular, may be riskier for health than remaining overweight (Powers, 1980).

Behavior therapists have also paid scant attention to what more medically- and dynamically-oriented weight researchers have pointed out, namely that there are negative consequences of dieting. Most behavioral researchers report a high initial dropout rate in their programs (20–25%), yet dropouts have not typically been studied. Stunkard (1957) also warns about dieting depression and more recently corroborates that 54% of overweight patients report negative symptoms during dieting—including nervousness, weakness, irritability, and fatigue (Stunkard, 1976).

4. Overweight Is Caused by Overeating, Excess Caloric Intake

The majority of behavioral programs assume that excess weight is caused by an excess caloric intake and a lessened caloric output. Central to this work has been the widespread acceptance of Schachter's theory, which emphasizes differences in eating styles between the obese and nonobese. This research has been critically reviewed by Gaul, Craighead, and Mahoney (1975), Leon and Roth (1977), Mahoney (1978) and Wooley, Wooley, and Dyrenforth (1979). Generally, there is agreement with Wooley and Wooley's conclusion that, "on the average the obese eat no more than the lean" (p. 4). Additionally, distinctive features of a presumed obese eating style have not been discovered.

In focusing on eating style and its measurement and control, behaviorists have in many respects ignored much of the medical literature. Constitutional factors (if both parents are obese, there is a very high risk of obesity), childhood environment (80% of overweight girls become overweight women) as well as hormonal and metabolic abnormalities may be more relevant than compulsive overeating for most overweight people (Powers, 1980).

5. One is Unattractive and Undesirable as an Overweight Woman

Most overweight women enter weight control programs not for health reasons, but to be more attractive (Stuart & Jacobson, 1976).

What we need to keep in mind is that our contemporary standards of thinness and desirability are culturally determined. Until early in this century, a somewhat ample, mature figure was favored. The nineteenth century was a "celebration of sumptuousness" (Reichman, 1977). Alexander Walker, the victorian expert on beauty, describes the feminine standards of beauty of that era as follows:

> Her face is round . . . her shoulders are softly rounded . . . her bosom, in its luxuriances, seems literally to protrude on the space occupied by her arms; her waist, though sufficiently marked, is as it were, encroached on by the (lushness) of all the contiguous parts . . . her thighs are large in proportion . . . the whole figure is soft and voluptuous in the extreme. . . . He then goes on to say . . . excessive leanness is repulsive (cited by Reichman, 1977, p. 23).

The Victorian female's weight might more realistically reflect the average woman's eating habits and the biological realities of accumulation of body fat as one ages. Today, however, sumptuousness is repulsive, and lean is desirable. The shift occurred somewhere in the 1920s at the beginning of the flapper era, with the utilization of fashion photography and mass distribution of women's magazines. Interestingly, the emancipation of women from restrictive clothing and mores during the 1920s may have led to its replacement by a new type of restriction. Rubens' models could not work today. The standard today is a very young, thin, flat-chested woman. Male body ideals, like male fashions, do not change so dramatically (Dyer, Feldman, & Mayer, 1970).

Behavior therapists have for the most part ignored the tremendous amount of social conditioning that has gone into the negative view of the overweight woman as unattractive and have rarely been willing to devise deprogramming methods to help overweight people learn to resist this negative conditioning and to construct an alternative program. In perusing this literature, one is reminded of some of the earlier work with homosexuals, where behavior therapists helped to devise programs to shape the homosexuals into heterosexuals instead of addressing the broader societal issues. We could learn from our errors with homosexuals, since a decade ago homosexuality in males was as unacceptable for our culture as overweight in females is today.

6. Anybody with Enough Will Power Can Learn to Control Overeating Behavior; Self-Regulation Is Good

> The failure of reducing diets is fat people's collective experience. . . . You can weigh less if you tried hard enough. If you failed, you were not motivated enough. (Alerbaran, p. 5, cited by Wooley and Wooley, 1980, p. 144).

By now, as the dismal results of our past decade's experiment with standard behavioral packages for the overweight are surfacing, we must begin to ask ourselves whether we are on the right track. Even if overweight were caused by the presumed overeating, we do not seem to have been successful in helping clients lose clinically significant amounts of weight or in helping them to maintain weight loss.

Built into behavioral self-regulation programs is another morality, that it is good to have self-control. Unlike phobics or even alcoholics, an overweight person has nowhere to hide. Mentioned previously is the prejudice doctors have toward the obese, particularly labeling them as weak-willed. Maddox and Liederman (1969), in an article on social deviance and disability, discuss the emphasis on Protestant ethic issues in our culture and its relation to self-control of impulses; hence, fatness suggests a kind of immorality, which invites retribution (p.21).

Certainly, failing at behavior modification is another addition to the low-self-esteem armor so many of our clients wear. It may be professional and unethical to continue to subject them to such failure when we really do not yet know how to help them progress toward their professed goal, to lose weight and become thinner.

CONSTRUCTING ALTERNATIVE PROGRAMS FOR MODERATELY OVERWEIGHT WOMEN

Primarily, one might ask whether behavior therapists should keep on trying the same behavior procedures with their unhappy, insistent clients instead of having the courage to face facts and to help the clients use their energy to work on self-acceptance of their body size and changing the societal prejudice against overweight. The following is an outline of a program devised to help moderately overweight women break out of the diet/self-hate/life-on-hold cycle so commonly seen in clinical practice. In many respects, this work can be viewed as a therapeutic reprogramming to counter personal/societal conditioning of overweight as abnormal, unhealthy, unattractive, and immoral. This work can be carried out individually or in group.

Although the program is designed for the large population of women who are moderately (20–30%) overweight, who represent the majority of clients in behavioral weight control programs, severely overweight women could benefit from some aspects of the program.

Phase I: Assessment

Since overweight is multifaceted, we must first do a careful assessment. Is the problem one of overeating or constitutional, developmental, or metabolic? How severe is the problem? How chronic? What are the psychological issues? Straw et al. have recently compiled a self-report measure of variables relevant to obesity that should prove useful to supplement the more standard interview procedures.

Phase II: Presentation of Choices

After a careful assessment, we need to make a realistic estimate of the likelihood that the client will reduce for the long term. If a client has a long history of chronic overweight, parents who were overweight, multiple experiences of dieting and weight gain, she is a poor candidate for another try at weight reduction, whether overeating is the major problem or not. However, if the weight gain is of recent origin (related to childbirth, nonreduction of caloric intake, reduction of physical activity, or recent stress) a behaviorally based program would appear to be a reasonable choice. In addition, one might be willing for those with poorer prognosis to attempt a behavior program for weight reduction if there is a real health hazard or sex, familial, and other related pressures.

BEGINNING THE PROGRAM

It may be necessary to help the clients in selecting goals to have some additional sessions in which they face facts. Such counseling might begin with a meditation on Stunkard's pessimistic statement. Recent reviews on the effects of behavioral and other treatments for overweight are handed out to be read, processed, and discussed. Many patients will be very angry at this opening approach. They might leave, still hoping to find a therapist to provide the "magic" for a cure. Perhaps, by paradoxical intention, a few will actually lose weight. One problem is that many clients have spent some time as thinner persons after a diet and may wish to go all out for another try. They sincerely believe that this time it may work. Unfortunately, many women who are chronic overeaters may have to make another attempt at weight loss before they are ready for an acceptance of overweight. The best one might be able to do with such clients is to help them to set a more realistic weight reduction goal. Whatever approach is used, therapy for women who fail to lose enough weight should be built into any well-designed program.

Phase III:
Consciousness Raising

Consciousness raising methods developed in the women's movement are utilized during this stage. The therapist teaches the client that the prejudices against overweight women can be viewed as "fatism" or "weightism" akin to sexism or racism. We proceed by examining the societal messages for women relevant to thinness, sexual desirability, health, and self-control in our culture. Clients are encouraged to bring their own examples and experience into therapy. Sources might include advertisements in magazines, expositions in film and on television, books, experiences in stores, and so forth. Readings are also assigned (Orbach, 1978; Flack & Grayer, 1975; Wooley & Wooley, 1979 a & b).

Phase IV:
Examination of Personal Belief Systems
Relevant to Body Size and Weight

The work in examination of personal belief systems evolves from first highlighting the societal messages and then translating these messages into the personal core beliefs that are unique to each woman. Examples include: "Any man who would want me fat, I wouldn't want," or "What's wrong with me, I must be very lazy not to change."

Phase V:
Cognitive Restructuring

The work in this phase involves cognitive restructuring that is challenging the maladaptive core beliefs and replacing them with more enhancing beliefs. The work, a variant of Ellis' (1962) RET, might proceed as follows: (1) *Belief:* If my body doesn't conform to that of my friends' or the charts, then I'm fat. (2) *Evalution of belief:* It is horrible to be fat. I am an undesirable person because I can't lose weight. I can't stand to be fat. I don't deserve to enjoy my life until I'm thin. (3) *Disputing techniques:* Where is the evidence that you don't deserve to enjoy life as a fat person? Why can't fat people be happy? The client begins to understand that it is not the "overweight" that is the problem, but the negative evaluation of the overweight and the feeling that they can't stand to be overweight or are horrible because they are overweight that perpetuates the unhappiness and preoccupation with dieting.

Positive strategies often need to be further explored at this point to move clients beyond disputing the negative beliefs. For example, this author has devised a "bill of rights for fat clients" (similar to the rights developed in the assertiveness area). Such items as I have a right to be overweight, not to have people comment on my appearance, a right to eat what I want without excusing myself, a right to a good job, a relationship, decent clothing, and so forth. Sometimes humor is used to help define rights. For example, Flack and Gaynor (1975) have devised a set of "tongue-in-cheek rules for fat people" in their groups. Such rules include the following: fat people should postpone living until they are thin, should never say no to demands and obligations, should not buy nice clothes, should not have needs, and so on.

We also examine positive aspects of being overweight. These include: beliefs that there is power in being large, strong, not able to be bowled over, not like other females, and so forth.

Phase VI: Reeducation to Love Oneself Fat

It is usually easier for overweight women to give themselves the same civil rights as thin women and more difficult really to accept and feel good about their bodies. This part of the program openly called "Let's Love Ourselves Fat" is one of the most controversial aspects and initially the part of the program to meet the most resistance. We train our clients to enjoy life with their body type and appetites. We do this via group discussion, books, bringing in role models, shopping expeditions, and so on. In many respects, the work in groups on this issue is similar to that of sex therapy groups for the inhibited woman, a form of sensuality training. Many overweight women are quite sensual and sexual, but they are ashamed of their bodies. Generally, there are so few positive role models for happy, healthy large women that the members of the groups are pioneers in trying to find people to bring to the groups. Specifically recommended are such books as S. Reichman's *Great Big Beautiful Doll* (1978), and trips to museums to look at Rubens' and others' paintings of voluptuous women. Excellent work in this area is being carried out by the National Association for Fat Americans, which parallels similar work in the Black Power and Gay Rights movements.

In addition, work with significant others, husbands, family, and so forth, is essential here. It is not unusual for clients to encounter resistance to their attempts to stop dieting or to have to handle remarks at parties about how wonderful they looked last year, when they were thinner. (We use assertive techniques for these issues.)

Phase VII: Follow-Up

Follow-up for this program involves continued support for the overweight woman to get on with her life; counseling is provided as needed.

EVALUATION

This work is still in the exploratory stage. It evolved out of this author's clinical work with approximately 50 overweight women, mainly dropouts and failures from her own and others' behavior modification programs over eight years. Many of the women, although still moderately overweight, are much more satisfied with their lives and are taking risks they never did before in business and in relationships.

Since moderately overweight women represent almost a quarter to a third of our female population, the mental health implications of this work are far-reaching.

SUMMARY

The time has come to design more effective behavioral programs to meet the realistic needs of moderately overweight women, who represent the majority of clients entering weight-reduction programs. Behavior therapists need to begin to acknowledge to themselves and their clients their failure as of this date in designing effective, long-lasting programs for weight reduction. Primarily, we might ask whether we should keep on trying the same behavioral procedures, which primarily focus on overeating behaviors, with our unhappy, insistent clients instead of having the courage to face facts and help our clients combat the obsession to be thin and compulsive dieting, by devising alternative programs for self-acceptance of overweight and setting more positive personal goals.

Little attention has been paid in the behavioral literature to the fact that we are mainly servicing a population of women who are typically 20 to 30% overweight and have been subjected to a massive program of negative conditioning about their weight. Further, many health professionals are prejudiced toward overweight people. Since most therapists and clients have been subjected to societal negative programming of overweight as undesirable, it is first necessary to examine some of the underlying assumptions behind that belief. The therapist and client need to challenge the assumption that there is a standard weight for each person, that moderate overweight is unhealthy and deadly, that self-control is easy, that overweight is related to overeating, and that women are unattractive and undesirable if they are moderately overweight. In challenging these assumptions, we lay the groundwork for behavior therapists to devise alternative programs for overweight women.

REFERENCES

Abramson, E. A review of behavioral approaches to weight control. *Behaviour Research and Therapy*, 1973, *11*, 547–556.

Altman, L. Researchers link obesity and chemical abnormality. *The New York Times*, October 30, 1980.

Bellack, A. Behavioral treatment for obesity: Appraisal and recommendations. In M. Hersen, R. Eisler & P. Miller (Eds.), *Progress in Behavior Modification*. New York: Academic Press, 1977.

Blechman, E. A. Behavior modification with women. In A. Brodsky and R. Hare-Mustin (Eds.), *Women and Psychotherapy*. New York: Guilford Press, 1980.

Bray, G. Obesity in perspective. DHEW Publ. No (NIH) 75–708, 1973.

Bray, G. *The obese patient*. Philadelphia: Saunders, 1976.

Ellis, Albert. *Reason and emotion in psychotherapy*. New York: Lyce Stuart, 1962.

Ferster, C. B., Nurnberger, J. L., & Levitt, E. G. The control of eating. *Journal of Mathetics*, 1962, *1*, 87–109.

Flack, R., & Grayer, E. D. A consciousness raising for obese women. *Social Work*, 1975, *20*, 484–487.

Fodor, I. G. A cognitive behavioral approach to helping the overweight woman (Abstract). *Scandinavian Journal of Behaviour Therapy*, 1977, *6*, Suppl. 4.

Fodor, I. G. Issues in treating the overweight women. Presentation at World Congress of Behaviour Therapy, Jerusalem, Israel, 1980.

Gaul, D. J., Craighead, W. E. & Mahoney, M. J. Relationship between eating rates and obesity. *Journal of Consulting and Clinical Psychology*, 1975, *43*, 123–126.

Goldblatt, P. B., Moore, N. E. & Stunkard, A. J. Social factors in obesity. *Journal of the American Medical Association*, 1965, *192*, 1039.

Glucksmore, M., Rand, C. & Stunkard, A. Psychodynamics of obesity. *Journal of the American Academy of Psychoanalysis*, 1978, *6*, 103–115.

Hall, S. M., & Hall, R. G. Outcome and methodological considerations in behavioral treatment for obesity. *Behavior Therapy*, 1974, *5*, 352–364.

Herman, M. W. Excess weight and sociocultural characteristics. *Journal of American Dietetic Association*, 1973, *63*.

Huenemann, R., Crawford, P., & Shapiro, L. Cultural factors in the development, maintenance and control of obesity. *Cardiovascular Reviews and Reports*, 1980, *1*.

Keys, A., & Grande, F. Body weight, body composition and calorie status. In R. S. Goodhart & M. E. Shils (Eds.), *Modern nutrition in health and disease* (5th ed.). Philadelphia, PA.: Lea and Febiger, 1973.

Leon, G. Current directions in the treatment of obesity. *Psychological Bulletin*, 1976, *83*, 557–578.

Leon, G., & Roth, L. Obesity: Psychological causes, correlations, and speculations. *Psychological Bulletin*, 1977, *84*, 117–139.

Maddox, G. L., & Liederman, V. Overweight as a social disability with medical implications. *Journal of Medical Education*, 1969, *44*, 214–220.

Mahoney, M. Fat fiction. *Behavior Therapy*, 1975, *6*, 416–418.

Mahoney, M. Behavior modification in the treatment of obesity. *Psychiatric Clinics of North America*, 1978, *1*.

Mahoney, M., & Mahoney, K. *Permanent weight control*. New York: W. W. Norton, 1976.

Mahoney, M., Mahoney, K., Rogers, T., & Straw, M. Assessment of human obesity: The measurement of body composition. *Journal of Behavioral Assessment*, 1979, *1*.

Mann, G. V. The influence of obesity on health. *New England Journal of Medicine*, 1975, *291*, 226–232.

Metropolitan Life Insurance Company. Frequency of overweight and underweight. *Statistical Bulletin*, 1960, *41*, 1–8.

Metropolitan Life Insurance Company. Trends in average weights and heights among insured men and women. *Statistical Bulletin*, 1977, *58*, 3–5. (a)

Metropolitan Life Insurance Company. Survival after midlife among nonwhites. *Statistical Bulletin*, 1977, *58*, 10–11. (b)

Metropolitan Life Insurance Company. Mortality differentials favor women. *Statistical Bulletin*, 1980, *61*, 2–3.

Orbach, S. *Fat is a feminist issue*. New York and London: Paddington Press, 1978.

Powers, Pauline. *Obesity: The regulation of weight*. Baltimore, MD: Williams and Wilkins, 1980.

Reichman, S. T. *Great big beautiful doll*. New York: Dutton, 1977.

Silverstone, J. T. Psychosocial aspects of obesity. *Proceedings of the Royal Society of Medicine*, 1968, *61*, 371–375.

Straw, M. K., Mahoney, M. J., Straw, R. B., Rogers, T., Mahoney, B. K., Craighead, L., & Stunkard, A. The master questionnaire: An obesity assessment device. Unpublished manuscript.

Stuart, R. Behavioral control of overeating. *Behaviour Research Therapy*, 1967, *5*, 357–365.

Stuart, R., & Davis, B. *Slim chance in a fat world.* Champaign, IL: Research Press, 1972.

Stuart, R., & Jacobson, B. Sex differences in obesity. In E. Gomberg and V. Franks, *Gender and disordered behavior: Sex differences in psychopathology.* Brunner/Mazel, 1979.

Stunkard, A. J. The dieting depression: Incidence and clinical characteristics of untoward responses to weight reduction regimes. *American Journal of Medicine*, 1957, *23*, 77–86.

Stunkard, A. J. The management of obesity. *New York State Journal of Medicine*, 1958, *58*, 79–87.

Stunkard, A. J. From explanation to action in psychosomatic medicine: The case of obesity. *Psychosomatic Medicine*, 1974, *37*.

Stunkard, A. J. *The pain of obesity.* Palo Alto, CA: Bull Publishing Company, 1976.

Stunkard, A. J., & Mahoney, M. J. Behavioral treatment of the eating disorders. In H. Leitenberg (Ed.), *Handbook of behavior modification and behavior therapy.* Englewood Cliffs, NJ: Prentice Hall, 1976.

Stunkard, A. J., & Mendelson, M. Obesity and the body image. I. Characteristics of disturbances in the body image of some obese persons. *American Journal of Psychiatry*, 1967, *123*, 1296–1300.

Stunkard, A. J., & Penick, S. B. Behavior modification in the treatment of obesity: The problem of maintaining weight loss. *Archives of General Psychiatry*, 1979, *36*, 801–806.

The hottest models in town. *New York Magazine*, September 29, 1980.

What's being written. *Obesity/Bariatric Medicine*, 1979, *8*, 1.

Wilson, G. T. Behavioral treatment of obesity: Maintenance strategies and long-term efficacy. In P. O. Sjoden, S. Bates, & W. Dockens (Eds.), *Trends in behavior therapy.* New York: Academic Press, 1979.

Wooley, S. C. & Wooley, O. W. Obesity and women, I: A closer look at the facts. *Women's Studies International Quarterly*, 1979, *2*, 69–79. (a)

Wooley, O. W. & Wooley, S. C. Obesity and women, II: A neglected feminist topic. *Women's Studies International Quarterly*, 1979, *2*, 81–92. (b)

Wooley, S. C. & Wooley, O. W. Women and weight: Toward a

redefinition of the therapeutic task. In A. Broadsky & R. Hare-Mustin (Eds.), *Women and psychotherapy: An assessment of research and practice.* New York: Guilford Press, 1980.

Wooley, S. C., Wooley, O. W. & Dyrenforth, S. R. Theoretical, practical and social issues in behavioral treatments of obesity. *Journal of Applied Behavioral Analysis*, 1979, *12*, 3–25.

Yates, A. *Theory and practice in behavior theory.* New York: Wiley, 1975.

PART IX

Systems, Social Factors, and Prevention

CHAPTER 21

The Contribution of Behavioral Economics to Behavior Modification

Robin C. Winkler, Ph.D.

Behavioral interventions are interventions within an interconnected whole such that a change in one part of the system affects behavior in other parts. These interdependencies occur with an intervention, and the intervention itself exists within a larger whole. Economics, because it makes interdependencies central to analysis, is able to correct errors in behavior modification resulting from a focus on target behaviors and isolation of the intervention process from relevant economic contexts. Examples are given of interdependencies within behavioral interventions, using research from token economies, alcohol and marijuana studies, and general behavior therapy. Economic and reinforcement theory are integrated to account for these systemic effects of target behavior changes. Examples of interdependencies external to behavioral interventions are given using research in domestic resource conservation and cost-benefit analysis in behavioral medicine. It is proposed that behavioral interventions be viewed as interventions in systems as a whole and that behavioral economics be used as a theoretical framework for such a view.

INTRODUCTION

This paper is about interdependencies between behaviors and interdependencies between consequences. It argues that all behavioral interventions are interventions in behavioral systems. Failure to consider interventions in this way may lead to negative clinical outcomes and misinterpretations. Recent theoretical developments that link reinforcement and economic theory provide a behavioral framework for viewing targeted behavioral interventions as interventions in behavioral systems. It will be argued that the phenomenon described by dynamic theorists as "symptom substitution" is in part quite consistent with a reinforcement theory account of behavior modification.

Two types of interdependencies will be discussed. The first set of interdependencies are *internal* to behavioral interventions. An analysis will be made of interdependencies encountered when carrying out target behavior interventions. The second set of interdependencies will be concerned with the way in which *interventions themselves* might be understood in relationship to other social and economic processes. Although this second group is *external* to behavioral interventions, these interdependencies, as the term implies, have a direct bearing on the interventions themselves. This section of the paper is based on the view that behavior modification must be reflexive, that is, behavior modifiers need to consider how their own work relates to the social/economic context in which they operate. We shall deal with the internal or microinterdependencies first.

INTERDEPENDENCIES WITHIN BEHAVIORAL INTERVENTIONS

Interventions aimed at modifying behavior have generally been conceptualized in behavior modification as modifications of target behavior(s). In the majority of applied behavior analysis studies, data is presented only for a target behavior. In others, multiple behaviors may be presented, but each is viewed as a target behavior, and the framework used remains focused on the concept of modifying target behaviors. Such an approach encourages specificity, focuses the intervention, and makes recording behavior easier.

But interventions focusing on target behaviors are much more than that. Any behavioral intervention is an intervention into a *system* of behavior and consequences. The intervention may be focused, but its effects are far greater than any change in target behavior(s). These effects may be positive or negative in terms of their relevance to therapeutic or other applied goals.

This problem has received some sporadic attention through the study of side-effects of primary interventions (Risley, 1968; Wahler, 1975; Sajwaj, Twardosz, & Burke, 1972). This kind of research, however, and the concept of side-effects still maintains the notion that the intervention is primarily one that affects target behavior.

What is being proposed here is that *every* intervention is an intervention into a system of behaviors and consequences and that a theoretical framework that conceptualizes systems of behavior and predicts effects of changes in those systems is needed. Interventions in such a framework remain specific, targeted, and focused, but they are always understood as having effects on behavioral systems, not just the targeted behaviors.

The very existence of systemic effects of target behavior interventions has been hotly debated in behavior modification and behavior therapy. The psychodynamic view of early behavioral approaches to therapy was that one could not isolate problem behaviors and change them without producing symptom substitution. Behavioral approaches to therapy were purely symptomatic, so the "real" problems would be untouched and would therefore surface in other forms. The loud chorus from behavior therapy was that symptom substitution does not exist (because the "real" problem lay in behavior, not somewhere "below" it). In the process, behavior modification denied the existence of systemic consequences of target behavior changes. It will be clear from this paper that a behavioral approach makes no such predictions at all. The problem lies in understanding, predicting, and controlling the systemic consequences that behavioral psychology clearly predicts, rather than simply denying their existence.

To understand, predict, and control systemic effects of target behavior changes one needs a body of theory that is itself systemic in approach. Behavioral economics is ideally suited to this task. Behavioral economics combines the method and theory of operant psychology with the theory of economics. As we shall see, behavioral economics extends operant psychology rather than contradicts it. It may seem unusual to go apparently so far afield to find a theoretical language to construe the systemic effects of behavioral interventions. Yet, by turning to economics, we are at the same time drawing operant psychology out of a narrow corner and using it to understand complex clinical phenomena that many clinicians are tempted to account for in nonbehavioral terms. We shall see that contemporary behavioral economics and operant psychology have far more to offer the clinician than introductory reinforcement principles.

Economics is fundamentally about interdependence. We have noted elsewhere, in referring to token economies,

> economists view an economic system as an interconnected whole in which a change in one part of the system may affect behavior in all parts. The interdependencies postulated can be conveniently divided into two categories. First, interdependencies exist between the variables of the system within any observation period. . . . For example, changing the wage rate (reinforcement rate) in a particular job (behavior), Job A, has an effect on both the frequency with which the target behavior A is performed and, via the changes in relative wages (reinforcement) and income (reinforcement received), also influences the performance of other jobs (behavior) and consumption (reinforcement-seeking) within the period of observation. Second, interdependencies exist across observation periods.

> The behavior during one time period affects behavior in future observation periods while anticipated conditions in future time periods feed back and affect present behavior (Battalio, Kagel, & Winkler, 1975, p. 90).

We went on to assert, again with respect to token economies:

> While it is apparent . . . that psychologists and psychiatrists are aware of these interdependencies, it is equally clear that these systemic effects do not form a central framework of analysis as they do for the economist. The secondary role given these interdependencies . . . leaves . . . many questions unanswered. . . . Further, the failure to consider these interdependencies fully has led to conclusions which are unwarranted on the basis of the experimental evidence presented. (Battalio, Kagel, & Winkler, 1975, p. 91)

The same observations apply to behavior therapy as a whole. For the moment, let us use token economy data to illustrate the argument, beginning with interdependencies within an observation period.

These token economy studies were carried out in a chronic ward of a large state psychiatric institution. In the first study, the token wage rate for a target behavior was varied between 5, 0, 1, 0, 5 tokens after a 4-week baseline of 0 tokens. (Battalio, Kagel, & Winkler, 1975). Each wage condition lasted a week. The behavior was toothbrushing, a self-care behavior that is typically problematic on chronic wards. In a target-behavior-oriented framework, the aim would be to increase the proportion of toothbrushing per opportunity to do so, and the behavior recorded would be chosen accordingly. As Figure 21-1 shows, the target behavior increased with increased wages, the increase being commensurate with the size of the wage increase.

But the change in wage for the target behavior also changes the *relative wage for all other behaviors.* The 5-token wage was quite high in that one third of all residents earned less than 25 tokens per week, an amount that could be earned by using all the opportunities for toothbrushing in a 5-token week. The wage change for the target behavior had systematic effects on the other token-earning behaviors. The effect of the 5-token wage on residents from four income classes (defined from baseline data) is shown in Figure 21-2. The two higher-income classes switch out of the relatively less well paid jobs while maintaining total income. The two lower-income classes do not switch out of other token earning behaviors and increase their total income largely through their increased time spent on the target behavior. The lower-income classes increased their consumption (rather than saving), while the higher-income classes maintained a constant consumption level.

If the aim of a target behavior change is to improve the overall behavior of the participants in the program, this aim was not achieved

Figure 21-1. Effect of 0, 1, and 5 Tokens on Target Behaviors, Tooth Brushing. (Reprinted from "Experimentation in controlled environment: its implications for economic behaviour and social policy making," edited by C. G. Miles and published by the Alcoholism and Drug Addiction Research Foundation, Toronto, Ontario, Canada, 1975)

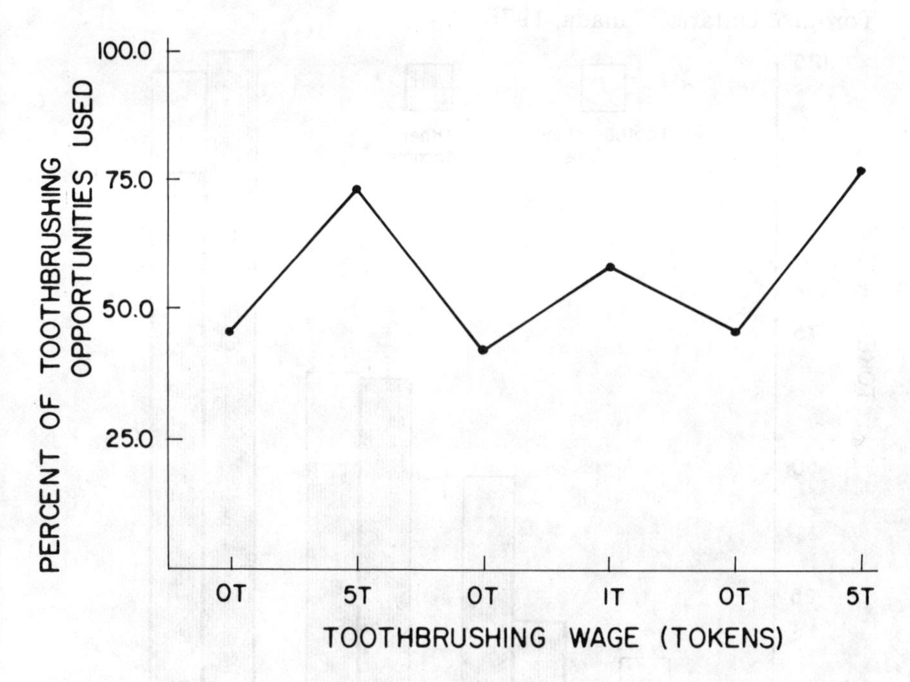

for the high-income earners. What may have been gained on the target behavior was lost with the other token-earning behaviors. On the other hand, gains in overall functioning for the low-income earners would have been hidden by focusing solely on the target behavior.

The same problem applies to changes in consumption of a single reinforcer. Reinforcer sampling (Ayllon & Azrin, 1968) has been offered as a procedure for increasing the attractiveness or potency of a reinforcer. The procedure involves providing a subject with free samples or unusually cheap samples, which increase subsequent consumption of that commodity. Such procedures also change the relative value of reinforcers and can be expected to have positive and negative systemic effects similar to those in the wage change study.

Let us now turn to interdependencies over time. One of the contributions behavior analysis has made to the understanding of alcohol and marijuana usage is to study heavy users of these drugs

Figure 21-2. Effect of Token Reinforcement for Target Behavior on Total Income Earning and Income from Target Behavior as a Function of Income Level of Residents. (Reprinted from "Experimentation in controlled environment: its implications for economic behaviour and social policy making," edited by C. G. Miles and published by the Alcoholism and Drug Addiction Research Foundation, Toronto, Ontario, Canada, 1975)

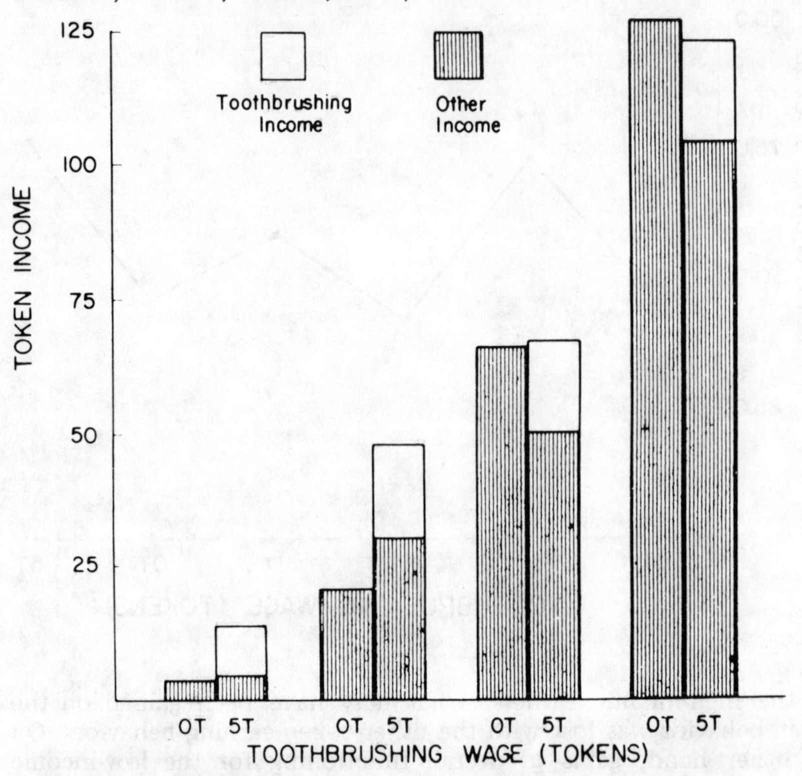

under controlled conditions in which some simple behavior earns points that may be exchanged for the preferred drug (Nathan, O'Brien, & Lowenstein, 1971; Mendelson & Meyer, 1972). These are essentially studies of drug consumption in token economies. Failure to consider interdependencies over time in these token economies has led to conclusions in this literature that are taken to reflect characteristics of the drug and its users when, in fact, they can be accounted for in terms of interdependencies over time.

Token economies differ in their economic structure. Compare two token economies: one an experimental token economy in which volunteer marijuana smokers lived for 98 days continuously and could earn points from simple construction tasks, which were exchangeable for marijuana and other goods (Miles et al., 1975); the other a standard chronic ward of a state psychiatric institution

(Winkler, 1980a). In the first economy, tokens saved could be exchanged for ordinary currency on leaving the token economy; participants knew the termination date and volunteered in order to earn money. In the second, tokens could not generally be exchanged for ordinary currency, and participants had no clear information on when they would leave the economy. Structural factors promoting saving were therefore restricted in the ward economy, whereas in the experimental economy, structural factors promoting saving in the national economy were present. Predictably, the pattern of saving (and therefore income and consumption, since these exist in a definitional relationship) differed substantially between the two token economies. Virtually all income in the experimental economy went to saving once a constant figure was exceeded, so that as income rose beyond this figure, saving rose proportionately (Winkler, 1980a). However, in the institutional token economy, almost all income went to consumption. In fact, over the seven weeks of one observation period, the total net saving for the 38 people in the economy was only +3 tokens. During that period, participants sequentially added and subtracted to a stock of savings, but over the period these canceled each other out (Winkler, 1980a).

With these differences in mind, we may return to the marijuana and alcohol studies using simple token economies. Mendelson and Meyer (1972), in reporting a study of marijuana smokers, conclude:

> The most significant feature of this (work) behavior was that, almost without exception, every subject earned the maximum number of reinforcements points every day in both studies. This finding is in marked contrast to results obtained in alcohol-related research in which alcoholics have periodic, complete cessation of work output when they are consuming alcohol (p. 94).

Marijuana smokers, they assert, work steadily while smoking, but alcoholics go on periodic sprees. The implication is that the differences are a function of alcohol versus marijuana consumption. But the economic interdependencies across time in these studies show that such conclusions are unwarranted. In the marijuana studies, points earned were exchangeable for usual currency on termination of the study, and point-earning was limited by an arbitrary ceiling. In the alcohol studies, points could not be cashed in at the end of the study, and there were no limits on earning. The difference is entirely consistent with the difference between income, consumption, and saving patterns in the experimental and institutional token economies noted above: steady earning to maximize saving in one and periodic adding to and subtracting from saving in the other. Similar conflicts in the evidence for spree behavior in alcoholics can be found in the work of Nathan, O'Brien, and Lowenstein (1971) and Mello, McNamee, and Mendelson (1968). The conflicts in these studies result from sequential experimental designs that fail to take economic interdependencies over time into consideration (Battalio, Kagel, & Winkler, 1975).

Do these interdependencies exist outside token economies, and can they be understood in terms of behavioral economics? The generality of these interdependencies is most powerfully demonstrated by considering the theoretical principles that are used to understand them.

Let us take the phenomenon of a differential effect of target wage increase on total income for high- and low-income earners. This finding is consistent with neoclassical labor supply theory in economics (Battalio, Green, & Kagel, 1979). The labor supplied to do a job, or time allocated to a reinforced behavior, is usually represented as a forward rising curve at low wages, which becomes vertical, then bends back at higher wages rates: a backward-bending or bitonic labor supply curve. The low-income people may be regarded as being on the rising end of the curve, and the high-income people on the falling or backward-bending end (Winkler, 1980b). The different positions on the labor supply curve may be regarded as reflections of different substitutabilities for labor (income) and leisure for the different income levels, that is, the trade-off between work (extra income) and not working varies with income.

This use of labor supply theory, which may at first seem remote from clinical psychology, is well supported by other research. In a second token economy study, we have shown the relevance of further principles. Labor supply theory asserts that labor supply is controlled by real wages, that is, wages divided by prices, rather than wages alone. This implies that with wages constant, price changes will have effects on labor supply according to the way in which price changes affect real wages. In the same token economy as that used in the wages study mentioned above, we found that price manipulations controlled labor supply. Price changes will affect labor supply to the extent subjects under normal (baseline) conditions purchase the goods the prices of which have changed. Price affects labor supply more where the price of preferred goods is altered. An index of these baseline preferences, combined with a series of price changes, showed that with raised real wages, labor supply increased, and with reduced real wages, controlled labor supply, labor supply decreased, and this again had a similar differential effect for high- and low-income earners (Kagel et al., 1977). Subsequently it has been shown that, in fact, labor supply theory does not go beyond behavior modification but rather represents a return to one of the basic foundations of the field. Labor supply theory may be interpreted in the more familiar language of reinforcement theory. Labor may be defined as key or lever responding, wage as rate of reinforcement, and price as, for example, time of drinking following a lever press. Interpreted in this way, it becomes possible to analyze labor supply theory experimentally within the paradigm of animal operant psychology. This may also seem a strange concept: studying economics with animals in laboratory experiments. The logic, however, is the same as that which led to the field of behavior modification itself. Laboratory experiments with animals generated much of the theoretical language that informs our applied field. Economics is in large part concerned with elucidating laws of human behavior (Kagel & Winkler, 1972). Experimental studies with animals may therefore be used in economics as they have been in psychology. Through these studies, experimental psychology and economics merge to become behavioral economics, and therefore the use of economic theory in behavior modification is, in effect, a return to basic experimental foundations in search of new and more powerful theory.

There are now numerous animal (and some human) studies that confirm the basic principles of labor supply theory used in the above analysis. Bitonic labor supply curves, substitution of labor and leisure as a function of wages and deprivation, and the role of real wages have all been confirmed in operant research (Battalio, Green, & Kagel, 1979; Winkler, 1980a).

The differential effect of real wages for high- and low-income earners might also be accounted for in terms of satiation, where satiation is defined in terms of the range of consumption goods available relative to income-earning activities (Battalio, Kagel, & Winkler, 1975). Viewed in this way, low-income earners have more room to increase consumption than high-income earners, who may be close to a ceiling of consumption, given the available goods in the economy. However, the two interpretations are not inconsistent. Green and Green (1979) show that labor/leisure tradeoffs are a function of satiation level. Pigeons at 95% body weight substitute leisure for income more often than pigeons at 70% body weight on schedules of VR50 and VR100. Income levels may be interpreted as relative deprivation levels, an interpretation also made by Green and Green. Viewing the total economy in terms of income/leisure tradeoffs has the advantage of greater generality.

Interpreted in this way, the token economy data is consistent with maximization theory as it has been used in both neoclassical labor supply theory and animal studies of that theory.

This and other research has led to new theories in operant psychology that incorporate concepts from economics (Rachlin, 1980; Allison, 1980; Staddon, 1980). It is through these theoretical developments that generalizations of behavioral economics beyond token economies to behavior modification in general are occurring. Before turning to these theoretical developments in more detail, let us consider a clinical situation that parallels the target behavior wage increase in the token economy.

Clients commonly present with a target behavior problem that the therapist assesses as being a function of insufficient positive reinforcement for either a positive alternative to the problem or for the problem itself. The therapist arranges for a target behavior to be rewarded more frequently by positive attention given by a parent, teacher, or attendant. To determine the effect of his intervention, he monitors the target behavior to see if the increased positive reinforcement is effective. The client, as well as the target behavior, has a range of other behaviors that are also maintained by attention or other consequences. This common clinical situation is identical to the token economy study described above. Accordingly, one would predict quite different results over the behavioral repertoire for clients who are generally well liked and reinforced by their parents, teachers, or attendants, and those who are not. In the former case, the target behavior may improve, but there will be a decline in other behaviors, particularly if the effort in maintaining attention by the other behaviors is considerable. For the attention-deprived person, however, one would predict a general increase in both target and nontarget behaviors.

These effects are more likely to be observed, predicted, and prevented by the adoption of newer approaches to reinforcement theory that draw upon economic concepts. Labor supply theory, maximization, and conservation theory have already been mentioned. Herrnstein (1974) has also developed reinforcement theory in terms of concepts based on interdependence between responses and reinforcers. Unlike maximization theory, Herrnstein does not draw explicitly upon economic concepts. However, Rachlin, Kagel, and Battalio (1980) have argued that Herrnstein's matching law may be regarded as a specific case of maximizing in that matching is found with multiple reinforcement schedules that have the subject choosing between perfectly substituable outcomes (such as food and food), but that where the multiple schedules involve a choice between less substitutable outcomes (such as food and water), maximizing theory, because it considers substitutability, provides a better fit to the data.

McDowell (1980) has indicated the value of Herrnstein's hyperbola for clinical work. Herrnstein's hyperbola (Herrnstein, 1974) quantifies response rate as a function of reinforcement rate (r), the total amount of behavior the organism can show (k), and extraneous reinforcement, or all the reinforcement available in the situation other than r (r_e). In this context, the key characteristic of Herrnstein's formulation is that target behavior is a function of all behavior and all reinforcers in the situation. Herrnstein's formulation has been supported by animal and human studies (McDowell, 1980). McDowell notes that Herrnstein would predict that varying the rate of reinforcement for a behavior that is an alternative to a target behavior will influence the target behavior. As he correctly points out, this is not an argument that one behavior is incompatible with another but rather that "extraneous" reinforcement affects target behavior response rate (or, in maximizing theory, utility is made up of a "package" of consequences to multiple behaviors). Procedures based on this argument have been used in clinical work before, but without the well-defined theoretical framework Herrnstein offers (McDowell,

1980). However, as Rachlin, Kagel, and Battalio (1980) note, allocation of time among behavioral alternatives depends on the substitutability of the outcome of the alternatives. The relevance of this observation for clinical work lies in the fact that one needs a procedure to determine which alternative consequences and which alternative behaviors one should vary to modify the target behavior. Obviously, not any other behavior or consequence will do. For this reason, maximization theory is potentially more relevant for clinical work in that it indicates a need to consider qualitative as well as quantitative tradeoffs among consequences (Rachlin, Kagel, & Battalio, 1980) and behaviors (Rachlin & Burkhard, 1978). In either case, however, relatively recent developments in reinforcement theory provide a theoretical framework for clinical work that has hitherto been guided more by clinical lore and "common sense."

Clinicians are aware of these problems. But behavior modification retains its focus on target behavior and a view that considers side-effects as an occasional nuisance. The newer reinforcement theories, which draw upon economic concepts, give interdependencies a central place. As such, they are more appropriate for clinical work.

These developments in behavioral economics and reinforcement theory are relatively new. At present, the clinician is best advised to assess clients within the general assumptions of such a model (allocation of time to multiple behaviors within contingency constraints; substitutability of behaviors) and to attend deliberately to estimating systemic effects of interventions. Some guidelines include:

1. mapping relevant behavioral repertoires relevant to the contingencies that maintain the problem or that are to be changed in the intervention;
2. assessing the substitutabilities of behaviors through an assessment of behaviors maintained by common contingencies, and assessment of the relative strength and attractiveness of those reinforcers;
3. applying the body of theory referred to above in predicting therapeutically relevant shifts in the allocation of behavior, given the data obtained in assessment;
4. maintaining an assessment system throughout the intervention and maintenance periods that looks for redistributions as a function of the intervention;
5. using this expanded assessment (which, of course, includes change in the target behavior) to feed back on the accuracy of initial predictions.

This approach can be illustrated through studies designed to influence domestic conservation of resources. Numerous studies have investigated various procedures designed to reduce household consumption of electricity (Winett, 1980). The target of these interventions has been total electricity usage measured by records taken from the household electricity meter. This measure is, of course, the final outcome of many behaviors by the various occupants of the house or apartment. How does one map the relevant behavioral repertoires? In American domestic electricity consumption, thermostat settings provide the greatest single source of variance for electricity usage in heating and cooling (Winkler & Winett, 1981). Inefficient and efficient strategies of thermostat setting may be defined as two repertoires: the first is typically characterized by fixed thermostat settings at high levels in winter and low levels in summer; the second, energy-efficient repertoire is characterized by different settings during the day and night, different settings when the house is occupied or unoccupied, and levels closer to outside temperatures in winter and summer. Utility for these two repertoires can be regarded as being made up of at least two types of consequence: monetary cost to the consumer and comfort. The mix of this package of consequences defines utility for the two repertoires. Allocation of time to these two repertoires depends on levels of the two consequences *and* tradeoffs or substitutabilities between these two consequences. (As cost rises, the less comfort may be chosen; as cost falls, more comfort is chosen; at two cost levels the one with more comfort will be chosen). This, in turn, is affected by the availability of behaviors other than the two mentioned, which might influence the utility as defined, such as different use of clothing, installation of insulation, use of natural ventilation, and so forth.

In this view, the intervention then becomes one that formulates clear specification of the alternative behavioral repertoire and other behaviors that influence utility as defined. The intervention is not simply a financial consequence contingent on meter records or feedback on such records (two commonly used intervention strategies, Winkler & Winett, 1981). Assessment of outcome is defined not only by meter records but by adoption of the two behavioral repertoires, other utility relevant behaviors, *and* measures of the consequences that make up utility. Accordingly, comfort is assessed throughout the intervention by installing hygrothermographs, which continuously record temperature and humidity in the home. Subject reports of comfort are related to these measures to determine how subjects have traded off comfort with financial costs during the intervention. By switching to the alternative (cheaper) repertoire, comfort was maintained at lower cost, and energy for cooling reduced by 34 to 45% in summer when households were informed about the alternative and given daily feedback and/or videotape program that modeled adoption of the repertoire while maintaining reports of comfort (Winkler & Winett, 1981).

Comfort and cost are not perfectly substitutable outcomes. If cost reduction is achieved at the expense of perceived deterioration in comfort, then appeals based on cost reduction will not be very effective, and vice versa. Obviously, as the levels of either factor vary, tradeoffs will also vary. The major point is, however, that intervention should be based on concepts of interdependence between multiple behaviors.

EXTERNAL INTERDEPENDENCIES AND BEHAVIORAL ECONOMICS

Behavioral interventions take place within an economic system. How behavioral interventions relate to the particular economic systems in which they exist is partially determined by how one evaluates the significance of those interventions. Failure to place the behavior change process itself within relevant economic contexts can lead to considerable distortions in appraising their significance.

The misleading nature of interpretations of behavior change that ignore economic context is clearly illustrated in studies concerned with the modification of electricity consumption. There are now numerous studies that show that monetary rebates contingent on reduced use produce conservation of electricity of between 15 and 30% (Winett, 1980). It is implied that such rebates might therefore be considered as a social policy instrument in programs to reduce national energy consumption. Certainly it is argued that the behavioral control produced by rebates shows their power in modifying an economically and socially important set of behaviors.

Rebates are not only reinforcers, they may also be conceptualized as changes in the price of electricity (Battalio et al., 1979). This means that rebate studies are experimental studies of the price elasticity of demand for domestic electricity (price elasticity being the relationship between price variation and consumption variation). Interpreted in this way, it is possible to calculate price elasticities from rebate studies carried out within a behavior modification framework. In a study of high and low rebates compared to feedback, information, and control conditions, we found that high rebates did control summer electricity consumption, but that the elasticity estimates were between -0.20 and -0.32 (Battalio et al., 1979). These figures were comparable to short-run price elasticity estimates obtained from the same sample using standard econometric procedures to analyze their response to "naturally occurring" price changes in the national economy. The experimentally based estimates were also comparable to commonly cited short-run price elasticity estimates in economic literature obtained from correlational studies in economics (Taylor, 1975). They indicate that the domestic demand for electricity is very price inelastic, that is, not very responsive to price—a conclusion in direct contradiction to the usual interpretation in the behavioral literature. The most reasonable conclusion from our data was not that we have a potentially useful policy in rebates but the exact opposite, that rebates are not likely to be, under the conditions of our study (and the studies reviewed by Winett, 1980), very effective.

The problem lies in the fact that the rebates used in the behavioral studies amount to price changes of 100 to 400%. In a further study of rebates we calculated a rebate size that was meaningful in terms of economic policy. This study was concerned with water conservation, a major problem in arid-zone cities. Using water supply authority data, it was possible to estimate the money saved in dam and mains construction (the major projected cost to the authority) that might result from a projected savings in consumption from a rebate. These estimates were used to calculate a rebate the size of which might be appropriate in terms of savings in capital construction cost. This economically realistic rebate failed to produce a reduction in household water usage that was greater than the reductions produced by weekly feedback inside or outside the home in summer either for high- or for low-income households (Nicol et al., 1979).

The purpose of these observations is not to decry behavioral programs in domestic resource conservation. Rather, it is to suggest that, rather than being assessed solely from within behavior modification, they be placed in the real economic contexts in which, if they are to be taken seriously, they must ultimately be meaningful. Two procedures drawing upon economic expertise may assist in achieving this aim. The first is to calculate price elasticities in rebate studies and the size of rebates in terms of relevant local policy concerns routinely. Although present data suggest that the short-term elasticity of domestic demand for electricity and water is low, these figures are themselves a function of context. It is likely that at higher prices, price elasticities will be higher and even more likely that a given rebate will be more effective at higher basic prices for the resource (see Winkler & Winett, 1982).

A second type of economic interdependency that is external to the behavioral intervention itself is perhaps the most familiar to psychologists. Cost-benefit analysis is concerned with assessing the significance of the gains produced by an intervention when considered against the increase in costs in making that intervention.

In behavioral medicine, cost-benefit analysis has a special relevance. Health care costs have risen steeply in recent years (McKinlay, 1979). There is now considerable questioning of the value for money represented in this expenditure, particularly when mortality rate reductions are related to health care costs (Ehrlich, 1975; McKinlay, 1979). This concern has led both to a call for cost-benefit evaluation of health care services and to a movement to promote self-responsibility in health care as a brake on escalating expectations of health care providers.

Behavioral medicine, with its emphasis on self-help, self-responsibility, and prevention might be regarded as a positive response to the cost problems in health care. If self-management in behavioral treatment and prevention programs are effective in changing behavior, then they become potential candidates for a larger policy of encouraging the community to see health as a product they themselves create rather than a product produced by experts, which they consume. Such a policy has its problems, insofar as it stresses individual self-help only at the expense of social determinants of health-related behavior, but it is a policy that is both timely and consistent with behavioral approaches to health care.

Viewed in this context, it is incumbent upon behavioral medicine not only to show that it is clinically effective but that it is cost-effective, particularly in terms of reductions in utilization of health care services. Just as in the resource conservation example, it is likely to be misleading to consider only whether target behaviors have changed. Accordingly, in our self-management program for chronic headache, we have been concerned with both clinical outcome and cost-effectiveness (Yates, 1979).

The 12-session program provides tension headache and migraine sufferers with the opportunity to learn stress management coping skills (relaxation, cognitive coping skills, and assertion) in a group setting (Winkler et al., 1981). Daily headache records taken for four weeks prior to treatment and periodically over a one-year follow-up period indicate that average hourly intensity of headache is significantly reduced for chronic headache sufferers (mean years of headache, 17 years) and initial improvement is maintained at one year (Winkler et al., 1981). The program has been tested successfully against waiting list controls and is equally effective for chronic migraine and tension headache sufferers (Winkler et al., 1981).

Effectiveness, with respect to costs, is assessed by having participants record daily (a) medication used, (b) any utilization of health costs, (c) time off from work or home duties. The dollar cost for each category is assessed on the basis of (a) pharmaceutical industry data on drug costs to government and consumer, (b) average professional service fees available from the professional societies, and (c) average wage for the relevant community of subjects and of housekeepers (for home duty costs). The cost of providing the intervention is assessed on the basis of the wage of the providers and the time they spend in treatment (infrastructure costs such as offices, telephones, and so forth were negligible in this example).

Eighteen chronic headache sufferers were seen in three groups for 12 sessions. Screening criteria for subjects were two or more headaches per month for the last year and no medical complications.

The cost-effectiveness of the self-management program was such that it paid for itself within six weeks of treatment termination (Bolton & Winkler, n.d.). Cost-effectiveness was aided considerably by the group nature of the program. This positive cost-benefit assessment for self-management of headache is, however, only a simple, first step. Ultimately relative clinical and cost-benefit assessments of self-management against traditional medical approaches will be the most useful in health policy.

All subjects in the above cost-effectiveness assessment had been suffering from headache for many years. By this time, health care utilization was low—they had given up on doctors. Cost savings would have been greater earlier in their headache careers, when diagnostic costs are higher and the search for costly "cures" is more vigorous. Cost-effectiveness considerations therefore suggest that consideration should be given to delivering behavioral medicine interventions as early as possible in the client's search for assessment and treatment. However, the effectiveness of self-help may be greatest after this period and minimal during it.

In both the above examples of external interdependencies, there is a common theme. Behavioral interventions must be evaluated not only in terms of criteria that are internal to behavior modification but also in terms of the criteria that already exist in the fields into which behavior modification has moved. In both examples, economists have been in the field well before the arrival of psychologists. By drawing upon the concepts and procedures economists have developed for use in the new field, behavior modification can make itself more relevant to the major policy issues in the field. Without such connections, behavior modification runs the risk of isolating itself and reducing its potential contribution.

REFERENCES

Allison, J. Economics and operant conditioning. In Pharzen & M. D. Zeiler (Eds.), *Advances in analysis of behavior, Vol. 2: Predictability, correlation, and contiguity*. Chichester, England: Wiley, 1980 (in press).

Ayllon, T., & Azrin, N. H. Reinforcer sampling: a technique for increasing the behavior of mental patients. *Journal of Applied Behavior Analysis*, 1968, *1*, 13–20.

Battalio, R. C., Green, L., & Kagel, J. H. Income-leisure tradeoffs for animal workers. Working Paper No. 79–08, Texas A & M University, 1979.

Battalio, R. C., Kagel, J. H., & Winkler, R. C. Analysis of individual behavior on controlled environments: an economist's perspective. In C. G. Miles (Ed.), *Experimentation in controlled environments: its implications for economic behavior and social policy making.* Toronto: Addiction Research Foundation, 1975, 89-102.

Battalio, R. C., Kagel, J. H., Winkler, R. C., & Winett, R. A. Residential electricity demand: an experimental study. *The Review of Economics and Statistics*, 1979, *61*, 180-189.

Bolton, B., & Winkler, R. C. *Cost-effectiveness of a self-management programme for chronic headache.* Unpublished manuscript, Department of Psychology, University of Western Australia.

Ehrlich, D. A. (Ed.). The health care cost explosion: Which way now? Bern: Hans Huber, 1975.

Green, J. K., & Green, L. The effect of deprivation level on labor supply in pigeons: An experimental analysis of economic behavior. Presented at the *5th Annual Convention Behavior Analysis.* Dearborn, MI: 1979.

Herrnstein, R. J. Formal properties of the matching law. *Journal of the Experimental Analysis of Behavior*, 1974, *21*, 159-164.

Kagel, J. H., Battalio, R. C., Winkler, R. C., & Fisher, E. B., Jr. Job choice and total labor supply: an experimental analysis. *Southern Economic Journal*, 1977, *44*, 13-24.

Kagel, J. H., & Winkler, R. C. Behavioral economics: areas of cooperative research between economics and applied behavior analysis. *Journal of Applied Behavior Analysis*, 1972, *5*, 335-342.

McDowell, J. J. On the validity and utility of Herrnstein's hyperbola in applied behavior analysis. In C. M. Bradshaw, E. Szabadi, & C. F. Lowe (Eds.), *Quantification of steady-state operant behavior.* Elsevier: North Holland Biomedical Press, 1980.

McKinlay, J. B. Epidemiological and political determinants of social policies regarding the public health. *Social Science and Medicine*, 1979, *13a*, 541-558.

Mello, N. K., McNamee, H. B., & Mendelson, J. H. Drinking patterns of chronic alcoholics: gambling and motivation for alcohol. In J. O. Cole (Ed.), *Clinical research in alcoholism.* Psychiatric Research Report No. 24, Washington, DC, American Psychiatric Association, 1968, 83-118.

Mendelson, J. H., & Meyer, R. E. Behavioral and biological concomitants of chronic marijuana smoking by heavy and casual users. In *Marijuana: a signal of misunderstanding.* Technical papers of the first Report of the National Commission on Marijuana and Drug Abuse, Vol. 1, US Government Printing Office, Washington, DC, 1972.

Miles, C. B., Congreve, G. R. S., Gibbons, R. J., Marsham, J., Devenyi, P., & Hicks, R. C. An experimental study of the effects of daily cannabis smoking on behaviour patterns. In C. G. Miles (Ed.), *Experimentation in controlled environments: its implications for economic behaviour and social policy making.* Toronto, Canada: Addiction Research Foundation, 1975, 1-44.

Nathan, P. E., O'Brien, J. S., & Lowenstein, L. M. Operant studies of chronic alcoholism: Interaction of alcohol and alcoholics. In M. K. Roach, W. M. McIssac, & P. J. Creaver (Eds.), *Biological aspects of alcohol.* Austin: University of Texas Press, 1971.

Nicol, M., Winkler, R. C., Haggard, A., & Syme, G. J. Experimental analysis of domestic resource consumption. Invited Address, Australian Behaviour Modification Association Annual Conference, Adelaide, 1979.

Rachlin, H. Economics and behavioral psychology. In J. E. R. Staddon (Ed.), *Limits to action: allocation of individual behavior.* New York: Academic Press, 1980.

Rachlin, H., & Burkhard, B. The temporal triangle: response distribution in instrumental conditioning. *Psychological Review*, 1978, *85*, 22-47.

Rachlin, H., Kagel, J. H., & Battalio, R. C. Substitutability in time allocation. *Psychological Review*, 1980, *87*, 355-374.

Risley, T. Effects and side-effects of punishing the deviant behavior of an autistic child. *Journal of Applied Behavior Analysis*, 1968, *1*, 21-34.

Sajwaj, T., Twardosz, S., & Burke, M. Side effects of extinction procedures in a remedial pre-school. *Journal of Applied Behavior Analysis*, 1972, *5*, 163-176.

Staddon, J. E. R. (Ed.). *Limits to action: The allocation of individual behavior.* New York: Academic Press, 1980.

Taylor, L. D., The demand for electricity: A survey. *The Bell Journal of Economics*, 1975, *6*, 74-110.

Wahler, R. G. Some structural aspects of deviant child behavior. *Journal of Applied Behavior Analysis*, 1975, *8*, 27-42.

Winnett, R. A. An emerging approach to energy conservation. In D. M. Glenwick & L. Jason (Eds.), *Behavioral Community Psychology.* New York: Praeger, 1980.

Winkler, R. C. Behavioral economics, token economies, and applied behavior analysis. In J. E. R. Staddon (Ed.), *Limits to action: the allocation of individual behavior.* New York: Academic Press, 1980. (a)

Winkler, R. C. Target behaviour changes in behavioural economics. In C. M. Bradshaw, E. Szabadi, & C. F. Lowe (Eds.), *Quantification of steady-state operant behaviour.* Amsterdam: Elsevier, 1980, 287-298. (b)

Winkler, R. C., Ray, P. A., Haggard, A., & Schwartz, S. Evaluation of a self-management programme for chronic headache. In J. W. G. Tiller & P. R. Martin (Eds.), *Behavioural Medicine.* Geigy, 1981.

Winkler, R. C., & Winett, R. A. Behavioral interventions in resource conservation: a systems approach based on behavioral economics. *American Psychologist*, 1982, *37*, 421–435.

Yates, B. T. How to improve, rather than evaluate, cost-effectiveness. *The Counselling Psychologist*, 1979, *8*, 72–76.

CHAPTER 22

Training for Ecobehavioral Technology

Edwin P. Willems, Ph.D.

INTRODUCTION

People everywhere are worried about behavioral problems. Everyday human behavior and its emergence into troubling forms is a serious threat to persons, to societies, and to the human species. We hear of uneasiness over crime and social disintegration; the deterioration of daily behavioral and social life; the feeling that things are not working or are coming apart; the sense of vulnerability to the acts of persons and to daily events which seem unintelligible and over which we have little control; and the vague awareness that our own behavior, our own choices, our own work habits, and our own life styles are visiting back upon us a torrent of behavioral problems and health problems ranging from the mild to the catastrophic. We hear a great deal of intense concern about the quality of life in old age, the welfare of children, the problems of work places, getting from one place to another, the increasing complexity, mystery, and elusiveness of well-being, the behavioral components of health problems, and new forms of deviance and pathology. It is only reasonable that persons worried about such problems would turn to psychology.

However, when persons turn to psychology for assistance, they confront an irony. Most research in psychology deals with relatively small and discrete problems and with modest objectives. When one tries to stretch these pieces to fit a comprehensive framework and use them to clarify everyday problems of behavior, the bits and pieces wear poorly on the larger canvas of real life. They wear poorly for those persons who try to use the understanding in treatments or technologies to solve some individual or community problem; they wear poorly for planners and designers who try to use the models in designing everyday systems for human living; and they wear poorly for policymakers. Human behavior—what persons *do*—is inextricably bound up in larger ecological systems. By and large, the fragments of our research domain have not begun to approach the scale and complexity of those systems. Simple ideas and simple findings seem to be easier for us to comprehend and to embrace than complex ones that may be much more appropriate.

Psychology must overcome its growing sense of futility about understanding and changing the seemingly pell-mell course of problems of human behavior and must develop the means to influence and shape that course in more reflective, purposeful, and humane directions. One necessary ingredient for these developments is to expand and complicate our models of the contexts in which behavior is embedded. A further comment is in order to clarify what "complicate" means.

In society's growing awareness of ecological phenomena, we are reluctant to introduce new biotic elements and new chemicals into our ecological systems, but we do not display the same judiciousness about intervening in social/behavioral/environmental systems. Almost every day, we hear of projects or technologies being changed, slowed down, stopped, or disapproved of on ecological grounds, because of the known complexity or delicacy of ecosystems. The location of a proposed factory is changed, a bridge is not built, a planned freeway is rerouted, a smokestack is modified, someone is restrained from introducing a new animal into an area, or a pesticide, pharmaceutical, or other chemical is taken off the market. How often has a program or a project whose target is human *behavior* been changed, slowed down, stopped, or disapproved of on *behavioral*/ecological grounds, because of the known complexity and delicacy of ecobehavioral systems? The answer should sober us quickly.

It is quite foreign to psychologists to think of the physical, social, and spatial environment as inextricable parts of the behavioral processes of organisms. Two results often follow from this disregard. One is relatively splintered, bit-like attempts to understand large-scale, complex phenomena, and the second is a rather blithe form of bit-like tinkering in complex interdependent systems. Every intervention, every human artifice has its price, no matter how well-intentioned the agent of intervention may be. The places, programs, and times for which this is true need to be documented and understood much better by psychologists. To illustrate what I mean here, let me present briefly a hierarchical series of examples.

Partly because of their rigor and partly because of the explicitness with which their intended effects can be spelled out, various programs of applied behavior analysis or behavior modification illustrate these problems very clearly for human behavior. Buell et al. (1968) used teacher attention to reinforce a withdrawn girl's use of play equipment in a preschool setting. The intervention was successful (the intended effect), but it also affected the girl's interactions with other children, such as touching, verbalizations, and cooperative play (positive unintended effects). Twardosz and Sajwaj (1972) found that increasing the rate of sitting in a retarded and hyperactive boy also decreased his rate of weird posturings and increased his rate of proximity to other children.

Unintended effects of a more unpleasant and pernicious sort also occur. Herbert et al. (1973) trained parents in the use of differential attention to increase appropriate behaviors and decrease deviant behaviors in six children. One child showed some improvement, and one showed no change. In the cases of four children, dramatic, intense, and *durable* (but unintended) effects showed up, both in the treatment setting and in other settings. Examples were assaulting mother, scratching self until bleeding, enuresis, and throwing furniture. Sajwaj, Twardosz, and Burke (1972) found various so-called "side-effects" of manipulating single behaviors in a preschool boy. They taught the teacher to extinguish the child's nagging, but the program produced systematic changes in other behaviors by the child in the same setting and in another setting as well. Some of the unintended effects were desirable, such as increasing speech initiated to children and increasing cooperative play; some were undesirable, such as decreasing task-appropriate behavior, and increasing disruptive behavior; and some were neutral, such as use of girl's toys. The investigators were able to show that the covarying effects were not due to differential attention by the teacher applied directly to those behaviors but were somehow, as yet mysteriously, a function of modifying the nagging in one setting.

These examples suggest that person/behavior/environment systems are quite complex and that the simplistic models and technologies of change often used by the behavior therapist are not comprehensive enough to lead to the understanding of complex human behavior or to predictable interventions. Extensive research should be conducted to ascertain which kinds of unintended effects occur most frequently and why they occur, so that practitioners can begin to predict such effects and plan their interventions with these effects in mind, in at least crude cost-benefit assessments.

There are other examples that fall higher on a hierarchy of setting size and complexity. In a mental hospital ward, Proshansky, Ittelson, and Rivlin (1970) used some amenities of interior design to increase the rate of sociable occupancy and use of a solarium, and they found that the rate of detached, withdrawn standing behavior went down. However, they had only succeeded in changing the *location* of the troubling behavior—a great deal of it now occurred at the other end of the corridor, by the nurses' station.

In 1974 and 1975, because of the energy crisis, administrators of a VA hospital decided to decrease the amount of electricity consumed (David M. Bailey, personal communication). They disconnected one-half to two-thirds of the fluorescent lights in several wards. When they did this, they found that the noise level in those wards decreased so much that they could cancel their plan to spend thousands of dollars to soundproof the wards. This was a simple intervention in a behavioral-environmental system that resulted in two positive unintended effects. We do not know whether there were other, less positive effects, such as a decrease in rates of activity and interactions.

Several years ago, a group of educators mobilized a new program of early intervention to train disadvantaged children in cognitive skills (Dale Johnson, personal communication). All available measures showed that the program achieved *none* of its *intended* effects on the children. However, community participation and political involvement by the childrens' families increased markedly.

According to a television news report, the police department in San Diego tried an experiment to reduce excessive automobile speed in an area in which the speed limit was 20 miles per hour. Without issuing tickets, the police gathered baseline data and found the average speed to be 23 miles per hour. In order to reduce the average speed, they then posted a new speed limit of 19 miles per hour, hoping, perhaps, to capitalize on the attention-getting value of unusual numbers on signs. After waiting for a period of time for stabilization of driving habits, the police found, to their surprise, that the new average speed had increased to *26 miles per hour!*

My major point here is two-fold. First, psychologists often believe that their favorite approaches to research will ultimately yield comprehensive understanding of human behavior. I think they are wrong in many cases because their conception of the research problems is too narrow and too simplistic. Second, in seeking to alleviate human problems, practitioners often believe that, in order to be successful, they need mainly to do more of what they are already doing and do it more intensely. Again, I think often they are wrong, and I think many of their best efforts will suffer because they do not understand the size and the complexity of the systems in which they are dabbling.

We often hear of severe and sometimes permanent damage being done by the very things we have been invited to use and consume. *Where are the scientists ahead of time?* That question and what we can do to answer it for techniques of social, behavioral, and psychological change represent major unfinished business for us. We should ask ourselves, "Where are *we* ahead of time, with some *anticipatory* understanding of the effects of our social-behavioral interventions and technologies?" Gaining such anticipatory, before-the-fact understanding provides the dim outlines of important work for us. Without it, we will often perpetuate the uncomfortable irony of producing pain through our efforts to produce good.

One of the significant features of many social, physical, and biological systems is that they function as integrated wholes; manipulation of any part of such a system will affect each of the other parts and change the whole. Even the most positively motivated intrusions into these systems can lead to all sorts of unanticipated effects, many of them unpleasant and pernicious. To label these unintended effects as "side effects" only compounds the problem. Anticipated and unanticipated effects are all functions of the system's processes. Side effects do not occur in the real world. They exist in our images of events because we *expect* some things and not others to result from our efforts.

One response by practitioners who focus on the person is a kind of fretful and piecemeal awareness of the importance of larger contexts, which leads them to say, in effect, "Oh yes. We must consider social environment, stressors, or cultural themes and the ways in which they affect our phenomenon of interest." However, this approach is only lip service at worst, or the accounting for a little more variance at best. I am advocating a more radical view, a truly alternative view about how human behavior works, how it develops into troubling forms, and how it leads to and results from health problems. On this view, the perspectives and findings of ethology, community studies, public policy research, sociology, sociobiology, and behavioral ecology are just as fundamental and central as are the perspectives and findings of learning theory, behavior analysis, clinical medicine, physiology, and neuroanatomy. In fact, the former may be *more* important because they deal with behavior as the major means by which persons and groups come to terms with the environmental systems.

IMPLICATIONS FOR TRAINING

In various contexts, other persons and I have discussed and fought about the shape of behavioral ecology, as well as the mutual implications of behavioral ecology and programs of intervention (Rogers-Warren & Warren, 1977; Willems, 1973, 1974, 1977a, 1977b; Willems & Stuart, 1980). Rather than to present more of that argument, I shall list a series of implications for behavior therapy. Some of the implications suggest primarily research and development, and some can be translated more directly into training.

First, as scientists and practitioners, we often accept the doctrine of the organization of the world in terms of levels. Then we become very precise at working *within* a level. Having picked the level of analysis that clusters very tightly around the person and his behavior, the behavior therapist and the applied behavior analyst tend to stick to that level, to work within it and not with it. That is, they do little to display its relations to the environment as it extends away from the person and over time. But this commitment to one level may fail to be heuristic; what is more, it may actually become *antiheuristic* and dysfunctional if it blinds us to phenomena that cut across levels.

Discussing success and failure in behavior therapy, Liberman (1980) says, "After almost 20 years of behavioral analysis and therapy, workers in the field must realize that political, personal, and social factors determine upwards of 90% of the success and survival of technical procedures" (p. 370). We must come to view and to study human behavior at levels of complexity that are quite atypical in behavior therapy and applied behavior analysis. This complexity lies in *systems*—relationships that link person, behavior, social environments, and physical environments. In other words, we must widen our conceptualizations.

Second, at some point we must come to see that such systems cannot be understood piecemeal. It is very likely that we will continue to study and manipulate pieces and components of these systems. However, we must conceptualize the interdependencies. Unfortunately, this recommendation runs against some important historical trends. According to a survey conducted by Hayes, Rincover, and Solnick (1980), research and clinical demonstrations in applied behavior analysis are becoming more narrow, less complex, more purely technical, and less conceptual (that is, less concerned with general principles).

Third, our programs of research and development as well as our programs of therapeutic follow-up must reflect the fact that behavior-environment systems have important properties that change, unfold, and become clear only over long periods of time. That is, our perspective and our methods must become truly longitudinal and should span longer time frames.

Fourth, psychologists often see descriptive research as worthless at worst and only tolerable at best. We must come to see systematic naturalistic description of organism/behavior/environment systems as a fundamental and integral part of our research enterprise, just as it is in more mature sciences.

Fifth, both our analytic and our therapeutic approaches to such systems must be based on the assumption of interdependence—that tampering with any part of such a system will likely affect the other parts and alter the whole.

Sixth, we must train ourselves, our colleagues, and our students to develop an ecological awareness of the many ways in which (a) simple intrusions can produce unintended effects, (b) indirect harm may follow from narrowly defined good, and (c) long-term harm may follow from short-term good.

Seventh, we must accept the challenge of understanding such systems, so that the effects of interventions and planned changes can be anticipated in comprehensive fashion. Stated generally, this means we must know much more about the ecobehavioral[1] systems in which we are increasingly inclined to intervene. Stated more concretely, this means that we should acquire the skill to write *ecobehavioral impact statements* for our therapeutic work. From our present vantage point, this sounds clumsy, mystifying, and onerous. However, shifting to that point of view will foster studies and approaches to intervention that will provide criteria for evaluating our practices, classifying them in terms of benefit and cost, and modifying or withholding those that are technically feasible but ecologically and socially objectionable.

Eighth, since no one person can do everything, we undoubtedly will have to train professionals to work therapeutically in altogether new partnerships and arrangements, in the new mode of ecobehavioral technology. Behavior, the principal means by which organisms carry on commerce with the environment, is embedded in and related to phenomena at many levels, which themselves form hierarchies: molecules, cells, tissues, organs, organ systems, organisms, settings, facilities, institutions, political systems, and economic systems. Behavior is a mid-range phenomenon here; what organisms *do* is the principal means by which they relate to the various levels of context. Thus, the full contextual understanding of behavior requires models and approaches developed by persons with expertise at the various levels of embeddedness. One step is to develop new forms of intensive, problem-oriented collaboration and cooperation in our work. In one sense, behavior therapists already work with persons from outside their discipline more frequently than most professionals. They work with teachers, parents, administrators, neighborhood organizers, medical personnel, and so on. In most cases, however, those other persons have been involved primarily in identifying and defining a problem to be solved or they have been consumers of the technology. I am speaking more of training and collaborative work that moves freely across the boundaries. In short, behavior therapy is far too important to be left to behavior therapists.

Ninth, we need to develop much more sophisticated understanding of the contexts of behavior. Frances Horowitz (1975) once noted that, "Behavior analysts are notorious for ignoring the nature of the organism with which they are working" (p. 14). This complaint implies that behavior analysts work primarily with organisms. I would argue that the behavior analyst does not work primarily with organisms. He works with behaviors and with the environments of those behaviors. He identifies a target *behavior* and sets up ways to manipulate the *environment* of that behavior in order to control it and change it. I would shift Horowitz's friendly complaint to make

[1] The adjective "ecobehavioral" is a shorter and more efficient form of the cumbersome phrase, "ecological-behavioral," or "behavioral-ecological."

a different friendly complaint: Behavior analysts are notorious for ignoring the nature of the environmental settings with which they work. They claim adherence to learning theories and to the principles of reinforcement, stimulus control, and environmental maintenance, but, *as therapists*, they are curiously person-oriented in their work.

Human behavior is astonishingly setting-dependent. Behavior that is appropriate to one setting may not be appropriate to another. Different settings have different task structures and behavioral requirements. What persons learn to do in one setting may not transfer to other settings. Thus, what the behavior therapist experiences as frustrating problems of intersetting generalization often may be client behaviors that are obeying basic principles of setting dependency. We need to delve into that aspect of behavior much more in order to produce the most effective, generalizable, and durable therapeutic changes. Stokes and Baer (1977) have reviewed the empirical literature on mechanisms of generalization in programs of behavior change. Setting dependencies of behavior are at the heart of the problem of generalization and of unanticipated effects.

Tenth, we need to develop new information systems and new approaches to monitoring, both for programs of research in ecobehavioral technology and for evaluating interventions. Without such development, the empirical effectiveness of ecobehavioral technology will be stunted. By and large, we have depended on data systems that are cost-inefficient. More cost-efficient and sustainable data systems are feasible. Furthermore, the typical approach to data gathering must be expanded to increase (a) the number of types of behavior observed, (b) the number of persons observed, (c) the dimensions of behavior observed, (d) the length of time, and (e) the number of settings observed. Very exciting work of this sort is coming out now, and we should watch it carefully.

A study by Spyker, Sparber, and Goldberg (1972) illustrates the importance of expanding data systems to study complex effects. Neurological dysfunction is the official criterion for recognizing a case of methylmercury poisoning and for setting allowable standards. Noting that, these investigators gave pregnant mice small injections of methylmercury or saline solution and later—two months after birth—conducted extensive neurological tests on the babies. There were no differences between the poisoned animals and animals whose mothers had received injections of saline solution. However, the investigators expanded their data system to include open-field and swimming tests. The poisoned group displayed significant decrements on these behavioral criteria.

In my research program, we have used data from our direct observations of spinal cord patients to assess the effects of changes in hospital treatments. In one case, we found no effect on the *kinds* of patient behavior, but there were large effects on other aspects of the behaviors, such as the number of settings entered and the rate at which they behaved without the direct, hands-on involvement of someone else.

SOME POSITIVE EXAMPLES

Is it possible to illustrate this complicated approach to behavior therapy more concretely? Fortunately, there are some examples to look at.

A Priori Prediction of Effects

It should be possible to develop the theoretical or a priori prediction of effects. My point here is that not all unanticipated effects need be unanticipated; probably, a significant portion of them can be predicted if we only put our minds to it. We need not start from scratch in puzzling out the complexities for every problem of intervention. Among us, we have more relevant collective wisdom, past experience, working models, existing data, and explicit theories than we give ourselves credit for. In some areas, we can use our accumulated experience and hypotheses to predict various effects that might occur with an intervention. At the very least, we can predict some and then monitor their occurrence.

Zelazo, Zelazo, and Kolb (1972) studied the infantile walking response and found that, if held under the arms with feet touching a flat surface, a newborn infant will perform coordinated walking movements. Usually, the response disappears by about the eighth week after birth. Stimulation (practice) of the response during the period from the second through the eighth week after birth resulted in significant reductions in the ages at which the infants began to walk alone. The investigators described a number of possible benefits that could result from the development of early mobility, particularly the promoting of competence and independence.

Based partly on prior developmental data and theory and partly on his own common sense, Gotts (1972) argued that to accelerate the onset of walking might prove undesirable because detrimental effects might result. For example, "at the naturally occurring mean age for solo walking . . . the average infant's posterior fontanel is closed and his anterior fontanel is closed or nearly closed. . . . To accelerate the onset of walking would . . . unnecessarily expose younger children, who have less complete fontanel closure, to possible central nervous system injury" (p. 1057). Gotts spelled out other possible effects. Whether or not we agree with Gotts is less interesting to me than the use of existing ideas, data, and intuitions to frame before-the-fact predictions of indirect and secondary effects. There should be many possibilities of this sort that would allow us to anticipate and measure a higher proportion of what are, at present, unanticipated effects.

Empirical Prediction of Effects

I suggest that we might use theories and collective wisdom to predict some intervention-produced effects. At a more empirical level, we can make the data-based predictions of "other" effects that will accompany our interventions. The best example of this strategy comes from the work of Robert Wahler's group and, to a lesser extent, from my own research program.

Wahler (1975), Lichstein and Wahler (1976), and Kara and Wahler (1977) suggest that if baseline data are extensive enough, both in time and array of measures, they can be used to predict complex changes in behaviors that are not manipulated directly in the subsequent treatment. For example, Kara and Wahler (1977) monitored 14 categories of a child's behavior during baseline. Through factor and cluster analysis, the investigators identified the clusters that occurred during baseline. One behavior was selected from one of the clusters to be put on an extinction schedule during the intervention phase, while the other behaviors in that cluster were maintained on their baseline schedules. As the focal behavior followed the extinction-reinstatement manipulation in the multiple reversal design, the other behaviors in the cluster increased *and* decreased in ways that were predicted from the directions of their interrelationships in the baseline cluster analysis. Behaviors that were related positively to the target behavior in the cluster decreased when the target behavior went on extinction. Behaviors that were related negatively to the target behavior *increased* when the target behavior went on extinction. By using some extensive baseline data and some unusual statistical operations on the data, the investigators were able to predict some intervention-produced effects that otherwise would have remained hidden and unanticipated. In our longitudinal research with spinal cord patients, we have been conducting similar cluster analyses as a basis for identifying key constituents of patient performance, for anticipating the specific ways in which performance will be affected by events such as illnesses, and for selecting the best predictors of post-hospital adjustment (Willems & Alexander, in press).

Larger Contexts

The examples of infantile walking and behavior clusters are most directly relevant to the issues of subtle relationships and unintended effects. The next example, also from the work of Wahler's group, illustrates some of the ways in which the larger context can affect the outcome of a therapeutic intervention. Wahler (1980) and Wahler et al. (1977) describe a program of parent training to treat oppositional and disturbed children. Across all client families, the program was successful during the time it was applied, but the degree of maintenance of the effects during follow-up was mixed. To make a long story short, the clinician-investigators found maintenance to be very low among insular families, families whose parents—primarily mothers—had few community contacts (friendships, etc.) and had mainly aversive contacts when they did occur.

The hypothesis that insularity led to the maintenance problems was supported by further investigation. For example, the relationship was so precise that the troubled behavior of the children went down on days when outside contacts went up for mothers, and vice versa. Aversive behavior by mothers toward children also decreased on days of higher outside contact, and vice versa. Across days, there were negative correlations between number of outside contacts on the one hand and rates of troubling behavior by children and aversive behavior by mothers on the other. These findings on the behavioral ecology of families support two more general inferences. First, the family problems appeared not to be a function of parents who were bad in some stylistic sense. Rather, both parents and children had bad days as a result of events in their social contexts. Second, it seems clear that, at times, our therapeutic targets and our degree of success and failure are affected by the larger context in which they embedded.

CONCLUSION

Enough of examples and abstract arguments. I know that behavior therapists *strive* to be effective. However, as a behavioral ecologist, I am concerned about those instances in which the therapist (a) is unsuccessful and does not know why, (b) is successful and does not know why, and (c) is successful or unsuccessful but produces something else not intended, and which may be troublesome in its own right. The perspective of behavioral ecology has much to offer the therapist. Behavior therapists should be trained to accept the likelihood of unintended effects as part of their work, so they can learn how to predict when and how such effects will occur, and so they can weigh such probabilities before the fact in their decisions about intervention. Then we will have achieved an effective ecobehavioral technology.

SUMMARY

In looking to psychology for ways to deal with complex behavior problems, society is looking to a discipline with narrow vision. The subtle interdependency of phenomena that is taken for granted by ecologists in other disciplines has not impressed the scientists and practitioners of behavior, and the conceptual scope of these scientists and practitioners is too restricted to take account of the larger contexts or systems in which persons and their behavior are embedded. Thus, while demonstrating ever greater mastery of units of behavior, behavior therapists continue to disregard demonstrable effects of larger systems and their interdependencies, even though those phenomena are very likely to affect the success or failure of therapeutic work.

Although they vary in their specificity and practicality, a number of implications for training can be spelled out for the training of behavior therapists. Finally, three examples point to some of the ways in which the perspectives of ecobehavioral technology can be brought to bear on the work of the behavior therapist: (a) a priori transformation of unancicipated effects into anticipated effects; (b) data-based predictions of complex effects; and (c) indirect effects of the larger social environment on the success of the therapist.

REFERENCES

Buell, J., Stoddard, P., Harris, F. R., & Baer, D. M. Collateral social development accompanying reinforcement of outdoor play in a preschool child. *Journal of Applied Behavior Analysis*, 1968, *1*, 167–173.

Gotts, E. E. Newborn walking. (Letter) *Science*, 1972, *177*, 1057-1058.

Hayes, S. C., Rincover, A., & Solnick, J. V. The technical drift of applied analysis. *Journal of Applied Behavior Analysis*, 1980, *13*, 275-285.

Herbert, E. W., Pinkston, E. M., Hayden, M. L., Sajwaj, T. E., Pinkston, S., Cordua, G., & Jackson, C. Adverse effects of differential parental attention. *Journal of Applied Behavior Analysis*, 1973, *6*, 15–30.

Horowitz, F. D. Living among the ABAs—Retrospect and prospect. In E. Ramp & G. Semb (Eds.), *Behavior analysis: Areas of research and application.* Englewood Cliffs, NJ: Prentice-Hall, 1975, pp. 3–15.

Kara, A., & Wahler, R. G. Organizational features of a young child's behaviors. *Journal of Experimental Child Psychology*, 1977, *24*, 24–39.

Liberman, R. B. Review of: *Psychosocial treatment for chronic mental patients* by Gordon L. Paul and Robert J. Lentz. *Journal of Applied Behavior Analysis*, 1980, *13*, 367–381.

Lichstein, K. L., & Wahler, R. G. The ecological assessment of an autistic child. *Journal of Abnormal Child Psychology*, 1976, *4*, 31–54.

Proshansky, H. M., Ittelson, W. H., & Rivlin, L. G. The influence of the physical environment on behavior: Some basic assumptions. In H. M. Proshansky, W. H. Ittelson, & L. G. Rivlin (Eds.), *Environmental psychology*. New York: Holt, Rinehart & Winston, 1970, pp. 27–37.

Rogers-Warren, A., & Warren, S. (Eds.). *Ecological perspectives in behavior analysis*. Baltimore, MD: University Park Press, 1977.

Sajwaj, T., Twardosz, S., & Burke, M. Side effects of extinction procedures in a remedial preschool. *Journal of Applied Behavior Analysis*, 1972, *5*, 163–175.

Spyker, J. M., Sparber, S. B., & Goldberg, A. M. Subtle consequences of methylmercury exposure: Behavioral deviations in offspring of treated mothers. *Science*, 1972, *177*, 621–623.

Stokes, T. F., & Baer, D. M. An implicit technology of generalization. *Journal of Applied Behavior Analysis*. 1977, *10*, 349–367.

Twardosz, S., & Sajwaj, T. Multiple effects of a procedure to increase sitting in a hyperactive, retarded boy. *Journal of Applied Behavior Analysis*, 1972, *5*, 73–78.

Wahler, R. G. Some structural aspects of deviant child behavior. *Journal of Applied Behavior Analysis*, 1975, *8*, 27–42.

Wahler, R. G. The insular mother: Her problems in parent-child treatment. *Journal of Applied Behavior Analysis*, 1980, *13*, 207–219.

Wahler, R. G., Berland, R. M., Coe, T. D., & Leske, G. Social systems analysis: Implementing an alternative behavioral model. In A. Rogers-Warren & S. Warren (Eds.), *Ecological perspectives in behavior analysis*. Baltimore: University Park Press, 1977, pp. 211–228.

Willems, E. P. Go ye into all the world and modify behavior: An ecologist's view. *Representative Research in Social Psychology*, 1973, *4*, 93–105.

Willems, E. P. Behavioral technology and behavioral ecology. *Journal of Applied Behavior Analysis*, 1974, *7*, 151–165.

Willems E. P. Behavioral ecology. In D. Stokols (Ed.), *Perspectives on environment and behavior*. New York: Plenum, 1977, pp. 39–68. (a)

Willems, E. P. Steps toward an ecobehavioral technology. In A. Rogers-Warren & S. Warren (Eds.), *Ecological perspectives in behavior analysis.* Baltimore: University Park Press, 1977, pp. 39–61. (b)

Willems, E. P. & Alexander, J. L. Behavioral indicators of client progress after spinal cord injury: An ecological-contextual approach. In T. Millon, C. J. Green, & R. B. Meagher, Jr. (Eds.), *Handbook of health care clinical psychology*. New York: Plenum, in press.

Willems, E. P. & Stuart, D. G. Behavioral ecology as a perspective on marriages and families. In J. P. Vincent (Ed.), *Advances in family intervention, assessment and theory*, *Volume 1.* Greenwich, CT: JAI Press, 1980, pp. 89–127.

Zelazo, P. R., Zelazo, N. A., & Kolb, S. "Walking" in the newborn. *Science*, 1972, *176*, 314–315.

CHAPTER 23

Principles of Behavior Change and Primary Prevention

Ernest G. Poser, Ph.D.

Paradoxical as it may seem, prevention—even primary prevention—has much in common with therapy. Like many treatment methods, preventive strategies seek to strengthen the resistance of the host by applying some form of intervention generally administered by a health professional. Both therapy and prevention deal extensively with man/environment interactions and both depend upon a goal, a process to achieve it, and criteria whereby to measure outcome. It is also true that both enterprises often lack some or all of these desiderata. When that happens, a curious difference between treatment and prevention becomes apparent. Treatment efforts continue to be mandated even without adequate evidence of their effectiveness, whereas preventive programs are discouraged because of that same lack of evidence (Bloom, 1979). Inconsistencies of this kind seem to stem from the fact that primary prevention, by definition, always takes place in a population free of the disorder being prevented, and it is never easy to show cause for the absence of an event. Nevertheless, reducing the prevalence of an undesirable state or condition by reducing its incidence remains to be the essence of primary prevention. So-called secondary prevention, by contrast, seeks to reduce prevalence by shortening the duration of a disorder, and, as such, it is often indistinguishable from treatment. Following Caplan (1961) some authors also speak of tertiary prevention, but that these three aspects of prevention are hard to distinguish was recently shown in an empirical study by Perlmutter et al. (1976). In what is to follow I

Preparation of this article was supported in part by a Leave Fellowship (Award No. 451-790619) granted by the Social Sciences and Humanities Research Council of Canada.

shall be concerned exclusively with primary prevention, fully recognizing that the boundary between it and early secondary prevention is often difficult to discern, particularly in children.

INTRODUCTION

Primary prevention has run the gamut from being a powerful reality in public health, a political slogan in government, a stepchild in research planning, and a fond hope in applied mental health work. Preventive psychiatry has been practiced for decades, at least at the conceptual level. Psychology still has no name for its part in the preventive enterprise, though community psychology, crisis intervention, and, more recently, ecological psychology sometimes deal with the subject. The first article on prevention in the *Annual Review of Psychology* appeared in 1975, and the most recent, two-volume report on health promotion and disease prevention by the Surgeon General of the United States (Richmond, 1979) represents perhaps the most comprehensive recognition thus far of the intimate link between health and behavior. Regrettably, it contains next to no information on the prevention of behavior disorders. The report notes that the National Academy of Sciences, which elaborated criteria for assigning priorities to various areas of prevention, could not identify "screening procedures for mental or emotional problems . . . for inclusion in the list because of lack of information or consensus on what mental problems and related interventions meet the criteria utilized" (Fielding, 1979). Even so the report suggests that methods for preventive behavior change are at hand and likely to be relevant to target problems other than coronary heart disease. The signal success achieved in reducing the incidence of that disorder by effecting large-scale changes in health-related life styles (Maccoby et al., 1977) has given new impetus to those concerned with behavioral aspects of mental health maintenance. In fact, the Stanford Heart Disease Project stands as a challenge to mental health researchers to identify behavioral risk factors that relate to psychological disorders in the way that smoking, diet, and exercise are now known to relate to specific physical dysfunctions, notably lung cancer and heart and respiratory disease. That finding derived from a research strategy fully recognizing that behavior change is most effective when taught in the social context in which it is later to occur. Accordingly it will be argued in this paper that the public health model of prevention may not be the best one to apply in the behavioral sphere, and that principles of behavior change derived from social learning theory offer a viable if not unique alternative.

The public health model, spectacularly successful in stamping out the major infectious diseases prominent in mortality statistics around 1900, made several justified assumptions: (1) That the diseases in question had a specific cause. (2) That knowledge of that cause was a necessary prerequisite to the instigation of preventive measures. (3) That in most instances all members of a population could benefit equally from the preventive intervention, and, lastly (4) that a disorder, once controlled, would generally not require continued, voluntary effort by those affected to maintain that control. Few if any of these assumptions are germane to the prevention of behavior disorders. In these, the cause is rarely known and likely to be multidimensional and to affect individuals differentially. Where preventive measures are available, as in specific life crises (Raphael, 1977), learned helplessness (Klee & Meyer, 1979), or child abuse (Gray et al., 1978), the focus of attention is not so much on predisposing factors within the individual but equally on precipitating factors arising from the individual's social and physical environment.

EXPERIMENTAL STUDIES

The extension of learning principles to the anticipatory modification of maladaptive behavior is a very recent development. In fact, a review of the literature bearing on behavioral concepts applied to prevention reveals less than a dozen controlled studies, most of which are in the nature of clinical analogs. At this stage, the contribution these studies have made is largely along conceptual and methodological lines. The major conceptual innovation has been the "single target" approach in which the behavior to be prevented is clearly specified and its antecedents and consequences are subjected to a behavioral analysis before an intervention is applied. Frequently the target problem is not the unwanted behavior itself but one or more of its precursors. Our work on preexposure of individuals to a "to-be-conditioned stimulus" is a case in point. It was originally suggested by the realization that English (1929) and Bregman's (1934) failure to replicate Watson's classical conditioning experiment with "Little Albert" (Watson & Rayner, 1920) could be attributed to the difficulty of conditioning avoidance responses to familiar objects. This led us to explore the phenomenon of latent inhibition, which Lubow (1965) defined as "the decremental effect of non-reinforced preexposure on subsequent conditioning." Poser, Baum, and Skinner (1970) tested the generality of that effect in albino rats preexposed for 30 minutes each day on 12 consecutive days to a cage in which they were later to acquire avoidance responses to painful electric shock. Animals in a control group were also removed from their home cages for an equivalent period of time, during which they were placed in a different cage but not the one in which avoidance learning was later to occur. As predicted from earlier work by Lubow, Markman, and Allan (1968), the animals in our study also showed delayed acquisition in learning to avoid shock in the familiar cage to which they had been preexposed. Furthermore, extinction of the response was markedly faster in the experimental group. Surwit (1972) in our laboratory later demonstrated similar effects in human subjects preexposed to a tone subsequently used as a CS. Using the electrodermal response as a dependent variable, preexposed subjects again showed lower rates of responding than control subjects preexposed to an auditory stimulus other than that subsequently paired with shock. Also under laboratory conditions with human subjects, Iwakami (1969) at the University of Illinois demonstrated that the provision of relaxation training to subjects prior to learning an escape or avoidance response increased trials to acquisition and reduced the number of responses during extinction.

These and other studies gave reason to believe that, at least under laboratory conditions, avoidance responses could be modified by anticipatory manipulation of fairly complex stimuli such as preexposure to potentially traumatic environments in animals or desensitizing experiences and other preparatory events in humans.

CLINICAL STUDIES

Speculating that these were reasonable analogs to the "orthogenic" or immunizing experiences that occur in natural environments and at least partially account for the ability of most people to withstand adverse life situations, we proceeded to a clinical trial (Surwit, 1972). In this, very young children scheduled for their first visit to a dentist were preexposed, on 10 occasions, to the locus and instrumentation of a dental clinic in which they were subsequently to suffer their first dental treatment. Videotapes of these treatment sessions were made both for preexposed and control subjects, so that independent judges, unaware of the children's prior experience, could attempt to distinguish experimental from control subjects. The treating dentist was asked to make the same discrimination, on the basis of the child's "in-chair" behavior. Analysis of the videotapes proved to be inconclusive for technical reasons, but the dentist's discrimination of the two groups was better than chance up to the third treatment session. After that, the two groups became indistinguishable, a good example of Bandura's point that evidence of successful induction and generalization of behavior change does not necessarily imply that maintenance of such change was also achieved (Bandura, 1978).

Clinical applications of preventive measures presuppose the availability of techniques for early detection—not necessarily in terms of chronological age—of "populations at risk." That phrase was defined by Garmezy (1975) as "the study of persons who are not as yet disordered, but who may have a higher probability of risk for future disorder as suggested by the presence of certain factors in their lives or person. . . ." Such efforts are not, as some people have argued, instances of secondary prevention. To quote Garmezy again: "These are primary prevention efforts which are largely directed toward skills training and reflect a link that exists between competence factors and prognostic potential in psychopathology." The population at risk to which Garmezy refers is, of course, that of children at risk for schizophrenia. Techniques of *behavioral* prevention are unlikely to compete in that arena, or any other where the major concern is with disorders thought to be largely biogenic. Instead, behaviorally oriented strategies are more likely to be directed at psychological immunization against the macro- and microstressors associated with daily living. It is well known that the number of people affected by relatively minor psychological impairments is infinitely greater than that of hospitalized victims of psychotic illness (Bandura, 1978). Quite apart from the erosion of well-being that common life crises are known to entail, inability to cope with them adequately may well lead to irrational fears, depression, child neglect, separation anxiety, and other disabilities sometimes severe enough to require hospitalization.

The work of Gray et al. (1978) illustrates this point. Having identified 100 mothers as being at high risk for abnormal parenting practices, various prenatal screening procedures such as interviews, questionnaires, and observations during labor and delivery were used. Two high-risk and a low-risk control group were selected. One high-risk group received intensive postnatal counseling by various health professions, while the other received only routine care. Two years later, 25 families in each of the three groups were evaluated in detail. Five children in the high-risk/no intervention group required hospitalization for abuse or neglect. No child in the other two groups suffered an injury thought to be secondary to abnormal parenting practices. The possible long-term effect of such practices was invesgated in two controlled studies of unwanted children whose mothers had applied for abortions that were refused. Both studies (Dytrych et al., 1975; Forssman & Thuwe, 1966) found children of unwilling mothers to be less well adjusted in childhood and young adulthood than were the children of mothers who had not applied for abortions. The implication for behavioral prevention of unwanted pregnancies is self-evident.

ASSESSMENT AND OUTCOME

There is some, though at present only sporadic, evidence that the virulence, if not the incidence, of many disabilities can be reduced. The distinction between virulence and incidence is an important one. As in therapy outcome research, controlled studies of primary prevention have generally adopted an all-or-none criterion of success. In studies of that kind, only nonoccurrence of the to-be-prevented disorder in the target population is seen as successful prevention.

Possible attenuation of the disorder resulting from preventive efforts is not taken into consideration. Conclusions drawn from studies neglecting to take account of "effect size" may be as misleading in the assessment of preventive interventions as they were recently reported to be in therapy outcome research (Shapiro, 1980). Studies by Melamed and Siegel (1975) on the preparation of children for hospitalization and the work of Wolfer and Visintainer (1975) on the related subject of cognitive rehearsal in preparing children for minor surgery clearly demonstrate that the "extent" of improvement rather than its occurrence or nonoccurrence are also at issue in these preventive enterprises.

Clearly not all attempts to apply behavioral principles to prevention have met with success. In our own recent work, designed to reduce anticipated clinical pain by use of cognitive behavior modification, preliminary results show no treatment effect whatsoever (Tan, 1980). Cradock et al. (1978) also reported the failure of an attempt to immunize children for speech anxiety. Another area wherein preventive efforts have consistently failed is that of juvenile delinquency and crime. The work of McCord (1978), Meyer, Borgatta, and Jones (1965), Goodman (1972), and O'Donnell et al. (1979), among others, has documented these unsuccessful attempts to prevent antisocial behavior. The best one can say for these comprehensive and well-controlled investigations is that most did succeed at accurately defining and selecting the population at risk. Procedurally, not all of them meet the criterion of primary prevention adopted in paper, nor were the interventions *behavioral* in all cases.

In behavioral prevention, the counterpart to pretherapy assessment is a functional analysis of the unwanted behavior, the population considered "at risk," and the social and physical setting in which the undesired behavior is expected to occur. The interventions used are often identical to those commonly employed in therapy. As indicated earlier, they include systematic desensitization, participant or symbolic modeling, stress management (biofeedback), cognitive restructuring, social skills training, and so forth. As in therapy, preventive efforts may aim to modify overt self-reported or physiological aspects of behavior.

To date most studies of behavioral prevention have provided satisfactory evidence that some degree of change was achieved (Poser, 1976; Poser & King, 1976); a few have reported generalization of that effect beyond the specific target response or stimuli used in training (Meichenbaum & Turk, 1976; Gray et al., 1978; Deffenbacher et al., 1979). To the author's knowledge, no study has thus far had a follow-up long enough to demonstrate unequivocally that immunizing effects were maintained.

Here again similarity to the current status of behavior therapy is compelling. Poser (1977) reported on the clinical outcome of clients

Figure 23–1. Different Manifestations of Some Childhood Disorders. (Adapted from Butollo, W. H. L., S. Meyer-Plath, and B. Winkler. Bedingungen der Entwicklung von Verhaltensstörungen, *Handbuch der Psychologie* 8:2, 1973, 3074–3101. By permission)

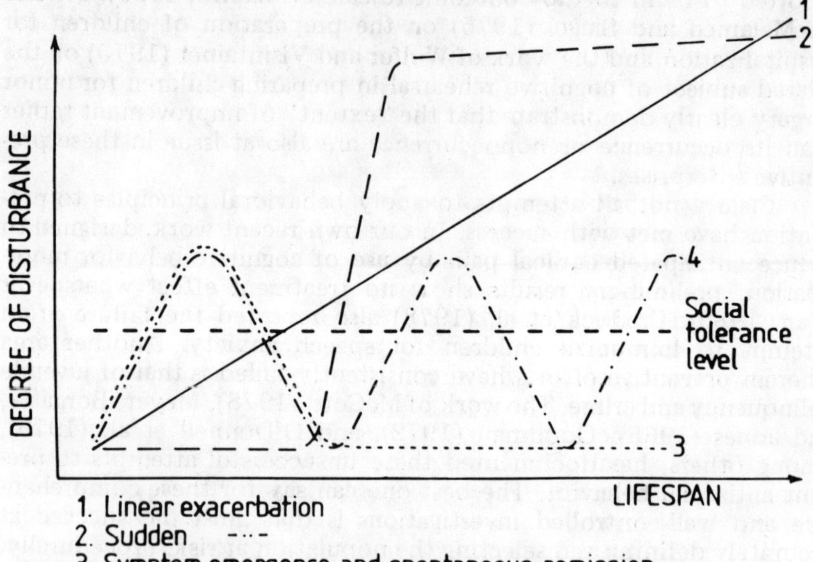

treated by various behavioral techniques. Some of these clients remained symptom-free for between 7 and 10 years, only to relapse at that time with symptoms identical to those presented at intake. There is no reason to suppose that the effect of preventive behavioral interventions in susceptible individuals is any more permant. Booster sessions may counteract that limitation; in fact it is unlikely that the effects of behavioral preventive interventions will be sustained ad infinitum unless the unwanted behavior is self-limiting as in some childhood disorders. From a preventive point of view, knowing the "course" of a disorder may be more crucial than understanding its cause. Figure 23-1 shows the course of maladaptive behaviors commonly seen in children. The broken horizontal line depicts a hypothetical tolerance level below which the deviation is either not recognized or not sufficiently bothersome to cause concern. All primary prevention is implemented below that level. In developmental terms, line 1 may represent delinquency or aggressive behavior starting at an early age and getting progressively worse. According to Robins (1966), Clarizio (1969), and others, these conditions are least likely to remit spontaneously as a function of age. By the same token, they are also difficult to prevent. Curve 2 shows the sudden onset of a condition, perhaps childhood schizophrenia, which rapidly exacerbates and levels out at a high degree of disturbance. Primary prevention in this instance may be totally impossible. The third curve might reflect shyness or withdrawal often seen in young children but generally regarded as self-limiting, while the fourth curve could represent behaviors such as truancy, school phobia, or bedwetting. The graph is merely intended to make two points. Firstly, that disorders of Type 1 and 2 are more difficult to prevent than those of Type 3 and 4, possibly because the former two are related to maturation and are rarely self-limiting. Secondly, the figure illustrates the point made earlier in this chapter that the outcome of prevention, like that of therapy, should not be judged simply in terms of success of failure. In a given preventive program, the degree of disturbance may have been modified whether or not it subsequently surpasses the hypothetical level of social tolerance shown on the graph.

Once again the magnitude of the preventive effect—not merely its presence or absence—should be evaluated. Indeed, it is important that "effect size" not be interpreted unidirectionally. Some changes following therapy are decremental (O'Donnell et al., 1979) not to say detrimental (McCord, 1978), and the same is true of prevention.

Efforts to deal preventively with the grief of bereaved families provide an example. Polak et al. (1975) conducted a controlled study in which families who had experienced the sudden death of a family member were given crisis intervention services for 2 to 6 sessions over a period of 10 weeks. Interventions made use of a social systems network, and treatment focused on increasing the effectiveness of the family in coping with feelings, decisions, and problems of adjustment related to death. At six months follow-up, there were no major statistical differences between the bereaved families who received the intervention and those who did not. In a subsequent paper, Williams and Polak (1979) provided an 18-month follow-up of the same group of bereaved families. The data indicate that a short-term crisis intervention service involving a person-centered cathartic approach and offered by mental health professionals had little or no impact upon postadjustment of the surviving family members. Worse than that, they found that short-term crisis service may actually have delayed or interfered with the natural adaptive bereavement process.

Yet in another study by Raphael (1977), also dealing with bereaved persons, the findings, 13 months after termination of treatment, showed a significant lowering of morbidity in the intervention group as compared to the control group. The more significant impact of intervention occurred with the subgroup of persons who perceived their social network as very nonsupportive during the bereavement crisis.

Though both of these preventive studies used intervention techniques that were more dynamically than behaviorally oriented, their design had much in common with other projects reviewed in this paper. Both investigations addressed populations known to be at risk for posttraumatic coping deficits, and in both a control group of persons, equally at risk but untreated, was used as a comparison group. They also attempted to specify what postbereavement consequences were to be prevented, though not perhaps as precisely as a more behavioral approach would have allowed. The two studies are comparable in that they provided roughly the same number of intervention sessions and similar lengths of follow-up. There were also some very salient differences, however, in the timing of interventions, homogeneity of target populations, and the selection criteria used. It is quite possible that interventions beginning within hours after the sudden death of an individual and aimed at the entire family, as in the Polak study, are less likely to succeed than those aimed at widows under the age of 60 seen within seven weeks of their husbands' death, as in Raphael's work. A seven-week posttraumatic time lapse may have given the newly-bereaved a chance to use their personal coping style, at least initially, and there is evidence to believe that interference with that process may account for the negative outcome of the study by Polak et al. (1975).

Contradictory findings of this sort must be expected at this early stage of the preventive enterprise. Regretfully, they are often taken to support the position of those who do not believe that preventive efforts in the mental health field are realistic at present (Lamb & Zusman, 1979; Cummings, 1972). On the positive side, it is the analysis of studies reporting conflicting results that could well lead to valuable insights concerning the specific variables that need to be taken into account when designing preventive interventions.

Though behavior-specific procedures of prevention are not necessarily superior in outcome to those more dynamically or globally oriented, they have the distinct advantage of being amenable to component analyses of the methods used. In the two bereavement studies just cited, it was clearly not possible to sort out the specific effect coping styles might have had on the bereaved persons. A behavioral design could have dealt with that particular variable. For instance, King (1975) in the context of preventing unnecessary avoidance behavior in young children, selected only those first-graders who had never had contact with a live snake. He carefully excluded those already snake-phobic as well as those clearly not afraid of harmless snakes. The remainder were exposed to symbolic modeling. The purpose was to discover whether children observing video films showing other children handling snakes would subsequently be less likely to avoid a live boa constrictor than would children in the control groups. The models emitted either a copy or a mastery style in handling the snake.

As expected, both modeling styles were superior to the two control conditions, that is, simply viewing films about snakes or receiving no treatment at all. Surprisingly, however, the mastery condition proved to be consistently superior to the coping one in helping children to approach the live snake in the behavioral test. Ratings by an independent observer and a physiological index of arousal pointed in the same direction, though differences between treatment groups were not, in all instances, statistically significant. Inasmuch as symbolic modeling can be viewed as a form of visual preexposure to stimuli later encountered when approaching a live snake, the outcome of this experiment appears to be consistent with laboratory studies on nonreinforced preexposure reviewed earlier. The King study illustrates that there is a distinct advantage to those preventive strategies amenable to component analyses. Such studies establish not only the outcome of the intervention but also permit identification of process variables crucial to bringing it about.

Much of the behavioral literature dealing with controlled studies of prevention concerns itself with the modification of antecedents of the target behavior to be prevented. Fewer are directed at the consequences of such behavior. The latter typically focus on confronting high risk populations with tangible evidence of the dire consequences specific behaviors are likely to entail, thereby seeking to discourage the undesired behaviors. Often the weakness of these strategies resides in the long delay between supposedly wrongful behaviors and problems to which they give rise. Failure to prevent juvenile delinquency or crime by deterrent measures may be partly due to that limitation.

Innovative attempts to circumvent the delay between noxious behavior and its consequences in preventive interventions were recently reported by Evans et al. (1978). Working with seventh-grade students, they used videotaped messages, focused discussion, feedback, and monitoring to defer the onset of smoking in children. Effective monitoring was achieved by first introducing subjects to mass spectrometric technique for determining the nicotine content of saliva. Before self-reports on smoking behavior were obtained, each child was asked to produce a specimen of saliva. Though these specimens were not in fact analyzed, an earlier study had shown that having to produce a specimen resulted in more accurate self-reports. The strategy seems promising in that onset rates for the treated groups at termination of the 10-week program were below 10%, whereas those in control groups were in excess of 18%.

Studies of this sort highlight two important variables relevant to other forms of prevention. One of these is the principle of immediacy, that is, the reduction of time lag between the desired behavior change and its salutary consequences. The other is proper sequencing of persuasion and skills training in the manner suggested by Berkanovic (1976). His analysis is based on the health belief model, which postulates that in the presence of certain cues or stimuli to take health action, the likelihood of taking action is dependent on the individual's beliefs about the seriousness of the health condition to which the action is addressed, his susceptibility to it, the efficacy of the proposed action, and the difficulties he may encounter in attempting to carry out the action (Berkanovic, 1976, p. 93–94). Work by Suchman (1967) dealing with the role of demographic variables in determining acceptance or rejection of preventive measures is quite consistent with Berkanovic's analysis.

FUTURE TRENDS

The distinction between health promotion and disease prevention (Richmond, 1979) is already well established. It suggests that the enhancement of physical and psychological well-being is a legitimate enterprise in its own right. Disease prevention may contribute to that end, but the quest to eliminate manifestations of pathology is not in itself coterminous with optimising a person's coping skills or general well-being.

In that sense, the target of contemporary health services has already evolved beyond disease prevention per se. In the psychological domain, concern with behavioral medicine (Schwartz & Weiss, 1978) is being extended to comprise behavioral health. In his definition of behavioral health, Matarazzo (1980) stresses individual responsibility in the application of behavioral and biomedical knowledge to the maintenance of health (p. 813). But if the exercise of individual responsibility is taken to include life-style changes intended to resolve persistent problems in living, a lot more than *health* maintenance is at stake. It may therefore be timely to recognize that traditional boundaries of health care delivery have already been surpassed. At this stage, the concern is no longer restricted to therapeutic or even health-related preventive measures, but also comprises behavioral prescriptions for the purpose of optimization.

The distinction is illustrated in Figure 23-2. Here optimization is used to describe the point at which an individual's control of his own behavior and environment optimally favors the achievement of specific goals. As such, the concept of optimization goes well beyond the attainment of physical or behavioral health. It may indeed be functionally independent of health-related parameters.

"Situational enhancement" is used to describe the process whereby optimization is achieved. It may refer to the acquisition or consolidation of social skills, increased assertiveness, or fear-reducing strategies. Alternatively, enhancement may result from the exercise of more effective control over environmental and ecological events: Examples would include the situational management of eating behavior or delinquency as well as the control of noise and air pollution. Such methods may at times be preventive, and they may or may not be behavioral. But in the sense here proposed they are not primarily health-related. For this reason they are not covered by the meaning currently assigned to behavioral health or behavioral medicine. In

Figure 23-2. A Two-Dimensional View of Disease Prevention and Optimization.

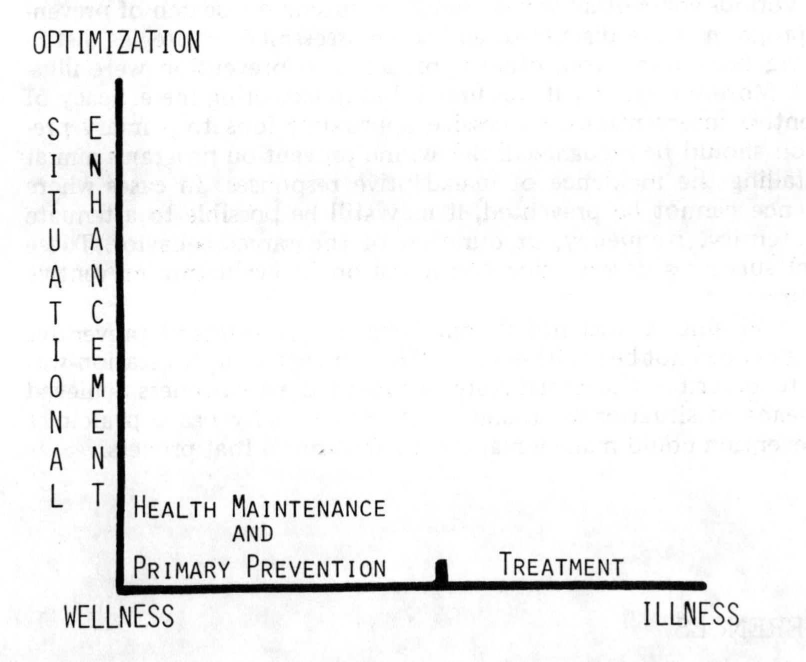

terms of Figure 23-2, both of these strategies address the Wellness/Illness rather than the Wellness/Optimization continuum. Established principles of behavior change, particularly those concerned with self-management (Mahoney & Thoresen, 1974), problem solving (D'Zurilla & Goldfried, 1971), and social skill acquisition (Twentyman & McFall, 1975), are likely to make signal contributions to the attainment of optimization. To be maximally effective, however, these interventions will have to be offered in a multidisciplinary context in which specialists in ecological and social change are also represented.

SUMMARY

It was the purpose of this paper to illustrate and encourage the use of behavioral principles in the context of preventive programs. Review of the relevant studies shows that treatment and prevention have many features in common, that principles of preexposure are applicable to preventive behavior change, and that preventive efforts need not necessarily await complete knowledge of etiological factors associated with the target problems to be averted. Beliefs to the contrary have, in the past, inhibited research in this area. Some critics have gone so far as to assert that "without knowledge of cause primary prevention programs can only be shots in the dark" (Lamb & Zusman, 1979).

Various conceptual issues crucial to outcome research of preventive programs were discussed, and some assessment strategies distinguishing behavioral from other approaches to prevention were illustrated. More specifically it was urged that in exploring the efficacy of preventive interventions, successive approximations to primary prevention should be recognized. Behavioral prevention programs aim at forestalling the incidence of maladaptive responses. In cases where incidence cannot be prevented, it may still be possible to attenuate the intensity, frequency, or duration of the target behavior. These partial successes deserve due consideration in evaluating preventive measures.

In closing it was noted that behaviorally oriented preventive strategies need not be health-related. The concept of optimization was used to describe a personal state of maximal effectiveness achieved by means of situational enhancement. Behaviorally based principles of prevention could make a major contribution to that process.

REFERENCES

Bandura, A. On paradigms and recycled ideologies. *Cognitive Therapy and Research*, 1978, *2*, 79–103.

Berkanovic, E. Behavioral science and prevention. *Revue of Medicine*, 1976, *5*, 92–105.

Bloom, B. L. Prevention of mental disorders: Recent advances in theory and practice. *Community Mental Health Journal*, 1979, *15*, 179-191.

Bregman, E. An attempt to modify the emotional attitudes of infants by the conditioned response technique. *Journal of Genetic Psychology*, 1934, *45*, 169–198.

Caplan, G. *Prevention of mental disorders in children.* New York: Basic Books, 1961.

Clarizio, H. F. Stability of deviant behavior through time. In H. F. Clarizio (Ed.), *Mental health and the educative process.* Chicago: Rand McNally, 1969.

Cradock, C., Cotler, S., & Jason, L. A. Primary prevention: Immunization of children for speech anxiety. *Cognitive Therapy and Research*, 1978, *2*, 389–396.

Cummings, E. Primary prevention—more cost than benefit. In H. Gottesfeld (Ed.), *The critical issues of community mental health.* Behavioral Publications, 1972, 161–176.

Deffenbacher, J. L., Mathis, H., & Michaels, A. C. Two self-control procedures in the reduction of targeted and non-targeted anxieties. *Journal of Counseling Psychology*, 1979, *26*, 120-127.

Dytrych, Z., et al. Children born to women denied abortion. *Family Planning Perspectives*, 1975, *7*, 165-171.

D'Zurilla, T. J., & Goldfried, M. R. Problem solving and behavior modification. *Journal of Abnormal Psychology*, 1971, *78*, 107-126.

English, H. B. Three cases of the "conditioned fear response". *Journal of Abnormal & Social Psychology*, 1929, *34*, 221-225.

Evans, R. I., Rozelle, R. M., Mittelmark, M. B., Hansen, W. B., Bane, A. L., & Havis, J. Deterring the onset of smoking in children: Knowledge of immediate physiological effects and coping with peer pressure, media pressure, and parent modeling. *Journal of Applied Social Psychology*, 1978, *8*, 126-135.

Fielding, J. E. Preventive services for the well population. In J. B. Richmond, *Healthy people: The Surgeon General's report on health promotion and disease prevention*, Washington, DC: U.S. Government Printing Office, 1979, 277-304.

Forssman, H., & Thuwe, I. One hundred and twenty children born after application for therapeutic abortion refused. *Acta Psychiatrica Scandinavica*, 1966, *42*, 71-88.

Garmezy, N. Intervention with children at risk for behavior pathology. *The Clinical Psychologist*, 1975, *28*, 12-14.

Goodman, G. *Companionship therapy*. San Francisco, CA: Jossey Bass, 1972.

Gray, J. D., Cutler, C. A., Dean, J. G., & Kempe, C. H. *Prediction and prevention of child abuse and neglect*. Proceedings: Third Annual Conference on Issues in Child Abuse and Neglect, Cornell University, 1978.

Iwakami, E. E. The effects of muscle relaxation on the acquisition and extinction of a conditioned avoidance response. *Dissertation Abstracts*, University of Illinois, 1970, *30*, 3386-3387.

King, M. *The prevention of maladaptive avoidance responses through observational learning: An analogue study*. Unpublished doctoral dissertation, McGill University, 1975.

Klee, S., & Meyer, R. G. Prevention of learned helplessness in humans. *Journal of Consulting & Clinical Psychology*, 1979, *47*, 411-412.

Lamb, H. R., & Zusman, J. Primary prevention in perspective. *American Journal of Psychiatry*, 1979, *136*, 12-17.

Lubow, R. Latent inhibition: Effects of frequency of nonreinforced preexposure of the CS. *Journal of Comparative & Physiological Psychology*, 1965, *60*, 454-457.

Lubow, R., Markman, R., & Allen J. Latent inhibition and classical conditioning of the rabbit pinna response. *Journal of Comparative and Physiological Psychology*, 1968, *66*, 688–694.

Maccoby, N., Farquhar, J. W., Wood, P. D., & Alexander, J. Reducing the risk of cardiovascular disease: Effects of a community-based campaign on knowledge and behavior. *Journal of Community Health*, 1977, *3*, 100–114.

Mahoney, M. J., & Thoresen, C. E. *Self-control: Power to the person.* Monterey, CA: Brooks-Cole, 1974.

Matarazzo, J. Behavioral health and behavioral medicine: Frontiers for a new health psychology. *American Psychologist*, 1980, *35*, 807–817.

McCord, J. A 30-year follow-up of treatment effects. *American Psychologist*, 1978, *3*, 284–289.

Meichenbaum, D., & Turk, D. The cognitive-behavioral management of anxiety, anger and pain. In P. O. Davidson (Ed.), *The Behavioral Management of Anxiety, Depression and Pain.* New York: Brunner/Mazel, 1976.

Melamed, B. G., & Siegel, L. J. Reduction of anxiety in children facing hospitalization and surgery by use of filmed modeling. *Journal of Consulting & Clinical Psychology*, 1975, *43*, 511–521.

Meyer, H. J., Borgatta, E. F., & Jones, W. C. *Girls at Vocational High.* New York: Russell Sage Foundation, 1965.

O'Donnell, C. R., Lydgate, T., & Fo, W. S. O. The buddy system: Review and follow-up. *Child Behavior Therapy*, 1979, *1*, 161–169.

Perlmutter, F. D., Vayda, A. M., & Woodburn, P. K. An instrument for differentiating programs in prevention—primary, secondary and tertiary. *American Journal of Orthopsychiatry*, 1976, *46*, 533–541.

Polark, P. R., Egan, D., Vandenbergh, R., & Williams, W. V. Prevention in mental health: A controlled study. *American Journal of Psychiatry*, 1975, *132*, 146–149.

Poser, E. G. Strategies for behavioral prevention. In P. O. Davidson (Ed.), *The behavioral management of anxiety, depression and pain.* New York: Brunner/Mazel, 1976.

Poser, E. G. *Behavior therapy in clinical practice: Decision making, procedure and outcome.* Springfield, IL: Charles C. Thomas, 1977.

Poser, E., Baum, M., & Skinner, C. CS preexposure as a means of "Behavioral prophylaxis": An animal paradigm. *Proceedings of the 78th Annual Convention of the American Psychological Association*, 1970, *78*, 521–522.

Poser, E. G., & King, M. Primary prevention of fear: An experimental approach. In I. G. Sarason & C. D. Spielberger (Eds.),

Stress and anxiety, Volume 3. New York: Wiley, 1976, 325–344.

Raphael, B. Preventive intervention with the recently bereaved. *Archives of General Psychiatry*, 1977, *34*, 1450–1454.

Richmond, J. B. *Healthy people: The Surgeon General's report on health promotion and disease prevention.* Washington, DC: U.S. Government Printing Office, 1979.

Robins, L. N. *Deviant children grow up.* Baltimore, MD: Williams & Wilkins, 1966.

Schwartz, G. E., & Weiss, S. M. Yale Conference on behavioral medicine: A proposed definition and statement of goals. *Journal of Behavioral Medicine*, 1978, *1*, 3–12.

Shapiro, D. A. Science and psychotherapy. *British Journal of Medical Psychology*, 1980, *53*, 1–10.

Suchman, E. A. Preventive health behavior: A model for research on community health campaigns. *Journal of Health & Social Behavior*, 1967, *8*, 197–209.

Surwit, R. *The anticipatory modification of the conditioning of a fear response in humans.* Unpublished doctoral dissertation, McGill University, 1972.

Tan, S. Y. *Acute pain in a clinical setting: Effects of cognitive-behavioral skills training.* Unpublished doctoral dissertation, McGill University, 1980.

Thomas, A., & Chess, S. Development in middle childhood. *Seminars in Psychiatry*, 1972, *4*, 331–341.

Twentyman, C. T., & McFall, R. M. Behavioral training of social skills in shy males. *Journal of Consulting & Clinical Psychology*, 1975, *43*, 384–395.

Watson, J. B., & Rayner, R. Conditioned emotional reactions. *Journal of Experimental Psychology*, 1920, *3*, 1–14.

Williams, W. V., & Polak, P. R. Follow-up research in primary prevention: A model of adjustment in acute grief. *Journal of Clinical Psychology*, 1979, *35*, 35–45.

Wolfer, J. A., & Visintainer, M. A. Pediatric surgical patients' and parents' stress responses and adjustment as a function of psychologic preparation and stress-point nursing care. *Nursing Research*, 1975, *24*, 244–255.

Name Index

Subject Index